The Genetics and Biology of
DROSOPHILA

VOLUME 1b

Edited by

M. ASHBURNER

Department of Genetics, University of Cambridge
Cambridge, England

and

E. NOVITSKI

Department of Biology, University of Oregon
Eugene, Oregon, U.S.A.

1976

ACADEMIC PRESS

LONDON NEW YORK SAN FRANCISCO

A Subsidiary of Harcourt Brace Jovanovich, Publishers

ACADEMIC PRESS INC. (LONDON) LTD.
24/28 Oval Road,
London NW1

United States Edition published by
ACADEMIC PRESS INC.
111 Fifth Avenue
New York, New York 10003

Library of Congress Catalog Number 75-19614
ISBN: 0 12 064902-0

Printed in Great Britain by
Billing & Sons Limited,
Guildford and London

Contributors

CHILDRESS, D., *Metabolism and Radiation Research Laboratory, U.S.D.A., Fargo, North Dakota, U.S.A.*

FINNERTY, V., *Department of Biology, University of Connecticut, Storrs, Connecticut, U.S.A.*

GREEN, M. M., *Department of Genetics, University of California, Davis, California, U.S.A.*

HARTL, D. M., *Department of Biological Sciences, Purdue University, West Lafayette, Indiana, U.S.A.*

HIRAIZUMI, Y., *Department of Zoology, The University of Texas, Austin, Texas, U.S.A.*

HOCHMAN, B., *Department of Zoology, University of Texas, Knoxville, Tennessee, U.S.A.*

HOLM, D. G., *Department of Zoology, University of British Columbia, Vancouver, British Columbia, Canada.*

ISING, G., *Institute of Genetics, University of Lund, Lund, Sweden.*

JUDD, B. H., *Department of Zoology, University of Texas, Austin, Texas, U.S.A.*

LEFEVRE, G., *Department of Biology, California State University, Northridge, California, U.S.A.*

LEIGH, B., *Department of Radiation Genetics and Chemical Mutagenesis, University of Leiden, Leiden, The Netherlands.*

NOVITSKI, E., *Department of Biology, University of Oregon, Eugene, Oregon, U.S.A.*

PARKER, D. R., *Department of Biology, University of California, Riverside, California, U.S.A.*

RAMEL, C., *Wallenberg Laboratory, University of Stockholm, Stockholm, Sweden.*

RITOSSA, F., *Instituto di Genetica, Universita di Bari, Bari, Italy.*

SCHALET, A., *Department of Radiation Genetics and Chemical Mutagenesis, State University of Leiden, Leiden, The Netherlands.*

WILLIAMSON, J. H., *Department of Biology, University of Calgary, Calgary, Alberta, Canada.*

ZIMMERING, S., *Division of Biological and Medical Sciences, Brown University, Providence, Rhode Island, U.S.A.*

Preface

The publication of the first volume of *The Genetics and Biology of Drosophila* occurs on the fiftieth anniversary of the publication of *The Genetics of Drosophila* by Morgan, Bridges and Sturtevant. Since that time over 20,000 papers have been published on aspects of the biology and genetics of this fly. Twenty-five years ago Demerec edited the now classic *Biology of Drosophila*—a volume that has been an invaluable source ever since. Apart from this no attempt has been made, since 1925, to publish any comprehensive account of the biology and genetics of *Drosophila*. This is perhaps surprising in view of the interest and significance of much *Drosophila* research for biology in general. Even a brief perusal of the most recent "Bibliography on the Genetics of *Drosophila*" should be sufficient to gain some idea of the breadth of current *Drosophila* research. It ranges from problems in "pure genetics", to sophisticated studies in neurobiology and ecology. In many, if not most, people's minds when they select *Drosophila* as an experimental organism is the fact that our knowledge of its genetics, and our ability to use this knowledge to experimental advantage, far exceeds that of the genetics of any other multicellular organism.

This, and subsequent volumes of *The Genetics and Biology of Drosophila* will, we hope, be of value both to the established *Drosophila* research worker and to biologists in general. In particular we hope that the individual chapters will help advanced students and postgraduates in gaining a "feel" for *Drosophila* showing them just what has, and more importantly what has not, been achieved so far.

We are very fortunate in having Pete Oliver write his personal history of *Drosophila* research as the first chapter in this volume. Oliver had the privilege of seeing *Drosophila* genetics grow from the preserve of a select few in the fly rooms of Columbia, Caltech and Texas to the world-wide activity it is today.

The remaining chapters of the first volume are individual reviews of topics in *Drosophila* genetics. The different contributors have approached their chosen topics in their own styles; this has been encouraged by us. In some cases the chapters are very complete reviews of a vast literature published during the last 50 or 60 years. In other cases the chapters are more restricted in scope, often the major contributions to the subject having been made by the authors themselves. The breadth of the coverage is not as extensive as might be wished. For various reasons certain subjects are not included, or not covered as fully as they might have been. We regret this but feel that to have delayed the publication of this volume, to ensure fuller coverage, could not be justified.

Many areas of *Drosophila* research are in a state of flux at the present time. In part this is a consequence of new fields of research opening up, itself partly a consequence of the impact of the success of molecular biologists. This impact has been twofold. Most importantly *Drosophila* biologists have had to assimilate the revolution that has occurred in our view of the nature and function of the genetic material since 1953. Secondly the technical successes of the molecular biologists, often forerunners or coincident with their theoretical successes, are being applied to *Drosophila*, and other eukaryotes, not least by molecular biologists moving from their favoured bacteriophage and bacteria to *Drosophila* itself. The rapid advances being made in many areas of *Drosophila* research have two consequences for an undertaking of this nature. In the first place the inevitable delays between pen and print mean that some chapters will be out of date. Secondly a consequence of rapid advancement in most fields of research is that controversies arise. Controversies are of the utmost importance for the advancement of any research since contrasting opinions, when strongly held and defended, sharpen the critical eye. As editors we have often had to appear to take sides in particular controversies. In fact we do not, at least in our guise of editors. Were these volumes to be the final chapter in the history of *Drosophila* genetics the fact that we may even appear to be partisan would be most regrettable. But these volumes are no such thing. They are one account of the state of the art in the mid nineteen-seventies. Doubtless when the next comprehensive coverage of *Drosophila* genetics is attempted, hopefully before 2025, many of the current problems and areas of disagreement will have vanished. If this volume in any way spurs on the forward progress of *Drosophila* biology we will be satisfied.

MICHAEL ASHBURNER
and
ED NOVITSKI
November 1975

Contents

Editorial Note

Despite the fact that these volumes are the first attempt to review the biology and genetics of *Drosophila* since 1925 there are several very valuable sources of information on *Drosophila* to which we would like to bring the reader's attention:

1. *The Genetics of Drosophila.* T. H. Morgan, C. B. Bridges and A. H. Sturtevant. Bibliographica Genetica, vol. II. Martinus Nijhoff, The Hague 1925.
   This reviews the achievements of the first fifteen or so years of Morgan's laboratory, and other investigators, and includes a bibliography of the *Drosophila* literature and a description of the mutants then known.
2. *The Mutants of Drosophila melanogaster.* C. B. Bridges, completed and edited by K. S. Brehme. Carnegie Institution of Washington Publication No. 552. Washington D.C. 1944.
   This volume, issued in draft by Bridges as *Drosophila Information Service No. 9* (1938), is a compilation and description of the mutants and other genetic variants known by December 1942.
3. *Genetic Variations of Drosophila melanogaster.* D. L. Lindsley and E. H. Grell. Carnegie Institution of Washington Publication No. 627. Washington D.C. 1968.
   This is a complete revision of Bridges and Brehme and is stated to be reasonably complete to 1966. In addition to a description of mutants, chromosome aberrations and special chromosomes it includes valuable comments upon the vexed problem of the nomenclature used by *Drosophila* geneticists.
4. *Drosophila Information Service* (DIS)
   This mimeographed bulletin is published approximately annually and distributed to *Drosophila* workers all over the world. It usually includes lists of stocks, new mutants, brief research reports, technical and teaching notes, bibliographies and a geographical directory of *Drosophila* workers.
   Number 1 was published in 1934 and was arranged by C. B. Bridges and M. Demerec. M. Demerec continued as editor until No. 33 (1959). Since then the editor has been E. Novitski, Department of Biology, University of Oregon, Eugene, Oregon, to whom inquiries may be directed.

No. 6 (1936) was a special issue devoted to methods and No. 9 (1938) was a draft list of mutants by C. B. Bridges. All except the ephemera of Nos. 1–14 and 15–24 have been reissued by E. Novitski as collected volumes.

5. *The Mutants of Drosophila melanogaster classified according to body parts affected.* N. B. Braver, Carnegie Institution of Washington, Publication No. 552A. Washington, D.C. 1956.

The following bibliographies of the *Drosophila* literature have been published (in addition to the bibliographies often contained in DIS).

6. In *The Genetics of Drosophila* (item 1 above). Covers the period to 1924 and includes approximately 500 titles.
7. *Bibliography on the genetics of Drosophila.* H. J. Muller. Imperial Bureau of Animal Breeding and Genetics. Oliver & Boyd, Edinburgh 1939.
   Covers the period from 1925 to 1939 and includes 2965 titles. Not indexed by Muller but indexed by Herskowitz together with part II (item 8 below).
8. *Bibliography on the genetics of Drosophila Part II.* I. H. Herskowitz. Bibliography No. 6 of the Commonwealth Bureau of Animal Breeding and Genetics. Commonwealth Agricultural Bureau, Farnham Royal, Bucks 1953.
   Covers the period from 1939 to 1950 (2841 titles). The index includes entries in Part I (item 7 above).
9. *Bibliography on the genetics of Drosophila Part III.* I. H. Herskowitz. Indiana University Publications, Bloomington 1958.
   Covers the period 1951–1956 (3100 titles).
10. *Bibliography on the genetics of Drosophila Part IV.* I. H. Herskowitz. McGraw-Hill Book Co., New York 1963.
   Covers the period 1957–1962 (3305 titles).
11. *Bibliography on the genetics of Drosophila Part V.* I. H. Herskowitz. Macmillan Co., New York 1969.
   Covers the period 1962–1967 (3775 titles).
12. *Bibliography on the genetics of Drosophila Part VI.* I. H. Herskowitz. Collier-Macmillan Co., New York 1974.
   Covers the period 1968–1972 (4821 titles).

Subsequent volumes of *The Genetics and Biology of Drosophila* will deal with the less strictly genetic aspects of this fly. The following monographs are often invaluable sources:

13. *Drosophila melanogaster Meig. Eine Einfuhrung in den Bau und die Entwicklung.* E. H. Strasburger. Julius Springer. Berlin 1935.

14. *The embryonic development of Drosophila melanogaster*. D. F. Poulson. Actualites Scientifiques et Industrielles 498. Hermann and Cie, Paris. 1937.
15. *The Biology of Drosophila*. Edited by M. Demerec. J. Wiley and Sons, New York. 1950. Reissued by Hafner Publishing Co., New York 1965.
16. *Evolution of the genus Drosophila*. J. T. Patterson and W. S. Stone. Macmillan Co., New York 1952.
17. *Systematic studies of the early stages of Drosophilidae*. T. Okada. Bunka Zugeisha Co., Tokyo 1968.
18. *Ovarian development in Drosophila melanogaster*. R. C. King. Academic Press, New York 1970.

The Department of Zoology, University of Texas at Austin occasionally publishes collections of papers which were once entirely, and largely still are, devoted to aspects of *Drosophila* biology and genetics. There are two series:

19. *Studies on the Genetics of Drosophila*. Directed by J. T. Patterson (Nos. I to VIII (1940–1954)) and edited by M. R. Wheeler (No. IX (1957)).
20. *Studies in Genetics*. Edited by M. R. Wheeler. Nos. II (1962) to VI (1971).

The following elementary introductions to the genetics of *Drosophila* have been published:

21. *Drosophila—a guide*. M. Demerec and B. P. Kaufmann. Carnegie Institute of Washington, Washington D.C. The latest edition is the 8th (1973).
22. *Practical heredity with Drosophila*. G. Haskell. Oliver and Boyd, Edinburgh 1961.
23. *Experiments in genetics with Drosophila*. M. W. Strickberger. Wiley and Sons, New York 1962.
24. *Drosophila*. B. Shorrocks. Ginn and Co. Ltd., London 1972.

Contents of Volume 1a

Contents of Volume 1c

Acknowledgements

During the gestation of these volumes we have received advice, not always taken, from many members of the *Drosophila* community. We wish to record our thanks to all those who have helped us on both specific and general matters, and for the diplomacy shown, and often needed, by our colleagues. Michael Ashburner wishes to thank Mel Green, in particular, for his great encouragement in the early stages of this project.

Without Roger Farrand and Jenny Mugridge, of Academic Press, London, these volumes would never have appeared. The cheerful confidence they showed in us, even during our darkest winters, was beyond the call of their duties. Both editors and contributors have benefited greatly from their wisdom and tact.

Thanks are due to our families. They have had to bear the brunt of our commitment and have suffered as a result. They, as well as the authors and editors, have long looked forward to the publication of these volumes although, perhaps, for rather different reasons.

11. Compound Chromosomes Involving the X and the Y Chromosomes

E. NOVITSKI

Department of Biology
University of Oregon
Eugene, Oregon, U.S.A.

and

D. CHILDRESS

Metabolism and Radiation Research Laboratory
U.S.D.A., Fargo, North Dakota, U.S.A.

I. Introduction

The syntheses of the various types of chromosomes detailed below represents one of the very elegant and aesthetically satisfying branches of *Drosophila* genetics. Most work concerned with the production of chromosome rearrangements involves the random breakage of chromosomes, usually by X-rays, followed by selection of types considered desirable for a specific purpose. Here, however, the emphasis is on the creation of a specific new chromosome type considered desirable for some experimental or stock-keeping application. The end result is then reached by a logical sequence of preliminary steps until the desired end-product is reached.

Besides the syntheses described in this chapter, this approach has also been applied to the construction of compound autosomes (see Chapter 13).

These chromosomes with altered structure yield information on meiotic processes which could not be obtained by studying normal chromosome behavior. Non-random disjunction, weak-strong centromere behavior and non-homologous pairing are examples of meiotic phenomena which have been discovered and characterized to a very sophisticated level through the study of compound chromosomes. In this discussion, brief summaries of the information obtained from each chromosome type follow the description of the synthesis in some of those cases when their study has led to the discovery of some new aspect of meiotic behavior, and the references cited provide more complete information on the behavior of the chromosomes and the methods of synthesis and recovery.

Most of these chromosomes were originally constructed by means of rare exchanges in the heterochromatic regions. The ability of *D. melanogaster* to tolerate the loss, gain, and repositioning of large blocks of heterochromatin from the X and Y chromosomes makes a considerable amount of manipulation possible. Many of the syntheses involve X chromosomes with long inversions which reposition the normally proximal X heterochromatin distally. Exchanges between the X and Y, and between the X and an X duplication, particularly the Bar–Stone duplication, are the basic steps in the construction of most of these chromosomes.

The diagrams represent general methods of construction; the markers used and the specific methods of recovery of the exceptions in each case are not shown; it is assumed that these details can be supplied at will by the reader. The examples given do not represent an exhaustive listing of all possible methods of synthesis since many variations, and even improvements, become obvious once the initial fact of synthesis has been realized. In our diagrams, euchromatin is represented by a single line, heterochromatin by the thicker blocked area, usually adjacent to the centromere, which is indicated in the traditional fashion by a small circle. For simplicity, chromosomes will be shown as single strands unless the analysis demands the full four strands, and acentric fragments and irrelevant crossover products are generally omitted from the diagrams. The marker yellow (*y*), which is normally located at the distal tip of the X chromosome, is used to indicate the arrangement of the euchromatin with respect to the centromere and the heterochromatin. The long and short arms of the Y chromosome are designated Y^L and Y^S, respectively.

The word compound was originally applied to combinations of whole chromosomes or chromosome arms when used in the context of *Drosophila* synthesis (Novitski, 1954) and should not be confused with the meaning of the word when applied to other cytological situations, to multiple sex-chromosomes, for instance. Furthermore, a few misguided workers have recently redefined the term to apply only to those combinations in which similar elements, as two X's, or two 2L's are joined together. We consider this definition too restrictive and unimaginative, and will continue to call combinations of the X-chromosome and the Y-chromosome compounds. In other words, we would prefer to define the word compound as a chemist would, rather than as a grammarian might.

II. The Compound X Chromosomes

The compound X chromosomes contain the genetic material from two X chromosomes attached to a single centromere. The centromere may be median (metacentric) or subterminal (acrocentric). The chromosome arms may be free or joined to form a ring, and in tandem or reversed order with respect to each other. All six possible types of compounds have been synthesized (Novitski, 1954): the reversed metacentric (RM), the tandem metacentric (TM), the reversed acrocentric (RA), the tandem acrocentric (TA), the tandem ring (TR), and the reversed ring (RR).

Following a system originally proposed by Muller (1936) for constructing attached-X (RM) chromosomes, Novitski (1954) and Lindsley and Sandler (1963) successfully developed systems for generating other compounds making use of the Bar^{S} duplication from *T(1;4)B*^{S}. These chromosomes, called by Lindsley and Sandler the reversed metacentrigenic (RMG), the tandem metacentrigenic (TAG), and the reversed acrocentrigenic (RAG), respectively, may be recovered from a heterochromatic exchange between an X chromosome and the *B*^{S} element. This system may be applied in reverse; if the compound chromosome is already available, the "compoundigenic" may be generated by euchromatic exchange between the compound and the duplication. At first sight it might seem pointless to break down a compound by allowing it to cross over with a duplication, thereby creating a chromosome that will readily give a compound again, but this is one of the few possible ways of introducing new markers into a compound once it has been found.

A. Reversed Metacentric (attached-X)

The reversed metacentric compound X consists of two X chromosomes in the same sequence joined to a median centromere. It may be recovered *de novo* as an exchange between a Y heterochromatic arm on an X chromosome and the proximal heterochromatin of a normal X (Fig. 1a). Genetically different reversed metacentrics may also be generated by the use of the reversed metacentrigenic (Muller, 1936; Lindsley and Sandler, 1963).

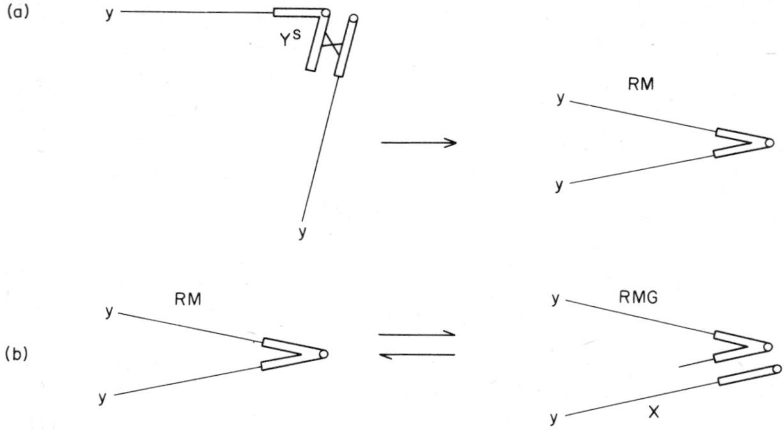

FIG. 1(a). Recovery of the reversed metacentric (attached-X) from heterochromatic exchange between an attached X–Y and a normal X. (b) Relationship between the reversed metacentric and reversed metacentrigenic chromosome (RMG). (Redrawn from Lindsley and Sandler, 1963.)

The RMG is an X chromosome with tne B^S duplication attached as a second arm by crossing over between the duplication attached and the RM. Figure 1b illustrates the method of generating both the RMG and the new RM.

B. Tandem Metacentric

This compound may be constructed by heterochromatic exchange between a normal X and the short arm of an attached X–Y with a complete euchromatic inversion. The two chromosome arms in the resulting compound are arranged in tandem, causing them to form a spiral during synapsis (Fig. 2a). The TMG, originally recovered by Novitski (1954) as a heterochromatic exchange between the B^S duplication and the Y^L arm of $Y^SX{\cdot}Y^L$, can be used to generate new tandem metacentrics (Fig. 2b). A simple ring X chromosome is also tandem metacentrigenic; if it is placed in a triploid along with two rod X-chromosomes, one in normal sequence and the other inverted, certain double crossovers, one of which is depicted in Fig. 2c, will produce a TM. This method has been used by Lindsley and Novitski (1959) for this purpose, and a modification of this procedure has successfully opened out an unstable ring (Hinton, 1957).

Synapsis. In many cases the inverted arm of the TM may carry some X heterochromatin at the distal tip derived from a scute inversion. Novitski and Braver (1954) studied such a TM, modified further by the presence of a heterozygous delta-49 inversion. The crossing over relationships

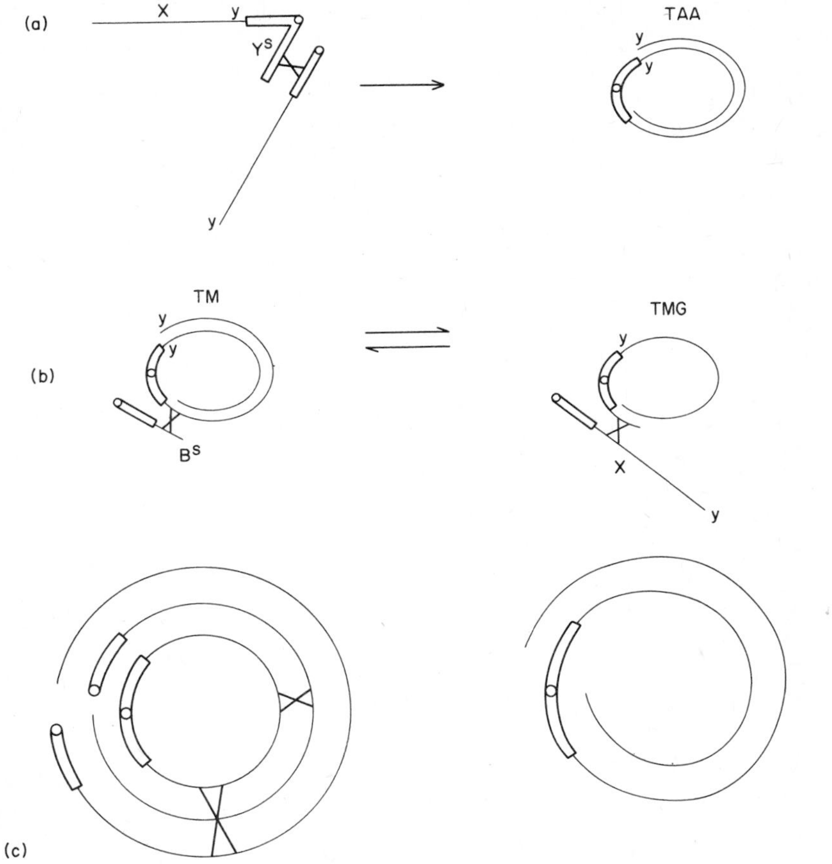

FIG. 2(a). Synthesis of the tandem metacentric by heterochromatic exchange between a normal X and an inverted attached X–Y. (b) Synthesis of the tandem metacentrigenic (TMG). (Redrawn from Lindsley and Sandler, 1963.) (c) The production of a tandem metacentric by double crossing over in a triploid with a ring chromosome, a chromosome in normal sequence, and an inverted chromosome.

between its arms, and the arms of its derivatives, made it seem likely that chromosome pairing was initiated in the heterochromatic regions with subsequent synapsis in the euchromatic regions.

1. Ring formation

Tandem metacentrics regularly generate ring chromosomes by crossing over. These rings are stable and do not seem to encounter the problems of intertwining and interlocking after replication, expressed by bridge formation at anaphase followed by loss from the daughter products, that one might reasonably expect of ring chromosomes, although Sandler (1965) has argued that they probably are lost to some degree. One TM studied by Pasztor (1971) produces unstable rings which are frequently lost at cell division. The unstable rings produced are similar in several respects to X^{c2}, w^{vC}, an X-ray-induced single ring analysed in detail by Hinton (1957). In particular, the source of the instability is located in or near the centric heterochromatin in both cases.

2. *Nonrandom disjunction*

Probably the most interesting meiotic phenomenon discovered through the study of the tandem metacentric compound chromosome is that of non-random disjunction (Novitski, 1951a, 1967). When two chromatids of unequal size are formed by crossing over within the tandem metacentric (see Fig. 3), the smaller chromatid is recovered with greater frequency than the long chromatid. The coefficient of non-randomness (c) is the probability of recovering the shorter chromatid when it separates from the longer at second anaphase. For the tandem metacentric, c is close to 1 if ring loss is taken into account (Lindsley and Sandler, 1965). The best

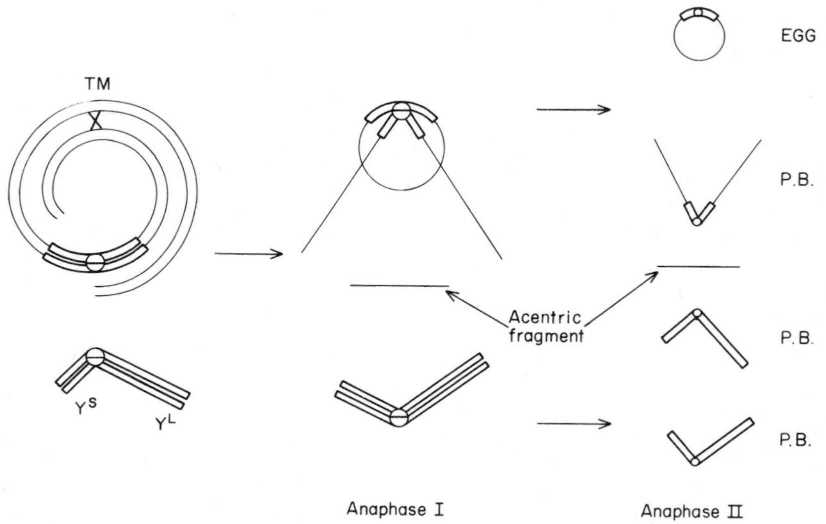

FIG. 3. Nonrandom disjunction. At first anaphase the TM separates from its homologue, the Y chromosome. The ring, which was generated by crossing over within the TM, is recovered more frequently in the functional egg nucleus. (Redrawn from Novitski, 1967.)

explanation for this non-random recovery is that the longer chromatid "drags", resulting in an orientation of the shorter chromatid toward the outer potential egg nucleus and placing the longer chromatid in one of the two inner polar bodies.

This phenomenon has also been observed in translocation heterozygotes (Zimmering, 1955), in rod chromosomes in situations in which asymmetrical dyads may be generated through crossing over (Novitski, 1951), in detachments of attached-X (RM) chromosomes (Lucchesi, 1965; Parker, 1954).

C. Reversed Acrocentric

The reversed acrocentric has the two arms of the X in reverse order with respect to each other and joined to a subterminal centromere. An exchange between the distal heterochromatin of an inverted X and the proximal heterochromatin of a normal X produces the RA (Fig. 4a; Novitski, 1954). Sandler (1954) observed that RA compounds were not recovered by this method unless Y^L was attached as a second arm to the normal X chromosome. This also appears to be the case for the synthesis of RA from RAG (Fig. 4b; Lindsley and Sandler, 1963). In addition, the RA shows a peculiar distribution of tetrads; there are very few single exchanges, and many double and no-exchange tetrads (Sandler, 1958). One of the most

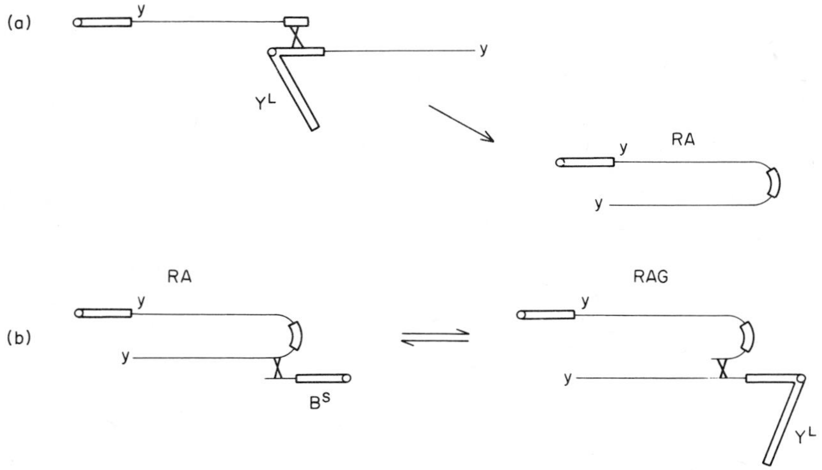

FIG. 4. (a) Synthesis of the reversed acrocentric from an exchange between the distal heterochromatin of an inverted X chromosome and the proximal heterochromatin of $X \cdot Y^L$. (b) The relationship between RA and the reversed metacentrigenic (RAG). (Redrawn from Lindsley and Sandler, 1963.)

commonly used reversed acrocentrics is that found accidentally by Muller (1943) and labelled *y f*:=.

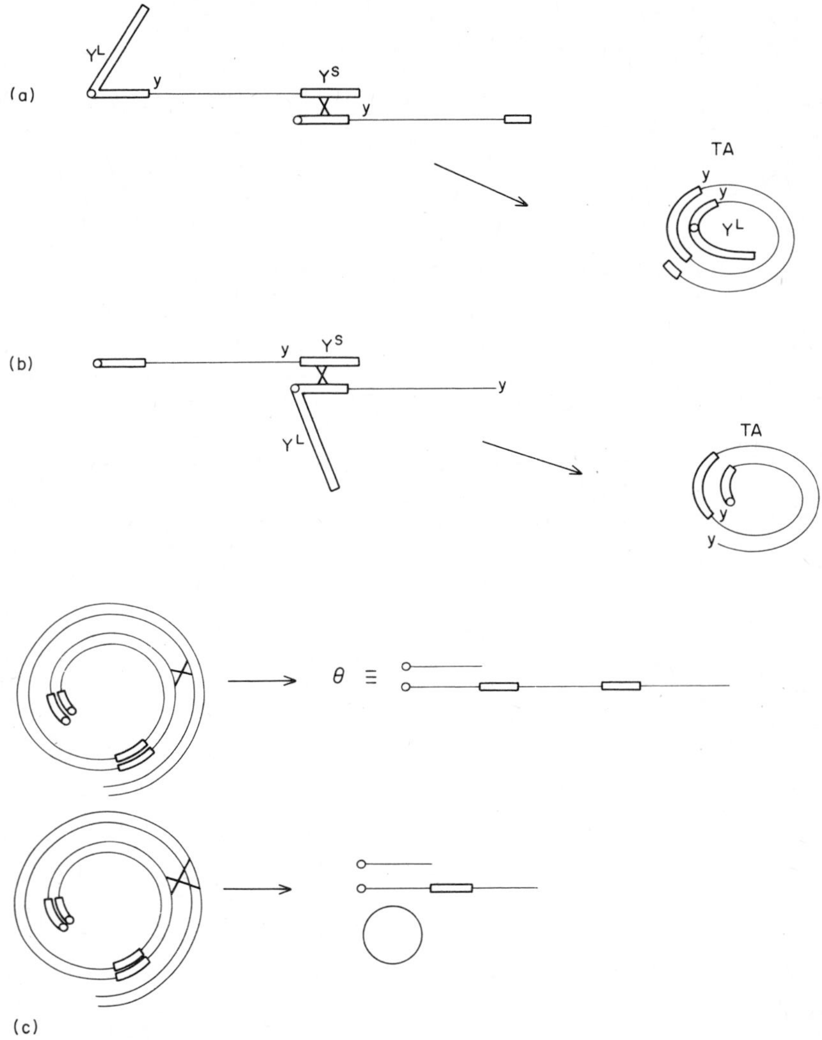

FIG. 5. Two methods of synthesis of the tandem acrocentric. (a) Exchange between the proximal heterochromatin of an inverted X and Y^S from an inverted attached X–Y chromosome ($Y^SX \cdot Y^L$) (Novitski, 1954). (b) Exchange between Y^S (XY^S) and the proximal heterochromatin of $X \cdot Y^L$ (Lindsley and Sandler, 1963). (c) Crossing over within a tandem acrocentric showing the production of three chromosomes in tandem in one case and an acentric ring in the other.

D. Tandem Acrocentric

The synthesis of the tandem acrocentric (Novitski, 1954) is shown in Fig. 5a, and a second method in Fig. 5b (Sandler and Lindsley, 1963). The TA has the two X chromosome arms connected in tandem and joined to a subterminal centromere. Besides generating single chromosomes after single exchange, the TA will also generate triple chromosomes. These have never been recovered experimentally. Since the data suggest that non-randomness is virtually completely in favor of the shorter chromosome over the TA, when the shorter is generated (i.e. $c = 1$) it seems reasonable that the short single generated at the same time as the long triple precludes the recovery of the triple.

E. Tandem Ring

The tandem ring was first synthesized by Novitski (1954) using the tandem acrocentric shown in Fig. 5a with the long arm of the Y replaced by the B^S duplication. Crossing over between the B^S segment and the most distal homologous region closes the ring (Fig. 6).

Crossing over within the tandem ring should give rise to single, double, and triple ring chromosomes, acentric rings and a number of different kinds of dicentrics. The behavior of the various kinds of dicentrics has

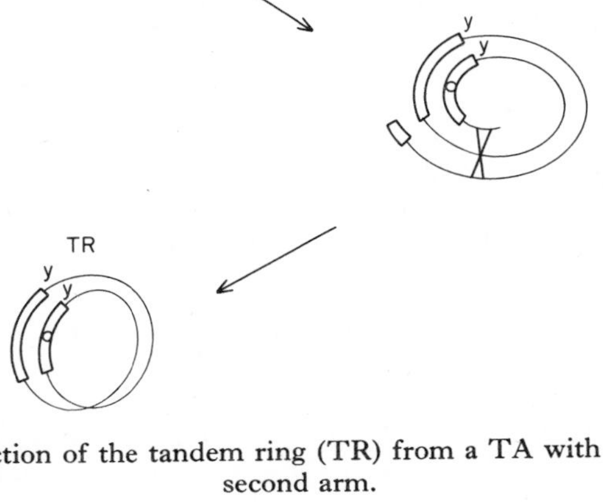

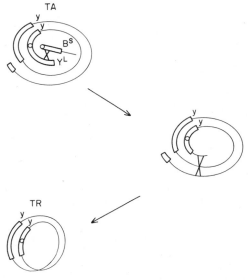

FIG. 6. Construction of the tandem ring (TR) from a TA with B^S attached as a second arm.

been interpreted in terms of centromere strength with relation to the lengths of the two strands connecting the centromeres (Novitski, 1955).

F. Reversed Ring

The recovery of the reversed ring was somewhat more fortuitous than that of the other X-chromosome compounds. Fig. 7 shows the probable events which led to the recovery of the reversed ring from the tandem ring (Novitski, 1954). The reversed ring may also be synthesized by using a

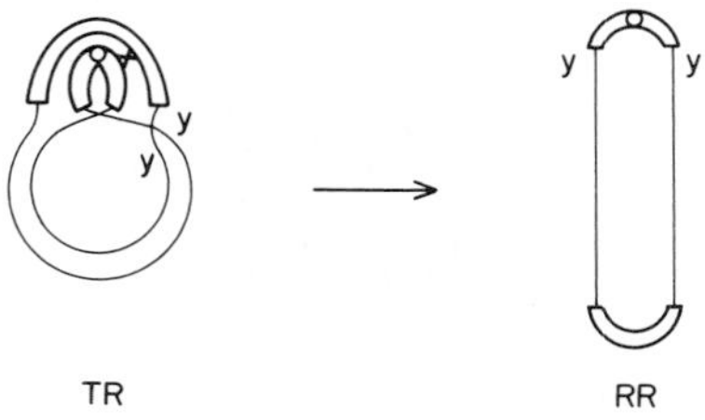

FIG. 7. Probable exchange event that led to the recovery of the reversed ring (RR) from the tandem ring (TR). (Redrawn from Novitski, 1954.)

reversed metacentric with heterochromatic regions at the distal tips (reversed ringigenic???). Exchange in these heterochromatic regions produces the closed ring (Sandler, 1957). Evaluation of crossing over within the RR shows that it has an abnormal tetrad distribution, similar to that observed for the RA (Sandler, 1957).

III. The Attached X–Y Combinations

A. Attached X–Y

It is possible to attach part or all of the Y chromosome to the X by breakage and reunion in the heterochromatic regions of these two chromosomes.

The first attached X–Y chromosome was synthesized by two consecutive exchanges between an opened out ring chromosome (*In(1)EN*) and the Y chromosome, placing Y^S distally and Y^L proximally (Fig. 8; Lindsley and Novitski, 1959). Because of the clear need for an X–Y chromosome in which the X segment is in normal rather than inverted order, variants of this chromosome were produced by irradiation, one of which was an X–Y chromosome in normal order (Novitski, 1951b). However, a simpler and more direct method of producing such X–Y chromosomes has been described by Parker (1954) by exchange between the Y chromosome and

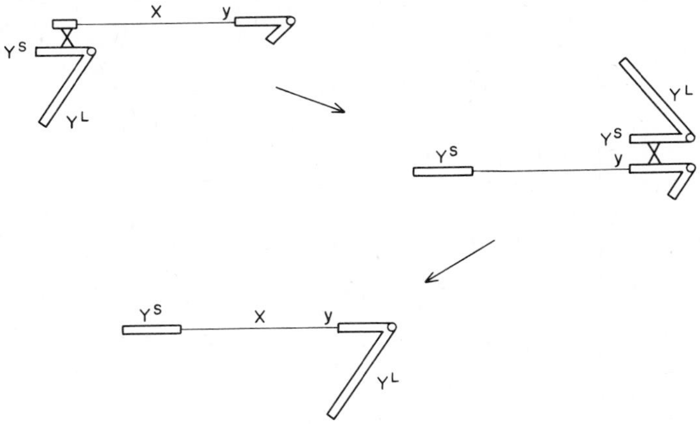

FIG. 8. Synthesis of the attached X–Y by X chromosome proximal and distal heterochromatic exchanges with the short arm of the Y chromosome. (Modified from Lindsley and Novitski, 1959.)

the heterochromatic region of a reversed metacentric. Either arm of the Y chromosome may be involved in the exchange, producing two different types of attached X–Y (Fig. 9).

1. Weak–strong centromere behavior at the first anaphase division in the female

In *Drosophila* females, the four meiotic products may be considered to be

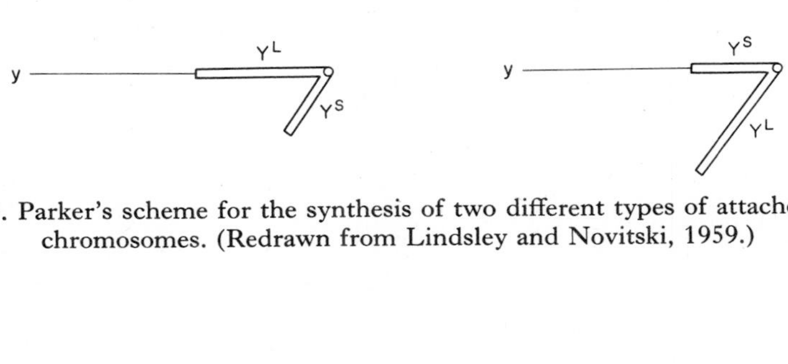

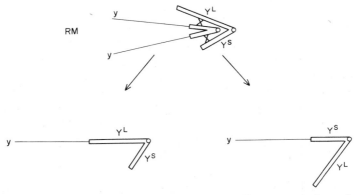

FIG. 9. Parker's scheme for the synthesis of two different types of attached X–Y chromosomes. (Redrawn from Lindsley and Novitski, 1959.)

linearly aligned, with one or the other of the two outermost products becoming the functional egg pronucleus. Bridges formed by four strand double crossing over within a heterozygous X chromosome inversion stall on the spindle at first anaphase, producing nullo-X gametes. These nullo-X eggs, when fertilized by X-bearing sperm, produce patroclinous males in a ratio of two for each three recovered double crossovers, a ratio that is the one theoretically expected (Sturtevant and Beadle, 1936). However, if one of the X chromosomes has the long arm of the Y attached proximally, nullo-X gametes are recovered only half as often (with relation to the doubles recovered) as when no Y chromosome is attached. The centromere associated with the long arm of the Y chromosome evidently pulls the dicentric resulting from crossing over within the heterozygous inversion to one of the outer nuclei, resulting in a chromosomal imbalance which kills the egg. If the long arm of the Y is appended proximally to both the X chromosomes, nullo-X gametes are recovered only rarely. This has been interpreted to indicate that an equal and opposite pull exerted by both centromeres at first anaphase results in fragmentation of the bridge, delivering lethal fragments to the potential egg nuclei (Novitski, 1952).

It has been determined that the strength of a centromere at meiosis is related to the adjacent heterochromatin (Lindsley and Novitski, 1958). As a general rule, those centromeres with the *bb* locus adjacent are strong when compared with X chromosome centromeres without attached-Y chromosome material. The use of compound autosomes (see Chapter 13) has made it possible to test the centromeres of the second chromosome; they behave as do the strong centromeres of the X-chromosome (Novitski, 1955).

2. *Weak–strong centromere behavior at second anaphase*

Females bearing $X \cdot Y^L$ chromosomes heterozygous for an inversion were used to demonstrate that the behavior of strong and weak centromeres at second anaphase is similar to that at first anaphase (Ptashne, 1960). Second anaphase bridges are formed by crossing over proximal to and within the inversion in the same tetrad. Since nullo-X gametes are not recovered from such heterozygotes, it is presumed that the bridges formed break at second anaphase, sending lethal fragments to the egg. When Y^L is not attached to the X chromosome, nullo-X gametes are recovered. Hence, it is concluded that the bridge stalls at second anaphase producing nullo-X eggs.

It is clear from this work on centromere strengths that the chromosomes are not just passively pulled to the poles at anaphase but they themselves make a detectable contribution to the division process.

B. Ring X–Y Compound Chromosome

Because of the obvious usefulness of a ring X–Y chromosome in certain kinds of irradiation experiments, and in serving as an X-chromosome balancer, attempts have been made by several investigators to derive such a chromosome. These efforts, which might be described as one-shot attempts, depended upon the fortuitous appearance of a ring X–Y after irradiation of a suitable precursor. In those cases in which the rings appeared, they lacked one or more fertility factors of the Y chromosome.

A scheme involving a number of steps was developed, such that at each stage it was possible to test for the presence of all the Y fertility factors. These steps are shown in Fig. 10. Basically, the problem is to attach a normal X to one Y arm, an inverted X to the other, each to be accomplished without the loss of Y fertility factors, after which the

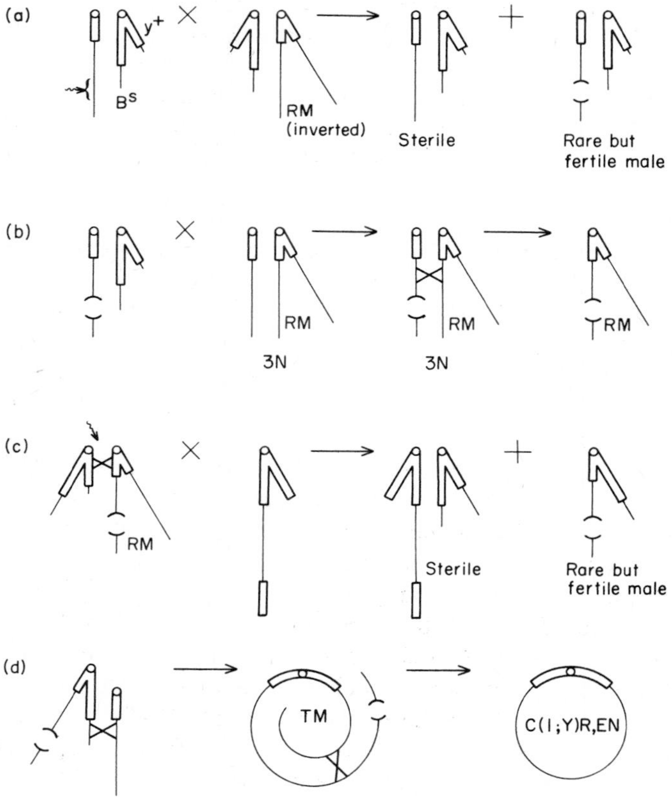

FIG. 10. Construction of the modified tandem metacentrigenic (TMG) which generates complete ring X–Y chromosomes.

compound so produced, a tandem metacentric, can then cross over to produce complete X and Y chromosomes joined together in a ring.

The Y chromosome to be used carries the B^S duplication, to be used later tandem metacentrigenically, and since this duplication sterilizes the male, it can be used in the male only if the X has a corresponding deficiency. Getting an inverted X chromosome with a deficiency such that a male with y^+ *YdupB*^{S} would be fertile is fairly simple (Fig. 10a). Males carrying a scute inversion and a normal Y chromosome were irradiated and mated to females with an attached-X and y^+ *YdupB*^{S}. From this mating, all F_1 males should be sterile, because of the presence of the B^S duplication, unless the F_1 male carried an X-ray-induced change, a deficiency for the region covered by the B^S duplication. Finding such changes, however rare, is very simple. All that needs to be done is to dump large numbers of F_1 together into bottles. Virtually all such cultures will be sterile and the occasional fertile bottle signals the desired event. A number of such deficiencies have been derived by this method.

The next series of steps involves putting the deficiency on an inverted attached-X. This was done (Fig. 10b) by mating males carrying one of the induced deficiencies (as well as y^+ *YdupB*^{S}) to 3N females with an inverted attached-X. In the F_1 triploids, a crossover between that compound and the deficient chromosome moved the deficiency to the compound, which was then recovered in diploid progeny.

Deficiency-bearing compound females with y^+ *YdupB*^{S} were irradiated to increase the frequency of detachment by which the deficient arm of the compound would be hooked onto the complete Y chromosome, the latter losing y^+ but retaining the B^S duplication. The requirements for this event, that the arm of the compound involved be the deficient and not the normal arm, that y^+ be lost from the Y and not B^S, and that the detachment involves the Y at precisely the right point so that no fertility factors are lost, all suggest a difficult-to-detect low frequency event. However, if such parental females are mated to X–Y males, all regular progeny will be sterile and only a few rare exceptional classes of males will be fertile, one of those being the desired type (Fig. 10c). Once again F_1 progeny may be dumped in quantity into culture bottles, virtually all of which will eventually prove to be completely sterile, with the few fertile ones yielding the detachment shown at the right of Fig. 10c.

Females with this detachment and an X in normal sequence can now, by ordinary crossing over in the B^S region, produce a TM with a complete Y chromosome, easily identified as an apparent non-disjunctional F_1 exception, but without the *B* marker. A female carrying such a TM mated to X–Y/0 males will produce male progeny which prove to be fertile, and which carry a ring chromosome. As every person who has examined

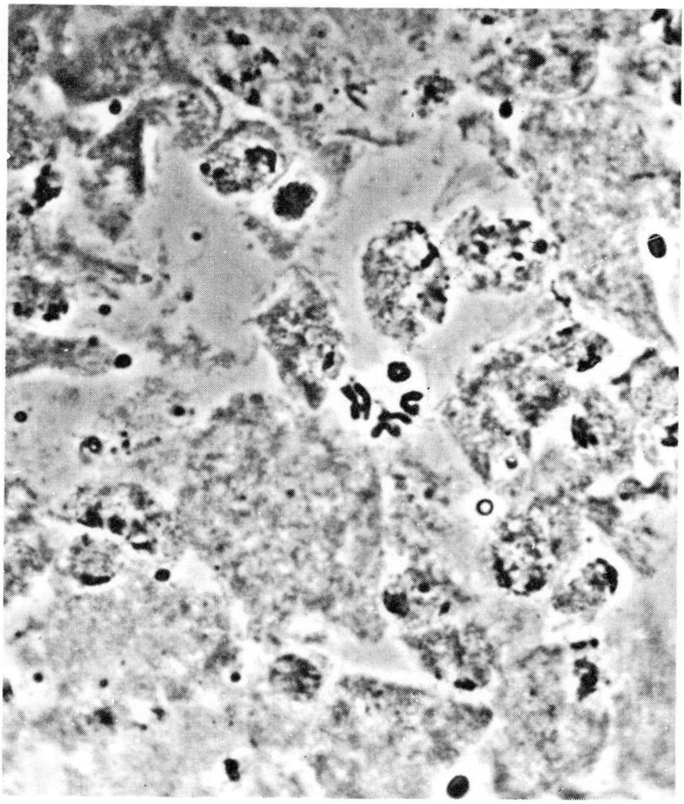

FIG. 11. Compound Ring X–Y chromosome (*C(1; Y)R, EN*) in a neuroblast cell.

X-chromosome variants in neuroblast cells knows, chromosomes with distal heterochromatin simulate rings in appearance (and rings often appear not to be rings!) so that the ring conformation seen in Fig. 11 must be verified genetically. This is done, first, by making heterozygotes of the ring with both normal and inverted chromosomes, and showing that only doubles are recovered in each case, a behavior which only a ring will show, and, second, by showing that the frequency of double crossovers recovered is only a third as great for the ring as for the rod chromosome (Novitski, 1952). From these tests we conclude that the derived chromosome is indeed a ring, viable and fertile in the male, without any additional X- or Y-chromosome material. Following standard practice, this chromosome is labelled *C(1; Y)R, EN*, that is, a compound (C) involving the X and Y chromosomes (1;Y), in ring conformation (R) and involving the entire (EN) essential components of each chromosome.

References

BROSSEAU, G. E. (Jr.) (1964). Non-randomness in the recovery of detachments from the reversed metacentric compound X in *D. melanogaster*. *Can. J. Genet. Cytol.* **6,** 201–206.

HINTON, C. W. (1957). An analysis of rod derivatives of an unstable ring chromosome of *D. melanogaster*. *Genetics* **42,** 55–65.

LINDSLEY, D. L. and NOVITSKI, E. (1958). Localization of the genetic factors responsible for the kinetic activity of X chromosomes of *D. melanogaster*. *Genetics* **43,** 790–798.

LINDSLEY, D. L. and NOVITSKI, E. (1959). Compound chromosomes involving the X and Y chromosomes of *D. melanogaster*. *Genetics* **44,** 187–196.

LINDSLEY, D. L. and SANDLER, L. (1963). Construction of the compound X chromosomes in *D. melanogaster* by means of the Bar Stone duplication. *In*: "Methodology in Basic Genetics" (Burdette, W. J., Ed.), pp. 390–403. Holden-Day, San Francisco.

LINDSLEY, D. L. and SANDLER, L. (1965). Meiotic behavior of tandem metacentric compound X chromosomes in *D. melanogaster*. *Genetics* **51,** 223–245.

LUCCHESI, J. C. (1965). The nature of induced exchanges between the attached X and Y chromosomes in *D. melanogaster* females. *Genetics* **51,** 209–216.

MULLER, H. J. (1936). Insertion of desired genes into attached X's. *Dros. Inf. Serv.* **6,** 8.

MULLER, H. J. (1943). A stable double X chromosome. *Dros. Inf. Serv.* **17,** 61.

NOVITSKI, E. (1951a). Non-random disjunction in *Drosophila*. *Genetics* **36,** 267–280.

NOVITSKI, E. (1951b). Useful derivatives of the X·Y chromosome. *Dros. Inf. Serv.* **25,** 122.

NOVITSKI, E. (1952). The genetic consequences of anaphase bridge formation in *Drosophila*. *Genetics* **37,** 270–287.

NOVITSKI, E. (1954). The compound X chromosomes in *Drosophila*. *Genetics* **39,** 127–140.

NOVITSKI, E. (1955). Genetic measures of centromere activity in *D. melanogaster Symposium on Genetic Recombination*, 1954. *J. cell. comp. Physiol.* **45,** Suppl. 2, 151–169.

NOVITSKI, E. (1967). Nonrandom disjunction in *Drosophila*. *Ann. Rev. Genet.* **1,** 71–86.

NOVITSKI, E. (1972). Strengths of autosomal centromeres. *Dros. Inf. Serv.* **49,** 61.

NOVITSKI, E. and BRAVER, G. (1954). An analysis of crossing over with a heterozygous inversion in *D. melanogaster*. *Genetics* **39,** 197–209.

NOVITSKI, E. and LINDSLEY, D. L. (1950). Construction of tandemly attached X chromosomes. *Dros. Inf. Serv.* **24,** 90.

PARKER, D. R. (1954). Role of the Y chromosome in induced detachment of attached X chromosomes in *D. melanogaster* (Abstr.). *Rec. Genet. Soc. Am.* **23,** 59, and *Genetics* **39,** 985.

PARKER, D. R. and MCCRONE, J. (1958). A genetic analysis of some rearrangements induced in oocytes of *Drosophila*. *Genetics* **43,** 172–186.

PASZTOR, L. M. (1971). Unstable ring-X chromosomes derived from a tandem metacentric compound in *D. melanogaster*. *Genetics* **68,** 245–258.

PTASHNE, M. (1960). The behavior of strong and weak centromeres at second anaphase of *D. melanogaster*. *Genetics* **45,** 499–506.

SANDLER, L. (1957). The meiotic behavior of reversed compound ring X chromosomes in *D. melanogaster*. *Genetics* **42,** 764–782.

SANDLER, L. (1965). The meiotic mechanics of ring chromosomes in female *D. melanogaster*. *Nat. Cancer Instit. Monogr.* **18,** 243–273.

STURTEVANT, A. H. and BEADLE, G. W. (1936). The relations of inversions in the X chromosome of *D. melanogaster* to crossing-over and disjunction. *Genetics* **21,** 554–604.

ZIMMERING, S. (1955). A genetic study of segregation in a translocation heterozygote in *Drosophila*. *Genetics* **40,** 809–825.

12. Ring Chromosomes and Radiation Induced Chromosome Loss

B. LEIGH

Department of Radiation Genetics and Chemical Mutagenesis
and *J. A. Cohen Institute of Radiopathology and Radiation Protection*
University of Leiden, Leiden, The Netherlands

I. Introduction

Ring X-chromosomes do not occur in wild populations of *Drosophila*, but they can be maintained in laboratory stocks. *R(1)1* (formerly X^{C1}) was discovered in 1922 and since then several ring X-chromosomes have been found and constructed. They are interesting because their spontaneous behaviour and response to radiation differ from rod X-chromosomes. Hypotheses about chromosome behaviour, in many cases, will lead to different expectations when applied to rod or ring chromosomes. Such hypotheses can then be tested by comparing the expectations with experimental data. It is also possible to work in the other direction and inquire whether an observed peculiarity associated with ring chromosomes is a more general property of all chromosomes, but which had not been identified earlier. Some aspects of ring chromosomes behaviour have been explained but others are only partially understood.

Many of the properties of ring X-chromosomes were described by L. V. Morgan (1933) in her detailed report on the first ring chromosome, *R(1)1*. This was isolated as a spontaneous product from a *C(1)RM,y* female. Heterozygous *ring/rod* females gave progenies with many X0 males and gynandromorphs. In a cross-over test, markers as far apart as *y* (0·0) and *f* (56·7) appeared to be closely linked. Cytological examination by Dobzhansky (see L. V. Morgan, 1933) showed that the new chromosome was a closed ring. No single cross-over products were recovered from ring/rod females and double cross-over rods were more than twice as frequent as double cross-over rings. In this paper, Mrs. Morgan also reports the first spontaneous opening of the ring to give a normal sequence rod X-chromosome.

The purpose of this chapter is to review what is known about ring chromosomes. During the preparatory work, the author found himself being drawn into a detailed consideration of the mechanisms of ring and rod chromosome loss induced by irradiation of male germ cells. This subject is covered briefly in the context of radiation genetics (Sankaranarayanan and Sobels, Chapter 26) and will be expanded here.

II. Origin and Structure

R(1)1 and *R(1)2* (formerly X^{C2}) both arose as spontaneous products of different reversed metacentric attached X chromosomes. These are generally described as stable ring chromosomes because they can be kept without much difficulty and also because they do not produce mosaics with a high enough frequency to warrant their being referred to as unstable. *R(1)2* has been used in more investigations because it is the more viable of the two chromosomes. Schultz and Catcheside (1938) described both of these chromosomes as having a duplication of the proximal region and a deficiency of the distal region of the X: *R(1)1* has a duplication for 20C–20D and is deficient for 1A, *R(1)2* has a duplication of all of section 20 and a deficiency for 1A1–1A*3*. Viinikka *et al.* (1971) found a great variation in the banding pattern of the proximal and distal centric regions of the salivary chromosomes of *R(1)2*. They were less positive than Schultz and Catcheside about the identification of the mirror-image duplication of section 20. Even the presence of a nucleolus-organizing region in both the proximal and distal members of the duplication appears to be open to question.

There are several known variants of the *R(1)2* chromosome. Hannah-Alava (personal communication) points out that any stock may become heterogeneous for different rings if unequal double crossing-over, between chromatids or between chromosomes, can occur in the centric region of the ring. The only limitation is that deficiencies should be covered by homologous regions in either the ring-X or in the Y-chromosome. Indeed, Hannah-Alava (unpublished observations) found that some rings derived from a common stock had different sized heteropycnotic blocks. It is clear that *R(1)2* chromosomes, although derived from one isolate, have "evolved" into a series of chromosomes. In practice, this means that the designation—*R(1)2*—does not provide a full description of any particular chromosome. The original *R(1)2* carried y^+ and was viable as an X0 male. An *R(1)2, y B* used by Ostertag (1963) and Leigh (1969) was not viable either as an X0 male or as a homozygous female. Females, heterozygous for this *R(1)2, y B* and a rod X-chromosome carrying $In(1)B^{M1}$, *bb*, have a bobbed phenotype (Schalet, unpublished observations). This ring is not deficient for the pairing site operative in males (Lindsley and Sandler, 1958) because segregation from the Y occurs regularly. Falk (1974) has described an *R(1)2, y f* which is viable in X0 males and homozygous females. No duplication of section 20 could be seen in the salivary chromosomes. One of the best known derivatives of *R(1)2* is $R(1)2, In\text{-}w^{vC}$ (Inversion white variegated of Catcheside). This is the first unstable ring chromosome which has been studied in detail (Hinton, 1955). Its usefulness is discussed by Hall *et al.* (Chapter 6). The history of $R(1)2, In\text{-}w^{vC}$ is very interesting (Novitski, personal communication). It has a radiation induced inversion and comes from the experiments of Catcheside and Lea (1945). It was soon used in the elementary biology course in Texas, for demonstrating gynandromorphs (half X0/half XX mosaics). Griffen and Lindsley (1946) describe the instability as frequent elimination during the cleavage mitoses and suggest that this might be useful for the study of sex-linked genes. Novitski obtained some of this stock and sent sub-cultures to several laboratories. Within a few years most of these stocks had stabilized, they no longer produced high frequencies of gynandromorphs. Novitski recovered an unstable line from Cornell and by careful selection has been able to maintain it for more than 20 years.

Single ring X-chromosomes are recovered as cross-over products from compound tandem metacentric (attached) X-chromosomes. Siderov *et al.* (1935, 1936), Sturtevant and Beadle (1936), and Muller (1944) were able to obtain single ring X-chromosomes in this way. All of these rings, however, were deficient for the distal region of the X up to and including *ac*. They were lethal in males unless the Y chromosome carried sc^8 or a similar duplication.

To construct a *C(1)TM* which will give single rings with good viability, it is necessary to start either with a ring chromosome or an inversion which has its distal break very close to the tip of the X chromosome. The inversion always used is *In(1)EN*, which is an opened out *R(1)1* (Novitski,

1949). A single cross-over between this chromosome and *In(1)sc*^{8} gives *In(1)sc*^{8L}–*EN*^{R}, which has the free distal end of *In(1)sc*^{8} marked with y^{+} and the centromeric end of *In(1)EN* marked with *y*. It also has a large block of heterochromatin at the distal end and another on the right arm. This makes it an ideal chromosome for building onto and it has been used to construct the $Y^{S}EN.Y^{L}$, $Y^{S}X.Y^{L}$, *C(1)TM*, and *C(1)TMB*^{S} chromosomes (Novitski and Lindsley, 1950; Lindsley and Novitski, 1959; Lindsley and Sandler, 1965). The last two types of chromosome give single rings as regular products of exchange. Novitski and Lindsley (1950) obtained a *C(1)TM* as a double cross-over product from a triploid female which carried a normal order rod X-chromosome, an *R(1)2*, and a rod X with a scute-type inversion (they used *In(1)sc*^{8L}–*EN*^{R}). A *C(1)TM* obtained in this way will consistently produce single rings which are structurally identical to the *R(1)* carried by the triploid female.

Compound tandem ring X's also generate single rings by crossing over (Novitski, 1954; Sandler and Lindsley, 1967). The heterochromatic content of the single ring derivatives of *C(1)TM*'s and *C(1)TR*'s is dependent on the composition of the centric heterochromatin of the parental compound chromosome. In at least one case (Pasztor, 1971), a *C(1)TM* consistently produces an unstable single ring—*R(1)5A*.

III. Behaviour

A. Somatic Tissues

Braver and Blount (1949), Hinton (1955), and Brosseau (1966) have examined brain preparations from larvae with stable and unstable ring chromosomes. Braver and Blount (1949) and Brosseau (1966) found interlocking rings and double dicentrics, while Hinton (1955) found clear examples of double dicentrics but no unequivocal figures of interlocking rings. As Hinton noted, this discrepancy may be due to the cytological techniques which were available. There were, however, also large differences in the frequencies of bridges recorded in the three investigations. Braver and Blount found 12% and 22% bridge configurations in the ganglion cells of *R(1)2/In(1)dl–49* and *R(1)2, In-w*^{vC}*/In(1)dl–49* females, respectively. Hinton found bridges in 10·1% of the ganglion cells of *R(1)2, In-w*^{vC} larvae and only 1·6% in material with a stabilized derivative of this chromosome. Brosseau observed 6% and 3% anaphases with bridge configurations in ganglia from *R(1)2, In-w*^{vC}*/In(1)dl–49* and *R(1)2/In(1)dl–49* females. A significant observation of Brosseau's is that the frequency of bridges in the neural ganglion cells is significantly increased when *R(1)2* males are mated to aged females. The discrepancies between the three sets of data may have several causes, including differences between ring chromosomes which are formally identical, different female stocks, and the age of the females to which the ring X males were mated.

All three reports agree that there was no obvious correlation between anaphase bridge formation and chromosome loss. Oster and Balaban (1962) report an increase in the frequency of bridge formation when larvae with ring X-chromosomes are exposed to radiation.

Ostertag (1963) extended a series of experiments first carried out by Muller and Oster (for references see Ostertag, 1963) on the killing of larvae by exposure to radiation. He irradiated third instar larvae and found that heterozygous *R(1)2*/rod X females are no more sensitive than homozygous rod X/rod X females. This, however, was changed when the female larvae were heterozygous for *R(1)2* and either of two rod X chromosomes which carried hemizygous lethal deficiencies. Such females are as sensitive as *R(1)2*/Y males. This evidence indicates that radiation causes loss of ring X-chromosomes in somatic tissue, but somatic cell lethality is not a direct consequence of this loss.

Somatic mosaicism may result from chromosome loss during cleavage divisions and will appear as a gynandromorph. This type of mosaicism will be discussed in the context of behaviour of ring X-chromosomes during zygote formation. Another type of mosaicism results from somatic crossing-over (Stern, 1936).

Mosaic spots, on ring X/rod X females, are produced through somatic crossing over and chromosome loss. They are not affected by maternal ageing (Brown and Welshons, 1955) and are smaller and more frequent than in homozygous rod X females (Stern, 1936; Brown and Welshons, 1955; Brown *et al.*, 1962). By using different combinations of markers, Brown *et al.* (1962) were able to estimate that about 60% of the small spots are a consequence of ring X-chromosome loss. Nevertheless, somatic crossing over accounts for five times as many spots on ring X/rod X females compared to homozygous rod X females. A probable explanation, suggested by Brown *et al.* (1962), is that somatic crossing over occurs at a later stage in heterozygous females. This temporal shift would be observed as a larger number of smaller spots. Walen (1964) has shown that the frequency of somatic crossing over is directly correlated to the heterochromatic content of the chromosomes involved, irrespective of whether these are ring or rod shaped.

There is an interesting discrepancy between the observations of Brown and Welshons (1955) and Brosseau (1966). The former found no effect of maternal ageing on small spot mosaicism and the latter found a significant maternal ageing effect on the frequency of dicentrics in neural ganglion cells. These are both late somatic effects, but one is in adult tissue and the other is in larval tissue. There may, however, be other reasons for the different response to maternal ageing.

B. Germ Line

All ring chromosomes are remarkably stable during the mitotic divisions in both the male and female germ lines.

During meiosis in males there is no crossing-over and no evidence to indicate that ring chromosomes have any peculiar problems. In a cytological study, of meiotic second division figures, Welshons and Hinton (1955) found bridges in 3·6% and 17·3% of the X-bearing cells in *R*(*1*)*2*/Y and *R*(*1*)*2*, *In-w*^{vC}/Y males, respectively. Some of the bridges could be identified as double dicentrics.

Ring X-chromosomes can open out in males and this probably results from exchange with the Y chromosome (Novitski, 1949; Muller, 1956). The rate of opening is very low (Hannah-Alava, personal communication), but opened rings are generally more viable than the parent chromosome. Hannah-Alava (personal communication) found that ring X chromosomes opened most frequently when kept in a stock as *R*(*1*)*2*/*R*(*1*)*2* females and *R*(*1*)*2*/Y males. The rate of opening was much lower when the rings were kept balanced over an attached X-chromosome or a doubly inverted chromosome such as *Basc*. This means that ring X chromosome stocks have to be checked periodically. Some opened rings may carry an entire arm of the Y chromosome, for example *In*(*1*)*EN2* has Y^S on the right arm (Muller, unpublished observations).

There are three ways of looking at ring X-chromosome behaviour during meiosis in females; firstly, to study the crossing-over relationships and stability of known rings, secondly, to investigate the behaviour of newly generated rings, and thirdly, to ask whether rings affect the meiotic process.

The first ring X-chromosome was noticed because of the unusual composition of the cross-over products from *R*(*1*)*1*/rod-X females (L. V. Morgan, 1933). Not only were there no single cross-overs, but the reciprocal double cross-over products were not recovered in equal frequencies. L. V. Morgan (1933) and Sturtevant and Beadle (1936) assumed that the inequality of classes was caused by viability differences. The explanation, however, was contained in Figure 7 of Sturtevant and Beadle's 1936 paper. This was shown by Novitski (1952a) who substituted a ring for the inversion and obtained the figure which is reproduced here (Fig. 1).

The origin of the double cross-over chromatids can be seen in the second and third lines of Fig. 1. The two-strand double cross-overs will yield equal numbers of double cross-over rings and rods. One of the two

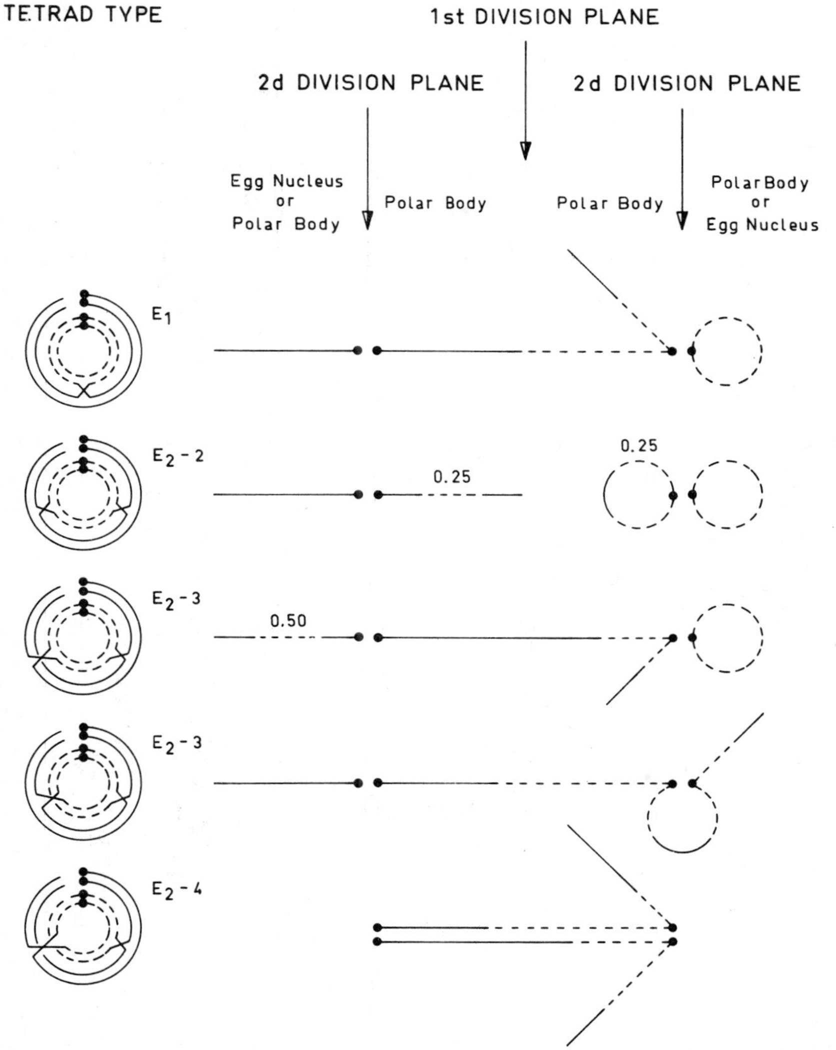

FIG. 1. The consequences of single and double crossing-over between a ring X and a rod X chromosome (after Novitski, 1952a). The probability of recovery in the egg nucleus is shown above each double cross-over chromatid.

types of three-strand-double crossing-over will yield double cross-over rods, but the other type will not yield double cross-over rings. The probability of recovery in the maternal gamete is shown above each double cross-over chromatid. Assuming that all types of double crossing over occur at the same frequency, these probabilities can be added together and it will be seen that there is an expected ratio of three double cross-over rods to one double cross-over ring. L. V. Morgan (1933), Novitski (1952a), and Sandler (1965) all found a ratio of 3·4:1 (Sandler, 1965, Table 7). This is very close to the expected value and the discrepancy may result from the higher rate of loss and the lower viability of the double cross-over rings.

The genetic test for a ring chromosome consists of making it heterozygous with a normal order chromosome on the one hand and an inverted chromosome on the other hand, both amply marked (particularly at the ends) in order to detect all, or virtually all, cross-overs. A ring chromosome will behave like an inversion in that the terminal markers appear to be linked in tests both with a normal and an inverted chromosome. Furthermore, as just mentioned, the ratio of cross-overs carrying the rod chromosomes to those carrying the presumptive ring will be about 3:1. However, if the ring has opened up, single cross-overs will appear in one of the two kinds of test, indicating the polarity of the new rod chromosome, and the ratio of recovered double cross-overs in the other test will be simply 1:1.

In addition to the increased frequency of opening out of the *R(1)2* chromosome in homozygous females (Hannah-Alava, personal communication), there are other peculiarities associated with ring chromosomes when in the homozygous state. L. V. Morgan (1933), Battacharya (1950), and Sandler (1965) found very high frequencies of patroclinous X0 males in the progenies of such females. This might be expected because crossing-over will tie the rings up into dicentrics. Battacharya, however, also noted high frequencies of gynandromorphs and it is therefore possible that much of the complete loss is post-meiotic.

Male-like triploids (intersexes) occurred at a rate of 5 in 24,000 in the progeny of homozygous *R(1)2,rb* females (Battacharya, 1950).

Single ring X-chromosomes affect crossing over on the third chromosome (Suzuki, 1962). *C(1)TM/0* and *C(1)TA/0*, however, caused a similar pattern of interference.

Fewer than expected ring X bearing progeny are recovered from heterozygous ring X/rod X females when either crossing over is suppressed by homozygosity for *c(3)G* (Sandler, 1965) or when females are *R(1)2/FM7* and homozygous for *mei-S332*, which causes precocious separation of sister centromeres (Sandler *et al.*, 1974). In the latter case, an analysis of the data indicated that the deficit is caused by dominant lethality and not chromosome loss.

The recovery of single ring cross-over products from a *C(1)TM* did not appear to be affected by homozygosity for *mei-S332* (Sandler *et al.*, 1974). When *C(1)TM* and *C(1)TR* females carry either a Y-chromosome or $y^+ Y^L$ there is an enhanced recovery of single rings in their progeny (Novitski and Sandler, 1956; Lindsley and Sandler, 1965; Sandler and Lindsley, 1967).

Sister strand crossing over has been considered as a process which may occur in *D. melanogaster*. When such exchanges occur in ring chromosomes, bridges will be produced at the second meiotic division and this will be expressed as a deficiency of ring bearing progeny (L. V. Morgan, 1933). To increase the probability of detecting such an effect, Mrs. Morgan compared the ratios of ring and rod X-bearing progeny from females which were heterozygous for *R(1)1* and either a normal rod X or *In(1)dl–49*. The ratio of non-cross-over ring and rod X-chromosomes was similar in the progeny of both types of female. Novitski (1955) repeated this experiment with *In(1)AB* and reached the same conclusion, that sister strand crossing over does not occur in the single ring X-chromosomes.

Green (1967) tested the possibility that the high mutability of white-crimson (w^c) might be associated with some kind of exchange between sister chromatids. He compared the rates of mutation in the progeny of *R(1)2*, w^c *spl f/X*, *y* w^c females. In a total progeny of about 35,000, there were 15 ring and 10 rod X-chromosomes with mutants of w^c. Sister strand exchange would have reduced the frequency of recoverable mutants in the ring X-chromosome. From the data obtained, this can be excluded as a possible mechanism causing mutation at w^c.

The data obtained from a study of females which carried tandem compound ring X-chromosomes could not be interpreted as being inconsistent with sister strand exchange (Novitski, 1955). Sandler (1957) studied crossing over in reversed compound ring X-chromosomes. He concluded that either sister strand crossing over does not occur or its occurrence is virtually undetectable.

C. Zygote Formation

Griffen and Lindsley (1946) state that unstable ring chromosomes are lost during the early cleavage divisions. Giesel (1968) scored the proportion of gynandromorphs which showed male tissue in a specific small area, such as the left foreleg. She found this in approximately half (0·47) of the gynandromorphs and concluded that the loss occurs in one of the first two cleavage nuclei. Similar observations are reported by Hall *et al.* (Chapter 6).

Hinton (1959) made a cytological study of embryos which had developed to between the third and eighth cleavage before being fixed. He found higher frequencies of anaphase bridges when the parental matings had involved either *R(1)2,In-*w^{vC} or an unstable rod derivative than when one of the parents carried *R(1)2* or a stable derivative of the unstable ring. In the *R(1)2,In-*w^{vC} material a relatively high number of embryos had one or two division figures with bridges, and a few embryos had many bridges. Both unstable chromosomes, the ring and the rod, were associated with embryonic nuclei showing gross anomalies—pycnosis, chromosome fragmentation, increased amounts of chromatin, and tripolar spindles. These nuclei were intermingled with normal nuclei and their frequency decreased with successive cleavage divisions. Hinton interprets the observation of a few embryos with many bridges as evidence of bridge-breakage-fusion cycles. It is, however, unlikely that the bridges seen by Hinton were in embryos which would have developed into X0 males or gynandromorphs. These would presumably have shown bridges during the first and second cleavage divisions and very rarely during the third division. One or two bridge-breakage-fusion cycles might give rise to the free duplications, *Dp(1:f)R*, which Hinton (1954) found as spontaneous derivatives of *R(1)2,In-*w^{vC} in the male tissue of gynandromorphs and X0 males. Five fragments were recovered in attached-X females and these are the ones which were analysed and found to be small unstable rings. Such fragments, arising spontaneously, have not yet been recovered from *R(1)5A* or the stable rings but this may be because they are rare and only detectable with the proper markers.

Brown and Hannah (1952) found an increase in the frequency of gynandromorphs when *R(1)2* males are mated to aged females. Hannah (1955) lists 12 factors which affect the frequencies of gynandromorphs, X0 males, and sex ratio shift. These include paternal age and maternal age, genotype, and nourishment. The stable ring *R(1)2* becomes unstable when introduced into an aged oocyte environment. Maternal ageing and irradiation of ring X males are two treatments which increase the frequencies of X0 males and decrease the frequencies of ring X bearing female progeny (Oster and Sobels, 1956), but the relationship between gynandromorph induction and radiation is not as clearly established as it is with maternal ageing (Leigh, 1969).

The mechanics of ring X-chromosome loss will be discussed later, but it will be assumed that the initiating event is chromosome breakage. The evidence cited above can be interpreted as indicating that ring X-chromosomes tend to break in the time interval between gamete formation and the first cleavage division. Unstable rings, and the unstable rods derived from them, have a higher probability of breaking at this time. This probability is also dependent on maternal age and genotype (Brown and Hannah, 1952). The effect of paternal age is more complicated (Hannah, 1955) and may in part be dependent on the amount of sperm transferred or differential sperm utilization.

Muller (1940) expounded the idea that chromosome breaks, induced by irradiation of mature sperm, are replicated to become double chromatid breaks before joining takes place. Novitski (1963a) interpreted data, from an experiment on induced loss and partial loss of a Y chromosome, as providing an indication that some individuals might be derived from only one of the first two cleavage nuclei. Leigh and Sobels (1970) combined both of these ideas to explain the origin of compound autosomes induced by irradiation of mature sperm. The change in radiosensitivity of the male pronucleus (Würgler and Ulrich, Chapter 28) may be related to the chromosomal replication. If this interpretation is correct, there must be a chromosomal replication in both the maternal and paternal pronuclei. These nuclei remain separate, although close to each other (Sonnenblick, 1950), and the nuclear membranes dissolve at the start of the first cleavage prophase (Dävring and Sunner, 1973). Thus the pronuclei are *haploid* when the chromosomes replicate. All other chromosome replications occur in *diploid* nuclei.

From the behaviour of free duplications derived from $R(1)2,In\text{-}w^{vC}$ (Hinton, 1955) and by replacement of different regions of *R(1)5A* (Pasztor, 1971), it has been shown that the loci of instability of both of these chromosomes are located in the centric heterochromatin. They presumably interfere with the pronuclear replication, causing the unstable ring to break. This may be an effect of the arrangement of the heterochromatic material, being analogous to position effect. On the other hand, it may be an expression of a duplication or partial deficiency of a specific segment of heterochromatin. All of these alterations could be "corrected" by unequal crossing-over.

There are no positively identified dicentric chromosomes in *Drosophila*. Instability, however, might result from 2 closely linked centromeres (Novitski, personal communication). These would usually act in harmony, but might have a high probability of being directed to opposite poles at the pronuclear division. Spontaneous stabilization would result from inactivation or loss of either centromere. This hypothesis explains why such chromosomes have arisen so rarely (only twice), after irradiation, and both in combination with ring chromosomes.

This hypothesis does not explain why stable rings become unstable when introduced into aged oocyte cytoplasm. It is also possible that many induced "unstable" chromosomes have not been recognized. The unstable rod derivatives of $R(1)2,In\text{-}w^{vC}$ cause dominant lethality but no chromosome loss. Such chromosomes, from a different origin, might easily be described as "having poor viability". Identification of the instability would depend on a cytological analysis of early embryos, neural ganglia, or spermatocytes.

IV. Radiation Genetics

A. Females

Parker and Williamson (Chapter 27) discuss the details of aberration induction in oocytes. Many complications are added by introducing a ring chromosome into such a system. It is not surprising, therefore, that few studies have been made on the effects of radiation on ring X bearing females. Fabergé (1952) and King *et al.* (1956) irradiated heterozygous ring/rod females and found increases in the frequencies of dominant lethality and X-chromosome loss.

B. Males; Mature germ Cell Stages

When ring X bearing males are irradiated and mature germ cells are sampled, the frequencies of sex chromosome loss and deficiencies of female progeny are significantly higher than when rod X bearing males are similarly treated. Bauer (1939, 1942) put forward the hypothesis that chromosome breakage may be followed by torsion of the chromatids (twisting through 180° or 360°) before joining of the broken ends. This will not change the structure of a rod chromosome but, at the next centromere division, a ring chromosome will become either a double dicentric bridge or two interlocked single rings (Fig. 2). Muller (1940) pointed out that breakage might be followed by sister-chromatid union. A broken rod chromosome, at the next division, would form a single-chromatid dicentric bridge and an acentric fragment. These could result in either chromosome loss or dominant lethality. Sister-chromatid fusion in a broken ring will result in the production of a dicentric double-chromatid bridge. Catcheside and Lea (1945), Baker (1957), and Hinton (1959) have described models based on these ideas. One version of the ring breakage model is shown in Fig. 2. It is assumed there is only one break in the ring chromosome, that this becomes a double chromatid break, and that pair-wise rejoining occurs between the four open chromatid ends. Interpretation of the consequences of bridge formation are based on ideas put forward by Novitski (1955).

Restitution will restore the original configuration and the chromosome will behave as though it had not been broken.

Chromatid fusion will lead to the production of an asymmetrical dicentric double-chromatid bridge. The difference between the lengths of the two arms will depend on the position of the break relative to the centromere. When this difference is significant such a bridge will effectively be two single-chromatid bridges—the short one breaking before the long one begins to stretch. The result will be dominant lethality.

Torsional restriction, twisting through 180°, will produce a symmetrical

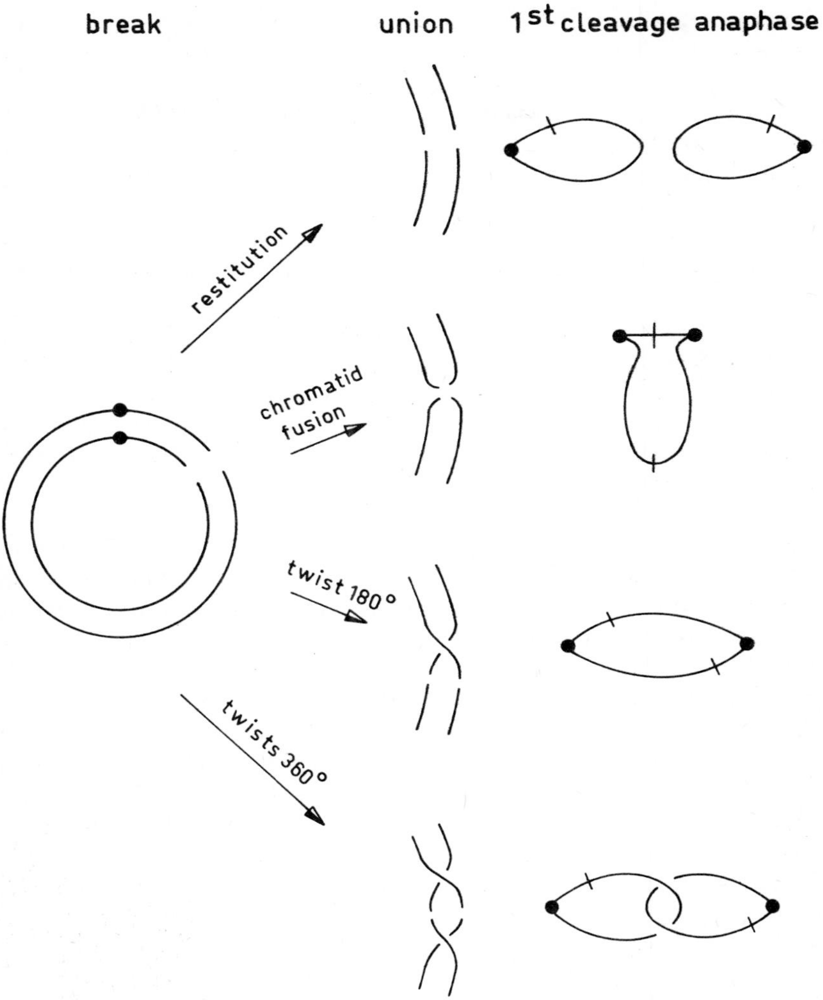

FIG. 2. The ways in which the chromatid ends of a broken ring may join and the configurations produced at the following division. On the anaphase configurations, the points of chromatid union are marked with short cross lines.

dicentric double-chromatid bridge. This is the configuration which is most likely to result in chromosome elimination.

Torsional restitution, twisting through 360°, will produce interlocked single rings, another symmetrical configuration. Breakage of one chromatid, however, will release one intact ring. The broken ring may then replicate and the end join in any of the four possible ways. This will determine the genotype of the adult fly. Elimination of this chromosome, at the second cleavage division, will produce an organism with equal amounts of X0 and XX tissue. Lethality will eliminate one of the first cleavage products and a normal female may be derived from the other one.

When chromatid fusion and torsional restitution occur, an unstable ring chromosome will express itself by high rates of total loss, dominant lethality, and gynandromorphs. On the other hand, an unstable rod derivative will yield an abnormal configuration only after chromatid fusion. According to Muller (1940) chromatid fusion should result in either chromosome loss or dominant lethality. Hinton (1957), however, found that at zygote formation unstable rod chromosomes only increase the frequency of dominant lethality. There is other evidence, obtained since 1940, which does not fit the chromatid fusion model of radiation induced chromosome loss. This is important because any conclusions, drawn from a comparison between ring and rod chromosomes, are dependent on the basic assumptions about the consequences of breakage.

Traut *et al.* (1970) irradiated rod X males and used genetic markers which enabled them to identify X0 larvae among their progeny. They examined the chromosome complements of the cells in neural ganglia and found that more than 90% of such larvae carried chromosome fragments. Many of these were presumably grossly deleted X chromosomes, which can only be detected genetically when they cover known markers. Either distal (Lüning, 1954; Lindsley and Sandler, 1958) or proximal (Falk, 1970) markers can be used for this purpose. Lindsley and Sandler (1958) and Falk (1973) found direct evidence of autosomal involvement in the production of about a quarter of the gross deletions of rod X-chromosomes. This suggests that the induction kinetics should show a multi-hit component, but X0 males have reduced viability and their recovery is also affected by such factors as genotype and larval density.

Von Borstel (1960) has shown that single chromatid bridges, formed at the first cleavage division, act as dominant lethals. This is in accordance with Hinton's (1957) evidence and arguments.

According to Traut *et al.*'s evidence (1970) most rod chromosome losses are partial losses. The less than 10% of total loss cases could result from multi-break events. In the simplest case loss of a rod X-chromosome will require two breaks, one of which must be proximal to any of the markers used in the test system. The other break may be either at the distal end of the X-chromosome or in an autosome. The latter case is shown in Fig. 3, which is a modification of the model proposed by Leigh and Sobels (1970) to account for the induction of compound autosomes when mature sperm are irradiated. There is one important change: the "lost" cleavage nucleus must contain either a dicentric bridge (Novitski, 1963a) or another

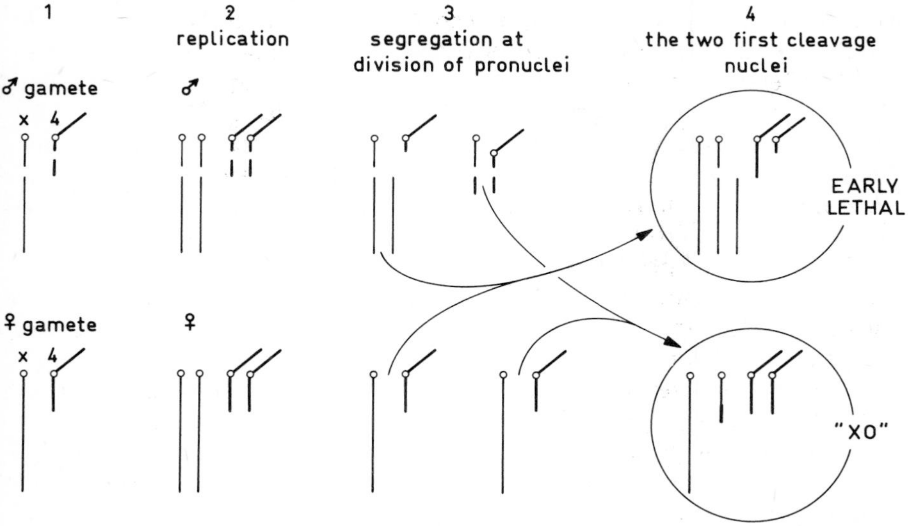

FIG. 3. Proposed mechanism of rod X-chromosome loss, following irradiation of mature sperm. 1. A break is induced at the centric end of the X chromosome and another near the tip of an autosome, a break in 4L is shown. 2. The chromosomes replicate in the pronuclei. 3. The pronuclei divide, union of the chromatid ends has presumably occurred before this time, but the breaks are shown open to clarify the segregation of the chromatids. 4. Diploid nuclei are formed at the end of the first cleavage division. One nucleus receives a complement which will cause early lethality. The other nucleus is viable and contains a centric fragment.

configuration which will cause early lethality. The products shown in the earlier figure (reproduced by Sankaranarayanan and Sobels, Chapter 26) would probably cause aneuploid lethality of the whole embryo at a late stage of development.

Induced breaks, one in the proximal X heterochromatin and the other in 4L, are shown in Fig. 3,1. The broken chromosomes replicate in the male pronucleus and the centric X fragment is capped by the free tip of 4L. When the other tip of 4L caps a centric 4, the deletional translocation *T(1:4:f)* can segregate with a complete 4 chromosome (Fig. 3,4) at the first cleavage division. An "X0" male may then develop from this nucleus. This model predicts that, when the fragment is capped by the tip of a major autosome, the capping segment will be recovered as a duplication. One of the limiting factors on the recovery of such deleted X-chromosomes may be the effect of the resulting trisomy in the first cleavage nucleus. There are other complications when the fourth chromosome is involved, because haplo-4 and triplo-4 flies are viable.

Models of the type shown in Fig. 2 are satisfying on paper but there are difficulties about applying them to experimental data. The sex ratio shifts in the progeny of irradiated ring X males, often show large variation. This may be between experiments carried out by different investigators (Lindsley *et al.*, 1963) or within sets of experiments (Würgler and Maier, 1972). From the model it is also expected that under a given set of conditions there should be a relationship between the induced frequencies of loss and sex-ratio shift. In at least one set of experiments (Leigh, 1969) no relationship could be established.

It would be simple if there was a clear distinction between the behaviour of ring chromosomes and that of rods. There is, however, some evidence which indicates that rod X-chromosomes can be divided into at least two classes, with respect to their response to radiation as expressed by loss, partial loss, and sex-ratio shift. Lüning (1954) irradiated Canton S and *Basc* males, mated them to homozygous *y* females, and scored the frequencies of hyperploid y^+ males in their progeny. Significantly higher frequencies were obtained from irradiated *Basc* males. Strangio (1966) compared normal rod X males and *Basc* males, for the induction of X0 males. Data are available for the fourth day after irradiation and show a much higher frequency of X0 males in the progeny of the treated *Basc* males. The *Basc* chromosome carries the free left end of *In(1)sc*^{S1}. This has a long sub-terminal block of heterochromatin. Lindsley *et al.* (1963) found significant sex-ratio shifts in the progeny of irradiated males whose X-chromosomes carried long sub-terminal heterochromatic blocks.

The frequencies of radiation induced loss of two ring chromosomes, *R(1)1* and *R(1)2*, and at least one rod chromosome, *In(1)EN* are not affected by oxygen tension (Baker, 1957; Leigh, 1968).

Muller (1954) discusses the problem raised by another set of observations. When there is a high probability that a break in the ring X-chromosome will cause loss or lethality, there should be a reduction in the frequencies of other types of genetic damage which also result from chromosome breakage. Offerman (Muller, 1940) found that the same frequencies of recessive sex-linked lethals were induced in ring X and rod X chromosomes. For doses up to 4000 R, this observation has since been repeated by Novitski (1952b), Oster (1956, 1957, 1958) and Edington (1956). Catcheside and Lea (1954) scored cytologically detectable changes in the salivary gland nuclei of F_1 larvae from irradiated males. With the exception of reciprocal translocations, they found the same frequencies of induced changes such as inversions, intercalations, and deficiencies, irrespective of whether the irradiated males carried ring or rod X-chromosomes. Muller (1940) reports an excess of multi-break exchanges involving ring X-chromosomes and points out that this may be due to an increased probability of recovery rather than a higher rate of primary induction.

In an extensive study which has only been partially reported (Valencia and Muller, 1949; Hannah, 1949), similar frequencies of "gene" mutations were induced in rod X, ring X, and attached X.Y chromosomes. An analysis of the *ct* mutations, induced in the ring X-chromosome (Hannah, 1949; Hannah-Alava, 1971), showed that many of them were associated with deficiencies, inversions, and deletion-insertion translocations.

C. Males: Spermatocytes

Spermatocytes are the most senstitive stage for the induction by radiation of deletions, losses, and partial losses of sex chromosomes (Chandley and Bateman, 1960; Strangio, 1961; Sävhagen, 1963; Zimmering and Wu, 1963; Sobels, 1963). Suter (1973) irradiated pupal spermatocytes, of ring X and rod X males carrying a $B^SY\ y^+$, and compared the induced frequencies of loss, partial loss, and inter-Y-arm exchange. The last type of change was induced at the same rate in both types of males and, therefore, should be excluded from any further comparison. When ring X spermatocytes are irradiated, high frequencies of complete loss of X or Y and low frequencies of single marker recovery from the Y are obtained. This relationship is reversed when rod X spermatocytes are irradiated, giving low frequencies of complete loss and high frequencies of single Y-marker recovery.

Zimmering and Wu (1963, 1964a, b) have shown that radiation induces high frequencies of exchange between the X and Y chromosomes. On the basis of this evidence and another observation, that there is no sex ratio shift in the progeny from irradiated ring X spermatocytes (Leigh, 1969), it can be argued that most of the complete losses are a consequence of exchange between the ring X and the Y-chromosome. The resulting dicentric bridges will eliminate equal numbers of both chromosomes.

When the markers of the paternal *R(1)* and Y chromosome are recovered in the same gamete, to give an XXY female, this is usually classified as a non-disjunctional event. By progeny testing, Strangio (1970) was able to show that some of these females carried newly induced attached X–Y chromosomes. In separate tests (Leigh, unpublished observations) it has been found that such X–Y chromosomes are produced as a consequence of chromatid exchanges.

Suter's (1973) data can be interpreted as indicating that when rod X spermatocytes are irradiated, most of the single Y-marker recoveries are also a consequence of X–Y exchange. When the X-chromatid break is in or close to the centric heterochromatin, an exchange with part of a Y arm will result in the formation of two heteromorphic dyads. One will consist of an unbroken X and a centric X fragment capped by the distal part of a Y arm. The other will consist of an unbroken Y and a Y with a break in one arm capped by the free euchromatic portion of the X chromosome. Zimmering and Bendbow (1973) have recently obtained evidence for the preferential recovery of the shorter element of heteromorphic dyads induced in spermatocytes. The exchange described above should therefore result in the preferential recovery of the Y-capped X-centric chromatid and the intact Y-chromatid. The reduced probability of recovering the respective sister centromeres, which both carry euchromatic X-chromatids, would account for the sex ratio shift observed by Hannah-Alava (1968).

V. Other Ring Chromosomes

Compound ring chromosomes, *C(1)TR* and *C(1)RR*, are useful for studies on crossing over (Novitski, 1954; Sandler, 1965). On the other hand, there is at least one compound ring chromosome which is useful because it gives no cross-over products. *C(1)A* (Lindsley and Grell, 1968) was recovered as a spontaneous stabilization of *C(1)TR* by H. Armentrout. Lindsley (personal communication) described it as the best compound for balancing purposes and included a drawing of it on page 405 of "Genetic Variations of *Drosophila melanogaster*" (Lindsley and Grell, 1968).

R(Y)L chromosomes are useful for balancing attached $X.Y^S$ and *C(1)RM* chromosomes (Muller, 1948), because all spontaneous crossing over will produce inviable dicentrics.

Complete *R(Y)* chromosomes, when introduced to some stocks via the male, may cause the death of almost all male progeny (Oster, 1964). As far as is known, the lethal embryos have not yet been analysed cytologically.

When male germ cells are irradiated, ring Y-chromosomes are lost more frequently than rod Y-chromosomes (Herskowitz *et al.*, 1957; Herskowitz, 1963). This confirms that it is the ring configuration, and not some other property of ring X-chromosomes, which results in the high rate of radiation induced loss.

By constructing *C(1)TM* chromosomes with different amounts of Y heterochromatin at the centric region (Novitski, 1963b), it has been possible to derive $R(1{:}Y^L)$ and $R(1{:}Y)$ chromosomes (Lucchesi, 1965; Novitski, see Chapter 11).

VI. Conclusion

It is difficult to separate many of the properties of ring chromosomes from those of rod chromosomes. This is partly because ring chromosomes were discovered early in the history of *Drosophila* genetics. It was then easy to ascribe most of their properties to ring-ness. This is justified with respect to their behaviour during meiosis in females, but is not as clear with other aspects of their behaviour. At present it is not possible to do more than attempt to define some of the problems. Their solution may only be possible when there is more knowledge about the behaviour of modified rod chromosomes.

Radiation studies are generally interpreted on the basis of models, used for example to derive the frequency of chromosome breakage from an observed frequency of chromosome loss. A new model of rod chromosome loss has been included. It can be used to explain the available data and makes predictions which can be tested experimentally.

Ring chromosomes will continue to be useful tools in genetic research. It is, however, important to realize the restrictions as well as the advantages of working with them.

Acknowledgements

I would like to thank Professor F. H. Sobels for his encouragement and Drs. A. Schalet, D. R. Parker, and K. Sankaranarayanan for useful discussion. Particular thanks are due to Drs. A. Hannah-Alava and E. Novitski for having made available unpublished data and background information and for their critical reading of the manuscript. The experimental work of the author and the writing of this chapter were supported by Euratom contracts No. 052–64–1 BIAN and 102–72–a–1 BIAN.

References

BAKER, W. K. (1957). Induced loss of a ring and a telomeric chromosome in *Drosophila melanogaster*. *Genetics* **42,** 735–748.

BATTACHARYA, P. (1950). Behaviour of the ring-chromosome in *Drosophila melanogaster*. *Proc. Roy. Soc. Edinb. B.* **64,** 199–215.

BAUER, H. (1939). Die Dosisabhängigkeit röntgeninduzierter Chromosomenmutationen im Ring-X-Chromosom von *Drosophila melanogaster*. *Naturwissenschaften* **27,** 821–822.

BAUER, H. (1942). Röntgenauslösung von Chromosomenmutationen bei *Drosophila melanogaster* II. Die Häufigkeit des primären Bruchereignisses nach Untersuchungen am Ring-X-Chromosom. *Chromosoma* **2,** 407–458.

BRAVER, G. and BLOUNT, J. L. (1949). Somatic eliminations of ring chromosomes in *Drosophila melanogaster*. (Abstr.) *Genetics* **35,** 98, 1950.

BROSSEAU, G. E. (1966). Some aspects of ring chromosome behaviour in *Drosophila*. *Dros. Inf. Serv.* **41,** 97–99.

BROWN, S. W. and HANNAH, A. (1952). An induced maternal effect on the stability of the ring-X-chromosome of *Drosophila melanogaster*. *Proc. Natl. Acad. Sci. U.S.A.* **38,** 687–693.

BROWN, S. W. and WELSHONS, W. (1955). Maternal aging and somatic crossing over of attached-X chromosomes. *Proc. Natl. Acad. Sci., Wash.* **41,** 209–215.

BROWN, S. W., WALEN, K. H. and BROSSEAU, G. E. (1962). Somatic crossing-over and elimination of ring X chromosomes of *Drosophila melanogaster*. *Genetics* **47,** 1573–1579.

CATCHESIDE, D. G. and LEA, D. E. (1945). Dominant lethals and chromosome breaks in ring X-chromosomes of *Drosophila melanogaster*. *J. Genet.* **47,** 25–40.

CHANDLEY, A. C. and BATEMAN, A. J. (1960). Mutagenic sensitivity of sperm, spermatids, spermatocytes, and spermatogonia in *Drosophila melanogaster*. *Heredity* **15,** 363–375.

DÄVRING, L. and SUNNER, M. (1973). Female meiosis and embryonic mitosis in *Drosophila melanogaster*. 1. Meiosis and fertilization. *Hereditas* **73,** 51–64.

EDINGTON, C. W. (1956). The induction of recessive lethals in *Drosophila melanogaster* by radiations of different ion density. *Genetics* **41,** 814–821.

FABERGÉ, A. C. (1952). Loss of ring chromosomes produced by X-rays in female *Drosophila*. (Abstr.) *Genetics* **37,** 579–580.

FALK, R. (1970). Induction of deletions in X-chromosomes of *Drosophila*. *Mutation Res.* **10,** 61–66.

FALK, R. (1973). The nature of chromosomal fragments in X-chromosomes of *Drosophila melanogaster*. *Mutation Res.* **20,** 437–439.

FALK, R. (1974). On the structure of the R(1)2, *y f* chromosome. *Dros. Inf. Serv.* **50,** 144.

GIESEL, B. J. (1968). Further studies of an unstable ring chromosome of *Drosophila melanogaster*. Ph.D. Thesis, University of Oregon.

GREEN, M. M. (1967). The genetics of a mutable gene at the white locus of *Drosophila melanogaster*. *Genetics* **56,** 467–482.

GRIFFEN, A. B. and LINDSLEY, D. L. Jr. (1946). The production of gynandromorphs through the use of unstable ring chromosomes in *Drosophila melanogaster*. (Abstr.) *Anat. Rec.* **96,** 555–556.

HANNAH, A. M. (1949). Radiation-mutations involving the cut locus in *Drosophila*. (Abstr.) *Proc. 8th int. Congr. Genet.* 1948 (*Stockh.*). Lund: Issued as a supplementary volume of *Hereditas*, 1949, pp. 588–589.

HANNAH, A. M. (1955). Environmental factors affecting elimination of the ring-X chromosome in *Drosophila melanogaster*. *Z. Vererbungslehre* **86,** 600–621.

HANNAH-ALAVA, A. (1968). Sex-ratio depression as a brood-pattern criterion of radiation damage in *Drosophila melanogaster*. *Genetics* **39,** 519–543.

HANNAH-ALAVA, A. (1971). Cytogenetics of nucleolus-transpositions in *Drosophila melanogaster*. *Molec. Gen. Genetics* **113,** 191–203.

HERSKOWITZ, I. H. (1963). An influence of maternal nutrition upon the gross chromosomal mutation frequency recovered from X-rayed sperm of *Drosophila melanogaster*. *Genetics* **48,** 703–710.

HERSKOWITZ, I. H., CARLSON, E. A. and MULLER, H. J. (1957). Sex chromosome loss following X-radiation of *D. melanogaster* sperm. (Abstr.) *Genetics* **42,** 367.

HINTON, C. W. (1954). The occurrence of fragments of the unstable w^{vC} chromosome. *Dros. Inf. Serv.* **28,** 124.

HINTON, C. W. (1955). The behaviour of an unstable ring chromosome of *Drosophila melanogaster*. *Genetics* **40,** 951–961.

HINTON, C. H. (1957). The analysis of rod derivatives of an unstable ring chromosome of *Drosophila melanogaster*. *Genetics* **42,** 55–65.

HINTON, C. W. (1959). A Study of w^{vC} chromosome instability in cleavage mitoses of *Drosophila melanogaster*. *Genetics* **44,** 923–931.

KING, R. C., DARROW, J. B. and KAYE, N. W. (1956). Studies on different classes of mutations induced by radiation of *Drosophila melanogaster* females. *Genetics* **41,** 890–900.

LEIGH, B. (1968). The absence of an oxygen enhancement effect on induced chromosome loss. *Mutation Res.* **5,** 432–434.

LEIGH, B. (1969). Radiation-induced loss of ring-X chromosomes in the germ cells of *Drosophila melanogaster* males. *Mutation Res.* **8,** 101–109.

LEIGH, B. and SOBELS, F. H. (1970). Induction by X-rays of isochromosomes in the germ cells of *Drosophila melanogaster* males. Evidence for nuclear selection in embryogenesis. *Mutation Res.* **10,** 475–487.

LINDSLEY, D. L. and GRELL, E. H. (1968). Genetic variations of *Drosophila melanogaster*. Carnegie Institution of Washington Publication No. 627.

LINDSLEY, D. L. and NOVITSKI, E. (1959). Compound chromosomes involving the X and Y chromosomes of *Drosophila melanogaster*. *Genetics* **44,** 187–196.

LINDSLEY, D. L. and SANDLER, L. (1958). The meiotic behaviour of grossly deleted X chromosomes in *Drosophila melanogaster*. *Genetics* **43,** 547–563.

LINDSLEY, D. L. and SANDLER, L. (1965). Meiotic behaviour of tandem metacentric compound X chromosomes in *Drosophila melanogaster*. *Genetics* **51,** 223–245.

LINDSLEY, D. L., EDINGTON, C. W. and VON HALLE, E. S. (1963). The effect of gametic genotype on the radiation sensitivity of *Drosophila* sperm. *In*: "Repair from Genetic Radiation Damage. (F. H. Sobels, ed.), pp. 63–76, Pergamon Press, Oxford.

LUCCHESI, J. C. (1965). The influence of heterochromatin on crossing over in ring/rod heterozygotes of *D. melanogaster*. *Dros. Inf. Serv.* **40,** 58–59.

LÜNING, K. G. (1954). Variations in the breakability of chromosomes in mature spermatozoa of *Drosophila melanogaster* at different modes of irradiation. *Heredity* **8,** 211–223.

MORGAN, L. V. (1933). A closed X chromosome in *Drosophila melanogaster*. *Genetics* **18,** 250–283.

MULLER, H. J. (1940). An analysis of the process of structural change in chromosomes of *Drosophila*. *J. Genet.* **40,** 1–66.

MULLER, H. J. (1944). Tandem attached X's producing ring chromosomes. *Dros. Inf. Serv.* **18,** 57–58.

MULLER, H. J. (1948). The construction of several new types of Y chromosomes. *Dros. Inf. Serv.* **22,** 73–74.

MULLER, H. J. (1954). The manner of production of mutations by radiation. *In*: "Radiation Biology", **1** (A. Hollaender, ed.) pp. 475–626, McGraw-Hill Book Co., New York.

MULLER, H. J. (1956). Another entire inversion formed by opening of a ring X. *Dros. Inf. Serv.* **30,** 140–141.

NOVITSKI, E. (1949). An inversion of the entire X chromosome. *Dros. Inf. Serv.* 23, 94–95.

NOVITSKI, E. (1952a). The genetic consequences of anaphase bridge formation in *Drosophila*. *Genetics* **37,** 270–287.

NOVITSKI, E. (1952b). X-ray-induced lethal rate in ring chromosomes. *Dros. Inf. Serv.* **26,** 115.

NOVITSKI, E. (1954). The compound X chromosomes in Drosophila. *Genetics* **39,** 127–140.

NOVITSKI, E. (1955). Genetic measures of centromere activity in *Drosophila melanogaster*. In: *Symposium on Genetic Recombination*, 1954. *J. Cell. Comp. Physiol.* **45,** Suppl. 2, 151–169.

NOVITSKI, E. (1963a). The origin of mosaics. *Dros. Inf. Serv.* **38,** 71.

NOVITSKI, E. (1963b). Construction of new chromosomal types in *Drosophila melanogaster*. *In*: "Methodology in Basic Genetics" (W. J. Burdette, ed.), pp. 381–389, Holden-Day, Inc., San Francisco.

NOVITSKI, E. and LINDSLEY, D. L. (1950). Construction of tandemly attached X chromosomes. *Dros. Inf. Serv.* **24,** 90.

NOVITSKI, E. and SANDLER, L. (1956). Further notes on the nature of non-random disjunction in *Drosophila melanogaster*. *Genetics* **41,** 194–206.

OSTER, I. I. (1956). The frequency of induced lethals in morphologically different chromosomes. (Abstr.) *Genetics* **41,** 655–656.

OSTER, I. I. (1957). Modification of X-ray mutagenesis in *Drosophila*. Relative sensitivity of spermatids and mature spermatozoa. *Proc. 5th Int. Conf. Radiobiol.*, Stockholm, 1956, *Adv. in Radiobiol.* 475–480.

OSTER, I. I. (1958). The consequences of X-irradiating morphologically dissimilar chromosomes. (Abstr.) *Rad. Res.* **9,** 163–164.

OSTER, I. I. (1964). Filicidal Y chromosomes. (Abstr.) *Genetics* **50,** 274.

OSTER, I. I. and BALABAN, G. (1962). Cytological demonstration of induced breakage in somatic chromosomes of *Drosophila*. (Abstr.) *Genetics* **47,** 974–975.

OSTER, I. I. and SOBELS, F. H. (1956). "Natural implantation" of a lethal mutation in *Drosophila melanogaster*. *Am. Nat.* **90,** 55–60.

OSTERTAG, W. (1963). The genetic basis of somatic damage produced by radiation in third instar larvae of *Drosophila melanogaster*. 1. Death before maturity. *Z. Vererbungslehre* **94,** 143–162.

PASZTOR, L. M. (1971). Unstable ring-X chromosomes derived from a tandem metacentric compound in *Drosophila melanogaster*. *Genetics* **68,** 245–258.

SANDLER, L. (1957). The meiotic behaviour of reversed compound ring X chromosomes in *Drosophila melanogaster*. *Genetics* **42,** 764–782.

SANDLER, L. (1965). The meiotic mechanics of ring chromosomes in female *Drosophila melanogaster*. *Nat. Cancer. Instit Monogr.* **18,** 243–273.

SANDLER, L. and LINDSLEY, D. L. (1967). Meiotic behaviour of tandem compound ring X chromosomes in *Drosophila melanogaster*. *Genetics* **55,** 645–671.

SANDLER, L., ROMANS, P. and FIGENSHOW, J. (1974). An effect of centromere function on the behaviour of ring-X chromosomes in *Drosophila melanogaster*. *Genetics* **77,** 299–307.

SÄVHAGEN, R. (1963). Cell stages and differential sensitivity to irradiation in males of *Drosophila melanogaster*. *In*: "Repair from Genetic Radiation Damage". (F. H. Sobels, ed.), pp. 343–357, Pergamon Press, Oxford.

SCHULTZ, J. and CATCHESIDE, D. G. (1938). The nature of closed X-chromosomes in *Drosophila melanogaster*. *J. Genet.* **35,** 315–320.

SIDOROV, B. N., SOKOLOV, N. N. and TROFIMOV, I. E. (1935). Forces of attraction of homologous loci and chromosome conjunction. *Nature, Lond.* **136,** 108–109.

SIDOROV, B. N., SOKOLOV, N. N. and TROFIMOV, I. E. (1936). Crossing-over in heterozygoten inversionen. I. Einfaches crossing-over. *Genetica* **18,** 291– 312.

SOBELS, F. H. (1963). Repair and differential radiosensitivity in developing germ cells of *Drosophila* males. *In*: "Repair from Genetic Radiation Damage", (F. H. Sobels, ed.), pp. 179–197, Pergamon Press, Oxford.

SONNENBLICK, B. P. (1950). The early embryology of *Drosophila melanogaster*. *In*: "Biology of Drosophila" (M. Demerec, ed.), pp. 62–167, John Wiley and Sons Inc., New York.

STERN, C. (1936). Somatic crossing-over and its genetic control in *Drosophila*. *Genetics* **21**, 625–730.

STRANGIO, V. A. (1961). Radiosensitive stages in the spermatogenesis of *Drosophila melanogaster*. *Nature, Lond.* **192**, 781–782.

STRANGIO, V. A. (1966). Brood sensitivity patterns after the irradiation of males bearing a rod, ring or inverted-X and a doubly marked Y-chromosome. *Dros. Inf. Serv.* **41**, 176.

STRANGIO, V. A. (1970). Sub-metacentric recombinant chromosomes recovered from irradiated males bearing a ring-X and a doubly-marked Y. *Dros. Inf. Serv.* **45**, 132.

STURTEVANT, A. H. and BEADLE, G. W. (1936). The relations of inversions in the X chromosome of *Drosophila melanogaster* to crossing over and disjunction. *Genetics* **21**, 554–604.

SUTER, K. E. (1973). Röntgeninduzierte mutationsspektren versheidener kiemzellstadien von *Drosophila*-männchen met einem doppelt markierten Y-chromosom und einem stab-X- oder einem ring-X-chromosom. *Mutation Res.* **19**, 83–98.

SUZUKI, D. T. (1962). Interchromosomal effects on crossing-over in *Drosophila melanogaster*. 1. Effects of compound and ring X chromosomes on the third chromosome. *Genetics* **47**, 305–319.

TRAUT, H., SCHEID, W. and WIND, H. (1970). Partial and total sex-chromosome loss induced by X-rays in mature spermatozoa of *Drosophila melanogaster*. *Mutation Res.* **9**, 489–499.

VALENCIA, J. I. and MULLER, H. J. (1949). The mutational potentialities of some individual loci in *Drosophila* .(Abstr.) *Proc. 8th Int. Congr. Genet.* 1948 (*Stockh.*). Lund: Issued as a supplementary volume of *Hereditas*, 1949, pp. 681–683.

VIINIKKA, Y., HANNAH-ALAVA, A. and ARAJÄRVI, P. (1971). A reinvestigation of the nucleolus-organizing regions in the salivary gland nuclei of *Drosophila melanogaster*. *Chromosoma* (*Berl.*) **36**, 34–45.

VON BORSTEL, R. C. (1960). Sulla natura della letalita dominante indotta dalle radiazioni. *Atti. Assoc. Genet. Ital.* **5**, 35–50.

WALEN, K. H. (1964). Somatic crossing over in relationship to heterochromatin in *Drosophila melanogaster*. *Genetics* **49**, 905–923.

WELSHONS, W. J. and HINTON, C. W. (1955). Bridges at anaphase II in ring-X males. *Dros. Inf. Serv.* **29**, 171.

WÜRGLER, F. E. and MAIER, P. (1972). Genetic control of mutation induction in *Drosophila melanogaster*. 1. Sex-chromosome loss in X-rayed mature sperm. *Mutation Res.* **15**, 41–53.

ZIMMERING, S. and BENDBOW, E. B. (1973). Meiotic behaviour of asymmetric dyads in the male *Drosophila*. *Genetics* **73**, 631–638.

ZIMMERING, S. and WU, C. K. (1963). Radiation induced X–Y exchange and nondisjunction in spermatocytes of the immature testis of *Drosophila*. *Genetics* **48**, 1619–1623.

Zimmering, S. and Wu, C. K. (1964a). X–Y nondisjunction and exchange induced by X rays in primary spermatocytes of the adult *Drosophila*. *Genetics* **49**, 499–504.

Zimmering, S. and Wu, C. K. (1964b). Meiotic X–Y exchange and nondisjunction induced by irradiation in the *Drosophila* male. *Genetics* **50**, 633–638.

13. Compound Autosomes

D. G. Holm

Department of Zoology
University of British Columbia
Vancouver, British Columbia, Canada

I. Introduction

In 1960 there appeared in that year's issue of *Drosophila Information Service* a report by I. E. Rasmussen announcing the availability of a new class of autosomal rearrangements. These rearrangements, available both for the second and the third chromosome, were viewed as structural analogues of the attached-X, and, therefore, were termed "attached-2R; 2L" and "attached-3R; 3L", respectively. Attached autosomes, now commonly referred to as compound autosomes (sometimes as isochromosomes), were basically designed as a mechanism, as stated by Rasmussen (1960), "to make use of a partial tetrad analysis . . . on the major autosomes".

During the ensuing years their worth in half-tetrad analysis was unquestionably recognized. But, in addition, their unexpected behaviour during meiosis in males disclosed a new system for studying exceptional meiotic events during oogenesis. The spectrum of uses for compound autosomes is still widening, and since these chromosomes are relatively new additions to our repertory of chromosomal rearrangements, the reader will encounter, in the following sections, a considerable degree of speculation along with some suggestions for possible future studies. Moreover, a few of the studies hereinafter reported, are still in progress. Therefore, some interpretations are based on incomplete data and, in view of future findings, may require considerable modifications. Nevertheless, I trust this review encompasses the present status of knowledge on the formation, the meiotic behaviour and the uses of compound autosomes, and hope it will serve as a practicable guide to those employing or considering compound autosomes as a basic genetic tool.

To put this subject in its proper perspective, the following discussion begins with a description of the procedures used by E. B. Lewis and collaborators (I. E. Rasmussen, E. Oreas, P. Deal, D. Shreffler and A. Roberts) for constructing and identifying the original autosomal attachments (Lewis, 1960).

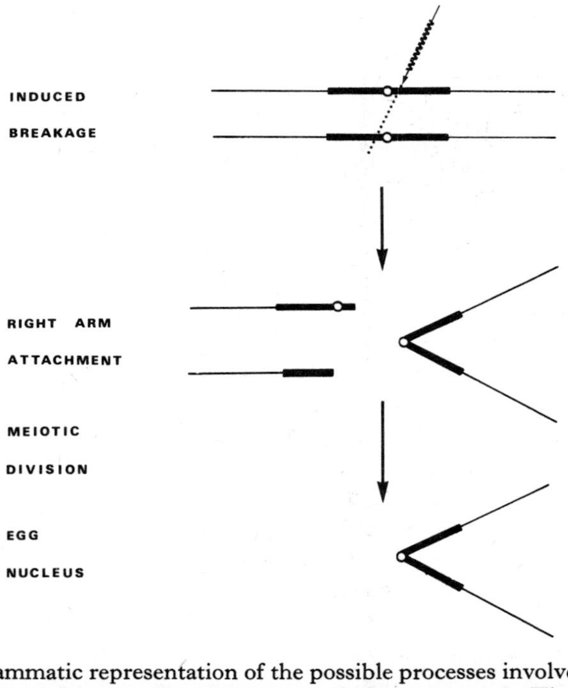

FIG. 1. Diagrammatic representation of the possible processes involved in generating an attachment between the right arms of chromosome 3. The mechanism, as illustrated, requires that a centric free arm join to the broken end of an acentric whole arm fragment.

II. Generation

A. Origin

The construction of compound autosomes was initiated by I. E. Rasmussen who focussed attention on the right arm of chromosome three. This choice was strictly based upon the availability of rearrangements. The plan was to induce, in females, attached-3R's through the use of X-rays. It was anticipated that the resultant eggs would lack altogether 3L (see Fig. 1). To "rescue" such eggs would require fertilization by sperm disomic for the left arm of chromosome 3 and nullosomic for the right arm. The problem, therefore, was to find a means of producing males which would yield an appreciable percentage (say over 10%) of this class of sperm, since it was anticipated that the proportion of eggs bearing attached-3R's would at best be very small, even after heavy doses of X-rays. Sperm of the desired type are expected to be produced by males doubly heterozygous for certain kinds of translocations. In general, the two translocations should

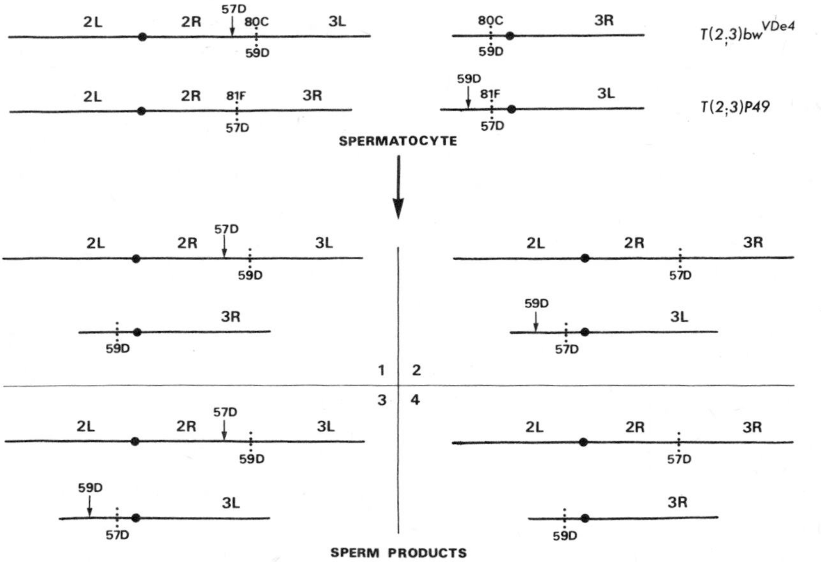

FIG. 2. The four sperm products from males doubly heterozygous for translocations, $T(2;3)bw^{VDe4}$ and $T(2;3)P49$. The derived translocation, represented as product 3, carries the necessary chromosomal constitution to rescue eggs deficient for 3L but disomic for 3R. Also note that product 3 carries a duplication of the region 57D to 59D on the second chromosome. Products 1 and 2 will be recovered in combination with a standard second and third; whereas, product 4 will be lethal.

share one break in common in a chromosome other than the third, while the other breaks should occur, in the case of one of the translocations, just to the left, and in the case of the other translocation, just to the right, of the centromere of the third chromosome. It may be seen from the diagram (Fig. 2) that males carrying this combination of translocations would be expected to produce up to 25% sperm of the desired type. Among existing rearrangements, two translocations between the second and third chromosome approximately fulfilled these conditions; namely, *T(2;3)bw*^{VDe4} (with points of breakage on the salivary chromosome map at 59D–E;80C) and *T(2;3)P49* (57D–E;81F). As represented by product 3, in Fig. 2, sperm essentially disomic for 3L and nullosomic for 3R are expected to be produced by such males, while the second chromosome carries only a small duplication for the region from 57D to 59D; since much larger duplications in this region of the second chromosome are known to be viable and fertile, no difficulties were anticipated from the presence of such a duplication.

Females that were genotypically *cv–c sbd*^{2} *bx sr gl e*^{s}*/st sbd gl*^{3} *e*^{4} *wo ro ca* were X-rayed and mated to males heterozygous for the above two translocations. Approximately five pairs of flies were placed in each culture bottle where egg laying was permitted for a nine-day period. The offspring were scored on the 14th and 17th day for the presence of any *sbd gl e* flies. Approximately 28,000 flies were screened in two separate irradiated groups. These offsprings included 18 *sbd gl e* flies that were then backcrossed to heterozygotes for the original two translocations. Among the eighteen, 4 proved to be the result of non-virginity; one was lost; eight were sterile; and the remaining five gave results consistent with the inheritance of an induced attached-3R, together with a translocation product. One of the latter five (designated stock number 4) was chosen for intensive cytological examination. Analysis of the salivary gland chromosome from this stock confirmed the presence of two normal-appearing, completely synapsed right arms of the third chromosome, and showed the presence of a second chromosome with attached-3L from the *T(2;3)P49* stock and an additional 3L from the *T(2;3)bw*^{VDe4} stock. Since salivary gland chromosomes do not reveal centromere position, it was necessary to make ganglion preparations to determine how the 3R's were constructed. Examination of ganglion cells by Lewis and Rasmussen showed somatic pairing of one of the autosomes, such as is seen in attached-X chromosomes in this organism, thus supporting the supposition that attached-3R's had been induced.

With the confirmed recovery of a strain of attached-3R's (which were designated "ATR1"; attached third right No. 1) the next procedure was to construct attached-3L's. This was achieved by simply X-raying females

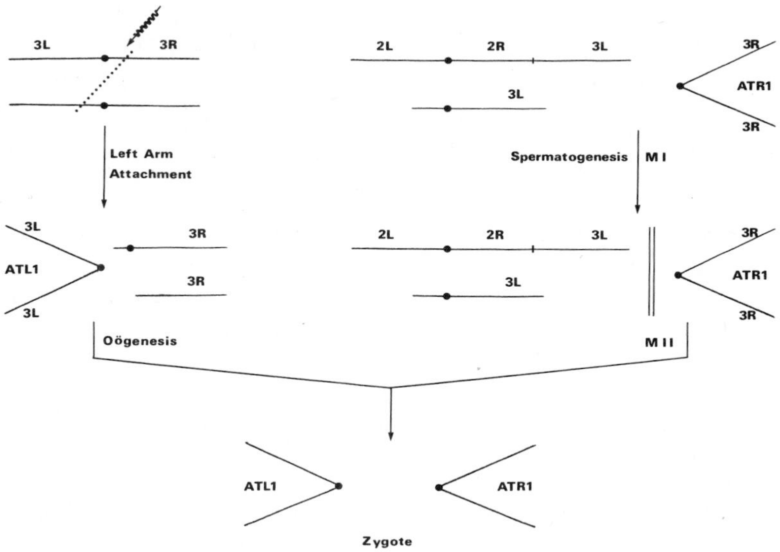

FIG. 3. Diagrammatic interpretation of the processes involved in generating *ATL1* and the recovery of the newly induced attachment in combination with a paternally derived *ATR1*.

of genetic constitution, *se h app*/h^2 *rs*, and mating them to males of the ATR1 stock. From this mating, all offspring die except those coming from eggs whose chromosomal constitution has been so altered as to compensate for the grossly unbalanced constitution of the sperm from ATR1 males (see Fig. 3). The mating produced several *h*/h^2 flies, one of which (designated ATL1), when backcrossed to the ATR1 stock, gave rise to a strain having attached-3L's and attached-3R's. Upon cytological analysis, the salivary gland chromosomes, as would be expected in such a stock, appeared completely normal. The condensed chromosomes in the ganglion cells, however, showed clear evidence for the existence of two pairs of attached autosomal arms; that is, somatic pairing of the arms of two large V-shaped chromosomes.

By completely analogous procedures, E. Orias and P. Deal were able to derive attached-2L's and 2R's. In this case the translocations chosen, *T(2;3)P3* (40;88B) and *(T2;3)P58* (41;89E), provided the appropriate sperm products for recovering attached-2L chromosomes generated in females. From X-ray treated *b el* rd^s *pr cn*/so^2 *b* females, an attached left arm was synthesized and maintained through backcrossing to the doubly translocated stock. Males from this attached-2L stock (ASL1), which contained the derived translocation product, were then mated to X-rayed females of various genotypes, including *pk cn; px;* and wildtype. Several instances of attached-2R's were constructed and combined in stock with ASL1. One of these when analysed cytologically was consistent with the observations on the attached-3 stock. No abnormalities were found in the salivary gland chromosomes, but the ganglion cells contained two large V-shaped chromosomes having somatically paired arms.

Attached fourth chromosomes, the last in this series, were constructed by D. Shreffler and A. Roberts. Here the procedure was somewhat simpler in that it suffices to use a single translocation, namely, one involving the fourth chromosome. For the purpose, *T(3;4)86D* was chosen, since a stock with a dominant marker (*Ubx*) on the third chromosome and a single free fourth chromosome (marked by the dominant mutant, ey^D), was already available. Males from this stock were mated to X-rayed females of the genotype, *ci* ey^R/*gvl* sv^n. In this way a number of derived products containing attached fourth chromosomes from the maternal parent were synthesized. Cytological studies confirmed the presence of a fourth chromosome about twice normal size. Presumably such lines containing attached-fourth chromosomes lack, in part or entirely, the very short and wholly heterochromatic left arm of chromosome four. Furthermore, the presence of two attached-fourth chromosomes results in a viable tetrasomic fly with exaggerated triple-IV characteristics; namely, there is no trident pattern and the body is long and slender in appearance.

B. Induced and Spontaneous Formation

While the construction of the original compound autosomes represents a major undertaking, generating additional compounds has proved to be a relatively simple and straightforward process. The past few years have witnessed the production of numerous compound-2 and compound-3 chromosomes homozygous and heterozygous for a variety of genetic markers and chromosomal aberrations, including deletions, duplications and paracentric inversions. The procedure commonly adopted involves the treatment of 3 to 4 day old virgin females, from a selected genotype, with gamma or X-radiation. The treated females are then crossed to either compound-2 or compound-3 males. The only progeny recovered from such a cross are those inheriting either a newly generated compound-left or compound-right from the female parent, with the complementary compound autosome from the male parent, and those receiving, through nondisjunction or loss of the treated chromosomes, either both standards from the mother or both compounds from the father. Because each newly generated compound may possess, as a function of their formation, peculiar intrinsic properties, care is taken to isolate each new attachment in a separate strain. It is essential, therefore, that the compounds, carried by the male parents, are appropriately marked. Once recovered, each compound is identified by a code letter and number, followed by the genotype. Generally, the code letter indicates the location at which the compound was generated, the number indicates the order. For example, *C(3L)RM P2,ri* indicates Compound-3L, reverse metacentric, Pasadena 2, homozygous for *ri*. Some codes include a second letter, which usually identifies the investigator.

Definitive studies on the kinetics of radiation induced compound formation as yet have not been reported. However, it is of interest to note some of the findings related to this problem. If treated females, mated to compound-2 males, are carried through a series of two day broods, the greatest recovery of *C(2L)* and *C(2R)* chromosomes is normally from brood 2, which suggests this event occurs during the first prophase of meiosis. Beyond days 7 and 8, the production appears to fall off rapidly, although compounds have been recovered as late as the fourteenth day of egg laying. The doses of gamma radiation used in most experiments ranged from 1000 to 4000 rads. Although the estimated frequency of compound formation was significantly increased at the higher levels of radiation, the total recovery per treated female appears to show only moderate change due to increased dominant lethality in the early broods (Gavin, 1971; Yeomans, 1972). Aside from radiation dose and duration of egg sampling, the genotype of the treated female is an important factor influencing the overall recovery of newly generated compounds. As a conservative estimate, it was recently demonstrated that from 30 to 50 newly generated compound-2 chromosomes could be expected from eggs laid during the first four days following the treatment of 1000 three-day-old virgin females with 2000 rads of gamma radiation (W. G. Gibson, personal communication). The estimated frequency of compound-2 formation, at 2000 rads, based on these initial results, is approximately 0·2 to 0·3%. It is also important to note that *C(2L)RM* and *C(2R)RM* chromosomes have been recovered as spontaneous occurrences (Chadov, 1970; Gavin, 1971; Yeomans, 1972). Comparable measurements on the formation of compound-thirds are not available. However, experience has shown that sufficient recovery can be obtained from eggs laid in the first six days by 1000 females that received 3000 rads of gamma radiation.

The induced formation of compound autosomes is not exclusive to the gametes of females. Newly generated compound-thirds (Leigh and Sobels, 1970; Gavin, 1971) have been recovered from X-ray treated males mated to compound-bearing females. It was found that compounds apparently were induced, not only in every stage of spermatogenesis, but also in spermatids. That compounds were recovered from spermatids presents a problem that is yet to be satisfactorily explained (Leigh and Sobels, 1970;

Sobels and Leigh, 1971; Sankaranarayanan and Sobels, Chapter 26 this volume). Nevertheless, regarding the events during spermatogenesis, since the treated males were heterozygous for a series of markers along the selected chromosomes, the results of these experiments clearly demonstrate that compounds can be generated in males through the attachment of either sister or nonsister chromatids. It is of further interest that following the initial recovery of nonsister attachments, which serves as a means of measuring the rate of sperm development, sister strand compounds continue to be recovered in relatively high proportions. These findings were interpreted (Leigh and Sobels, 1970) to indicate a common mechanism involved in the formation of both types of compound autosomes.

Similar results had been obtained in experiments where compound-3 chromosomes homozygous for proximally located recessive visible markers were constructed in heterozygous females (Holm *et al.*, 1969; Holm, unpublished data). Even though these compounds, at the time, were viewed as possible sister-strand attachments, it could not be ignored that they might have resulted from induced exchange in the proximal heterochromatin simultaneous with the attachment of nonsister chromatids. If, however, the generation of compound arms in primary oocytes involved the random association of any two chromatids in the tetrad, then one-sixth of the compounds generated in heterozygous females should be homozygous for any given marker, regardless of its map position. The first quantitative approach to this problem was reported by Bateman (1968) for a series of compound-2 chromosomes constructed in *dp b vg*/*b pr cn bw* females. The frequency of homozygosis for the proximal markers was somewhat less than the theoretical expectation, but the proportion of compounds homozygous for the distal markers, *dp* and *bw*, was in good agreement with the model of random association. These results promoted further studies using females heterozygous for markers closely linked to the centromere (Gavin, 1971; Yeomans, 1972). Although only a total of 101 compounds were generated in the two experiments, the frequency of putative sister-strand attachments was sufficiently high to support the basic assumption. The convincing demonstration of induced sister-strand attachments in females was provided by the recovery of *C*(*2L*)*lt* and *C*(*2R*)*stw* chromosomes from *lt stw*/*In*(*2LR*)*SM1*,*Cy* heterozygotes (Gavin, 1971). Because the *SM1* chromosome includes, together with paracentric inversions in each arm, a large pericentric inversion, attachments between this chromosome and a standard homologue result in dominant lethal products.

C. The Nature of Formation

The above observations establish three major features of compound formation in *Drosophila*: (1) compound autosomes can be induced in both male and female germ cells; (2) they arise as products of either sister strand or nonsister strand attachments; and (3) they can occur, with low frequency, as products of spontaneous events. The next obvious question concerns the mechanism by which these processes come about. Of historical significance is the model of centromere misdivision proposed by Darlington (1939). In his studies on the meiotic events in *Fritellaria*, Darlington noted that where bivalents did not form, the plane of division occasionally transversed the centromere of the univalent. This "centromeric misdivision" apparently resulted in the attachment of half centromeres of the sister chromatids, thus forming what was referred to as isochromosomes. Giles (1943) observed, in a single plant of the genus *Gasteria*, that isochromosomes were frequently generated during meiosis between both sister and nonsister chromatids of a specific pair of cytologically marked homologues. He suggested that exchanges between centromeric fibres, where adjacent rather than opposite ends reattached, brought about the production of isochromosomes. This model was recently challenged by Brandham (1970) who speculates that the high incidence of apparent isochromosome formation of both arms arose through normal crossing over within a region in which the homologues were heterozygous for a pericentric inversion. It is interesting to find that Bateman (1968) also proposed misdivision and exchange within the centromeres as possible modes of compound formation. These models, he argues, are supported by the fact that the standard chromosomes he reconstituted from the compounds were all homozygous viable.

A third model, also suggested by Bateman, describes compounds arising through "illegitimate exchange". This is comparable to the translocation type model originally described by Rasmussen (1960) and later supported by Leigh and Sobels (1970). The latter model suggests that asymmetric breaks occur on opposite sides of homologous centromeres. The repair of these breaks, through the joining of the acentric fragment to the homologous centric free arm, would produce a compound autosome that is heterozygous for a deficiency and carries a small duplication for the proximal region of the opposite arm.

Although all the above models remain open to debate, experimental evidence weighs strongly in favour of a translocation or unequal exchange event. First we note that induced attached-X formation during oogenesis (Herskowitz *et al.*, 1962) and during spermatogenesis (Neuhaus, 1936; Leigh, 1972), apparently requires that one of the X-chromosomes in females, and the single X in males, carries a duplication attached to the short arm. This implies that the formation of compounds is not independent of target size on either side of the centromere. We also note that radiation induced reversions of attached-X chromosomes are translocation events involving either the Y (Parker and Hammond, 1958) or one of the autosomes (Abrahamson *et al.*, 1956).

The features of compound formation that support this model were first recognized through the construction of *C*(*2L*) and *C*(*2R*) chromosomes in *SD–72* heterozygous females (Kowalishyn, 1971). The *SD–72* allele is inseparable from a small pericentric inversion whose break points 39–40 on the left, and *42A* on the right (Lewis, 1962), flank the recessive visible markers *lt* and *rl*. This was verified genetically by showing that flies carrying the combination of *C*(*2L*)*RM,lt;* (*C2R*)*RM,SD–72*/+ were phenotypically lt^+, and flies carrying *C*(*2L*)*RM,SD–72*/+; *C*(*2R*)*RM,rl* were phenotypically rl^+. These observations clearly demonstrate that compounds carrying deficiencies and duplications that include these markers are viable, and that the recovery of any newly formed compound is not absolutely dependent on the genetic constitution of the complementary attachment. With this in view, all available *C*(*2L*) chromosomes were combined with one of the *C*(*2R*)*RM,rl* chromosomes in stock whereupon it was found that approximately one half of the *C*(*2L*) chromosomes carried a rl^+ allele (Holm, Gavin, Kowalishyn and Yeomans, in preparation). Likewise, the *C*(*2R*) chromosomes were tested against a *C*(*2L*),*lt* which revealed that 1 out of 30 had a duplication of lt^+. In addition, it was noted that one of the three available *C*(*2R*),*rl* chromosomes in combination with approximately one half of those *C*(*2L*)'s that did not cover rolled, expressed a phenotype indistinguishable from heterozygotes of *rl* over the proximal deficiency on 2R, *Df*(*2R*)*M–S2*^{10}. This observation suggests that the *rl*-bearing compound in question is hemizygous for the proximal heterochromatic region up to and including the rolled locus.

With regard to comparing the mechanics of generating sister-strand and nonsister-strand attachments, it should be noted that a number of gamma ray induced *C*(*2L*),*lt* chromosomes recovered from *lt stw*/*In*(*2LR*)*SM1,Cy* females also covered the expression of rolled on *C*(*2R*). Furthermore, upon testing two *C*(*2L*) chromosomes that arose spontaneously, one was found to carry a duplication for rl^+. It would appear, therefore, that not only the induced formation of sister and nonsister attachments, but also the spontaneous formation of compounds, occurs as the result of a common mechanism; namely, as a translocation-like event.

D. Reversion

The stability of compound autosomes is realized through the absence of reverted chromosomes appearing in stocks, even those maintained over a number of years. This is not to say spontaneous reversion will not occur, as revertants have been found, although infrequently, from matings of compound-bearing females to normal males (Leigh and Sobels, 1970; Gavin, 1971). But, the possibility that this event will occur simultaneously in both of the gametes forming a zygote is considered extremely remote. On the other hand, when compound-bearing females are treated with either gamma or X-rays, detachments are frequently recovered (Bateman, 1968; Chovnick *et al.*, 1970; Baldwin and Suzuki, 1971; Hilliker, 1972a, b; Yeomans, 1972).

In contrast to the findings of Bateman (1968), a significant proportion of the detachments obtained in more recent investigations have carried recessive lethals. The work of Baldwin and Suzuki (1971) was the first to demonstrate that the majority of those lethals arise in association with the breakage and rejoining of the autosomal arms. Out of the 162 fertile reconstituted third chromosomes, 96 were homozygous viable; the remaining 66 were homozygous lethal. 53 of the recessive lethals were assigned to two main clusters, the remaining 13 represented mutations induced independent of the detachment event. One cluster was represented by 12 non-complementary lethals; the second cluster, containing the remaining lethals, was divided into at least 2 complementation groups, but 22 of the lethals failed to complement any of the mutations within the cluster. Crossover analysis revealed that the lethals were in the centromeric region flanked by the proximal markers *ri* on the left and p^p on the right. It was considered that the two main clusters represented deletions to either side of the centromere and that they were generated as a consequence of the asymmetrical exchanges that produced the reverted chromosomes. Since none of the known proximally located recessive markers showed pseudodominance over any of the deletions, the clusters could not be assigned a position with respect to the left or right side of the centromere.

Reverted compound-2 chromosomes produced a similar pattern as described for chromosome-3; namely, two main nonoverlapping clusters of lethals were induced as a consequence of detaching the compounds (Hilliker, 1972a, b). From a total of 84 revertants derived from irradiated females carrying the same combination of compound-2 chromosomes, 28 were homozygous lethal. Three lethals arose from secondary hits, the remaining 25 belonged to the two major clusters. On the basis of complementation and pseudodominance tests, the clusters of lethals were subdivided into groups. One cluster was represented by two groups, designated as groups A and B. The 17 lethals in group A were characterized by not complementing each other nor the large heterochromatic deficiency, $Df(2R)M\text{–}S2^{10}$, on the right arm. They were further characterized by uncovering the marker rolled, but they were not lethal with *M(2)S2*, nor did they uncover straw. The group B lethal did not complement any group A lethals, nor $Df(2R)M\text{–}S2^{10}$, but it did cover the marker *rl*.

That the second cluster of lethals represented deletions of the proximal region of the left arm was realized from a group of two noncomplementing lethals that were deficient for the locus *lt* and lethal with all other lethals in the cluster. The remaining 5 lethals fell into two complementing subgroups, neither of which were deficient for *lt* nor any of the markers more distal to light. The latter groups were interpreted as deletions between the centromere and the light locus.

It is noted that none of the revertants carried lethals for both arms. The absence of such doubles suggests that the pairs of compounds from which the reconstituted standard autosomes were generated did not carry deficiencies for any functional loci in the proximal region. The recovery of nonoverlapping deficiencies in 2L, however, suggests that *C(2R)* was heterozygous for a duplication of the proximal region in 2L. The recovery of overlapping deficiencies that extend varying distances in a distal direction supports the concept that the detachment of compound autosomes. as well as attachment, represents a translocation event.

III. Meiotic Behaviour

From the previous discussion on compound formation, we recall that included with the progeny carrying newly attached arms, progeny arose as a result of nondisjunction or chromosome loss. In fact, with rare exception, the majority of the recovered progeny inherited either the paternal set of compounds or the corresponding maternal pair of homologues. Since previous crosses between males and females with differently marked compound autosomes rarely produced exceptional progeny, it was decided that a closer examination of the meiotic behaviour of these chromosomes was in order. The results from initial studies on compound-3 meiotic behaviour revealed that; (1) in the absence of structurally rearranged heterologues, over 95% of the products of oogenesis carry either a *C(3L)* or a *C(3R)*, (2) when compound-3 females carry either an inverted second or a compound-X chromosome, the recovery of nonsegregational compound-3 gametes is greatly increased, and (3) the production of nonsegregational compound-3 gametes in males is a regular and frequent event (Baldwin and Chovnick, 1967; Holm *et al.*, 1967). These findings led to further studies, the results of which are reviewed below.

A. In Females

Progeny that arise from crosses involving compound-3 (or compound-2) parents are recovered in two distinct genetic classes. To define these two classes of progeny, those receiving one compound autosome from the female parent and the complementary compound from the male shall be referred to as segregational progeny; and those inheriting both compounds from the mother (the matroclinous progeny) or from the father (the patroclinous progeny), as the nonsegregational progeny.

In those crosses where compound-3 (or compound-2) females are structurally homozygous for the standard arrangement of all chromosomes, other than the compounds, the nonsegregational events are clearly the exceptions. Nevertheless, the frequency does vary for the different strains of females tested. The basic or spontaneous frequency of any given strain can be viewed as a function of some intrinsic property of the compounds involved for two reasons (Holm, 1969; Holm and Chovnick, 1975): (1) the distribution of exceptional events, comparing all crosses in a given sample, are relatively homogenous; and (2) where unusually high spontaneous events occur (at times approaching 5% nonsegregation) it is associated with the presence of some particular compound chromosome.

If the meiotic assortment of compounds is viewed as a function of distributive pairing, then spontaneous nonsegregation may reflect the frequency with which compounds nonhomologously pair with other chromosomes available to the "distributive pairing pool" (R. F. Grell, 1962). As demonstrated by R. F. Grell (1964) the fourth chromosomes are regular members of the distributive pairing pool, and, as realized from secondary nondisjunction (Bridges, 1916), nonexchange X-chromosomes comply with the rules of distributive pairing (Roberts, 1962).

In keeping with the "size rule" of the distributive pairing model (R. F. Grell, 1967) it would be argued that the fourth chromosomes do not serve as competitive pairing partners for the compound autosomes. However, as demonstrated in recent studies (Harger and Holm, in preparation), there is a high correlation between the spontaneous level of nonsegregation and the frequency of X-chromosome nondisjunction. Moreover, progeny patroclinous for the compounds are frequently matroclinous for the nondisjunctional X-chromosomes.

In view of the previous observations, it is not surprising that in combination with rearranged heterologues, a compound-X chromosome or a free Y chromosome, compound autosomes show a marked increase in nonsegregation. Some specific examples serve to demonstrate this point. With the presence of a compound-X (and one, or possibly two, free Y chromosomes) the percent nonsegregational progeny produced by compound-3 females ranged from 20% to 27% depending on the pair of compound autosomes involved (Holm, 1969; Holm and Chovnick, 1975). It is interesting to note that 33% nonsegregation would be expected from random nonhomologous pairing of the compound-X, Y and compound autosomes. That this is not realized may imply some degree of either

TABLE I. Distribution of compound autosomes recovered in maternally derived gametes.

Genotype of Female parent[a]	Gametic classes								Percent Nonsegregation	Percent Assortment of *Cy* from *C(3L)*; *C(3R)*
	Segregational				Nonsegregational					
	C(3)L; 0		*0; C(3R)*		*C(3L); C(3R)*		*0; 0*			
	+[b]	*Cy*	+	*Cy*	+	*Cy*	+	*Cy*		
+/+;P5;P5	6634	—	6497	—	40	—	34	—	0·6	—
+/*Cy*;P5;P5	3128	2831	2896	2917	605	311	310	559	13·2	65·2
+/*Cy*;P2;P2	1271	1172	1174	1267	170	107	59	136	8·8	64·8
+/*Cy*;SH2;SH21	2386	1829	2854	2980	281	326	270	194	9·6	44·4
+/*Cy*;SH2;SH21	1760	1639	1810	1715	212	243	155	110	9·4	44·7
bw^{V1}/*Cy*;SH2;SH21	1144	1095	1203	1201	153	39	33	131	7·1	79·8

[a] *Cy* represents *In(2LR)SM1,Cy*; bw^{V1} designates *In(2LR)*bw^{V1}. The compound autosomes [*C(3L)*;*C(3R)*] are indicated by their specific code letters and numbers. [b] In the sixth cross, the wild-type chromosome was replaced by *In(2LR)*bw^{V1}.

preferential pairing or selective distribution from a pairing complex. It was also demonstrated that heterozygosity for *In(2LR)SM1,Cy* (a multiple break inversion on chromosome two) occasioned a relatively high frequency of nonsegregational events as compared to the spontaneous level (see Table I). Similarly, structural heterozygosity on the third is accompanied by increased nonsegregation between *C(2L)* and *C(2R)* (Holm, 1969; E. H. Grell, 1970; Holm and Chovnick, in preparation). In a series of four experiments involving compound-2 females carrying a marked-Y chromosome, E. H. Grell (1970) found that 24 to 31% of the recovered progeny were nonsegregational for the compounds. Grell further demonstrated that when two free arms are substituted for one of the compound autosomes, the remaining compound autosome and the Y, which constitute the only regular members of the distributive pairing pool other than the fourths, are recovered separately in 95–98% of the progeny.

The meiotic behaviour of compound autosomes, as revealed by the experimental results cited above, is in keeping with the general model for distributive pairing (see R. F. Grell, Chapter 10, in this volume). However, it should be emphasized at this point that "distributive pairing" is being used strictly as an operational term that refers to a property of meiosis which influences the distribution of those chromosomes not engaged in exchange pairing with independent homologues. Within this context, nonhomologous compound autosomes are viewed as pairs of heterologues and, therefore, are believed to form (in addition to the fourths) regular members of the distributive pairing pool. While the size rule of distributive pairing appears to hold true with respect to the fourths, the exceptional (spontaneous) events that occur in the absence of heterologous rearrangements appear to be a function of nonhomologous pairing between the compounds and nonexchange X-chromosomes. By replacing one or more standard chromosomes with structurally heterozygous or attached chromosomes, what can be inferred as competitive distributive pairing, involving the compounds, becomes a regular event. This is witnessed, indirectly, in the distribution of chromosomes in the nonsegregational class of progeny. When the distributive pairing alternative is a Y chromosome, or when both a Y and a compound-X are in the pairing pool, the heterologues are most frequently recovered independent of the compound autosomes in the nonsegregational gametes. However, when competitive distributive pairing involves two compound autosomes and a pair of structurally heterozygous autosomes, increased nonsegregation will be realized only where one standard and two compound autosomes migrate to the same anaphase pole. Examples from studies involving compound-3 chromosomes (Holm, 1969) are included in Table I.

The features of the results recorded in Table I are consistent with those obtained in other experiments. There is generally a uniform recovery of the four classes of segregational progeny. The exception recorded on line 4 of Table I was assumed to be the result of poor viability for the particular combination of the maternally derived *C(3L)* with the paternally derived *C(3R)*. Therefore, this experiment was repeated (line 5) using male parents taken from a different compound-3 strain. It will be noted that the distribution of compound autosomes in the four nonsegregational classes is unquestionably nonrandom with respect to the structurally heterozygous second chromosomes. However, the *SM1,Cy* chromosome and its homologue are recovered in relatively equal proportions in each test. If the distribution of the maternal set of nonsegregating compounds is compared with that of one of the two heterologues (in this instance *SM1,Cy*) we discover that: (1) the nonrandom distribution was reproducible in repeat runs using the same female parents (lines 4 and 5); (2) the distribution varied as a function of the pair of compounds used, as well as the structural nature of the rearranged heterologue; and (3) the greatest degree of nonrandomness occurred when one of the rearranged heterologues was an acrocentric chromosome (line 6).

Since there is no apparent recombination between *SM1,Cy* and its normal homologue (MacIntyre and Wright, 1966), we might assume (even for Experiment 5 where a low frequency of exchange between *SM1,Cy* and bw^{v1} was observed) that, in experiments recorded in Table I, the four major autosomes were regular members of the distributive pairing pool. There arises from these, and similar observations, the unsolved problems of how many chromosomes engage in a single pairing complex and what regulates the preferential distribution of certain heterologues. Previous studies on nonexchange chromosomes (Cooper, 1948; R. F. Grell and Grell, 1960; R. F. Grell, 1962; Moore and Grell, 1972) clearly imply the formation of trivalent pairing complexes. Based on the present set of data, however, it is difficult to determine whether or not similar multichromosomal pairing complexes are involved; although it is tempting to interpret the results with this possibility in view. Regarding the preferential assortment of nonhomologues, since the four major autosomes are similar in size (keeping in mind that the attached arms of the compounds can freely engage in exchange pairing) it is important to acknowledge that properties other than size might regulate the distributive pairing behaviour of these chromosomes. It is interesting to note, especially in connection with distribution of the acrocentric inverted second, bw^{V1}, that Moore and Grell (1972b) found chromosomal arm length to influence the assortment of chromosomes from the distributive pairing pool. We might find, for example, that centromeric displacement weakens the distributive pairing forces, thereby frequently excluding such chromosomes where there is distributive pairing competition. Unfortunately, this does not serve as an explanation for unequal assortment where all distributively pairing chromosomes are structurally similar. It is hoped that future investigations along these lines might provide a better insight into the meiotic events involving competitive distributive pairing of three or more major chromosomes.

B. In Males

In the studies reported above, the recovery of nonsegregational gametes from females did not appear to be limited by the availability of sperm carrying the complementary non-segregational products. This regular and frequent production of sperm disomic and nullosomic for compound autosomes is most easily explained by assuming that attached left arms share no male-specific pairing properties with the attached right arms, and therefore assort independently. If this assumption is correct, then one-quarter of the zygotes produced by compound-bearing strains will carry a normal complement of chromosomes. If, in addition, it is assumed that all aneuploid combinations of compound autosomes lead to embryonic lethality no greater than 25% of the fertilized eggs will be expected to hatch. This argument is illustrated in the form of a Punnett Square in Fig. 4.

As shown by Fig. 4, only four of the sixteen possible combinations of gametes form a normal complement of chromosomes, and, because the frequency of each sperm type is set at 0·25, the proportion of total viable zygotes (25%) remains constant, regardless of the changes in frequency (x) of segregational gametes produced by the female. It must also be assumed that: (1) the four classes of gametes are equally viable; and (2) all other chromosomes disjoin regularly; and if nondisjunction occurs, the percent hatch decreases accordingly.

One series of experiments designed to test this model (Holm, 1969; Holm and Chovnick, 1975) involved crosses between different combinations of males and females from four separate compound-3 strains. Each run included 25 to 30 separate egg laying chambers containing one female and two males. Eggs were scored daily for 5 or 6 days, subsequent to the first day that hatched eggs appeared. In the absence of structural heterozygosity for chromosome-2 in females, the lowest frequency of hatched eggs (648 out of 3123) was 20·8%, the highest (1646 out of 6429) was 25·6%. Structural heterozygosity of chromosome-2 in males had no measurable effect on egg hatchability, but, as predicted, rearrangements of the second chromosome in females occasioned a considerable increase in the frequency of embryonic lethality. Additional results from different sources (Scriba,

♂ / ♀	3L' 0.25	3R' 0.25	3L'; 3R' 0.25	O ; O 0.25	Viable Zygotes Distribution Frequency
3R X/2	3L'; 3R .25X/2				.25X/2
3L X/2		3L ; 3R' .25X/2			.25X/2
O ; O 1−X/2			3L'; 3R' .25(1−X)/2		.25(1−X)/2
3L ; 3R 1−X/2				3L ; 3R .25(1−X)/2	.25(1−X)/2
Viable Zygotes Total Frequency					0.25

FIG. 4. The use of a Punnett Square to illustrate the frequency of viable zygotes produced in a cross involving *C(3L);C(3R)* males and females. Note that although the distribution frequency is dependent on the value (X) of compound-autosome segregation in females, the total frequency of viable zygotes is fixed at a theoretical 0·25 as a function of random assortment of *C(3L)* and *C(3R)* in males.

1969; Evans, 1971; Lutolf, 1972; Fitz-Earle *et al.*, 1973) are in agreement with these findings.

The evidence, at least for the strains tested, rather convincingly supports the concept that during spermatogenesis *C(3L)* and *C(3R)* assort independently. However, in a series of six experiments involving different combinations of males and females from four compound-2 strains, the mean frequency of egg hatchability was consistently greater than 25% (Holm, 1969; Holm and Chovnick, in preparation). The frequencies ranged from a low of 26·1% (1841 from a total of 7051 eggs) to a high of 29·9% (1214 from a total of 4063 eggs). Although the 95% confidence interval included the theoretical value (0·25) in three of the crosses, adjusting for embryonic lethality from causes other than aneuploidy for compound-2 chromosomes would bring all values above the 25% level.

To determine whether or not some of the embryos aneuploid for compound-2 chromosomes might develop beyond the hatching stage, thereby producing the unexpected increase, a number of broods from five compound-2 hatchability tests were carried through to eclosion. Only those progeny advancing to at least the stage of eye pigment development were scored. Since, on the average, 96% of the larvae developed to mature pupae, or adults, and noting further that death in a few progeny occurred at early pupal or late third instar stages, death in early larval stages was insufficient to account for the increased hatch encountered in the compound-2 strains. From this, it could be argued that aneuploidy for compound autosomes results in embryonic lethality. Apart from these results, the developmental studies of Scriba (1967, 1969) convincingly demonstrate that the various forms of aneuploidy for compound autosomes lead to developmental arrest during the embryonic stages. It is also interesting to note, however, that in crosses of compound-2 males to standard females, a small proportion of the eggs hatched, whereupon death occurred in the early larval stages (Würgler *et al.*, 1972). These larvae were believed to be either monosomic or trisomic for both arms of the second.

In contrast to the close agreement obtained by different investigators on egg hatch studies involving compound-third chromosomes, the hatch values reported for compound-2 strains cover a considerable range. For example, Scriba (1967) reported, in line with values obtained with compound-thirds, a hatch value of approximately 20%. Clark and Sobels (1973), who crossed males from two different compound-2 strains to females from a third strain, observed 29·6% hatch in one cross and 32·0% in the other. And the highest frequency thus far obtained was reported by Evans (1971) who discovered, with one of the compound-2 strains employed in his studies, that 41% of the eggs developed into adults. This latter result implies a very low degree of meiotic nonsegregation between *C(2L)* and *C(2R)* in the males.

It is interesting to consider these findings in view of the following: (1) a number of compound-2 chromosomes (both attached-left and attached-rights) are known to carry rather extensive duplications for the proximal region of the opposite arm; and (2) male-specific pairing sites on the X were shown cytologically (Cooper, 1949) and genetically, through the deletion in the sc^4sc^8 chromosome (Sandler and Braver, 1954), to occupy a position in the proximal heterochromatin. From this, it might be inferred that the frequency of hatch over 25% is a function of pairing recognition, which in turn is a measure of homology shared by the complementary pair of compound seconds. That this has not yet been discovered for any combination of compound-thirds, might indicate that male-specific pairing sites on chromosome three are outside the limits of the duplications (and deficiencies) that can be tolerated by the compound-3 chromosomes. The solution to this problem may best be obtained in using the proximal deletions generated through reverting compound autosomes (Baldwin and Suzuki, 1971; Hilliker, 1972b).

IV. Manipulation

Many of the stocks used for the studies described in the previous section possessed, in addition to the compound autosomes, some combination of structually rearranged and genetically marked heterologues. In consideration of the meiotic properties of the compound autosomes in males, and in view of the rules governing the meiotic distribution of nonexchange and compound chromosomes in females, it becomes quite apparent that the mechanics of manipulating compound stocks present little difficulty. Nonetheless, as a guide, this section is included to describe some of the procedures that have been followed for introducing rearranged or marked heterologues into, or their removal from, compound autosome strains.

Probably the easiest chromosome to place into, but the most difficult to remove from, a compound autosome stock is the compound-X. Females, bearing a compound-X in combination with structural heterozygosity for the autosomes corresponding to the pair of compound autosomes carried by the males, produce a high proportion of compound-X, nullo-autosome gametes. For example, *C(1)RM/Y;In(3LR)TM3/+* females mated with *C(3L);C(3R)* males will produce, through the fusion of *C(1)RM*, nullo-3 eggs with a Y-bearing disomic-3 sperm, *C(1)RM/Y;C(3L);C(3R)* progeny. The occurrence of autosomal nondisjunction in such females is sufficiently frequent that from 25 to 50 pairs of parents will produce an adequate number of compound females to establish a new line. It should also be noted that this same procedure offers an easy method for inserting a marked Y chromosome into a compound strain. The Y chromosome may be recovered in the compound male progeny, although it frequently accompanies the compound-X in such crosses.

Introducing a standard or inverted X-chromosome, or an attached X·Y, follows the same general procedure, noting that the X-chromosomes, as well as the autosomes, must be structurally heterozygous. The interesting feature of such a cross (which is in keeping with the distributive pairing model) is that the progeny inheriting the paternal set of compounds usually inherit both maternally derived X-chromosomes.

The following example will relate the general procedure for constructing a compound-bearing stock with structural heterozygosity in the second pair of autosomes. Females of the constitution *In(2LR)SM1/+;In(3LR) TM3/+* are crossed to *C(3L);C(3R)* males. Although the total number of viable progeny produced per female parent is considerably lower in this case than with the compound-X females, or with females structurally heterozygous for the X-chromosome, sufficient progeny are recovered from 100 pair matings to establish the required stock.

Removing a standard autosome, or a standard X-chromosome, can also be accomplished in a single cross. However, in this case, compound males bearing the chromosome in question are mated with females heterozygous for inversions on the X and on the autosome corresponding to the compounds carried by the males. Regardless of whether an autosome or an X-chromosome is to be removed, the same combination of chromosomes can be used in the female.

If it is desired that a compound-X be transferred back into a standard strain, the following two-step procedure, which is a very efficient method of producing triploids, has been successfully employed. We will consider, as an example, the *C(1)RM/Y;C(3L);C(3R)* constructed above. The females are mated with males carrying compound-seconds and standard thirds. (To prevent crossing out of any markers that might be carried on the attached-X chromosome, it is advisable to use males that carry an inverted X.) The triploid females recovered in the F_1 generation are then crossed to standard males. The F_2 generation will contain, in addition to triploid females, triploid intersexes, diploid males, and females with normal X chromosomes, diploid females carrying the compound-X.

Attention has been given to compound-3 stocks in the specific examples described above. However, the same rules hold true for replacing chromosomes in compound-2 strains. One can also accomplish chromosome replacement by using meiotic mutants (Sandler *et al.*, 1968), but where the selected strain also carries a chromosome bearing the segregation mutant, there is the added inconvenience of removing this mutation from the stock. It also will be realized that a desired heterologue can be introduced simultaneous with the generation of a new compound. This method, however, should be avoided as it may very well result in an induced alteration of the selected heterologue.

V. Applications

Through their structural and associated meiotic properties, compound autosomes provide a curious set of germ products that serve as a valuable tool for genetic analysis. These properties, which have been discussed in the foregoing sections of this paper, can be summarized as follows: (1) in the absence of structurally aberrant heterologues in females, compound autosomes are infrequently recovered in the same female gamete; (2) from females carrying structurally complexed heterologues, in particular a compound-X, or carrying a free Y, a large proportion of the recovered gametes are either nullosomic or disomic for the attached autosomes; and

(3) in compound males, nonsegregational gametes are regular products, the frequency of which, for compound thirds at least, is indicative of random assortment. In addition, it is realized that any newly generated compound autosome can be carried exclusively in either a male or a female line and, because of the structural nature of the chromosomes, there is an almost complete genetic barrier between compound-bearing and standard strains of this species. Throughout the remainder of this paper, we shall examine how compound autosomes have been used to widen our scope of knowledge on some basic problem areas in genetics, and speculate, correspondingly, on their role in future studies.

A. Nondisjunction and Nonhomologous Pairing

Basically, our appreciation of nondisjunction in association with nonhomologous pairing derives from a history of investigations of the X chromosome (Bridges, 1916; Sturtevant and Beadle, 1936; Cooper, 1948; Cooper *et al.*, 1955; Sandler and Novitski, 1956; R. F. Grell, 1962a, b) as well as chromosome four (Sturtevant, 1936; Sandler and Novitski, 1956; R. F. Grell, 1964; R. F. Grell and Grell, 1960; Moore and Grell, 1972a, b). That the major autosomes also engage in nonhomologous pairing was made evident from crosses where females carried, in addition to either a free Y or some complex rearrangement of the X chromosome, a reciprocal 2:3 translocation and an inverted autosome (Oksala, 1968; Forbes, 1960; R. F. Grell, 1962; E. H. Grell, 1963; Miller and Grell, 1963); but demonstrations of nondisjunction of independent, nonexchange autosomes have been limited to indirect observations based on increased egg mortality (Cooper *et al.*, 1955; Terzaghi and Knapp, 1960) or to rather infrequent recoveries of matroclinous products using X-ray induced chromosome loss in sperm (Ramel, 1962). Since the proportion of aneuploid gametes produced by compound-bearing males can be as high as 50%, we have, at hand, a very suitable genetic assay system for expanding this area of investigation.

Initial studies, using compound bearing males to recover nondisjunctional products of oogenesis, give clear support to the notion that nondisjunction of the major autosomes arises as a consequence of nonhomologous pairing. For example, when females are heterozygous for inversions in both the X and second chromosome, progeny, matroclinous for chromosome two, are generally patroclinous for the X (Chadov *et al.*, 1970). When, in addition to an inverted X, females carry a free Y, nondisjunction of structurally heterozygous seconds is most frequently correlated with segregation of the nondisjoining pair from the Y chromosome (Chadov, 1969). In a study involving inversion heterozygosity for chromosome three, Evans (1971) found a similar nondisjunctional response to free Y chromosomes.

Other lines of investigation for which compound-bearing males might be employed, include: (1) an expansion of the studies by Ramel (1962) on the effects of compound-X chromosomes on autosomal nondisjunction in females with, and in females without, a free Y; (2) in view of the influence centromeric position might have on distributive pairing (Moore and Grell, 1972b), a consideration of possible preferential nonhomologous pairing using the diversity of autosomal inversions already available; and (3) a look at the possibility that deletions in the proximal heterochromatin might alter distributive pairing properties. It is interesting to note, in connection with the last point, that Baldwin and Suzuki (1971), in determining the properties of their reconstituted third chromosomes which carried proximally located recessive lethals, found some that caused a measurable increase in chromosome three nondisjunction. These lethals, it was noted above, were believed to reflect the presence of deletions in the proximal heterochromatin.

There is also considerable potential, engaging compound-bearing females, for examining departures from the normal meiotic behaviour of autosomes in males. Recalling that a compound-X (Holm and Chovnick, 1975) or a free Y (E. H. Grell, 1970) will increase the frequency of compound autosome nonsegregation to approximately 30%, it is immediately apparent that sperm, nondisjunctional for an autosome, can be readily recovered. Although the meiotic distribution of autosomes in males appears remarkably refractory to rearrangements (Stern, 1934; Frost, 1961), the present system may uncover subtle differences not revealed by the previously available systems. And in view of the effect the sc^4sc^8 inversion has upon X–Y segregation in males (Sandler and Braver, 1954) we recognize the potential in testing the various autosomal deletions, particularly those in the proximal heterochromatin.

B. Induced Nondisjunction and Chromosome Loss

X-rays were shown to invoke nondisjunction and chromosome loss even before this source of radiation was known to be a mutagenic agent (Mavor, 1924). Considerable attention has since been given to the effects of radiation on the distribution and recovery of the X chromosome, with a view to showing the sensitivity of progressive stages in germ cell development and the kinetics of radiation induced damage (for example, see Traut, 1964, 1967, 1970, 1971; Traut and Scheid, 1969; and for a review see Sobels, 1972). With the introduction of compound autosomes, chromosome-2 (but thus far, not chromosome-3) has become the subject of similar investigations.

Bateman (1968) reported that approximately two-thirds of the exceptional progeny, produced by irradiated females mated to compound-2 males, were patroclinous for chromosome two. He also noted that only 10% of the progeny arose through induced nondisjunction, while the remainder carried newly generated compound autosomes. These results, however, are based on a heterogeneous sampling of gametes with respect to stages of oogenesis. Focusing attention upon events postfertilization, Würgler *et al.* (1972) discovered induced loss but no nondisjunction of chromosome two following X-ray treatment, up to 6 hours after deposition, of eggs from a standard female fertilized by sperm from a compound-2 male. Induced dicentric anaphase bridge formation between sister chromatids was considered the possible cause. Studies on radiation induced nondisjunction of compound-2 chromosomes at oocyte stages 7 and 14 showed, in contrast to the findings for the X chromosome (Traut, 1970), no threshold of induced nondisjunction, even at 250 R of X-irradiation (Sobels and Clark, 1972; Clark and Sobels, 1973).

One aspect of induced nondisjunction and chromosome loss, which has received rather little attention, concerns the effect of radiation upon structurally heterozygous chromosomes and upon nonhomologous pairing. For the X-chromosome, Day and Grell (1966) found an insignificant difference for either induced loss or nondisjunction in comparing structural homozygotes with structural heterozygotes. However, chromosome loss was found to be greater for the exchange paired X-chromosomes than it was for the distributively paired complex of chromosome-4 with a free-X duplication (R. F. Grell *et al.*, 1966), although nondisjunctional frequencies were the same in both cases. In contrast, initial studies on chromosome two indicate a marked difference between structural homozygotes and heterozygotes (Gavin, 1971; Gavin and Holm, 1972; Gibson and Holm, unpublished data). For example, at doses of 1000 and 2000 rads of gamma radiation, the progeny recovered from homozygous females mated with compound-2 males arose, primarily, as the result of chromosome loss. For structurally heterozygous *SM1,Cy/+* (or *SM1,Cy/lt stw*) females, on the other hand, the frequency of induced nondisjunction was greatly increased and exceeded, by far, the frequency of chromosome loss. Even though the staging of oogenesis was quite heterogeneous in these tests, the results certainly imply that the effects of radiation upon distributive pairing are independent from those responsible for chromosome loss. It should be noted that studies on induced nondisjunction of autosomes also can be conducted in males since, as pointed out in the previous section, significant proportions of nullosomic and disomic gametes are available through the use of appropriate strains of compound-bearing females.

C. Meiotic Mutants

Mutants that alter the normal meiotic processes in females have been realized since the discovery of *c(3)G*, a recessive crossover suppressor on chromosome three (Gowan and Gowan, 1922; Gowan, 1933). Also, on chromosome three, there is the recessive meiotic mutant, ca^{nd} (claret nondisjunctional), first discovered by Sturtevant (1929) in *D. simulans*, and later by Lewis and Gencarella (1952) in *D. melanogaster*. More recently, Sandler *et al.* (1968) uncovered additional loci on both chromosome 2 and 3 that exercise an influence on either reductional or equational division. Mutations at these sites have been designated the *mei* mutants. (See Chapter by Baker and Hall for a full discussion.)

As with studies on spontaneous or induced autosomal nondisjunction, the compound autosomes have served an important role during the analysis of properties of meiotic mutants. Granted, much information has been derived from observations on the X and fourth chromosome, as well as from the recovery of triploid progeny and studies on egg lethality. However, such studies do not allow for comparisons of nondisjunction and nonhomologous pairings involving the major autosomes. As shown by Sandler *et al.* (1968), nonhomologous pairing is an important consideration in defining the properties of meiotic mutants. Subsequent investigations in which the regular nonsegregation of compounds in males was used to aid in describing the properties of meiotic mutants include the studies on; claret nondisjunctional (D. G. Davis, 1969), the *mei* mutants (Robbins, 1971; Baker and Carpenter, 1972) and the alleles of *c(3)G* (Hall, 1972).

D. Half-tetrad Analysis

Like the attached-X chromosomes, compound autosomes provide a means of recovering two, instead of only one, of the four meiotic products from females. Consequently, this system permits half-tetrad analysis of autosomal crossing over and provides a useful method for studying genetic fine structure. From the classic studies on attached-X chromosomes (Anderson, 1925; Emerson and Beadle, 1935; Beadle and Emerson, 1935; Welshons, 1955) the rules governing recombination were established. The value of the attached-X system, however, is severely limited in that, following the synthesis of a single attached-X heterozygous for a series of markers, recombination generates a population of females phenotypically identical but genotypically heterogeneous. This necessitates, therefore the analysis of single females to establish the coupling relationship of the markers on the attached arms. Such a system, with the exception of the unique condition provided by the complementing *ma–l* alleles (Smith *et al.*, 1970), cannot provide the high resolution required for the systematic analysis of genetic fine structure and gene conversion. Newly generated compound autosomes, in contrast, can be recovered and maintained exclusively in a male line. Thus a system is provided for generating homogeneous populations of compound autosomes heterozygous for a given distribution of genetic markers. As required, numerous females can be produced for large scale half-tetrad analysis.

In preparation for studies on gene conversion in higher organisms, Baldwin and Chovnick (1967) examined recombination between the attached arms of compound-3R using mass matings. Their results were in complete agreement with the rules established through half-tetrad analysis of single attached-X females. In addition, they found crossing over within the *C(3R)* chromosome to be influenced by the interchromosomal effect (Lucchesi and Suzuki, 1968). Following this (Holm, 1969) it was revealed that, in accordance with the finding of E. H. Grell (1963) for the attached-X chromosome, exchange pairing between the attached arms of *C(3R)* is independent of those events regulating the meiotic distribution of this chromosome.

The systematic investigations that led to the confirmation of gene conversion in higher organisms are described in another chapter of this volume (Finnerty, Chapter 8). However, included in this section is a brief account of those aspects of the investigation in which compound autosomes served a major role. The *ry* (rosy) cistron, for which the order of several alleles had been defined in an internally consistent fine structural genetic map (Chovnick *et al.*, 1964; Chovnick, 1966), provided the focal point of these studies. Half-tetrad analyses were conducted using compound-3R chromosomes heterozygous for alleles of the *ry* cistron, as well as for outside markers flanking the rosy region (Chovnick *et al.*, 1970). According to the rules of crossing over, the surviving ry^+ progeny would be equally distributed into two phenotypic classes—(1) those in which the exchange was between alleles on nonsister chromatids attached to a common centromere, and (2) those in which recombination occurred between alleles on nonsister chromatids attached to different centromeres. But, in sharp contrast to this, the majority of the ry^+ half-tetrads were phenotypically representative of the class displaying no exchange for outside markers. Detachment of the compounds and analysis of the distribution of markers in the latter group of ry^+ half-tetrads revealed that, although one-third could be explained as classical single exchanges, the remaining two-thirds arose as exceptional events operationally defined as gene conversions. Complete analysis of the rosy alleles on the mutant strands from these half-tetrads (Ballantyne and Chovnick, 1971) established rigorous confirmation that gene conversion represents a non-reciprocal event. Supported by the evidence obtained from the half-tetrad system, extensive studies involving a variety of heterozygous rosy alleles on free thirds provided an interpretation of gene conversion that related it to linked exchange (Chovnick *et al.*, 1971).

In addition to the investigations on the rosy cistron, half-tetrad analyses were carried out at two other loci on the right arm of chromosome three. Hexter *et al.* (1967) examined crossing over between alleles of the spineless-aristopedia locus, and Lewis (1967) recovered a series of recombinant products from females heterozygous for all five pseudoalleles of the bithorax complex. The bithorax study warrants particular note as it represents the first analysis of reciprocal products recovered from recombinations between closely linked markers carried on compound autosomes.

One final comment on half-tetrad analysis concerns the possible use of compound autosomes for examining induced exchange during spermatogenesis. It is interesting that the tetrads of a compound do not segregate until the second meiotic division; whereas, homologues of standard chromosomes disjoin at meiosis I. This should, in theory, provide a means of separating events at the two meiotic stages by simultaneously inducing exchange in standard and compound chromosomes. Moreover, although only reciprocal exchanges could be recovered, it also should be possible to measure induced exchanges in spermatids and sperm.

VI. Summary

This review was prepared, primarily, to introduce to the reader the possible uses of compound autosomes, as well as relate the current concepts on their formation and intrinsic meiotic behaviour. Compounds have unquestionably opened new avenues of investigation and it is expected that considerable progress will be made in the future. In the work that has been done with compound autosomes, we note two areas in which significant contributions have been made: (1) distributive nondisjunction and (2) half-tetrad analysis. The latter has been most rewarding in providing a means of demonstrating gene conversion; the former has rather clearly shown that the meiotic behaviour of compound autosomes in females is in general agreement with the distributive pairing hypothesis.

Possibly of greater interest, especially in view of future investigations, is the random assortment of compound autosomes in males. Spermatozoa generated by compound-bearing males provide the means of capturing nondisjunctional products of oogenesis as well as newly induced rearrangements and genetic lesions that alter the normal meiotic processes in females.

Because investigations dealing with compound autosomes are still in their early stages, speculation has been a rather constant theme throughout the foregoing discussion; and there is at least one additional area of speculation that deserves consideration, mainly because it stems from the earliest studies on the application of compound autosomes.

McCloskey (1966) used compound autosomes to examine the chromosomal requirements of functional sperm. His study clearly demonstrated that a complete complement of autosomal material was not essential to sperm activity. Three years later, Lindsley and Grell (1969) reported that, in fact, a sperm could function while carrying only chromosome four. A single sperm of this nature was rescued from a compound-2; compound-3 male. In view of the meiotic properties of compound autosomes in males, if, in addition to the compounds, each male carried an attached X·Y chromosome, all chromosomes but the pair of fours should assort relatively at random. This system should produce a chromosomally heterogeneous population of sperm cells in which some predictable proportion is devoid of all but a single fourth chromosome. There remains, however, the problem of freeing the sperm nuclei on the basis of chromosomal content. If accomplished, the potential *in vitro* studies are open to the speculations of the reader.

Acknowledgements

I am indebted to Dr. E. B. Lewis who kindly made available the material on the procedures he and his collaborators used to construct the original compound autosomes, and who provided helpful criticism of the manuscript. For valuable assistance during the preparation of this manuscript, I wish to thank my wife, Barbara. Studies carried out in my laboratory were supported by the National Research Council of Canada (A5853).

References

Abrahamson, S., Herskowitz, I. H. and Muller, H. J. (1956). Identification of half-translocations produced by X-rays in detaching attached-X chromosomes of *Drosophila melanogaster*. *Genetics* **41**, 410–419.

Anderson, E. G. (1925). Crossing-over in a case of attached-X chromosomes in *Drosophila melanogaster*. *Genetics* **10**, 403–417.

Baker, B. S. and Carpenter, A. T. C. (1972). Genetic analysis of sex chromosomal meiotic mutants in *Drosophila melanogaster*. *Genetics* **71**, 255–286.

Baldwin, M. and Chovnick, A. (1967). Autosomal half-tetrad analysis in *Drosophila melanogaster*. *Genetics* **55**, 277–293.

Baldwin, M. C. and Suzuki, D. T. (1971). A screening procedure for detection of putative deletions in proximal heterochromatin of *Drosophila*. *Mutation Res.* **11**, 203–213.

BALLANTYNE, G. H. and CHOVNICK, A. (1971). Gene conversion in higher organisms: Non-reciprocal recombination events at the rosy cistron in *Drosophila melanogaster*. *Genet. Res.* **17,** 139–149.

BATEMAN, A. J. (1968). Nondisjunction and isochromosomes from irradiation of chromosome *2* in *Drosophila*. Pp. 63–70. *In*: "Effects of Radiation on Meiotic Systems". International Atomic Energy Agency, Vienna.

BEADLE, G. W. and EMERSON, S. (1935). Further studies on crossing-over in attached-X chromosomes of *Drosophila melanogaster*. *Genetics* **20,** 192–206.

BRANDHAM, P. E. (1970). The consequences of crossing-over in pericentric inversions in acrocentric chromosomes. *Heredity* **25,** 125–129.

BRIDGES, C. B. (1916). Non-disjunction as proof of the chromosomal theory of heredity. *Genetics* **1,** 1–52; 107–163.

CHADOV, B. C. (1969). Preliminary data on 2 chromosome aneuploidy in XXY females of *D. melanogaster*. *Dros. Inf. Serv.* **44,** 111.

CHADOV, B. F. (1970). The spontaneous formation of the second isochromosomes in female *Drosophila melanogaster* with a normal and structurally altered genotype. *Genetika* **6,** (9), 170–172 (in Russian).

CHADOV, B. F., CHADOVA, E. V. and GAPONENKO, A. K. (1970). Nonhomologous pairing and nondisjunction of chromosomes of the first and second pairs in oogenesis of *Drosophila melanogaster* XX-females. *Genetika* **6,** (10), 79–90 (in Russian).

CHOVNICK, A. (1966). Genetic organization in higher organisms. *Proc. Roy. Soc. London,* **B164,** 198–208.

CHOVNICK, A., SCHALET, A., KERNAGHAN, R. P. and KRAUSS, M. (1964). The rosy cistron in *Drosophila melanogaster*: Genetic fine structure analysis. *Genetics* **50,** 1245–1259.

CHOVNICK, A., BALLANTYNE, G. H., BAILLIE, D. L. and HOLM, D. G. (1970). Gene conversion in higher organisms: half-tetrad analysis of recombination within the rosy cistron of *Drosophila melanogaster*. *Genetics* **66,** 315–329.

CHOVNICK, A., BALLANTYNE, G. H. and HOLM, D. G. (1971). Studies on gene conversion and its relationship to linked exchange in *Drosophila melanogaster*. *Genetics* **69,** 179–209.

CLARK, A. M. and SOBELS, F. H. (1973). Studies on non-disjunction of the major autosomes in *Drosophila melanogaster*. I. Methodology and rate of induction by X-rays for the compound second chromosome. *Mutation Res.* **18,** 47–61.

COOPER, K. W. (1948). A new theory of secondary non-disjunction in female *Drosophila melanogaster*. *Proc. Natl. Acad. Sci. U.S.A.* **34,** 179–187.

COOPER, K. W. (1949). The cytogenetics of meiosis in *Drosophila*. *J. Morph.* **84,** 81–121.

COOPER, K. W., ZIMMERING, S. and KRIVSHENKO, J. (1955). Interchromosomal effects and segregation. *Proc. Natl. Acad. Sci. U.S.A.* **41,** 911–914.

DARLINGTON, C. D. (1939). Misdivision and the genetics of the centromere. *J. Genet.* **37,** 341–364.

DAVIS, D. G. (1969). Chromosome behaviour under the influence of claret nondisjunctional in *Drosophila melanogaster*. *Genetics* **61,** 577–594.

DAY, J. W. and GRELL, R. F. (1966). Radiation induced nondisjunction and loss of chromosomes in *Drosophila melanogaster* females II. Effects of exchange and structural heterozygosity. *Mutation Res.* **3,** 503–509.

EMERSON, S. and BEADLE, G. W. (1935). Crossing-over near the spindle fiber in attached-X chromosomes of *Drosophila melanogaster*. *Z. Indukt. Abstamm. Vererb.* **65,** 129–140.

EVANS, W. H. (1971). Preliminary studies on frequency of autosomal nondisjunction in females of *D. melanogaster*. *Dros. Inf. Serv.* **46,** 123–124.

FITZ-EARLE, M., HOLM, D. G. and SUZUKI, D. T. (1973). Genetic control of insect populations. I. Cage studies of chromosome replacement by compound autosomes in *Drosophila melanogaster*. *Genetics* **74,** 461–475.

FORBES, C. (1960). Nonrandom assortment in primary nondisjunction in *Drosophila melanogaster*. *Proc. Natl. Acad. Sci. U.S.A.* **46,** 222–225.

FROST, J. N. (1961). Autosomal nondisjunction in males of *Drosophila melanogaster*. *Genetics* **46,** 39–54.

GAVIN, J. A. (1971). The effect of gamma radiation and alkylating agents on the recovery of nondisjunctional and compound autosomes in *Drosophila melanogaster*. B.Sc. Thesis, University of British Columbia.

GAVIN, J. A. and HOLM, D. G. (1972). Gamma ray induced nondisjunction and chromosome loss of chromosome 2 in females. *Dros. Inf. Serv.* **48,** 143–144.

GILES, N. H. (1943). The origin of iso-chromosomes at meiosis. *Genetics* **28,** 512–524.

GOWAN, J. W. (1933). Meiosis as a genetic character in *Drosophila melanogaster*. *J. Expl. Zool.* **65,** 83–106.

GOWAN, M. S. and GOWAN, J. W. (1922). Complete linkage in *Drosophila melanogaster*. *Am. Nat.* **56,** 286–288.

GRELL, E. H. (1963). Distributive pairing of compound chromosomes in females of *Drosophila melanogaster*. *Genetics* **48,** 1217–1229.

GRELL, E. H. (1970). Distributive pairing: mechanism for segregation of compound autosomal chromosomes in oocytes of *Drosophila melanogaster*. *Genetics* **65,** 65–74.

GRELL, R. F. (1962a). A new model of secondary nondisjunction: the role of distributive pairing. *Genetics* **47,** 1737–1754.

GRELL, R. F. (1962b). A new hypothesis on the nature and sequence of meiotic events in the female of *Drosophila melanogaster*. *Proc. Natl. Acad. Sci. U.S.A.* **48,** 165–172.

GRELL, R. F. (1964). Distributive pairing: the size dependent mechanism for regular segregation of the fourth chromosome in *Drosophila melanogaster*. *Proc. Natl. Acad. Sci. U.S.A.* **52,** 226–232.

GRELL, R. F. (1967). Pairing at the chromosomal level. *J. Cell. Physiol.* (Suppl.) **70** 1, 89–112.

GRELL, R. F. and GRELL, E. H. (1960). The behavior of nonhomologous chromosomal elements involved in non-random assortment in *Drosophila melanogaster*. *Proc. Natl. Acad. Sci. U.S.A.* **46,** 51–57.

GRELL, R. F., MUNOZ, E. R. and KIRSCHBAUM, W. F. (1966). Radiation induced nondisjunction and loss of chromosomes in *Drosophila melanogaster* females. I. The effect of chromosome size. *Mutation Res.* **3,** 494–502.

HALL, S. C. (1972). Chromosome segregation influenced by two alleles of the meiotic mutant *c(3)G* in *Drosophila melanogaster*. *Genetics* **71,** 367–400.

HERSKOWITZ, I. H., SCHALET, A. and REUTER, M. DEL VAL (1962). Induced changes in female germ cells of *Drosophila*. VII. Exchanges induced in different X-chromosome regions after X-raying oocytes and oogonia. *Genetics* **47,** 1663–1678.

HEXTER, W. M., LOZNER, E. C. and BUNN, Jr., P. A. (1967). Genetic recombination at the spineless-aristopedia locus in *Drosophila melanogaster*. *Genetics* **56,** 565.

HILLIKER, A. J. (1972a). Deficiency mapping of the proximal heterochromatic region of chromosome 2 of *Drosophila melanogaster* with radiation induced detachments of compound second autosomes. B.Sc. Thesis, University of British Columbia.

HILLIKER, A. J. (1972b). Deficiency mapping of the proximal region of chromosome 2 of *Drosophila melanogaster*. *Can. J. Genet. Cytol.* **14,** 729.

HOLM, D. G. (1969). The meiotic behavior of compound autosomes in *Drosophila melanogaster*. Ph.D. Thesis, University of Connecticut.

HOLM, D. G. and CHOVNICK, A. (1975). The compound autosomes of *Drosophila melanogaster*: The meiotic behavior of compound-3. *Genetics* **81** (in the press).

HOLM, D. G., DELAND, M. and CHOVNICK, A. (1967). Meiotic segregation of C(3L) and C(3R) chromosomes in *Drosophila melanogaster*. *Genetics* **56,** 565–566 (Abstr.).

HOLM, D. G., BALDWIN, M., DUCK, P. and CHOVNICK, A. (1969). The use of compound autosomes to determine the relative centromeric position of chromosome three. *Dros. Inf. Serv.* **44,** 112.

KOWALISHYN, F. J. (1971). The meiotic behaviour of segregation distorter in compound-2 chromosomes of *Drosophila melanogaster*. B.Sc. Thesis, University of British Columbia.

LEIGH, B. (1972). Induction of attached-X chromosomes in spermatozoa by X-irradiation. *Dros. Inf. Serv.* **48,** 107.

LEIGH, B. and SOBELS, F. H. (1970). Induction by X-rays of isochromosomes in the germ cells of *Drosophila melanogaster* males: Evidence for nuclear selection in embryogenesis. *Mutation Res.* **10,** 475–487.

LEWIS, E. B. (1960). Personal communication.

LEWIS, E. B. (1962). Salivary gland chromosome analysis of segregation distorter lines. *Dros. Inf. Serv.* **36,** 87.

LEWIS, E. B. (1967). Genes and gene complexes. *In*: "Heritage from Mendel" (R. A. Brink, ed.) pp. 17–47. University of Wisconsin Press, Madison.

LEWIS, E. B. and GENCARELLA, W. (1952). Claret and nondisjunction in *Drosophila melanogaster*. *Genetics* **37,** 600–601.

LINDSLEY, D. L. and GRELL, E. H. (1968). Genetic variations of *Drosophila melanogaster*. Carnegie Institute of Wash. Pub. No. 627.

LINDSLEY, D. L. and GRELL, E. H. (1969). Spermiogenesis without chromosomes in *Drosophila melanogaster*. *Genetics* **61,** (Suppl. 1), 69–78.

LUCCHESI, J. C. and SUZUKI, D. T. (1968). The interchromosomal control of recombination. *A. Rev. Genet.* **2,** 53–86.

LUTOLF, H. V. (1972). Meiotic segregation of compound-3 chromosomes in Drosophila. *Genetica* **43,** 431–442.

MACINTYRE, R. J. and WRIGHT, T. R. F. (1966). Recombination in FM4/ ;SM1/ ;Ubx^{130}/ heterozygotes. *Dros. Inf. Serv.* **41,** 141–143.

MAVOR, J. W. (1924). The production of non-disjunction by X-rays. *J. Expl. Zool.* **39,** 381–432.

MCCLOSKEY, J. D. (1966). The problem of gene activity in the sperm of *Drosophila melanogaster*. *Am. Nat.* **100,** 211–218.

MILLER, B. A. and GRELL, R. F. (1963). Nonrandom assortment of chromosome 3 and a Y. *Dros. Inf. Serv.* **38,** 65–66.

MOORE, C. M. and GRELL, R. F. (1972a). Factors affecting recognition and disjunction of chromosomes at distributive pairing in female *Drosophila melanogaster*. I. Total length *vs.* arm length. *Genetics* **70,** 567–581.

MOORE, C. M. and GRELL, R. F. (1972b). Factors affecting recognition and disjunction of chromosomes at distributive pairing in females of *Drosophila melanogaster*. II. The effect of a second arm. *Genetics* **70,** 583–593.

NEUHAUS, M. J. (1936). Production of attached-X chromosomes in *Drosophila melanogaster* males. *Nature, Lond.* **137,** 996–997.

OKSALA, T. (1958). Chromosome pairing, crossing over, and segregation in *Drosophila melanogaster* females. *Cold Spring Harb. Symp. Quant. Biol.* **23,** 197–210.

PARKER, D. R. and HAMMOND, A. E. (1958). The production of translocations in *Drosophila* oocytes. *Genetics* **43,** 92–100.

RAMEL, C. (1962). Interchromosomal effects of inversions in *Drosophila melanogaster*. II. Non-homologous pairing and segregation. *Hereditas* **48,** 59–82.

RASMUSSEN, I. E. (1960). Reports on new mutants. *Dros. Inf. Serv.* **34,** 53.

ROBBINS, L. G. (1971). Nonexchange alignment: A meiotic process revealed by a synthetic mutant of *Drosophila melanogaster*. *Molec. Gen. Genetics* **110,** 144–166.

ROBERTS, P. (1962). Interchromosomal effects and the relation between crossing-over and nondisjunction. *Genetics* **47,** 1691–1709.

SANDLER, L. and BRAVER, G. (1954). The meiotic loss of unpaired chromosomes in *Drosophila melanogaster*. *Genetics* **39,** 365–377.

SANDLER, L. and NOVITSKI, E. (1956). Evidence for genetic homology between chromosomes I and IV in *Drosophila melanogaster*, with a proposed explanation for the crowding effect in triploids. *Genetics* **41,** 189–193.

SANDLER, L., LINDSLEY, D. L., NICOLETTI, B. and TRIPPA, G. (1968). Mutants affecting meiosis in natural populations of *Drosophila melanogaster*. *Genetics* **60,** 525–558.

SCRIBA, M. E. L. (1967). Embryonale Entwicklungsstorungen bei Defizienz und Tetraploidie des 2. Chromosoms von *Drosophila melanogaster*. *Roux' Archiv. Entwment.* **159,** 314–345.

SCRIBA, M. E. L. (1969). Embryonale Entwicklungsstorungen bei Nullosomie und Tetrasomie des 3. Chromosoms von *Drosophila melanogaster*. *Devl. Biol.* **19,** 160–177.

SMITH, P. D., FINNERTY, V. G. and CHOVNICK, A. (1970). Gene conversion in *Drosophila:* Nonreciprocal events at the maroon-like cistron. *Nature, Lond.* **228,** 441–444.

SOBELS, F. H. (1972). The role of *Drosophila* in the field of mutation research. *Archiv. Genetik* **45,** 101–125.

SOBELS, F. H. and CLARK, A. M. (1972). The induction of autosomal nondisjunction by X-rays of stage-7 oocytes of *Drosophila melanogaster*. *Intl. J. Rad. Biol.* **23,** 195–196.

SOBELS, F. H. and LEIGH, B. (1971). The induction of X-rays of double mosaics involving the Y-chromosome, supporting first cleavage segregation in *Drosophila melanogaster*. *Mutation Res.* **12,** 100–101.

STERN, C. (1934). On the occurrence of translocations and autosomal nondisjunction in *Drosophila melanogaster*. *Proc. Natl. Acad. Sci. U.S.A.* **20,** 36–39.

STURTEVANT, A. H. (1929). The claret mutant type of *Drosophila simulans*: a study of chromosome elimination and cell lineage. *Z. Wiss. Zool.* **135,** 325–356.
STURTEVANT, A. H. (1936). Preferential segregation in triple-IV females of *Drosophila melanogaster*. *Genetics* **21,** 444–466.
STURTEVANT, A. H. and BEADLE, G. W. (1936). The relations of inversions in the X chromosome of *Drosophila melanogaster* to crossing over and disjunction. *Genetics* **21,** 554–604.
TERZAGHI, E. and KNAPP, D. (1960). Pattern of chromosome variability in *Drosophila pseudoobscura*. *Evolution* **14,** 347–349.
TRAUT, H. (1964). The dose dependence of X-chromosome loss and nondisjunction induced by X-rays in oocytes of *Drosophila melanogaster*. *Mutation Res.* **1,** 157–162.
TRAUT, H. (1967). X-chromosome loss induced by low X-ray doses in mature and immature oocytes of *Drosophila melanogaster*. *Mutation Res.* **4,** 510–513.
TRAUT, H. (1970). Nondisjunction induced by X-rays in oocytes of *Drosophila melanogaster*. *Mutation Res.* **10,** 125–132.
TRAUT, H. (1971). The influence of the temporal distribution of the X-rays dose on the induction of X-chromosomal nondisjunction and X-chromosome loss in oocytes of *Drosophila melanogaster*. *Mutation Res.* **12,** 321–327.
TRAUT, H. and SCHEID, W. (1969). The dose dependence of X-chromosome loss induced by X-rays in mature oocytes of *Drosophila melanogaster*. *Mutation Res.* **7,** 471–474.
WELSHONS, W. J. (1955). A comparative study of crossing over in attached-X Chromosomes of *Drosophila melanogaster*. *Genetics* **40,** 918–936.
WÜRGLER, F. E., RUCH, P. and GRAF, U. (1972). X-ray-induced loss of the maternal second chromosome in inseminated eggs of *Drosophila melanogaster*. *Mutation Res.* **15,** 31–40.
YEOMANS, T. C. (1972). Induced exchange and compound autosome formation in females of *Drosophila melanogaster*. B.Sc. Thesis, University of British Columbia.

Appendix to Chapter 13

THE CONSTRUCTION OF AN ENTIRE COMPOUND TWO CHROMOSOME

E. NOVITSKI

Department of Biology, University of Oregon
Eugene, Oregon, U.S.A.

Joining chromosome arms together with no loss of essential euchromatic material in acrocentric compounds generally implies the availability and use of heterochromatic regions as attachment points (Fig. 1a). The recovery of a reversed acrocentric compound X chromosome by Muller in 1943, during the course of an X-ray experiment, was possible only because one of the chromosomes carried a scute inversion with distal heterochromatin. A small amount of essential euchromatic material beyond that heterochromatin was lost during the formation of the reversed acrocentric; this was not important because the deficiency was covered by the other normal arm.

The most primitive compounds are the metacentrics, since these do not require any joining of arms end to end, but a simple reattachment, spontaneous or induced, at the centromere region (Fig. 1b). Just as the attached-X (the reversed metacentric) is the simplest compound X-chromosome to produce, so are the compound autosomes (described in the preceding chapter), with one autosomal arm on either side of the centromere, the basic autosome compounds (Figure 1c). By analogy with the X chromosome compounds, what is ideally needed for the synthesis of the complete set of autosomal compounds is a heterochromatic attachment point at the tips of the autosomal arms, to serve the same function with the autosomes that *In(1)EN* (Novitski, 1949) served for the X compounds (Figure 1d).

There are several ways of seeking such attachment points, bits of non-essential heterochromatic material capped by a dispensable marker placed distally on some autosomal arm without the simultaneous loss of essential distal genes. In the first place, tests might be made of reciprocal

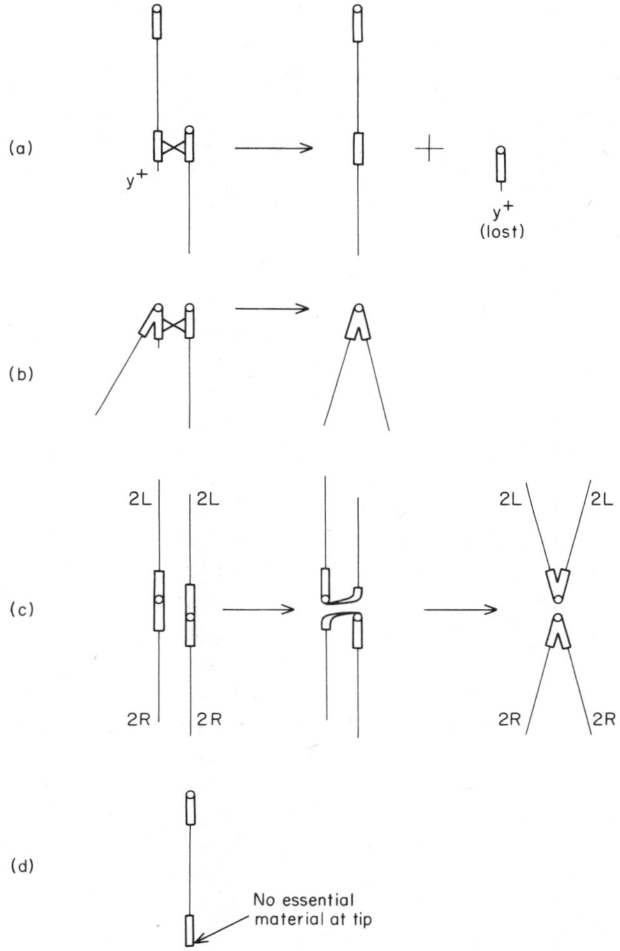

FIG. 1. The requirements for the formation of compounds. (a) The formation of an acrocentric compound using subterminal heterochromatin as an attachment point. (b) The origin of a simple metacentric, as an attached-X. (c) The formation of autosomal compounds. (d) An ideal chromosome for the formation of acrocentric compounds.

Y-autosome translocations to determine whether the autosomal segment by itself is viable and fertile when homozygous. Positive results in such a test would suggest the desirable prerequisite—an autosome with a useable attachment point (Fig. 2). (An autosomal segment viable and fertile in the heterozygous state in the absence of the other half of the translocation,

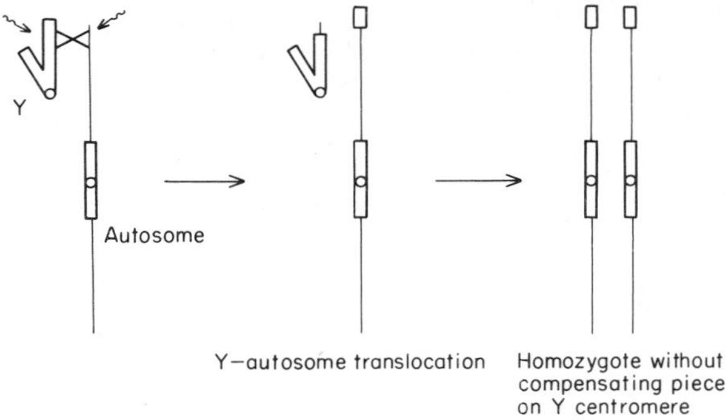

FIG. 2. The principle of manufacturing a precursor to compounds: the distal attachment of a piece of heterochromatin to the tip of the autosome, followed by the testing of the homozygote autosome, without the remainder of the translocation, for viability and fertility in the homozygote.

might be useful in limited applications, in the same sense that a scute inversion is useful in making up reversed acrocentric X compounds, but a chromosome of such limited usefulness should be avoided if possible. Certainly the compound described in this Appendix could not have been synthesized with such a chromosome.) In any case, appropriate tests of all Y-autosomal translocations available in 1972, including the array induced by the Lindsley, Sandler *et al.* (Lindsley *et al.*, 1972) collaboration, do not fit the simple requirements of viability and fertility when homozygous.

The second method depends on the experimental production of such a chromosome. This has now been accomplished (Novitski *et al.*, 1971). Briefly females carrying the $y^+ Y B^S$ of Brosseau were irradiated and F_1 progeny were selected which had either y^+ or B, but not both or neither, and which were not simple detachments of the compound used in the female. Such exceptions, it was reasoned, might include translocation-like rearrangements in which the half of the translocation with an autosome carrying one of the markers was recovered and the complementary piece, the Y carrying the autosomal segment was lost (Fig. 3). Translocations of this sort, unless insertional, would have to involve a break fairly close to the tip of the autosome in order to be viable as a heterozygous deficiency. When such losses were found, tests were made for linkage to the second and third chromosomes. In two cases, Bar was linked to the second chromosome and a simple crossover test placed it, in each case, to the left of aristaless, which is itself at 0·1 on the linkage map. In one case (B3), but not the other (B5), the second chromosome with the new tip carrying Bar is viable and fertile in the homozygote. The attachment on B5 is quite obvious cytologically (Novitski *et al.*, 1971) (Fig. 4); quinacrine staining reveals the brightly staining region of the Y at the tip of 2L.

With this attachment point at the tip of 2L, it is now possible to make up

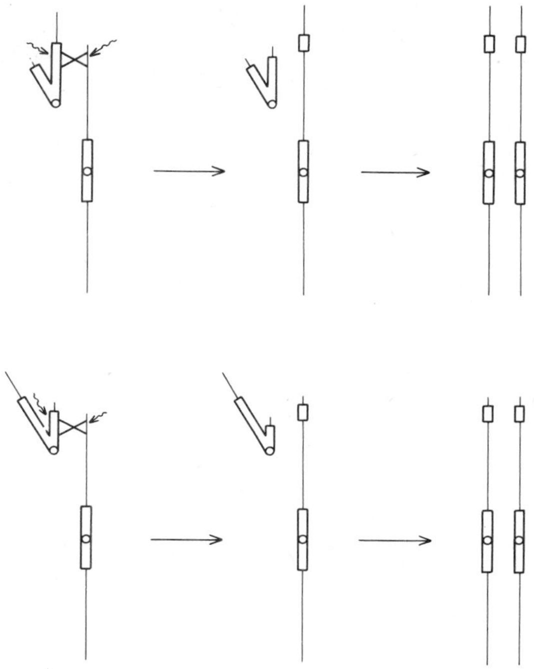

FIG. 3. The production of distally marked precursors, using a Y chromosome marked with either the normal allele at the tip of one arm or B^S at the tip of the other.

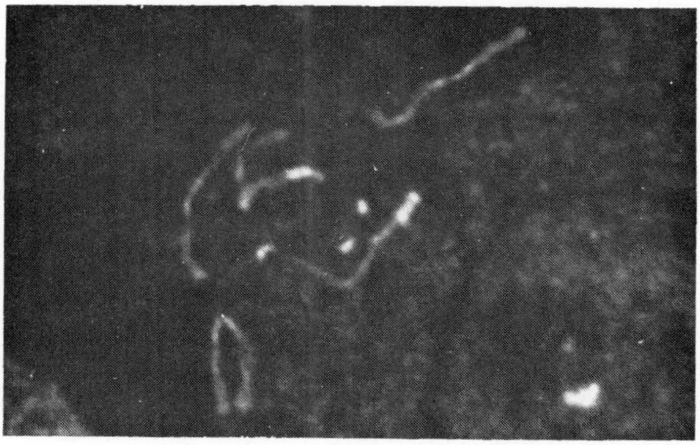

FIG. 4. Quinacrine stained ganglion metaphase showing the attachment of part of the Y chromosome to the tip of 2L.

any number of additional compounds at will, the only additional element needed being some incentive for doing so, since the specific procedures for attaching the X chromosome, or any of the autosomal or Y-chromosome arms, are straightforward enough. Our first interest was in joining together all four arms of the second chromosome found in the diploid, with one centromere. The configuration of such a chromosome would be *2R2L.2L2R*.

This was accomplished by way of the steps illustrated in Fig. 5. Females carrying *Dp(1;2)*B^S were mated to *C(2L)*, *C(2R)*; *C(3L)*, *C(3R)* males (Fig. 5a). Such a mating produces a sizable number of triploids (Novitski, 1973). Figure 5b shows the second chromosome composition of such triploids.

In the triploid female, a cross over will transfer the duplication to *C(2L)* as in Fig. 2c. A cross over in the four strand stage will make the duplication homozygous (Fig. 5d), readily recognized since the original is

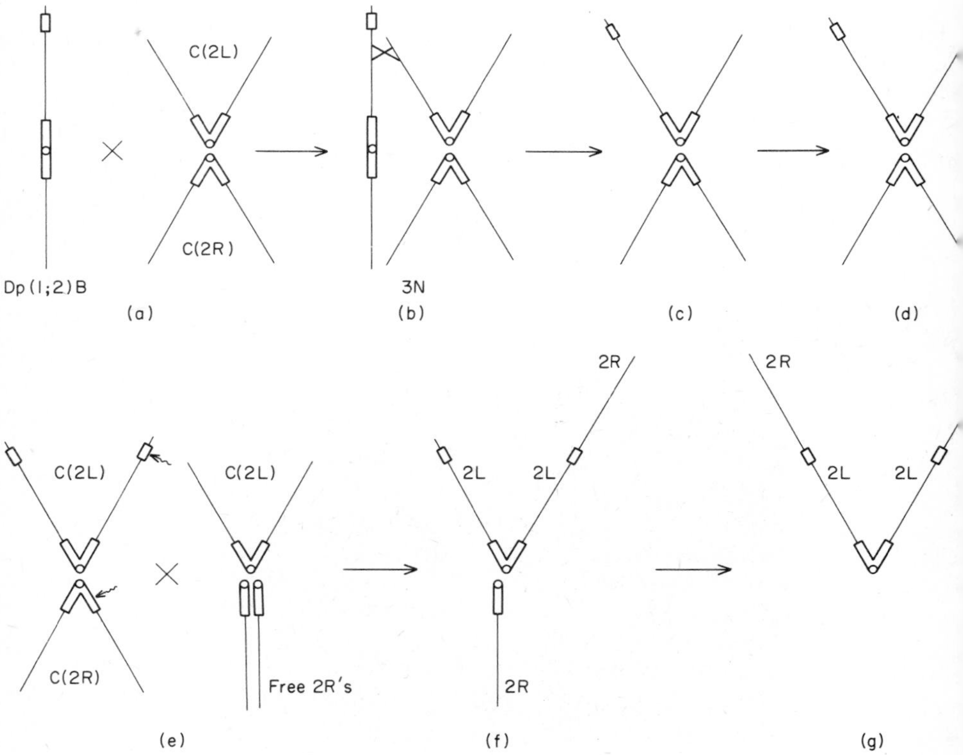

FIG. 5. The production of C(2)EN from a second chromosome with heterochromatin distally placed on 2L.

heterozygous Bar and the latter homozygous Bar. Females homozygous for the duplication, on each arm of *C(2L)*, are irradiated and mated to males carrying *C(2L)* but with two free right arms (Fig. 5e). Such a mating will ordinarily produce no progeny, or, at best, a very small number of unusual types, since none of the combinations of *C(2R)* [or no *C(2R)*] with a single free 2R are viable. The event desired, an exchange involving the region of the heterochromatin between the tip of 2L and the B^S marker and the region between the centromere and the euchromatin of 2R (marked with squiggly arrows in Fig. 5e), will give rise to the chromosome in Fig. 5f, one of the very few viable types that can result from this otherwise sterile mating. The loss of the Bar marker from one of the two left arms helps identify the desired event.

Theoretically, the next step is simple and self-generating, since a single crossover between the 2L arms can change the chromosome from *2R2L.2L* *Dp(1;2)*B^S to *2R2L.2L2R*. This would be identified by the loss of Bar. In practice, the conversion is more difficult because at the same time that the desired compound is generated, the complementary product, which is *Dp(1;2)*B^S *2L.2L Dp(1;2)*B^S, is also produced and these two compete at second anaphase, with the latter chromosome, the shorter and unwanted one being preferentially recovered (Novitski, 1954). In practice this difficulty can be circumvented by mating females carrying the compound shown in Fig. 5f to *C(2L)*, *C(2R)* males. This is, once again, basically a progeny-less mating because of the incompatibility of a free 2R with either a *C(2R)* or no 2R. However, if the appropriate exchange occurs in 2L in the compound, and the egg does not get the free 2R (which should be about half of the cases) then a viable progeny, of the right sort, will be produced, i.e. a compound with the structure *2R2L.2L2R* as in Fig. 5g. A photograph of a neuroblast cell showing this compound is found in Fig. 6.

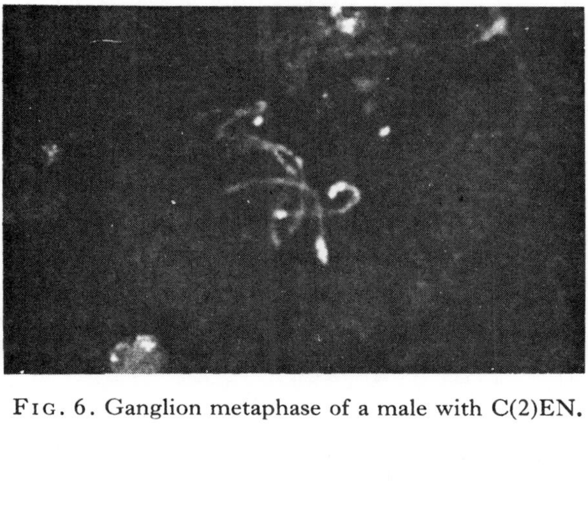

FIG. 6. Ganglion metaphase of a male with C(2)EN.

The nomenclature of this compound is *C(2)EN*, the latter two letters signifying the presence of entire second chromosomes in the compound.

ACKNOWLEDGEMENT

Supported by NIH Grant GM18678.

References

LINDSLEY, D. L., SANDLER, L., BAKER, B. S., CARPENTER, A. T. C., DENELL, R. E., HALL, J. C., JACOBS, P. A., MIKLOS, G. L. G., DAVIS, B. K., GETHMANN, R. C., HARDY, R. W., HESSLER, A., MILLER, S. M., NOZAWA, H. PARRY, D. M. and GOULD-SOMERO, M. (1972). Segmental aneuploidy and the genetic gross structure of the D. genome. *Genetics* **71,** 157–184.

NOVITSKI, E. (1949). An inversion of the entire X chromosome. *Dros. Inf. Serv.* **23,** 94–95.

NOVITSKI, E. (1954). The compound X chromosomes in D. *Genetics* **39,** 127–140.

NOVITSKI, E. (1972). Strengths of autosomal centromeres. *Dros. Inf. Serv.* **49,** 61.

NOVITSKI, E., EHRLICH, E. and BECKER, H. J. (1971). A terminal attachment region on 2L. *Dros. Inf. Serv.* **47,** 91–92.

14. Genetic and Cytogenetic Aspects of Altered Segregation Phenomena in *Drosophila*

S. Zimmering

Division of Biological and Medical Sciences
Brown University
Providence, Rhode Island, U.S.A.

I. Introduction

At germ cell formation in *Drosophila*, homologous chromosomes usually pair at prophase I, and separate at anaphase I; sister centromeres then separate at anaphase II and a chromatid is delivered to each of the four products. In the female, one of the outer products of a linear array of four becomes the functional egg and represents a random sample of the four chromatids; in the male, it is generally considered that all four products function. In the absence of crossing over, complementary noncrossover egg and sperm types are produced in equal frequency. Following crossing over, reciprocal crossover products are formed in equal frequency as are reciprocal noncrossovers after separation of the chromatids of the crossover dyads at anaphase II. Some exceptional cases include (1) the failure of homologues to separate at anaphase I (primary and secondary nondisjunction); (2) the failure of sister chromatids to separate at anaphase II (most readily detected in the male as the production of patroclinous daughters); and (3) the unequal production of reciprocal gametic types following separation of genetic alternatives at meiosis I and at meiosis II: in the former case, genetic alternatives segregate at anaphase I and functional gametes carrying one of these alternatives are produced in excess of the other; in the latter, crossing over occurs between homologues (or chromatid interchange between heterologues), chromatids of the dyads separate at anaphase II and gametes carrying one type of chromatid are produced in excess of the other. The former includes the typical cases of meiotic drive in the male and the latter those in the female and in special cases in the male where crossing over occurs (spontaneous or induced).

Section II of the present chapter reviews some aspects of meiotic nondisjunction in the female and male *D. melanogaster* (not including genetic control). Section III considers cases of meiotic drive in the male not involving crossing over, and Section IV those cases of drive in females and males requiring crossing over. One of the cases described in Section II, segregation-distorter, *SD*, is provided extensive treatment in the final section. Earlier reviews by Zimmering *et al.* (1970a, b) and Novitski (1967) have covered some of the material to be presented below.

II. Meiotic Nondisjunction in *D. melanogaster*

A. Primary Nondisjunction in the Female

From matings in *D. melanogaster* of females homozygous for the X-linked gene *v* (vermilion eye color) with wild type males, Bridges (1916) noted the appearance of occasional vermilion daughters and wild type sons. He suggested that "if [the] two X chromosomes fail to disjoin from one another . . . both remain in the egg or both pass out into the polar body; in the former case, the egg will be left with two X chromosomes and in the latter with no X. . . . The fertilization of such XX and zero eggs by the X and the Y spermatozoa will result in four new types of zygotes: (1) the XX egg fertilized by the X sperm gives an XXX zygote which might be expected to develop into a female. No females of this class have been found, and it is certain that they die; (2) the fertilization of the XX egg by the Y sperm gives rise to a female having an extra Y chromosome

(XXY); since both of the X chromosomes came from the vermilion-eyed mother, this daughter must be a vermilion matroclinous exception; (3) the fertilization of the zero egg by the X sperm gives rise to a male which has no Y chromosome (X0) and whose X coming from his red-eyed father brings in the red gene which makes the son a patroclinous exception; these X0 males are viable but are completely sterile; (4) the zero egg by the Y sperm gives a zygote (0Y) which is not viable."

From crosses of w^e $v/+$ $+$ or y w^e $v/+$ $+$ $+$ females with B males, Bridges (1916) reported finding two classes of non-Bar exceptional daughters: "regular primary exceptions" carrying a noncrossover chromatid of each maternal X, and "equational primary exceptions" bearing a crossover and a noncrossover chromatid and thus homozygous for some loci originally heterozygous in the mother. Since most equational exceptions were homozygous for w^e (or y w^e) and not v, and at that time y and w^e were thought to occupy proximal positions in the X, Bridges argued that regular primary exceptions arose from a failure of separation at the first division (reductional) in the absence of genetic exchange, and that equational primary exceptions resulted from failure of sister centromere separation at the second division (equational) following genetic exchange at the first. However, in the light of Anderson's (1925) work with attached-X's demonstrating that y was, in fact, located at the far distal end of X, Bridges' suggestion on the origin of equational exceptions was brought into question. It became clear that, since genes at the distal end of X showed increasing frequencies of homozygosis and those at the proximal end decreasing frequencies, nondisjunction giving rise to regular and equational exceptions occurs at the reduction division (Anderson, 1929). Sturtevant (1929) similarly interpreted the origin of equational exceptions in *D. simulans* and Moriwaki (1938) a case in *D. ananassae*. Figures 1 and 2 show the origin of equational exceptions according to Bridges and to Anderson, respectively.

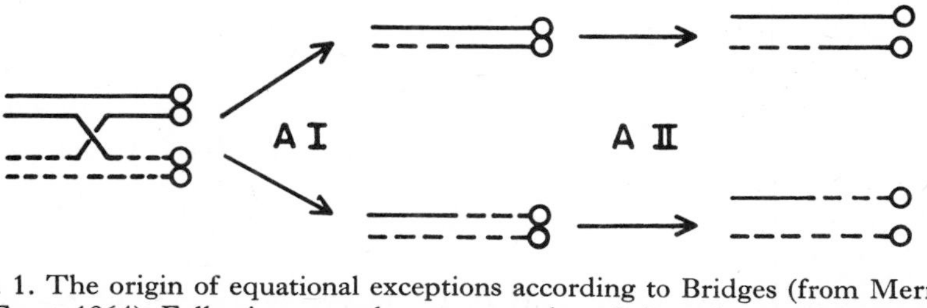

FIG. 1. The origin of equational exceptions according to Bridges (from Merriam and Frost, 1964). Following an exchange at prophase I, homologous chromosomes separate at anaphase I, but sister centromeres fail to separate at anaphase II giving rise to equational exceptions the majority of which are homozygous for proximal genes.

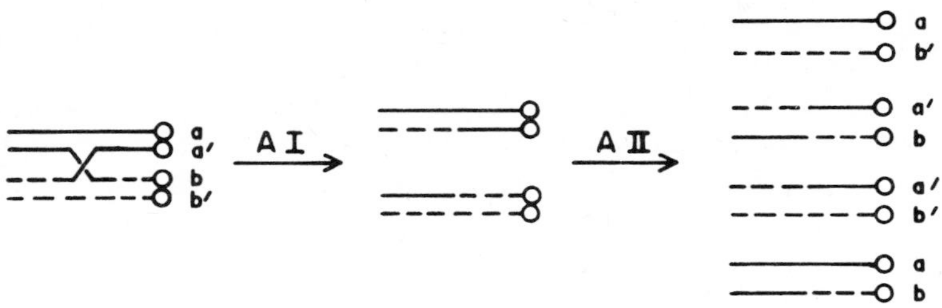

FIG. 2. The origin of equational exceptions according to Anderson (from Merriam and Frost, 1964). Following an exchange at prophase I, homologous chromosomes proceed to the same pole at anaphase I and random assortment of the chromatids at anaphase II gives rise to equational exceptions the majority of which are homozygous for distal genes.

Measurements of the spontaneous frequency of primary nondisjunction in *D. melanogaster* females carrying normal X's and under standard conditions usually give values of between 0·05% and 0·1% (Bridges, 1916; Safir, 1920; Merriam and Frost, 1964; Traut, 1970; Tokunaga, 1970a). In large-scale experiments where reliable comparisons may be made, the frequency of male exceptions exceeds that of female exceptions in ratios of some 3–7:1 (Safir, 1921; Mavor, 1924; Patterson *et al.*, 1932; Uchida, 1962; Tokunaga, 1970a). This discrepancy has been shown not to be related to a depression in the viability of XXY females as compared with X0 males (see, for example, Cooper *et al.*, 1955).

The question of the genetic composition of primary exceptional females has been explored extensively by Merriam and Frost (1964). Tetrad analysis of regular progeny showed that 4·6% came from no-exchange tetrads (E_0), 65·7% from single exchange (E_1), 28·7% from double exchange (E_2) and 1·0% from triple exchange (E_3) tetrads. From exceptional daughters the respective frequencies were 25·9% (E_0), 24·5% (E_1), 47·5% (E_2) and 1·9% (E_3). Surprisingly, therefore, some 74% of all primary exceptions were derived from exchange tetrads and a clear disproportionality from double exchange tetrads. They noted that crossing over was not noticeably different in females yielding or not yielding exceptions, and that crossovers carried by exceptions were not clustered in any region, the recombinant frequencies for each region under study being approximately equal in regular females and equational exceptions.

Summarizing the major characteristics of primary nondisjunction to be taken into account in proposing possible mechanisms Merriam and Frost (1964) list the following: (1) nondisjunction results from a failure of the reduction division; (2) exceptions may arise from exchange tetrads; and (3) exceptional males are recovered more frequently than females. Bridges

(1916) suggested "perhaps the cause of initial aberrant reduction . . . is a mechanical entanglement . . . of the two X chromosomes resulting in a delayed reduction. In such cases, the formation of the cell boundaries would catch the lagging X's and include them in one or the other cell and perhaps very often prevent their leaving the middle of the spindle to form either daughter nucleus. If such an occurrence were common there should be more zero than XX eggs and consequently more primary exceptionals should be males than females." This hypothesis accounts for the excess of patroclinous males, and, as Merriam and Frost suggest, if entanglements are due to occasional unresolved chiasmata, they should be more frequent among multiple exchanges and could account for the excess of doubles among their exceptions. They point out that an increase in triples would also be expected but this has not been observed. On the other hand, their data suggest at least a difference in the expected direction; the E_3 in regulars was 1·0% and in exceptionals 1·9%. Unaccounted for, then, would be the source of E_0's. However, if entanglements leading to nondisjunction occur in the absence of exchange, E_0's would be accounted for (this is the sense in which Bridges originally used the suggestion of entanglement). It should be noted that the suggestion of Sturtevant and Beadle (1939), that regular exceptions arise as a result of pairing failure, coupled with the suggestion of Sandler and Braver (1954), that asynapsis could lead to meiotic loss of one or the other X, could account for regular primary exceptions and the excess of exceptional males. As pointed out by Merriam and Frost, however, since most exceptions come from exchange tetrads, a disproportionately high frequency of loss from a smaller number of no-exchange tetrads would have to be assumed. The possibility cannot be denied at present (because of the cytological intractability of female meiosis) that an excess of patroclinous males arises from events unrelated to nondisjuncton, for example, via appropriate events leading to chromosome loss following spontaneous breakage of X at meiosis, adding to the zero class of sperm arising from nondisjunction.

Firm data on spontaneous nondisjunction in major autosomes should be forthcoming shortly as a result of the availability of the special compound autosomes. If the frequencies in the females are like those in the male (Frost, 1961), they will turn out to be as low as X nondisjunction; nondisjunction of chromosome 4 in the female is known to resemble X (Morgan *et al.*, 1925). Since nondisjunctional autosomes recovered from crosses with compound-autosome bearing males may be tested for their genetic composition, it will be possible to determine if the exchange frequency distribution inferred from nondisjunctional X's holds for autosomes and thus if the mechanism(s) of nondisjunction operating in the two cases is the same.

1. Factors affecting nondisjunction

(a) *Aging*. Whereas no significant effect of aging of females was found when aging was carried out at normal temperatures (Patterson *et al.*, 1932; Uchida, 1962; Kelshall, 1963), Hildreth and Ulrichs (1969) reported one following aging at 10°C. In the first two-day brood following treatment, they found 0·33 % nondisjunctionals from females aged at 10°C as compared with 0·09 % from those aged at 25°C. No eggs were laid during the cold treatment and normal numbers at 25°C. They suggested that earlier attempts failed because whereas the females were aged, their oocytes were not, egg laying having been largely uninterrupted at the normal temperatures.

Restricting the first brood to one day following the aging of females at 10°C, Tokunaga (1970a) found some 15–20 % X-nondisjunctionals. Furthermore, large numbers of triploid intersexes, some triploids and haplo 4's were observed, demonstrating that nondisjunction in retained mature eggs may extend to the entire diploid genome (Tokunaga, 1970b). Females aged at 25°C showed no such effect on the first day, but both kinds of females (aged at 10°C or 25°C) showed in later broods (6th–13th brood from single-day broods) similar patterns of elevated nondisjunction. Tokunaga suggests that eggs deposited on the first day from females aged at the cold temperature may be compared to vertebrate eggs exposed to overripeness yielding higher than normal frequencies of triploid and aneuploid embryos (see, for example, Yamamoto and Ingalls, 1972), and that the aging effects found in later broods could be compared to factors operating to bring about nondisjunction in earlier stages (dictyotene) where the majority of cases of chromosome 21 nondisjunction in humans not related to overripeness occur (see, for example, Matsunaga and Maruyama, 1969). The genetic composition of the X's of the first day exceptions was checked to some extent, sufficient to suggest to Tokunaga that nondisjunction occurred at the first division and that the exceptional females appear to have been derived from a random sample of oocytes. To what extent exceptionals in the later broods are comparable in their origin to those recorded by Merriam and Frost (1964) from females undergoing uninterrupted oogenesis remains to be determined.

(b) *High temperature*. R. F. Grell (1971) has shown an effect of high temperature on nondisjunction of X's. Exposure of developing females to 35°C at a stage where germ cells consisted predominantly of late oogonia and early oocytes resulted in a significant increase in X nondisjunction and a marked increase in no-exchange X's from a control value of 7 % to 45 % at the higher temperature. On the other hand, no increase in autosomal nondisjunction or autosomal no-exchange tetrads was found. Grell interprets her data as suggesting (1) that heat increases the production of no-exchange tetrads which is a prerequisite for the increase in non-disjunction of X's, and (2) that heat must also affect some component of the "distributive" mechanism [a mechanism R. F. Grell (1962a) has proposed which provides for the regular separation of no-exchange X's] since despite no-exchange frequencies of some 45% or greater, the frequency of nondisjunction in females heterozygous for multiple X inversions is much lower than that induced by heat treatment (about 2·5% in this experiment, as compared with 0·4% in females heterozygous for *Ins(1)dl–49*, B^{M1} where E_0's = 75%; Cooper, 1945). The effect on the "distributive" mechanism is presumed to be indirect since segregation occurs some six days following treatment.

(c) *X-irradiation.* Whereas ionizing radiation is known to increase the frequency of XX and nullo-X eggs, the latter rises more sharply than the former with increasing doses (see, for example, Kiriazis and Abrahamson, 1968); the disproportionately high frequency of nullos is generally attributed to breakage events leading ultimately to "chromosome loss' and unrelated to nondisjunction (see, for example, Muller, 1940). The discussion in paragraphs (a), (b), (c) and (d) below will be limited, therefore, to the effects of X-rays in producing XX eggs expressed as the recovery of exceptional females. The work of earlier investigators (Mavor, 1922; Anderson, 1925, 1931; Patterson *et al.*, 1932) provided evidence of an increase in the frequency of exceptional females following X-irradiation of oocytes in XX mothers. Anderson (1931) found, upon analysis of the genetic constitution of primary exceptional females, a rate of homozygosis for proximal genes relatively high in relation to distal genes, and suggested this to be due to nondisjunction occurring at both divisions after X-ray treatment. As far as is known, no further work along this line has been reported.

More recent work, employing controlled doses, more sophisticated genetic techniques and based on a considerably better understanding of oogenesis, has provided additional information on certain aspects of the nondisjunction phenomenon.

(a) In experiments testing relative radiosensitivity of oocytes at various stages of oogenesis (stages described in King *et al.*, 1956) major emphasis has been placed on the mature oocyte, stage 14, in late prophase or meta-phase I, and on the less mature stage 7, in earlier prophase. At doses up to 400–500 R to stage 14 oocytes, no increase in nondisjunction of X's (Kiriazis and Abrahamson, 1968; Traut, 1970) or chromosome 4 (Kiriazis and Abrahamson, 1968) was observed. These results are in sharp contrast to the findings that such doses induce at this stage a frequency of some 50% dominant lethals, and a frequency X-chromosome loss (X0 males) some 60X higher than controls, both phenomena involving considerable chromosome breakage (Parker, 1959; Traut and Scheid, 1969). In stage 7 oocytes, no continuous increase in nondisjunction was found up to a dose of 1000 R but there was a significant dose effect from 1000 R to 1800 R, suggesting a threshold effect at about 1000 R (Traut, 1970). Additionally, Traut (1971) reported a decline in nondisjunction after protraction of the dose but not fractionation as compared with a single acute dose. In view of these responses, Traut suggests that radiation-induced nondisjunction is not likely to be the result of damage to "targets" (i.e. centromere, centrosome) suggested earlier (Muller, 1954). Referring to the finding of R. F. Grell *et al.* (1966, to be described more fully later) that radiation-induced nondisjunction is not related to chromosome length, Traut argues that chromosome "stickiness" (Lea, 1956; Bacq and Alexander, 1961; Traut, 1964) must be regarded with reservation as a probable cause. As an alternative, he suggests that X-rays induce disturbances of processes leading to the formation of the spindle apparatus. Damage to the spindle itself would be assumed to cause nondisjunction in stage 14 oocytes although testing this would be difficult since doses large enough to cause nondisjunction in stage 14's would at the same time lead to their elimination via dominant lethality. On the other hand, failure to observe an increase in nondisjunction in stage 14's has been explained rather simply by Kiriazis and Abrahamson (1968) as suggesting that chromosomes at stage 14 have past the point in meiosis at which X-rays will cause aberrant segregation (see also Busby, 1971, below). Furthermore, Clark and Sobels (1973) have reported that following X-irradiation (presumably to stage 7 oocytes) nondisjunction of autosomes (using attached-autosomes in the male) shows a linear dose-effect relationship for radiation exposures from 250 R–2000 R providing no evidence of a threshold effect (whereas the abstract fails to report separately the recovery of nullo- and disomic products, it is presumed that the conclusions are based on the latter).

(b) The findings of R. F. Grell *et al.* (1966) mentioned above concerning the effects of X-irradiation on chromosomes of different lengths were derived from experiments in which induced nondisjunction was followed in two pairs of chromosomes bearing a length ratio of 10:1 to each other. No significant difference was found for any daily brood over the 12-day period followed and no difference in the average nondisjunction frequency. A trend, however, was observed in that a somewhat higher frequency of nondisjunction of the smaller pair was observed in days 1–7 than in days 8–12 (nondisjunction of the larger remained sensibly the same over the entire period). They suggested the possibility that the first 8 broods represent treated oocytes and the later ones oogonia (R. F. Grell and Chandley, 1965) and that the decrease in later broods could be characteristic of early premeiotic interphase and oogonia. In any event, finding that induced nondisjunction showed no correlation with the 10:1 difference in length suggested the possibility that each chromosome represents a more or less equivalent target for the induction of events leading to nondisjunction and that the centromere or adjacent regions could represent such a target.

(c) That X-ray induced nondisjunction is independent of exchange in the X's undergoing nondisjunction has been demonstrated by Day and Grell (1966) who observed about 1·6% nondisjunction for X's homozygous for multiple inversions with 90% exchange tetrads and X's heterozygous for these inversions with a maximum exchange frequency of some 24%.

(d) It has been recently demonstrated that following X-ray induced heterologous interchange, the interchange heterologues regularly separate leading to frequent nondisjunction from normal pairing partners (Parker, 1965, 1969; Parker and Williamson, 1970). For example, when attached-X (reversed metacentric) females carrying a doubly marked Y chromosome (B^SYy^+) were irradiated in stage 7 oocytes, Y chromosome fragments (carrying either B^S or y^+), bearing a Y chromosome centromere and derived from interchange with chromosome 4, assorted at random with respect to the attached-X chromosome, being recovered equally in male and female progeny; if such fragments disjoined regularly from the attached-X, they would be recovered in males only (Parker, 1965). Following irradiation of attached-X females lacking a Y chromosome, detachments of the attached-X chromosome following interchange with chromosome 4 were recovered. Among the capped detachments, i.e. those bearing the centromere of the attached-X, (1) some 85% were accompanied by the normal homologue of chromosome 4 and only 10% by the sister of the 4 involved in the exchange (Parker, 1965) and (2) diplo-4 oocytes representing nondisjunction of the normal 4 and the normal sister of the affected 4 were included 30 times more frequently into nullo-X gametes (recovered as triplo-4 males) than into attached-X gametes (recovered as triplo-4 females) (Parker and Williamson, 1970). These latter two observations are compatible with the idea that the broken 4 and broken X separate with a high degree of regularity and the free chromosome 4 assorts at random with respect to its normal synaptic partner. On the other hand, Busby (1971) found that induced interchange between attached-X and 4 in stage 14 oocytes does not lead to separation of the interchange heterologues; in this case the sister chromatid of the broken 4 was recovered with the capped detachment in 15 of 23 cases. Busby points out that these findings are consistent with those of Kiriazis and Abrahamson (1968) who found no evidence of induced nondisjunction in stage 14 oocytes and lends support to their suggestion concerning the reason for the failure of X-rays to induce nondisjunction at this stage of oogenesis.

2. *Other factors*. Inversion heterozygosity in X is known to lead to an increase in X nondisjunction (Sturtevant and Beadle, 1936) and according to R. F. Grell (1962b) may result from an effect of inversions in reducing "distributive pairing" between noncrossover X's. Still greater increases are achieved when X's and a pair of autosomes are heterozygously inverted (Sturtevant, 1944), imagined as resulting from nonhomologous pairing of noncrossover X's and autosomes (Cooper *et al.*, 1955; see R. F. Grell, 1962a, but later Novitski, 1964). Anderson (1929) reported high X nondisjunction in females heterozygous for an X;3 translocation, the break in X being at vermilion. The presence of an extra chromosome or chromosome element may cause an increase in X nondisjunction, e.g. an extra fourth chromosome (Sandler and Novitski, 1956; note also their extension of this finding to explain the "crowding effect" related to chromosome segregation patterns in triploid females), a small free second chromosome fragment (R. F. Grell, 1970), fragments of X (Lindsley and Sandler, 1957) and Y (Neuhaus, 1941) chromosomes, and most effectively, the complete Y (Bridges, 1916). [Nondisjunction in XXY females, i.e. secondary nondisjunction, is covered in detail below.] Finally, suggestive evidence of an increase in nondisjunction has been obtained following treatment with certain chemicals such as some organic mercury compounds (Ramel, 1967; Ramel and Magnusser, 1969), actinomycin D (Felix, 1969), and monosodium glutamate (De la Rosa *et al.*, 1972). An earlier report by Mottram (1930) that anoxia (CO_2) increases nondisjunction was not confirmed in experiments of either Kelsall (1963) or Smoler (1965).

B. Secondary Nondisjunction in the Female

Bridges (1916) demonstrated that the presence of a Y chromosome in females increases significantly the frequency of nondisjunction of X's. Nondisjunction in XXY females was termed "secondary nondisjunction". Virtually all secondary exceptional females were noncrossovers (a few are equational exceptions not related to the presence of the Y; Bridges, 1916; Sturtevant and Beadle, 1936; Merriam and Frost, 1964); this observation has been confirmed in many experiments. Since, in contrast, regular progeny were predominantly crossovers, Bridges suggested that secondary exceptions arise from events prior to crossing over and involve XY rather than XX synapsis. From the former situation four kinds of gametes are produced in equal frequency, XX, Y, XY and X. Whereas this suggestion predicted that the frequency of secondary nondisjunction (XX–Y segregations) could not exceed 50% and the frequency of exceptional offspring 33% (half XX gametes are lost as XXX females and half Y gametes as YY zygotes), these frequencies were clearly exceeded in tests where XXY females were heterozygous for certain X chromosome inversions; for example, *In(1)dl–49/+/Y* (Sturtevant and Beadle, 1936) and *In(1)dl–49/In(1)AM/Y* females (Cooper, 1948) produced respectively 45·6% and 67% secondary exceptions among female progeny. (Frequencies of secondary exceptions from females heterozygous for X inversions are generally based on female progeny only since exceptional males may arise through the production of nullo-X eggs generated by 4-strand double exchanges; Sturtevant and Beadle, 1936; Novitski, 1952.) From experiments testing crossing over and nondisjunction in XX and XXY females heterozygous for a variety of inversions and combinations thereof, Sturtevant and Beadle (1936) reported a strong negative correlation between secondary nondisjunction and crossing over. Since crossing over was not greatly affected by the presence of a Y whereas nondisjunction was, they suggested (in line with Anderson's (1929) notion) that "the frequency of secondaries is dependent on the occurrence of noncrossover tetrads rather than the reverse". Further, Sturtevant and Beadle determined that since *In(1)dl–49/+/Y* females gave 45·6% nondisjunctional daughters implying 62·6% XX–Y segregations [100((2 x 0.456)/(1 + 0.456))] and the frequency of noncrossover tetrads was about 70%, then 90% or so of noncrossover tetrads gave rise to nondisjunctional gametes. The frequency of noncrossover tetrads (Cooper, 1949) and XX–Y segregations (Cooper, 1948) in females heterozygous for *Ins(1)dl–49,B^{M1}*, were both reported to be about 75%.

An alternative to Bridges' model was proposed by Cooper (1948) who suggested that the mechanism of secondary nondisjunction in the *Drosophila* female "is a case of imposed nonrandom segregation from an XYX trivalent each arm of the Y assuming to pair with a different X"; ". . . sequential differences between X chromosomes in effect emphasize their likenesses to the Y chromosomes", Y becomes a more attractive partner to X so that "conjunction becomes more frequent in those regions of X wherein pairing with Y normally occurs". XY–X segregations may occur from the trivalent when the elements are arranged linearly on the metaphase I plate whereas from alternate coorientation, XX–Y (nondisjunctional) segregations occur, the latter orientation permitting 100% nondisjunction

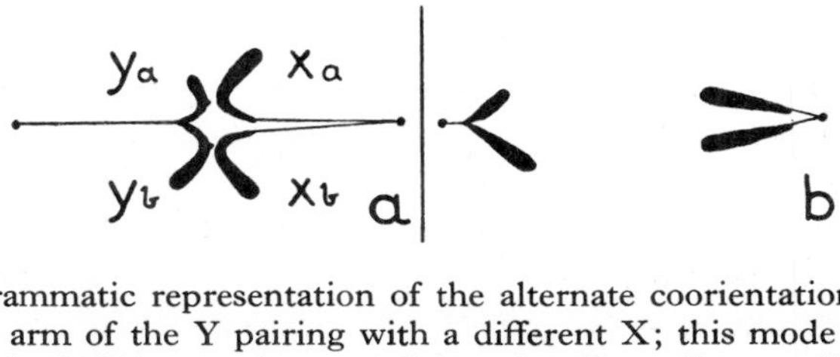

FIG. 3. Diagrammatic representation of the alternate coorientation of the XYX trivalent, each arm of the Y pairing with a different X; this mode of orientation permits 100% secondary nondisjunction (from Cooper, 1948).

(Fig. 3). Cooper envisions the cytological features of secondary nondisjunction as similar to directed segregation in the male of *D. miranda* (MacKnight and Cooper, 1944; Cooper, 1946). The requirement of a two armed Y was demonstrated by showing that whereas *In(1)dl49*,$B^{M1}/+/$Y females gave 77% XX–Y segregations, substitution of the complete Y by the short arm of Y only gave 24%.

Oksala (1957) proposed a series of events preceding secondary nondisjunction. He assumes that the chromosomes are polarized at meiosis, that the distal ends of chromosomes concentrate at the same area of the nuclear membrane, and that pairing begins at these ends. The proximal regions containing large heterochromatic blocks lie at the top of the bouquet and the Y, as with other totally heteropycnotic elements, remains at the base. A euchromatic inversion in one X causes loop formation which does not permit the proximal parts to rise to the top of the bouquet, but retains them at the base where they can pair with Y. More complex heterozygosity results in slower and more difficult pairing providing each arm of the Y with a greater opportunity to pair with different X's.

In her "distributive pairing" hypothesis, R. F. Grell (1962a, see Chapter 10) postulated that chromosomes, whether homologues or heterologues, not involved in exchange may pair "distributively" and separate. The Y does not undergo exchange and is consequently always available for distributive pairing. Since Y pairs with X's that have failed to undergo exchange, yet does not cause an increase in noncrossover tetrads (R. F. Grell, 1962b, 1970), R. F. Grell (1962b) imagines that Y does not serve as a potential pairing partner with X's during the period that X's undergo "exchange pairing", but pairs selectively with noncrossover X's subsequent to exchange at "distributive pairing".

Commenting on Sturtevant and Beadle's finding of a high correlation between non-crossover tetrads and nondisjunctional gametes, R. F. Grell (1962b) observed that with normal X's, the correlation is not as good, some 5% non-crossover X's giving rise to but 2% nondisjunctional gametes. Grell interprets these findings as suggesting that heterozygous rearrangements may reduce "distributive pairing" between noncrossover homologues permitting "distributive pairing" with Y. She cites findings of an increase in primary nondisjunction in the presence of heterozygous inversions as support for this suggestion.

Several factors have been shown to depress the frequency of secondary nondisjunction. These include (1) the substitution of a complete Y with a one armed Y^S (Neuhaus, 1941; Cooper, 1948), or with a one armed Y^L (Neuhaus, 1941); (2) the presence of effectively one armed free X duplications (Lindsley and Sandler, 1957) where secondary nondisjunction was reduced to virtually primary nondisjunction rates when the free duplication did not carry bb^+; (3) addition of a Y to XXY females (Cooper, 1948); (4) an increase in meiotic crossing over following heat treatment (R. F. Grell, 1967); and (5) the presence of autosomal heterozygosity (Sturtevant, 1944; Zimmering, 1958; Cooper, unpublished observations); in this case it is not certain to what extent the reduction is brought about by increases in X crossing over [the "interchromosomal effect" of inversions on crossing over, see, for example, Schultz and Redfield (1951) and Chapter 7) or through pairing between Y and noncrossover autosomes (R. F. Grell, 1962a)]. As indicated above, the Y chromosome does not increase the frequency of non-crossover tetrads. On the other hand, it is not without effect on X crossing over. Recognized since Bridges' (1916) work is the now well documented effect of Y in causing a depression in crossing over in the proximal region, and visualized as resulting from competitive pairing of the two X's and Y in the proximal regions at the time of exchange (Sturtevant and Beadle, 1936; Dobzhansky, 1931). R. F. Grell (1970) has observed that since depressions in X crossing over caused by the presence of X duplications were related entirely to the amount of euchromatin present distally and unrelated to the amount of heterochromatin contained proximally (R. F. Grell, 1967), that heterochromatin may fail to undergo "exchange pairing" as well as exchange. Thus, to account for the proximal decrease in the presence of a Y, she has suggested the possibility that the effect of Y on crossing over may be physiological rather than mechanical.

C. Primary Nondisjunction in the Male

Commenting on the detection of products of primary nondisjunction in the male, Bridges (1916) observed, "If primary nondisjunction occurred in the male, XY and zero sperm would be formed, but the zygotes from them would not differ in their sex-linked characters from regular offspring, so that such an occurrence could not be detected immediately. However, the XY sperm would give rise to XXY daughters, and these in turn would produce secondary exceptions which could be observed." Since that time identification of the presence (or absence) of a Y chromosome has been greatly facilitated as a result of findings that position-effect variegation is suppressed toward wild type upon the addition of a Y and conversely enhanced toward the mutant phenotype upon deletion of this element (Gowen and Gay, 1933) and, more recently, as a result of the synthesis of special Y chromosomes to which are appended wild type alleles of X chromosome genes. Most commonly used are the y^+Y (sc^8.Y of Muller, 1948) and the B^SY (Brosseau and Lindsley, 1958) where y^+ and B are appended to the long arm of Y, Y^L, and the $B^S Y y^+$ (Brosseau *et al.*, 1961) where B is appended to Y^L and y^+ to the short arm Y^S. Experiments

(Frost, 1961; Kelsall, 1961; Zimmering and Wu, 1963, 1964a, b) suggest that primary exceptions are recovered with a frequency of some 0·01–0·05% or so and that primary exceptional males outnumber females about 3–8:1, thus this is not too different from primary nondisjunction in ordinary XX females.

It should be noted that in making accurate measurements of XY nondisjunction in males carrying a singly marked Y, i.e. y^+Y, exceptional daughters carrying the y^+ gene must be tested to determine if the gene is still associated with the Y or is linked with X; the former indicates a nondisjunctional event, the latter X–Y interchange (interchange between Y and autosomes is rare, Zimmering and Kirshenbaum, 1964). Such testing is necessary because a considerable proportion of such exceptional females are, in fact, derived from X–Y interchange. Judging from the experiments of Zimmering and Wu (1964b), a minimum of one-third of all daughters carrying the y^+ allele from y^+Y-bearing fathers arise from X–Y interchange rather than nondisjunction. Furthermore, Smith (1964) found that of two exceptional females from bw^+Y fathers (bw^+ is inserted in Y^L; Dempster, in Muller, 1951), one arose through X–Y interchange and the other through XY nondisjunction, and Zimmering and Wu (1963, 1964a) found seven cases of interchange (six involving interchange between X and Y^S) and three of nondisjunctional females from $B^S Y y^+$-bearing males. In the latter case, direct examination of progeny phenotypes permits a distinction between the two. Arguments have been presented that such recombinants are a result of interchange during gonial mitosis (Cooper, 1949; Lindsley, 1955).

As is the case in the female, the source(s) of the excess of the zero gametic class remains in question. While chromosome loss following XY pairing failure is a formal possibility, extensive cytological work by Cooper (1952a, 1964) and Peacock (1965) has provided no evidence of meiotic loss of unpaired chromosomes in the male. Peacock (1965) found in a male "high nondisjunction line" that whereas exceptional sons vastly exceeded exceptional daughters, anaphase II cells with zero and XY complements were present in equal frequency. It appears at this time that the two kinds of sperm arising through nondisjunction in this line may not participate equally in fertilization (see later discussion of cytogenetics of the sc^4–sc^8 male); the same explanation could account for the deficiency of recovery of XY *vs.* zero sperm arising from nondisjunction in ordinary XY males. Alternatively, spontaneous breakage events in Y (or X) leading to subsequent elimination, and unrelated to pairing, would add to the zero sperm arising through nondisjunction thus affecting the observed discrepancy. Special mechanisms for different Y's could be invoked such as (1) in y^+Y males, spontaneous interarm exchange at a four strand stage resulting in homozygosis for the y^+ gene in one dyad and homozygosity for its absence in the other, and (2) in $B^S Yy^+$ males, breakage proximal to the markers and a resultant ring chromosome carrying neither marker (as Oster, 1964, has reported from irradiation studies). In any case, the contribution of these special mechanisms to the zero class are experimentally ascertainable.

Regarding nondisjunction frequencies of major autosomes, estimates suggest that they are low and on the order of XY nondisjunction (Stern, 1934; Pontecorvo, 1940; Frost, 1961). Frost (1961) reported higher than expected frequency of simultaneous nondisjunction of XY and chromosome 2 and suggested that nondisjunction of one bivalent reflects localized conditions which favor the occurrence of nondisjunction of other bivalents as well.

Hall (1970) reported on results from his experiments and extracted those from the work of others bearing on this question, concluding that in the majority of cases and for all experiments summed, the frequency of double nondisjunction of the sex chromosomes and chromosome 4 was much greater than would be expected if they occurred independently and that this appears to hold in both males and females.

From large scale X-irradiation experiments where critical distinction could be made between nondisjunction and interchange, Zimmering and Wu (1963; 1964a, b) demonstrated that the vast majority of females previously classified as arising by nondisjunction following irradiation in primary spermatocytes (Strangio, 1962; Sävhagen, 1961) originate through induced interchange between X and Y. After irradiation with 1000 R of primary spermatocytes in $B^S Yy^+$ males, 112 interchange and 5 nondisjunctional daughters were recovered (Zimmering and Wu, 1963); and from y^+Y males, 117 y^+ daughters were interchanges and 36 nondisjunctionals (Zimmering and Wu, 1964b; Wu, 1964; in the latter case, only interchanges between X and Y^L are detectable). A reasonable estimate would be that a dose of 1000 R to primary spermatocytes, prior to anaphase separation, probably induces no more than about 0·01% XY nondisjunction. Thus, the high rate of exchange relative to nondisjunction would simply represent another example of the efficacy of X-rays in causing chromosome breakage in primary spermatocytes (see for example, Sävhagen, 1961 and Bateman, 1957) and its inefficacy in causing nondisjunction.

It was indicated above that heterologous interchange in stage 7 oocytes results in regular separation of the interchange elements leading to frequent nondisjunction from normal synaptic partners. Golden and Zimmering (1972) have reported preliminary results suggesting similar behaviour in primary spermatocytes. Of 26 Y-autosome interchanges recovered following irradiation of primary spermatocytes, 10 were recovered in zero or

XY sperm, and 16 in X and Y sperm. Since the unusually large number of exceptional relative to regular gametes is not observed under conditions of ordinary segregation, the results have been taken to suggest that following induced Y-autosome interchange, the Y and autosome separate regularly and X moves at random with respect to Y. Presumably such interchanges were derived from primary spermatocytes at a stage (perhaps analogous with stage 7 oocytes) where segregation patterns had not as yet been irrevocably determined.

High nondisjunction rates are known when the X is deficient for some 80% of the basal heterochromatin and thus lacking material necessary for Y chromosome pairing (Gershenson, 1933; this system is discussed in detail in the section on meiotic drive). The effect of the addition of an extra Y to ordinary XY males has been known, since Bridges (1916), to increase markedly the frequency of XY sperm, although Cooper (1949) has suggested that this may simply reflect a random assortment of the three elements from XYY trivalent. Mittler *et al.* (1967) have reported a significant effect of caffeine on nondisjunction and chromosome loss in ring-bearing XY males. On the other hand, Zettle (personal communication) while confirming the effect on chromosome loss finds no evidence of an increase in nondisjunction.

Equational exceptions: Finally, some cases may be mentioned demonstrating that nondisjunction of X chromatids may occur in the male. This gives rise to 2X sperm, which are recovered as patroclinous daughters, and are referred to as "equational exceptions". Neuhaus (1937) recovered patroclinous attached-X daughters from males carrying an X to which was attached Y^S or Y^L, suggesting as its origin a crossover at a four strand stage between the Y arm and the proximal heterochromatin of X. L. V. Morgan (1938) reported several cases of 2X sperm. Some arose through XY exchange followed by nondisjunction of the dyads at meiosis I (see also Zimmering, 1962), others from a failure of X's to separate following centromere splitting at meiosis II, and a few from a failure of centromere splitting at meiosis II. Schultz (1934) reported a stock giving a high rate of equational nondisjunction (some 30% of F_1 females were derived from 2X sperm) due to the presence of a gene in the X heterochromatin; later generations gave 1–2% equational exceptions. Lamy (1949) reported an average frequency of 0·42% equational exceptions from a stock of white males crossed with yellow attached-X females and a marked effect of age, frequencies ranging from 0·06% for the first 14 days of mating, to 1·6% from days 35–38. Whether this reflected a high frequency of XY exchange followed by nondisjunction was not reported. He alluded to Slyzynska's finding of patroclinous females from ring-X-bearing males; in this case, XY exchange would be precluded as a cause since simple exchange would give rise to a dicentric bridge which would be eventually eliminated Cooper (1952b) reported a frequency of $0{\cdot}09 \pm 0{\cdot}05\,\%$ for an X chromosome carrying *Ins(1)dl–49*, B^{M1}, a frequency in line with Lamy's early broods and perhaps not too different from the spontaneous rate of XY nondisjunction. Estimates in the female of equational exceptions not associated with crossing over appear to be lacking, although simple experiments involving X's heterozygous for appropriate multiple inversions would provide such information.

III. Meiotic Drive in the Male *Drosophila* not involving Crossing Over

As indicated briefly in the introduction, instances of unequal production of reciprocal gametic types have been found following separation of genetic alternatives at meiosis I and at meiosis II; in the former, the absence of crossing over results in the separation of genetic alternatives at anaphase I and in the latter crossing over occurs and the genetic alternatives separate from the crossover dyads at anaphase II. The former includes typical cases of meiotic drive in the male and the latter those in the female and in special cases in the male where crossing over occurs. The term "meiotic drive" was coined by Sandler and Novitski (1957) to describe any alteration of the normal process of meiosis such that a heterozygote for two genetic alternatives produces an effective gametic pool with an excess of one type.

It should be recalled that only one product of oogenesis is functional and occupies an outer position in a linear array of four products; thus, an excess of gametes carrying one of the two genetic alternatives may be achieved by any mechanism causing preferential segregation of that alternative into the functional product. In the male, on the other hand, (1) cytological analysis provides no evidence of an ordered arrangement of four products (see Cooper, 1951), and (2) it is generally considered that sperm function depends mainly or entirely on the diploid genotype of the male and little if at all on the genotype of the sperm (Muller and Settles, 1925, 1927; McCloskey, 1966; Lindsley and E. Grell, 1969), and that all four products of spermatogenesis are functional. Thus cases of meiotic drive in the male require new interpretations. The present section traces the development of our understanding of four well studied cases of meiotic drive in the male where genetic alternatives separate at anaphase I, followed by a description of others of this type, and concludes with a discussion of cases of meiotic drive in females and males where genetic alternatives separate at anaphase II from crossover dyads.

The four well-studied cases are (a) "sex-ratio" (Gershenson, 1928);

(b) the sc^4–sc^8 system (Gershenson, 1933); (c) the Bar–Stone translocation (Novitski and Sandler, 1957); and (d) Segregation-distorter, *SD* (Sandler *et al.*, 1959). Each case is characterized by the production of highly distorted segregation ratios subject to modification by genetic and environmental factors. Originally, each was uniquely interpreted. Subsequently, an attractive unifying hypothesis was proposed, suggested by the work on the Bar–Stone system (Novitski and I. Sandler, 1957) and formalized later by Peacock and Erickson (1965) as the "functional-nonfunctional poles" model. Later, genetic data in disagreement with this model, and upon which much of the strength of the model rests, were reported (Hartl *et al.*, 1967; Zimmering and Fowler, 1968; Hartl, 1969). More recently electron micrography has provided a firm basis in the case of "sex-ratio" (Policansky and Ellison, 1970) and *SD* (Tokuyasu *et al.*, 1972), and a preliminary suggestive basis in the case of sc^4–sc^8 (Beuregard and Zimmering, unpublished observations) for the conclusion that the "functional–nonfunctional" poles hypothesis is not applicable, but that they should rather be described in terms of failures in spermiogenesis. For convenience, the material will be presented in the sequence (a) a description and interpretation of the early work carried out on these systems; (b) the re-investigation of the *SD* system which led to the formulation of the "functional–nonfunctional" poles hypothesis; (c) the re-investigations of the "sex-ratio" and the sc^4–sc^8 systems and their interpretation according to that model; (d) later genetic data not in support of this hypothesis, culminating in recent electron micrography implicating sperm dysfunction as causing drive in these cases.

A. Early Work on "Sex Ratio" in *D. pseudoobscura*

Probably the earliest reported instance of meiotic drive in the male was the case of "sex-ratio" (*sr*) in the *D. obscura* group (Gershenson, 1928); *sr* is now known in other *Drosophila* groups (Stalker, 1961). Males carrying an *sr*-bearing X (always associated with inversions—Wallace, 1948; Stalker, 1961) produce mainly or only female progeny. Since there is little evidence of extreme post-fertilization mortality, it is clear that such males produce mostly or only X-bearing sperm (Gershenson, 1928). From cytological studies of meiosis and spermiogenesis in *sr* males of *D. psuedoobscura*, Sturtevant and Dobzhansky (1936) reported the following observations. At diakinesis, X and Y were unpaired (the three autosomes formed regular bivalents), the X possessed an additional equational split (i.e. consisted of four chromatids) and consistent with this observation, an X passed to each pole at anaphase I. The Y was located at random on the spindle, subsequently formed a micronucleus in the cytoplasm of one daughter cell and then degenerated. Meiosis II was normal and an X was found in virtually all telophase II cells. They reported that examination with light microscopy of immature and mature sperm gave no evidence of abnormalities in number or appearance. Sturtevant and Dobzhansky concluded that the "sex ratio" effect resulted from the extra replication of the *sr*-bearing X and the concomitant degeneration of the Y.

B. Early Work on the sc^4–sc^8 System in *D. melanogaster*

It is known in a variety of organisms that chromosomes failing to pair at meiosis I are frequently "lost"; that is, they are not included in the meiotic products. Gershenson (1933) and later Sandler and Braver (1954) described the segregation of X and Y in males carrying the sc^4–sc^8 X chromosome, an X deficient for some 80–90% of the basal heterochromatin and thus lacking many of the pairing sites at which X and Y normally conjoin (Cooper, 1964). Data from an experiment of Sandler and Braver (1954) illustrate the kinds of results from such males. From crosses of sc^4–sc^8 males with ordinary females, the frequencies of the classes of progeny representing the recovery of X, Y, X + Y, and zero gametes were approximately 0·47, 0·27, 0·03, and 0·23. Sandler and Braver suggested that (a) the high frequency of primary nondisjunction is due to a failure of pairing and consequent random segregation of X and Y at anaphase I; (b) the deficiency in recovery of X + Y types is a function of the loss of one or both of these chromosomes; and (c) since the X chromosome was recovered with approximately normal frequency and the Y with only half-normal frequency, the Y was lost more frequently. Subsequently, Zimmering (1963) showed that if sc^4–sc^8 males develop at 18°C, the relative frequencies of the four gametic types are markedly altered. For example, for X, Y, X + Y, and zero, these were approximately 0·48, 0·42, 0·04 and 0·06, respectively, compared with 0·49, 0·24, 0·02, and 0·25 for the corresponding classes at 26°C. In view of the striking similarity in the magnitude of increase in frequency of the Y class and the depression in the zero class at 18°C, he suggested that the effect of the lower temperature was simply to regularize the transmission of the Y. It was then shown that in males carrying a modified Bar–Stone translocation where a Y chromosome was appended to the proximal element, X^P (see Fig. 4), the univalent was recovered with near normal frequency when males were raised at 18°C, although highly depressed when such males developed at 26°C. This observation prompted the argument that it was unnecessary to invoke any change in the frequency of synapsis and that the temperature effect in the sc^4–sc^8 system could be interpreted solely on the assumption that meiotic

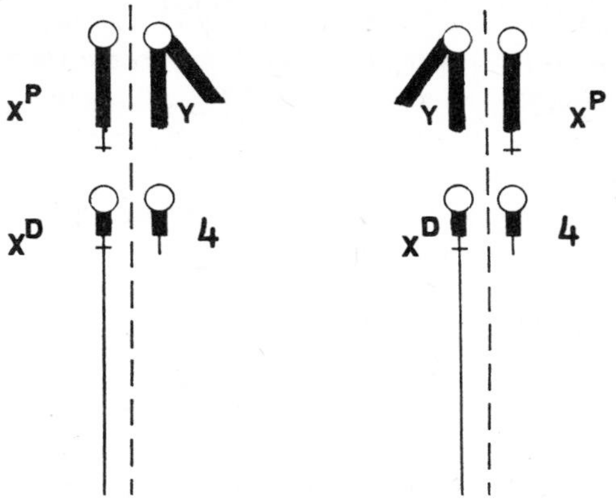

FIG. 4. The two kinds of orientation of the paired homologues of the male Bar–Stone translocation giving rise to the four gametic types $X^D + X^P$ and $4 + Y$ (left) and $X^D + Y$ and $4 + X^P$ (right).

loss of the Y occurs at a relatively high frequency at 26°C, and at a markedly lower frequency at 18°C.

C. The Bar–Stone Translocation in *D. melanogaster*

Novitski and I. Sandler (1957) obtained information on the relative frequencies of the different kinds of gametes produced by males carrying *T(1;4)B^S* (Stone, 1934), a translocation between the X and the minute fourth chromosome. Let X^D represent the distal end of X carrying the centromere of the fourth chromosome, and X^P the proximal end of X, capped by the telomere of chromosome 4 (Fig. 4). Because in heterozygous males X^D regularly separates from chromosome 4 and X^P from the Y, four kinds of sperm are produced: $X^D + X^P$, $4 + Y$, $X^D + Y$, and $4 + X^P$. Whereas equality of the four types is expected, the observed frequencies were, respectively: 26·5%, 19·1%, 11·6%, and 42·8%. A relation between the frequencies of the gametic types was arrived at by deriving the overall frequency of recovery of each of the four components and computing, by cross-multiplying, the expected frequencies of the four combinations. The values for the components were: $X^D = 0{\cdot}391$; $4 = 0{\cdot}619$; $X^P = 0{\cdot}693$; and $Y = 0{\cdot}307$. The expected frequencies of each of the four gametic types were 0·264, 0·190, 0·117, and 0·429, respectively. This excellent agreement between the observed and expected values indicated no deviation from random assortment of the two bivalents despite distortions in individual segregation ratios. On the basis of direct experimental tests, the possibility of differential zygotic mortality was ruled out. It was argued that sperm competition after storage in the ventral receptacle was unlikely as the distance covered by the sperm from the storage organs to the egg is very short. While gametic lethality in the conventional sense was a possibility, Novitski and Sandler argued that this would be contrary to the well-known capacity of sperm to function independently of gene content. Moreover it was pointed out that sperm types $X^D + X^P$ and $4 + Y$ are recovered with frequencies of 26·5% and 19·1%, respectively, and are genetically normal; the former is, however, recovered 39% more frequently than the latter. Further, if either were abnormal it would be the type carrying the translocation, yet it is recovered the more frequently of the two. As a last resort they suggested the possibility that not all products of spermatogenesis are functional, and that the smaller elements of each bivalent, 4 and X^P, preferentially segregate into the functional products. This situation is superficially similar to the phenomenon of nonrandom disjunction in the *Drosophila* female (Novitski, 1951) although the latter requires genetic exchange, an event not occurring spontaneously in the male.

The finding by Zimmering (1960) that raising Bar–Stone males at 18°C rather than 26°C resulted in all gametic types being recovered with virtually normal frequencies provided a means of determining the stage(s) of germ cell formation implicated in this phenomenon (Zimmering and Perlman, 1962). The method employed consisted of placing males at 18°C in successively older stages of development and correlating the disappearance of distorted ratios with the types of germ cells present at the time of exposure to the lower temperature. The results showed clearly that only the meiotic divisions were involved. It was shown further (Zimmering, 1959, 1960) that gametic ratios may be markedly different depending upon the genetic background, in that substitution of Y chromosomes and autosomes from different laboratory stocks caused high, intermediate, or no distortion; an age effect was also observed, older males exhibiting considerably less distortion than younger ones (Zimmering and Barbour, 1961). Striking effects of autosomal modifying genes on sex-chromosome segregation ratios had been reported earlier by Lindsley and Sandler (1957) studying the meiotic behavior in males of bivalents consisting of the attached-XY chromosome and small duplications consisting largely of the basal heterochromatin of the X. Experiments determining whether the same modifiers operate in the two systems are yet to be carried out.

D. Early Work on Segregation-distorter in *D. melanogaster*

The features of the *SD* system described earlier and which are of interest for the purposes of the present discussion are the following (Sandler *et al.*, 1959): (a) *SD*, located in or near the centromeric heterochromatin in the right arm of chromosome 2 acts in the heterozygous male but not in the heterozygous female; *k*, the proportion of recovered *SD*-bearing progeny, may be as high as 1·0 from heterozygous males but is uniformly 0·5 from heterozygous females; (b) the phenomenon is not the result of differential zygotic mortality of SD^+-bearing individuals; (c) for *SD* to operate, some special synaptic condition is required which is disturbed by a breakpoint in the immediate vicinity of the *SD* region. To account for these findings, Sandler *et al.* proposed that *SD* could cause some sort of break at SD^+. The fragment bearing sister centromeres would undergo sister-strand fusion at the first division or could be delayed until the second division at which time an anaphase bridge is formed. The bridge or its breakage products would then cause the dysfunctioning of SD^+-bearing sperm. Attempts at confirmation by direct cytological analysis, however, proved inconclusive.

E. Re-investigation of "Sex-ratio"

A re-investigation of "sex-ratio" from the point of view of the "functional-nonfunctional" pole model was carried out by Novitski *et al.* (1965). Their description of meiotic events differs critically from Sturtevant and Dobzhansky (1936). They reported that at the first meiotic division, the X and Y chromosomes usually pair and disjoin normally, with equal numbers of X- and Y-bearing cells being found in secondary spermatocytes. In the latter, the Y shows "degeneration" at metaphase II or anaphase II. Analysis of complete anaphase II cysts showed that X-bearing cells were normal while Y-bearing cells had only autosomes at the poles; the Y showed no centromeric activity, remaining as a chromatin mass at the equator. In none of the males examined were there any indications that all second division cells contained an X chromosome. Counts were made with light microscopy on spermatid and sperm bundles in *sr* and normal males; no differences in number or evidence of degeneration or abnormal development was detected. Since Schultz (1933) had shown that XY and zero sperm are recovered following nondisjunction in *sr* males and that the zero class which did not carry a degenerate Y is nonetheless depressed (in contrast with results from nondisjunction in ordinary males where zeros exceed XY gametes), Novitski *et al.* argued that the degenerate Y very likely does not play a direct role in the sex-ratio effect. In view of these findings, they suggested that the "sex ratio" effect could be explained by the "functional-nonfunctional poles" model, a preferential movement of the X chromosome to the "functional pole" ensuring an all female progeny.

F. Re-investigation of the sc^4–sc^8 System

Combining genetic and cytological studies, Peacock (1965) reported the following observations on the behavior of X and Y in sc^4–sc^8 males: (a) Pairing of X and Y is followed by normal separation at anaphase I. (b) When X and Y are unpaired, both chromosomes move to the same pole; thus, the frequency of metaphase I pairing approximates that of anaphase I disjunctional segregations, and the frequency of cases of unpaired X and Y is equivalent to the frequency of anaphase I nondisjunctional cases; no meiotic loss of either X or Y was observed (see also Cooper, 1964). (c) Cytological and genetic determinations of the proportion of nondisjunctional gametes were in good agreement, invalidating the suggestion (Zimmering, 1960) that the excess of zero gametes and the depression in the Y-bearing class were related. (d) A strict equality of reciprocal cell types is found at the second division of meiosis, i.e. X = Y and X + Y = zeros. Yet (e) genetic data indicate characteristic discrepancies between reciprocal classes; i.e. a large excess of X over Y and zero over X + Y.

To account for these results, Peacock suggested that the sc^4–sc^8 system is a valid case of meiotic drive comparable to *SD* and Bar–Stone and explainable on the assumptions that synapsis is followed by a preferential movement of X to the functional pole and that failure of synapsis is followed by the nonrandom movement of both chromosomes to the nonfunctional pole. Peacock suggested further that Zimmering's (1963) data on the temperature effect in sc^4–sc^8 males (where at 18°C, the frequency of nondisjunction is reduced 50% or more and reciprocal classes from disjunctional and nondisjunctional events approach equality) is explainable if, at the cooler temperature, (a) movement of paired chromosomes is random with respect to the poles, and (b) movement of unpaired chromosomes is random with respect to each other. Peacock cited preliminary evidence in support of the fact that the proportion of X + Y and 0 cells at the second division approximates half the frequency of metaphase I synapsis failures. He suggested that the oriented anaphase movement of the unpaired X and Y could explain the behavior of other univalents that had been investigated, i.e. the depression in recovery of the sc^4–sc^8 chromosome in XYY males, where Y's form a bivalent and the X a univalent (Gershenson, 1933), the reduced recovery of the modified Y used by Zimmering (1963), and the deficiency in recovery of the attached-XY in XY/0 males (Sandler and Braver, 1954). The more normal rates of recovery at cooler temperatures of the modified Y (Zimmering, 1963) and the sc^4–sc^8 X in XY males (Zimmering and Green, 1965) would presumably reflect a more random movement of these chromosomes to the two poles, according to this model.

Additional data on segregation in sc^4–sc^8 males appeared to lend support to this model. Peacock and Erickson (1964) reported that first division spermatocytes in early pupae of some strains of *Drosophila* frequently contain a mass of granules, later identified by Erickson and Acton (1969) as probably rickettsia, which respond to an intracellular differentiation associated with meiosis. From cytological examination of granule-infected spermatocytes in sc^4–sc^8 and normal males, and comparison with genetic data from similar males, Yanders *et al.* (1968) found that in disjunctional anaphase I in the sc^4–sc^8 male, the X was seen far more frequently at the granule-free pole, and the genetic data showed that the X was recovered more frequently than the Y; similarly, in the nondisjunctional cases, the nullo-pole was usually granule free, and the nullo-class had a higher genetic recovery than X + Y. In the normal male, X and Y segregated at random with respect to the poles and genetic data indicated equal recovery. Since the characteristic discrepancies between reciprocal classes from the sc^4–sc^8 males are unaltered in the presence of the granules, they concluded that the granules and sex chromosomes in such males were responding independently to a pre-existing gradient in meiotic cells.

G. Re-investigation of *SD*

On cytogenetic re-analysis of the *SD* system, Peacock and Erickson (1965) reported that whereas the genetic consequences of *SD* were in complete agreement with the account of Sandler *et al.* (1959), the cytology of meiosis was entirely normal. Furthermore, under light microscopy, sperm development appeared normal, the number of sperm per sperm bundle compared favorably with normal males, and all sperm appeared motile. Experiments on the transfer, storage, and utilization of sperm showed that males aged 1–2 days transfer to the female 300–400 sperm, about the same number is stored, and about half the number stored are utilized in the production of progeny, that is, the progeny:sperm ratio is 0·5. Since all progeny are *SD*, they suggested that all nonfunctioning sperm are SD^+. Further, since they found progeny:sperm ratios of 0·5 from normal males, they predicted that both *SD* and normal males would produce the same number of progeny. On the original model by Sandler *et al.* (1959) *SD* males would produce only half the progeny of normal males. Results from experiments comparing the daily productivity of *SD* and SD^+ males showed a striking correspondence between the two over the period of nine days sampled. From other experiments where brooding periods were longer and the male tested over a period of some 30 days, it was found that *SD* males had a noticeably shorter period of fertility. It was suggested that the extended period of fertility of the control males reflected an extended period of gamete production rather than an accumulation from earlier production.

To account for these observations, they proposed the following explanation: (a) only half the sperm produced by the *Drosophila* male are functional, i.e. capable of fertilizing eggs; (b) the determination of the functional and nonfunctional classes of sperm occurs at the first division of meiosis, where an inequality of spindle poles is proposed (i.e. a "functional pole" and a "nonfunctional pole"—the former giving rise ultimately to two functional sperm, the latter to two nonfunctional sperm); and (c) the mode of operation of *SD* involves a preferential orientation of the *SD*-bearing chromosome to the functional pole at meiosis I. This model is a special case of that proposed by Novitski and I. Sandler (1957).

H. Results from more Recent Experiments and Alternatives to the "Functional–Nonfunctional Poles" Model

Two critical observations upon which Peacock and Erickson based their hypothesis that half the products of male meiosis are normally nonfunctional were (a) that progeny: sperm ratios approximate 0·5 from matings with both *SD* and normal males; and (b) *SD* and normal males produce equal numbers of progeny except for overall fertility differences. Regarding the significance of progeny:sperm ratios of 0·5, Zimmering and Fowler (1968) showed that under conditions yielding a progeny:sperm ratio of about 0·5 from matings of Oregon-R males with yellow females, in excellent agreement with results from similar experiments reported by Peacock and Erickson, significant departures toward a ratio of 1·0 were observed from mating of Oregon-R males with Oregon-R females. Progeny:sperm ratios from three experiments of matings of Oregon-R males with yellow and Oregon-R females were as follows: 0·42 and 0·62; 0·48 and 0·77; and 0·38 and 0·75. These results (and others, see Zimmering *et al.*, 1970b) argue that progeny:sperm ratios provide no useful information on the question of the production of nonfunctional sperm by the male *Drosophila*; such ratios may be explained as simply reflecting the relative efficiencies with which different females utilize sperm.

In connection with the question of the fertility of *SD* as compared with normal males, Hartl *et al.* (1967) and Hartl (1969) found that *SD* males show a reduction in fertility which is correlated with the degree of distortion of their segregation ratio, the higher the *k* value, the greater the infertility, suggesting a direct relation between the two and arguing that *SD* causes sperm dysfunction. The general term "gametic dysfunction" was coined by Lindsley and Sandler (1957) to describe some unique property of sperm representing one genetic alternative conferred upon it by reason of that genetic alternative having been heterozygous with another at meiosis. Finally, Tokuyasu *et al.* (1972) examined testes of heterozygous *SD* males (k = 1·0) with the electron microscope and have observed that spermatids often fail to individualize—i.e. the syncytial organization of the spermatid bundle remains intact—and that the number of spermatids failing to individualize may be as high as 32 per bundle. More cogently they find that invariably half the sperm in each bundle contain nuclei with incompletely condensed chromatin, and suggest that these are the SD^+ sperm.

Novitski (1970), reviewing briefly the concept of gamete dysfunction, took note of the finding of Hartl *et al.* (1967) and tested the fertility of Bar–Stone males compared with wild-type sibs (both derived from heterozygous Bar–Stone translocation mothers). A great difference between the fertility of the two males was found, the reduction in fertility of Bar–Stone males being much too great to be accounted for by the production of inviable aneuploid zygotes. He suggests that whereas it cannot be categorically ruled out that translocation males are less fertile because the translocation has accumulated sterility factors independent of the translocation itself, it is likely that a mechanism like sperm dysfunction is responsible for the depression in fertility. Furthermore, combining in a single male both *SD* and the Bar–Stone translocation, Novitski and Peacock (1970) reported that the recovery of the translocation components is different depending on whether or not the sperm also carries *SD*. When it does not, the homologues in the translocation approach a 50% recovery, with approximately 25% recovery of each of the four products, whereas with *SD*, the recoveries are grossly unequal. They suggest that these observations can be interpreted to mean that the same condition which leads to the preferential recovery of the *SD* chromosome also provides the basis for the preferential recovery of the translocation components. Moreover, preliminary electron micrography of testes of modified Bar–Stone males, $X^D/4$; $X^PY^L{\cdot}Y^S/0$ (Hogan and Zimmering, unpublished observations; see Zimmering, 1963, for genetic data) gives unmistakable evidence of too few normal sperm per bundle and the presence of considerable numbers of myelin bodies presumably occupying sites of degenerated sperm.

Only preliminary observations are available from electron micrography of testes of sc^4–sc^8 males (Beauregard and Zimmering, unpublished observations), but in this case also obvious ultrastructural abnormalities are observed reflected as failures of spermatid individualization (as in *SD*). It seems likely, therefore, that the reduced frequency of Y as compared with X, and XY as compared with zero gametes will turn out to be related to gametic dysfunction. If this turns out to be the case, the significance of the finding of Yanders *et al.* (1968) as it bears on the mechanism of meiotic drive in sc^4–sc^8 males would become more difficult to assess.

Finally, Policansky and Ellison (1970) reported that whereas they were able to confirm previous findings of nearly normal numbers of spermatids per bundle in *sr* ("sex-ratio") *D. pseudoobscura* males, only half of these were represented as mature sperm. For this study electron microscopy was necessary since, as the authors reported, great difficulties are encountered in counting mature sperm in this species using ordinary squash techniques. Electron micrographs showed that the mean number of mature sperm per bundle in sr^+ males was about 112 and in *sr* males about 55. The failure of half the spermatids to develop into normal sperm was confirmed in several *sr* lines. These findings provide a basis for an understanding of the sex-ratio effect on the assumption that those cells which undergo spermiogenic failure in *sr* males would form functional Y-bearing sperm in normal males.

I. Additional Cases of Meiotic Drive in the Male not involving Crossing Over

The X-linked "sex-ratio" phenomenon is evidently a very old feature of *Drosophila* populations as evidenced by its widespread occurrence in natural populations (Stalker, 1961), and by the modifications that have evolved: these include a gene *msr* (*msr* = male sex ratio) that reverses the action of *sr*; that is, *sr*; *msr* males produce mostly male offspring (Novitski, 1947), and the evolution of a variety of "sex-ratio" X chromosomes and a variety of Y chromosomes of differing sensitivity to the various "sex-ratio" X's (Stalker, 1961). The *msr* gene causes the production of a large excess of male offspring and is due to the action of an autosomal recessive which operates only in the presence of the X-linked *sr* gene. Significantly whereas no obvious effects on fertility were reported for *sr* or *msr/msr* males, those of the composition *sr*; *msr/msr* are almost completely sterile. Dissection of the ventral receptacle of females revealed copious quantities of sperm; hence, sperm are transferred and stored, yet such females produced no or few progeny. Presumably this is a case of "double dysfunction", but its details have yet to be worked out.

A gene causing an abnormal sex-ratio but clearly not *sr*, has been found in a natural population of *D. simulans* (Faulhaber, 1967). In this case the aberrant sex-ratio, an excess of females, is caused by a recessive factor on chromosome 3. Males raised at 14°C produced unisexual female progenies and these were analysed cytologically; it was observed that half of the 64 spermatids were morphologically abnormal, although they develop into sperm that were transferred to the female and stored. Evidently, however, these sperm were not able to participate in fertilization.

Finally, there is the case of "Recovery Disrupter" (symbol: *RD*) isolated from an irradiated population of *D. melanogaster* (Novitski and Hanks, 1961), but very likely common in natural populations (Hanks, 1968b). The gene, *RD*, is located proximally on the X chromosome, has no effect in females, but in males causes a preponderance (about two-thirds) of female offspring (Hanks, 1964). Temperature-sensitivity studies indicate that the mutant exerts its effect at meiosis (Erickson and Hanks, 1961). Cytologically, *RD* can be seen to cause fragmentation of the Y chromosome with a frequency sufficient to account for the abnormal sex-ratio if it is assumed that the Y chromosome fragmentation leads to sperm lethality (Erickson, 1965). Moreover, direct observation revealed that *RD* males contain sperm bundles with 48 elements rather than the usual 64. As with meiotic drive systems found in nature, modifiers of *RD* also are found (Kuhn and Hanks, 1967; Remondini and Hanks, 1966).

Clearly, the cases of meiotic drive discussed above represent marked deviations from normal and are thus rendered easier to detect and explore experimentally. Less easy to detect but nonetheless demonstrable departures from 1:1 have been reported, for example, in secondary sex-ratio. Hanks (1965), who examined two normal strains of *D. melanogaster*, presents evidence that the sex-ratios of the two lines are different, that this difference is not the result of early zygotic mortality, and that it is a genetic property of the male parent. Thus it seems possible that the primary sex-ratio is generally different from 1:1 and that this is the result of meiotic drive of the sex-chromosomes in the heterogametic sex (Novitski, 1951, 1953; Hanks, 1965).

A paternal age effect on secondary sex-ratio has been reported by Yanders (1965) who provided evidence that the aging of *Drosophila* males produces a shift in sex ratio in the same direction as that noted in man (Novitski, 1953), i.e. towards a greater proportion of females.

It should be noted that other interesting cases of "sex-ratio" have been found in natural populations of *Drosophila* such as those whose expression requires the presence of extra-chromosomal elements (see, for example, Malogolowkin, 1958). In these cases, however, the cause of the departure from a 1:1 sex ratio is the death of the male zygotes. Additionally it has been reported by Minamori (1969, 1970) that in the presence of an extra-chromosomal element, delta, zygotes are killed carrying certain second chromosomes which by all other criteria are normal chromosomes.

IV. Meiotic Drive in the Female and Male *Drosophila* following Crossing Over

Novitski (1951) suggested that "the generalization that disjunction of chromatids at the second meiotic division is random does not appear to be completely valid when chromatids are structurally dissimilar". The phenomenon has been termed nonrandom disjunction and is visualized as involving the establishment of an asymmetric dyad, a dyad composed of structurally unlike chromatids, generated by crossing over in females of special constitutions, and the preferential inclusion of one or the other of these chromatids into the functional egg. The simplest demonstration comes from the work of Novitski (1951) where crossing over and subsequent recovery of crossover products was followed in females possessing a pair of rod-shaped homologues differing in length by virtue of a large block of heterochromatin located distally in one (sc^8) and absent in the other (sc^4–sc^8). He found that following exchange the shorter chromatid was recovered about twice as often as the longer; that is, *c*, the coefficient of nonrandomness or the degree of recovery of the preferred chromosome, was about 0·67 (*c* from symmetrical dyads is 0·5). Novitski's interpretation was as follows. An exchange in this heteromorphic bivalent gives rise to asymmetric dyads. These pass to opposite poles and the longer chromatid "drags" relative to the shorter creating an orientation of the centromere region. Thus upon centromere splitting at meiosis II, the longer chromatid will be present in the two inner products which ultimately become polar bodies while the shorter will be found in the outer nuclei, one of which will become the functional egg, the other the third polar body. It is obvious that the longer chromatid is not always eliminated in the middle polar bodies in the sc^4–sc^8 case since it is recovered in about one-third of the offspring. (Evidence against the notion that the large heterochromatic blocks at the tips of the chromosomes tend, following exchange, to separate later, thus giving the same overall effect as dragging, has been provided by Novitski and L. Sandler, 1956, and Weltman, 1954.)

Historically, the suggestion of nonrandom disjunction was first invoked to explain the unusually high recovery of crossover ring X's from females carrying the tandem metacentric compound X chromosome (Novitski, 1951). This compound X possessing the order ABCD·ABCD (the raised dot indicates the position of the centromere) pairs as a circle and produces, upon certain kinds of exchange, an asymmetric dyad consisting of a compound X chromatid equivalent to the length of two X's and a single X ring chromosome. The value of *c* for the ring is very high (Novitski, 1951, including Novitski's calculations based on the data of Sturtevant and Beadle, 1936, and of Sidirov *et al.*, 1936; Novitski and L. Sandler, 1956), and is probably close to unity (Lindsley and Sandler, 1965). Other compound X's generating asymmetric dyads upon crossing over are the tandem acrocentric and the tandem ring. The tandem acrocentric compound X having the order ·ABCDABCD pairs spirally and depending upon the stands involved in the exchange, the asymmetric dyad may be a double length rod chromatid attached to a single length rod or a triple length attached to a single length. Novitski and L. Sandler (1956) reported an overall *c* value for the single rod of about 0·9. Sandler and Lindsley (1963) reported a *c* value of about 1·0 for the recovery of the single rod from the triple, and judged from previous experience with ordinary rod asymmetric dyads (Novitski, 1951; Zimmering, 1955) that *c* for the single rod separating from the double was about 0·67. Finally, the tandem ring, essentially a tandem metacentric compound X where the two free ends have become attached, will generate following certain exchange a double ring attached to a single or a triple ring attached to a single ring (Novitski, 1954). Consistent with findings for the two other compound X's, *c* for the single ring is equal to about 1·0 (Sandler and Lindsley, 1967). It should be noted that in their studies on compound X's, the authors have observed a depression in recovery of newly generated single chromosomes (rings and rods) in females lacking a Y chromosome; the reason for this is unknown. The reader is referred to Chapter 11 which provides appropriate diagrams

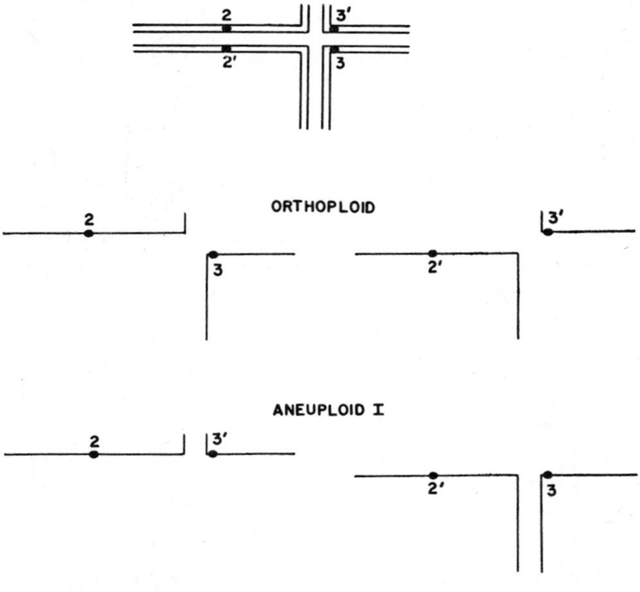

FIG. 5. The presumed pairing configuration of the bw^{V4} translocation heterozygote in the female and the products derived from alternate disjunction (orthoploid gametes) and from adjacent I disjunction (aneuploid I gametes) in the absence of crossing over in the interstitial region (between the centromere of chromosome 2 and the breakpoint). The numbers 2 and 3 stand for the centromere regions of the normal second and third chromosomes respectively and 2′ and 3′ for the homologous regions of the translocated chromosomes.

and a more detailed description of the origin and crossover mechanics in compound X's.

Novitski (1951) proposed that nonrandom disjunction could provide a solution to the problem of unequal recovery of complementary segregation products in certain translocation heterozygotes reported by Glass (1934, 1935). Glass studied three translocations between chromosomes 2 and 3, all described as having similar breakpoints and attachments, i.e. a break in 2R at the *bw* locus and one in the proximal heterochromatin of 3L, with re-attachment of all of 3L to the tip of 2L, and the tip of 2L to 3R. The presumed pairing configuration is shown in Fig. 5. From each of

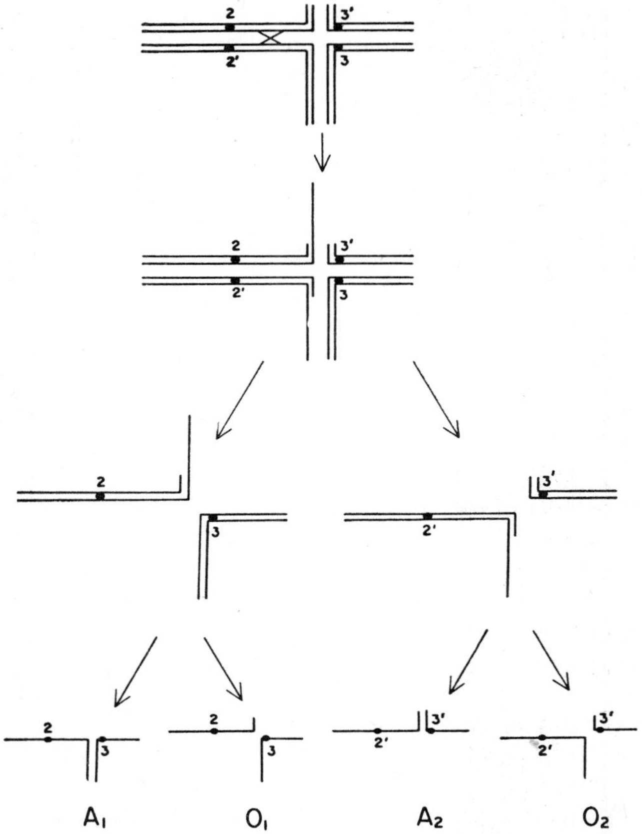

FIG. 6. The events leading to the production of aneuploid I gametes (A1 and A2) following alternate disjunction at the first division where A2, carrying the shorter crossover chromatid is expected to be produced more frequently than A1 which bears the longer.

these three translocations, Glass reported a discrepancy in the recovery of complementary aneuploid I products, 2 + 3′ being recovered about twice as frequently as 2′ + 3. As an explanation Novitski suggested the following. Crossing over in the interstitial region (between the centromere and the breakpoint, Fig. 6) results in the production of asymmetric dyads. Following alternate disjunction four kinds of gametes are produced, two of which, A1 and A2, are complementary aneuploid I's. Since A1 represeets the inclusion into the egg of the longer chromatid of the asymmetric dyad and the A2 the shorter, it is expected that nonrandom disjunction would result in a preferential inclusion of the shorter resulting in an excess of A2 as compared with A1. Zimmering (1955a) tested this possibility in one of these translocations, *T(2;3)*bw^{V4}, and from crosses of appropriately marked heterozygous translocation females by heterozygous translocation males provided conclusive evidence that the inequality in recovery of A1 and A2 could be entirely accounted for as resulting from the operation of nonrandom disjunction. It was further predicted that following crossing over and the establishment of an asymmetric dyad, adjacent I disjunction (Fig. 7) would lead to the production of orthoploid (balanced) crossover gametes 03 and 04, and 03 would be recovered more frequently than 04. The prediction was clearly born out, 03 being recovered more than twice as frequently as 04. Additional evidence of nonrandom disjunction has been reported in other translocation heterozygote females where crossing over in the interstitial region gives rise to asymmetric dyads (Zimmering, 1955b; Chandley, 1965), and from asymmetric dyads created upon X-ray induced chromatid interchange at meiosis I in stage 7 oocytes (Parker and McCrone, 1958; Brosseau, 1964; Lucchesi, 1965). Results from tests of females heterozygous for the bw^{V4} translocation and sc^8/sc^4–sc^8 showed that the two asymmetric dyads produced by crossing over behave independently of each other (Zimmering and Fanucci, 1965) suggesting that nonrandom disjunction may occur in all meioses rather than preferentially in some since the latter would lead to an excess of cases of nonrandom disjunction of both elements (Novitski, 1967).

Zimmering (unpublished observations) has carried out experiments determining the meiotic behavior of asymmetric dyads induced by X-rays in primary spermatocytes of male *Drosophila* heterozygous for the bw^{V4} translocation. From matings of heterozygous bw^{V4} males with homozygous nontranslocation females, crossovers in the interstitial region and i5 the region to the left of the centromere (in 2L) were recovered; the former are derived from asymmetric dyads and the latter from symmetric dyads (see Fig. 7). In each of three experiments, gross inequalities in recovery of reciprocal crossover classes was found following induced crossing over in the interstitial region and no evidence of such inequalities following

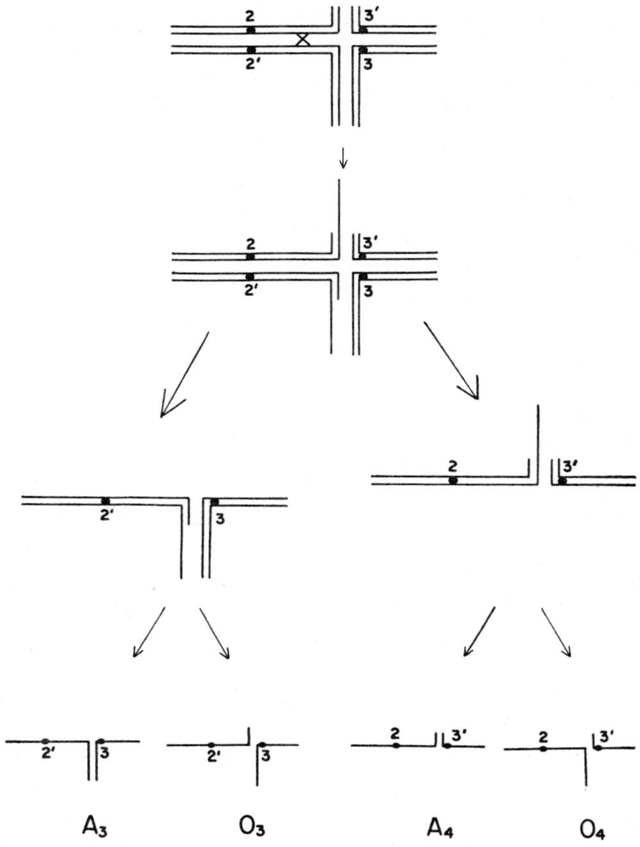

FIG. 7. The consequences of adjacent I disjunction following an exchange in the interstitial region. In this case, the orthoploid gamete 03 carrying the shorter crossover chromatid should be recovered more frequently than 04 carrying the longer.

crossing over outside the limits of the interstitial region, or in noncrossovers. The numbers of shorter/longer crossover chromosomes recovered following crossing over in the interstitial region were 32/17, 53/30, and 34/10, and the numbers in the reciprocal classes from crossing over outside the interstitial region 63 and 73, 121 and 111, and 96 and 92. The average *c* value for the shorter chromatid from the male was 0·67, and was 0·65 for the shorter chromatid from spontaneous crossing over in heterozygous bw^{V4} females serving as controls. The simplest formal possibilities would appear to be (1) half the time a sperm receives the longer chromarid from the asymmetric dyad, but not the symmetric dyad, it dysfunctions; if so, the dysfunctioning could be related to (or identical with) factors operating in the Bar–Stone male bringing about a depression in the recovery of the longer homologues; or (2) the nonrandom inclusion of the longer crossover chromatid into regularly produced nonfunctional sperm, the nonfunctionality being set up at the second division and distinguishing second division daughter cells. A search for evidence of gametic dysfunction in the male through analysis of ultrastructure is not a profitable approach in this case since a dose of 1000 R is necessary to bring about 1% crossing over in the interstitial region; nonetheless further information bearing on the mechanism operating in the male bw^{V4} is obtainable through genetic means.

Finally, Mukherjee and Das (1971) have reported a case of aberrant segregation in a laboratory stock of *D. ananassae*. The distortion occurs following crossing over, is expressed as a gross departure from equality in recovery of complementary crossover products, and occurs in both males and females (the distortion is somewhat greater in males than females; spontaneous crossing over occurs in the *D. ananassae* male; Moriwaki, 1938). Egg hatch data from reciprocal crosses of distorting lines with tester stocks showed clearly that the effect is not relatable to differential mortality of zygotes. It was noted that in contrast with cases of nonrandom in the female reviewed above, for example, sc^4–sc^8/sc^8, the distortion is not found in the noncrossover classes despite uncorrected crossover frequencies as high as 33%. The formal possibilities mentioned above to explain the results from the bw^{V4} male would apply here also, i.e. the presence of the "defective" crossover chromatid in the sperm causing dysfunction (but leaving sufficient numbers of normal sperm to effect normal egg hatch, as in *SD*), or the preferential inclusion of this chromatid into a nonfunctional product. In this case, analysis of ultrastructure would be a useful approach as a means of distinguishing between the two possibilities. Whatever the details of the mechanism in the female, it would presumably include as one feature the nonrandom inclusion of the "defective" crossover chromatid into a nonfunctional meiotic product. It should be noted that if, in the female, the presence of the "defective" chromatid in the meiotic product caused its dysfunctioning, then a mechanism ensuring highly selective inclusion of the dysfunction-causing chromatid into regularly nonfunctional products would have to be invoked.

V. Summary and Concluding Remarks

Instances of departures from the usual rules of chromosome behavior and gametogenesis have been reviewed, principally those reflected as failures of chromosome separation and of the unequal production of complementary gametic types after separation of genetic alternatives at anaphase I and at anaphase II. It is clear now that spontaneous primary nondisjunction of the acrocentric X's in XX *D. melanogaster* females occurs at the reduction division, that a large majority arise from exchange tetrads and that zero gametes exceed XX gametes. Attempts to provide a unified hypothesis accounting for all these observations have been largely unsuccessful. Furthermore it is not as yet known, for example, if crossover events preceding nondisjunction of the large metacentric autosomes or of autosomal acrocentrics like X are similar to those preceding X nondisjunction.

Some of the agents increasing nondisjunction in females and discussed in some detail include aging at a low temperature, high temperature treatment, X-rays, and the presence of a Y chromosome. Retention ("aging") of mature eggs (post-crossovers) by means of aging females at a low temperature has been shown to result in high X and autosomal nondisjunction; retention of earlier stages gives evidence of a small but significant elevation in X nondisjunction. Additionally, exposure of very early oocytes (pre-crossovers) to brief periods of high temperature results in a sharp increase in no-exchange tetrads and a significant increase in nondisjunction of X's. X-rays have been shown to increase nondisjunction of X's in stage 7 but not in stage 14 oocytes. To account for these increases, mechanisms including effects on the centromere or centrosome, and disorientation of spindle and/or pre-spindle elements have been variously considered but not as yet tested. Finally, recent experiments demonstrate that nondisjunction in stage 7 oocytes may come about when, following X-ray induced heterologous interchange, the interchange heterologues regularly separate from each other, leaving their normal pairing partners to assort randomly. Such events do not occur in stage 14 oocytes following heterologous interchange, suggesting that segregation patterns are already determined. Similar reasoning had been used to explain the failure of X-rays to induce nondisjunction in stage 14 oocytes. The presence of a Y in XX females has been known to increase nondisjunction of X's (secondary nondisjunction). Since a model postulating XY rather than XX synapsis permits a maximum of 50% XX–Y segregations and this value rises to some 70–80% in females heterozygous for certain multiple X inversions, new models have been sought. One which can account for such high nondisjunction postulates the conjunction of noncrossover X's (secondary exceptions are noncrossovers) with the Y chromosome, each arm of the Y pairing with a different X, and an alternate co-orientation of the three elements of the trivalent on the metaphase I plate, an orientation permitting 100% nondisjunction. Assuming the principle of a trivalent to be correct, important questions relating to events leading to such XYX conjunction remain to be settled.

In the male *D. melanogaster*, primary nondisjunction of X and Y probably occurs at a rate about as low as that of X's in the female, and, as in the female, diplo gametes are recovered less frequently than zeros. Cytogenetic data from a special high nondisjunction line in the male has demonstrated that XY pairing failure at prophase I leads to XY nondisjunction at anaphase I, that XY and zero cells are present in equal numbers at anaphase II but that zero gametes are recovered in the progeny more frequently than XY. It is quite possible that XY gametes in this line undergo dysfunction and that this could explain the results in the ordinary male; thus, the frequency of exceptional females, representing the recovery of XY gametes would effectively underestimate the nondisjunction rate, and if zeros arose only as a product of nondisjunction, it would represent the more accurate measure of nondisjunction. In critical experiments testing for spontaneous XY nondisjunction, it has been clearly demonstrated that a sizable proportion of exceptional females (30% or more) are derived from X–Y interchange, not XY nondisjunction. From critical X-irradiation experiments, the contribution of X–Y interchange females to the exceptional female class has been shown to be even more considerable, interchanges outnumbering nondisjunctionals 10–20:1, suggesting, in line with the data from the female, that X-rays are effective in causing breaks (precedent to interchange) and relatively less effective in causing nondisjunction. On the basis of preliminary evidence, heterologous interchanges induced sometime during the primary spermatocyte stage may behave as those induced in stage 7 oocytes, leading to nondisjunction.

Finally, cases of meiotic drive have been reviewed reflecting unequal recovery of reciprocal products following separation of genetic alternatives at anaphase I and at anaphase II, the latter following crossing over. Recent studies based on electron micrography have suggested the strong likelihood that cases such as "sex-ratio", *SD*, the sc^4–sc^8 system, and the Bar–Stone translocation are explicable on the basis of gametic dysfunction. Experiments demonstrating quantitative changes in the proportion of ultrastructurally abnormal sperm commensurate with changes in the degree of genetic distortion would lend support to his idea. A case in *D. melanogaster* was reviewed showing that following crossing over in a heteromorphic bivalent, giving rise to asymmetric dyads each consisting of a longer and shorter chromatid, the shorter is recovered more frequently. This was demonstrated earlier in the female and more recently following X-ray induced crossing over in the male. The mechanism in the female very likely involves a nonrandom inclusion of the shorter chromatid into the functional egg (nonrandom disjunction); in the male, two formal possibilities are suggested: (1) a proportion of sperm carrying the longer crossover chromatid derived from the asymmetric dyad undergoes dysfunction, or

(2) the longer chromatid is preferentially included into regularly produced nonfunctional sperm, the nonfunctionality set up at the second division and distinguishing second division daughter cells. In principle, the mechanisms described above would cover the case in *D. ananassae* where complementary crossover types in both females and males are recovered unequally. Since crossing over occurs spontaneously at a high rate in the male of this species, it may in this case be possible with the aid of electron microscopy to distinguish between the alternatives suggested as operating in the male.

References

ANDERSON, E. G. (1925). The proportion of exceptions in the offspring of exceptional females from X-ray treatment in *Drosophila*. *Papers Mich. Acad. Sci.* **4,** 523–525.

ANDERSON, E. G. (1929). Studies on a case of high non-disjunction in *Drosophila melanogaster*. *Z. indukt. Abstamm. VererbLehre.* **51,** 397–441.

ANDERSON, E. G. (1931). The constitution of the primary exceptions obtained after X-ray treatment of *Drosophila*. *Genetics* **16,** 386–396.

BACQ, Z. M. and ALEXANDER, P. (1961). "Fundamentals of Radiobiology", Pergammon Press, New York, pp. 245–248.

BATEMAN, A. J. (1957). Mutagenic sensitivity of maturing *Drosophila* sperm. II. Deleted X's. *J. Genet.* **55,** 467–475.

BATEMAN, A. J. (1965). X-irradiation of heterozygous attached-X. *Dros. Inf. Serv.* **40,** 79.

BRIDGES, C. B. (1916). Non-disjunction as proof of the chromosome theory of heredity. *Genetics* **1,** 1–52, 107–163.

BROSSEAU, G. E. (1964). Non-randomness in the recovery of detachments from the reversed metacentric compound X chromosome in *D. melanogaster*. *Can. J. Genet. Cytol.* **6,** 201–206.

BROSSEAU, G. E. and LINDSLEY, D. L. (1958). A dominantly marked Y chromosome: YB^S. *Dros. Inf. Serv.* **32,** 116.

BROSSEAU, G. E., NICOLETTI, B., GRELL, E. H. and LINDSLEY, D. L. (1961). Production of altered Y chromosomes bearing specific sections of the X chromosome in *Drosophila*. *Genetics* **46,** 339–346.

BUSBY, N. (1971). Segregation following interchange induced by irradiating mature oocytes of *D. melanogaster*. *Mutation Res.* **11,** 391–396.

CHANDLEY, A. C. (1965). Application of the "distributive pairing" hypothesis to problems of segregation in translocation heterozygotes of *D. melanogaster*. *Genetics* **52,** 247–258.

CLARK, A. M. and SOBELS, F. H. (1973). Section on Environmental Mutagenesis and related subjects. *Mutation Res.* **21,** 26.

COOPER, K. W. (1945). Normal segregation without chiasmata in female *D. melanogaster*. *Genetics* **30,** 472–484.

COOPER, K. W. (1946). The mechanism of non-random segregation of sex chromosomes in male *D. miranda*. *Genetics* **31,** 181–194.

COOPER, K. W. (1948). A new theory of secondary non-disjunction in female *D. melanogaster*. *Proc. Nat. Acad. Sci. U.S.A.* **34,** 179–187.

COOPER, K. W. (1949). The cytogenetics of meiosis in *Drosophila*: mitotic and meiotic autosomal chiasmata without crossing-over in the male. *J. Morph.* **84,** 81–121.

COOPER, K. W. (1951). *In*: "Biology of Drosophila" (M. Demerec, ed.), pp. 1–61. John Wiley & Sons, New York.

COOPER, K. W. (1952a). Studies on spermatogenesis in *Drosophila*. *Am. Phil. Soc. Yrbk.* 1951, 146–147.

COOPER, K. W. (1952b). The rate of equational nondisjunction of the X chromosome in male *Drosophila*. *Dros. Inf. Serv.* **26,** 96.

COOPER, K. W. (1964). Meiotic conjunctive elements not involving chiasmata. *Proc. Nat. Acad. Sci. U.S.A.* **52,** 1248–1255.

COOPER, K. W., ZIMMERING, S. and KRIVSHENKO, J. (1955) Interchromosomal effects and segregation. *Proc. Nat. Acad. Sci. U.S.A.* **41,** 911–914.

DAY, J. W. and GRELL, R. F. (1966). Radiation-induced nondisjunction and loss of chromosomes in *D. melanogaster* females. II. Effects of exchange and structural heterozygosity. *Mutation Res.* **3,** 503–509.

DE LA ROSA, M. E., DE JIMÉNEZ, J. G., OLVERA, R. and FELIX, R. (1972). Monosodium glutamate effects on X chromosome loss and nondisjunction in *D. melanogaster*. *Dros Inf. Serv.* **48,** 97–98.

DOBZHANSKY, TH. (1931). The decrease of crossing-over observed in translocations and its probable explanation. *Am. Nat.* **65,** 214–232.

ERICKSON, J. (1965). Meiotic drive in *Drosophila* involving chromosomal breakage. *Genetics* **51,** 555–571.

ERICKSON, J. and ACTON, A. B. (1969). Spermatocyte granules in *D. melanogaster*. *Can. J. Genet. Cytol.* **11,** 153–168.

ERICKSON, J. and HANKS, G. D. (1961). Time of temperature sensitivity of meiotic drive in *D. melanogaster*. *Am. Nat.* **95,** 247–250.

FAULHABER, S. H. (1967). An abnormal sex ratio in *D. simulans*. *Genetics* **56,** 189–213.

FELIX, R. (1969). *In*: "Programa de Genetica y Radiobiologica" Comision Nacional de Energia Nuclear, IX Informe Anual, pp. 30–31.

FROST, J. N. (1961). Autosomal nondisjunction in males of *D. melanogaster*. *Genetics* **46,** 39–54.

GERSHENSON, S. (1928). A new sex ratio abnormality in *Drosophila obscura*. *Genetics* **13,** 488–507.

GERSHENSON, S. (1933). Studies on the genetically inert region of the X-chromosome of *Drosophila*. I. Behaviour of an X-chromosome deficient for a part of its inert region. *J. Genet.* **28,** 297–313.

GLASS, H. B. (1934). The effect of lethal genes on the nondisjunctional classes in mutual translocations of *Drosophila*. *Z. indukt. Abstamm. VererbLehre* **67,** 254–258.

GLASS, H. B. (1935). A study of factors influencing chromosomal segregation in translocations of *D. melanogaster*. *Univ. Missouri Res. Bull.* **231,** 1–28.

GOLDEN, B. R. and ZIMMERING, S. (1972). Behavior of quasi-bivalents formed by heterologous interchange at meiosis in the male *Drosophila*. *Mutation Res.* **16,** 222–224.

GOWEN, J. W. and GAY, E. H. (1933). Eversporting as a function of the Y-chromosome in *D. melanogaster*. *Proc. Nat. Acad. Sci. U.S.A.* **19,** 122–126.

GRELL, R. F. (1962a). A new hypothesis on the nature and sequence of meiotic events in the female of *D. melanogaster*. *Proc. Nat. Acad. Sci. U.S.A.* **48,** 165–172.

GRELL, R. F. (1962b). A new model for secondary nondisjunction. The role of distributive pairing. *Genetics* **47,** 1737–1754.

GRELL, R. F. (1966). The meiotic origin of temperature-induced crossovers in *D. melanogaster* females. *Genetics* **54,** 411–421.

GRELL, R. F. (1967). Pairing at the chromosomal level. *J. Cell. Physiol. Suppl.* 1, 119–146.

GRELL, R. F. (1970). The time of initiation of segregational pairing between nonhomologues in *D. melanogaster*: a re-examination of w^{m4}. *Genetics* **64,** 337–365.

GRELL, R. F. (1971). Induction of sex chromosome nondisjunction by elevated temperature. *Mutation Res.* **11,** 347–349.

GRELL, R. F. and CHANDLEY, A. C. (1965). Evidence bearing on the coincidence of exchange and DNA replication in the oocyte of *D. melanogaster*. *Proc. Nat. Acad. Sci. U.S.A.* **53,** 1340–1346.

GRELL, R. F., MUNOZ, E. R. and KIRSCHBAUM, W. F. (1966). Radiation-induced nondisjunction and loss of chromosomes in *D. melanogaster* females. I. The effect of chromosome size. *Mutation Res.* **3,** 494–502.

HALL, J. C. (1970). Non-independence of primary nondisjunction for the sex and fourth chromosomes in *D. melanogaster*. *Dros. Inf. Serv.* **45,** 160.

HANKS, G. D. (1964). The analysis of a case of meiotic drive in *D. melanogaster*. *Genetics* **50,** 123–130.

HANKS, G. D. (1965). Are deviant sex ratios in normal strains of *Drosophila* caused by aberrant segregation? *Genetics* **52,** 259–266.

HANKS, G. D. (1968a). RD (Recovery Disrupter) activity associated with various wild type X chromosomes. *Dros. Inf. Serv.* **43,** 98.

HANKS, G. D. (1968b). Rate of recovery of products from nondisjunction of the 4th chromosome in RD strain males. *Dros. Inf. Serv.* **43,** 98.

HARTL, D. L. (1969). Dysfunctional sperm production in D.m. males homozygous for the segregation distorted elements. *Proc. Nat. Acad. Sci. Wash.* **63,** 782–789.

HARTL, D. L., HIRAIZUMI, Y. and CROW, J. F. (1967). Evidence for sperm dysfunction as the mechanism of segregation distortion in *D. melanogaster*. *Proc. Nat. Acad. Sci. U.S.A.* **58,** 2240–2245.

HILDRETH, P. E. and ULRICHS, P. C. (1969). A temperature effect on nondisjunction of the X chromosomes among eggs from aged *Drosophila* females. *Genetica* **40,** 191–197.

KELSALL, P. J. (1961). Nondisjunction of the sex-chromosomes in the male of *D. melanogaster*. *Nature, Lond.* **190,** 1035–1036.

KELSALL, P. J. (1963). Nondisjunction and maternal age in *D. melanogaster*. *Genet. Res.* **4,** 284–289.

KING, R. C., RUBINSON, A. C. and SMITH, R. F. (1956). Oogenesis in adult *D. melanogaster*. *Growth* **20,** 121–157.

KIRIAZIS, W. C. and ABRAHAMSON, S. (1968). The effectiveness of varying doses of X-rays in the production of X chromosome loss and nondisjunction in stage 14 oocytes of *D. melanogaster*. *Genetics* **60,** 193.

KUHN, D. T. and HANKS, G. D. (1967). Suppression of RD effect due to a 4th chromosome carrying minute. *Dros. Inf. Serv.* **42,** 79.

LAMY, R. (1949). Production of 2–X sperm in males. *Dros. Inf. Serv.* **23,** 91.

LEA, D. E. (1956). Action of radiation on living cells. Cambridge Univ. Press pp. 192–197.

LINDSLEY, D. L. (1955). Spermatogonial exchange between the X and Y chromosomes of *D. melanogaster*. *Genetics* **40,** 24–44.

LINDSLEY, D. L. and GRELL, E. (1969). Spermiogenesis without chromosomes in *D. melanogaster*. *Genetics* **61,** Suppl. 69–78.

LINDSLEY, D. L. and SANDLER, L. (1957). The meiotic behavior of grossly deleted X chromosomes in *D. melanogaster*. *Genetics* **43,** 547–563.

LINDSLEY, D. L. and SANDLER, L. (1965). Meiotic behavior of tandom metacentric compound X chromosomes in *D. melanogaster*. *Genetics* **51,** 223–245.

LUCCHESI, J. C. (1965). The nature of induced exchanges between the attached-X and Y chromosomes in *D. melanogaster* females. *Genetics* **51,** 209–216.

MCCLOSKEY, J. D. (1966). The problem of gene activity in the sperm of *D. melanogaster*. *Am. Nat.* **100,** 211–218.

MACKNIGHT, R. H. and COOPER, K. W. (1944). The synapsis of the sex chromosomes of *D. miranda* in relation to their directed segregation. *Proc. Nat. Acad. Sci. U.S.A.* **30,** 384–387.

MALOGOLOWKIN, C. (1958). Maternally inherited "sex-ratio" conditions in *D. willistoni* and *D. paulistorum*. *Genetics* **43,** 274–286.

MATSUNAGA, E. and MARYUMA, T. (1969). Human Sexual Behavior, Delayed Fertilization and Down's Syndrome. *Nature, Lond.* **221,** 642–644.

MAVOR, J. W. (1922). The production of nondisjunction by X-rays. *Science, N.Y.* **55,** 295–297.

MAVOR, J. W. (1924). The production of nondisjunction by X-rays. *J. Expl. Zool.* **39,** 381–432.

MERRIAM, J. R. and FROST, J. N. (1964). Exchange and nondisjunction of the X chromosomes in female *D. melanogaster*. *Genetics* **49,** 109–122.

MINAMORI, S. (1969). Extrachromosomal element delta in *D. melanogaster*. I. Gene dependence of killing action and of multiplication. *Genetics* **62,** 583–596.

MINAMORI, S. (1970). Extrachromosomal element delta in *D. melanogaster*. III. Induction of one-sided gamete recovery from male and female heterozygotes. *Genetics* **66,** 505–515.

MITTLER, S., MITTLER, J. E. and OWENS, S. L. (1967). Loss of chromosomes and nondisjunction induced by caffeine in *Drosophila*. *Nature, Lond.* **214,** 424.

MORGAN, L. V. (1938). Origin of attached-X chromosomes in *D. melanogaster* and the occurrence of nondisjunction of X's in the male. *Am. Nat.* **72,** 434–446.

MORGAN, T. H., BRIDGES, C. B. and STURTEVANT, A. H. (1925). The genetics of *Drosophila*. *Bibliogr. Genet.* **2,** 1–262.

MORIWAKI, D. (1938). A probable case of equational nondisjunction in *Drosophila ananassae*. *Cytologia* **9,** 347–351.

MOTTRAM, J. C. (1930). Nondisjunction produced by carbon dioxide. *Nature, Lond.* **125,** 275–276.

MUKHERJEE, A. S. and DAS, A. K. (1971). Segregation distortion and crossing over in males of *D. ananassae*. I. Preliminary genetic analysis. *Genetics* **67,** 521–532.

MULLER, H. J. (1940). An analysis of the process of structural change in chromosomes of *Drosophila*. *J. Genet.* **40,** 1–66.

MULLER, H. J. (1948). The construction of several new types of Y chromosomes. *Dros. Inf. Serv.* **22,** 73.

MULLER, H. J. (1951). Homosexual copulation in the male of *Drosophila,* and the problem of the fate of sperm of males isolated from females. *Dros. Inf. Serv.* **25,** 118–119.

MULLER, H. J. (1954). The nature of the genetic effects produced by radiation. *Radiation Biology*, **1,** Chap. 7, 351–473. McGraw-Hill, New York.

MULLER, H. J. and SETTLES, F. (1925). The nonfunctioning of the genes in spermatozoa. *Anat. Res.* **31,** 347.

MULLER, H. J. and SETTLES, F. (1927). The nonfunctioning of the genes in spermatozoa. *Z. indukt. Abstamm. VerebLehre.* **43,** 285–312.

NEUHAS, M. (1937). Additional data on crossing-over between X and Y chromosomes in *D. melanogaster. Genetics* **22,** 333–339.

NEUHAS, M. (1941). The influence of separate arms of the Y chromosome on secondary nondisjunction in the females of *D. melanogaster. Dros. Inf. Serv.* **15,** 16.

NOVITSKI, E. (1947). Genetic analysis of an anomalous sex ratio condition in *D. affinis. Genetics* **32,** 526–234.

NOVITSKI, E. (1951). Non-random disjunction in *Drosophila. Genetics* **36,** 267–180.

NOVITSKI, E. (1952). The genetic consequences of anaphase bridge formation in *Drosophila. Genetics* **37,** 270–287.

NOVITSKI, E. (1953). The dependence of the secondary "sex ratio" in humans on the age of the father. *Science, N.Y.* **117,** 531–533.

NOVITSKI, E. (1954). The compound X chromosomes in *Drosophila. Genetics* **39,** 127–140.

NOVITSKI, E. (1964). An alternative to the distributive pairing hypothesis in *Drosophila. Genetics* **50,** 1449–1451.

NOVITSKI, E. (1967). Nonrandom disjunction in *Drosophila. Ann. Rev. Genet.* **1,** 71–86.

NOVITSKI, E. (1970). The concept of gamete dysfunction. *Dros. Inf. Serv.* **45,** 87–88.

NOVITSKI, E. and HANKS, G. D. (1961). Analysis of irradiated *Drosophila* populations for meiotic drive. *Nature, Lond.* **190,** 989–990.

NOVITSKI, E. and PEACOCK, W. J. (1970). Results from the combination of B^S and SD in the male. *Dros. Inf. Serv.* **45,** 95–96.

NOVITSKI, E. and SANDLER, I. (1957). Are all products of spermatogenesis regularly functional? *Proc. Natl. Acad. Sci. Wash.* **43,** 318–324.

NOVITSKI, E. and SANDLER, L. (1956). Further notes on the nature of non-random disjunction in *D. melanogaster. Genetics* **41,** 194–206.

NOVITSKI, E., PEACOCK, W. J. and ENGEL, J. (1965). Cytological basis of "sex ratio" in *D. pseudoobscura. Science* **148,** 516–517.

OKSALA, T. A. (1957). Chromosome pairing, crossing over, and segregation in meiosis in *D. melanogaster* females. *Cold Spr. Harb. Sympos. Quant. Biol.* **23,** 197–210.

OSTER, I. I. (1964). Filicidal Y chromosomes. *Genetics* **50,** 274.

PARKER, D. R. (1959). Dominant lethal mutation in irradiated oocytes. *Univ. Texas Publ.* **5914,** 113–127.

PARKER, D. R. (1965). Chromosome pairing and induced exchange in *Drosophila. Mutation Res.* **2,** 523–529.

PARKER, D. R. (1969) Heterologous interchange at meiosis in *Drosophila.* II. Some disjunctional consequences of interchange. *Mutation Res.* **7,** 393–407.

PARKER, D. R. and MCCRONE, J. (1958). A genetic analysis of some rearrangements induced in oocytes of *Drosophila*. *Genetics* **43,** 172–186.

PARKER, D. R. and WILLIAMSON, J. H. (1970). Heterologous interchange at meiosis in *Drosophila*. III. Interchange-mediated nondisjunction. *Mutation Res.* **9,** 273–286.

PATTERSON, J. T., BREWSTER, W. and WINCHESTER, A. M. (1932). Effects produced by aging and X-raying eggs of *D. melanogaster*. *J. Hered.* **23,** 325–333.

PEACOCK, W. J. (1965). Nonrandom segregation of chromosomes in *Drosophila* males. *Genetics* **51,** 573–583.

PEACOCK, W. J. and ERICKSON, J. (1964). An indicator of polarity in the spermatocyte? *Dros. Inf. Serv.* **39,** 107–108.

PEACOCK, W. J. and ERICKSON, J. (1965). Segregation-distortion and regularly nonfunctional products of spermatogenesis in *D. melanogaster*. *Genetics* **51,** 313–328.

POLICANSKY, D. and ELLISON, J. (1970). "Sex ratio" in *D. pseudoobscura*: Spermiogenic failure. *Science* **169,** 888–889.

PONTECORVO, G. (1940). Further investigations on the scY^L chromosome. *Dros. Inf. Serv.* **13,** 74.

RAMEL, C. (1967). Genetic effects of organic mercury compounds. *Hereditas* **57,** 445–447.

RAMEL, C. and MAGNUSSON, J. (1969). Genetic effects of organic mercury compounds II. Chromosome segregation in *D. melanogaster*. *Hereditas* **61,** 231–254.

REMONDINI, D. J. and HANKS, G. D. (1966). Location of a second chromosome factor RD2, as one of the recovery disrupter components. *Dros. Inf. Serv.* **41,** 91.

SAFIR, S. R. (1921). Genetic and cytological examination of the phenomena of primary nondisjunction in *D. melanogaster*. *Genetics* **5,** 459–487.

SMITH, C. A. M. (1964). Induced X–Y exchange and nondisjunction in $B^S Yy^+$ and bw^+Y males. *Dros. Inf. Serv.* **39,** 126.

SANDLER, L. and BRAVER, G. (1954). The meiotic loss of unpaired chromosomes in *D. melanogaster*. *Genetics* **39,** 365–377.

SANDLER, L. and LINDSLEY, D. L. (1963). The meiotic behavior of tandem acrocentric compound X chromosomes in *D. melanogaster*. *Genetics* **48,** 1533–1543.

SANDLER, L. and LINDSLEY, D. L. (1967). Meiotic behavior of tandem compound ring X chromosomes in *D. melanogaster*. *Genetics* **55,** 645–671.

SANDLER, L. and NOVITSKI, E. (1956). Evidence for genetic homology between chromosomes I and IV in *D. melanogaster*, with a proposed explanation for the crowding effect in triploids. *Genetics* **41,** 189–193.

SANDLER, L. and NOVITSKI, E. (1957). Meiotic drive as an evolutionary force. *Am. Nat.* **91,** 105–110.

SANDLER, L., HIRAIZUMI, Y. and SANDLER, I. (1959). Meiotic drive in natural populations of *D. melanogaster*. I. The cytogenetic basis of segregation-distortion. *Genetics* **44,** 233–250.

SÄVHAGEN, R. (1961). The relation between X-ray sensitivity and stages of development of treated cells in spermato- and spermio-genesis of *D. melanogaster*. *Hereditas* **47,** 43–68.

SCHULTZ, J. (1933). X-ray effects on *Drosophila pseudo obscura*. *Genetics* **18** 284–291.

SCHULTZ, J. (1934). Report of investigations on the constitution of the germinal material in relation to heredity. *Carnegie Inst. Wash. Yrbk.* **33,** 280.

SCHULTZ, J. and REDFIELD, H. (1951). Interchromosomal effect on crossing-over in *Drosophila. Cold Spr. Harb. Symp. Quant. Biol.* **16,** 175–197.

SIDIROV, B. N., SOKOLOV, N. N. and TROFIMOV, I. E. (1936). Crossing-over in heterozygoten Inversionen. I. Einfaches Crossing-over, *Genetica* **18,** 291–312.

SMOLER, M. H. (1965). The ineffectiveness of anoxia in promoting nondisjunction. *Dros. Inf. Serv.* **40,** 87.

STALKER, H. D. (1961). The genetic systems modifying meiotic drive in *D. paramelanica. Genetics* **46,** 177–202.

STERN, C. (1934). On the occurrence of translocations and autosomal nondisjunction in *D. melanogaster. Proc. Nat. Acad. Sci. U.S.A.* **20,** 36–19.

STONE, W. S. (1934). Linkage between X and IV chromosomes in *Drosophila melanogaster Genetica* **16,** 506–520.

STRANGIO, V. A. (1962). Radiosensitivity during spermatogenesis in *D. melanogaster. Am. Nat.* **96,** 145–149.

STURTEVANT, A. H. (1929). The claret mutant type of *Drosophila simulans*: a study of chromosome elimination and of cell-linkage. *Z. Wiss. Zool.* **135,** 325–355.

STURTEVANT, A. H. (1944). Maintenance of a Drosophila stock center, in connection with investigations on the constitution of the germinal material in relation to heredity. *Carnegie Inst. Wash. Yrbk.* **43,** 164.

STURTEVANT, A. H. and BEADLE, G. W. (1936). The relations of inversions in the X chromosome of *D. melanogaster*, to crossing-over and disjunction. *Genetics* **21,** 554–604.

STURTEVANT, A. H. and BEADLE, G. W. (1939). "Introduction to Genetics". Saunders, Philadelphia & London.

STURTEVANT, A. H. and DOBZHANSKY, TH. (1936). Geographical distribution and cytology of "sex ratio" in *Drosophila pseudoobscura* and related species. *Genetics* **21,** 473–490.

TOKUNAGA, C. (1970a). The effects of low temperature and aging on nondisjunction in *Drosophila. Genetics* **65,** 75–94.

TOKUNAGA, C. (1970b). Aspects of low-temperature-induced meiotic nondisjunction in *Drosophila* females. *Genetics* **66,** 653–661.

TOKUYASU, K. T., PEACOCK, W. J. and HARDY, R. W. (1972). Dynamics of spermiogenesis in *D. melanogaster*. I. Individualization process. *Z. Zellforsch.* **124,** 479–506.

TRAUT, H. (1964). The dose-dependence of X-chromosome loss and nondisjunction induced by X-rays in oocytes of *D. melanogaster. Mutation Res.* **1,** 157–162.

TRAUT, H. (1970). The resistance of mature oocytes of *D. melanogaster* to the induction of nondisjunction by X-rays. *Mutation Res.* **10,** 156–158.

TRAUT, H. (1971). The influence of the temporal distribution of the X-ray dose on the induction of X-chromosomal nondisjunction and X-chromosome loss in oocytes of *D. melanogaster. Mutation Res.* **12,** 321–327.

TRAUT, H. and SCHEID, W. (1969). The dose-dependence of X-chromosome loss induced by X-rays in mature oocytes of *D. melanogaster. Mutation Res.* **7,** 471–474.

UCHIDA, I. A. (1962). The effect of maternal age and radiation on the rate of disjunction in *D. melanogaster. Canad. J. Genet. Cytol.* **4,** 402–408.

WALLACE, B. (1948). Studies on "sex ratio" in *D. pseudoobscura*. I. Selection and "Sex ratio". *Evolution* **2,** 189–217.

WELTMAN, A. A. (1954). Nonrandom disjunction in attached-X females. *Dros. Inf. Serv.* **28,** 166.

WU, C. K. (1964). X-ray induced exchange and nondisjunction in *Drosophila* spermatocytes. *Dros. Inf. Serv.* **39,** 126–127.

YAMAMOTO, M. and INGALLS, T. H. (1972). Delayed fertilization and chromatid anomalies in the Hamster embryo. *Science, N.Y.* **176,** 518–521.

YANDERS, A. F. (1965). A relationship between sex ratio and paternal age in *Drosophila*. *Genetics* **51,** 481–486.

YANDERS, A. F., BREWEN, J. G., PEACOCK, W. J. and GOODCHILD, D. J. (1968). Meiotic drive and visible polarity in *Drosophila* spermatocytes. *Genetics* **59,** 245–253.

ZIMMERING, S. (1955a). A genetic study of segregation in a translocation heterozygote in *Drosophila*. *Genetics* **40,** 809–825.

ZIMMERING, S. (1955b). The effect of the Y chromosome and Y chromosome fragments on crossing over in the autosomes of *Drosophila*. *Dros. Inf. Serv.* **29,** 174.

ZIMMERING, S. (1958). A simultaneous measure of inter-chromosomal effects on autosomal crossing over and sex chromosome nondisjunction in *Drosophila*. *Genetics* **43,** 354–361.

ZIMMERING, S. (1959). Modification of abnormal genetic ratios. *Science, N.Y.* **130,** 1426.

ZIMMERING, S. (1960). Modification of abnormal gametic ratios in *Drosophila*. I. Evidence for an influence of Y chromosomes and major autosomes on gametic rations from Bar-Stone translocation males. *Genetics* **45,** 1253–1268.

ZIMMERING, S. (1962). Genetic evidence of X-ray induced exchange occurring at a four-strand stage in *Drosophila* spermatocytes. *J. Hered.* **53,** 254–256.

ZIMMERING, S. (1963). The effect of temperature on meiotic loss of the Y chromosome in the male *Drosophila*. *Genetics* **48,** 133–138.

ZIMMERING, S. and BARBOUR, E. (1961). Modification of abnormal gametic ratios in *Drosophila*. II. Evidence for a marked shift in gametic ratios in early vs. later sperm batches from A-type Bar-Stone translocation males. *Genetics* **46,** 1253–1260.

ZIMMERING, S. and GREEN, R. E. (1965). Temperature-dependent transmission rate of a univalent X chromosome in the male *D. melanogaster*. *Can. J. Genet. Cytol.* **7,** 453–456.

ZIMMERING, S. and FANUCCI, A. J. (1965). Assortment of non-randomly disjoining chromatids. *Can. J. Genet. Cytol.* **7,** 250–253.

ZIMMERING, S. and FOWLER, G. (1968). Progeny:sperm ratios and non-functional sperm in *D. melanogaster*. *Genet. Res. Camb.* **12,** 359–363.

ZIMMERING, S. and KIRSHENBAUM, G. (1964). Radiation induced deletions in spermatids and spermatocytes of *Drosophila*. *Z. Vererbungsl.* **95,** 301–305.

ZIMMERING, S. and PERLMAN, M. (1962). Modification of abnormal gametic ratios in *Drosophila*. III. Probable time of the *A*-type effect in Bar–Stone translocation males. *Can. J. Genet. Cytol.* **4,** 333–336.

ZIMMERING, S. and WU, C. K. (1963). Radiation induced X–Y exchange and nondisjunction in spermatocytes of the immature testis of *Drosophila*. *Genetics* **48,** 1619–1623.

ZIMMERING, S. and WU, C. K. (1964a). X–Y nondisjunction and exchange induced by X-rays in primary spermatocytes of the adult *Drosophila. Genetics* **49,** 499–504.

ZIMMERING, S. and WU, C. K. (1964b). Meiotic X–Y exchange and nondisjunction induced by irradiation in the *Drosophila* male. *Genetics* **50,** 633–638.

ZIMMERING, S., SANDLER, L. and NICOLETTI, B. (1970a). Mechanisms of meiotic drive. *Ann. Rev. Genet.* **4,** 409–436.

ZIMMERING, S., BARNABO, J., FEMINO, J. and FOWLER, G. L. (1970b). Progeny:sperm ratios and Segregation-Distorter in *D. melanogaster. Genetica* **41,** 61–64.

Note in Proof:

Since completion of the writing of this article (1972) a lengthy review covering in detail some of the male meiotic drive systems described herein was published by Peacock and Miklos (1973, *Advan. Genet.* **17**: 361–409). A major contribution of the paper involved presentation of a new model, *Pairing-Dysfunction,* which provides an explanation for distorted segregation ratios in sc^4–sc^8/Y males, and accounts for sex chromosome behavior in sc^4–sc^8/Y/Y, $X.Y$/0, and X^D,B^S $Y^L.Y^S$/0 males. Briefly, Peacock and Miklos propose that (1) several pairing sites exist in the conjunctive regions of X and Y, (2) pairing of a sufficient number of these sites allows for normal segregation of X and Y and for normal spermiogenesis, and (3) the *presence* of a chromosome possessing unpaired sites leads ultimately to dysfunction, the degree of dysfunction depending on the effective number of sites unpaired. The authors suggest that other systems exhibiting meiotic drive, i.e. *SD*, $T(X;4)B^S$, be reexamined in the light of the possible importance of the disruption of pairing.

15. Segregation Distortion

DANIEL L. HARTL*

Department of Biological Sciences
Purdoe University, West Lafayette, Indiana, U.S.A.

and

YUICHIRO HIRAIZUMI†

Department of Zoology
The University of Texas, Austin, Texas, U.S.A.

* Supported by National Science Foundation grant GB–18786, National Institutes of Health grant GM21732 and Research Career Award GM2301. † Supported in part by National Science Foundation grant GB–17986.

I. Introduction: Properties of *SD* Chromosomes

The discovery of segregation distorter in 1956 in a natural population of *Drosophila melanogaster* was quite by accident. In their study of the heterozygous effects on fitness of chromosomes that carry recessive lethals, Hiraizumi and Crow (1960) extracted from the Madison, Wisconsin, population a total of 183 second chromosomes which were made heterozygous with the recessive markers *cn* and *bw* in males and then backcrossed to *cn bw* females. Departures from the expected one-to-one ratio in the F_1 were measured, and, by and large, all chromosomes segregated according to expectation. Six very striking exceptions were noted, however. The exceptional chromosomes all turned out to manifest the same phenomenon, and in the first detailed report of the phenomenon (Sandler *et al.*, 1959) they were called *SD* chromosomes. The *SD* chromosomes were characterized by the observation that the mating *SD/cn bw* ♂♂ × *cn bw* ♀♀ produced 90% or more of *SD*-bearing progeny. Five of the 6 (*SD-1*, *SD-5*, *SD-8*, *SD-9*, and *SD-36*) appeared to be identical; these were called the *SD-5* type chromosomes. All 5 carried an allelic recessive lethal; all 5 had in the right arm of chromosome 2 a proximal inversion [*In*(*2R*) *45c–F; 49A*] and a nonoverlapping distal inversion that was later identified as *In*(*2R*) *NS* = *In*(*2R*) *52A2–B1; 56F9–13*. The remaining *SD* (*SD-72*), by contrast, was lethal-free and lacked the proximal inversion, but in addition to *In*(*2R*) *NS* it carried a small pericentric inversion [*In*(*2LR*) *39–40; 42A*] that involved essentially all the centric heterochromatin (Sandler *et al.*, 1959; Lewis, 1962; Lindsley and Grell, 1968). Recombination in the left arm of all 6 *SD*'s was normal, and the results of standard tests for translocations between chromosome 2 and the other chromosomes were negative.

Although *SD* chromosomes were first discovered in the Madison population, they also occur elsewhere. Indeed, most natural populations appear to harbor *SD*, it having now been found in several states of the upper Midwest U.S.A. (Greenberg, 1962), in Mexico (Mange, 1961), in Japan (Hiraizumi and Nakazima, 1965), in Italy (Nicoletti and Trippa, 1967; Trippa *et al.*,1972), and elsewhere. In only one natural population examined extensively, that in Austin, Texas, has *SD* not been found. In addition to *SD* itself, suppressors of *SD* also occur at appreciable frequencies in natural populations (Hiraizumi *et al.*, 1960; Kataoka, 1967; Hartl, 1970). Furthermore, as experimental studies of *SD* began in earnest, several additional phenomena associated with *SD* were discovered. *SD* sometimes appears to be unstable (Sandler and Hiraizumi, 1959, 1960a; Miklos and Smith-White, 1971; Miklos, 1972a); it may induce specific mutations upon the X chromosome and upon its homologue (Sandler and Hiraizumi,

1959, 1961a; Sandler, 1962; Sandler and Rosenfeld, 1962; Hiraizumi, 1961); it has a pronounced aging effect (Sandler and Hiraizumi, 1961b; Hiraizumi and Watanabe, 1969); it affects the sex ratio (Hiraizumi and Nakazima, 1967; Denell *et al.*, 1969; Denell and Miklos, 1971); its segregation ratio changes with brood and may be affected by the genotype of the females (Hiraizumi and Watanabe, 1969; Denell and Judd, 1969; Hartl and Childress, 1972; Hartl, 1973a).

The many observations that bear on *SD* can conveniently be classified under four headings: (1) the mechanism of *SD*—how it happens that an *SD* chromosome is recovered in excess over its homologue; (2) the genetic structure of *SD* chromosomes—how many loci are involved, where they are on the chromosome, and how they interact with one another; (3) the associated phenomena—a veritable grab-bag of observations, understood to varying degrees, that bear indirectly on the questions raised above; and (4) the *SD* system as it exists in natural populations—including here both *SD* and the suppressors, with primary emphasis on the contemporary effects of *SD* and on its long-term evolutionary implications.

The population biology of *SD* is most appropriately considered in relation to other cases of non-Mendelian segregation that exist in natural populations of *Drosophila*, and we will defer consideration of these issues except for those aspects of the population studies that bear directly on mechanistic or genetic points. We will here first discuss the early data on *SD* that localized to an extent the region of chromosome 2 responsible for the segregation distortion and narrowed somewhat the hypothetical mechanisms of action of *SD* that were plausible. Then we will discuss the experiments that bear directly on the mechanism of *SD*, following this with a detailed examination of the genetic structure of *SD* chromosomes, and after that a review of the phenomena associated with *SD* and their postulated mechanisms. Within each of these areas of discussion the development will be more or less chronological.

II. Initial Observations of Segregation Distortion

As mentioned previously, the operational definition of a segregation distorter (*SD*) chromosome is that the mating *SD/cn bw* ♂♂ × *cn bw* ♀♀ produces a greater than expected proportion of *SD/cn bw* progeny. The observed proportion of *SD/cn bw* progeny from such a cross is a useful and widely employed metric of distortion. In general, the amount of distortion is measured by a value usually called *k*, which is computed as the proportion of *SD*-bearing progeny recovered from any mating in which one of the parents is heterozygous for *SD*, or for any of the derivatives of *SD*.

The six *SD*'s originally recovered from the Madison population—*SD-1*, *SD-5*, *SD-8*, *SD-9*, *SD-36*, *SD-72*—produced *k*-values of 0·97, 0·93, 0·99, 0·94, 0·97, and 0·97, respectively, in the mating *SD/cn bw* ♂♂ × *cn bw* ♀♀. The reciprocal crosses, by contrast, produced *k*-values of 0·51, 0·52, 0·55, 0·53, 0·53, and 0·53, where each of the numbers given is based on well over 1000 progeny (Sandler *et al.*, 1959). Thus *SD* is a chromosome that grossly distorts the segregation ratio in males but not in females. This assumes, of course, that the distortion can be attributed to *SD* and not to some peculiarity of the *cn bw* chromosome. The latter possibility is excluded by the observation that whereas the *cn bw* chromosome segregates normally when it is heterozygous with non-*SD* chromosomes, the *SD* chromosomes distort the second chromosomes from most laboratory strains as well as non-*SD* chromosomes isolated from natural populations. Sandler *et al.* (1959) made *SD-5* heterozygous with the second chromosomes from 4 laboratory strains and with 3 wild-type chromosomes from the Madison population, and observed *k*-values ranging from 0·75 to 0·92. Several *SD* chromosomes were also made heterozygous with chromosomes carrying various structural abnormalities, inversions or translocations, with the result that some of these were distorted and some were not, a result interpreted as meaning that the distortion of the segregation ratio by *SD* required synapsis, an hypothesis that will be discussed in detail later. Nevertheless, the activity of *SD* against a structurally normal homologue implies that it is the *SD* chromosome that causes the distortion of the segregation ratio in heterozygous males.

The region of the *SD* chromosome that is responsible for the effect is in or near the centric heterochromatin. Owing to the pair of inversions in 2R of the *SD-5* type chromosomes, recombination between *cn* and *bw* in the cross *SD/cn bw* ♀♀ × *cn bw* ♂♂ is extremely rare. Only one recombinant, deriving from *SD-36* and in later papers called *R(SD-36)-1*^{bw}, was recovered; this recombinant carries both inversions in 2R, the recessive lethal, and the marker *bw*. It is a distorter with an average *k*-value of about 0·85. Recombinants from *SD-72* are somewhat easier to obtain. Sandler *et al.* (1959) obtained 11. Seven of these were *bw* recombinants, and all lacked *In(2R) NS* but were distorters. The other 4 recombinants were *cn* and carried the inversion but were nondistorters. Thus the distortion is not due to the recessive lethal or to the proximal inversion in the *SD-5* type chromosomes, because *SD-72* lacks these, nor is the distortion due to the pericentric inversion in *SD-72*, because the *SD-5* type chromosomes do not carry it. *In(2R) NS* can be eliminated as the cause of the distortion because of the *bw* recombinants that distort although they lack the inversion. Moreover, since the region of the *SD-72* chromosome that is responsible for the distortion seems to segregate from *cn* (*cn* is about 2·5 map units to the right of the centromere), one infers that segregation distortion is caused by a genic, as opposed to a gross chromosomal, element that is located in the region of the *SD* chromosome in or near the centric heterochromatin. This inference was supported by the finding that the one cn^+-bearing nondistorter recovered from the cross of *R*(*SD*)–*4*/*pr cn* ♀♀ × *cn bw* ♂♂, where *R*(*SD*)–*4* is one of the *bw*-bearing derivatives of *SD–72*, also carried the marker *pr*, which is about 3 map units to the left of *cn*, whereas none of the cn^+-bearing distorters carried this marker (Sandler *et al.*, 1959).

The question of whether the distortion of the segregation ratio in *SD*/*cn bw* males is attributable to the lack of fertilization of eggs by sperm bearing the *cn bw* chromosome or to the lethality of zygotes that arise from *cn bw*-bearing sperm can be settled by direct experiment by comparing the number of eggs laid by females that have been inseminated by *SD*/*cn bw* males with the number of adults that arise from the eggs. The experiments of Sandler *et al.* (1959) were sufficient to show that matings of females with *SD*/*cn bw* males produced no greater zygotic loss than matings with non-*SD* males, but the experiments were complicated by the fact that the hatchability of eggs from *cn bw* females is low (about 50%) irrespective of the males they are mated with, and by the additional fact that the only genetic marker on the *SD–5* chromosome was the lethal it carried. A more recent experiment illustrates the same point (Hartl, unpublished observations): The dominant marker *Cy* (map position 6·1) was placed by recombination onto the left arm of *SD–72* and onto the left arm of the second chromosome of the wild type *Tokyo* strain. Males of the constitution *Cy SD–72*/*cn bw* or *Cy Tokyo*/*cn bw* were mated with females from the *Tokyo* strain, and the eggs laid and the progeny arising from these eggs were tabulated. Eighty-nine per cent of 228 eggs obtained from females inseminated by *Cy SD–72*/*cn bw* males gave rise to adults, and among the adults the proportion that were *Cy SD–72* was 0·97; 86% of 247 eggs obtained from females inseminated by *Cy Tokyo*/*cn bw* males gave rise to adults, and the proportion that were *Cy Tokyo* was 0·48. The results of Sandler *et al.* (1959), more extensive than those above, showed that the mechanism of distortion of the segregation ratio by *SD* is prezygotic.

III. The Mechanism of Distortion

The earliest hypothesis put forward as the mechanism of *SD* was that *SD* induced upon its homologue a gross chromosomal abnormality that would interfere with the behavior of its homologue during meiosis to such an extent that the non-*SD*-bearing sperm would be either not formed or not functional (Sandler *et al.*, 1959). This hypothesis received indirect support from the observation that males heterozygous for *SD* and a translocation between the Y chromosome and the homologue of *SD* produced *SD*-bearing progeny that were almost exclusively female, a result that would not occur if the homologue of *SD* were being eliminated during meiosis and *SD* were undergoing an extra replication, as was at the time thought to be the mechanism of distortion of sex ratio in *D. pseudoobscura* (Sturtevant and Dobzhansky, 1936—later shown not to be the case by Novitski *et al.*, 1965; Policansky and Ellison, 1970). Although the observation demonstrated that the non-*SD*-bearing products of meiosis were not included in functional sperm, it left open the question of their fate. On the one hand, Novitski and I. Sandler (1957) had proposed on the basis of their studies of the segregation distortion of *T(1;4)* B^S that males of *D. melanogaster* regularly produce from each primary spermatocyte two functional and two nonfunctional sperm. Applied to *SD*, this hypothesis implies that *SD* would orient itself during meiosis in such a way as to consign its homologue to the nonfunctional sperm. On the other hand, there remained the possibility that *SD* did not utilize a pre-existing function–nonfunctional polarity to bring about its effect, but rather induced directly the elimination of the non-*SD*-bearing sperm.

A. Breakage Hypothesis

The *breakage hypothesis* was proposed as a specific cytogenetic mechanism to bring about the latter (Sandler *et al.*, 1959). In this model, one supposes that during prophase I the homologue of *SD* suffers a physical break at some specific location, which after chromosome replication undergoes a reversed sister strand reunion, thereby producing an acentric fragment and a dicentric; at anaphase II the dicentric becomes a chromatid bridge, and this causes the death or nonfunction of the cells it ties together. The tantalising preliminary report that dicentrics and bridges could be observed cytologically in heterozygous *SD* males (Sandler *et al.*, 1959) could not be verified, however (Thomas, unpublished observations), so the literal version of the breakage hypothesis had to be abandoned. Indeed, the meiotic divisions in heterozygous *SD* males appear to be normal (Peacock and Erickson, 1965). This by no means excludes the possibility that *SD* causes some kind of physical alteration in its homologue, too small or too subtle to be observed cytologically. On the contrary, the results of two sets of experiments have been offered in support of this viewpoint.

Crow *et al.* (1962) reasoned that if *SD* induces a physical break in its homologue, then a single additional break induced by X-irradiation at the appropriate site on the *SD* chromosome would be sufficient to produce an apparent recombination, whereas the production of a similar recombinant in normal males would require two induced breaks. Accordingly, males of the constitution *In(2L)Cy, Cy cn bw/SD-5* or *In(2L)Cy, Cy cn bw/ Canton S* were exposed to 1500 R of X-rays and mated with *cn bw* females 9–10 days later in order to sample those chromosomes that were in the meiotic stages at the time of treatment. The rate of induced recombination between the rightmost breakpoint of *In(2L)Cy*, in salivary gland chromosome region 33F5–34A1 and near 48 on the genetic map (Lindsley and Grell, 1968), and the locus of *cn* was about twice as high in *SD*'s as in controls. Furthermore, when the experiment was carried out with *In(2L + 2R)Cy, Cy bw* as the homologue of *SD*, the rate of induced recombination was no higher than in controls, an observation whose significance arises from the fact that *In(2L + 2R)Cy* is one of the inverted chromosomes that is not distorted, and therefore presumably not broken, by *SD* (Sandler *et al.*, 1959).

Suggestive evidence for chromosome breakage by *SD* also came from Hiraizumi's (1961) preliminary report that the small percentage of *cn bw* chromosomes recovered from *SD/cn bw* males, when made homozygous, have severely reduced viabilities and occasionally carry recessive lethals that map near the region of the centromere. The results of both Crow *et al.* (1962) and Hiraizumi (1961), however, could arise in the absence of physical breakage of the homologue by *SD* if *SD* merely caused its homologue to have enhanced sensitivity to irradiation or spontaneous breakage.

B. Functional Pole Hypothesis

An alternative to the breakage hypothesis was proposed by Peacock and Erickson (1965), who invoked the functional pole hypothesis of Novitski and I. Sandler (1957) and suggested that the mechanism of *SD* was to orient its homologue in the direction of an anaphase pole that was predetermined to be nonfunctional. The evidence for this point of view came from a comparison of the number of progeny obtained from females inseminated by *SD/cn bw* or Oregon R males with the number of sperm stored in the seminal receptacles and spermathecae of similarly inseminated females. The mean number of progeny per female was about half as great as the mean number of stored sperm in the comparable females, irrespective of whether the males were *SD* or wild type. The only exceptions to this occurred when the level of insemination was very high or very low, in which case nearly all the sperm appeared to be capable of fertilization. These results were interpreted as meaning that the nonfunctional sperm were morphologically normal and motile, and were stored in the female, except when they were displaced by competition with normal sperm. This could occur in the males when the number of sperm was small or in the females when the number of sperm was large.

Several years later, Zimmering and Fowler (1968) reported experiments that cast doubt on this interpretation. The ratio of the mean number of progeny from one set of females to the mean number of stored sperm in a comparable set of females (called the progeny:sperm ratio) was found to depend on the genotype of the females. This ratio in the *y* females used by Peacock and Erickson was indeed about 0·5, but in Oregon R females it was nearer to 0·8. In a later series of experiments, Zimmering *et al.* (1970a) examined the progeny: sperm ratios obtained from females of several different genotypes when they were mated with *SD–72/cn bw* males, and observed ratios from a low of 0·31 in an *Ins(1)*sc^{S1}*49*sc^{8} strain to a high of 0·88 in an Oregon-R/*y* hybrid. Thus it appeared on the one hand that progeny:sperm ratios could not be used to infer what proportion of sperm in an ejaculate was functional, and on the other hand that the *cn bw*-bearing sperm from *SD–72/cn bw* males are often not ejaculated because the maximum progeny:sperm ratio observed was substantially above 0·5. All of which left the mechanism of *SD* up in the air, because the functional pole hypothesis of Peacock and Erickson could still have been correct even though specific evidence for it was unavailable.

C. Sperm Dysfunction

On the other hand, it was established that under the appropriate conditions the number of functional sperm could be the limiting factor in the number of progeny produced by a mating (Duncan, 1930; Lefevre and Jonsson, 1962; Lefevre and Parker, 1963; Peacock and Erickson, 1965). Since a clear prediction of the functional pole hypothesis is that *SD* males will produce no fewer functional sperm than normal males—only the genotypic distribution among the functional sperm is altered—the way was opened up for a direct test of the functional pole hypothesis by measuring the fecundity of heterozygous *SD* and control males under conditions in which sperm was limiting. This approach had been tried by Peacock and Erickson (1965), and for reasons still not completely understood gave results indicating that the fecundity of heterozygous *SD* males was normal. A contrary result was obtained by Hartl *et al.* (1967) and independently by Nicoletti *et al.* (1967). The main finding was that when very young males were mated for a short interval with females, and the females were brooded until they ceased to lay fertilized eggs, the total number of progeny produced by heterozygous *SD* males was roughly half as great as the number produced by comparable non-*SD* males (Hartl *et al.*, 1967).

Furthermore, this reduction in fecundity occurred only in conjunction with segregation distortion. When the action of *SD* was suppressed, either by an insensitive homologue, or by a suppressor-bearing X-chromosome, or by raising the males at low temperatures, the fecundity of males was normal (Hartl, 1968). Even within a single *SD* strain, one with an average *k*-value sufficiently low to allow an appreciable male-to-male variance, there was a strong negative correlation between the number of progeny produced by a male and his degree of distortion (Hartl *et al.*, 1967; Hartl, 1968). Similar results were obtained when the males were mated exhaustively until they became sterile (Hartl *et al.*, 1967; Nicoletti *et al.*, 1967; Hartl, 1968; Hiraizumi and Watanabe, 1969). The interpretation of the latter experiments is rendered somewhat ambiguous, however, because *SD* males become sterile more quickly than normal males (Sandler and Hiraizumi, 1961b; Peacock and Erickson, 1965; Hiraizumi and Watanabe, 1969). Nevertheless, the data indicate that the non-*SD*-bearing sperm are being rendered dysfunctional by the action of *SD*, an hypothesis called the *dysfunctional sperm* hypothesis, which includes the breakage model as a special case but does not necessarily imply that *SD* induces a physical break in its homologue.

D. Evidence from Electron Microscopy

Although the meiotic divisions in heterozygous *SD* males are normal (Peacock and Erickson, 1965), a characteristic abnormality in spermatogenesis associated with *SD* has recently been described (Tokuyasu *et al.*, 1972; Peacock *et al.*, 1972). The male of *D. melanogaster* has two testes, each a blind tube about 2 mm long and 0·1 mm in diameter. In normal spermatogenesis, the spermatogonia at the apical end of the testis undergo four synchronous mitotic divisions giving rise to a syncytium of 16 primary spermatocytes that is surrounded by cyst cells. As this is happening, the cyst is migrating down the inside wall of the testis. The spermatocytes undergo meiosis in the middle region of the testis, and the resulting 64 spermatids begin to elongate symmetrically, eventually to attain a length of 80–90% of the testis, oriented with the heads near the base, and all interconnected by cytoplasmic bridges except for the head region in which such bridges are rarely seen. After elongation, a spindle-shaped *cystic bulge* initiates the process of individualization. Beginning in the head region, the bulge traverses through the entire length of the bundle, eliminating the syncytial bridges as it progresses, removing unneeded organelles, parts of the nuclear membrane, nucleoplasm, and cytoplasm, and leaving behind 64 sperm tails, each invested in its own membrane. When the bulge, now 30–35 μ in diameter, reaches the apical end of the bundle, the coiling of the bundle begins. This commences in the basal region. As the bundle is coiled the tail tips are pulled from the apex of the testis to the base, and the cystic bulge is pulled along. Once in the basal region, the bulge is detached from the tail tips and, now called the *waste bag*, is slowly degraded (Tokuyasu *et al.*, 1972; Stanley *et al.*, 1972). Two abnormalities in spermatogenesis associated with *SD* have been described. One abnormality that has been observed in all *SD*'s so far examined is the incomplete condensation of the chromatin in the heads, causing the heads to appear larger than normal. In *SD*'s that have *k*-values close to 1 the number of abnormal heads per bundle is very nearly 32, the number expected to carry the homologue of *SD* (Tokuyasu *et al.*, 1972; Peacock *et al.*, 1972). A second aberration associated with *SD* involves the individualization process, but this aberration occurs to different extents in different *SD*'s. In *SD–72* (Canberra), for example, which is derived from the original *SD–72* (Madison), the sperm destined to be dysfunctional are often not individualized. The cystic bulge leaves behind it at least 32 spermatids invested in their own membranes, and a large number, up to 32, of spermatids still interconnected (Peacock *et al.*, 1972; these structures apparently correspond to those described in *SD*(*ROMA*)*–1* by Nicoletti, 1968, as degenerating sperm). The spermatids left in the syncytium are evidently unable to coil properly, and they come to be included in the waste bag at the base of the testis and are degraded, never to be ejaculated. In *SD–72* (Madison), by contrast, the number of spermatids that fail to be individualized is much smaller, though somewhat variable, and in this case the dysfunctional sperm that are individualized do appear to be ejaculated (Peacock *et al.*, 1972). In any case, the success or failure of individualization of a spermatid appears to depend on whether or not individualization occurs normally in the head region, as if this were the crucial step allowing or disallowing the normal "polymerization" of the precursor subunits all the way up the tail (Tokuyasu *et al.*, 1972).

The discovery of a morphological concomitant of *SD* action along with the reduced fecundity of *SD* males would appear to be convincing evidence that the mechanism of distortion is sperm dysfunction. Two clear alternatives can still be distinguished concerning the action of *SD* during spermatogenesis. One possibility is that the homologue of *SD* causes the dysfunction of the sperm that carry it; another possibility is that *SD* induces an abnormality in one of the anaphase I poles that causes the affected pole to give rise to dysfunctional sperm, and then *SD* consigns its homologue to the dysfunctional pole. Pertaining to this, Sandler and Carpenter (1972) have shown that when *SD* is heterozygous with a translocation that segregates in such a way that *SD* and its homologue are often included in the same telophase I nucleus, the sperm that carry the homologue of *SD* are rendered dysfunctional whether or not they also carry *SD*. Thus, the homologue of *SD* is that which causes the sperm dysfunction. It is still not known, however, whether *SD* induces a physical break in its homologue. Nevertheless, the firm indications of the major features of the mechanism of *SD* allow the next important question to be brought into focus, what it is on the *SD* chromosome that causes the dysfunction of sperm bearing its homologue, and how this effect is brought about.

IV. The Genetic Structure of SD Chromosomes

The genetic structure of *SD* chromosomes is most conveniently discussed by splitting the issue into two parts that are more or less distinct. The first pertains to genetic elements on the right arm of *SD* chromosomes that modify segregation distortion. Owing to the inversions in 2R of most *SD* chromosomes, the *bw*-bearing recombinants from the cross *SD*/*cn bw* ♀♀ × *cn bw* ♂♂ are almost always segregation distorters. The average degree of distortion of these chromosomes varies, ranging from 0·80 to 0·95, but the degree of distortion of any one of the recombinants has a consistent and reproducible mean. More to the point, when a large number of males heterozygous for any one of the recombinant *SD*'s is tested, the variance in the segregation ratio from male to male is significantly greater than would be predicted from the binomial distribution (Sandler and Hiraizumi, 1960a; 1961b). This larger than binomial variance is called "instability", and it will be discussed in the next section. The subject of this section is the second aspect of the genetic structure of *SD* chromosomes, the nature of the *SD* region itself.

A great deal of ambiguity surrounds some of the earlier experiments because in several instances one or another of the complexities of the *SD* system has intruded to produce countercurrents of confusion and contradiction that make a rigorous interpretation of the data well-nigh impossible. The initial recombination studies were performed with a *bw*-bearing derivative of *SD–72*, which at the time was not known to be carrying the pericentric inversion mentioned previously (Sandler and Hiraizumi, 1960b). A subsequent study was made of $R(SD\text{–}36)\text{–}1^{bw}$, which lacks the pericentric inversion, but here ambiguities arise because one of the strains employed is known to carry a partial suppressor of *SD* (Hiraizumi and Nakazima, 1967). The most straightforward results are those of Crow *et al.* (1962) who induced recombinants from *SD–5*, but in this case only the recombinants carrying a selected marker were analysed, the reciprocal products were ignored. A more recent experiment (Hartl, 1974) serves to remove some of the ambiguities of the earlier experiments; this will be discussed in its proper chronology.

The organization of this section will be to present a summary of the results of the recombination experiments on *SD* and to discuss the principal inferences about the genetic structure of the *SD* region that emanate from the data. Some of the results are inconsistent, most likely because of the technical complications discussed above, and the interpretations of the results are likewise at variance. The more recent data remove some of the ambiguities, and some of the earlier interpretations have now been superceded. Our primary aim in this section is to recount the tortuous history of this aspect of the studies of segregation distortion.

In all, three distinct interpretations of the genetic structure of the *SD* region have been offered. Common to all three interpretations is the assertion that at least two major loci on the *SD* chromosome are involved. One of these has consistently been called *SD*, although in a subsequent paper (Hartl, 1969) this locus is called *Sd* in order to distinguish between a locus on an *SD* chromosome and the chromosome itself, and this terminology will be used in the present article. The second locus has several aliases, each one introduced to correspond with the analogy that seemed most useful at the time. First called Activator (*Ac*), by analogy with McClintock's (1951, 1956) *Ac–Ds* system in maize (Sandler and Hiraizumi, 1961b; Hiraizumi and Nakazima, 1967), the locus became a Director (*Dr*) in Hartl (1969) and a Receptor (*Rc*) in Sandler and Carpenter (1972), and has recently been demoted by Miklos (1972a), who considers it to be a mere enhancer of *Sd* with no extraordinary properties. Later on in this review the locus will be called *Rsp* (for Responder), as in recent literature.

A. Recombinants from *R(SD–72)–4/pr cn*

Sandler and Hiraizumi (1960b) examined recombination in the cross *R(SD)–4/b pr cn en* ♀♀ × *b pr cn en* ♂♂, where *R(SD)–4* is a *bw*-bearing derivative of *SD–72* that lacks *In(2R)NS* but carries the pericentric inversion, and has a *k*-value of about 0·96 (Sandler *et al.*, 1959). The amounts of crossing over in the controls in the region *b–pr*, *pr–cn*, and *cn–en* were, respectively, about 3%, 1·5%, and 5%. In *R(SD)–4*, although recombination in the *b–pr* region was essentially normal, recombination in the *pr–cn* region was reduced to about one-tenth of the control value, and in the *cn–en* region it was reduced to about half the control value. Ten *b* and ten *en* recombinants were tested for distortion, and all were segregation distorters. Thus the distortion of *R(SD)–4* can be attributed to some gene or genes either in or close to the *pr–cn* region.

Further analysis was carried out by examining the *pr* and *cn* recombinants from *R(SD)–4/pr cn* ♀♀ × *pr cn* ♂♂ (Sandler and Hiraizumi, 1960b). Again, recombination in the *pr–cn* region was reduced to one-tenth of the control value, a reduction that could be attributed to the pericentric inversion. If this were the case, then some of the recombinants from *R*(*SD*)*–4* should have lost the pericentric, and the rate of recombination in these derivatives should have been normal. In point of fact, none of the recombinants had normal recombination in the *pr–cn* region. One class of *cn* and one class of *pr* recombinants was recovered in which the frequency of recombination in the *pr–cn* region was about 0·1 %, compared to the control value of 1 %. These recombinants presumably carried the inversion intact. All the other recombinants, *cn* and *pr* alike, had recombination values in the *pr–cn* region of about 0·67 %, which suggests that either *R*(*SD*)*–4* carried a chromosome abnormality in the centromeric region in addition to the inversion, or that non-homologous exchange was occurring in the region covered by the inversion, which would lead to small duplications or deficiencies that would be expected to decrease the rate of recombination when subsequently tested. In any case, the reason that Sandler and Hiraizumi (1960b) failed to obtain any recombinants with normal amounts of recombination in the *pr–cn* region is still not understood.

As for the properties of the recombinants with respect to segregation distortion, Sandler and Hiraizumi (1960b) examined 25 each of *cn* and *pr* recombinants in terms of (1) whether the segregation ratio was normal when these chromosomes were heterozygous with *cn bw*, and (2) whether the segregation ratio was normal when these chromosomes were heterozygous with *SD–5*. The first criterion is the operational definition of segregation distortion; the second criterion is the operational definition of sensitivity to distortion—if the segregation ratio in the second test is 0·5, then the homologue of *SD–5* is said to be "insensitive", if the segregation ratio is biased in favor of *SD–5* (or any other tester *SD*), then the homologue is said to be "sensitive". We emphasize the operational definition of sensitivity in terms of the segregation ratio to make the point that an insensitive homologue of *SD* is not necessarily one that is never included in dysfunctional sperm. This is, to be sure, one mechanism of insensitivity: if a chromosome has the effect, when heterozygous with *SD*, of suppressing *SD* or of preventing by some other means the production of dysfunctional sperm, then the homologue of *SD* will be insensitive according to the definition above. But insensitivity will also come about if it happens that whenever a primary spermatocyte becomes predisposed to produce dysfunctional sperm, the *SD* chromosome is as likely to be included in the dysfunctional sperm as the homologue of *SD*. The assay of sensitivity based on the segregation ratio does not distinguish between these possibilities, although insensitive chromosomes that behave according to the latter mechanism have been derived from *SD* chromosomes by recombination (Hiraizumi and Nakazima, 1967; Hartl, 1969).

Using the criteria of distorting ability and sensitivity, Sandler and Hiraizumi (1960b) were able to distinguish three classes of *cn* recombinants and two classes of *pr* recombinants. The *cn*-bearing recombinants were denoted SD^a (active), SD^{sa} (semiactive), and SD^{in} (inactive). The SD^a type is a segregation distorter that is insensitive: SD^a *cn*/*cn bw* males have an average *k*-value of 0·82; *SD–5*/SD^a *cn* males have an average *k*-value (defined here as the proportion of *SD–5* among the progeny) of 0·52. The SD^{sa} type is a weak segregation distorter that is sensitive: the average *k*-values of SD^{sa} *cn*/*cn bw* and *SD–5*/SD^{sa} *cn* males are 0·59 and 0·91, respectively. The SD^{in} type is a nondistorter that is sensitive: SD^{in} *cn*/*cn bw* males have an average *k*-value of 0·53; *SD–5*/SD^{in} *cn* males have an average *k*-value of 0·97. The two classes of *pr*-bearing recombinants are conveniently denoted as *pr Sens* (Sensitive) and *pr Ins* (Insensitive). Both are nondistorters, but the *k*-value of *SD–5*/*pr Sens* males is 0·75 whereas the *k*-value of *SD–5*/*pr Ins* males is 0·56. The sensitivity of the *pr Sens* chromosome, incidentally, is very close to that reported for the *pr cn* chromosome itself (Sandler and Hiraizumi, 1960b).

The isolation of insensitive recombinants that are segregation distorters (SD^a) as well as insensitive recombinants that are nondistorters (*pr Ins*) suggests that *SD* chromosomes carry two functions that are separable by recombination, one of them being associated with the segregation distortion and the other with insensitivity. Since no *cn* recombinants are recovered that behave like *pr Ins*, it follows that the insensitivity function is located on the chromosome to the right of the segregation distorter function (Sandler and Hiraizumi, 1960b). The insensitivity was considered to have its genetic basis in the dramatic reduction in recombination frequency in the centromeric region of *Ɍ(SD)–4*. This reduction was thought to be due to a duplication or an insertion, and the insensitivity of any recombinant was assumed to depend on the length of the chromosome aberration carried by the recombinant chromosome. But this hypothesis ran into difficulty as soon as it was found that the chromosome abnormality was not necessary for either distortion or insensitivity (Lewis, 1962; Hiraizumi and Nakazima, 1967). The segregation distortion itself was assumed to be due to a gene, called *Sd*, that required a second gene, *Ac*, located just to the right of *Sd*, in order to be "activated" or "switched on". The nondistorting *cn* recombinant, SD^{in}, in this model is *Sd* Ac^+, whereas both SD^{sa} and SD^a are *Sd Ac*. But the latter two chromosomes exhibit grossly different amounts of distortion, and to account for this Sandler and Hiraizumi (1960b) proposed that the SD^{sa} chromosomes carried an aberrant *Sd* locus that had somehow been altered by the occurrence of a crossover in its immediate vicinity.

The details of the hypothesis aside, the most important inference—that the distortion and insensitivity functions are separable—can be tested directly. The obvious prediction is that males heterozygous for a sensitive distorter (SD^{sa}) and an insensitive nondistorter (*pr Ins*) will produce a deficiency of SD^{sa}-bearing progeny brought about by the SD^{sa} chromosome causing its own dysfunction. Since the *k*-value of SD^{sa} *cn*/*cn bw* is about 0·59, one would expect the recovery of SD^{sa} *cn* from SD^{sa} *cn*/*pr Ins* males to be about 0·31. The actual value obtained was 0·36 (based on about 35,000 progeny—Sandler and Hiraizumi, 1960b). This was, and still is, a critical observation.

Various combinations of *cn* and *pr* recombinant chromosomes were also made heterozygous in females, and wild type re-recombinants from the females were tested to determine whether *SD* had been reconstituted (Sandler and Hiraizumi, 1960b). Of the four genotypes tested, SD^{in} *cn*/*pr Sens*, SD^{in} *cn*/*pr Ins*, SD^{sa}/*pr Sens*, and SD^{sa}/*pr Ins*, only one—SD^{sa}/*pr Ins*—gave rise to a wild type segregation distorter, this one having an average *k*-value of 0·83. That the *pr Sens* chromosome cannot supply elements that SD^{sa} and SD^{in} have lost comes as no surprise, because the *pr Sens* chromosome behaves essentially like the original *pr cn*. But to explain why SD^{in} *cn*/*pr Ins* females do not give rise to SD^{a}'s requires that the SD^{in} chromosome must be missing some element that cannot be supplied by *pr Ins*, hence the hypothesis of *Ac*. It is to be noted, on the other hand, that only 5 wild type re-recombinants from this genotype were tested, so there remains the possibility that SD^{a}'s can be generated but happened by chance not to be obtained.

B. Recombinants from *R*(*SD–36*)*–1*/*pr cn*

An experiment to be considered in juxtaposition to that of Sandler and Hiraizumi (1960b) is the one of Hiraizumi and Nakazima (1967), who derived *cn* and *pr* recombinants from *R*(*SD–36*)*–1*^{bw}, which lacks the pericentric inversion, and tested these recombinants for distortion and sensitivity in the manner described previously. The results were quite different. Whereas Sandler and Hiraizumi (1960b) had obtained 11 SD^{a}, 5 SD^{sa}, and 9 SD^{in} recombinants, Hiraizumi and Nakazima (1967) obtained 3 SD^{a}, 12 SD^{sa}, and 0 SD^{in}. The difference in the proportions of SD^{a} and SD^{sa} in the two experiments may be due to a change in the effective linkage relationships in *R*(*SD*)*–4* brought about by the pericentric inversion. A similar explanation may be offered for the absence of SD^{in} in the second experiment, although it may also be that SD^{in} is a peculiar duplication or deficiency produced only by *SD*'s carrying the inversion. As for the *pr* recombinants, whereas Sandler and Hiraizumi (1960b) had recovered 13 *pr Ins* and 12 *pr Sens* chromosomes, Hiraizumi and Nakazima (1967) recovered 9 *pr Ins* and 0 *pr Sens*, the absence of the latter class being attributed to the small number of chromosomes tested.

We have in this paper been using the symbols SD^a, SD^{sa}, SD^{in}, *pr Ins*, and *pr Sens* only as a shorthand notation for recombinant chromosomes that have certain operationally defined properties of segregation distortion and sensitivity. One of the real conundrums raised by the experiments of Hiraizumi and Nakazima (1967) is the suggestion that the two criteria used for identification are not sufficient to uniquely specify a chromosome's behavior. In particular, the SD^{sa} and *pr Ins* of Hiraizumi and Nakazima (1967) do not behave like the SD^{sa} and *pr Ins* of Sandler and Hiraizumi (1960b). In the latter case, as we have mentioned previously, the recovery of SD^{sa} from SD^{sa} *cn*/*pr Ins* males was 0·36, as if SD^{sa} were distorting itself; in the former case, by contrast, the recovery of SD^{sa} from SD^{sa} *cn*/*pr Ins* males was 0·46, as if no distortion at all were occurring (this value is again based on more than 30,000 progeny). So here, lurking in the shadows of the minor discrepancies was a stark contradiction. The contradiction, we should add, has not been completely resolved, but it does seem to relate to a peculiarity of the *pr cn* chromosome. This matter will be returned to in a moment.

Based on these results, Hiraizumi and Nakazima (1967) proposed a model of the genetic structure of the *SD* region that was similar in notation to that of Sandler and Hiraizumi (1960b), but which differed in several important particulars. Gone from this model is the peculiar mutability of *Sd* that distinguishes SD^{sa} from SD^a; gone also is the assumption that *Ac* "turns on" the *Sd* locus. In the model of Hiraizumi and Nakazima (1967), *Sd* is a locus much like before, but *Ac* is now a bifunctional locus whose two functions are (1) that it is an enhancer of *Sd*, and (2) that it confers insensitivity on the chromosome that carries it. Thus SD^a is in this hypothesis genotypically *Sd Ac*, SD^{sa} is *Sd* Ac^+, *pr Ins* is Sd^+ *Ac*, and *pr Sens*, if one were found, would be Sd^+ Ac^+. The only additional assumption required to account for the data is that the enhancing effect of *Ac* is exerted only when *Sd* and *Ac* are in *coupling*, otherwise the recovery of SD^{sa} from SD^{sa} *cn*/*pr Ins* males should have been on the order of 0·15.

Miklos (1972a) has recently re-examined these data and has come to conclusions very similar to those of Hiraizumi and Nakazima (1967). He has considered only the *cn*-bearing recombinants, and argues that they can be accounted for by assuming three loci in the *SD* region, the first being *Sd*, the second being an enhancer of *Sd* immediately to its right, and the third being another enhancer of *Sd* somewhat further to the right. If one calls these enhancers *En–1* and *En–2*, respectively, and calls their normal alleles $En\text{–}1^+$ and $En\text{–}2^+$, then Miklos's (1972a) hypothesis is that

SD^{in} is genotypically *Sd En–1*$^+$ *En–2*$^+$, SD^{sa} is *Sd En–1 En–2*$^+$, and SD^a is *Sd En–1 En–2*. The assumption here is that Hiraizumi and Nakazima (1967) obtained no SD^{in} recombinants because of the very close linkage between *Sd* and *En–1*. Also, the enhancer function of *Ac* is associated with *En–2*. The hypothesis does not deal specifically with the issue of insensitivity, but the experimental results require that the insensitivity function be near *En–2* or perhaps identical to *En–2*.

One ambiguity in all these results concerns the meaning of "insensitivity". The genotype SD^a *cn*/*pr Ins* has a normal segregation ratio but a fecundity characteristic of SD^a *cn*/*cn bw* (Hartl, 1969). This suggests that sperm dysfunction is still occurring in the males and that the specific chromosome included in the dysfunctional sperm is random. The full implication of this has not been resolved, but it certainly implies that the "insensitivity" function is more subtle than the mere inability to be affected by *SD*.

A more important issue that arises is that none of the interpretations of the data take into account the fact that the *pr cn* chromosome used in the studies of Sandler and Hiraizumi (1960b) and Hiraizumi and Nakazima (1967) carries a partial suppressor of *SD*. The recovery of *SD–5* from *SD–5*/*pr cn* males was reported in the former paper to be about 0·80. But *SD–5* is an *SD* that when heterozygous with *cn bw* produces a segregation ratio of 0·98 or more. Thus there is something on the *pr cn* chromosome that reduces the degree of segregation distortion. One question which may be asked is: What effect does this chromosome have on an SD^a, which when heterozygous with *cn bw* has an average *k*-value of about 0·85? Here the effect is much more dramatic and can be approached quantitatively, with considerable elegance, by the method of probit analysis used first in connection with *SD* by Miklos and Smith-White (1971). The method will be discussed in detail in the next section, but the primary argument is that whereas enhancers and suppressors of *SD* have nonlinear effects on *k*, they should have linear effects on the probits of $(2k - 1)/k$. Applied to the data in hand, the analysis implies that a supressor that reduces the *k*-value of *SD–5* from 0·98 (corresponding to 7·04 probits) to a value of 0·80 (5·67 probits), will reduce the *k*-value of an SD^a from 0·85 (5·93 probits) to a value of 0·60 (4·57 probits) because the reduction in the number of probits is in both cases the same (1·37 probits). This implies that the SD^{sa} recombinants may actually be SD^a's that also carry the suppressor from the *pr cn* chromosome. On the other hand, Miklos (1972a) has shown that the predictions based on this method are not always verified, so some skepticism is in order. Nevertheless, the suggestion that the culprit in the previous experiments was the *pr cn* chromosome stimulated a re-analysis of the *SD* region by recombination, using as a homologue of *SD* a chromosome known to be suppressor-free (Hartl,

1974). The data provoke a significant reappraisal of the earlier results, and they will be briefly summarized.

C. Recombinants from *R(SD–36)–1/Tft cn*

A chromosome sensitive to *SD* and carrying the markers *Tft* (53·2 on the chromosome map) and *cn* (57·5) was constructed. The *k*-value of $R\text{–}1^{bw}/Tft$ *cn* males was 0·95. Females of the genotype $R\text{–}1^{bw}/Tft$ *cn* were mated with *cn bw* males and *Tft* and *cn* recombinants were selected. The overall rate of recombination in the *Tft–cn* region was 1·1%, somewhat less than the expected frequency of 4·3%, probably because of the two inversions in 2R of $R\text{–}1^{bw}$ (see Hiraizumi and Nakazima, 1967).

The *Tft* and *cn* recombinants were examined for distortion by ascertaining their segregation ratio when heterozygous with *cn bw*; the recombinants were examined for sensitivity by ascertaining the segregation ratio of another *SD*, either *SD(NH)–2* or $SD\text{–}72^{bw}$, when heterozygous with them. In the data below the recovery of the recombinant from *cn bw* heterozygotes is denoted as *k*; the symbol *s* denotes the recovery of the *SD(NH)–2* or $SD\text{–}72^{bw}$ chromosome in the tests for sensitivity.

Eleven *Tft* recombinants were examined and these fell into three classes: (1) Five recombinants were insensitive distorters with $\bar{k} = 0{\cdot}88$ and $\bar{s} = 0{\cdot}46$. These are by inference *Sd Rsp*. (*Rsp* is here used synonymously with *Ac*.) (2) Five recombinants were insensitive nondistorters with $\bar{k} = 0{\cdot}54$ and $\bar{s} = 0{\cdot}47$. These are presumably + *Rsp*. (3) One recombinant was a sensitive nondistorter with $k = 0{\cdot}56$ and $s = 0{\cdot}97$. This would be genotypically + +. The recovery of the three classes of recombinants implies that (a) *Sd* is to the right of and separable from *Tft*, and (b) *Rsp* is to the left of and separable from *cn*.

Twenty-one *cn* recombinants were examined and these fell into three classes: (1) Four recombinants were insensitive distorters with $\bar{k} = 0{\cdot}75$ and $\bar{s} = 0{\cdot}54$. These are by inference *Sd Rsp*. (2) Seventeen recombinants were sensitive nondistorters with $\bar{k} = 0{\cdot}52$ and $\bar{s} = 0{\cdot}99$. Class (2) could be further subdivided into two groups based on the recovery of the *cn* recombinant when it was heterozygous with a + *Rsp*-bearing *Tft* recombinant. One subclass of (2) produced a *deficiency* of *cn* progeny, the average proportion of *cn* progeny being about 0·09. These are by inference *Sd* +. The other subclass of (2) segregated normally, the average proportion of *cn* progeny being about 0·46. These are presumably + +.

Three conclusions warrant emphasis: (a) the *Sd* +/+ *Rsp* males produce a gross *deficiency* of *Sd*-bearing progeny, (b) no dramatic *cis-trans* differences are apparent, and (c) sensitive recombinants with $k \simeq 0{\cdot}60$ (SD^{sa}) are not recovered and may arise only when the *pr cn* chromosome is employed as the homologue of *SD*. These data, therefore, suggest that the relationship and interactions between *Sd* and *Rsp* (or *Ac*) are rather straightforward and uncomplicated. The snarls and tangles in the previous results may well arise from modifiers and inversions and other technical pitfalls in the system that are unrelated to the genetic structure of the *SD* region itself.

D. Recombinants from *SD–5/In(2L)Cy, Cy cn bw*

The properties of the *Tft* recombinants studied by Hartl (1974) confirm an earlier result obtained by Crow *et al.* (1962) in their study of the radiation induced recombinants from *SD–5/In(2L)Cy, Cy cn bw* males. In this experiment, the *In(2L)Cy, Cy cn bw* chromosome was known to be highly sensitive to *SD* action, the *k*-value of *SD–5/In(2L)Cy, Cy cn bw* males being about 0·97. Three kinds of *Cy* cn^+ bw^+ recombinants were obtained. Four of them were virtually identical in behavior to *SD–5* itself, 10 were nondistorters ($k = 0{\cdot}51$) that were "insensitive", and 6 were identical in behavior to *In(2L)Cy, Cy cn bw*. The reciprocal products of recombination could unfortunately not be examined.

V. The Associated Phenomena

A great many phenomena associated with segregation distortion have been discovered. Some of these, such as the instability of *SD*, have been described in detail (Sandler and Hiraizumi, 1959; 1960a; Miklos and Smith-White, 1971; Miklos, 1972a); others, such as the effects of translocations on *SD*, have only been sketched (Novitski and Ehrlich, 1970). Some of the associated phenomena, for example the time during spermatogenesis that *SD* is temperature sensitive (Mange, 1968), have an obvious bearing on the molecular mechanism of action of *SD*; other of the associated phenomena, for example the brooding effect (Hiraizumi and Watanabe, 1969), have no such obvious connection. We have deferred discussing the associated phenomena until now because in many of them it is too much a matter of taste where in the foregoing discussion the observations would best be fitted in. No particular significance should be attached to the order in which the phenomena are discussed; we have chosen the order only for convenience.

A. The Instability of Segregation Distortion

When *SD*'s derived directly from nature—these will for convenience be denoted SD^o (*o* for *original*)—are used to generate *bw*-bearing recombinants by means of the mating *SD°/cn bw* ♀♀ × *cn bw* ♂♂, several kinds of *bw*-bearing recombinants are recovered (Sandler and Hiraizumi, 1959, 1960a). These recombinants can be distinguished from one another because their average *k*-values differ, and, indeed, each recombinant may be unique, but by and large the recombinants can be separated into two groups, one having an average *k*-value of about 0·85 and the other having an average *k*-value of about 0·97. The *SD°* chromosome from which the recombinants are generated has an average *k*-value of about 0·99.

Not only do strains carrying *SD°* or either of the types of recombinant differ from one another in their average degrees of distortion, but they also differ in the male-to-male variance in the segregation ratio: the strain having the greatest male-to-male variance is the recombinant with an average *k* of about 0·85; the strain having an intermediate variance is the recombinant with an average *k* of 0·97; the strain having the smallest variance is that carrying *SD°*. These differences in the variance prompted the *SD* chromosomes in the strains to be called "unstable" ($k = 0{\cdot}85$), "semistable" ($k = 0{\cdot}97$), and "stable" (*SD°*, $k = 0{\cdot}99$). Here there is a serious confounding effect, however. Since the segregation ratio has a binomial distribution, the variance in the segregation ratio in a strain is expected to be $k(1 - k)/N$ where N is the number of progeny tested per male and k is the characteristic *k*-value of the strain. This variance will attain its maximum at $k = 0{\cdot}50$ and will decrease monotonically as k increases. Therefore *SD*'s with a low *k*-value will have a larger variance than strains with a high *k*-value simply because of the nature of the binomial distribution.

The real question is whether a component of variation can be detected in the *SD* lines that cannot be attributed to the variance of the binomial distribution. This issue was resolved by Sandler and Hiraizumi (1961b), who examined the variance in the distributions of $\theta = \text{arc sin}\sqrt{k}$, because the variance in θ is independent of k, and found that indeed there is an extra-binomial component of variance in the *SD* lines. The question then becomes one of accounting for the differences in variability of the *SD* lines.

Sandler and Hiraizumi (1960a) had observed that every recovered recombinant of *SD°* that had undergone recombination in 2R was less stable than the *SD°* from which it was derived, and that no semistable or unstable lines could be obtained from original *SD*'s without recombination in 2R. They concluded from this that there was somewhere in 2R a modifier of *SD* whose absence caused *SD* to be either semistable or unstable, the modifier being present in *SD°* but lost by recombination. Furthermore, since every recombinant *SD* had reduced stability, the modifier, called "stabilizer" (*St*), would have to be near or possibly distal to *bw*, close to the tip of 2R. Thus every *cn*-bearing recombinant from the cross *SD°/cn bw* ♀♀ × *cn bw* ♂♂, though not itself *SD*, should carry *St* and therefore should be able to confer additional stability upon semistable and unstable *SD*'s. Accordingly, the distribution of *k*-values of males that were heterozygous for a semistable *SD* and a *cn*-carrying recombinant was examined, and this distribution was found to be stable, like the original *SD*^{o}. The effect of the *cn*-bearing recombinant upon the unstable *SD*'s, by contrast, was not to confer complete stability but only to cause an enhancement of stability (Sandler and Hiraizumi, 1960a). In any case, the *cn*-bearing recombinant had an effect that could be operationally defined, and the finding of Denell and Judd (1968) that a derivative of *SD–72* arising from a rare spermatogonial recombination still carried *St* led them to conclude that *St* was between the rightmost breakpoint of *In*(*2R*)*NS* and the locus of *bw*, which places *St* in salivary gland chromosome region 56F–59E.

All this leaves open the question of how semistable *SD*'s differ from unstable *SD*'s. They do not differ from one another by modifiers on the *SD* chromosome because unstable lines can be obtained from semistable lines in the absence of crossing over merely by selecting as the fathers of each succeeding generation the males in the previous generation that had the lowest *k*-values. The converse experiment does not succeed: unstable lines cannot be made more stable by selection. Sandler and Hiraizumi (1960a) were able to account for these results by assuming that instability was a reflection of the ability of *SD* to exist in a number of different "states" with an exceptionally high rate of transition or mutation from one state to another. Unstable lines were therefore envisioned as lines in which the *SD* was more mutable to lower *k* states than the *SD* in semistable lines, and the overall rate of transition from one *SD* state to another was assumed to be under the control of, or at least influenced by, the *St* locus. This hypothesis was rather nebulous and, although it adequately explained the data, it led to no firm predictions. Furthermore, it was unprecedented in its assumption of *SD* "states" and of mutability between them, but this seemed to fit rather well with other information that at the time was interpreted to mean that *SD* had the ability to induce specific mutations of several kinds (Sandler and Hiraizumi, 1959; Sandler, 1962; Sandler and Rosenfeld, 1962).

The whole question of stability and instability has been reopened recently by Miklos and Smith-White (1971) and Miklos (1972a) who have ingeniously employed probit analysis in examining the distribution of *k*-values from a set of males. Not only is the hypothesis of highly mutable *SD* "states" unnecessary to account for stability, semistability, and instability, but the actual differences between stable, semistable, and unstable lines turn out to be quite unprofound. The basic assumption in the analysis is that each primary spermatocyte has a certain amount of "potency" or "make" that determines whether or not the non-*SD*-bearing sperm will be rendered dysfunctional: if the amount of make in a primary spermatocyte is above a certain threshold, then the non-*SD*-bearing sperm will dysfunction; otherwise they will not. If the primary spermatocytes in a male have a distribution of make so that a fraction, p, of the meiocytes have make above the threshold level, then the relationship between p and the k-value of the male can be easily obtained. Each primary spermatocyte in the male will, on the average, produce a number of functional sperm equal to $4(1 - p) + 2p = 4 - 2p$, because each meiocyte in which distortion occurs produces only two functional sperm. Furthermore, each primary spermatocyte in the male will produce 2 functional *SD*-bearing sperm whether distortion occurs in the meiocyte or not. Since the k-value of a male is the ratio of functional *SD*-bearing sperm to the total number of functional sperm, one has that $k = 2/(4 - 2p) = 1/(2 - p)$, or $p = (2k - 1)/k$. When the number of functional sperm produced by a male limits the number of progeny produced by a mating, then the fecundity of an *SD* male will be proportional to $4 - 2p = 1/(2k)$ (Hartl *et al.*, 1967).

Suppose now that in the primary spermatocytes of a male, the amount of make is normally distributed with mean μ and variance σ^2. What is the relationship between this distribution and p? By definition, p is the proportion of meiocytes in which the amount of make is above a threshold, t, so $p = \int_t^\infty N(\mu,\sigma^2)dx$, where $N(\mu,\sigma^2)$ represents $1/(\sigma\sqrt{2\pi})\ exp[-(x-\mu)^2/2\sigma^2]$. Expressing the level of make as a deviation from its mean in units of standard deviation, we have $p = \int_{(t-\mu)/\sigma}^{\infty} N(0,1)dx = \int_{-\infty}^{(\mu-t)/\sigma} N(0,1)dx$, the last equality following from the symmetry of the normal distribution. Call $(\mu - t)/\sigma = m$, and one has $p = \int_{-\infty}^{m} N(0,1)dx$. The number m is the difference between the mean make level in a male and the threshold level, expressed in units of standard deviation. For any p, the corresponding value of m can be obtained from tables of the area under the normal curve, but this will often result in negative values of m. To avoid these, the number 5 is conventionally added to m, and the number $m + 5$ is called the ***probit*** of p (Fisher and Yates, 1963).

The k-values from a set of males can therefore be transformed to p's and then, with the aid of tables, to m's. The mean of the m's is the mean difference between the amount of make and the threshold, expressed in units of the within-male standard deviation of make. The variance in the m's is the variance in mean make between males. (We are here assuming that the binomial sampling variance of the individual k-values is small.) When the number of tested males is large, however, then this method of analysis becomes quite tedious because each k must first be transformed to p [$= (2k - 1)/k$], and then p to m. To facilitate matters we have supplied in the Appendix a table of probits of $(2k - 1)/k$. These were obtained by repeatedly integrating $\int_{-\infty}^{m} N(0,1)dx$ numerically, searching for the m giving $p = \int_{-\infty}^{m} N(0,1)dx$ to sufficient accuracy. The numbers in the body of the table are the values of $m + 5$. (Using the table in the Appendix rather than the probit tables of Fisher and Yates, 1963, will avoid the need for interpolation.)

Several interesting results emerge when the distribution of make in the males of a given *SD* strain is considered as a whole. Suppose that make is distributed normally with mean M and variance V_M, and let the mean (or median) k-value of the whole set of males be K. The relationship between K and M is that $(2K - 1)/K = p = \int_{-\infty}^{M} N(0,1)dx$, and $dK/dM = (dK/dp)\,(dp/dM) = K^2N(0,1)|_M$ where $N(0,1)|_M$ represents the ordinate of the standardized normal density evaluated at M. The relationship between the empirical variance in the k-values, V_K, and V_M is $V_K = V_M(dK/dM)^2$. This is the important result. It shows that the variance in K is not independent of M because V_K is a function of (dK/dM). The results are presented graphically in Fig. 1. The left-hand curve is dK/dM

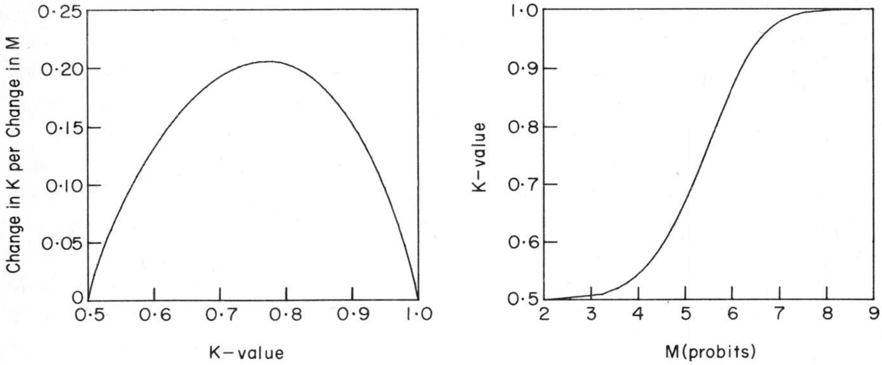

FIG. 1. The left-hand curve is dK/dM versus K where $dK/dM = K^2(1/\sqrt{2\pi})\exp(-M^2/2)$ and $(2K-1)/K = \int_{-\infty}^{M} (1/\sqrt{2\pi})\exp(-x^2/2)dx$. The right-hand curve is K versus M from the second expression above. The curve on the right is redrawn after Miklos and Smith-White (1971).

plotted as a function of K. This is a hump-shaped curve, slightly skewed, with its maximum at approximately $K = 0{\cdot}66$. For values of K near 0·50 or 1·0, V_K will be small because dK/dM is close to 0; for $0{\cdot}52 < K < 0{\cdot}62$ or $0{\cdot}91 < K < 0{\cdot}95$, the shoulders of the hump, V_K will change with K and will be moderately large; for $0{\cdot}62 < K < 0{\cdot}91$, the top of the hump, V_K will be approximately constant and maximal. Thus the five regions of the curve: 0·50–0·52, 0·52–0·62, 0·62–0·91, 0·91–0·95 and 0·95–1·0 represent *SD*'s whose variance in k-values would make them appear stable, semistable, unstable, semistable, and stable, respectively. But the fundamental difference in the *SD*'s is not in their variances; it is in the mean amount of make, and the differences in stability are a simple consequence of this.

The five regions of the dK/dM *vs* K curve are shown in slightly different forms in the right-hand curve in Fig. 1, which exhibits K as a function of M. The regions of stability are the upper and lower asymptotic regions, instability is represented by the approximately linear region in the middle of the curve, and semistability corresponds to the curvilinear regions.

The distributions of k-values of recombinant *SD*'s derived by Sandler and Hiraizumi (1960a) have been re-examined by Miklos and Smith-White (1971), who have shown that the observed distributions are astonishingly like those predicted from the relationships between M and K. By examining the segregation ratios of F_1 males of a cross between an *SD* and several laboratory strains, Miklos and Smith-White (1971) have also shown that the relationship between (dK/dM) and K (Fig. 1, left) can be empirically verified. Moreover, the variance in make, V_M, is approximately constant in inbred, homogeneous strains of *SD*, and has a value of about 0·3–0·4. In outbred strains, however, V_M increases, sometimes reaching values as great as 1·0 or 2·0. This suggests that the main source of variation in make between males is genetic, and that there are a large number of modifiers, each of small effect, that increase or diminish the mean level of make.

What, then, is *St*? Miklos (1972a) has examined several *SD*'s derived by recombination in the right arm of *SD–72*. The reduction in the mean probit level of the recombinants ranges from 0·3 to 1·8, presumably depending on where in the chromosome the recombination occurred; this also suggests a number of modifiers in 2R, each of small effect. So the action of "*St*" appears to be the cumulative effect of minor enhancers of mean make level, and the "position" of *St* becomes, in some sense, the entirety of 2R. Although this is the overall picture, some modifiers have greater effects than others, and these can be detected. Miklos (1972b) has localized one of the more potent modifiers to the region of *cn–c* (region 57·5 to 75·5 on the genetic map) and another to the region of *c–px* (75·5 to 100·5). Miklos (1972b) believes that some of the enhancers produce significant effects only when in coupling with the *SD* region.

B. Suppressors of Segregation Distortion

The model of segregation distortion developed by Miklos and Smith-White (1971) provides an explanation of the variability of *SD* in terms of mean level of make and suggests that the mean level of make is influenced by many modifiers, each of small effect. Equally important, in its use of the probit transformation the method provides a metric of distortion that circumvents some of the statistical drawbacks of *k*-values. In particular, a modifier of *SD* can now be said to increase or decrease make by 1·4 probits, say, and this value will be relatively independent of the *k*-value of the *SD* the modifier is tested against. There remains a question of whether all modifiers of *SD* are genes that increase or decrease "make" by a certain amount. Here we are limited to examining genetic systems that cause the *k*-value of *SD* to be lower than some standard value, because systems that enhance *SD*, other than "*St*", have not been adequately studied. We agree to call genetic systems that decrease the average *k*-value "suppressors of *SD*" irrespective of whether the suppression is complete or partial and irrespective of the mechanism of the suppression. Several suppressor systems have been examined, and not all of them can be accounted for on the basis of "make".

Suppressors of *SD* are known on the X-chromosome and on both major autosomes, and they exist at relatively high frequencies in natural populations as well as in laboratory strains (Sandler *et al.*, 1959; Kataoka, 1967; Hartl, 1970; Waddle, 1973). Sandler *et al.* (1959) were the first to discover that the *In(2LR)Cy* chromosome, when heterozygous with *SD*, led to a normal segregation ratio. This is the effect of *In(2LR)Cy* on all *SD*'s so far tested, and in the *SD/In(2LR)Cy* genotypes sperm dysfunction does not occur as evidenced by the fact that the fecundity of the males is normal (Hartl *et al.*, 1967; Hartl, 1968). The effect of *In(2LR)Cy* has been called both "suppression" and "insensitivity". Which is preferable is entirely a matter of taste because in this instance the effects are operationally confounded. Whichever it is called, the mechanism of action of *In(2LR)Cy* is still controversial. Because *In(2LR)Cy*, $In(2LR)Pm^2 = In(2LR)bw^{V1}$, and several translocations with breakpoints in the vicinity of the *SD* region suppressed *SD*, Sandler *et al.* (1959) suggested that synapsis in the *SD* region was required for distortion to occur and that the absence of synapsis in the *SD* region was responsible for the lack of distortion in these genotypes. The reservations about the validity of the synapsis hypothesis arise not so much from hard evidence against the hypothesis as from the circumstantial nature of the evidence for it.

The circumstantial underpinnings of the synapsis hypothesis can be pulled away one by one. Synapsis in the *SD* region of *SD–72/cn bw* males cannot be very good in the first place: recombination in the *SD* region of the females is only one-tenth of normal (Sandler and Hiraizumi, 1960b). Nevertheless, the *k*-value of *SD–72/cn bw* males is about 0·99. Secondly, the suppression of *SD* by $In(2LR)Pm^2$ is not likely to be mechanical. $In(2LR)Pm^2$, although it completely suppresses *SD–72*, only partially suppresses *SD–5*, and only slightly suppresses *SD(NH)–2*, though the males in the latter case are somewhat sterile. The *k*-values of *SD–72/In(2LR)Pm*^{2}, *SD–5/In(2LR)Pm*^{2}, and *SD(NH)–2/In(2LR)Pm*^{2} are 0·54, 0·66, and 0·98, respectively (Hartl, 1968), but the inversions in *SD(NH)–2* are fully as extensive as those in *SD–72*, including the pericentric (Hiraizumi and Nakazima, 1965). Thirdly, Novitski and Ehrlich (1970) have shown that the relationship between the breakpoint of a translocation and its effect on *SD* is by no means simple, and it is certainly not the case that a break in the *SD* region always causes suppression. Therefore, although synapsis may in fact be important in segregation distortion, the evidence for it is no longer as unassailable as it once appeared.

A second type of suppressor of *SD* is the *pr*-carrying recombinant from *R(SD–36)–1*^{bw}*/pr cn* femlaes. This recombinant is thought to carry *Ac* (Hiraizumi and Nakazima, 1967). Like *In(2LR)Cy*, when *pr Ac* is in combination with any *SD* the segregation ratio is normal. Unlike suppression by *In(2LR)Cy*, however, sperm dysfunction still seems to occur in *SD/pr Ac* males because their fecundity is no greater than that of *SD/cn bw* (Hartl, 1969). It is as if *SD* carried a locus that when homozygous caused the specificity, but not the action, of *SD* to be unexpressed, as if in meiocytes in which *SD* were active either *SD* or its homologue would with equal probability be rendered dysfunctional. What to call the site of specificity in *SD* is again a matter of taste. The locus with the postulated property is called "activator" in Hiraizumi and Nakazima (1967), "director" in Hartl (1969), "receptor" in Sandler and Carpenter (1972), and a "locus of 'sensitivity' " in Miklos (1972a). We have used "*Ac*" only to avoid a proliferation of names for the same or similar functions. In any case, neither the properties of the locus nor its mechanism of action are adequately understood. Whoever writes the play can name the characters.

Although suppressors like *In(2LR)Cy* and *pr Ac* are rather difficult to understand on the basis of the "make" hypothesis of Miklos and Smith-White (1971), some suppressors of *SD* may fit nicely into this framework. Among these may be the autosomal suppressors of *SD* found in natural populations (Hiraizumi *et al.*, 1960; Kataoka, 1967; Hartl, 1970), the suppressor on the *pr cn* chromosome (Hiraizumi and Sandler, 1960b), and the suppressors on chromosome 3 studied by Waddle (1973). These suppressors are characterized by the peculiar property that their effect on the *k*-value of *SD*'s with a high *k*-value is far smaller than their effect on the *k*-value of *SD*'s with a slightly lower *k*-value (Hiraizumi *et al.*, 1960; Hartl, 1970). The best example of this arises from Kataoka's (1967) study of an X-linked suppressor of *SD* found in a natural population in Japan. She tested the effect of this chromosome on four different *SD*'s, having average *k*-values of 0·988, 0·982, 0·961, and 0·869. The effect of the suppressor on these *SD*'s was 0·19, 0·99, 2·87, and 2·17 probits, respectively.

That is, the suppressor is more than 10 times as effective in suppressing some *SD*'s as others. This example makes it worthwhile to emphasize a further point: elegant as probit analysis may be, predictions of mean *k*-value based on the method should be regarded with some skepticism.

We have so far catalogued three classes of suppressors of *SD*, the *In*(*2LR*)*Cy* type, the *Ac* type, and the *pr cn* type. A fourth kind of modification of segregation distortion has been described by Novitski and Ehrlich (1970, see also Thompson and Yamazaki, 1967). In examining a series of translocations for their effect on the segregation distortion of *SD–72*, Novitski and Ehrlich (1970) could detect no relationship between the degree of modification of the segregation ratio and the position of the breakpoints of the translocation. *SD–72* in combination with many of the translocations produced *k*-values that were nearly normal (Mendelian), or slightly above normal, indicating some kind of "suppression" of *SD*. Indeed, several Y–3 translocations with no involvement of chromosome 2 were found to suppress or partially suppress *SD–72*. Most striking of all were the Y–2 translocations that reversed the effect of *SD*, so that the *SD* chromosome was recovered less frequently than would be expected, presumably because the Y–2 translocations were somehow causing the *SD* chromosome to be included in its own dysfunctional sperm. This effect does not depend on whether *SD* or its homologue is involved in the translocation. *T*(*Y;2*), *SD*, *j–4**, for example, has a *k*-value of 0·34 and *SD* is involved in the translocation, its breakpoint being near the centromeric heterochromatin of 2L at 37B. *SD–72* in combination with *T*(*Y;2*),*11–26A* has a *k*-value of 0·24, though this time the homologue of *SD* is the structurally abnormal chromosome, broken at 36F, again near the centromeric heterochromatin of 2L. The reversal of *SD* is not limited to breakpoints in this region, however, because *SD–72* in combination with *T*(*Y;2*),*11–11N* has a *k*-value of 0·18, although the translocated chromosome is broken in the middle of 2L at 34A. The reversal of *SD* was also found associated with some translocations that had breakpoints near the centromeric heterochromatin of 2R. The mechanism of this phenomenon is not understood, but it may not be limited to translocations. Hartl (1970) has recovered a second chromosome from a natural population that seems to reverse *SD*, although this chromosome is not likely to be involved in a translocation.

As mentioned previously, Kataoka (1967) has analysed a type of X-chromosome that has a suppressing effect on *SD*. This chromosome is of interest because of its high frequency—about 85%—in natural populations and because its frequency is about the same in populations in Madison as in Japan (Hartl, 1970). An X-chromosome marked with several mutants and not carrying a suppressor of *SD* was made heterozygous with the suppressor-X and the recombinants were tested for their effect on *SD*

(Kataoka, 1967). The data are somewhat ambiguous, but they do suggest that at least two loci are involved in the suppressor system. One of these is located somewhere between the loci of *cv* and *f* [Kataoka interprets her data as implying the suppressor is between *v* and *f*, while Miklos (1972a), examining the same data, places the suppressor between *cv* and *v*]. The other modifiers on the suppressor-X have effects that are too small to be unambiguously detected. Thus the suppressor-X chromosome is essentially a polygenic system, but one major locus can be detected.

The genotype of *SD* males with respect to their Y-chromosome constitution can also influence segregation distortion. *SD* males that are XYY, for example, have lower *k*-values than males that are XY (Hiraizumi, 1969). Small duplications of the Y-chromosomes in attached X–Y males may also alter the segregation ratio of *SD* (Enns, 1970). The mechanism of these effects has not been adequately investigated, but Enns (1970) has suggested that the suppressing effect is attributable to a region near *KL–2*, a region known to be involved in the suppression of variegated position effects (Brosseau, 1964).

C. The Induction of Mutations by Segregation Distorter

Many of the early experiments involving *SD* gave results that were interpreted as meaning that *SD* was somehow associated with an extraordinary ability to induce mutations. This was, of course, an assumption of the breakage hypothesis (Sandler *et al.*, 1959), but the idea was extended to include other observations as well. The finding that most laboratory strains carry modifiers of *SD* led to a re-examination of many of these experiments, with the result that what was often interpreted as "mutation" could now be accounted for by the segregation of modifiers in the background genotype. A few observations are not so easily explained, however. The "instability ' of segregation distortion (Sandler and Hiraizumi, 1959, 1960a) as well as the phenomena of "conditional distortion" (Sandler and Hiraizumi, 1959, 1961a; Sandler, 1962; Sandler and Rosenfeld, 1962) and "translocal modification" (Sandler and Hiraizumi, 1959) can be satisfactorily accounted for by the segregation of modifiers rather than by the induction of mutations (Miklos and Smith-White, 1971; Miklos, 1972a, b). The results of Hiraizumi (1961) and Crow *et al.* (1962) are not so easily interpreted.

We have discussed the issue of stability and instability of *SD* in an earlier section and have shown how Miklos and Smith-White (1971) could account for the phenomenon by assuming a large number of minor modifiers of *SD* that alter the mean level of "make". "Translocal modification" (Sandler and Hiraizumi, 1959) can be explained on much the same basis. In studies of a bw^D chromosome that was "insensitive" to *SD*—operationally, bw^D behaves like a suppressor of *SD*—Sandler and Hiraizumi (1959) noticed that the *SD–5/cn bw* sons of the mating *cn bw/*bw^D ♂♂ × *SD–5* ♀♀ had lower *k*-values than *SD–5/cn bw* males whose *cn bw* chromosome had not been previously heterozygous with bw^D. Similarly, the *SD–5/cn bw* sons of the mating *SD–5/*bw^D ♂♂ × *cn bw* ♀♀ had reduced degrees of distortion. This was interpreted as due to directed mutations at or near the "locus" of *SD*, because in recombination tests the locus on the bw^D chromosome responsible for the suppression of *SD* seemed to be linked to *cn*. The bw^D chromosome was envisioned as causing to appear on the *cn bw* chromosome an "allele" of *SD* less sensitive to distortion, and as causing on the *SD* chromosome an allele of *SD* that was a less efficient distorter. Miklos and Smith-White (1971) have argued that precisely these results would be expected if the chromosomes in the bw^D strain carried modifiers of *SD*. Crossing *SD* or *cn bw* with the bw^D strain would have the effect of "contaminating" the genetic background with minor suppressors. Thus, although translocal modification may indeed occur, the evidence for it is unfounded. What would be required to re-introduce the phenomenon would be a demonstration that it occurs under experimental conditions in which the genetic background of all the strains is rigorously controlled.

Another phenomenon that invites re-interpretation in the light of more recent information is that known as "conditional distortion", in which *SD* was envisioned as being able to induce on the X-chromosome a specific suppressor or inhibitor of its own action (Sandler and Hiraizumi, 1959, 1961a; Sandler, 1962). The basic observation (Sandler and Hiraizumi, 1959) is that when *SD/cn bw* males are mated with *In(2LR)Cy/cn bw* females and the *SD/In(2LR)Cy* daughters are mated with *cn bw* males, then when the *SD/cn bw* sons of this latter mating are tested for distortion two kinds of sibships are found. In one of these, all the sons are distorters, and the *SD/In(2LR)Cy* mother of the sibship is said to be "unconditioned"; in the other type of sibship half the males show distortion of the segregation ratio and the other half do not. The *SD/In(2LR)Cy* mother of the latter type of sibship is said to be "conditioned". The element causing the suppression of *SD* was shown to be X-linked by mating *C(1)DX, y f/Y; SD/In(2LR)Cy* females to *cn bw* males and finding that all of the patroclinous *SD/cn bw* males were distorters. Further evidence for the location of the suppressor came from matings of *SD/cn bw* ♂♂ × *C(1)DX, y f/Y; cn bw* ♀♀, and in this case either all the sons of a given male were distorters or all had the distortion suppressed. Thus, a "conditioned" female is simply one that is heterozygous for the X-linked suppressor of *SD*.

Where does the suppressor come from? Sandler and Hiraizumi (1961a) argued that it could not have been segregating in the genetic background, and therefore it must have been induced specifically by *SD*. They argued that all the strains used in the study had been repeatedly backcrossed to *cn bw* in order to make the genetic background of the strains uniform. Another argument was that matings of *SD*/*cn bw* ♂♂ × *cn bw* ♀♀ produced no *SD*-bearing sons that failed to distort whereas the reciprocal mating, in which one of the maternal X's is descended from the X in an *SD* male, does produce some *SD*-bearing nondistorters. Finally, the *SD*/*cn bw* males that sire nondistorting sons when mated with *C(1)DX*/*Y; cn bw* females are themselves distorters.

Be that as it may, the element on the "conditioned" X chromosome responsible for the suppression of *SD* looks for all the world like Kataoka's (1967) suppressor. One should note initially that the suppressor discovered by Kataoka is so common in natural populations and in laboratory strains that stocks having X chromosomes that completely lack the suppressor are actually rather rare. Moreover, all the known properties of the "conditioned X" and Kataoka's suppressor are identical. Several peculiar anomalies in the experiments on conditional distortion can also be explained by postulating that the suppressor-X was segregating at some low frequency in the backcrossed laboratory strains.

In the first place, the suppressor could be detected only in the presence of some *SD*'s but not others. *R*(*SD*)*–4*, for example, and *R*(*SD–5*)*–32* seemed to be able to "induce" the suppressor whereas *SD–72* and *SD–5* could not (Sandler and Hiraizumi, 1961a). The first two *SD*'s have average *k*-values of about 0·90 whereas the other two have *k*-values of 0·99 or more. This is consistent with the observation that Kataoka's suppressor has a much more dramatic effect on *SD*'s with *k*-values of about 0·90 than it has on *SD*'s with higher *k*-values (Kataoka, 1967). Another way to state the argument is that both the "conditioned" X and Kataoka's suppressor are able to suppress only those *SD*'s that lack "*St*". Third, the "conditioned" X was found to be "induced" by the SD^{in} *cn* recombinants from *R*(*SD*)*–4*/*pr cn* females, but these recombinants do not appear to be segregation distorters inasmuch as their segregation ratio is normal. Fourth, Sandler and Hiraizumi (1961a) experienced some difficulty in repeating the experiments. The suppressor-X was occasionally found quite frequently, sometimes rather rarely, and for some periods it could not be found at all. Miklos's (1972a) attempt to repeat the observations was utterly without success. Finally, the map position of the suppressor on the conditioned X and the map position of Kataoka's suppressor seem to be the same. Sandler (1962) found that the suppressor on the conditioned X was some $8{\cdot}8 \pm 1{\cdot}7$ units from 57·0, the position of Bar on the chromosome map. This is entirely consistent with the region, *v–f*, in which Kataoka places her suppressor. Kataoka's data, taken at face value, would put her suppressor at approximately 47 on the chromosome map. Sandler's (1962) data, taken with the same naiveté, would place the suppressor on the conditioned X at about 48. The agreement seems just too remarkable to be coincidence.

Thus, the instability of *SD*, translocal modification, and conditional distortion can all be accounted for on bases other than the induction of mutations by *SD*, and therefore these phenomena, in retrospect, fail to support the contention that *SD* is associated with the induction of specific mutations of various kinds. This is not to imply that *SD* does not induce mutations or chromosome aberrations that may be detected by other methods. Indeed, two studies designed specifically to detect aberrations induced by *SD* have both yielded positive results. We have already mentioned in connection with the breakage hypothesis how Crow *et al.* (1962) argued that if, as an integral part of the mechanism of segregation distortion, the *SD* chromosome were to induce a physical break in its homologue in the vicinity of the *SD* region, then irradiating males should produce a rate of induced recombination that is higher in males with an *SD* that causes distortion of the segregation ratio than it would be in controls or in *SD* males whose distortion had been suppressed, because in the males with an "active" *SD* the irradiation would have to produce only one break in order to give rise to a recombinant, this break being in the *SD* chromosome itself in a position roughly homologous to the *SD*-induced break, whereas in the other males two breaks would be required to produce a recombinant. The results were in good agreement with this suggestion. Young males were exposed to 1500 R of X-rays and mated 9 days later in order to sample those cells that were in the meiotic stages at the time of treatment. The rate of induced recombination between the rightmost breakpoint of *In(2L)Cy* and the locus of *cn* in *SD–5/In(2L)Cy, Cy cn bw* males was about 0·43%; in *Canton S/In(2L)Cy, Cy cn bw* males it was about 0·24%; and in *SD–5/In(2L + 2R)Cy, Cy bw* males, in which distortion does not occur, the rate was 0·21%.

We have also pointed out a second experiment that implicates *SD* as causing mutations. Hiraizumi (1961) studied the viability, when homozygous, of the *cn bw* chromosomes derived from *SD/cn bw* males. The homozygous viability of the *cn bw* chromosomes—measured as the proportion of *cn bw/cn bw* progeny from the mating *In(2LR)Cy/cn bw* ♀♀ × *In(2LR)Cy/cn bw* ♂♂—was 27·5% in those chromosomes derived from an *SD* with a *k*-value of about 0·98, 28·6% in those chromosomes derived from an *SD* with a *k*-value of about 0·90, and 30·7% in the controls. Only 148 *cn bw* chromosomes from the *SD* males were examined, however, but among these were 3 that carried recessive lethals, as opposed to none among the 86 control chromosomes. The lethals were mapped, and all fell within 5% of the *SD* region. The nature of the low viability mutations and lethals is not known, but Hiraizumi (1961) suggests that they are small deficiencies.

D. The Aging Effect on Segregation Distortion

By two procedures it can be shown that the degree of distortion of the segregation ratio in *SD* males is reduced as a consequence of aging (Sandler and Hiraizumi, 1961b; Hiraizumi and Watanabe, 1969). Males that are mated repeatedly produce lower *k*-values in each successive brood; males that are aged in isolation from females produce, when they are finally mated, a segregation ratio that is lower than that of unaged males. These seem to be equivalent observations because males of *Drosophila* do not store sperm even in the absence of females (Lüning, 1952). The aging effect, expressed in terms of the *k*-value, is most pronounced in *SD*'s that have *k*-values of about 0·85, but a small effect can also be detected in *SD*'s with *k*-values near 1·0 or around 0·60 (Hiraizumi and Watanabe, 1969). This is consistent with the dK/dM curve on the left of Fig. 1. If the mean level of "make" in a male decreases with age—for whatever reasons—then the *SD*'s with intermediate *k*-values will be most strongly affected. The decrease in the degree of distortion, expressed in terms of the probit transformation, is about 0·05 probits per day over a 20-day period irrespective of the initial *k*-value of the *SD* (Hiraizumi and Watanabe, 1969). The overall change is therefore about 1 probit (Miklos, 1972a). The aggregate of modifiers in 2R called "*St*" does not exhibit an aging effect, nor does the recombinant from *R(SD–36)–1* that carries *Ac* (in the terminology of Hiraizumi and Nakazima, 1967). Hiraizumi and Watanabe (1969) have shown that the aging effect represents a true decrease in the degree of distortion rather than, say, a decrease in the relative viability of *SD* progeny. The critical observation is that the number of *SD*-bearing progeny produced by *SD* males, relative to the total number of progeny produced by normal males, is constant over the entire aging period, whereas the relative number of non-*SD*-bearing progeny from the *SD* males increases. The mechanism of the aging effect is not known, but the phenomenon is obviously similar to the aging effect on the meiotic drive of $T(1;4)B^S$ studied by Zimmering and Barbour (1961).

Among the most peculiar phenomena noted in connection with the aging effect is its apparent heritability. Not all *SD* males in a given line have exactly the same aging effect. In some males the segregation ratio declines rather rapidly, in others it declines more slowly. Old males that have low *k*-values by virtue of the aging effect produce sons whose average *k*-value is slightly lower than that of sons of fathers that did not age so rapidly. This procedure can be repeated over several generations by selecting as the fathers of each generation the males in the previous generation that had the most pronounced aging effect. With each generation of selection the average *k*-value becomes slightly lower, and this has been interpreted as meaning that the aging effect is associated with a permanent, heritable change in the *SD* chromosome itself (Sandler and Hiraizumi, 1961b). As an alternative it may be argued that in a heterogeneous strain the males exhibiting the most pronounced aging effect will be precisely those with *k*-values closest to 0·75 because of the shape of the *dK*/*dM* curve. Thus the apparent heritability of the aging effect will be due to the inadvertent selection of minor modifiers that decrease the mean level of "make". A similar explanation can be offered for the finding that the *SD*-bearing sons of old mothers or old *SD*/*In*(*2LR*)*Cy* fathers have slightly lower *k*-values than the *SD*-bearing sons of young mothers or young *SD*/*In*(*2LR*)*Cy* fathers (Sandler and Hiraizumi, 1961b). Heterogeneity in the genetic background can also account for the apparent heritability of the suppression of *SD* by the *Muller-5* chromosome (Sandler and Rosenfeld, 1962), a chromosome that carries a suppressor of *SD* that may be identical with the X linked suppressor described by Kataoka (1967).

E. The Effect of *SD* upon the Sex Ratio

One of the early questions involving the *SD* second chromosome was its effect on the segregation frequencies of other chromosomes in the complement. Although Sandler *et al.* (1959) had shown that the second chromosome itself was the only chromosome in *SD* males to exhibit marked departures from one-to-one segregation, Hiraizumi and Nakazima (1967) noticed a consistent deficiency of males in the class of progeny not receiving the *SD* chromosome. The effect of *SD* on the sex ratio is dependent on the occurrence of distortion; suppression of the distortion of *SD* by either a sex linked suppressor, *In*(*2LR*)*Cy*, or *In*(*2LR*)Pm^2 leads to a disappearance of the sex ratio effect (Hiraizumi and Nakazima, 1967; Hiraizumi, 1969). Similarly, *Sd*/*cn bw* males produce a deficiency of males among their *cn bw* bearing progeny, but this is not observed in *Ac*/*cn bw* or *St*/*cn bw* males (Hiraizumi and Nakazima, 1967). The magnitude of the effect also depends on the degree of distortion. *SD*'s that have average *k*-values of 0·99, for example, produce about 29% males in their non-*SD*-bearing progeny; *SD*'s that have average *k*-values of 0·90 produce about 42% males in the corresponding class; and *SD*'s with *k*-values of 0·60 produce about 48% males in the non-*SD*-bearing progeny (Hiraizumi and Nakazima, 1967). The distortion of the sex ratio by *SD* can be amplified by chromosome rearrangements involving the X and Y. The proportion of males in the *cn bw*-bearing progeny of $Y^SX.Y^L$, *In(1)EN, y B/0; SD–72/cn bw*, for example, is only 6% (Denell and Miklos, 1971).

In any case, the proportion of males in the *cn bw*-bearing progeny of *SD/cn bw* males is very much reduced. On this there is general agreement and consistency. As for the sex ratio in the *SD*-bearing progeny of *SD/cn bw* males, however, contradictory reports have appeared. Hiraizumi and Nakazima (1967) have consistently found in this class of progeny a very slight *excess* of males, and this has been observed even in the progeny of *Ac/cn bw* and "*St*"/*cn bw* males. On the strength of this observation, Hiraizumi and Nakazima (1967) have proposed that the *SD* and the X chromosome share a region of homology that sometimes results in partial synapsis or at least co-orientation of the chromosomes during meiosis so that the *SD* and the X chromosome would proceed to opposite poles at anaphase I. This mechanism would produce a deficiency of males in the non-*SD*-bearing progeny with a concomitant excess of males in the *SD*-bearing progeny. The observed deficiency of males in the former class is much greater than the excess in the latter, however, but this can easily be explained by assuming that the probability of distortion is smaller in meiocytes in which the *SD* and the X "disjoin".

The slight excess of males in the *SD*-bearing progeny of *SD/cn bw* males, the finding on which the hypothesis of partial synapsis depends, was not observed in the experiments of Denell *et al.* (1969), although they did observe a deficiency of males in the *cn bw*-bearing progeny that was quantitatively in agreement with the earlier reports. Denell *et al.* (1969) point out that their observations are most easily explained by the simple hypothesis that Y; *cn bw*-bearing sperm are more likely to undergo dysfunction than X; *cn bw*-bearing sperm. In terms of the probit transformation, this implies that the threshold of "make ' above which dysfunction occurs is lower in Y-bearing sperm than in X-bearing sperm (Denell and Miklos, 1971). The analysis has been further carried out by Denell and Miklos (1971) who have found that the proportion of males in the *cn bw*-bearing progeny of $Y^SX.Y^L/Y$*; SD–72/cn bw* males is about 28% whereas in $Y^SX.Y^L/0$*; SD–72/cn bw* males it is about 6%. Thus it appears that the threshold of dysfunction is highest in $Y^SX.Y^L$ sperm, these being the most frequently recovered, lowest in nullo-XY sperm, and intermediate in X-bearing and Y-bearing sperm. (This has also been observed by Enns, 1969.)

All of this can be accounted for on the hypothesis of Hiraizumi and Nakazima (1967) by assuming that when the $Y^SX.Y^L$ chromosome lacks a normal pairing partner, as it does in $Y^SX.Y^L/0$ males, then the chromosome will more frequently "disjoin" from *SD* than it otherwise would in the presence of a free Y (Denell and Miklos, 1971). In short, no critical data are available for distinguishing between the two hypotheses.

F. Effects involving Sperm Utilization

The results of Mange (1968) and those of Tokuyasu *et al.* (1972) imply that the primary events leading to sperm dysfunction occur while the sperm are still in the *SD* males. In some *SD*'s the dysfunctional sperm are not even ejaculated. An important question is whether this tells the whole story. In one view, three kinds of non-*SD*-bearing sperm can be distinguished, those that are dysfunctional and are not ejaculated, those that are dysfunctional and are ejaculated, and those that are fully functional. The segregation ratio of an *SD* male and the number of sperm he transfers will be determined by the relative proportions of these three types, and the segregation ratio will be fixed at ejaculation. A second view (Denell and Judd, 1969; Hartl and Childress, 1972) holds that there is actually a continuum of effects induced by *SD*, the most extremely affected sperm being dysfunctional, whether they are ejaculated or not, and the least affected being functional. Beteween these lies a class of sperm, actually rather small in number, that are functional under some conditions but dysfunctional under others.

Denell and Judd (1969) have suggested that conditions in the reproductive tract of the female can determine whether a sperm will be functional or dysfunctional. As evidence, they have shown that *SD* males mated to a series of females of different genotypes produce different segregation ratios. The effect is quantitatively rather small, about 0·5 probits, and in a replicated experiment the variance in segregation ratio within genotypes between replicates was actually greater than the variance between genotypes within replicates, though both were statistically significant. The segregation ratio of *SD–72/cn bw*, measured when the males were mated to the different strains of females, ranged from 0·93 to 0·99; the range of segregation ratios of $R(SD\text{–}36)\text{–}1^{bw}/cn\ bw$ was 0·67 to 0·75. These differences appear too large to be accounted for by small differences in viability because control matings with males carrying the same visible markers as the *SD* chromosomes produced no differences in recovery ratio in the different strains of females.

A related phenomenon has been described by Hiraizumi and Watanabe (1969). When a set of females is permitted a single copulation with a set of *SD* males and the females are brooded, the recovery of the *SD* chromosome increases in the successive broods. The magnitude of this effect is about the same as that of Denell and Judd (1969), roughly 0·5 probits. The brooding effect requires the occurrence of segregation distortion because *SD* males in which the distortion is suppressed exhibit no brooding effect (Hartl and Childress, 1972; Hartl, 1973a). The phenomenon does not depend on physiological changes in the females as they age, however, because the brooding effect is independent of the age at which the females are first mated. Furthermore, when females allowed to exhaust their sperm supply are remated, the brooding effect in the second mating is the same as if the females had been virgin all along. Simple sperm competition between *SD*-bearing and non-*SD*-bearing sperm can be eliminated from consideration because the change in the segregation ratio occurs whenever the sperm are stored in the female, even when the females are maintained under conditions that discourage egg laying. All this suggests that the brooding effect is caused by a class of sperm, small in number, that are destined to dysfunction eventually but are able to fertilize eggs if the opportunity presents itself at or soon after the time of mating. A further indication that the brooding effect involves a change in the functional ability of the non-*SD*-bearing sperm is that temperature shocks of 29°C or 18°C applied to mature sperm result in an immediate increase in the segregation ratio with no subsequent brooding effect, whether the sperm are treated in the females or while they are still in the males.

G. The Time of Action of *SD*

Whenever the final events leading to sperm dysfunction occur, the primary event induced by *SD* seems to take place quite early in spermatogenesis. Mange (1968) has studied a temperature sensitivity of *SD* that is similar in many respects to the temperature sensitivity of the meiotic drive of *RD* (Erickson and Hanks, 1961), $T(1;4)B^{S}$ (Zimmering and Perlman, 1962), and $sc^{4}\ sc^{8}$ (Zimmering, 1963). *SD* males raised at temperatures of 30°C or 19°C have *k*-values lower than those raised at 23°C by about 1·5 probits. Temperature shocks of males for 24 hours at different stages of development cause a reduction in *k*-value that is greatest in the progeny obtained from the males 8–9 days following treatment. This is consistent with the view that the temperature sensitive period of *SD* is in early meiosis, possibly in the primary spermatocytes (Mange, 1968). Denell *et al.* (1969) have found that the sex ratio in the non-*SD*-bearing progeny is also altered by temperature treatment, and the effect of temperature on the sex ratio is commensurate with the effect on segregation distortion. Irradiating *SD–72* males with 450 R of X-rays causes a decrease in the segregation ratio of about 0·5 probits 7–10 days after treatment, suggesting that the stage of irradiation sensitivity coincides with the stage of temperature sensitivity.

The greatest frequency of X-ray induced recombination occurs in those broods with the greatest decrease in the segregation ratio, again suggesting that the action of *SD* is in early meiosis (Murnik, 1971).

The results of Mange (1968) have been confirmed by Hihara (1971), who also studied the temperature sensitivity of Kataoka's (1967) X-linked suppressor. This suppressor is less effective when the males carrying it are raised at 17°C. In contrast to the results indicating that the temperature sensitive period of *SD* is in early meiosis, the temperature sensitive period of the suppressor appears to be in the early spermatids.

H. Effects of Homozygous *SD* on Male Fertility

One of the strongest arguments for sperm dysfunction as the mechanism of segregation distortion is the reduced fecundity of heterozygous *SD* males (Hartl *et al.*, 1967; Nicoletti *et al.*, 1967). In a heterozygous *SD* male, the *SD* chromosome renders the sperm carrying its homologue dysfunctional. If a similar mechanism were operating in males carrying two *SD* chromosomes, then the one *SD* would bring about the dysfunction of sperm carrying the other and the other would bring about the dysfunction of sperm carrying the one, and the upshot would be sterility, or near sterility, of the males. This issue was addressed in the early studies of *SD*, and the apparent fertility of *SD–72/SD–5* males led to the idea that an *SD* chromosome carries an "immunity" to its own action or to the action of any other *SD* (Sandler *et al.*, 1959). Mange (1961) and Nicoletti and Trippa (1967) reported the male fertility of two other SD_i/SD_j combinations. (In the terminology of this section SD_i and SD_j represent *SD* chromosomes that are different in the sense of being derived from different natural populations or carrying different inversions or lethals or whatever. Most SD_i/SD_i combinations cannot be examined directly because they are lethal in both sexes.)

On the other hand, Hartl (1969) found that two SD_i/SD_j combinations involving *SD(NH)–2* were virtually sterile in males, although the fertility of the females was normal. This would suggest that an *SD* chromosome is not resistant to the action of another *SD*. The evident contradiction in the results led to an examination of the male fertility of all 55 combinations of 11 *SD* chromosomes (Hartl, 1973b). Of these 55 combinations, 36 were sterile in males, or nearly sterile, with the fertility in the females being normal, 15 were partially fertile, and 4 were lethal. Sterility or quasi-sterility is defined in these experiments as the production by an SD_i/SD_j male of only 0–5% as many progeny as normal males under conditions in which the functional sperm are sampled exhaustively. The nearly sterile males produce substantial numbers of motile sperm that are transferred to the females during copulation, and these sperm are stored in the seminal receptacles and spermathecae of the females. Few progeny result, however (Hartl, 1969, 1973b). Miklos (1972c) has studied this question quantitatively in one nonlethal SD_i/SD_i combination and has found that the males transfer about 33% as many sperm as normal males, but they produce only 0·5% as many progeny.

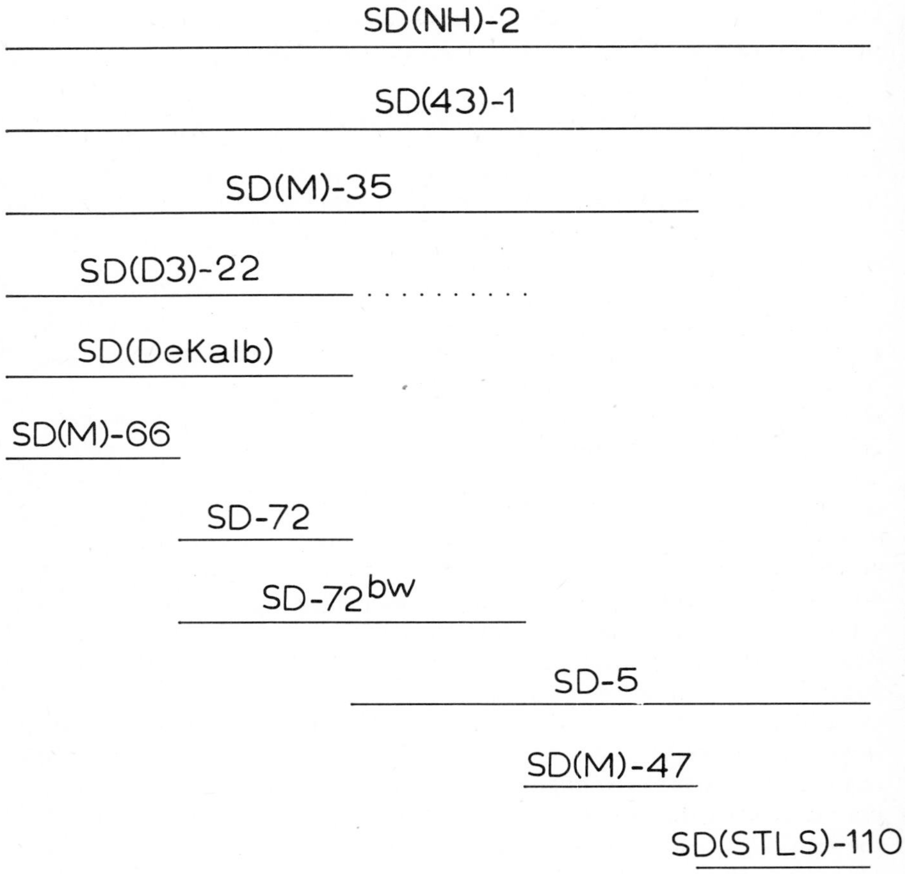

FIG. 2. Complementation map of male fertility of *SD* combinations. Males carrying two overlapping *SD* chromosomes are sterile or nearly sterile; males carrying two nonoverlapping *SD* chromosomes are partially fertile, up to 50% of the fecundity of wild type. The ambiguity represented by the dotted segment on *SD(D3)–22* arises from *SD(D3)–22* and *SD–5* having a recessive lethal in common. *SD–72* is *SD–72* (Madison), *SD–72*^{bw} is *SD–72* (Canberra). From Hartl (1973b).

What fertility there is among the SD_i/SD_j combinations that are not quasi-sterile is, at best, partial fertility. The males produce 10–50% as many progeny as normal males, and no combination has been found with a fecundity of more than half the normal level. Taken as a whole, an SD_i/SD_j combination is either very nearly sterile or quite fertile, with very little in between.

The quasi-sterility and partial fertility of SD_i/SD_j combinations falls into a simple pattern (Fig. 2). An *SD* chromosome is represented as a line segment; SD_i/SD_j combinations whose segments overlap are nearly sterile; SD_i/SD_j whose segments are nonoverlapping are partially fertile. This assumes that the true homozygous *SD*'s, SD_i/SD_i, are nearly sterile, an issue on which there is little evidence other than three combinations that have been examined. Two derivatives of *SD–36*, *R*(*SD–36*)–1^{bw} and *R*(*cn*)–*14*, are nearly sterile in combination (Hartl, 1969); a homozygous nonlethal recombinant from *SD–72* is nearly sterile (Miklos, 1972c); and *SD–72*^{bw}/*SD–72* is nearly sterile (Hartl, 1973b).

The pattern of interaction in Fig. 2 is of the familiar kind for intracistronic complementation (Fincham, 1966), remarkable only in its simple linearity and typified by the inclusion of two "alleles", *SD*(*NH*)–*2* and *SD*(*43*)–*1*, that fail to complement with any others. These chromosomes allow one to distinguish whether either *Sd* or *Ac*, in the terminology of Hiraizumi and Nakazima (1967), is responsible for the near sterility of SD_i/SD_j males. The evidence points to *Sd* as the locus at which the complementation occurs. Although *SD*(*NH*)–*2*/*Ac* males have a fecundity of about half the normal level, this is expected from the presence in the genotype of *SD*(*NH*)–*2* alone. By contrast, *SD*(*NH*)–*2*/*Sd* males are quite infertile (Hartl, 1973b).

The usual interpretation of a map such as Fig. 2 is that complementation represents the interaction of defective polypeptide subunits in a multimeric molecule. If the defects in the constituent polypeptides occur at different positions along the chain, then the polypeptides can sometimes interact in such a way as to confer an amount of enzyme activity upon the multimer, although the amount of activity produced is usually much less than the normal amount (Crick and Orgel, 1964).

VI. A Proposal for the Molecular Mechanism of *SD*

To account for the complementation leading to partial male fertility in some SD_i/SD_j combinations, Hartl (1973b) has suggested that the mechanism of *SD* involves two mutually compatible defects in a regulatory mechanism important in the genetic control of spermatogenesis. Of the two major loci in the *SD* system, *Sd* may be thought of as the controller, and the locus usually called *Ac* is better regarded for purposes of this hypothesis as a Responder (*Rsp*). The regulatory hypothesis assumes that a necessary condition for a sperm to undergo spermatogenesis without dysfunction is that the *Rsp* locus be complexed with the product of the *Sd* locus, which is assumed to be a multimeric regulatory protein. Three kinds of regulatory multimers can be distinguished: Sd^+/Sd^+ homomultimers, which are assumed to be able to interact with both Rsp^+ and *Rsp*; Sd^+/Sd heteromultimers, which can complex only with *Rsp*; and *Sd*/*Sd* homomultimers, which can complex with neither Rsp^+ nor *Rsp*. The predominating form of the regulatory protein in Sd^+/Sd males is assumed to be the Sd^+/Sd heteromultimer.

By assigning these functions to the two major loci of the *SD* system, the regulatory hypothesis accounts for the distortion in $Sd\ Rsp/Sd^+\ Rsp^+$ males, because the Sd^+/Sd heteromultimer interacts only with *Rsp*; it accounts for the lack of distortion of the segregation ratio in $Sd\ Rsp/Sd^+\ Rsp$ males, because the specificity of the Sd^+/Sd heteromultimer is directed only to *Rsp*; it accounts for the reduced fecundity of $Sd\ Rsp/Sd^+\ Rsp$ males, provided the amount of the regulatory protein is limiting; and it accounts for the near sterility of *Sd Rsp*/*Sd Rsp* males because of the lack of specificity of the *Sd*/*Sd* homomultimer for *Rsp*. An attractive feature of the hypothesis is that it provides a mechanism for the complementation of some SD_i/SD_j combinations based on the argument that some Sd_i/Sd_j heteromultimers may have a small amount of activity not possessed by either Sd_i/Sd_i or Sd_j/Sd_j homomultimers. The hypothesis also suggests that *SD* will be sensitive to many kinds of genetic and environmental modifiers because anything that lessens the stability of the Sd/Sd^+ heteromultimer will increase the relative amount of the Sd^+/Sd^+ homomultimers in an *SD* male, and this will appear as partial suppression.

The suggestion that a *Sd–Rsp* complex is required for normal spermatogenesis has obvious similarities with a known mechanism of enzyme repression in bacteria (Beckwith and Zipser, 1970). It may indeed be the case that the *Sd–Rsp* complex is required to repress mRNA synthesis which, if allowed to proceed unchecked, would lead to sperm dysfunction. One arrives at this extension of the hypothesis almost by elimination. In a purely formal sense, the action of *SD* is to convert its homologue into a sperm lethal. Lethality in somatic cells often arises from a defect in one or more cistrons, either because the products of these cistrons are not produced at all or, if they are produced, they are defective. The situation is different in spermatogenesis in *Drosophila*. The bulk of gene activity occurs in primary spermatocytes when the nuclei are still diploid, as inferred from the failure to detect incorporation of tritiated uridine in later stages of spermatogenesis (Olivieri and Olivieri, 1965; Hennig, 1967).

The situation is further complicated by the syncytial nature of the immature sperm in a cyst (Meyer, 1961). The shared cytoplasm would argue for uniformity of the sperm, although it is perhaps significant that the sperm heads are not included in the syncytium (Tokuyasu *et al.*, 1972). In any case, sperm all but devoid of chromosomes can complete spermatogenesis and function in fertilization (Muller and Settles, 1927; McCloskey, 1966; Lindsley and Grell, 1969), and there seems no simple way that the non-*SD* chromosome can be induced to produce a defective product that causes lethality of the sperm, because the other results suggest that the genes in the sperm are inactive anyway. Stating the paradox in this manner leads to the obvious alternative, however, that the defect in the non-*SD* chromosome involves the continued synthesis of a normal gene product, or products, when the synthesis in normal cells would have been repressed. The non-*SD* chromosome behaves, in this hypothesis, like an i^- or an o^c mutation (Beckwith and Zipser, 1970).

The hypothesis of Hartl (1973b) is not as *ad hoc* as it may first appear because it has become increasingly apparent that the inactivation of genes, or the lack of it, during spermatogenesis is an extremely important process. This whole subject received an airing at the Edinburgh Symposium (1972). Lifschytz (1972) stressed the role of X-chromosome inactivation in spermatogenesis and Auerbach (see the Discussion to Sandler and Carpenter, 1972) wondered whether gene inactivation could somehow be involved in the case of segregation distortion. The specific mechanism proposed by Hartl (1973b) argues that the events involved in segregation distortion are more concerned with the genetic control of spermatogenesis than they are with the interaction of chromosomes on a purely mechanical level.

One caveat regarding this hypothesis should be entered. Like all proposals concerning *SD*, it should be regarded with some skepticism until more detailed information is available. The *SD* system has been a merciless destroyer of otherwise elegant hypotheses, as the pages of this review recount, and it would be too much to expect that the present hypothesis will fare much better. As a working model, however, the hypothesis has much to commend it.

VII. Interactions of *SD* with other Systems of Meiotic Drive

We emphasize here the use of the word *interaction* rather than *similarity*. The latter, a comparison between *SD* and other systems of meiotic drive, has been presented by Zimmering *et al.* (1970b) and Hartl and Childress (1972). With one exception we will confine ourselves in this discussion to cases in which both *SD* and a second system of meiotic drive have been studied in the same males so that interactions between the two systems could be detected. Novitski and Peacock (1970) have reported a curious interaction between *SD* and *T(1; Y;4)*B^S. This is a translocation that has as one element the distal segment of the X chromosome from the region of Bar to the tip appended to the centromere of chromosome 4 (this element is referred to as X^D), and as the other element a Y chromosome that has incorporated into it the basal segment of the X from the centromere to Bar (we will refer to this piece as B^S *Y*). The *T(1; Y;4)* B^S males have, in addition, a normal Y chromosome. Ordinarily, X^D disjoins from 4 and B^S *Y* from Y, and from the $X^D \leftrightarrow 4$ bivalent the relative frequencies of functional X^D- and 4-bearing sperm are 0·43 and 0·57, respectively, versus the expected one-to-one. From the B^S $Y \leftrightarrow$ Y bivalent the relative frequencies of B^S *Y*- and Y-bearing sperm are 0·39 and 0·61, respectively. The relative frequencies of sperm carrying $X^D + B^S$ *Y*, $X^D +$ Y, 4 + B^S *Y*, or 4 + Y can be obtained to a good approximation by multiplying the probabilities of recovery of each chromosome in the sperm taken separately (Novitski and Sandler, 1957; Novitski and Peacock, 1970). The mechanism of the meiotic drive in *T(1; Y;4)* B^S is not known with assurance, but sperm dysfunction has been suggested (Novitski, 1970; Hartl and Childress, 1972).

When *SD* and *T(1; Y;4)* B^S are segregating in the same male the relative frequencies of the four sperm types from the translocation differ according to whether the sperm also carry *SD*. Among the progeny that receive *SD* the relative frequencies of the segregants from the translocation are as those given above, virtually the same as the frequencies recovered when the translocation is segregating in the absence of *SD*. Among the progeny receiving the non-*SD* chromosome, however, the relative frequencies of the four sperm types are nearly equal, as if in those meiocytes in which *SD* was "inactive" the meiotic drive of the translocation also did not occur. Novitski and Peacock (1970) have suggested on this basis that the same condition that leads to the preferential recovery of *SD* also leads to the preferential recovery of the components of the translocation.

Although the mechanisms of distortion of *SD* and of *T(1; Y;4)* B^S are clearly related, they are not identical. This follows from the fact that the segregation distortion of *SD* does not occur in the presence of *T(1;4)* B^S although the unequal recovery of the components of the translocation is still observed (Hartl and Childress, 1972) (*T(1;4)* B^S differs from *T(1;Y;4)* B^S in that the B^S *Y* element is replaced with the basal segment of the X capped by the tip of chromosome 4). Were the mechanisms of distortion identical, it would not be possible to observe distortion of one without concomitant distortion of the other.

Miklos *et al.* (1972) have studied the interactions of *SD* and *In(1)* sc^{4L}

sc^{8R}, an X chromosome that carries a large heterochromatic deficiency. Four gametic types are recovered from sc^4 sc^8/Y males, X-bearing and Y-bearing, and two nondisjunctional types, XY-bearing and nullo. The amount of distortion of sc^4 sc^8 depends somewhat on the amount of nondisjunction; when the frequency of nondisjunction is 25 %, as an example, the recovery of X-bearing sperm among the regular segregants is about 0·65, and the relative frequency of nullo sperm among the nondisjunctants is about 0·90. *SD* interacts with sc^4 sc^8 in a manner similar to its interaction with *T(1;Y;4)* B^S. Among the *SD*-bearing progeny of sc^4 $sc^8/Y;SD/cn\ bw$ males the recovery of the segregants from sc^4 sc^8 is virtually identical to that found when *SD* is absent from the system. Among the non-*SD*-bearing progeny the X- and Y-bearing sperm are found with frequencies that are more nearly equal, and similarly for the XY- and nullo segregants (Miklos *et al.*, 1972).

It should be mentioned that a case of non-Mendelian segregation very similar to *SD* occurs in the house mouse. The *t*-alleles in the mouse are autosomal segregation distorters that distort the segregation ratio only in males (Chesley and Dunn, 1936). Like *SD*, the *t*-alleles are found in virtually all natural populations, usually associated with abnormalities that tend to suppress crossing over and frequently carrying a recessive lethal. The crossover suppressors and the lethal can be separated by crossing over from the region responsible for the distortion (Lyon and Meredith, 1964). The *t*-alleles also exhibit several associated phenomena that are shared with *SD*: males heterozygous for the *t*-alleles have a pronounced heterogeneity in the segregation ratio from ejaculate to ejaculate (Dunn, 1956); an apparent effect of the female on the recovery ratio has been described (Bateman, 1960), the recovery ratio obtained from an ejaculate is affected by the length of time between ejaculation and fertilization (Braden, 1958, 1972; Yanagisawa *et al.*, 1961). These parallelisms could be fortuitous, of course, but taken together with the similarity in phenotype between t_i/t_j and SD_i/SD_j males they suggest that the mechanisms of distortion may be much the same. Some t_i/t_j combinations are sterile; other combinations are quite fertile, and this suggests a kind of complementation (Dunn, 1956; Dunn *et al.*, 1962; Dunn and Bennett, 1969). The sterile t_i/t_j combinations produce sperm that in the light microscope appear to be of normal morphology and motility; the sperm are ejaculated and swim up the uterus, but they are dysfunctional because they cannot traverse the utero-tubal junction (Braden and Gluecksohn-Waelsch, 1958; Olds, 1970). The mechanisms of distortion of *SD* and the *t*-alleles are probably not identical—spermatogenesis in mammals and insects is sufficiently different to render the hypothesis immediately suspect. But the phenomenological similarities of the two cases surely suggest an underlying mechanistic resemblance, perhaps having more to do with the genetic control of spermatogenesis than with the details of the process itself. Additional information on the similarity between *SD* and the *t*-alleles can be found in Gluecksohn-Waelsch and Erickson (1970), Zimmering *et al.* (1970b), Braden *et al.* (1972), and Hartl and Childress (1972).

VIII. Summary

Fifteen years of study of segregation distortion have revealed a system that is not as complex as originally thought. Complexities there are in abundance, but they are not insurmountable. The mechanism of *SD* is to render dysfunctional those sperm that carry its homologue. The genetic structure of *SD* involves two major loci in the centromeric region of chromosome 2, but there are also a great many modifiers of *SD*, most having small effects, scattered throughout the genome. *SD* can be suppressed by any of several different mechanisms, and certain genetic situations can be contrived in which *SD* distorts itself. Many of the early experiments that were interpreted as meaning that *SD* was uncommonly mutable or had an extraordinary ability of inducing specific mutations appear, in retrospect, to be attributable to the segregation of modifiers of *SD* in the background genotype. Nevertheless, *SD* may be involved in the induction of viability mutations or chromosome breaks in its homologue. The time of action of *SD* is in early meiosis, and the complementation leading to partial male fertility of some SD_i/SD_j combinations suggests that the molecular mechanism of distortion involves two complementary defects in the normal mechanism of genetic control of spermatogenesis. *SD* interacts with the meiotic drive of $T(1;Y;4)\ B^S$ and $sc^4\ sc^8$ in a way that suggests the basis of sperm dysfunction is similar in all three cases. The phenomenological similarity between *SD* and the *t*-alleles in the house mouse suggests the same.

Acknowledgements

Our thanks to Drs. L. Sandler and E. Novitski for their helpfulness and for their careful reading of the manuscript.

References

Bateman, N. (1960). Selective fertilization at the T-locus of the mouse. *Genet. Res.* (*Camb.*) **1,** 226–238.

Beckwith, J. R. and Zipser, D. (1970). "The Lactose Operon." Cold Spring Harbor Laboratory.

BRADEN, A. W. H. (1958). Influence of time of mating on the segregation ratio of alleles at the T-locus in the house mouse. *Nature, Lond.* **181,** 786–787.

BRADEN, A. W. H. (1972). T-locus in mice; segregation distortion and sterility in the male. *In*: "Edinburgh Symposium on the Genetics of the Spermatozoon" (Eds. R. A. Beatty and S. Gluecksohn-Waelsch). Bogtrykkeriet Forum, Copenhagen. Pp. 289–305.

BRADEN, A. W. H. and GLUECKSOHN-WAELSCH, S. (1958). Further studies of the effect of the T-locus in the house mouse on male fertility. *J. Expl. Zool.* **138,** 431–452.

BRADEN, A. W. H., ERICKSON, R. P., GLUECKSOHN-WAELSCH, S., HARTL, D. L., PEACOCK, W. J. and SANDLER, L. (1972). A comparison of effects and properties of segregation distorting alleles in the mouse (*t*) and *Drosophila*(*SD*). *In*: "Edinburgh Symposium on the Genetics of the Spermatozoon" pp. 310–312 (Eds. R. A. Beatty and S. Gluecksohn-Waelsch). Bogtrykkeriet Forum, Copenhagen.

BROSSEAU, G. E., Jr. (1964). Evidence that heterochromatin does not suppress V-type position effect. *Genetics* **50,** 237.

CHESLEY, P. and DUNN, L. C. (1936). The inheritance of Taillessness (anury) in the house mouse. *Genetics* **21,** 525–536.

CRICK, F. H. C. and ORGEL, L. E. (1964). The theory of inter-allelic complementation. *J. Molec. Biol.* **8,** 161–165.

CROW, J. F., THOMAS, C. and SANDLER, L. (1962). Evidence that the segregation-distortion phenomenon in *Drosophila* involves chromosome breakage. *Proc. Nat. Acad. Sci. U.S.A.* **48,** 1307–1314.

DENELL, R. E. and JUDD, B. H. (1968). Segregation distortion in *D. melanogaster*; the location of stabilizer of SD. *Dros. Inf. Serv.* **43,** 119.

DENELL, R. E. and JUDD, B. H. (1969). Segregation distorter in *D. melanogaster* males: An effect of female genotype on recovery. *Molec. Gen. Genet.* **105,** 262–274.

DENELL, R. E. and MIKLOS, G. L. G. (1971). The relationship between first and second chromosome segregation ratios from *Drosophila melanogaster* males bearing segregation distorter. *Molec. Gen. Genetics* **110,** 167–177.

DENELL, R. E., JUDD, B. H. and RICHARDSON, R. H. (1969). Distorted sex ratios due to *segregation distorter* in *Drosophila melanogaster*. *Genetics* **61,** 129–139.

DUNCAN, F. N. (1930). Some observations on the biology of the male *Drosophila melanogaster*. *Am. Nat.* **64,** 545–551.

DUNN, L. C. (1956). Analysis of a complex gene in the house mouse. *Cold Spring Harb. Symp. Quant. Biol.* **21.** 187–195.

DUNN, L. C. and BENNETT, D. (1969). Studies of effects of *t*-alleles in the house mouse on spermatozoa. II. Quasi-sterility caused by different combinations of alleles. *J. Reprod. Fert.* **20,** 239–246.

DUNN, L. C., BENNETT, D. and BEASLEY, A. B. (1962). Mutation and recombination in the vicinity of a complex gene. *Genetics* **47,** 285–303.

Edinburgh Symposium on the Genetics of the Spermatozoon. (1972). (Eds. R. A. Beatty and S. Gluecksohn-Waelsch.) Bogtrykkeriet Forum, Copenhagen, 406 pp.

ENNS, R. E. (1969). Unpublished Ph.D. thesis. University of Oregon, Eugene.

ENNS, R. E. (1970). Segregation in males with XY–X chromosomes with and without free Y's and the segregation distorter chromosome, *SD–72. Dros. Inf. Serv.* **45,** 136.

ERICKSON, J. and HANKS, G. D. (1961). Time of temperature sensitivity of meiotic drive in *Drosophila melanogaster. Am. Nat.* **95,** 247–250.

FINCHAM, J. R. S. (1966). "Genetic Complementation". W. A. Benjamin, New York.

FISHER, R. A. and YATES, F. (1963). "Statistical Tables for Biological, Agricultural and Medical Rèsearch." 6th ed. Oliver and Boyd, Edinburgh.

GLUECKSOHN-WAELSCH, S. and ERICKSON, R. (1970). The T-locus of the mouse: Implications for the mechanisms of development. *Current Topics in Developmental Biology* **5,** 281–316.

GREENBERG, R. (1962). Two new cases of *SD* found in nature. *Dros. Inf. Serv.* **36,** 70.

HARTL, D. L. (1968). Evidence that the mechanism of segregation distortion in *Drosophila melanogaster* involves the production of dysfunctional sperms. Ph.D. Thesis, University of Wisconsin, Madison.

HARTL, D. L. (1969). Dysfunctional sperm production in *Drosophila melanogaster* males homozygous for the segregation distorter elements. *Proc. Nat. Acad. Sci. U.S.A.* **63,** 782–789.

HARTL, D. L. (1970). Meiotic drive in natural populations of *Drosophila melanogaster*. IX. Suppressors of *segregation distorter* in wild populations. *Can. J. Genet. Cytol.* **12,** 594–600.

HARTL, D. L. (1973a). The mechanism of a brooding effect associated with segregation distortion in *Drosophila melanogaster. Genetics* **74,** 619–631.

HARTL, D. L. (1973b). Complementation analysis of male fertility among the segregation distorter chromosomes in *Drosophila melanogaster. Genetics* **73,** 613–629.

HARTL, D. L. (1974). Genetic dissection of segregation distortion. I. Suicide combinations of *SD* genes. *Genetics* **76,** 477–486.

HARTL, D. L. and CHILDRESS, D. (1972). Genetic studies of sperm function and utilization in *Drosophila melanogaster. In*: "Edinburgh Symposium on the Genetics of the Spermatozoon" (Eds. R. A. Beatty and S. Gluecksohn-Waelsch). Bogtrykkeriet Forum, Copenhagen. Pp. 269–288.

HARTL, D. L., HIRAIZUMI, Y. and CROW, J. F. (1967). Evidence for sperm dysfunction as the mechanism of segregation distortion in *Drosophila melanogaster. Proc. Natl. Acad. Sci. U.S.A.* **58,** 2240–2245.

HENNIG, W. (1967). Untersuchugen zur struktur und Funktion des Lampbursten-Y-chromosoms in der Spermatogenese von Drosophila. *Chromosoma* **22,** 294–357.

HIHARA, Y. K. (1971). Genetic analysis of modifying system of segregation distortion in *Drosophila melanogaster*. I. Active stage of the *SD*—suppressor and the reconfirmation of the dysfunctional sperm model. *Jap. J. Genet.* **46,** 75–82.

HIRAIZUMI, Y. (1961). Lethality and low viability induced by the segregation distorter locus (symbol *SD*) in *Drosophila melanogaster. Ann. Rep. Natl. Inst. Genet. Jap.* **12,** 1–2.

HIRAIZUMI, Y. (1969). Nonrandom assortment in *SD* heterozygous XYY males of *Drosophila melanogaster. Jap. J. Genet.* **44,** 97.

HIRAIZUMI, Y. and CROW, J. F. (1960). Heterozygous effects on viability, fertility, rate of development and longevity of Drosophila chromosomes that are lethal when homozygous. *Genetics* **45,** 1071–1084.

HIRAIZUMI, Y. and NAKAZIMA, K. (1965). *SD* in a natural population of *D. melanogaster* in Japan. *Dros. Inf. Serv.* **40,** 72.

HIRAIZUMI, Y. and NAKAZIMA, K. (1967). Deviant sex ratio associated with segregation distortion in *Drosophila melanogaster*. *Genetics* **55,** 681–697.

HIRAIZUMI, Y. and WATANABE, S. S. (1969). Aging effect on the phenomenon of segregation distortion in *Drosophila melanogaster*. *Genetics* **63,** 121–131.

HIRAIZUMI, Y., SANDLER, L. and CROW, J. F. (1960). Meiotic drive in natural populations of *Drosophila melanogaster*. III. Populational implications of the segregation-distorter locus. *Evolution* **14,** 433–444.

KATAOKA, Y. (1967). A genetic system modifying segregation-distortion in a natural population of *Drosophila melanogaster* in Japan. *Jap. J. Genet.* **42,** 327–337.

LEFEVRE, G. and JONSSON, U.-B. (1962). Sperm transfer, storage, displacement and utilization in *Drosophila melanogaster*. *Genetics* **47,** 1719–1736.

LEFEVRE, G. and PARKER, D. M. (1963). Male fertility as a function of the number of females available for mating. *Dros. Inf. Serv.* **37,** 98.

LEWIS, E. B. (1962). Salivary gland chromosome analysis of segregation distorter lines. *Dros. Inf. Ser.* **36,** 87.

LIFSCHYTZ, E. (1972). X-chromosome inactivation: an essential feature of normal spermiogenesis in male heterogametic organisms. *In*: "Edinburgh Symposium on the Genetics of the Spermatozoon" (Eds. R. A. Beatty and S. Gluecksohn-Waelsch). Bogtrykkeriet Forum, Copenhagen. Pp. 223–232.

LINDSLEY, D. L. and GRELL, E. H. (1968). Genetic variations of *Drosophila melanogaster*. Carnegie Inst. Wash. Publ. No. 627. 471 pp.

LINDSLEY, D. L. and GRELL, E. H. (1969). Spermiogenesis without chromosomes in *Drosophila melanogaster*. *Genetics* **61,** Supplement 1, 69–78.

LÜNING, K. G. (1952). X-ray induced dominant lethals in different stages of spermatogenesis in *Drosophila*. *Hereditas* **38,** 91–107.

LYON, M. F. and MEREDITH, R. (1964). Investigations on the nature of *t*-alleles in the house mouse. I. Genetic analysis of a series of mutants derived from a lethal allele. *Heredity* **19,** 301–312.

MANGE, E. J. (1961). Meiotic drive in natural populations of *Drosophila melanogaster*. VI. A preliminary report on the presence of segregation-distortion in a Baja California population. *Am. Nat.* **95,** 87–96.

MANGE, E. J. (1968). Temperature sensitivity of segregation-distortion in *Drosophila melanogaster*. *Genetics* **58,** 399–413.

MCCLINTOCK, B. (1951). Chromosome organization and genic expression. *Cold Spring Harb. Symp. Quant. Biol.* **16,** 13–47.

MCCLINTOCK, B. (1956). Controlling elements and the gene. *Cold Spring Harb. Symp. Quant. Biol.* **21,** 197–216.

MCCLOSKEY, J. D. (1966). The problem of gene activity in the sperm of *Drosophila melanogaster*. *Am. Nat.* **100,** 211–218.

MEYER, G. F. (1961). Intercellulare Brucken (Fusome) in Hoden und in Ei-Nahrzellverband von *Drosophila melanogaster*. *Z. Zellforsch. mikrosk. Anat.* **54,** 238–251.

MIKLOS, G. L. G. (1972a). An investigation of the components of *segregation-distorter* systems in *Drosophila melanogaster*. *Genetics* **70,** 405–418.

MIKLOS, G. L. G. (1972b). The genetic structure of chromosomes carrying *segregation-distorter*. *Can. J. Genet. Cytol.* **14,** 235–243.

MIKLOS, G. L. G. (1972c). Properties of males homozygous for segregation distorter. *Dros. Inf. Serv.* **48,** 117–119.

MIKLOS, G. L. G. and SMITH-WHITE, S. (1971). An analysis of the instability of segregation-distorter in *Drosophila melanogaster*. *Genetics* **67,** 305–317.

MIKLOS, G. L. G., YANDERS, A. F. and PEACOCK, W. J. (1972). Multiple meiotic drive systems in the *Drosophila melanogaster* male. *Genetics* **72,** 105–115.

MULLER, H. J. and SETTLES, F. (1927). The non-functioning of the genes in spermatozoa. *Z. Indukt. Abstamm. Vererblehre* **43,** 285–312.

MURNIK, M. R. (1971). Environmental effects on *segregation-distorter* in *Drosophila melanogaster*: Irradiation of *SD–72* at the onset of spermatogenesis. *Genetica* **42,** 457–465.

NICOLETTI, B. (1968). Il Controllo genetico della meiosi. *Atti Assoc. Genet. Ital.* **13,** 1–71.

NICOLETTI, B. and TRIPPA, G. (1967). Osservazioni citogenetiche su di un nuovo caso di "segregation distortion" (*SD*) rinvenuto in una popolazione naturale di *Drosophila melanogaster*. *Atti Assoc. Genet. Ital.* **12,** 361–365.

NICOLETTI, B., TRIPPA, G. and DEMARCO, A. (1967). Reduced fertility in *SD* males and its bearing on segregation distortion in *Drosophila melanogaster*. *Atti Acad. Naz. Lincei* **43,** 383–392.

NOVITSKI, E. (1970). The concept of gamete dysfunction. *Dros. Inf. Serv.* **45,** 87–88.

NOVITSKI, E. and EHRLICH, E. (1970). Suppression of SD by Y; autosome translocations. *Dros. Inf. Serv.* **45,** 102.

NOVITSKI, E. and PEACOCK, W. J. (1970). Results from the combination of B^S and *SD* in the male. *Dros. Inf. Serv.* **45,** 95–96.

NOVITSKI, E. and SANDLER, I. (1957). Are all products of spermatogenesis regularly functional? *Proc. Nat. Acad. Sci. U.S.A.* **43,** 318–324.

NOVITSKI, E., PEACOCK, W. J. and ENGEL, J. (1965). Cytological basis of "sex ratio" in *Drosphila pseudoobscura*. *Science, N.Y.* **148,** 516–517.

OLDS, P. J. (1970). Effect of the T locus on sperm distribution in the house mouse. *Biol. Reprod.* **2,** 91–97.

OLIVIERI, G. and OLIVIERI, A. (1965). Autoradiographic study of nucleic acid synthesis during spermatogenesis in *Drosophila melanogaster*. *Mutation Res.* **2,** 366–380.

PEACOCK, W. J. and ERICKSON, J. (1965). Segregation-distortion and regularly nonfunctional products of spermatogenesis in *Drosophila melanogaster*. *Genetics* **51,** 313–328.

PEACOCK, W. J., TOKUYASU, K. and HARDY, R. W. (1972). Spermiogenesis and meiotic drive in *Drosophila*. *In*: "Edinburgh Symposium on the Genetics of the Spermatozoon" (Eds. R. A. Beatty and S. Gluecksohn-Waelsch). Bogtrykkeriet Forum, Copenhagen. Pp. 247–268.

POLICANSKY, D. and ELLISON, J. (1970). "Sex ratio" in *Drosophila pseudoobscura*: Spermiogenic failure. *Science, N.Y.* **169,** 888–889.

SANDLER, L. (1962). A directed, permanent, genetic change involving the segregation-distortion system in *Drosophila melanogaster*. *Am. Nat.* **96,** 161–166.

Sandler, L. and Carpenter, A. T. C. (1972). A note on the chromosomal site of action of *SD* in *Drosophila melanogaster*. *In* "Edinburgh Symposium on the Genetics of the Spermatozoon" (Eds. by R. A. Beatty and S. Gluecksohn-Waelsch). Bogtrykkeriet Forum, Copenhagen. Pp. 233–246.

Sandler, L. and Hiraizumi, Y. (1959). Meiotic drive in natural populations of *Drosophila melanogaster*. II. Genetic variation at the segregation-distorter locus. *Proc. Nat. Acad. Sci. U.S.A.* **45,** 1412–1422.

Sandler, L. and Hiraizumi, Y. (1960a). Meiotic drive in natural populations of *Drosophila melanogaster*. IV. Instability at the segregation-distorter locus. *Genetics* **45,** 1269–1287.

Sandler, L. and Hiraizumi, Y. (1960b). Meiotic drive in natural populations of *Drosophila melanogaster*. V. On the nature of the *SD* region. *Genetics* **45,** 1671–1689.

Sandler, L. and Hiraizumi, Y. (1961a). Meiotic drive in natural populations of *Drosophila melanogaster*. VII. Conditional segregation distortion: A possible nonallelic conversion. *Genetics* **46,** 585–604.

Sandler, L. and Hiraizumi, Y. (1961b). Meiotic drive in natural populations of *Drosophila melanogaster*. VIII. A heritable aging effect on the phenomenon of segregation-distortion. *Can. J. Genet. Cytol.* **3,** 34–46.

Sandler, L. and Rosenfeld, A. (1962). A genetically induced, heritable modification of segregation-distortion in *Drosophila melanogaster*. *Can. J. Genet. Cytol.* **4,** 453–457.

Sandler, L., Hiraizumi, Y. and Sandler, I. (1959). Meiotic drive in natural populations of *Drosophila melanogaster*. I. The cytogenetic basis of segregation-distortion. *Genetics* **44,** 233–250.

Stanley, H. P., Bowman, J. T., Romrell, L. J., Reed, S. C. and Wilkinson, R. F. (1972). Fine structure of normal spermatid differentiation in *Drosophila melanogaster*. *J. Ultrastruct. Res.* **41,** 433–466.

Sturtevant, A. H. and Dobzhansky, T. (1936). Geographical distribution and cytology of "sex-ratio" in *Drosophila pseudoobscura* and related species. *Genetics* **21,** 473–490.

Thompson, P. E. and Yamazaki, T. (1967). Translation and nonhomologous activity of Segregation-distorter (*SD*) in males of Drosophila. *Genetics* **56,** 592–593.

Tokuyasu, K. T., Peacock, W. J. and Hardy, R. W. (1972). Dynamics of spermiogenesis in *Drosophila melanogaster*. I. Individualization process. *Z. Zellforsch.* **124,** 479–506.

Trippa, G., Lovere, A., Micheli, A. and Miola, I. (1972). Frequencies of *SD* chromosomes in natural populations of *Drosophila melanogaster*. *Dros. Inf. Serv.* **49,** 81.

Waddle, F. (1973). Unpublished Ph.D. thesis, Bowling Green State University, Bowling Green, Ohio.

Yanagisawa, K., Dunn, L. C. and Bennett, D. (1961). On the mechanism of abnormal transmission ratios at the T locus in the house mouse. *Genetics* **46,** 1635–1644.

Zimmering, S. (1963). The effect of temperature on the meiotic loss of the Y chromosome in the male Drosophila. *Genetics* **48,** 133–138.

Zimmering, S. and Barbour, E. (1961). Modification of abnormal gametic ratios in Drosophila. II. Evidence for a marked shift in genetic ratios in early vs. later sperm batches from A-type Bar-stone translocation males. *Genetics* **46,** 1253–1260.

Zimmering, S. and Fowler, G. L. (1968). Progeny: sperm ratios and non-functional sperm in *Drosophila melanogaster*. *Genet. Res.* (*Camb.*) **12,** 359–363.

Zimmering, S. and Perlman, M. (1962). Modification of abnormal gametic ratios in Drosophila. III. Probable time of the A-type effect in Bar-stone translocation males. *Can. J. Genet. Cytol.* **4,** 333–336.

Zimmering, S., Barnabo, J. M., Femino, J. and Fowler, G. L. (1970a). Progeny: sperm ratios and segregation-distorter in *Drosophila melanogaster*. *Genetica* **41,** 61–64.

Zimmering, S., Sandler, L. and Nicoletti, B. (1970b). Mechanisms of meiotic drive. *A. Rev. Genet.* **4,** 409–436.

Appendix

The table provides the probits of $(2k-1)/k$ for various values of k. The increments on k are 0·001 for $0{\cdot}500 < k < 0{\cdot}999$ and 0·0001 for $k > 0{\cdot}9990$. The probit of $(2k-1)/k$ is defined as $m + 5$ where m is the number such that

$$\frac{2k-1}{k} = \int_{-\infty}^{m} \frac{1}{\sqrt{2\pi}} e^{-\frac{x^2}{2}} dx.$$

The procedure used to obtain m is discussed in the text.

k	0·000	0·001	0·002	0·003	0·004	0·005	0·006	0·007	0·008	0·009
0·50	$-\infty$	2·3473	2·5896	2·7406	2·8524	2·9421	3·0176	3·0829	3·1408	3·1928
0·51	3·2401	3·2837	3·3241	3·3617	3·3971	3·4304	3·4619	3·4919	3·5205	3·5478
0·52	3·5739	3·5990	3·6232	3·6465	3·6690	3·6908	3·7119	3·7324	3·7522	3·7716
0·53	3·7904	3·8087	3·8265	3·8439	3·8610	3·8776	3·8938	3·9098	3·9253	3·9406
0·54	3·9554	3·9703	3·9848	3·9990	4·0128	4·0264	4·0399	4·0531	4·0661	4·0789
0·55	4·0915	4·1040	4·1162	4·1283	4·1402	4·1519	4·1635	4·1749	4·1862	4·1974
0·56	4·2084	4·2192	4·2300	4·2406	4·2511	4·2614	4·2717	4·2818	4·2919	4·3018
0·57	4·3116	4·3214	4·3310	4·3405	4·3500	4·3593	4·3686	4·3778	4·3869	4·3959
0·58	4·4048	4·4137	4·4225	4·4312	4.4398	4·4484	4·4569	4·4653	4·4736	4·4819
0·59	4·4902	4·4983	4·5064	4·5145	4·5225	4·5304	4·5383	4·5461	4.5539	4·5616
0·60	4·5693	4·5769	4·5844	4·5920	4·5994	4·6069	4·6142	4·6216	4·6288	4·6361
0·61	4·6433	4·6504	4·6576	4·6646	4·6717	4·6787	4·6856	4·6926	4·6994	4·7063
0·62	4·7131	4·7199	4·7266	4·7333	4·7400	4·7466	4·7533	4·7598	4·7664	4·7729
0·63	4·7794	4·7858	4·7923	4·7987	4·8050	4·8114	4·8177	4·8240	4·8302	4·8365
0·64	4·8427	4·8489	4·8550	4·8612	4·8673	4·8734	4·8794	4·8855	4·8915	4·8975
0·65	4·9034	4·9094	4·9153	4·9212	4·9271	4·9330	4·9388	4·9446	4·9505	4·9562
0·66	4·9620	4·9678	4·9735	4·9792	4·9849	4·9906	4·9962	5·0019	5·0075	5·0131
0·67	5·0187	5·0243	5·0298	5·0354	5·0409	5·0464	5·0519	5·0574	5·0629	5·0684
0·68	5·0738	5·0792	5·0846	5·0900	5·0954	5·1008	5·1062	5·1115	5·1168	5·1222
0·69	5·1275	5·1328	5·1381	5·1434	5·1486	5·1539	5·1591	5·1644	5·1696	5·1748
0·70	5·1800	5·1852	5·1904	5·1956	5·2007	5·2059	5·2110	5·2162	5·2213	5·2264
0·71	5·2315	5·2366	5·2417	5·2468	5·2519	5·2570	5·2620	5·2671	5·2721	5·2772
0·72	5·2822	5·2872	5·2923	5·2973	5·3023	5·3073	5·3123	5·3173	5·3223	5·3272

Appendix—(*continued*)

k	0·000	0·001	0·002	0·003	0·004	0·005	0.006	0·007	0·008	0·009
0·73	5·3322	5·3372	5·3422	5·3471	5·3521	5·3570	5·3620	5·3669	5·3718	5·3768
0·74	5·3817	5·3866	5·3915	5·3964	5·4013	5·4062	5·4112	5·4160	5·4209	5·4258
0·75	5·4307	5·4356	5·4405	5·4454	5·4503	5·4551	5·4600	5·4649	5·4698	5·4746
0·76	5·4795	5·4844	5·4892	5·4941	5·4990	5·5038	5·5087	5·5136	5·5184	5·5233
0·77	5·5281	5·5330	5·5379	5·5427	5·5476	5·5524	5·5573	5·5622	5·5670	5·5719
0·78	5·5768	5·5816	5·5865	5·5914	5·5962	5·6011	5·6060	5·6108	5·6157	5·6206
0·79	5·6255	5·6304	5·6353	5·6402	5·6450	5·6500	5·6548	5·6598	5·6647	5·6696
0·80	5·6745	5·6794	5·6843	5·6893	5·6942	5·6991	5·7041	5·7090	5·7140	5·7189
0·81	5·7239	5·7288	5·7338	5·7388	5·7438	5·7488	5·7538	5·7588	5·7638	5·7688
0·82	5·7738	5·7789	5·7839	5·7890	5·7940	5·7991	5·8042	5·8092	5·8143	5·8194
0·83	5·8245	5·8296	5·8348	5·8399	5·8450	5·8502	5·8554	5·8606	5·8657	5·8709
0·84	5·8761	5·8814	5·8866	5·8918	5·8971	5·9024	5·9076	5·9129	5·9182	5·9236
0·85	5·9289	5·9342	5·9396	5·9450	5·9504	5·9558	5·9612	5·9666	5·9721	5·9776
0·86	5·9830	5·9886	5·9941	5·9996	6·0052	6·0107	6·0163	6·0220	6·0276	6·0332
0·87	6·0392	6·0446	6·0503	6·0560	6·0618	6·0676	6·0734	6·0792	6·0850	6·0909
0·88	6·0968	6·1027	6·1087	6·1146	6·1206	6·1267	6·1327	6·1388	6·1449	6·1510
0·89	6·1572	6·1634	6·1696	6·1759	6·1822	6·1885	6·1949	6·2012	6·2077	6·2141
0·90	6·2206	6·2272	6·2338	6·2404	6·2470	6·2537	6·2604	6·2672	6·2741	6·2809
0·91	6·2878	6·2948	6·3018	6·3089	6·3160	6·3231	6·3303	6·3376	6·3449	6·3523
0·92	6·3597	6·3672	6·3748	6·3824	6·3901	6·3978	6·4056	6·4135	6·4215	6·4295
0·93	6·4376	6·4458	6·4541	6·4624	6·4709	6·4794	6·4880	6·4967	6·5055	6·5144
0·94	6·5234	6·5325	6·5417	6·5510	6·5605	6·5701	6·5798	6·5896	6·5995	6·6096
0·95	6·6199	6·6302	6·6408	6·6515	6·6624	6·6734	6·6847	6·6961	6·7078	6·7196
0·96	6·7317	6·7440	6·7565	6·7693	6·7824	6·7957	6·8094	6·8233	6·8376	6·8523
0·97	6·8673	6·8828	6·8986	6·9150	6·9318	6·9491	6·9670	6·9856	7·0048	7·0247
0·98	7·0454	7·0670	7·0895	7·1132	7·1380	7·1641	7·1918	7·2211	7·2525	7·2862
0·99	7·3226	7·3623	7·4060	7·4547	7·5100	7·5741	7·6507	7·7468	7·8775	8·0899
k	0·0000	0·0001	0·0002	0·0003	0·0004	0·0005	0·0006	0·0007	0·0008	0·0009
0·999	8·0899	8·1211	8·1557	8·1944	8·2387	8·2904	8·3527	8·4315	8·5400	8·7190

16. The Genetics of the Y Chromosome

JOHN H. WILLIAMSON*

Department of Biology
The University of Calgary
Calgary, Alberta, Canada

I. The Y Chromosome

A. Cytology

The Y chromosome of *Drosophila melanogaster* first received attention during the consideration of the importance of chromosomes in genetic systems and of sex determination in Diptera. The occasional presence of a Y chromosome in females and absence in males were noted by Bridges (1916) in his classic paper on the chromosome theory of heredity. As the meiotic divisions of *Drosophila* are not ideal for cytological analyses early descriptions of the genome were usually obtained from mitotic (gonial) divisions in the ovary and from mitotic prophase in neuroblasts. In metaphase figures the Y chromosome is J-shaped and was described by

* Supported by the National Research Council of Canada.

Heitz (1933) as completely heterochromatic. Consistent with this description is the observation that in salivary gland cells the Y chromosome resides in the heterochromatic chromocenter (Hannah, 1951). Muller and Painter (1932) compared the heterochromatic (proximal) region of the X chromosome with the Y chromosome and concluded that these regions were genetically inert. On the assumption, however, that heterochromaticity is a *phase* and not a *kind* of chromatin, it is probable that in such cells as oogonia and neuroblasts the Y is heterochromatic, but becomes euchromatic at least in part in the primary spermatocyte (see Section IV). The major cytological characteristics of the Y chromosome are diagrammatically represented in Fig. 1 (after Cooper, 1959). The long arm of the Y (Y^L) is

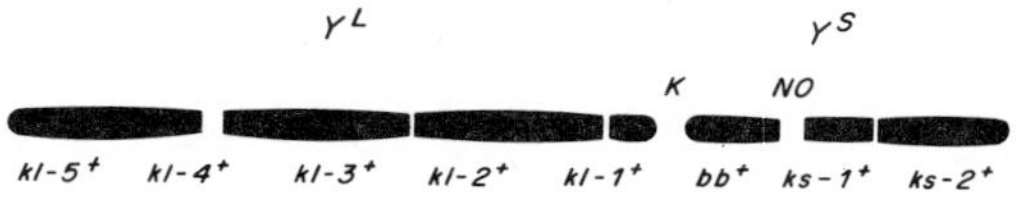

FIG. 1. A cytogenetic map of the Y chromosome (after Cooper, 1959). Y^L and Y^S: the long and the short arms of the Y chromosome; K: the centromere; NO: nucleolus organizer; bb^+: the locus of *bb* alleles; $kl\text{-}1^+$—$kl\text{-}5^+$: male fertility factors in Y^L; $ks\text{-}1^+$—$ks\text{-}2^+$: male fertility factors in Y^S. The order of the fertility factors are as indicated; their cytological location is not precisely known. The NO and *bb* locus are probably the same.

approximately 1·5 times as long as the short arm (Y^S). Y^L consists of four major heterochromatic blocks while Y^S consists of three major blocks. Implicit in this scheme is that each major block is probably an aggregate of several smaller units. There are three other major cytological landmarks on the Y, namely, the centromere, the nucleolar organizer region (NO) and a major constriction in Y^L. More recent data, discussed in subsequent sections, place two male fertility genes in Y^S distal to the NO and five male fertility genes in Y^L. Consideration of position-effect variegation in some rearrangements suggest that some of these five loci are located in the distal half of Y^L. The locus of bobbed (*bb*) alleles, assigned to the immediate vicinity of NO, has been considered the same as NO, i.e. the locus of those genes coding for ribosomal RNA (see Chapter 20 by Ritossa).

B. Genetics of Male Fertility

The Y chromosome of *D. melanogaster* is relatively large compared with the remainder of the genome, yet it carries very few known genetic loci. All but one of these function in the male, controlling differentiation of spermatids into functional sperm; the remaining locus is the bobbed locus. The Y chromosome is refractory to classical genetic techniques and has required unique genetic manipulation for its analysis. The presence of a Y chromosome in females and its absence in males is correlated with no immediately obvious phenotypic effect except that X0 males are completely sterile (Bridges, 1916). Cytological studies by Safir (1920) and Shen (1932) revealed that meiosis is regular in X0 males. They also described the processes of differentiation of spermatids in X0 males as being normal. However, these spermatids do not complete maturation nor do they become motile; instead they degenerate in the posterior regions of the testes and very few, if any, sperm enter the vasa efferentia. That each arm of the Y chromosome carries genetic information necessary for male fertility was demonstrated by Stern (1927, 1929) by separating the arms of the Y chromosome and demonstrating that male fertility requires the presence of both arms. Spontaneous exchange between the X and the Y chromosomes produced X chromosomes with an arm of the Y attached ($X \cdot Y^L$; $X \cdot Y^S$) and partial Y chromosomes, Y^S, Y^L, $Y^S \cdot Y^S$ ($= Y''$). Males of the genotypes X/Y^L, X/Y^S, $X \cdot Y^L$, $X \cdot Y^S$, $X \cdot Y^L/Y^L$ and $X \cdot Y^S/Y^S$ were completely sterile while $X \cdot Y^L/Y^S$ and $X \cdot Y^S/Y^L$ males were fully fertile. The male fertility factors in $\mathrm{Y^L}$ and $\mathrm{Y^S}$ were termed K_1 and K_2, respectively, with the *K* referring to complex; these are now known as *KL* and *KS* (Brosseau, 1960). Although Stern's experiments treated the arms of the Y chromosome as units, his choice of the term *complex* was fortunate.

The male fertility system on the Y chromosome was analysed in greater detail by Neuhaus (1938, 1939). He used a series of X-ray-induced Y;4 translocations to separate each fertility complex into several component parts. Only *T(Y;4)*'s demonstrating position-effect variegation of the normal allele of cubitus interruptus (ci^+) were utilized. The *T(Y;4)*'s were recovered and maintained in stock cultures with $X \cdot Y^S$ or $X \cdot Y^L$ chromosomes. Each *T(Y;4)* was tested to determine the presence of a complete set of Y chromosome fertility genes; those that did were not used. Neuhaus made crosses producing some males which carried one element from each of two *T(Y;4)*'s. If these two elements collectively carried the equivalent of a complete Y chromosome, the carrier male was fertile. If less than a complete Y chromosome was carried within the two elements, the carrier male was sterile. Complementation tests of this type led Neuhaus to postulate that ten male fertility genes are carried on the Y chromosome, five in each arm. One of the loci assigned to $\mathrm{Y^L}$ was postulated to have a homologous locus on the X chromosome. Neuhaus assumed that *T(Y;4)*'s exhibiting ci^+ variegation have breakpoints in distal regions of the arms of the Y chromosome (see Khovostova, 1939) and in his genetic map of the Y chromosome he thus placed the male fertility loci towards the end of each arm. The interstitial 85% of the Y chromosome he considered inert.

The experimental scheme and data of Neuhaus contain several intrinsic difficulties and inconsistencies as pointed out by Brosseau (1960) and Hess and Meyer (1968). The production of males carrying heterologous elements of Y;4 translocations required nondisjunctional events of low probability and these males could not be distinguished from regular males. In addition, there are several inconsistencies in the main table of results of the complementation tests. Neuhaus' contribution, however, was of major importance. Working with a dearth of genetic stocks and having to test very large numbers of males in a large series of combinations, he was able to demonstrate what Stern had predicted by the choice of the term "complex". Neuhaus had demonstrated that Stern's K_1 and K_2 were indeed complexes of genes. The absolute number was relatively unimportant.

A reinvestigation of the male fertility loci in the Y chromosome was undertaken by Brosseau (1960). He induced, by X-irradiation of y/y^+Y males, a series of Y chromosomes deficient for one or more of the male fertility factors. The mutant Y chromosomes were tested for complementation with both $X{\cdot}Y^L$ and $X{\cdot}Y^S$ chromosomes. Males that carried $X{\cdot}Y^L$ and a y^+Y chromosome mutant in Y^L but not in Y^S were fertile whereas this same y^+Y in combination with $X{\cdot}Y^S$ was sterile. Mutants in Y^S of the y^+Y were sterile in combination with $X{\cdot}Y^L$ and fertile with $X{\cdot}Y^S$. Sterility in both types of males identified Y chromosomes with mutants in each arm. Thirty-three of the deficient y^+Y chromosomes were mutant in Y^L and twelve were mutant in Y^S. Within each group, each mutant Y was tested for complementation in males carrying two mutant y^+Y chromosomes ($X/y^+Y^-/y^+Y^-$). Fertility of these males indicated that the two Y chromosomes collectively carried a complete set of male fertility loci. They would thereby not be deficient for the same locus. Sterility of $X/y^+Y^-/y^+Y^-$ males indicated that the two Y chromosomes share overlapping deficiencies. Brosseau's data are consistent with the model of a linear sequence of five fertility loci in the long arm of the Y chromosome and two fertility loci in the short arm. The difference between the numbers of loci in Neuhaus' and Brosseau's experiments is unimportant. One basic conclusion from both sets of data is that the Y chromosome is not an inert chromosome.

A series of the Brosseau mutant Y chromosomes has proven extremely useful in mapping Y chromosome breakpoints in rearrangements recovered from various experimental procedures. Prior to the establishment of these stocks, generally known as the "Brosseau-tester-Y-chromosomes", one could only determine if a rearrangement carried all of the Y chromosome fertility loci, a complete Y^L or a complete Y^S. This series of mutant Y chromosomes allows much more precision in determining which components of *KL* or *KS* are missing.

The male fertility loci in the Y chromosome can be altered by chemical mutagens and respond to such treatment in a manner not different from loci in euchromatic chromosomes (Williamson, 1968a, 1969a, 1970c). When males carrying the B^SYy^+ chromosome were fed ethyl methanesulfonate, male-sterility mutants in the Y chromosomes were recovered with a frequency of 2–2·5% of all tested Y chromosomes. As with loci in euchromatic chromosomes a high frequency of incomplete (mosaic) mutants could be recognized. Complementation tests with the Brosseau tester chromosome revealed that each of the seven male fertility loci mutated regularly as a consequence of treatment with EMS.

Complementation tests with the Brosseau stocks divided the sample of EMS-induced mutants into seven groups corresponding to the seven known loci. Each of these groups were tested for *intragenic* complementation in $X/B^SY^-y^+/B^SY^-y^+$ males where the two Y chromosomes are mutant in the same locus but are of different origin. Each of the seven male fertility loci were subdivided into more than one functional subunit (Williamson, 1972). The response of loci in the Y chromosome to EMS and the observed functional complementation of alleles tends to equate, at least partially, the Y chromosome genetic systems with those systems in euchromatic chromosomes. Obviously it is no longer appropriate to consider the Y chromosome basically different from any other chromosome.

Temperature-sensitive mutants in the male fertility loci of the Y chromosome can also be induced by chemical mutagens (Ayles *et al.*, 1973; Williamson, 1969a). Males carrying mutants of this type are fertile when reared at the permissive temperature (20–22°C) and sterile when reared at the restrictive temperature (28–29°C). The developmental aspects of *ts*-mutants are described by Ayles *et al.* (1973).

The cytological and genetic properties of the Y chromosome in *D. hydei* are described extensively by Hess in this volume.

In summary, the Y chromosome carries a genetic system controlling male fertility. This system is composed of at least seven genes, each of which is necessary for fertility; the linear sequence of these loci has been determined by deletion mapping. Chemical mutagens induce mutants in these loci, some of which are temperature-sensitive. Allelic complementation between mutants in all seven of the known loci has been observed.

II. Spermatogenesis

The formation of gametes in the male of *D. melanogaster* has now been described in detail both at the level of the light microscope and ultrastructurally. A definitive spermatogonium, after four mitotic divisions (the last three of these being synchronous), gives rise to a cyst of sixteen interconnected primary spermatocytes. Synchronous meiotic divisions in these cysts produce a syncytium of sixty-four spermatids. The synchrony observed during spermatogenesis continues throughout spermiogenesis, with the sixty-four spermatids differentiating into bundles of sixty-four sperm. Cooper (1950) has given an excellent, detailed description of the testis and of the various processes taking place in the testis of *D. melanogaster*.

III. Spermiogenesis

A. Normal Males

In *D. melanogaster* the meiotic divisions convert the sixteen-cell cysts of spermatocytes to cysts of sixty-four spermatids. Immediately after second-division cleavage the nucleus of the spermatid experiences a rapid increase in volume. The mitochondria coalesce to form a spheroid mass, the nebenkern, approximately the size of the nucleus. The centriole is located between the nucleus and the nebenkern. According to Cooper (1950) the center of the nucleus, the centriole and the center of the nebenkern define the axis of elongation of the spermatid. The centriole divides to form a pair, the proximal centriole near the nucleus and the distal centriole which elongates and initiates formation of the axial fiber. An acroblast forms apically from components of the Golgi apparatus while the nebenkern divides into two components between which the axial fiber grows. The axial fiber and nebenkern derivatives continue to elongate into a long sperm tail too thin to be observed with the light microscope as more than thread-like. During elongation of the spermatid the nuclear components combine to form a long, thin sperm head; drastic reduction of the amount of nuclear cytoplasm occurs concomitantly with nuclear condensation. The mature sperm measures 1·7–1·8 mm in length with the sperm head being less than 1/200th of the total length (Cooper, 1950). Hess and Meyer (1968) have divided the process of spermatid morphogenesis into eight stages. Although admittedly arbitrary, with no sharp cytological demarcation between stages, their subdivision of spermiogenesis has proved useful in comparative studies of the effects of Y chromosome deficiencies on spermiogenesis.

Ultrastructural descriptions of spermiogenesis in *Drosophila* and other insects have been given by Anderson (1967), Bairati (1967), Behne and Forer (1967), Daems *et al.* (1963), Kiefer (1966, 1969, 1970), Meyer (1968, 1972), Perotti (1969), Phillips (1970), Stanley *et al.* (1972), Tokuyasu *et al.* (1972a, b) and Yasuzumi *et al.* (1958). A typical cross section of a mature sperm from *D. melanogaster* reveals two major elements of the sperm tail. These are the paracrystalline derivatives of the nebenkern and the axial fiber complex. The axial fiber complex is made up of a pair of central microtubules and nine pairs of peripheral microtubules, generally considered typical of flagellar structures. In addition, the axial fiber complex contains paired satellites peripheral to the nine pairs of tubules, nine pairs of secondary fibers between the central pair and the peripheral pairs of tubules, and "spokes" of dense material joining these (Fig. 2).

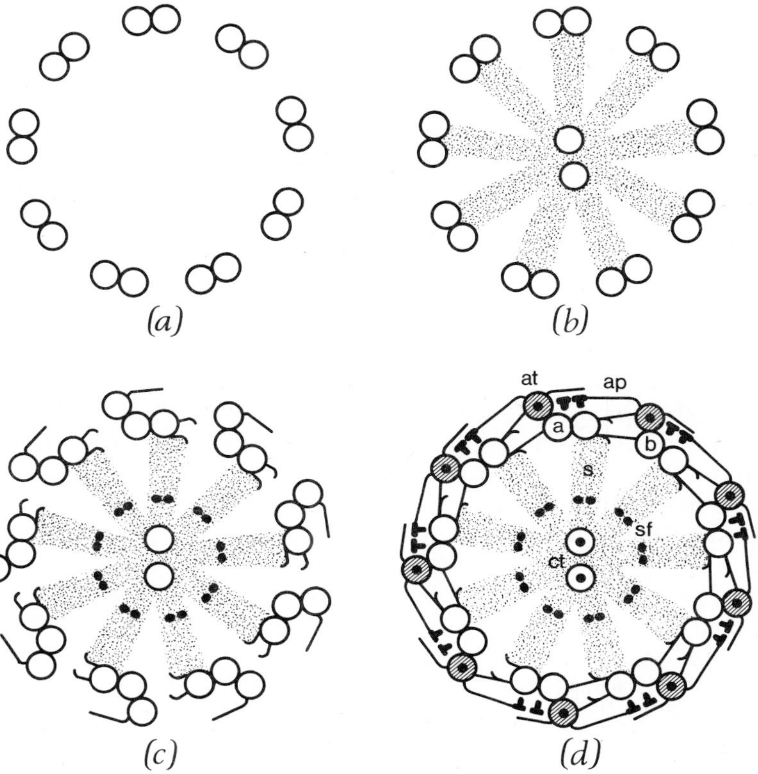

FIG. 2. Diagrammatic cross-section of the axial filament of immature and mature sperm. After Kiefer (1970) and Meyer (1968).

Development of the axial fiber complex appears to be an extension of, or initiated by, the distal centriole. The nine pairs of peripheral tubules are the first observed components of the developing axial fiber complex. Slightly later the central pair of microtubules are present and the material forming spokes between the central and peripheral tubules becomes visible. The accessory microtubules, which later form part of the satellites, are formed from one member of a pair of peripheral microtubules (the B fiber) while the other tubule forms a connecting fiber (the A fiber) between it and the adjacent pair of tubules. By the time of completion of the accessory tubules the spokes and secondary fibers are clearly defined and dense material forms adjacent to each accessory tubule. The accessory tubules and the central tubules become quite dense. The accessory tubules and the adjacent dense material form the satellites seen in cross sections of mature sperm. The accessory tubules and the central pair may contain a fiber along their inner axis (Kiefer, 1970).

The two nebenkern components of the early spermatid differentiate into paracrystalline material and form major and minor mitochondrial derivatives. The paracrystalline material of the nebenkern derivatives is regularly cross-striated with an average periodicity of 260 Å (Meyer, 1964; Perotti, 1969). The paracrystalline bodies parallel the longitudinal plane of the axial fiber complex and apparently contain respiratory proteins (Meyer, 1964).

The final stages of maturation of spermatids into functional spermatozoa have been detailed by Tokuyasu *et al.* (1972a, b). Spermatids contain a variety of cytoplasmic organelles that are not found in mature sperm (Hess and Meyer, 1968; Kiefer, 1969, 1970; Perotti, 1969). Tokuyasu *et al.* have described the mechanism of exclusion of these structures as one of the last events in maturation; the other final events are coiling of the sperm bundles in the terminal testicular regions and liberation of mature sperm from the bundles.

In the sixteen-cell-cyst stage of spermatogenesis the primary spermatocytes appear to be interconnected syncytially by interspermatocyte bridges as a consequence of incomplete cleavages during the synchronous mitotic divisions which result in the cysts of sixteen primary spermatocytes (King and Akai, 1971; Meyer, 1968). During spermiogenesis extensive networks of interspermatid bridges are observed (Bairati, 1967; Kiefer, 1966, 1969, 1970; Meyer, 1968). These interspermatid bridges probably are not related to the interspermatocyte bridges. The latter number only fifteen (or one less than the number of cells in the cyst) and are morphologically homogeneous while the interspermatid bridges are numerous and are morphologically quite variable. The process of individualization begins at the head region of the sperm bundle and traverses the length of the bundle. This morphogenetic process transforms the syncytial bundle of spermatids into bundles of mature spermatozoa each vested in its own membrane. During this process the syncytial bridges are removed, along with excess membranes, nucleoplasm and cytoplasm, unneeded organelles and abnormal spermatids. The cytological visualization of these processes of individualization of spermatids is a fusiform swelling of the bundle approximately 100 *micra* in length; this swelling is called the cystic bulge. The discarded material is contained at the distal end of the sperm bundle by the final form (waste bag) of the cystic bulge. After the sperm bundle is coiled this discarded material degenerates and is apparently ingested by the terminal epithelium of the testes.

This very precise ultrastructural description of the process of terminalization causes one to wonder if the processes that occur in the cystic bulge are the processes that are controlled by the male fertility genetic system of the *D. melanogaster* Y chromosome. Certainly in Y-deficient males of this species these processes are missing.

B. Y-deficient Males

Mature sperm are not found in the testes of males lacking a Y chromosome. Maturation of spermatids in these males does not proceed past stage 5 of spermiogenesis (Meyer, 1968) and reach a length of approximately 1·2 mm as compared with 1·7 mm for mature sperm. Developmental defects fall into two general classes, those affecting the differentiation of the mitochondrial derivative and those affecting the axial fiber complex. The spatial relationship between these two components of the sperm tail are often disorganized. In some cases a fiber complex is not attached to a nebenkern derivative, in some cases two complexes may be attached to one nebenkern derivative, while in still other cases a complex may be associated with more than one nebenkern derivative. The transformation of the nebenkern into paracystalline bodies normally begins at the junction of the axial complex and the nebenkern, but in X0 males transformation may begin at several points producing several paracrystalline bodies.

Axial fiber complexes in X0 males are surprisingly regular compared with the array of irregularities of the mitochondrial derivatives (Kiefer, 1970; Meyer, 1968, 1972). Most complexes contain all of the components of a normal axial fiber. Irregular complexes may be missing only the central pair of tubules or only a pair of peripheral tubules or sometimes both. Abnormal complexes, however, are at the same "stage" of development as the "regular" complexes.

Degeneration of the spermatid begins soon after it reaches stage 4 or 5 of maturation. Early degenerative processes result in disorganization of the axial fiber complex. The first observable consequences of degeneration begin with the separation of adjacent satellites, often resulting in loss of cylindrical organization of the complex. Next the integrity of the A and B fibers is lost, followed by the loss of the spokes and secondary fibers. Lastly the two central fibers, the accessory fibers and the non-tubular remains of the satellites are lost at approximately the same time. The observation of adjacent pairs of central fibers from degenerating fiber complexes led Kiefer (1970) to propose that the two central fibers are physically connected.

Complete deficiency of the Y chromosome apparently does not result in the inability to form the major components of normal spermatozoa. All of the observed effects appear to be consequences of loss of morphogenetic ability to properly assemble the structural components of the spermatid into a mature flagellum (Kiefer, 1969; Meyer, 1968, 1972). Thus the male fertility system of the Y chromosome functions in the morphogenesis of the sperm tail from components which must themselves be under the control of other genetic systems.

IV. Site of Y Chromosome Function

The genetic system of male fertility factors on the Y chromosome obviously functions during the processes of differentiation of spermatids into mature spermatozoa. In *D. melanogaster* the absence of one male fertility locus is essentially as detrimental to spermiogenesis as is the absence of the complete Y chromosome, although relatively minor differences have been reported (Kiefer, 1969; Meyer, 1969). The Y chromosome system appears to direct morphogenesis of pre-existing components of the mature sperm and does not code for their synthesis. There is no direct evidence as to the cell in which the primary function, transcription, of the male fertility system occurs. Indirect evidence strongly suggests that the Y chromosome functions in the primary spermatocyte. If the Y chromosome were considered to function after the first meiotic division one would have to explain the subsequent maturation of half the spermatids, those carrying an X chromosome but not a Y. Supporting this *a priori* argument that the Y chromosome must function in a diploid cell is the observation that spermatids are synthetically inactive (Olivieri and Olivieri, 1965). In addition, gametes lacking both an X and a Y are fully functional; indeed 50% of the gametes of males carrying a compound-XY and no free Y chromosome are of this class. Such considerations lead to the conclusion that the male fertility genes of the Y chromosome must be transcribed in diploid cells prior to meiosis and that the gene products, primary or secondary, are masked in some way and distributed more or less equally during the ensuing meiotic divisions to be utilized during spermiogenesis.

Two different lines of experimental evidence strongly imply that the primary spermatocyte is the cell in which the Y chromosome functions. The first of these is the "lampbrush-like" loops observed in primary spermatocytes. These have been described extensively in *D. hydei* where they are especially distinct and in more than 50 other species (Hess and Meyer, 1963, 1968). These loops are considered as cytological observations of functioning male fertility factors of the Y chromosome. Even more convincing are the data from temperature-sensitive mutations induced in several of the male fertility genes (Ayles *et al.*, 1973). Males carrying a Y chromosome with a temperature sensitive mutant in a fertility factor were fertile when reared at a low temperature (18–22°C) but were sterile when reared at 28–29°C. Males that were reared at the permissive temperature and exposed to the restrictive temperature for 24–48 hours became infertile within 5–6 days. Returning these males to the permissive temperature allowed a return of fertility after several days of sterility. Conversely sterile males reared at the restrictive temperature and maintained at the permissive temperature became fertile after 8–10 days. Consideration of the sequence of events that occur in the testes of *D. melanogaster* (Hannah-Alava, 1965) leads to the conclusion that the cell in which sensitivity to temperature is expressed must be the primary spermatocyte.

The possibility that the Y chromosome functions in the so-called "nutritive-cell" described by Guyénot and Naville (1929) should perhaps be considered. During maturation the sixty-four sperm occur in compact bundles with the sperm heads closely associated at one end and easily observed in orcein-stained preparations. With phase-contrast microscopy the sperm heads often appear to be embedded in a large cell, one bundle per cell. What appears to be actual fusion of the cytoplasm of the "nutritive cell" and that of the spermatids has been described (Hess and Meyer, 1968; Kaplan and Gugler, 1969). Maturation of sperm bundles occurs in the distal regions of the testes and, correspondingly, the "nutritive cells" are reportedly found in those regions. As maturation of the sperm bundle advances the "nutritive cell" becomes smaller and degenerates into a mass of cellular debris (Olivieri and Olivieri, 1965). As sperm of Y deficient males fail to attain motility Stern (1936) and Stern and Hadorn (1938) suggested that the attribute of motility, and thereby functionality, may be conferred to sperm by extra-spermatocytic factors. This suggestion may be restated to imply that the Y chromosome functions in the "nutritive cell".

That the "nutritive cell" is not the site of function of the Y chromosome can be concluded from the results of several experiments. Stern and Hadorn's transplantation experiments, wherein larval testes from Y-deficient genotypes were transplanted into larvae of fertile genotypes, failed to generate recovery of gametes of the transplanted tissue although tissue fusion occurred resulting in the mosaic testes in adults. The reciprocal experiment of transplantation of larval testes of fertile genotypes into larvae of sterile genotypes also produced adults with mosaic gonads but did not allow recovery of gametes from the transplanted genotypes. If the "nutritive cell" were the site of function of the Y chromosome, one might expect that sperm from sterile genotypes might develop under the influence of "nutritive cells" of fertile genotypes, producing functional gametes. Of course such would not be the case if the "nutritive cell" were always of direct cell lineage as is the sperm bundle. This, however, seems unlikely since cysts of spermatocytes are generated in the apical portion of the testis and move distally, while "nutritive cells" are found in the distal half of the testes. That "nutritive cells" do not synthesize RNA (Olivieri and Olivieri, 1965) implies that these cells are not the site of transcription of the Y chromosome (or that the technique used was not sensitive enough to recognize such synthesis). In X0 males of *D. hydei* spermatogenesis is blocked in prophase of meiosis I; in males with partial Y chromosomes the stage of morphogenesis attained by spermatids is directly dependent on how much of the Y chromosome is present (Meyer, 1969). Both of these observations argue that the "nutritive cell" is not the cell in which the Y chromosome male fertility genes function. Likewise, the temperature shift studies using *ts*-male-sterility mutants deny the suggestion that the "nutritive cells" convey motility on spermatozoa. Finally, capitalizing on the characteristic of "incompleteness" of mutants induced by chemical mutagens, genetic tests demonstrated that males mosaic for male-sterility mutants in the Y chromosome could be recognized when the tested males carried an additional complete Y chromosome (Williamson, 1970b). Mosaicism for male sterility mutants could not be recognized in regular (X/Y) males.

The very existence of "nutritive cells" is questioned by Tokuyasu *et al.* (1972a). They describe a fusiform swelling which traverses the spermatid bundle individualizing spermatids (Section III, A). They suggest that the so-called "nutritive cell" is in fact their "cystic bulge". It seems reasonable to assume that the "nutritive cells", which are described as being limited to the distal half of the testes, are very fragile, are not synthetically active, and which degenerate at the completion of spermatid maturation and are observed for only a few sperm bundles in a preparation, do not in fact exist and that these observations were really concerned with the cystic bulges of Tokuyasu *et al.*

V. Model of Y Chromosome Function

There now exists rather extensive genetic (Williamson, 1970a, b, 1972; Ayles *et al.*, 1973), cytological (Hess and Meyer, 1968) and biochemical (Hennig, 1967, 1968) evidence that the Y chromosome of *Drosophila* functions in the primary spermatocyte. The high frequency of mutations induced by EMS and the recovery of temperature-sensitive mutations in the male fertility genes of the Y chromosome suggest that these loci are unique sequences of genetic information. The argument is that genetic loci that respond frequently to mutagens that primarily induce missense mutations, as does EMS, are not expected to be composed of repetitive sequences. An even stronger argument, made by Ayles *et al.*, is that it is highly unlikely that recessive temperature-sensitive mutants would be induced in reiterated loci. Yet Hennig's experiments clearly demonstrated species of RNA limited to the male, indeed limited to the testes, that are complementary to the DNA of the Y chromosome. The conditions of his experiments were such that one can only conclude that there are functional regions in the Y chromosome made up of reiterated sequences.

A model of function of the Y chromosome male fertility factors based on these considerations was recently suggested (Williamson, 1972). The model proposes that in mature sperm the fertility factors are unique sequences. Therefore treatment of sperm with EMS will produce a high frequency of sterility mutants. In the primary spermatocyte, that cell in which the fertility factors function, these unique sequences are amplified prior to transcription. The lampbrush-like loops in the primary spermatocyte may be cytological consequences of amplification. The experiments of Hennig measured hybridization of these amplified sequences and the male specific species of RNA. After transcription the fertility loci return to the unique sequence condition. Admittedly this model is overly simplified and makes several gross assumptions. More extensive biochemical and developmental data will be required for a definitive description of the function of the male fertility loci during spermiogenesis.

VI. The Y Chromosome in other Genetic Systems

A. Bobbed Mutants

The bobbed (*bb*) locus is covered in detail in this volume by Ritossa (Chapter 20) and will be only briefly mentioned here as it applies to the Y chromosome. The *bb* locus in the Y is in the proximal half of the short arm of the Y chromosome. Alleles of *bb* can be found in Y chromosomes from wild populations (Barbour and Zimmering, 1961), in laboratory stocks (Barr, 1970), and can be induced by chemical mutagens (Williamson, 1970b). As is the case in the X chromosome, *bb* mutants in the Y are usually deletions for parts of the DNA that codes for the production of ribosomal RNA (Ritossa and Spiegelman, 1965; Ritossa, 1968, 1972). Two temperature-sensitive *bb* mutants in the Y chromosome have been shown to be partial deletions of the rDNA of the NO region (Procunier, unpublished observations); in both cases the restrictive temperature is low (18°C). The phenomenon of magnification (Ritossa, this volume) of *bb* mutants in the Y is reported to occur as it does in *bb* mutants in the X chromosome (Boncinelli *et al.*, 1972 Ritossa *et al.*, 1971; Ritossa, 1972) There is, however, some question as to whether the control of gene multiplicity in the NO region of the Y chromosome is exactly the same as in the X chromosome (Tartof, 1971, 1973; Williamson, Procunier and Church, 1973).

B. Quantitative Traits

Effects of the Y chromosome on polygenic traits have been reported although in no instance are the data convincing. Biometric analysis of seven characteristics were carried out by Neuhaus (1938) comparing males deficient for an arm of the Y chromosome with males carrying a complete Y chromosome. In only one trait, the length of the third longitudinal wing vein, was there a significant difference between genotypes. An effect of the Y chromosome on the frequency of particular classes of chaetae was reported by Mather (1944); however, Cooper (1945) pointed out major deficiencies in the genetic regime employed by Mather. The effects of the Y chromosome on cell size and wing hair numbers (Barigozzi, 1948a, b; Barigozzi and DePasquale, 1953) are likewise equivocal. The essence of this criticism, and that of Cooper towards Mather's data, is simply that adequate genetic controls were not established. Even if the Y chromosome does carry systems of "polygenes" these systems must of necessity be relatively unimportant since X0 males are morphologically quite normal.

C. Position-effect Variegation

One of the genetic effects of the Y chromosome is the modification of expression of position-effect variegation. Variegation is the production of a somatically mosaic pattern of a phenotype and is reviewed in this volume by Spofford. In *Drosophila* most variegated position effects are associated with chromosomal rearrangements, although rearrangements are not an absolute prerequisite of variegation (Lewis, 1930; Cooper, 1956; Steinberg, 1943). Variegating mutants may behave either as recessives or as dominants and in both classes the degree of expression of a mutant phenotype may be modified by cultural conditions and by genetic background. Suppression of variegation of the white locus, R(w^+), by the Y chromosome was first reported by Gowen and Gay (1933); XXY females and XYY males carrying a variegating R(w^+) have much less mutant tissue in their eyes than do regular females and males of otherwise similar genotype. The absence of the Y chromosome in X0 males caused a marked increase in the amount of mutant tissue in the eye of R(w^+) males (Schultz, 1936). Suppression of variegation by the addition of the Y chromosome to the genome, appears to be a general phenomenon (see R. F. Grell, 1959; Altorfer, 1967). The only definite exception is the light gene, mutants of which dilute the pigments in the eye to approximately 10% of normal. The presence of an extra Y chromosome enhances variegation of R(lt^+), while X0 males demonstrate suppressed variegation of R(lt^+) (Schultz, 1936). In a study that may well be used as a model for control of genetic and environmental backgrounds, R. F. Grell (1959) demonstrated that expression of R(ci^+) was suppressed by a supernumerary Y chromosome and suppressed even more by two supernumerary Y chromosomes. Y-suppressed lethals behave in a similar manner, some are suppressed by one Y chromosome while a few are suppressed by two Y chromosomes (Lindsley *et al.*, 1960).

A series of Y chromosome fragments were tested by Baker and Spofford (1959) for their effects on the expression of mottled eyes in flies carrying *Dp*(w^m) [=$T(1;3)N^{264-58}$]. Variegation was scored both visually and by chromatographic analysis of pigments. The Y chromosome fragments differed markedly in their ability to suppress variegation of the R(w^+), some being even more effective than the complete Y chromosome. Baker and Spofford speculated that the Y chromosome may be subdivided into several functional units. Brosseau (1964) suggested that a locus near $kl\text{-}2^+$ in Y^L and another proximal to $ks\text{-}1^+$ in Y^S were responsible for the suppression of position-effect variegation by the Y chromosome. However, a rather extensive analysis by Benner (1971) strongly suggests that there are no regions of the Y chromosome which specifically suppress variegation.

In his analysis of segregation in complex hyperploids Cooper (1956) observed that some individuals of both sexes had pale, washed-out areas in the posterior 20% of both eyes. Genetic and cytological observations revealed that this "blotching" of the eye was a consequence of two supernumerary Y chromosomes. Associated with this mottling caused by Y chromosome hyperploidy was frequent crippling due to developmental anomalies of the legs as well as coarseness and reduced transparency of the wings. Males with three Y chromosomes were sterile, as Schultz had reported earlier (Morgan *et al.*, 1934); such males copulated but did not transfer sperm to the female. Morphologically the testes and genitalia appeared normal and meiosis was regular; bundles of normal-appearing spermatozoa were produced but did not become motile and degenerated in the posterior regions of the testes. Thus the phenotype of sterility in males with three Y chromosomes parallels that in males deficient for a Y chromosome. Apparently the presence of two supernumerary Y chromosomes upsets the genetic balance of the male genome. Indeed, Cooper suggested the imbalance caused by three supernumerary Y chromosomes is lethal.

The fertility of females varies inversely with Y chromosome hyperploidy (R. F. Grell, 1959). Females with one Y chromosome were approximately 60% as productive as those with no Y chromosome while females with two Y chromosomes were only 15% as productive as the controls. Grell's data may be complicated by the fact that the tested females were also homozygous for five recessive mutants and heterozygous for an autosomal translocation. Some stocks of females with two Y chromosomes are quite fertile, although comparative studies have not been made.

D. Nucleic Acids

The metabolism of nucleic acids in the oocyte of *D. melanogaster* is affected by the presence of a Y chromosome. The effects of Y chromosome hyperploidy is greater than the addition of its own constitutive components. Microspectrophotometric measurements of the cytoplasm of immature oocytes in XX and XXY females revealed that absorption at 257 mμ was approximately 27% greater in XXY oocytes than in XX oocytes (Caspersson and Schultz, 1938). This difference was rather consistent regardless of the size of the oocytes. Caspersson and Schultz proposed that the XXY oocyte contained greater amounts of pentose-nucleic-acids than did the XX oocyte. This conclusion was questioned by Callan (1948) who measured the RNA contents of fertilized eggs from XX and XXY females by the rather imprecise furfural reaction.

Chemical determinations of DNA and RNA in mature salivary gland cells of XX and XXY females and XY and X0 males were made by Patterson *et al.* (1954). Females were found to have higher levels of both DNA and RNA than did males, presumably due to the second X chromosome. The addition or deficiency of a Y chromosome had no measurable effect on the content of either class of nucleic acids in salivary gland cells. This is consistent with the fact that in salivary gland cell nuclei the Y chromosome is found in the chromocenter and does not undergo polytenization (Hannah, 1951). Obviously one cannot compare these results with those from immature oocytes, the two types of cells being very different. There is also no apparent quantitative effect of the Y chromosome on RNA content in the adult (Altrofer, 1953; Kiefer, 1968).

The Y chromosome can be detected cytologically in the nurse cells of XXY females as a discrete heterochromatic body (Schultz, 1941, 1956; Freed and Schultz, 1956). The size of the Y-chromatin body increases during vitellogenesis but at a much slower rate than does the remainder of the genome which undergoes endopolyploidy to 1024-ploid. However, the effects of the Y chromosome on DNA content of the nurse cells do not correspond to its relative cytological size in these cells. Its presence increases the DNA levels of nurse cell nuclei by 11% in *C(1)RM*/Y females to 35% in X/$Y^S EN{\cdot}Y^L$ females; in either case the increase is greater than the DNA in the Y chromosome.

Not only does the Y chromosome increase the amount of DNA in the nurse cell nuclei, but it induces changes in base composition of the RNA extracted from the cytoplasm of mature unfertilized oocytes (Levenbook *et al.*, 1958). The total amount of RNA is not different in XX and XXY eggs, but the proportion of adenine is greater in XXY eggs. This is the apparent explanation of the early observation of Caspersson and Schutz that UV-absorption is greater in immature XXY oocytes compared with XX immature oocytes. Thus Callan's objections were correct, although not necessarily for the right reasons. Probably the amounts of RNA are not different in the two types of immature oocytes; instead the XXY oocytes have higher levels of adenine which account for the observed increase in UV absorption.

The total content of pyrimidines in XX and XXY oocytes is the same; however, cytosine is found only in trace amounts in XXY eggs but in sizeable amounts in XX eggs (Travaglini *et al.*, 1958). The converse is true for thymine. That the Y chromosome has effects on nucleic acid metabolism in the oocyte is obvious from these studies. However, the hypothesis that "heterochromatin" acts as a controlling factor in nucleic acid metabolism remains highly speculative.

In *D. melanogaster* the copolymer of deoxyadenylate and deoxythymidylate, dAT, has a very low buoyant density in CsCl gradients ($\rho = 1{\cdot}669$) and is a mixture composed of 83% alternating dAT, 15% apposed dAT and 2% poly dG·dC (Travaglini *et al.*, 1968; Fansler *et al.*, 1970). This unusual DNA comprises approximately 4% of the total DNA of wild type embryos, 2–16 hours into development, while similar embryos carrying an extra Y chromosome contain approximately 6% dAT (Blumenfeld and Forrest, 1971). Adult X0 males contain approximately 2% dAT. Blumenfeld and Forrest suggested that the Y chromosome carries a high concentration of dAT. They also determined the proportion of dAT in embryos carrying partial Y chromosomes [Y^S, $Y^S{\cdot}Y^S$, $sc{\cdot}Y^L$ ($=Y^L{\cdot}sc)^{S1}$]; the proportion of dAT varied from 5·4% to 6·5% of the embryonic DNA. Their choice of partial Y chromosomes to manipulate the genome resulted in manipulation, not just of arms of the Y chromosome, but of the number of NO regions in the tested genomes. All of the tested Y-fragments carry bb^+, including $sc{\cdot}Y^L$. Thus Blumenfeld and Forrest's highly speculative hypothesis may be altered to suggest that poly dAT is associated with the NO regions of the X and Y chromosomes. The dAT in *D. melanogaster* is differentially under-replicated in polytene cells (Blumenfeld and Forrest, 1972). This observation is consistent with their suggestion that the Y chromosome is dAT-rich, for in polytene cells the Y chromosome is located in the chromocenter and does not participate in polytenization.

In their characterization of the classes of DNA in *D. melanogaster*, Travaglini *et al.* (1972a) found in the unfertilized egg, which has no Y chromosome, that 30% of the total DNA is dAT. After fertilization the percentage of dAT decreases and in the pre-larval embryo is only 3·8% of the total DNA. In addition, they found that the proportion of dAT varied from 3·8% to 6% of the total DNA in pre-larval embryos of different wild type strains. On the basis of these data they suggested that the dAT in the *Drosophila* embryo is not uniquely associated with the Y chromosome. The dAT found in different species of *Drosophila* differs in a phylogenetic manner; indeed, *D. hydei* has no detectable dAT (Travaglini *et al.*, 1972b).

E. MISCELLANEOUS

Meiotic conjunction of the X and the Y chromosomes in males occurs between specialized regions of these chromosomes and not merely as a consequence of general pairing capabilities of heterochromatic regions (Cooper, 1964). These localized regions of conjunctive competence, called collochores, may be considered as chromosomal organelles dividing the heterochromatic regions of these chromosomes into conjunctively active and inert regions. That collochores are differentiated regions of the chromosomes remains somewhat hypothetical as no corresponding morphological features of chromosomes can be observed.

Interaction of the Y chromosome in several other genetic systems has been reported. The rate of meiotic loss of the Y chromosome depends on the temperature at which males are reared (Zimmering, 1963). The *k* value of *SD–72* (Segregation distorter) varies with Y chromosomes of different origins (Enns, 1970). In another meiotic mutant system, *RD* (Recovery disrupter) the *R* value (= sex ratio) varies with different Y chromosomes (Hanks, 1970; Williamson, unpublished observations). In compound-X females carrying two different Y-chromosome-fragments distinct disjunctional properties could be assigned to specific fragments (Brown, 1969).

VII. Marked Y Chromosomes

Conventions used to describe marked Y chromosomes were established by Brosseau *et al.* (1961). The long arm of the Y chromosome is considered its left arm such that the symbol Y infers the order: the long arm, the centromere and the short arm ($Y^L \cdot Y^S$). The symbol Y in combination with the genetic symbol of the marker used denotes a specific marked Y chromosome. If the marker is located on Y^L its symbol will precede the symbol Y (a^+Y); if the marker is on Y^S its symbol follows Y (Ya^+). Information concerning the origin and the relative position of genetic components is not conveyed by this system. The genetic composition of a normal Y chromosome is expressed as $KL \cdot bb^+ KS$ and that of the marker segment as $a^+\text{–}b^+$ where a^+ and b^+ are outside loci included in the heterologous segment. If the order of $a^+\text{–}b^+$ is not known these symbols are enclosed in parentheses, e.g. $KL\ a^+\text{–}b^+ \cdot bb^+\ KS$ *vs* $KL\ (a^+\text{–}b^+)\cdot bb^+\ KS$.

The relatively minor effects of hyperploidy for the Y chromosome allow its use in a variety of experimental designs not available for other chromosomes. Marked Y chromosomes carry normal alleles of small heterologous segments of the genome. Not only do they allow one to follow the meiotic behavior of the Y chromosome, but they have been very useful in intensive studies of the segment of the genome covered by the marked Y (Lifschytz and Falk, 1969a, b), in selective "kill" systems and in selective recovery systems wherein the male with a normal Y may be inviable.

The first of the marked Y chromosomes were the X-ray-induced bw^+Y of Dempster and the y^+Y ($=sc^8Y$) of Muller (1948). Lindsley and Grell (1968) describe the y^+Y chromosome as being X-ray-induced although Muller's original note leads one to believe that it arose spontaneously. Cooper (1952) speculated that the original Y chromosome giving rise to y^+Y may have had a history of irradiation. As is obvious from Fig. 3 these two marked Y chromosomes were used extensively in the derivation of a variety of marked Y chromosomes and of Y chromosome fragments, both marked and unmarked.

The precise origin of the bw^+Y was not recorded although it is known to be X-ray-induced and that a segment of the right arm of chromosome 2 was translocated to Y^L. Baker (1955) suggested that this segment was inserted in Y^L proximal to the *KL* fertility complex. The translocated segment reportedly carries salivary gland chromosome bands 59E1–2 through 60E3 (Gersh, 1956). This is probably an underestimate since the *bw* locus was placed in bands 59D9–59E2 by Slatis (1955). Genetically the insertion includes bw^+ (104·5) to ba^+ (107·4), inclusively (Brosseau *et al.*, 1961). The bw^+Y is thus designated $KL(bw^+\text{–}ba^+) \cdot bb^+KS$. Brosseau *et al.* claim that the meiotic behavior of bw^+Y is normal, that viability is not affected, but that two doses of bw^+Y are lethal. In my experience stocks carrying this Y chromosome are not as healthy as wild type stocks and are easily lost.

The y^+Y chromosome occurred as a recombinant in the progeny of males carrying $In(1)sc^8$ and an unmarked Y chromosome (Muller, 1948).

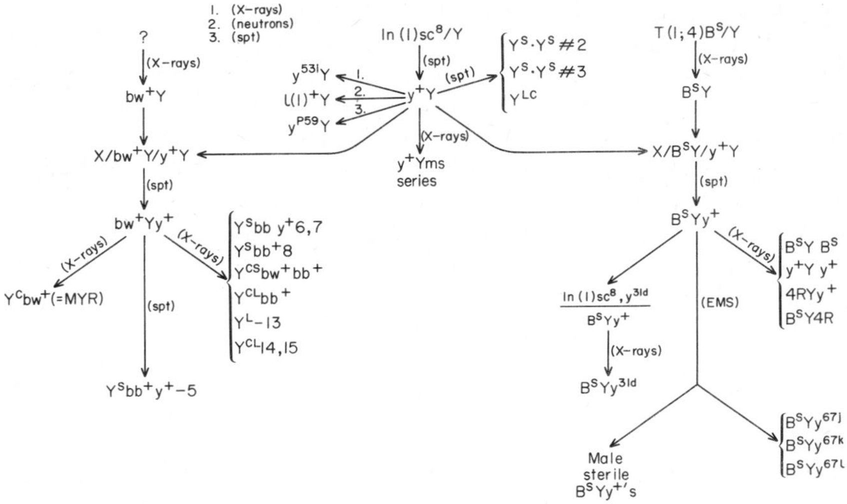

FIG. 3. A pedigree of marked Y chromosomes and Y chromosome fragments derived from the *bw*$^+$ *Y* and the *y*$^+$ *Y* chromosomes; spt = spontaneous; X-rays = X-ray-induced; neutrons = neutron-induced; EMS = ethyl methanesulfonate induced. All genetic symbols are described in detail in Lindsley and Grell (1968).

The exchange event occurred between the distally displaced hetero chromatic region of *In(1)sc*^{8}, distal to *bb*$^+$, and the long arm of the Y chromosome distal to the *KL* fertility complex. The long arm of the y^+Y chromosome was described by Muller as longer than a normal Y^L, being about as long as the somatic metaphase X chromosome. The y^+Y carries the tip of the X chromosome including *l(1)J1*$^+$, y^+, *ac*$^+$ and *Hw*$^+$ but not *sc*$^+$. The *Hw*$^+$ locus variegates; two doses of the *sc*^{8} duplication produces the Hairy-wing phenotype (Williamson, 1968b). In the same report describing y^+Y Muller described a partial Y chromosome $sc^{V1}{\cdot}Y^S$, carrying *KS* and y^+, a recombinant recovered from *In(1)sc*^{V1}/Y males.

A variety of complete and partial Y chromosomes have been generated from the y^+Y, some occurring spontaneously and some induced. The partial Y chromosomes Y^S, $Y^S{\cdot}Y^S$#2 and #3, and Y^{LC}[=*R(Y)L*], recognized by loss of y^+, were recovered by Muller (1948) as spontaneous recombinants from $X{\cdot}Y^S/y^+Y$ males. An X-ray-induced *y* mutant, $y^{53i}Y$, was recovered by Lüning (1953) and a spontaneous *y* mutant, $y^{P59}Y$, was recovered by Meyer (1959). Muller treated males carrying the y^+Y with neutrons and induced the *l(1)J1*$^+$*Y* chromosome, presumably deficient for the loci of y^+ and *ac*$^+$ (Muller, 1954).

The first Y chromosome carrying two genetic markers (other than the male fertility loci) was recovered by Cooper (1952) as a product of spontaneous recombination in males carrying both the bw^+Y and the y^+Y chromosomes. The bw^+Yy^+ arose as a consequence of the sc^8 duplication on Y^L of the y^+Y moving to the short arm of the bw^+Y. Cooper suggested that the sc^8 duplication in bw^+Yy^+ may be interstitial in Y^S. That y^+ is carried by Y^S was demonstrated by testing a series of spontaneous detachments of *C(1)RM, y ct f/bw⁺ Yy⁺* females. Since spontaneous detachments usually carry one or the other fertility complexes of the Y chromosome Cooper's detachments carried either bw^+ or y^+; males carrying the y^+ detachment and Y^{LC} were fertile while those carrying a y^+ detachment and Y^S or $Y^S \cdot Y^S$ were sterile.

Treatment of males carrying the $bw^+ Yy^+$ with X-rays induced a ring Y chromosome carrying complete male fertility complexes and bw^+ but not y^+ (Oster and Iyengar, 1955). This ring Y chromosome is $Y^C bw^+$, originally labelled MYR (marked Y ring). Baker (1955, 1957) generated a variety of partial Y chromosomes by irradiating the $bw^+ Yy^+$. Some carried bw^+ and some carried y^+ while others carried neither marker. Both Y^L and Y^S were recovered as rods and as rings. The most useful of these has been those that carry both bb^+ and y^+. At least one spontaneous Y^S fragment marked with y^+, $Y^S\ bb^+\ y^+$ –5, was recovered by Baker.

A different marked Y chromosome was induced by X-rays by Muller and Edmundson (1957). In this case a transposition of the euchromatic arm of chromosome 4 into the long arm of the Y was recovered as a fully functional Y chromosome. Two doses of this Y chromosome, *4Y* (=*Tp4; Y*), is fully viable and fertile in both sexes in the absence of free fourth chromosomes. Whether 4R is actually inserted into the Y chromosome or is carried distally on Y^L has not been demonstrated. *4Y* may be similar to the Y–4R interchange products discussed by Parker and Williamson (Chapter 27). Genetically *Tp4·Y* is $[KL(ci^+–spa^+)] \cdot bb^+\ KS$.

The usefulness of all of these marked Y chromosomes requires that the remainder of the homologous loci be mutant, i.e. either *y* or *bw*, or both (if *4Y* is used then ey^R or *spa* would be appropriate). Brosseau and Lindsley (1958) constructed a Y chromosome marked with the dominant eye mutant Bar–Stone (B^S), alleviating the problem of homozygosing all experimental stocks for *y*, *bw*, etc. The scheme used to generate the B^SY is shown in Fig. 4. They first produced a female heterozygous for $T(1;4)B^S$ and an attached XY chromosome (108–9 of Parker). $T(1;4)B^S$ is a translocation with the break in the X chromosome immediately distal to spa^+, the distal-most known locus on the fourth chromosome. One of the segregation classes was recovered in males carrying the $X^D4^P\cdot$ element of $T(1;4)B^S$ and a crossover product involving the attached-XY and the $4^DX^P\cdot$ element of $T(1;4)B^S$. These males, $X^D4^P\cdot$; $4^DX^PY^L\cdot Y^S/0$, carry the equivalent of a complete X and a complete Y chromosome. The males were then mated to compound-X females carrying no free Y chromosome to increase the number of X^D4^P·; $4^DX^PY^L$·Y^S/0 males. These were irradiated and mated to compound-X females. Progeny females carrying the dominant marker B^S were recovered and mated to regular males. The male progeny, carrying B^S, were tested for fertility. One fertile male carried a complete Y chromosome marked with B^S. The major part of X^P in the $4^DX^PY^L$·Y^S element had been deleted. Genetically the B^SY is 4^DB^S–(*su*)f^+KL·bb^+KS (Zimmering, 1959); its meiotic behavior is regular. Both males and females carrying a supernumerary B^SY are viable and fertile.

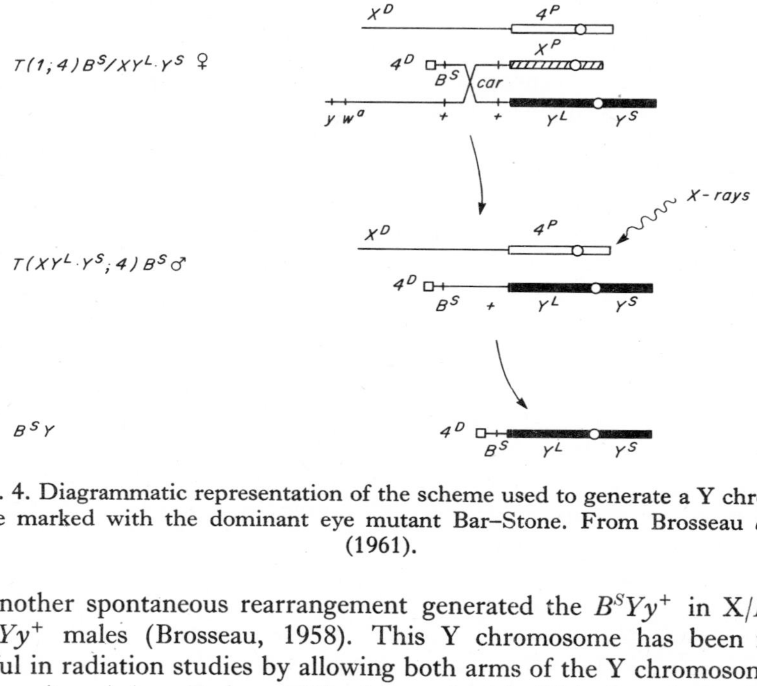

FIG. 4. Diagrammatic representation of the scheme used to generate a Y chromosome marked with the dominant eye mutant Bar–Stone. From Brosseau *et al.* (1961).

Another spontaneous rearrangement generated the B^SYy^+ in X/B^SY/bw^+Yy^+ males (Brosseau, 1958). This Y chromosome has been most useful in radiation studies by allowing both arms of the Y chromosome to be monitored (see Parker, 1968a for methods). This first derivative of this marked Y chromosome, B^SYy^{31d}, was obtained by irradiating females carrying both B^SYy^+ and $In(1)sc^8$, y^{31d} (Brosseau *et al.*, 1961). Irradiation of the B^SYy^+ has generated isomarked Y chromosomes and Y chromosome fragments, B^SY B^S and y^+Yy^+, in addition to $4RYy^+$ and B^SY4R chromosomes (Parker, 1965, 1967; Williamson, 1969b, 1970a). Treatment of the B^SYy^+ chromosome with the chemical mutagen ethyl methanesulfonate changed y^+ to y alleles and induced mutants in the male fertility loci (Williamson, 1970b).

Probably the most useful marked Y chromosomes other than the B^SYy^+ are the male sterile y^+Y's induced by Brosseau (1960). Brosseau (1964), Lucchesi (1965), Parker (1965, 1967, 1968a), Williamson (1969b, 1970a, 1972) and Benner (1971, 1972) have used the Brosseau tester stocks extensively. Prior to the establishment of the Brosseau deficient Y chromosomes rearrangements could only be identified as carrying a complete set of the Y chromosome fertility factors, a complete *KL* or a complete *KS*. Breaks in the Y chromosome separating the loci within *KL* or *KS* could not be precisely localized. Detachments of compound X chromosomes are readily recognized by linkage of a Y chromosome marker, either B^S or y^+, with X chromosome markers. Complementation tests using deficient Y chromosomes will determine the location of the induced break in the Y chromosome. Males carrying the detachment and a free Y chromosome are first crossed to compound-X females carrying no Y chromosome, e.g. *C(1)RM*/0, and the male progeny tested. Fertility of these males means that a complete complement of Y fertility genes are carried by the detachment. In such cases the break in the Y chromosome occurred distal to the distal-most fertility gene in the arm identified by the marker that was lost. If the males of this initial cross were sterile, then the detachment carried less than a complete set of fertility genes. Crosses of detachment-bearing males from stock culture are then made with females carrying a compound X chromosome and a partial Y chromosome, either Y^L or Y^S. For example, a detachment carrying B^S from the B^SYy^+ would be tested in $X{\cdot}B^S/Y^S$ males. Fertility of these males reveals that the $X{\cdot}B^S$ has a complete *KL* and this detachment would be tested against the *KS* deficient y^+Y chromosomes. Sterility of the $X{\cdot}B^S/Y^S$ males would indicate less than complete *KL* and this detachment would be tested in $X{\cdot}B^S/y^+Y^-$ males, the y^+Y^- representing the tester series deficient for genes in Y^L. The other class of detachments, $X{\cdot}y^+$ would be treated in a similar manner.

Another class of rearrangements recovered from irradiation experiments is the partial Y chromosomes, recognized by loss of a Y chromosome marker without linkage of the retained marker and the X chromosome. Such Y chromosome fragments are tested for a full complement of fertility genes by producing X/Y-fragment males. Sterile males indicated that the Y chromosome lost one marker and one or more of the fertility genes. These Y-fragments are then tested in $X{\cdot}Y^L$/Y fragment and $X{\cdot}Y^S$/Y fragment males. Fertility indicates the presence in the fragment of a complete set of fertility genes of the arm *not* carried by the X chromosome. The tests to determine the presence in the Y-fragment of one or more of the fertility genes of an incomplete set of *KL* or *KS* genes requires the testing of X/Y-fragment/y^+Y^- males. If the Y-fragment carries the locus for which the y^+Y^- is deficient these males will be fertile. Sterility reveals that both Y chromosomes are deficient for a common locus.

All fertility tests may be carried out in mass matings of the males to be tested so long as those that indicate fertility are retested by single-male tests. This is necessary since some of the deficient Y's are "leaky" and to insure that fertile nondisjunctional exceptions are not included in the mass-tested males.

VIII. Methods of Marking Y Chromosomes

Two methods of producing marked Y chromosomes have been described by Brosseau *et al.* (1961) and are presented in Figures 5–7. The generalized method requires use of a translocation with a break immediately distal to that region to be incorporated into a Y chromosome. A second requirement is that hyperploidy for the distal tip of the second element of the transloca-tion not be overly detrimental to viability. (This tip is that component

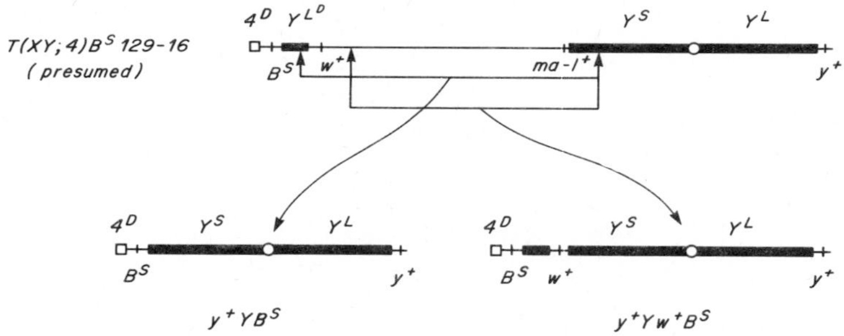

FIG. 5. The scheme used to generate the $y^+ YB^S$ and $y^+ Yw^+B^S$. The arrows indicate X-ray-induced break points deleting most of the X chromosome of $T(XY;4)B^S$ 129–16. The listed order $XY^S.Y^Ly^+$ was assumed by Brosseau *et al.*, 1961. See Fig. 6.

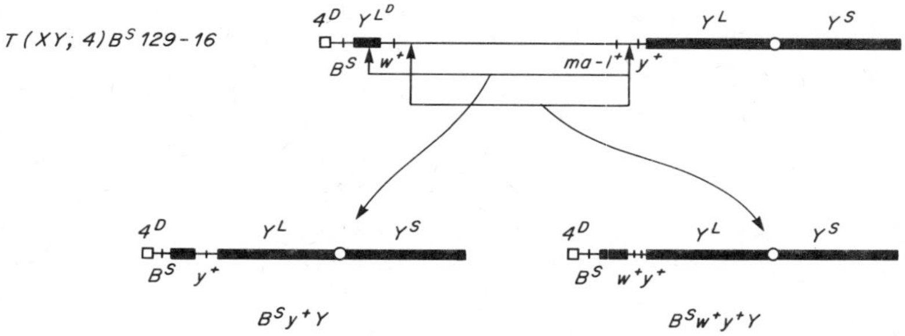

FIG. 6. The same scheme as in Fig. 5 but showing the correct order of 129–16.

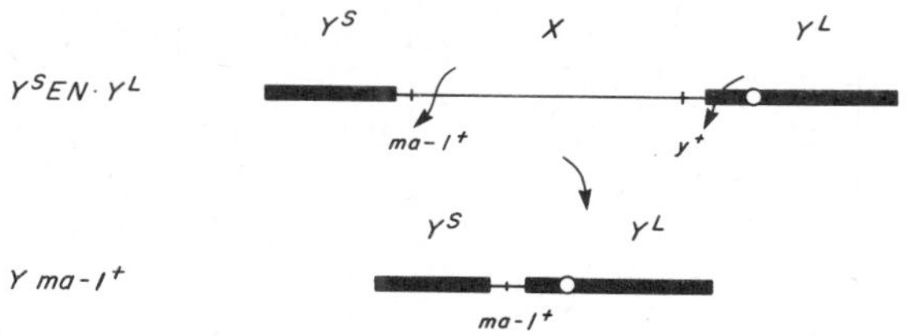

FIG. 7. The scheme used to generate Y chromosomes marked with X chromosome segments by irradiating $Y^SEN \cdot Y^L$. From Brosseau *et al.* (1961).

capping the broken end of the first element.) These requirements in addition to the male sterility frequently associated with *T(X;2)*'s and *T(X;3)*'s (Nicoletti and Lindsley, 1960) restrict this method. Putting X chromosome markers on the Y chromosome is, however, relatively easy. The use of *T(2;Y)* and *T(3;Y)* translocations may enhance the efficiency of the method for putting autosomal markers on the Y chromosome.

The first step in marking a Y chromosome with an X-chromosome marker is to select a translocation with appropriate breakpoints. The second step is to put the translocation in a female with a relatively simple attached-XY such as 108–9. A cross over between the translocation element carrying the desired marker and the attached-XY generates a Y chromosome carrying the proximal region of the X chromosome. This newly generated *T(1;Y)* and the second element of the translocation can be recovered in viable, fertile males without an additional Y chromosome. These males are then mated to compound-X females without a free Y chromosome and the progeny males irradiated. The irradiated males are mated to appropriately marked compound-X females (mutant at the desired locus). Female progeny carrying the marker from the translocation element putatively carry the desired Y chromosome. This putative marked Y chromosome is recovered in male progeny of the exceptional females. If these males are fertile and the marker segregates with the Y chromosome one has generated the desired marked Y chromosome.

The scheme in Figure 4 is the one used by Brosseau and Lindsley (1958) to generate the B^SY chromosome. The same scheme was used to generate the B^Sw^+Y chromosome. Figure 5 is the scheme used by Brosseau *et al.* (1961) to generate the $y^+Y\ B^S$ and $y^+Y\ w^+B^S$ chromosomes. (The $y^+Y\ B^S$ chromosome was presumably the reciprocal of the B^SYy^+ chromosome.) The $y^+Yw^+B^S$ chromosome lost B^S to generate the y^+Yw^+ chromosome; this latter chromosome subsequently lost y^+ to generate the Yw^+ chromosome. Once mastered conceptually, this scheme is relatively straight forward. As is often the case, however, fate played a important role in this experiment. Brosseau *et al.* used an attached-XY chromosome marked with y^+ recovered by Parker and McCrone (1958) from irradiated *C(1)RM*, y^2 *(su)*w^a w^a/y^+Y females. A *C(1)*–Y interchange product composed of a complete X chromosome, a complete Y chromosome and retaining y^+ would reasonably be considered to be y^2 *(su)*w^a w^a $Y^S{\cdot}Y^L$ y^+, as was assumed by Parker and McCrone and by Brosseau *et al.* and as shown in Fig. 5. In fact, however, such was not the case and attached-XY 129–16 is in reality y^2 *(su)*w^a w^a $y^+Y^L{\cdot}Y^S$ (Parker, 1968b) with the (unlikely) break in the y^+Y chromosome distal to y^+ and proximal to *l(1)J1*$^+$. Therefore the derived Y chromosomes are not as described by Brosseau *et al.* but are in reality B^Sy^+Y, $B^Sw^+y^+Y$, w^+ y^+Y and w^+Y (Fig. 6). If one is using the markers simply to follow the Y chromosome this creates no special problems. If, however, one's experimental scheme requires that the arms of the Y chromosome be differentially marked one should insure that the correct Y chromosome is being used; otherwise much effort can be wasted (Parker, 1968b).

Chovnick (1968b) used the method in Fig. 5 to produce Y chromosomes marked with the normal allele of *v* (vermilion). He used *T(1;Y)124* of Nicoletti and Lindsley (1960) and recovered three Y chromosomes presumed to be $B^Sv^+Yy^+$. If, as is likely, he also used the attached-XY 129–16 these chromosomes are then not as desribed but are $B^Sv^+y^+Y$. Chovnick irradiated one of these marked Y chromosomes to remove B^S and recovered two Y chromosomes marked with v^+ and y^+. One of the original chromosomes carried a rather large X chromosome segment covering *l(1)Q54*$^+$ to dy^+ (Schalet, 1969).

The second method of marking Y chromosomes with X chromosome markers is less versatile, but is effective for markers near either end of the euchromatic portion of the X. This method involves irradiating males carrying the attached-XY that is $Y^SEN{\cdot}Y^L$ and no free Y chromosome. Deletion of all of the X except the distal or the proximal-most markers produces Y chromosomes carrying a segment of the X chromosome interstitially. The *Yma-l*$^+$ chromosomes were induced in this manner (Fig. 7). A y^+*Yma-l*^{2} chromosome was induced by Chovnick (1968a) by irradiating a *y v mal*^{2} $Y^S{\cdot}Y^L$ y^+ chromosome. Here again the attached-XY may have been a derivative of 129–16 in which case the correct symbolism would be *ma-l*^{2} y^+Y.

Two Y chromosomes marked with *y* and sc^+ were recovered by Masterson (1968); the marked arm is unknown in both cases.

IX. Conclusion

This review of the genetics of the Y chromosome in *Drosophila melanogaster* must lead to the conclusion that the Y chromosome should no longer be considered an inert chromosome composed of "heterochromatin". It should instead be considered as a very complex genetic system, heteropycnotic in some cells, for which the analyses of genetic and cytological properties have only begun.

References

ALTORFER, N. (1953). Teneur en acide ribonucléique de différents génotypes chez *Drosophila melanogaster*. *Experimentia* **9,** 463–465.

ALTORFER, N. (1967). Effect of the absence of the Y chromosome on the expression of the *cubitus interruptus* phenotype in various translocations in *Drosophila melanogaster*. *Genetics* **55,** 755–767.

ANDERSON, W. A. (1967). Cytodifferentiation of spermatozoa in *Drosophila melanogaster*: The effect of elevated temperature on spermiogenesis. *Molec. Gen. Genet.* **99,** 257–273.

AYLES, G. B., SANDERS, T. G., SUZUKI, D. T. and KIEFER. B. I. (1973). Temperature-sensitive mutations in *Drosophila melanogaster* XI. Male sterile mutants of the Y chromosome. *Devl. Biol.* 32: 239–257.

BAIRATI, A. (1967). Struttura ed ultrastruttura dell apparato genitale maschile di *Drosophila melanogaster* Meig. *Z. Zellforsch. Mikrosk. Anat.* **76,** 56–99.

BAKER, W. K. (1955). On the structure of the $sc^{8}\cdot Y{:}bw^{+}$ chromosome of *D. melanogaster*. *Dros. Inf. Serv.* **29,** 101–102.

BAKER, W. K. (1957). Induced loss of a ring and a telomeric chromosome in *Drosophila melanogaster*. *Genetics* **42,** 735–748.

BAKER, W. K. and SPOFFORD, J. B. (1959). Heterochromatic control of position-effect variegation in Drosophila. *Univ. of Texas Publ.* **5914,** 135–154.

BARBOUR, E. and ZIMMERING, S. (1961). Preliminary analysis of a Y chromosome from nature carrying a mutant allele of *bobbed*. *Dros. Inf. Serv.* **35,** 71.

BARIGOZZI, C. (1948a). Role of the Y chromosome in the determination of cell-size in *D. melanogaster*. *Nature, Lond.* **162,** 30–31.

BARIGOZZI, C. (1948b). The influence of the Y chromosome on quantitative characters in *D. melanogaster*. *Heredity* **5,** 415–432.

BARIGOZZI, C. and DEPASQUALE, A. (1953). Heterochromatic and euchromatic genes acting on quantitative characters in *Drosophila melanogaster*. *Heredity* **7,** 389–399.

BARR, H. J. (1970). Analysis of a putatively *bb* lethal Y chromosome. *Dros. Inf. Serv.* **45,** 83.

BEHNE, O. and FORER, A. (1967). Evidence for four classes of microtubules in individual cells. *J. Cell Sci.* **2,** 169–192.

BENNER, D. B. (1971). Some evidence against the presence of suppressors of variegation on the Y chromosome. *Dros. Inf. Serv.* **47,** 72.

BENNER, D. B. (1972). Some properties of Y-fourth chromosome translocations. *Dros. Inf. Serv.* **48,** 122–123.

BLUMENFELD, M. and FORREST, H. S. (1971). Is Drosophila dAT on the Y chromosome? *Proc. Nat. Acad. Sci. U.S.A.* **68,** 3145–3149.

BLUMENFELD, M. and FORREST, H. S. (1972). Differential under-replication of satellite DNAs during Drosophila development. *Nature New Biol.* **239,** 170–172.

BONCINELLI, E., GRAZIANI, F., POLITO, L., MALVA, C. and RITOSSA, F. (1972). rDNA magnification at the *bobbed* locus of the Y chromosome in *Drosophila melanogaster*. *Cell Differentiation* **1,** 133–142.

BRIDGES, C. B. (1916). Non-disjunction as proof of the chromosome theory of heredity. *Genetics* **1,** 1–52, 107–163.

BROSSEAU, G. E., Jr. (1958). Crossing over between Y chromosomes in male Drosophila. *Dros. Inf. Serv.* **32,** 115–116.

BROSSEAU, G. E. (1960). Genetic analysis of the male fertility factors on the Y chromosome of *Drosophila melanogaster*. *Genetics* **45,** 257–274.

BROSSEAU, G. E. (1964). Non-randomness in the recovery of detachments from the reversed metacentric compound X chromosome in *Drosophila melanogaster*. *Can. J. Genet. Cytol.* **6,** 201–206.

BROSSEAU, G. E., Jr. (1964). Evidence that heterochromatin does not suppress V-type position effect. *Genetics* **50,** 237.

BROSSEAU, G. E., JR. and LINDSLEY, D. L. (1958). A dominantly marked Y chromosome: YB^S. *Dros. Inf. Serv.* **32,** 116.

BROSSEAU, G. E., NICOLETTI, B., GRELL, E. H. and LINDSLEY, D. L. (1961). Production of altered Y chromosomes bearing specific sections of the X chromosome in Drosophila. *Genetics* **46,** 339–346.

BROWN, D. E. (1969). Disjunction of some Y chromosome fragments in compound X females of *Drosophila melanogaster*. M.A. Thesis, Univ. of California, Riverside.

CALLAN, H. G. (1948). Ribose nucleic acid in the *Drosohpila* egg. *Nature, Lond.* **161,** 440.

CASPERSSON, T. and SCHULTZ, J. (1938). Nucleic acid metabolism of the chromosomes in relation to gene reproduction. *Nature, Lond.* **142,** 294–295.

CHOVNICK, A. (1968a). A $ma\text{-}l^2$ marked Y chromosome. *Dros. Inf. Serv.* **43,** 148–149.

CHOVNICK, A. (1968b). Generation of a series of Y chromosomes carrying the v^+ region of the X. *Dros. Inf. Serv.* **43,** 170.

COOPER, K. W. (1945). Normal segregation without chiasmata in female *Drosophila melanogaster*. *Genetics* **30,** 472–484.

COOPER, K. W. (1950). Normal spermiogenesis in *Drosophila*. *In*: "Biology of Drosophila" (M. Demerec, ed.) pp. 1–61. J. Wiley & Sons, New York, reprinted by Hafner Pub. Co., N.Y. 1965.

COOPER, K. W. (1952). On the location of y^+ and ac^+ in $sc^8 \cdot$Y. *Dros. Inf. Serv.* **26,** 97.

COOPER, K. W. (1956). Phenotypic effects of Y chromosome hyperploidy in *Drosophila melanogaster* and their relation to variegation. *Genetics* **41,** 242–264.

COOPER, K. W. (1959). Cytogenetic analysis of major heterochromatic elements (especially Xh and Y) in *Drosophila melanogaster* and the theory of "heterochromatin". *Chromosoma* **10,** 535–588.

COOPER, K. W. (1964) Meiotic conjunctive elements not involving chiasmata. *Proc. Nat. Acad. Sci. U.S.A.* **52,** 1248–1255.

DAEMS, W. T., PERSIJN, J.-P. and TATES, A. D. (1963). Fine-structural localization of ATPase activity in mature sperm of *Drosophila melanogaster*. *Expl. Cell Res.* **32,** 163–167.

ENNS, R. E. (1970). Segregation in males with XY–X chromosomes with and without free Y's and the segregation distorter chromosome, *SD–72*. *Dros Inf. Serv.* **45,** 136.

FANSLER, B. S., TRAVAGLINI, E. C., LOEB, L. A. and SCHULTZ, J. (1970). Structure of *Drosophila melanogaster* dAT replicated in an *in vitro* system. *Biochem. Biophys. Res. Commun.* **40,** 1266–1272.

FREED, J. J. and SCHULTZ, J. (1956). Effect of the Y chromosome on the DNA content of ovarian nuclei in *Drosophila melanogaster* females. *J. Histochem. Cytochem.* **4,** 441–442.

GRESH, E. S. (1956). Salivary analysis of Y: bw^+. *Dros. Inf. Serv.* **30,** 15.

GOWEN, J. W. and GAY, E. H. (1933). Eversporting as a function of the Y-chromosome in *Drosophila melanogaster. Proc. Nat. Acad. Sci. U.S.A.* **19,** 122–126.

GRELL, R. F. (1959). The Dubinin effect and the Y chromosome. *Genetics* **44,** 911–922.

GUYÉNOT, E. and NAVILLE, A. (1929). Les chromosomes et la réduction chromatique chez *Drosophila melanogaster. Cellule* **39,** 25–82.

HANKS, G. D. (1970). Frequency changes of marked Y chromosomes with *RD* background. *Dros. Inf. Serv.* **45,** 139.

HANNAH, A. (1951). Localization and function of heterochromatin in *Drosophila melanogaster. Adv. Genetics* **4,** 87–125.

HANNAH-ALAVA, A. (1965). The premeiotic stages of spermatogenesis. *Adv. Genetics* **13,** 157–226.

HEITZ, E. (1933). Cytologische Untersuchungen an Dipteren. III. Die somatische Heteropyknose bei *Drosophila melanogaster* and ihre genetische Bedeutung. *Z. Zellforsch.* **20,** 237–287.

HENNIG, W. (1967). Untersuchungen zur Struktur und Funktion des Lampenbürsten-Y-Chromosomes in der Spermatogenese von Drosophila. *Chromosoma* **22,** 294–357.

HENNIG, W. (1968). Ribonucleic acid synthesis of the Y-chromosome of *Drosophila hydei. J. Mol. Biol.* **38,** 227–239.

HESS, O. (1965). Struktur-Differenzierungen im Y-Chromosom von *D. hydei* und ihre Beziehungen zu Gen-Aktivitäten. III. Sequenz und Lokalisation der Schleifen-Bildungsorte. *Chromosoma* **16,** 222–248.

HESS, O. (1966). Structural modifications of the Y-chromosome in *Drosophila hydei* and their relation to gene activity. *Chromosomes Today* **1,** 167–173.

HESS, O. (1967). Complementation of genetic activity in translocated fragments of the Y chromosome in *D. hydei. Genetics* **56,** 283–295.

HESS, O. (1970a). Genetic function correlated with unfolding of lampbrush loops by the Y chromosome in spermatocytes of *Drosophila hydei. Molec. Gen. Genet.* **106,** 328–346.

HESS, O. (1970b). Independence between modification of genetic position effects and formation of lampbrush loops by the Y chromosome of *Drosophila hydei. Molec. Gen. Genet.* **107,** 224–242.

HESS, O. and MEYER, G. F. (1963). Chromosomal differentiation of the lampbrush type formed by the Y chromosome in *D. hydei* and *D. neohydei. J. Cell Bill.* **16,** 527–593.

HESS, O. and MEYER, G. F. (1968). Genetic activities of the Y chromosome in Drosophila during spermatogenesis. *Adv. Gen.* **14,** 171–223.

KAPLAN, W. D. and Gugler, H. D. (1969). Nutritive cells in the testes of Drosophila males. *Dros. Inf. Serv.* **44,** 64.

KHVOSTOVA, V. V. (1939). The role of the inert regions of chromosomes in the position effect of the *cubitus interruptus* gene in *Drosophila melanogaster* (in Russian). *Izv. Akad. Nauk. SSSR, Otd. Mat-est., Ser. biol.*, 541–574.

KIEFER, B. I. (1966). Ultrastructural abnormalities in developing sperm of X/O *Drosophila melanogaster. Genetics* **54,** 1441–1452.

KIEFER, B. I. (1968). Dosage regulation of ribosomal DNA in *Drosophila melanogaster. Proc. Nat. Acad. Sci. U.S.A.* **61,** 85–89.

KIEFER, B. I. (1969). Phenotypic effects of Y chromosome mutations in *Drosophila melanogaster* I. Spermiogenesis and sterility in *kl-1*$^{+}$ males. *Genetics* **61,** 157–166.

KIEFER, B. I. (1970). Development, organization and degeneration of the Drosophila sperm flagellum. *J. Cell Sci.* **6,** 177–194.

KING, R. C. and AKAI, H. (1971). Spermatogenesis in *Bombyx mori* I. The canal system joining sister spermatocytes. *J. Morphol.* **134,** 47–56.

LEVENBOOK, L., TRAVAGLINI, E. C. and SCHULTZ, J. (1958). Nucleic acids and their components as affected by the Y chromosome of *Drosophila melanogaster.* I. Constitution and amount of the ribonucleic acids in the unfertilized egg. *Expl. Cell. Res.* **15,** 43–61.

LEWIS, E. B. (1950). The phenomenon of position effect. *Adv. Gen.* **3,** 73–115.

LIFSCHYTZ, E. and FALK, R. (1969a). A system for screening of rare events in genes of *Drosophila melanogaster. Genetics* **62,** 343–352.

LIFSCHYTZ, E. and FALK, R. (1969b). A genetic analysis of the killer-prune (*K-pn*) locus of *Drosophila melanogaster. Genetics* **62,** 353–358.

LINDSLEY, D. L., EDINGTON, C. W. and von HALLE, E. S. (1960). Sex-linked recessive lethals in Drosophila whose expression is suppressed by the Y chromosome. *Genetics* **45,** 1650–1670.

LINDSLEY, D. L. and GRELL, E. H. (1968). Genetic Variations of *Drosophila melanogaster.* Carnegie Inst. Publ. 627.

LUCCHESI, J. C. (1965). The nature of induced exchanges between the attached-X and Y chromosomes in *Drosophila melanogaster* females. *Genetics* **51,** 209–216.

LÜNING, K. G. (1953). Report of K. G. Lüning. *Dros. Inf. Serv.* **27,** 58.

MASTERSON, J. (1968). A method for procuring certain X–Y duplications. *Dros. Inf. Serv.* **43,** 161.

MATHER, K. (1944). The genetical activity of heterochromatin. *Proc. Roy. Soc. Lond.* **132,** 308–332.

MEYER, G. F. (1963). Die Funktionsstrukturen des Y-chromosoms in den Spermatocytenkernen von *Drosophila hydei, D. neohydei, D. repleta* und einigen anderen Drosophila-arten. *Chromosoma* **14,** 207–255.

MEYER, G. F. (1964). Die parakristallinen Korper in den Spermienschwänzen von Drosophila. *Z. Zellforsch.* **62,** 762–784.

MEYER, G. F. (1968). Spermiogenese in normalen und Y-defizienten männchen von *Drosophila melanogaster* und *D. hydei. Z. Zellforsch.* **84,** 141–175.

MEYER, G. F. (1969). Experimental studies of spermiogenesis in Drosophila. *Genetics* (*Supplement*) **61,** 79–92.

MEYER, G. F. (1972). Influence of Y chromosome on fertility and phenotype of Drosophila spermatozoa. "Proc. Int. Symp. The Genetics of the Spermatozoon, Edinburgh, (R. A. Beatty and S. Gluecksohn-Waelsch, eds.) pp. 387–405.

MEYER, H. U. (1959). Report of Helen U. Meyer. *Dros. Inf. Serv.* **33,** 97.

MORGAN, T. H., BRIDGES, C. B. and SCHULTZ, J. (1934). Constitution of the germinal material in relation to heredity. *Carnegie Inst. Wash. Yearbook* **33,** 274–280.

MULLER, H. J. (1948). The construction of several new types of Y chromosomes. *Dros. Inf. Serv.* **22,** 73–74.

MULLER, H. J. (1954). A semi-automatic breeding system (Maxy) for finding sex-linked mutations at specific "visible" loci. *Dros. Inf. Serv.* **28,** 140–141.

MULLER, H. J. and EDMUNDSON, M. (1957). Transposition of entire 4- euchromatin into a fully functional Y. *Dros. Inf. Serv.* **31,** 140–141.

MULLER, H. J. and PAINTER, T. S. (1932). The differentiation of the sex chromosomes of Drosophila into genetically active and inert regions. *Z. indukt. Abstamm. VererbLehre* **62,** 316–365.

NEUHAUS, M. E. (1938). A cytogenetic study of the Y-chromosome in *Drosophila melanogaster* (in Russian). *Biol. Zhurnal.* **7,** 335–358.

NEUHAUS, M. J. (1939). A cytogenetic study of the Y chromosome in *Drosophila melanogaster*. *J. Genetics* **37,** 229–254.

NICOLETTI, B. and LINDSLEY, D. L. (1960). Translocations between the X and the Y chromosomes of *Drosophila melanogaster*. *Genetics* **45,** 1705–1722.

OLIVIERI, G. and OLIVIERI, A. (1965). Autoradiographic study of nucleic acid synthesis during spermatogenesis in *Drosophila melanogaster*. *Mutation Res.* **2,** 366–380.

OSTER, I. I. and IYENGAR, S. V. (1955). A marked ring-Y. *Dros. Inf. Serv.* **29,** 159.

PARKER, D. R. (1965). Chromosome pairing and induced exchange in Drosophila. *Mutation Res.* **2,** 523–529.

PARKER, D. R. (1967). Induced heterologous exchange in Drosophila I. Exchanges between Y and fourth chromosomes. *Mutation Res.* **4,** 333–337.

PARKER, D. R. (1968a). A survey of methods for the induction of aberrations in meiotic stages in Drosophila females and for observation of their disjunctional properties in the ensuring meiotic divisions. In Effects of Radiation on Meiotic Systems, pp. 209–218. Internat. Atomic Energy Agency, Vienna.

PARKER, D. R. (1968b) On the sequence of elements in compound-XY #129–16 and in some of its derivative marked Y chromosomes. *Dros. Inf. Serv.* **43,** 156.

PARKER, D. R. and MCCRONE, J. (1958). A genetic analysis of some rearrangements induced in oocytes of Drosophila. *Genetics* **43,** 172–186.

PATTERSON, E. K., LANG, H. M., DACKERMAN, M. E. and SCHULTZ, J. (1954). Chemical determinations of the effect of the X and Y chromosomes on the nucleic acid content of the larval salivary glands of *Drosophila melanogaster*. *Expt. Cell Res.* **6,** 181–194.

PEROTTI, M. E. (1969). Ultrastructure of the mature sperm of *Drosophila melanogaster*. Meig. *J. Submicro. Cytol.* **1,** 171–196.

PHILLIPS, D. M. (1970). Insect sperm: Their structure and morphogenesis. *J. Cell Sci.* **44,** 243–277.

RITOSSA, F. M. (1968). Nonoperative DNA complementary to ribosomal RNA. *Proc. Nat. Acad. Sci. U.S.A.* **59,** 1124–1131.

RITOSSA, F. (1972). Procedure for magnification of lethal deletions of genes for ribosomal RNA. *Nature New Biol.* **240,** 109–111.

RITOSSA, F. M. and SPIEGELMAN, S. (1965). Localization of DNA complementary to ribosomal RNA in the nucleolus organizer region of *Drosophila melanogaster*. *Proc. Nat. Acad. Sci. U.S.A.* **53,** 737–745.

RITOSSA, F., MALVA, C., BONCINELLI, E., GRAZIANI, F. and POLITO, L. (1971). The first steps of magnification of DNA complementary to ribosomal RNA in *Drosophila melanogaster*. *Proc. Nat. Acad. Sci. U.S.A.* **68,** 1580–1584.

SAFIR, S. R. (1920). Genetic and cytological examination of the phenomena of primary non-disjunction in *Drosophila melanogaster*. *Genetics* **5,** 459–487.

SCHALET, A. (1969). A Y chromosome carrying the v^+ to dy^+ region of the X. *Dros. Inf. Serv.* **44,** 123.

SCHULTZ, J. (1936). Variegation in Drosophila and the inert chromosome regions. *Proc. Nat. Acad. Sci. U.S.A.* **22,** 27–33.

SCHULTZ, J. (1941). The function of heterochromatin. *Proc. 7th Intern. Congr. Genetics, J. Genetics* (Suppl.) 257–262.

SCHULTZ, J. (1956). The relation of the heterochromatic chromosome regions to the nucleic acids of the cell. *Cold Spring Harb. Symp. Quant. Biol.* **21,** 307–328.

SHEN, T. H. (1932). Zytologische Untersuchungen über Sterilität bei Männchen von *Drosophila melanogaster* und bei F1-Männchen der Kreuzung zwischen *D. simulans*-Weibchen und *D. melanogaster*-Männchen. *Z. Zellforsch.* **15,** 547–580.

STANLEY, H. P., BOWMAN, J. T., ROMRELL, L. J., REED, S. C. and WILKINSON, R. R. (1972). Fine structure of normal spermatid differentiation in *Drosophila melanogaster*. *J. Ultrastruct. Res.* **42,** 433–466.

SLATIS, H. M. (1955). Position effect at the brown locus in *Drosophila melanogaster*. *Genetics* **40,** 5–23.

STEINBERG, A. G. (1943). Is a chromosomal aberration necessary for a position effect? *Dros. Inf. Serv.* **17,** 65.

STERN, C. (1927). Ein genetischer und zytologischen Beweis fur Vererbung im Y-Chromosom von *Drosophila melanogaster*. *Z. Indukt. Abstamm. Vererbhere.* **44,** 188–231.

STERN, C. (1929). Untersuchungen uber Aberrationen des Y-Chromosoms von *Drosophila melanogaster*. *Z. Indukt. Abstamm. VererbLehre.* **51,** 253–353.

STERN, C. (1936). Interspecific sterility. *Am. Nat.* **70,** 123–142.

STERN, C. and HADORN, E. (1938). The determination of sterility in Drosophila males without a complete Y chromosome. *Am. Nat.* **72,** 42–52.

TARTOF, K. D. (1971). Increasing the multiplicity of ribosomal RNA genes in *Drosophila melanogaster*. *Science, N.Y.* **171,** 294–297.

TARTOF, K. D. (1973). Regulation of ribosomal RNA gene multiplicity in *Drosophila melanogaster*. *Genetics* **73,** 57–71.

TOKUYASU, K. T., PEACOCK, W. J. and HARDY, R. W. (1972a). Dynamics of spermiogenesis in *Drosophila melanogaster*. I. Individualization process. *Z. Zellforsch.* **124,** 479–506.

TOKUYASU, K. T., PEACOCK, W. J. and HARDY, R. W. (1972b). Dynamics of spermiogenesis in *Drosophila melanogaster*. II. Coiling process. *Z. Zellforsch.* **127,** 492–525.

TRAVAGLINI, E. C., LEVENBOOK, L. and SCHULTZ, J. (1958). Nucleic acids and their components as affected by the Y chromosome of *Drosophila melanogaster*. II. The nucleosides and related compounds in the acid soluble fraction of the unfertilized egg. *Expl. Cell. Res.* **15,** 62–79.

TRAVAGLINI, E. C., PETROVIC, J. and SCHULTZ, J. (1968). Two satellite cytoplasmic DNA's in Drosophila. *J. Cell. Biol.* **39,** 136A.

TRAVAGLINI, E. C., PETROVIC, J. and SCHULTZ, J. (1972a). Characterization of the DNA in *Drosophila melanogaster*. *Genetics* **72,** 419–430.

TRAVAGLINI, E. C., PETROVIC, J. and SCHULTZ, J. (1972b). Satellite DNAs in the embryos of various species of the genus Drosophila. *Genetics* **72,** 431–439.

WILLIAMSON, J. H. (1968a). The induction of sterile Y chromosomes in *Drosophila melanogaster* with ethyl methanesulfonate. *Genetics* **60,** 288.

WILLIAMSON, J. H. (1968b). Identification of Y fragments with two doses of y^{+} or B^{S}. *Dros. Inf. Serv.* **43,** 157.

WILLIAMSON, J. H. (1969a). EMS-induced mutants in the Y chromosome of *D. melanogaster*. *Dros. Inf. Serv.* **44,** 68.

WILLIAMSON, J. H. (1969b). On the nature of Y chromosome fragments induced in *Drosophila melanogaster* females. I. Immature oocytes. *Mutant Res.* **8,** 327–335.

WILLIAMSON, J. H. (1970a). On the nature of Y chromosome fragments induced in *Drosophila melanogaster* females. II. Mature oocytes. *Mutation Res.* **9,** 85–90.

WILLIAMSON, J. H. (1970b). Mutagenesis and cell interactions. Site of Y chromosome function in *Drosophila melanogaster*. *Mutation Res.* **10,** 503–506.

WILLIAMSON, J. H. (1970c). Ethyl methanesulfonate-induced mutants in the Y chromosome of *Drosophila melanogaster*. *Mutation Res.* **10,** 597–605.

WILLIAMSON, J. H. (1972). Allelic complementation between mutants in the fertility factors of the Y chromosome in *Drosophila melanogaster*. *Molec. Gen. Genetics* **119,** 43–47.

WILLIAMSON, J. H., PROCUNIER, J. D. and CHURCH, R. B. (1973). Does the rDNA in the Y chromosome of *Drosophila melanogaster* magnify? *Nature* **243,** 190–191.

YASUZUMI, G., FUJIMURA, W. and ISHIDA, H. (1958). Spermatogenesis in animals as revealed by electron microscopy. V. Spermatid differentiation of *Drosophila* and grasshopper. *Expl. Cell. Res.* **14,** 268–285.

ZIMMERING, S. (1959). Presence of the normal allele of *su-f* in the B^{S} segment of sc^{8}: Y: B^{S}. *Dros. Inf. Serv.* **33,** 175–176.

ZIMMERING, S. (1963). The effect of temperature on meiotic loss of the Y chromosome in the male of *Drosophila*. *Genetics* **48,** 133–138.

17. Recombination Between the X and Y Chromosomes

JOHN H. WILLIAMSON*

Department of Biology
University of Calgary
Calgary, Alberta, Canada

and

DEAN R. PARKER

Department of Biology
University of California
Riverside, California, U.S.A.

I. Introduction

We use the term "exchange" to denote spontaneous recombination involving X and Y chromosomes and the term "interchange" to denote induced recombination. Some major differences between these two types of events are known and it would require much more critical analyses than have heretofore been accomplished to demonstrate that a single

* Supported by the National Research Council of Canada.

common mechanism is operative in cases where differences in the products of induced *vs* spontaneous recombination are not evident. To avoid the pitfall of implying a common mechanism, we prefer to avoid using a common term for spontaneous and induced events.

A variety of terms are found in the literature designating processes and products of exchange and interchange. Spontaneous exchange between the X and the Y was first noted by Stern (1927, 1929) in males and was termed "translocation" until it was found that spontaneous "detachment" (Kaufmann, 1933; Neuhaus, 1935, 1936) and "re-attachment" (Neuhaus, 1936, 1937) of attached-X chromosomes [=reversed metacentric compound X = *C(1)RM*] and the generation of fragments of the Y chromosome all involved exchanges between heterochromatic regions of X and of Y and that the frequencies of such exchanges in males and in females were not appreciably different (Neuhaus, 1937). Radiation-induced interchange can also lead to "detachment" of a *C(1)RM* and its two-hit kinetics led to the conclusion that it is a translocation-like process (Herskowitz, 1954; Kutschera, 1954; Parker, 1954). The products of induced detachments have been called "half-translocations" (Abrahamson *et al.*, 1956), translocations (Parker and McCrone, 1958) and "induced crossovers" (Lucchesi, 1965). The first term recognizes the recovery of only one element of a reciprocal translocation, the second stresses the breakage-and-rejoining nature of the event, while the third is based on presumed pairing relationships of the *C(1)RM* and the Y. However, to be descriptive the concept of the term "induced crossover" would require broadening to include interchange between heterologues (e.g., Y–4 interchange) or else a more precise definition of the "pairing" relationships in the oocyte nucleus. The term "induced crossing over" is itself ambiguous in that its occurrence in heterochromatic regions of chromosomes appears to be a translocation-like process, not involving identical breakpoints in the two involved homologues (Williamson *et al.*, 1970a, b) and hence may not differ from Herskowitz and Abrahamson's (1957) term, "pseudo-crossing over". It is because of these ambiguities that we limit "exchange" to spontaneous recombinational events and "interchange" to induced events.

II. Spontaneous Exchange

A. Males

The analysis of exchange between the X and the Y chromosomes in males began when Stern (1927, 1929; Stern and Ogura, 1931) recovered X chromosomes with an arm of the Y chromosome attached proximally as well as a rearranged Y chromosome with two short arms ($Y^S \cdot Y^S$). Males carrying $X{\cdot}Y^L$ or $X{\cdot}Y^S$ and a complete Y chromosome were fertile, whereas either class of male without a Y chromosome was sterile; males carrying $X{\cdot}Y^L$ and the $Y^S{\cdot}Y^S$ were fertile. Stern concluded that each arm of the Y chromosome carries a male fertility factor (or complex) and that males lacking one arm of the Y chromosome are sterile. The complex in the long arm he designated as K_1 and the complex in the short arm he designated as K_2. In males carrying a two-armed X chromosome [*Dp(1;1)Th, Theta*] (Stern and Doan, 1936) exchange with the Y chromosome involved either arm of the X and the separated arms were always associated with one or the other of the arms of the Y chromosome. Exchange in males between a two-armed X such as *Dp(1;1)Th* and the Y chromosome theoretically involves either arm of either chromosome; the recovered products do not allow the exclusion of one arm of the Y chromosome in the exchange process. The recovery of clusters of exchange products from individual cultures suggested that the exchange events occurred in premeiotic cells.

The occasional loss of the distal end of $In(1)sc^8$, marked with y^+ and ac^+, during spermatogonial divisions was shown by Lindsley (1955, 1958) to be a consequence of exchange between the distally displaced heterochromatic region of the X chromosome and the short arm of the Y. In seven cases of recovery of recombinant Y chromosomes all were products of eucentric exchange between the inverted distal heterochromatic region of $In(1)sc^8$ and the short arm of the Y. Of ten tested recombinant-X chromosomes, those that had lost y^+ and ac^+, all carried Y^S distally. Of the recombinants recovered from males carrying $In(1)sc^{8L}EN^R$, which has a proximal heterochromatic second arm, few (4/22) could be demonstrated to be products of exchange between the inverted X and the Y chromosome. From the analysis of these recombinants Lindsley inferred as many as six different regions of "uninterrupted eucentric homology" within the heterochromatic region of the X chromosome. Lindsley recognized that the occurrence of exchange is not by itself adequate proof of strict homology in the region of exchange. He proposed that X–Y exchange is conditioned by non-homologous associations of regions of chromosomes. These non-homologous associations may be "heterochromatin" specific.

B. FEMALES

Compound-X chromosomes had scarcely been recognized and appreciated before it was observed that the two X's attached to a common centromere sometimes separated (Morgan, 1922; Anderson, 1925). In Anderson's data detachment of the *C(1)RM* occurred with a frequency of one in 1300 progeny. Kaufmann (1933) analysed seven detachment-X chromosomes and observed two classes, either V-shaped or J-shaped. The four V-shaped detachments were composed of an X chromosome and the long arm of the Y attached to a common centromere. The three J-shaped detachments were composed of an X chromosome with the short arm of the Y attached proximally. Part of the corroborative evidence that the attached arms were either Y^L or Y^S came from observations of somatic pairing between the presumptive Y-arm of the detachment chromosome and the homologous arm of the intact Y chromosome. Genetic evidence was obtained by testing males carrying the V-shaped detachments and the short arm of the Y ($Y'' = Y^S \cdot Y^S$). Such males were fertile indicating that the detachment chromosome carried the male fertility complex from the long arm of the Y chromosome.

Neuhaus (1936) confirmed the cytological observations of Kaufmann that detached-X chromosomes carry, proximally, an arm of the Y chromosome and, in addition, correctly assigned the bobbed locus to the short arm of the Y chromosome. He recognized the recovery of clusters of exchange products and that such clusters implied that some exchange occurs in premeiotic cells. Two additional observations of significance were made by Neuhaus. He recovered no detachments of the *C(1)RM* in females without a Y chromosome and of 138 spontaneous detachments tested in no case was a free Y chromosome recovered. His interpretation of the failure to recover a free Y chromosome in detachment-bearing progeny, of the fertility of some detachment males ($X \cdot Y^L$) with Y'' and of the absence of detachments in *C(1)RM*/0 females was exchange occurring between homologous regions in the X and the Y chromosome.

C. Reconstruction of Compound-X Chromosomes

If exchange between a compound-X chromosome and the Y chromosome can yield detached-X chromosomes carrying an arm of the Y, then the reverse situation should also occur. Neuhaus (1935) tested this assumption. From $X \cdot Y^L/X \cdot Y^L$ females he recovered no compound-X's in 24,000 progeny, while he recovered two compound-X's from 27,000 progeny of $X \cdot Y^S/X \cdot Y^L$ females. When he looked at this event in males he obtained 66 compound-X chromosomes from 80,000 progeny of $X \cdot Y^S$/Y males but only 2 compound–X's from 88,000 progeny of $X \cdot Y^L$/Y males (Neuhaus, 1936). Some of the 66 compound-X's from $X \cdot Y^S$/Y males were recovered in clusters. Apparently in both sexes exchange between the X and Y^S occurs more frequently than does exchange between the X and Y^L. In the above experiments complementary exchange products were recovered from both sexes. These included Y^S rods, Y^L rods and $Y^S \cdot Y^S$ V-shaped fragments;

no $Y^L \cdot Y^L$ fragments were recovered. Whether this chromosome is not generated or simply is not recovered is not known.

The recovery of clusters of compound-X chromosomes from males poses an interesting question. Can a diplo-X cell, generated premeiotically, successfully complete spermatogenesis? Such cells would presumably form a patch of female tissue in the male gonad and would be expected to carry a complete Y chromosome, at least in $X \cdot Y^S$/Y males. The meiotic generation of a compound-X chromosome should not preclude its recovery via functional sperm. This may be a situation in which recovery of clusters of a rare recombinant does not demand its premeiotic origin.

D. Derived Y Chromosomes

The early experiments of Stern and of Neuhaus allowed the recovery of useful combinations of the X chromosome and the arms of the Y chromosome as well as partial Y chromosomes separating the two arms of the Y. These combinations have proved useful in various situations, the first being Stern's demonstration that each arm of the Y chromosome contains genes necessary for male fertility.

Other useful partial Y chromosomes have since been derived as consequences of exchange between the X and the Y chromosomes. As the reciprocal product of exchange between *In(1)sc*^{8} and the short arm of the Y, producing Y^S*In(1)sc*^{8}, Sidorov (1941) recovered the $sc^8 \cdot Y^L$, a partial Y chromosome marked with y^+. A similar Y^S recombinant was recovered by Crew and Lamy (1940) from *In(1)sc*^{S1} males ($Y^S \cdot sc^{S1}$). Muller (1948) used this process to generate three new Y chromosomes. From males carrying *In(1)sc*^{VI} and a normal Y chromosome he recovered the X centromere carrying the sc^{VI} duplication and Y^S. Thus an acrocentric Y^S marked with y^+ was generated. From *In(1)sc*^{8}/Y males Muller recovered the sc^8Y (y^+Y) chromosome carrying the fertility complexes of Y^L and Y^S plus part of the distally displaced heterochromatic region of the *In(1)sc*^{8} chromosome, including y^+, attached to Y^L. This marked Y chromosome was further modified, spontaneously, to give rise to Y^{LC}, a ring chromosome carrying only the male fertility genes of Y^S, bb^+, K_2, and y^+ being lost. Many other Y chromosomes carrying genetic markers from both X chromosomes and autosomes have been recovered and are described in Lindsley and Grell (1968).

E. Combinations of X and Y Chromosomes

From the experiments of Stern, of Neuhaus and of Kaufmann various useful combinations of the X and the Y chromosomes were recovered. These include $X \cdot Y^S$, $X \cdot Y^L$, $Y^S \cdot Y^S$ and Y^L. Their usefulness was first demonstrated in the early studies of the event that generated them, namely exchange between X and Y, in both males and females. They were also useful in Stern's partial analysis of the male fertility complexes of the Y and, later, in generating other X–Y combinations.

Two other very useful classes of rearranged chromosomes have been derived using the phenomenon of exchange between the X and the Y chromosomes. These are the compound-X chromosomes (Novitski, 1954) and the compound-XY chromosomes (Lindsley and Novitski, 1959). This latter type of chromosome contains, connected to one centromere, all of the genetic material necessary for male viability and fertility. The compound-X chromosomes and the compound-XY's have been extremely useful in manipulating the sex-chromosome complement of both males and females. In addition, the compound-XY's have been useful in the production of marked Y chromosomes (Brosseau *et al.*, 1961).

There are two general types of compound-XY chromosomes. The Lindsley and Novitski type is $Y^{S}EN{\cdot}Y^{L}$ with Y^{S} attached distally by spontaneous exchange in $In(1)sc^{8L}EN^{R}/Y$ males; Y^{L} was attached subsequently, and spontaneously, in $Y^{S}EN{\cdot}/sc^{8}Y$ males. Several variations of this chromosome exist, including $Y^{S}EN{\cdot}$ and $EN{\cdot}Y^{S}$. The other classes of compound-XY chromosome are either $XY^{L}{\cdot}Y^{S}$ or $XY^{S}{\cdot}Y^{L}$, derived from irradiated occytes detaching a *C(1)RM* (section III.A.1), the breakpoint in the Y chromosome being distal to all of the fertility loci in the involved arm of the Y chromosome (Parker and McCrone, 1958). These chromosomes are maintained as XY males with or without a free Y chromosome with females homozygous for the compound XY or with females carrying a compound-X chromosome.

F. X–Y Exchange: a Meiotic or Mitotic Process?

1. Time of occurrence

The origin of spontaneously occurring recombinants between the X and Y chromosomes remains an unanswered question. The recovery of recombinant chromosomes does not insure the occurrence of meiotic crossing over in precisely homologous regions of the X and the Y chromosomes. Premeiotic X–Y exchange is suggested by the recovery of relatively large clusters of rare rearrangements from individual males or females. Conversely, the unequal recovery of $X{\cdot}Y^{S}$ *vs* $X{\cdot}Y^{L}$ detachments of compound-X chromosomes in Neuhaus' (1935) data suggests that meiotic exchange is responsible, since chromatid exchange would generate heteromorphic dyads and would lead to anaphase-II nonrandomness (Section III.A.3) which would distort the ratio in the direction observed. Neuhaus recovered $X{\cdot}Y^{S}$ and $X{\cdot}Y^{L}$ in a ratio of 2:1 which is precisely the same ratio observed by Brosseau (1964) for radiation-induced detachments where genetic analysis confirmed breakpoints in the region of the centromere of the Y chromosome and where the experimental methods make it certain that the X–Y interchanges were induced in the primary oocyte. In comparison, when females heterozygous for *In(1)sc*^{VI} are irradiated two types of rearrangements are recovered—compound-X chromosomes and free duplications marked with y^+. The free duplications are much smaller than the compound-X chromosomes and are preferentially recovered in early broods, derived from irradiated primary oocytes (Roberts, 1969). In later broods, derived from cells which were treated premeiotically (cystocytes, cystoblasts or stem cells), recoveries of the two types of rearrangements occur equally frequently. These considerations require that both exchange and interchange can occur in premeiotic as well as in meiotic cells and tend to confirm the meiotic nature of exchanges characterized by nonrandom recovery of reciprocal products.

Clusters of recombinant chromosomes have been recovered from males of various genotypes by Stern, by Neuhaus and by Lindsley. X–Y exchange in males was considered by Lindsley as primarily a premeiotic process. Transmission of exchange products would simply require the presence of the equivalent of a complete Y chromosome in each bundle of spermatids. However, the generation of compound-X chromosomes recovered from males would, *a priori*, seem to be a meiotic event. It is difficult to imagine a diplo-X stem cell, even one containing a Y chromosome, completing spermatogenesis unless the X-chromosomes are inactivated, as suggested by Lifschytz and Lindsley (1972). Although evidence on the origin of X–Y exchange in males is meager, it seems likely that it may occur both meiotically and premeiotically.

2. *The role of homology*

Evidence that exchange involving Xh and Y is not necessarily based on specific homology is given by the variability of size and of content of the recovered recombinant chromosomes. Neuhaus (1937) noted that of six X·Y^{L} chromosomes recovered from *bb*/Y males, four were bb^+ and two were *bb*, indicating at least two regions in the Y chromosome where exchange with the X can occur. There is a distinctly higher frequency of induced detachment of *C(1)RM* when $Y^S{\cdot}Y^S$–2 is present than with $Y^S{\cdot}Y^S$ (Parker, unpublished observations). These two $Y^S{\cdot}Y^S$ recombinant chromosomes give different segregation ratios in *C(1)RM*/$sc^{VI}{\cdot}Y^S/Y^S{\cdot}Y^S$ females (Brown, 1969).

The most convincing evidence that specific homology is not the basis for X–Y exchange is that derived by Lindsley (1955, 1958) for the loss of the distal end of *In(1)sc*^{8}. Since the recovery of chromosomes in which Y^S has been attached distally requires either a *reversed* pairing relationship or a U-type exchange, and since the content of the recovered y^+-marked Y^L fragments as well as of distal attachments of Y^S to the X show considerable variation, it would require that there be several regions of "uninterrupted eucentric homology" if this were the necessary condition for exchange. Similarly, other kinds of heterochromatic exchange occur when the right end of the *EN* inversion has been substituted for the right end of *In(1)sc*^{8}. One could make the circular argument that exchange can occur between homologous segments, therefore exchange requires that segments be homologous, therefore the occurrence of exchange is evidence of homology. However, if sequential similarity is the basis for exchange it may be that these are reiterated sequences and, furthermore, that exchange may occur between sequences inverted with respect to each other. The finding that spontaneous exchange does not break up the fertility complexes, *KL* and *KS*, argues that nonhomologous exchange is not a uniform property of heterochromatic regions. On the other hand, it could be argued that identifying these segments of the Y as "heterochromatin" is a fallacy based on the specialized genetic properties of *KS* and *KL*, these being heteropycnotic in neuroblasts but not in primary spermatocytes where they function.

III. Induced Interchange

Drosophila oocytes undergo a marked increase in radiation sensitivity with age (Patterson *et al.*, 1932). Mature oocytes (Stage 14 of King *et al.*, 1956) are more sensitive to the induction of dominant lethals and show greater frequencies of genetic damage of all types that have been studied. Chromosome breaks induced in mature oocytes remain open for extended periods while breaks in immature oocytes rejoin in about 10–15 minutes (Parker, 1963; Parker and Hammond, 1958). Reciprocal translocations are recovered very infrequently from irradiated immature oocytes (Patterson and Muller, 1930; Glass, 1955) but quite easily from mature oocytes (Traut, 1967) while gross deficiencies likewise are more often obtained from mature oocytes (Parker and McCrone, 1958). Because of these differences, interchanges producing detachments of compound-X chromosomes in these two classes of oocytes will be treated separately in the following discussion.

A. Detachment of Compound-X Chromosomes

1. Immature oocytes

Very soon after the demonstration that compound-X chromosomes sometimes detach spontaneously, Muller and Dippel (1925) reported that the frequency of detachment was higher in females treated with X-rays than in the unirradiated controls. Later Rapoport (1940, 1941) reported that the induction of detachments of the compound-X chromosomes does not involve the Y chromosome. This was contrary to the observation that spontaneous detachment always involved the Y (Neuhaus, 1935, 1936). Rapoport's conclusion was based on the observation that radiation-induced detachments were recovered from females carrying no Y chromosome as frequently as from females with a Y chromosome. He postulated that after breakage by X-rays the broken ends of the centric-X chromosome healed by restitution of the telomere.

That Rapoport's conclusions were erroneous was reported independently from three laboratories (Herskowitz, 1954; Muller and Herskowitz, 1954; Kutschera, 1954; Parker, 1954). Parker demonstrated that the frequencies of induced detachments are not basically different in females with or without a Y chromosome (in agreement with Rapoport's observations), although in some cases the frequencies of detachments varied according to which Y chromosome or Y chromosome fragment was used. If detachments induced in females with a Y chromosome are products of interchange between the compound-X chromosome and the Y chromosome, what then is the nature of those detachments induced in females without a Y chromosome?

Parker (1954), Parker and McCrone (1958) and Abrahamson *et al.* (1956) tested detachments in analyses of the events producing these rearranged chromosomes. By testing fertility of males carrying a detachment chromosome and no Y chromosome, the detachment and Y^L, and the detachment and Y^S the presence of a complete Y chromosome, a complete Y^S or a complete Y^L, respectively, could be detected. Detection of less than a complete Y arm, or of a complete Y arm and a portion of the other arm, was not then possible, although there now exist stocks which allow such analysis (see Chapter 16). By back-crossing detachment carrying individuals to stocks homozygous for appropriate (distal) autosomal recessive markers one can determine if a detachment carried the tip of an autosome, carrying the normal allele of one of the test-markers. Detachments induced in females with a Y chromosome and in females without a Y chromosome were found to be X·4R, i.e. showed linkage of X and fourth chromosome markers, in approximately 15% and 60% of the cases, respectively, when immature oocytes were treated. Since in the first case some 80% of the detachments involved the Y chromosome, approximately 90% of the detachments could be classified as to the type of interchange event that was induced. Better systems of marking and of testing now available should increase this figure substantially.

Abrahamson *et al.* (1956) analysed detachments obtained by irradiating compound-X females without a Y chromosome. At least half of their detachments could be shown to have arisen by interchange with the autosomes; as in Parker's data X·4R detachments predominated.

Brosseau (1964) induced and analysed 115 X–Y detachments using the doubly-marked Y chromosome, B^SYy^+, which has on the end of each arm a marker derived from the X chromosome (Brosseau, 1958). When a compound-X chromosome is homozygous for the mutant *y* (yellow body color) any detachment involving the B^SYy^+ can be recognized by recovery of one of the two markers on the Y but not of both. Brosseau then used the male-sterile mutant Y chromosomes (Brosseau, 1960) to analyse the region of the Y chromosome in which a break had been induced to yield the detachment. He could determine if the detachment had retained the X centromere or the Y centromere in approximately 80% of the detachments. Approximately 20% of the breaks in the Y chromosome occurred in the centromere region proximal to the male fertility genes, while some 55% of the breaks occurred between the most distal male fertility gene of each arm and the terminal markers. These latter regions share homology with the X chromosome as does some part of Y^S around the nucleolar organizer region. These three regions of presumed homology accounted for some 70–80% of the breaks induced in the B^SYy^+, suggesting to Brosseau that these regions were synapsed at the time of interchange. However, it is quite possible that these regions are relatively long regions, providing long segments where breaks can occur, or they may be regions of high breakability. They may even be associated in a chromocentral arrangement such that fortuitous associations occur. There are no existing data capable of discriminating between these various possibilities.

Lucchesi (1965) induced and analysed a series of detachments and Y chromosome fragments using the same B^SYy^+. The distribution of breakpoints in the Y chromosome differed in the two classes of rearrangements. He argued that interchanges between the X and the Y chromosomes are influenced by homologies shared by these chromosomes and that the detachments are the result of induced crossing over. The Y chromosome fragments he suggested to be the result of translocations and deletions not dependent on homology. The data of Brosseau and Lucchesi demonstrate a very basic difference between exchange and interchange between the X and the Y. Spontaneous events apparently occur in the centromeric region of the Y chromosome but do not occur interstitially. Induced events involve breaks all along the Y chromosome. Seemingly exchange is a more precise process than is interchange.

After analysing a new set of Y chromosome fragments generated from the B^SYy^+, Parker (1965) re-examined Lucchesi's data and compared them with his own. In his set of fragments he found that approximately 50% of the Y chromosome fragments were derived from Y–4 interchange, i.e. they were Y–4R. He suggested that most interchanges induced in immature oocytes are "pairing" dependent. It should be emphasized here that in this report as in subsequent reports from Parker's laboratory (Parker 1967, 1969; Parker and Williamson, 1970; Williamson 1969, 1970), the term *pairing* is used to denote nonrandom spatial relationships between chromosomes in the oocyte nucleus and not to imply synapsis. There is as yet no evidence that interchanges of any type occur in immature oocytes that are not dependent on regular association of chromosomes in the oocyte nucleus.

2. *Mature oocytes*

Mature oocytes are some ten times more radiosensitive than are immature oocytes (Stage 7 and earlier) when dominant lethals are measured (Patterson *et al.*, 1932; King, 1957; Parker, 1959). In addition, rearrangements induced in mature oocytes differ both quantitatively and qualitatively from those induced in immature oocytes (Busby, 1971; King *et al.*, 1956; Parker and Hammond, 1958; Parker and McCrone, 1958; Traut and Scheid, 1969; Sankaranarayanan, 1969; Williamson, 1969, 1970). The relative frequency of detachments involving the Y chromosome and the fourth chromosome decreases while the frequency of interchange between the compound-X and the tips of the major autosomes increases from almost zero to an appreciable frequency.

The absence of dose fractionation effects in mature oocytes has previously been explained by postulating delayed rejoining of broken chromosome ends. That at least some breaks rejoin prior to division I was confirmed by Parker and Busby (1972) who recovered interchange products from a reversed acrocentric compound-X chromosome and the Y, chromosomes that usually segregate at division I. Anaphase II nonrandomness was found to influence the recovery of the reciprocal products of interchange with preferential recovery of the shorter element, the same as when interchange is induced in immature oocytes. A comparison of the distribution of breaks in captured detachments [the distal-X in the *C(1)RA*], revealed marked differences. In the capped detachments a majority (32/48) of the breakpoints in the Y were distal to *kl-5* or to *ks-2*, while in captured detachments fewer of the breaks in the Y chromosome were distal to the fertility loci (4/15). A more extensive analysis of Y chromosome breakpoint distribution will be necessary before firm conclusions can be made about these observations.

Several gaps occur in the existing information concerning the genetics of rearrangements induced in mature oocytes. One glaring deficiency is the lack of data on the distribution of breakpoints in the Y chromosome derived from detachments of a *C(1)RM* induced in mature oocytes. It would be interesting to have such data to compare with Brosseau's and Lucchesi's data from immature oocytes. In addition, breakpoint analysis using the *C(1)RA* in both mature and immature oocytes should be interesting, especially since ready identification of capped *vs* captured detachments can be made.

3. Division II nonrandomness

One question of major significance concerns the status of the meiotic chromosomes at the time that X–Y interchange occurs. If interchange is a chromosomal event the frequency of recovery of detachments of compound-X chromosomes with Y^S attached should approximate the recovery of detachments with Y^L attached. If, however, such interchange involves *chromatids* heteromorphic dyads are generated and anaphase II nonrandomness (Novitski, 1951, 1967) would lead to recovery of the shorter of the chromatids comprising the asymmetrical dyads. If, in addition, one arm of the Y is preferentially involved in the interchange event, then anaphase II nonrandomness would insure preferential recovery of one class of detachment.

Nonrandom recovery of complementary interchange products is observed when ionizing radiations are employed to induce detachments of compound-X chromosomes in females with or without a Y chromosome (Parker and McCrone, 1958; Brosseau, 1964; Lucchesi, 1965; Parker, 1969; Parker and Williamson, 1970). The inequality in recovery of complementary classes is one basis for the conclusion that induced interchange involves chromatids. In a series of detachments involving the sc^8Y, Parker and McCrone (1958) recovered 21 detachments with y^+ linked to the X and only 4 detachments of the complementary class, $XY^L{\cdot}Y^S$. In the same experiment the ratio of $X{\cdot}Y^L$: $X{\cdot}Y^S$ was 9:19. Similar inequalities were observed in experiments using other Y chromosomes marked such that complementary classes of interchange products could be recognized. From a series of detachments breaking the doubly-marked Y chromosome, B^SYy^+, Brosseau (1964) estimated coefficients of nonrandomness (*c* values) of recovery of capped-X's in the range of 0·75–0·90. He calculated similar *c* values for the data of Parker and McCrone. However, calculations of *c* values from these data are not reliable since each X–Y interchange produces *two* heteromorphic dyads, each of which would have its own characteristic *c* value.

Abrahamson *et al.* (1956) suggested that preferential recovery of capped detachments as opposed to captured detachments may be due to differences in aneuploidy between these two classes of detachments. Capped detachments are usually hyperploid while captured detachments are usually hypoploid for some part of the genome. However, aneuploidy for parts of the Y chromosome, and, indeed, for parts of the proximal, heterochromatic, region of the X chromosome, has little effect on viability, especially when detachments are recovered in females with a second, complete, X chromosome; yet nonrandom recovery of complementary classes is characteristic in such experiments. In addition, the argument of differential viability of aneuploids is inconsistent with the data from experiments using a *C(1)RA* (Parker and McCrone, 1958; Parker and Busby, 1973). Problems of X-chromosome hypoploidy should be the same in the proximal-X as in the distal-X, yet the proximal-X is preferentially recovered as detachments. The model of nonrandom recovery of the shorter chromatid from asymmetrical dyads, however, adequately explains these observations, and, indeed predicts just such results.

A more direct proof that interchanges induced in oocytes involve chromatids comes from the simultaneous recovery of a detachment carrying a Y chromosome marker and an unaltered Y chromosome. Chromosomal interchanges can not result in such events. Parker and McCrone (1958) reported recovery of $X{\cdot}Y^S$ chromosomes along with an entire Y chromosome; their analysis was not based on simple phenotypic scoring but on genetic analysis of exceptional progeny. Similar recoveries have been recorded resulting from X–Y, X–4R and Y–4R interchanges (Parker, 1965, 1969; Parker and Williamson, 1970; Rinehart and Ratty, 1968; Williamson, 1969, 1970). In addition analyses of Y chromosome fragments which have lost a marker from the doubly-marked B^SYy^+ revealed that many were consequences of anisobrachial interchange between opposite arms of sister chromatids (Williamson, 1969). Genetic data confirming that at least some induced interchanges in males involve chromatids have been reported by Zimmering (1962). Spontaneous interchange between Y chromosomes in X/Y/Y males also involves chromatids (Brosseau, 1958).

B. Interchange Involving only the Y Chromosome

1. *Immature oocytes*

When compound-X females carrying the doubly-marked Y chromosome, B^SYy^+, are irradiated interchange involving the Y, but not the X, yields Y chromosomes or partial Y chromosomes which are detected by loss of one of the terminal markers. Lucchesi (1965) performed the first major analysis of Y chromosome fragments and concluded that marker loss could occur by translocation, gross deletion or single-hit deletion. That the induction of this class of rearrangements was not pairing dependent was questioned by Parker (1965). From a new set of Y fragments he showed that linkage with fourth chromosome markers occurred in approximately 50% of the fragments, implying regular association of the Y and fourth chromosomes in the oocyte nucleus. In addition, Y–4R fragments were recovered as frequently in females as in males; indeed, nearly all Y chromosome fragments recovered in females are Y–4R fragments (37/39; Parker, 1965; Williamson, 1969). These observations imply that interchange directs disjunction of involved centromeres irrespective of their normal disjunctional behavior. Analysis of the Y–4R fragments revealed a different distribution of breakpoints than that found in the remaining fragments. When 4R was linked to the Y fragment many of the breaks in the Y were clustered in the long arm of the Y proximal to *kl–2*. In those fragments not showing linkage with 4R, breaks occurred more frequently towards the ends of the Y chromosome. Since interchange between the Y and the fourth chromosomes can account for only about half of the loss of markers from the B^SYy^+, random breakage events have not been excluded in the induction of Y fragments. However, in all cases that have been tested pairing relationships have been implicated.

Since the induction of interchange in oocytes involves chromatids one type of rearrangement that could account for some Y-fragments would be anisobrachial interchange between the two arms of the Y chromosome. This event could lead to "homozygosis" of the distal marker, producing isomarked Y fragments (y^+Yy^+ or B^SYB^S). This event presumably could not occur unless the arms of the Y were associated spatially so as to allow interchange of parts. Such interarm interchange would not alter segregational properties of the Y and isomarked fragments would be preferentially recovered in males. Recognition of isomarked fragments was accomplished by the "Hairy-wing" position effect of two doses of the sc^8 duplication and by the extreme reduction in eye size by two doses of B^S, and in some cases was confirmed by detachment analysis (Williamson, 1968, 1970). These isomarked fragments accounted for some 45% of all fragments recovered in males. There was no evidence of involvement of major autosomes in the induction of Y fragments. Thus some 75% of all Y chromosome fragments induced in immature oocytes have been shown to be Y–4R or isomarked.

2. *Mature oocytes*

When Y chromosome fragments induced in mature oocytes were analysed Y–4R linkage was found in less than 10% of the cases; approximately 35%

were isomarked and an estimated 20–25% were consequences of Y-major autosome interchange (Williamson, 1970). These data comparing Y chromosome fragments induced in immature and mature oocytes parallel those data on detachments induced in these two classes of oocytes. Both types of rearrangements show a major shift in the involvement of major autosomes in the two types of oocytes. Analysis of fragments induced in both classes of oocytes strengthen the hypothesis that induced interchange routinely involves chromosomes, or regions of chromosomes, that are regularly associated in the oocyte nucleus.

C. Comparison of Interchange in Immature and Mature Oocytes

In all cases in which spontaneous detachments have been analysed the obvious conclusion was that Y chromosome participation in the event was essential: females without a Y chromosome yield no spontaneous detachments. On the other hand, approximately 80% of the detachments induced in immature oocytes can be shown to be consequences of X–Y interchange, and of the remaining 20% about half can be shown to result from X–4 interchange. Only a very few have been shown to involve the major autosomes. Conversely, analysis of detachments induced in oocytes of females without a Y chromosome reveal that a majority are consequences of X–4 interchange, the fourth chromosome in some way mimicking the involvement of the Y chromosome. Again the analyses reveal little involvement of the major autosomes.

The frequent involvement of chromosome four in interchange with X and Y does not necessarily imply special relationships between these chromosomes. Such frequent involvement could be interpreted to imply genetic homology between X and 4 and between Y and 4 or preferential non-homologous associations between X and 4 and between Y and 4. However, the involvement of 4 in interchange with X and Y may be a consequence of its small size such that in a chromocentral-like arrangement of chromosomes in the oocyte it may occupy a position that allows frequent interchange. The relatively minor effects of fourth chromosome hyperploidy does not seriously hinder its recovery and when genetic schemes are devised to analyse interchange of major autosomes the fourth chromosome may be found to be frequently involved.

The treatment with radiation of mature oocytes of females with or without a Y chromosome produces a different array of events from the treatment of immature oocytes. In oocytes with a Y chromosome the Y is much less often involved in interchange. In both classes of females demonstrable involvement of interchange involving the major autosomes occurs.

The distribution of breakpoints in the Y chromosome determined from analyses of detachments recovered from irradiated mature oocytes is basically different from the distribution of breaks obtained from detachments induced in immature oocytes (Brosseau, 1964; Lucchesi, 1965; Parker and Busby, 1972a). A majority of detachments of a *C(1)RA* induced in mature oocytes have breakpoints in the Y chromosome which are distal to all fertility factors, whereas a majority of the detachments of a *C(1)RM* induced in immature oocytes have breakpoints in the Y chromosome located more proximally. Although this comparison is inconclusive because two different compound X chromosomes were used, comparable differences in distributions of breakpoints were observed when Y chromosome fragments were induced in the two classes of oocytes (Williamson, 1969, 1970). These observations have led to the conclusions that the spatial orientation of the chromosomes in the two classes of oocytes are markedly different with centromeric regions being closely associated in immature oocytes while in mature oocytes the centromeric regions have moved apart, bivalents being associated at their ends. These conclusions are based, in part, on the assumption that breaks can only rejoin if broken ends are closely associated and in part on the observation of dispersal of label over the karyosome of the oocyte during stages 12 and 13 (Chandley, 1966).

D. Interchange Induced by Chemicals

The antibiotic mitomycin-C has been reported to induce interchanges between the X and the Y chromosomes as well as between the arms of the Y chromosome (Schewe *et al.*, 1971). Products of X–Y interchange were recognized as detachments of compound-X chromosomes; anisobrachial interchanges in the Y chromosome, were recognized by loss of a marker from the $B^{S}Yy^{+}$. However, the analyses of these detachments and Y chromosome fragments were incomplete and no information is available concerning Y chromosome breakpoints. A complete analysis of the rearrangement induced by mitomycin-C would be desirable.

IV. Summary

There are three classes of genetic recombination involving the X and the Y chromosomes of *D. melanogaster*. The first of these is ordinary crossing over in euchromatic segments. This event is restricted to the female and is a very precise exchange between synapsed homologous segments. Except in rare cases this precision applies to intracistronic as well as intercistronic recombination. Secondly, there is heterochromatic recombination, discussed here as exchange between X and Y. This type of recombination is rare and restricted to regions of chromosomes or entire chromosomes which experience only limited recombination. It apparently occurs equally frequently in the two sexes. The third class of genetic recombination is induced interchange, the occurrence of which is not necessarily based on mutual genetic sequences. It can occur between homologues or between heterologues. The induction of interchange is dependent on chromosomal associations which may be fortuitous or which may be the results of structural order within the nucleus. Interchange can be induced in either sex and is less precise than is spontaneous heterochromatic exchange.

References

ABRAHAMSON, S., HERSKOWITZ, I. H. and MULLER, H. I. (1956). Identification of half-translocations produced by X-rays in detaching attached-X chromosomes of *Drosophila melanogaster*. *Genetics* **41,** 410–419.

ANDERSON, E. G. (1925). Crossing over in a case of attached X-chromosomes in *Drosophila melanogaster*. *Genetics* **10,** 403–417.

BROSSEAU, G. E., Jr. (1958). Crossing over between Y chromosomes in male Drosophila. *Dros. Inf. Serv.* **32,** 115–116.

BROSSEAU, G. E., Jr. (1960). Genetic analysis of the male fertility factors on the Y chromosome of *Drosophila melanogaster*. *Genetics* **45,** 257–274.

BROSSEAU, G. E., Jr. (1964). Non-randomness in the recovery of detachments from the reversed metacentric compound X chromosome in *Drosophila melanogaster*. *Can. J. Gent. Cytol.* **6,** 201–206.

BROSSEAU, G. E., Jr., NICOLETTI, B., GRELL, E. H. and LINDSLEY, D. L. (1961). Production of altered Y chromosomes bearing specific sections of the X chromosome in *Drosophila*. *Genetics* **46,** 339–346.

BROWN, D. E. (1969). Disjunction of some Y chromosome fragments in compound-X females of *Drosophila melanogaster*. M.A. Thesis, Univ. of California, Riverside.

BUSBY, N. (1971). Segregation following interchange induced by irradiating mature oocytes of *Drosophila melanogaster*. *Mutation Res.* **11,** 391–396.

CHANDLEY, A. C. (1966). Studies on oogenesis in *Drosophila melanogaster* with ^{3}H-Thymidine Label. *Expl. Cell Res.* **44,** 201–215.

CREW, F. A. E. and LAMY, R. (1940). Spontaneous inverted exchange between X and Y in *Drosophila melanogaster*. *J. Genet.* **39,** 273–284.

GLASS, B. (1955). A comparative study of induced mutation in the oocytes and spermatozoa of *Drosophila melanogaster*. I. Translocations and inversions. *Genetics* **40,** 252–267.

HERSKOWITZ, I. H. (1954). The relation between X-ray dosage and the frequency of simulated healing of chromosome breakages in *Drosophila melanogaster* females. *Proc. Natl. Acad. Sci. U.S.A.* **40,** 576–585.

HERSKOWITZ, I. H. and ABRAHAMSON, S. (1957). Induced changes in female germ cells of Drosophila. IV. Dependence of induced crossover-like exchanges in oocytes and oogonia upon X-ray intensity. *Genetics* **42,** 444–453.

KAUFMANN, B. P. (1933). Interchange between X- and Y-chromosomes in attached X females of *Drosophila melanogaster*. *Proc. Natl. Acad. Sci. U.S.A.* **19,** 830–838.

King, R. C. (1957). The problem of dominant lethals in *Drosophila melanogaster.* females. *Proc. Natl. Acad. Sci. U.S.A.* **43,** 282–285.

King, R. C., Rubinson, A. C. and Smith, R. F. (1956). Oogenesis in adult *Drosophila melanogaster. Growth* **20,** 121–157.

Kutschera, G. (1954). Die Strahleninduzierte trennung des attached-X-verbandes bei *Drosophila melanogaster. Chromosoma* **6,** 371–380.

Lifschytz, E. and Lindsley, D. L. (1972). The role of X-chromosome inactivation during spermatogenesis. *Proc. Nat. Acad. Sci. U.S.A.* **69,** 182–186.

Lindsley, D. L. (1955). Spermatogonial exchange between the X and Y chromosomes of *Drosophila melanogaster. Genetics* **40,** 24–44.

Lindsley, D. L. (1958). Spermatogonial exchange involving the X but not the Y chromosome in *Drosophila melanogaster. Z. Indukt. Abstamm. Vererblehre* **89,** 103–122.

Lindsley, D. L. and Grell, E. H. (1968). "Genetic Variations of *Drosophila melanogaster.*" *Carnegie Inst. Wash. Publ.* 627.

Lindsley, D. L. and Novitski, E. (1959). Compound chromosomes involving the X and Y chromosomes of *Drosophila melanogaster. Genetics* **44,** 187–196.

Lucchesi, J. C. (1965). The nature of induced exchanges between the attached-X and Y chromosomes in *Drosophila melanogaster* females. *Genetics* **51,** 209–216.

Morgan, L. V. (1922). Non-criss-cross inheritance in *Drosophila melanogaster. Biol. Bull. Woods Hole* **42,** 267–274.

Muller, H. J. (1948). The construction of several new types of Y chromosomes. *Dros. Inf. Serv.* **22,** 73–74.

Muller, H. J. and Dippel, A. L. (1925). Chromosome breakage by X-rays and the production of eggs from genetically male tissue in Drosophila. *Br. J. Exp. Zool.* **3,** 85–122.

Muller, H. J. and Herskowitz, I. H. (1954). Concerning the healing of chromosome ends produced by breakage in *Drosophila melanogaster. Am. Nat.* **88,** 177–208.

Neuhaus, M. E. (1935). Data concerning crossing over between the X and Y chromosomes in females of *Drosophila melanogaster. C.R.* (*Dokl.*) *Acad. Sci. U.R.S.S.* **3,** 41–44.

Neuhaus, M. (1936). Crossing over between the X and Y chromosomes in the females of Drosophila melanogaster. *Z. Indukt. Abstramm. Vererblehre* **70,** 265–275.

Neuhaus, M. (1937). Additional data on crossing over between X and Y chromosomes in *Drosophila melanogaster. Genetics* **22,** 333–339.

Novitski, E. (1951). Non-random disjunction in Drosophila. *Genetics* **36,** 267–280.

Novitski, E. (1954). The compound X chromosomes in Drosophila. *Genetics* **39,** 127–140.

Novitski, E. (1967). Nonrandom disjunction in Drosophila. *A. Rev. Genetics* **1,** 71–86.

Parker, D. R. (1954). Radiation-induced exchanges in Drosophila females. *Proc. Natl. Acad. Sci. U.S.A.* **40,** 795–800.

Parker, D. R. (1959). Dominant lethal mutation in irradiated oocytes. *Biological Contributions Univ. Texas Publ.* **5914**, 113–127.

Parker, D. R. (1963). *In* "Repair from Genetic Radiation Damage" (F. H. Sobels, Eds.), pp. 11–19. Pergamon, Oxford.

PARKER, D. R. (1965). Chromosome pairing and induced exchange in Drosophila. *Mutation Res.* **2,** 523–529.

PARKER, D. R. (1967). Induced heterologous exchange at meiosis in Drosophila I. Exchanges between Y and fourth chromosomes. *Mutation Res.* **4,** 333–337.

PARKER, D. R. (1969). Heterologous interchange at meiosis in Drosophila II. Some disjunctional consequences of interchange. *Mutation Res.* **7,** 393–407.

PARKER, D. R. (1970). Co-ordinated nondisjunction of Y and fourth chromosomes in irradiated compound-X female Drosophila. *Mutation Res.* **9,** 307–322.

PARKER, D. R. and BUSBY, N. (1972). Chromosomal interchange in mature oocytes of Drosophila. *Mutation Res.* **16,** 49–58.

PARKER, D. R. and BUSBY, N. (1973). Observations concerning the effects of radiations on the segregation of chromosomes. *Mutation Res.* **18,** 33–46.

PARKER, D. R. and HAMMOND, A. E. (1958). The production of translocations in Drosophila oocytes. *Genetics* **43,** 92–100.

PARKER, D. R. and MCCRONE, J. (1958). A genetic analysis of some rearrangements induced in oocytes of Drosophila. *Genetics* **43,** 172–186.

PARKER, D. R. and WILLIAMSON, J. H. (1970). Heterologous interchange at meiosis in Drosophila III. Interchange-mediated nondisjunction. *Mutation Res.* **9,** 273–286.

PATTERSON, J. T. and MULLER, H. J. (1930). Are "progressive" mutations produced by X-rays? *Genetics* **15,** 495–578.

PATTERSON, J. T., BREWSTER, W. and WINCHESTER, A. M. (1932). Effects produced by aging and X-raying eggs of *Drosophila melanogaster*. *J. Hered.* **23,** 325–333.

RAPOPORT, I. A. (1940). Proof of chromosome fragmentation. *Compt. rend.* (*Doklady*) *Acad. Sci. U.R.S.S.* **29,** 612–615.

RAPOPORT, I. A. (1941). Mutations restituting the telomere. *Compt. rend.* (*Doklady*) *Acad. Sci. U.R.S.S.* **31,** 266–269.

RINEHART, R. R. and RATTY, F. J. (1968). Further evidence that exchange occurs between chromatids in X–Y detachments. *Dros. Inf. Serv.* **43,** 142.

ROBERTS, P. A. (1969). Some components of X ray-induced crossing over in females of *Drosophila melanogaster*. *Genetics* **63,** 387–404.

SANKARANARAYANAN, K. (1969). The effects of oxygen and nitrogen post treatments on the survival of irradiated stage-14 oocytes of *Drosophila melanogaster*. *Mutation Res.* **7,** 369–383.

SCHEWE, M. J., SUZUKI, D. T. and ERASMUS, U. (1971). The genetic effects of mitomycin-C in *Drosophila melanogaster* I. Induced mutations and X–Y chromosomal interchanges. *Mutation Res.* **12,** 255–267.

SIDOROV, B. N. (1941). Spontaneous mutations in the scute^{8} inversion in *Drosophila melanogaster*. *C.R. Acad. d. Sci. U.S.S.R.* **30,** 248–249.

STERN, C. (1927). Ein genetischer und zytologischer Beweis fur Verberung im Y-Chromosom von *Drosophila melanogaster*. *Z. Indukt. Abstamm. Vererblehre* **44,** 187–231.

STERN, C. (1929). Untersuchungen uber Abberatronen des Y-chromosoms von *Drosophila melanogaster*. *Z. Indukt. Abstamm. Vererblehre* **51,** 253–353.

STERN, C. and DOAN, D. (1936). A cytogenetic demonstration of crossing over between X- and Y-chromosomes in the male of *Drosophila melanogaster*. *Proc. Natl. Acad. Sci. U.S.A.* **22,** 649–654.

STERN, C. and OGURA, S. (1931). Neue Untersuchungen uber Abberationen des Y-Chromosoms von *Drosophila melanogaster*. *Z. Abstgsi* **58,** 81–121.

Traut, H. (1967). X-ray induction of 2;3 translocations in mature and immature oocytes of *Drosophila melanogaster*. *Genetics* **56,** 265–272.

Traut, H. and Scheid, W. (1969). The dose-dependence of X-chromosome loss induced by X-rays in mature oocytes of *Drosophila melanogaster*. *Mutation Res.* **7,** 471–474.

Williamson, J. H. (1968). Identification of Y fragments with two doses of y^+ or B^S. *Dros. Inf. Serv.* **43,** 157.

Williamson, J. H. (1969). On the nature of Y chromosome fragments induced in *Drosophila melanogaster* females I. Immature oocytes. *Mutation Res.* **8,** 327–335.

Williamson, J. H. (1970). On the nature of Y chromosome fragments induced in *Drosophila melanogaster* females II. Mature oocytes. *Mutation Res.* **9,** 85–90.

Williamson, J. H., Parker, D. R. and Manchester, W. G. (1970a). X-ray-induced recombination in the fourth chromosome of *Drosophila melanogaster* females I. Kinetics and brood patterns. *Mutation Res.* **9,** 299–306.

Williamson, J. H., Parker, D. R. and Manchester, W. G. (1970b). X-ray-induced recombination in the fourth chromosome of *Drosophila melanogaster* females II. Segregational properties of recombinant fourth chromosomes. *Mutation Res.* **9,** 299–306.

Zimmering, S. (1962). Genetic evidence of X-ray-induced exchanges occurring at a four-strand stage in Drosophila spermatocytes. *J. Hered.* **53,** 254–256.

18. Genetic Units of *Drosophila*—Simple Cistrons

V. FINNERTY

Department of Biology
University of Connecticut
Storrs, Connecticut, U.S.A.

I. The rosy locus

A. INTRODUCTION

Of central importance to the development of current ideas concerning the organization and structure of the genetic material in higher eukaryotes was the early work with *Drosophila*—that inspired by Sutton and Wilson and carried out by Morgan, Stern, Sturtevant, Bridges and Muller. The weight of their work greatly reinforced Mendel's findings. And well it might; for once linkage, an apparent violation of the law of independent assortment, was understood, no repudiation of the Mendelian principles could be found. So imposing was this conceptual framework that when recombinants between mutant alleles of a given gene were first recovered they were viewed not as recombinants but as exceptional progeny associated with crossing over. They were exceptional in that they clearly violated the law of segregation. Indeed, assuming that true alleles must always segregate during meiosis, those which did not were then termed "pseudo-alleles", and a locus represented by an array of mutant alleles which would infrequently recombine was termed a pseudoallelic locus. Quite often various mutant homozygotes of such a cluster would display similar but not identical phenotypes, and mutant heterozygotes were often seen to complement to some degree. It was therefore reasonable that such clusters (better termed complex loci) were thought to consist of a finite number of distinct but functionally related units which were separable one from another by recombination. In some cases the spatial discreteness of the alleles was paralleled by a functional distinction but in other instances a complex behaved as a single unit of function (see reviews by Carlson, 1959 and Stadler, 1954). Studies with microorganisms had uncovered a series of closely linked genetic units controlling enzymes involved in physiologically related reactions, and heterozygotes involving different units in such series were complementary. The spatial clustering of these genetic units was intimately involved with the fact that they were coordinately regulated (Ames and Martin, 1964). Such clusters, operons, then appeared to parallel the complex loci of *Drosophila* (Demerec and Hartman, 1959; Lewis, 1951, 1967).

From studies of bacteriophage, Benzer's operational definition of three types of genetic units included a clear demonstration that one, a cistron, was a unit of function consisting of a linear array of smaller recombinational and mutational units. He speculated that such organization need not be restricted to prokaryotes but may be observed more readily in bacteriophage simply because sampling extraordinarily large numbers of offspring permitted a degree of resolution far greater than that possible with higher organisms (Benzer, 1957). On the other hand, it was suggested that either the mechanism of recombination or the organization of the chromosome in higher organisms could be such as to preclude intracistronic recombination (Green, 1955; Hexter, 1958).

In order to ask whether a functional unit in higher organisms would yield to recombination and reveal a pattern of organization identical to that seen in microbial forms two requirements must be satisfied: first, the resolving power of the recombinational analysis must be made comparable to that seen in microbial forms. Second, the unit must be clearly defined in terms of its function. Thus, evidence must be presented to demonstrate that the array of mutants to be analysed are true lesions of a single unit rather than lesions of several closely linked functionally similar or related genetic units. Investigations addressed to the question of intracistronic recombination in *Drosophila* (Chovnick *et al.*, 1962, 1964; Chovnick, 1966) utilized the rosy series of eye color mutants located at 3–52·0.

B. Fine Structural Analysis

1. *Structural and phenotypic definition of the rosy locus*

The rosy (*ry*) mutants were chosen for this study because they were found to represent lesions of a single functional unit. A complete account of the studies which led to the structural and phenotypic definition of the *ry* locus is given in a report by Schalet *et al.* (1964).

Eighty *ry* mutants have been described (Lindsley and Grell, 1968), the majority of which were X-ray induced, while only a few are spontaneous alleles. Rosy mutants possess only 35% of wild type amounts of the red eye pigments (Nolte, 1955) and thus display a dull brown eye color when homozygous. All of these *ry* heterozygotes are non-complementary (mutant) with respect to eye color. Further, *ry* homozygotes lack activity for the enzyme xanthine dehydrogenase (XDH) (Forrest *et al.*, 1956). Some of the reactions catalysed by XDH are given in a report by Forrest *et al.* (1961). Of particular interest is the finding that extracts of ry^1, completely lacking XDH activity, are incapable of converting 2-amino-4-hydroxypteridine (AHP) to isoxanthopterin, whereas extracts from a large array of eye color mutants and wild type could do so (Forrest *et al.*, 1956). As expected, rosy flies (and maroon-like, also lacking XDH activity) accumulate AHP and are deficient for isoxanthopterin (Glassman and Mitchell, 1959a). Rosy (and maroon-like) homozygotes are further seen to possess reduced amounts of drosopterins and increased amounts of biopterin (Hubby and Forrest, 1960). A relationship between isoxanthopterin, the hydroxypteridines and the red eye pigments is strongly inferred but its nature is not unequivocally established (Ziegler and Harmsen, 1969). When heterozygous with wild type neither rosy nor maroon-like show a reduction in drosopterins or in isoxanthopterin (Ursprung, 1961), and display a wild type eye color. In fact flies with only 5–10% of wild type levels of XDH activity will also display a wild type eye color (Glassman and Pinkerton, 1960; Glassman and Mitchell, 1959b). Nevertheless, the eye color defect appears to be related to the lack of XDH activity since hydroxypyrazolopyrimidine, a competitive inhibitor of XDH *in vivo* (Pomales *et al.*, 1963), when fed to wild type larvae can cause them to become *ry* phenocopies (Keller and Glassman, 1965). Rosy mutants (and maroon-likes) due to their XDH deficiency are also unable to catalyse the excretory conversions of hypoxanthine to xanthine to uric acid and this is reflected by their lack of uric acid and accumulation of hypoxanthine (Mitchell *et al.*, 1958), and as expected, they excrete hypoxanthine instead of uric acid. Both rosy and maroon-like mutants have abnormally shortened and malformed malphigian tubules which contain large pteridine globules and presumably accumulations of hypoxanthine; it is assumed that these morphological abnormalities are ultimately related to the enzymatic defect.

In contrast to their similarities rosy mutants differ from those at maroon-like in several respects: (1) Extracts of ry^2 (and wild type) can catalyse the conversion of 4-hydroxypteridine to 2,4-dihydroxypteridine.

Maroon-like extracts are unable to make this conversion (Forrest *et al.*, 1961). (2) At 29°C *ry*, but not maroon-like behaves as a late pupal lethal (Hadorn and Schwinck, 1956). (3) When maroon-like flies are bred from *ma-l*$^+$/*ma-l*$^+$ or *ma-l*$^+$/*ma-l* mothers, the offspring display a non-heritable wild type eye color. Offspring of the reciprocal cross will not show this "maternal effect" (Glassman and Mitchell, 1959a; Chovnick and Sang, 1968), nor is any such effect associated with *ry* mutants. The biochemical basis for these latter three differences between the two loci are unknown. Other differences between the two loci are better understood and are discussed in the following section.

To obtain *ry* mutants, X-rayed adult males were mated to *ry*^{2} females and their progeny visually screened for the mutant eye color. Those *ry* mutants which upon further testing proved to be lethal as homozygotes were also selected by this scheme since they too display the brown eye color when heterozygous with *ry*^{2}.

The *ry* mutants found to behave as homozygous lethals were crossed in such a way as to permit the lethal effect to separate from the *ry* phenotype by recombination. In all of those cases where the lethal effect was not easily separable from the *ry* phenotype it was possible to show a reduction in crossover values somewhere in the area adjacent to *ry*. The inference drawn from these observations was that such *ry* lesions were associated with chromosomal deletions or rearrangements involving that region. A cytological examination of such lethals, *kar*^{3l}, *ry*^{27}, *ry*^{54}, *ry*^{74}, *ry*^{75} and *ry*^{76} (Lefevre, 1971) demonstrated that this was indeed the case. Since the rosy lethals were found to behave either as deficiencies or as double mutants of *ry* and a separable lethal site, the conclusion was drawn that under routine culture conditions there is no lethality intrinsic to lesions involving only the *ry* locus.

In order to delineate an area in which to search for new genetic units which might bear a functional relationship to *ry*, a *ry* region was chosen as that portion of the right arm of chromosome 3 extending from karmoisin (*kar*, 3–51·7) at the left of *ry* to lethal 26 (*l*(3) 26, 3–52·2) to the right of *ry*. Then, adult wild type males were X-rayed and mated so that a mutagenized third chromosome was made heterozygous with a deficiency for the *ry* region (*Df(3)ry*^{27}). Of the 24 rosy-like eye color mutants selected over the *ry* deficiency all later proved to be non-complementary with *ry*^{2}. If the *ry* region contained any additional functional units concerned with XDH activity, hypomorphic mutations of such units would be expected to appear rosy-like when heterozygous for a deficiency for those units. Mutants within such units should then complement mutants of the *ry* functional unit. Since all 24 of the rosy-like mutants were non-complementary with *ry*^{2}, they must be lesions in the *ry* functional unit. Therefore, by these criteria no other loci concerned with XDH activity are believed to exist in the region immediately adjacent to *ry*. Strictly speaking, if adjacent to *ry* there were other functional units which, even if completely deleted, would only lead to a partial loss of XDH activity and a wild type eye color, they would not have been selected over ry^2 or a *ry* deletion. Leaky mutants of *ry* would similarly escape detection since even a small amount of XDH activity leads to a wild type eye color (Glassman and Pinkerton, 1960). It is, nevertheless, most probable that there are no functional units in the *ry* region similar to *ry* in that when mutated they are not lethal and lead to a rosy-like eye color.

A second experiment was designed with the purpose of detecting non-rosy recessive visible and lethal mutations in the *ry* region. Mutagenized third chromosomes were selected both over a deficiency for the *ry* region and over ry^2. Nineteen of these new mutants were crossed *inter se* and with the extant *ry* deficiencies in order to construct a complementation map of the region. Two new sites were found to the left of *ry* and four new sites to the right of *ry*. The linkage relationships were established by standard recombination experiments. The basic relations of these sites as established prior to the fine structural analysis of *ry* are given at the top of Fig. 1. In the course of a later study (Deland, 1971) EMS mutagenesis

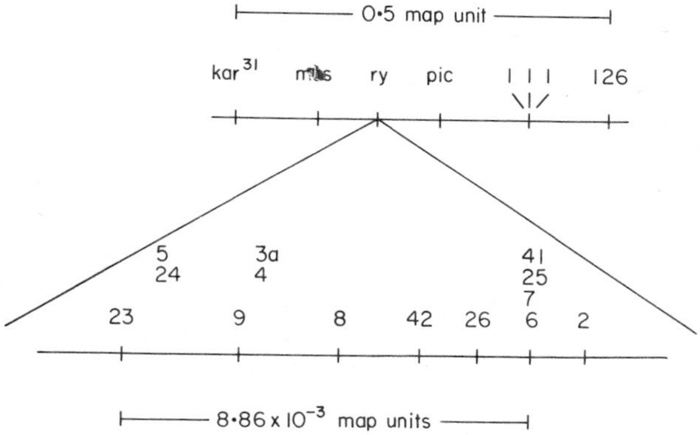

FIG. 1. Map of the rosy region and the rosy cistron.

followed by selection over ry^2 and a *ry* deficiency was employed to induce new visible and lethal recessive mutations in the *ry* region. The 41 new EMS mutations and the extant mutants of the *ry* region were crossed *inter se* to yield the complementation map given in simplified form at the middle of Fig. 1. Although the number of functional groups known in the region contiguous to *ry* was increased threefold, no new rosy-like functional groups were recovered. Thus, rather precise spatial limits are placed upon the *ry* locus.

2. *The lethal selective system*

A selective system patterned after that proposed by Whittinghill (1950) was used throughout the fine structural analysis. The scheme is outlined in Fig. 2; for any pair of *ry* mutants two series of crosses are used in which the female parents differ with respect to the distribution of the recessive

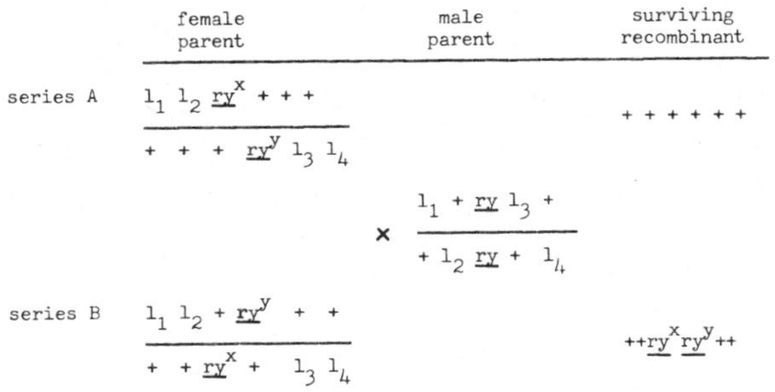

FIG. 2. Basic selective system for a pair of rosy mutants where ry^x is located to the left of ry^y.

lethal markers, l_1, l_2, l_3 and l_4. In both crosses all non-crossovers die, and survivors represent the following recombination classes: 1/4 of the crossovers between l_1 and l_2, 1/4 of the crossovers between l_3 and l_4, and 1/2 of the crossovers between l_2 and l_3. These crossovers are used to provide an estimate of the total number of zygotes sampled in each cross. By mating selective system females to selective system males, wild type males and ry^2/ry^2 males, it was ascertained that the mating to selective system males allows the survival of only 5% of the zygotes produced. Thus, the number of zygotes sampled in a given cross would equal the number of survivors ×20. Further, it was noted that ry/ry flies survive as well as ry/ry^+ under routine culture conditions, at 26°C, and that egg hatchability in all cases was >95%. Estimates of egg hatchability are important in considering the relative merits of various selective systems because a selective procedure which does not allow for cultures rich in larval growth may have the unfortunate result of also selecting against the extremely rare recombinants which might emerge. The selective efficiency of such a system as is outlined in Fig. 2 depends upon the frequency of recombination between the lethals and may therefore be improved by placing lethals even closer to the *ry* cistron. Finally, the efficiency of this system was increased to 99·4% by placing the cultures at 29°C when late in development. Thus a temperature unfavorable only for *ry* zygotes (Hadorn and Schwinck, 1956) was superimposed upon the lethal selective system.

If, as illustrated in Fig. 2, ry^x is located to the left of ry^y, then the series A cross will allow the survival of ry^+ crossovers, but the ry^x ry^y doubly mutant crossover will die. In the series B cross, the ry^+ crossovers die but the doubly mutant recombinants survive. If, however, ry^y is located to the left of ry^x, then the reciprocal results may be expected. In that case, the series B cross would produce ry^+ survivors, and the series A would produce doubly mutant survivors. It is not possible to phenotypically distinguish single from double mutants. Further, the failure to recover ry^+ survivors may either reflect a situation such as the series B cross of Fig. 2, or it may simply be a function of the extreme closeness of two sites, so that the paired reciprocal experiments must be carried out, only one of which yields ry^+ recombinants. If non-selective markers are used in conjunction with the lethal selective markers, a positive conclusion may be

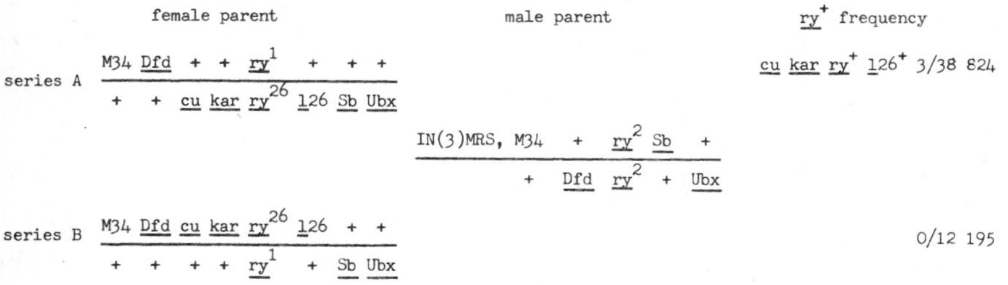

FIG. 3. Recombination analysis of ry^1–ry^{26}.

drawn in the absence of the reciprocal cross. This scheme is outlined in Fig. 3. In series A, ry^1 is tested against ry^{26} so that if ry^1 were located to the left of ry^{26}, then ry^+ individuals would survive as a function of crossing over between the rosy mutant sites. The lethal selective markers in this cross are Minute 34 (*M*(3)34, 3–44·4), Deformed (*Dfd*, 3–47·5), Stubble (*Sb*, 3–58·2) and Ultrabithorax (*Ubx*, 3–58·8), while curled (*cu*, 3–50·0), *kar* and *l26* are non-selective markers. Thus, any marker with a recessive lethal effect may be used as either a selective or non-selective marker, simply depending upon whether the genotype of the male parent allows for homozygosity of that marker.

3. *Mapping Procedures*

Considering again the cross outlined in Fig. 3, 3 ry^+ individuals, all marked with *cu* and *kar*, were recovered indicating that ry^1 lies to the left of ry^{26}. A small scale sampling of the reciprocal cross (series B) gave no ry^+ survivors, consistent with the conclusion from the series A cross. A frequency of 3 ry^+ recombinants in an estimated sample of 776,480 zygotes would give a map distance of $7{\cdot}73 \times 10^{-4}$ map units, since

$$d = \frac{2\ (ry^+ \text{ recombinants}) \times 100}{(\text{total surviving offspring})}$$

In this manner, ry^2 was found to lie $2{\cdot}6 \times 10^{-4}$ map units to the right of ry^{26}, thus establishing the order ry^1 — ry^{26} — ry^2. Using ry^{26} as a reference point, 13 other *ry* mutants were tested; the results of these experiments are given in Table I. Along with ry^2, four other mutants were found to lie to the right of ry^{26}, and the data are shown at the right of Table I. In the left portion of Table I are listed those recombination tests in which the mutants fell to the left of ry^{26}. This left cluster was examined in *inter se* recombination experiments so that four new sites were identified.

TABLE I. Summary of recombination data of an unselected sample of 15 independent mutations of rosy tested against ry^{26} in selective recombination tests.

Mutants tested	Frequency of ry^+ recombinants	Map distance	Mutants tested	Frequency of ry^+ recombinants	Map distance
ry^1–ry^{26}	3/776,480	$7{\cdot}73 \times 10^{-4}$	ry^{26}–ry^2	2/1,538,290	$2{\cdot}60 \times 10^{-4}$
ry^{3a}–ry^{26}	7/238,460	$5{\cdot}87 \times 10^{-3}$	ry^{26}–ry^6	1/633,820	$3{\cdot}16 \times 10^{-4}$
ry^4–ry^{26}	8/688,420	$2{\cdot}32 \times 10^{-3}$	ry^{26}–ry^7	1/701,120	$2{\cdot}85 \times 10^{-4}$
ry^5–ry^{26}	21/821,100	$5{\cdot}12 \times 10^{-3}$	ry^{26}–ry^{25}	1/238,710	$8{\cdot}38 \times 10^{-4}$
ry^8–ry^{26}	4/285,320	$2{\cdot}80 \times 10^{-3}$	ry^{26}–ry^{41}	3/188,520	$3{\cdot}18 \times 10^{-3}$
ry^9–ry^{26}	2/155,000	$2{\cdot}58 \times 10^{-3}$			
ry^{23}–ry^{26}	14/620,490	$4{\cdot}51 \times 10^{-3}$			
ry^{24}–ry^{26}	9/426,720	$4{\cdot}22 \times 10^{-3}$			
ry^{42}–ry^{26}	3/354,150	$1{\cdot}69 \times 10^{-3}$			
ry^{45}–ry^{26}	5/322,920	$3{\cdot}10 \times 10^{-3}$			

TABLE II. Summary of recombination data involving the left cluster of rosy mutants.

Mutants tested	Frequency of ry^{+} recombinants	Map distance $\times 10^{3}$
ry^{23}–ry^{4}	5/701,220	1·43
ry^{23}–ry^{8}	2/468,210	0·85
ry^{23}–ry^{9}	3/436,380	1·37
ry^{23}–ry^{3a}	2/348,420	1·15
ry^{9}–ry^{8}	2/1,129,950	0·35
ry^{24}–ry^{5}	0/168,120	—
ry^{5}–ry^{8}	3/833,280	0·72
ry^{24}–ry^{8}	1/388,800	0·51
ry^{5}–ry^{23}	0/1,397,440	—
ry^{23}–ry^{5}	0/1,018,560	—
ry^{24}–ry^{23}	0/235,830	—
ry^{5}–ry^{8}	0/1,146,960	—
ry^{24}–ry^{9}	0/523,320	—
ry^{3a}–ry^{9}	0/873,450	—
ry^{9}–ry^{3a}	0/597,610	—
ry^{3a}–ry^{9}	0/609,750	—
ry^{3a}–ry^{5}	0/229,290	—
ry^{24}–ry^{3a}	1/331,140	0·60
ry^{8}–ry^{4}	0/597,540	—
ry^{4}–ry^{8}	0/243,530	—
ry^{9}–ry^{4}	0/913,710	—
ry^{4}–ry^{9}	0/373,140	—
ry^{3a}–ry^{4}	0/957,840	—
ry^{4}–ry^{42}	4/352,530	2·27

Table II presents some of the data used to ascertain the existence of those four sites. In the first column are listed mutant pairs in which the distribution of lethal markers was such as to permit the survival of ry^{+} recombinants if the relative position of the pair was as indicated, i.e. ry^{23} to the left of ry^{4}, and so forth. Briefly then, to the right of ry^{23} (but to the left of ry^{26}, Table I) were ry^{4}, ry^{8}, ry^{9} *and* ry^{3a}; ry^{9} was found to lie to the left of ry^{8}, so that the order was ry^{23} – ry^{9} – ry^{8} – ry^{26} – ry^{2}. Other members of the left cluster, ry^{5} and ry^{24}, were inseparable and are placed together between ry^{53} and ry^{2}, since both fell to the left of ry^{8} and were inseparable from ry^{23} and from ry^{9}; ry^{3a} is placed between ry^{8} and ry^{9} since it failed to recombine with either one of them or with ry^{5} but fell to the right of ry^{24}. The mutant ry^{4} is placed with ry^{3a} on the basis of its failure to recombine with ry^{8}, ry^{8} or ry^{3a}. The last site, ry^{42}, fell so far to the right of ry^{4} (but to the left of ry^{26}) that it is most probably not a member of that left cluster. The *rosy* cistron has presently been resolved to six sites;

the ry^5 and ry^{24}, and ry^{3a} and ry^4 groups are not considered separate sites since absolute left-right positions for them were not determined. Results obtained in a later study placed ry^2 to the right of ry^{41} (Chovnick *et al.*, 1971). The lowest portion of Fig. 1 presents the genetic map of the rosy cistron. It is important to note that the various failures to separate pairs of *ry* mutants are not significant. From the smallest distance resolved at the *ry* cistron, that between ry^{26} and ry^2, it may be estimated (Chovnick *et al.*, 1962) that 10^7 failures of recombination are needed to permit the conclusion that two mutants are inseparable. None of the recombination tests sampled more than 10^6 zygotes.

4. Nature of the recombinants

At first, the fine structure experiments involved the testing of an array of independent *ry* alleles against a single randomly selected reference marker. The rationale for this was simply that if the resolving power of recombinational analysis in higher organisms was comparable to that of microorganisms, then such recombination tests should separate the mutants from the reference site. The data of Table I demonstrate that using ry^{26} as a reference site this could be accomplished. Furthermore, choosing a second *ry* reference site, an array of *ry* alleles should similarly be separable from it. The ry^1 allele was chosen as the second reference site against which to test 13 members of the left cluster. All of these recombination tests failed (Chovnick *et al.*, 1964), so that the *inter se* combinations given in Table II were then tried. The members of that left cluster undoubtedly behave as site mutants, since they recombine quite readily with one another.

It should be noted that the failures of recombination with ry^1 did not involve large enough sample sizes to permit the conclusion of inseparability. The earlier inference (Chovnick *et al.*, 1964) that ry^1 may be an intracistronic rearrangement is not borne out by the more recent studies demonstrating recombination with ry^1 (Chovnick *et al.*, 1971).

The rarity of the ry^+ survivors obtained from the fine structure crosses emphasizes the importance of ascertaining whether their appearance is indeed a function of crossing over, or whether they might be ascribed to spontaneous reverse mutations, linked or unlinked suppressors, or to some other unusual event. All ry^+ survivors were recovered as rare single individuals in a culture vessel, and therefore are not the result of either a premeiotic recombinational event or gonial mosaicism in either parent.

The origin of the rare ry^+ offspring was analysed in an experiment wherein the sexes of the parents used for the analysis of the ry^1/ry^2 heterozygote were reversed. Since crossing over in *Drosophila* occurs at significantly lower frequencies in males compared to females, the expectation would be that ry^+ survivors resulting from crossing over would only appear at a detectable rate if the female parent was heterozygous for *ry*. In the case where the female parent was heterozygous, ry^1/ry^2, the series A cross (with ry^1 carrying the left lethals and ry^2 the right lethals, see Fig. 2) yielded 8 ry^+ recombinants in 20,235 surviving offspring. The series B cross (where the arrangement of the lethals is reversed) gave no ry^+ recombinants in 11,940 surviving offspring. The efficiency of that selective system was about 95% so that the series A cross sampled 404,000 (20 $\times$ 20,235) zygotes and the series B cross sampled about 239,000 (20 $\times$ 11,940) zygotes. The male parent was homozygous ry^2 as in Fig. 2. When the sexes of the parents were reversed, under identical culture conditions, only 15 adult offspring emerged from an estimated 600,000 zygotes sampled. All 15 of the offspring were *ry* and were classed via the distribution of outside markers as being the result of extraordinarily rare crossover events in either the male or female parent (Chovnick *et al.*, 1962). The drastic reduction in the number of *ry* survivors (from about 32,000 to 15) and the absence of ry^+ survivors are taken as evidence that the ry^+ (and *ry*) survivors arise as a function of crossing over. Since spontaneous reverse mutation is expected to occur independently of recombinational events, this experiment also provides evidence that the ry^+ survivors did not arise as reversions of *ry* to ry^+. If, as in the case of the ry^1/ry^2 cross, the ry^+ survivors were "reversions", then they appeared in the series A cross at a rate of 1 ry^+/2500 *ry* survivors (8 ry^+/20,235 survivors). Such a rate of sponaneous mutation is extraordinarily high and furthermore was not seen in the series B cross. Moreover, all heterozygotes tested in this study which yielded ry^+ survivors did so in either the series A or the series B cross but never in both cases. If we were to consider the ry^+ individuals as reverse mutations occurring in the survivors of a cross there would be no explanation for the absence of ry^+ individuals in one of the mating series. Further, it is unlikely that spontaneous reverse mutation accounts for the origin of the ry^+ survivors, since their very presence and outside marker distribution was used to construct a perfectly consistent linear map of the *ry* cistron. Those considerations leading to the rejection of spontaneous reverse mutation would similarly lead to the rejection of spontaneous suppressor mutations as an explanation for the origin of the ry^+ individuals.

Finally, it should be emphasized that classes of wild type survivors unaccompanied by outside marker exchange expected in cases of intragenic recombination (Mitchell, 1955; Chovnick *et al.*, 1971) could not have been recovered in these studies since survival depended upon a non-parental configuration of the flanking lethals.

5. *Significance of the genetic analysis*

The fine structural studies of the rosy mutants offer a clear demonstration that there is a mechanism for intracistronic recombination in *Drosophila*. In addition, the organization of the rosy cistron was shown to be identical to that seen in microbial forms: a cistron consists of a linear order of separable sites each capable of independent mutation.

With this as a framework questions concerning the nature of intracistronic recombinational events now become pertinent. Experiments specifically addressed to such questions are discussed in Chapter 8.

C. The Rosy Function

1. *A structural gene for xanthine dehydrogenase*

The first evidence indicating that the rosy locus was a structural gene for XDH came from studies which demonstrated that the level of XDH activity in flies was dependent upon the number of ry^+ genes present (E. H. Grell, 1962). A ry^+ duplication was used to obtain flies with three doses of ry^+ and such individuals possessed 3 times the XDH activity of those having 1 ry^+ gene. An individual with two doses of ry^+ has twice the XDH activity of ry^+/ry. The proportional relationship between the level of XDH activity and the number of ry^+ genes was interpreted as an indication that the production of messenger RNA at the ry^+ locus is the limiting factor in the synthesis of the enzyme (Glassman, 1965). In contrast to this, a parallel study with *ma-l* demonstrated that the level of XDH activity does not bear a proportional relationship (gene dosage) to the number of $ma\text{-}l^+$ genes present, since $ma\text{-}l/ma\text{-}l^+$ has the same XDH activity as $ma\text{-}l^+/ma\text{-}l^+$ or $ma\text{-}l^+/ma\text{-}l^+/ma\text{-}l^+$ (E. H. Grell, 1962; Glassman, *et al.*, 1962). Similarly, lxd/lxd^+ has the same XDH activity as lxd^+/lxd^+ (Keller and Glassman, 1964a). The question of the validity of interpretations of dosage phenomena is presently difficult to resolve. The low xanthine dehydrogenase (*lxd*) locus (Keller and Glassman, 1964a) serves as an example: there is no gene dosage effect with respect to XDH activity since lxd^+/lxd has the same activity as lxd^+/lxd^+ (Keller and Glassman, 1964b). Yet lxd/lxd^+ has about 50% of the aldehyde oxidase and pyridoxal oxidase activities found in lxd^+/lxd^+ (Courtright, 1967; Collins and Glassman, 1969). Furthermore, *lxd* does not appear to be a structural gene for aldehyde oxidase (Courtright, 1967; Dickenson, 1970) or for xanthine dehydrogenase (Karam, 1965). The case of the *lxd* mutation serves to illustrate that dosage phenomena *per se* are really not useful criteria for deciding whether or not a locus is the site of a particular structural gene.

A more direct line of evidence comes from studies of electrophoretic variants for XDH which could be localized to the rosy mutant site (Yen and Glassman, 1965). Their experiments demonstrated that parental flies bearing differing electrophoretic variants of XDH produce hybrid progeny having an XDH with a mobility intermediate between those of the parents, along with the two expected parental forms. However, the XDH produced by several different *ry*/*ry*$^+$ hybrids has an electrophoretic mobility resembling only that form present in the *ry*$^+$ parent. The fact that the presence of a *ry* mutant allele does not affect the mobility of the XDH produced by such hybrids clearly indicates that a lesion at *ry* leads to either a lack of XDH or the production of a defective XDH molecule.

Of further interest is a second series of experiments (Yen and Glassman, 1965) wherein *ry*$^+$ flies bearing a given electrophoretic variant of XDH were crossed to *ma-l*, thereby producing hybrid progeny with an electrophoretic variant of XDH different from the *ry*$^+$ parent. Here then is the evidence that although the *ma-l* mutant lacks XDH activity, it does contain a structural gene for XDH. When *ry*/*ry* parents are crossed to *ma-l* mutants, their progeny bear only that XDH variant previously found in the *ma-l* stock, serving to further eliminate *ma-l* as a structural gene for XDH. Similar experiments with *lxd* led to the same conclusion: it has little to do with the structure of XDH.

A third line of investigation involved the preparation of antibodies to the XDH produced by wild type flies which were used to detect the presence of inactive XDH molecules (cross reacting material or CRM) in various mutant genotypes. One might expect missense mutants in a structural gene to produce such inactive molecules capable of some reaction with antibody to the wild type protein, whereas molecules identical to wild type XDH would be more highly reactive with that antibody. The *ry* homozygotes and *ma-l*/*ma-l*; *ry*/*ry* flies produce a small amount of CRM, while *ma-l*/*ma-l* and *lxd*/*lxd* produce near normal quantities of inactive XDH molecules (Glassman and Mitchell, 1959a; Karam, 1965). This indicates that the *ry* mutation results in the production of far fewer or relatively different XDH molecules compared to the wild type situation, and the presence of mutations at the *ma-l* or *lxd* loci has little effect on the production of wild type quantities of XDH CRM.

2. *Other loci interacting with rosy*

There are presently other loci known to be involved with the production and/or function of the XDH molecule. For one, maroon-like (*ma-l*) there exists an array of independent mutations, all of which like *ry* are completely deficient for XDH when homozygous (see the following section). Another locus, *lxd* (3–33) having 25% of the XDH activity of Oregon-R, is represented by a single allele extracted from an inbred but otherwise wild type population (Keller and Glassman, 1964a). Early studies with these mutants demonstrated that the lack of XDH activity in either rosy, maroon-like or low xanthine dehydrogenase is not due to the presence of a simple inhibitor (Glassman and Mitchell, 1959a; Glassman *et al.*, 1964). Since then a considerable amount of work has been directed toward understanding the relationship of the three loci, and this is discussed in the following section. The available evidence suggests that rosy is a major structural gene for XDH and that maroon-like produces a molecule intimately associated with XDH which is necessary for its activity. Glassman (1965, Glassman, *et al.*, 1968) has speculated that *lxd* may produce still another molecule necessary in some way for the function of XDH, or it may be involved in controlling the maroon-like product. There is at present no evidence to suggest that either maroon-like or low xanthine dehydrogenase are related to each other via a specific control mechanism. Further, there is no reason to suspect that these three loci are the only ones involved in the final expression of XDH activity (see the following section).

II. The maroon-like locus

A. Introduction

The original lesion of the maroon-like locus (*ma-l*, 1–64·8±) was reported in 1935, and remained its sole representative for 25 years (Lindsley and Grell, 1968; Schalet and Finnerty, 1968a). There was understandably little interest in the mutant until a survey of a large number of eye color mutants revealed that *ma-l*, along with rosy, lacked xanthine dehydrogenase (XDH) activity (Forrest *et al.*, 1956). Later came the finding that $ma\text{-}l^1/ma\text{-}l^{F1}$ heterozygotes display a wild type eye color but only a small restoration of XDH activity (Glassman and Pinkerton, 1960). To add to its fascination, *ma-l* was found to lack activity for two other enzymes, pyridoxal oxidase (PO) (Forrest *et al.*, 1961) and aldehyde oxidase (AO) (Courtright, 1967). The three enzymatic activities reside in separable molecular species (Courtright, 1967; Collins, *et al.*, 1971) and appear to catalyse metabolically unrelated reactions. The functional relationship of $ma\text{-}l^1$ to $ma\text{-}l^{F1}$ and the obviously complex relationship of maroon-like and rosy to XDH activity initially prompted studies of the complementation behavior and genetic organization of the locus. At first those studies revealed an elaborate pattern of complementation (Chovnick *et al.*, 1969) which, when considered with its biochemical pleiotropy, are typically seen in cases of complex loci (Lewis, 1967). Despite its apparent complexity, further biochemical and genetic studies provided independent lines of evidence to indicate that *ma-l* functions as a single cistron (Chovnick *et al.*, 1969; Finnerty and Chovnick, 1970).

B. Mapping Procedures

1. Description of mutants

Maroon-like and rosy mutants (see the previous section) are morphologically indistinguishable. Of the 37 known *ma-l* mutations 18 are lethal as homozygotes or hemizygotes and in all possible heterozygous combinations *inter se*. These X-ray induced *ma-l* mutants were judged to be deficient for *ma-l* and some of the surrounding genetic material on the basis of their non-complementarity both with viable *ma-l* mutants and with various other lethal and visible mutants in the *ma-l* region. The extent of the deficiency borne by each of the lethal *ma-l* mutants is fully described elsewhere (Schalet and Finnerty, 1968b; Chovnick *et al.*, 1969). Cytological analysis of some of these deficiencies proved that they are indeed chromosomal deletions (Schalet and Lefevre, 1973). No lethality appears to be associated with *ma-l* locus *per se* since a deletion involving only the *ma-l* locus is not lethal (Schalet and Finnerty, 1970).

The 19 non-lethal *ma-l* mutants were recovered from separate mutational events induced by X-rays and a variety of chemical mutagens. These fully viable *ma-l* mutants, together with their mutagenic origin are listed in Table III. As with the rosy studies, the first question of interest involved placing spatial limits upon those genes in the vicinity of *ma-l* which might bear a functional relationship to the *ma-l* locus. An extensive study of the proximal region of the X-chromosome (see Chapter 21) revealed a single eye color mutation, melanized, which is morphologically dissimilar from *ma-l* and is relatively distant from the *ma-l* locus. Complementation mapping utilizing both *ma-l* and non-*ma-l* deletions demonstrated that the viable *ma-l* mutations were restricted to a small portion of the proximal X chromosome (Schalet and Finnerty, 1968b).

All of the extant *ma-l* mutants were selected on the basis of a dull brown eye color, and as was the case for the rosy mutants, probably represent a rather limited array of the mutational lesions possible at these loci. The exact nature of the relationship of XDH activity to the synthesis of eye pigments is unknown, but is probably concerned with the ability of the enzyme to catalyse certain pteridine reactions. The evidence for the relationship of XDH activity to eye color (see the section on rosy) does not preclude the possibility that mutations affecting XDH (at *ma-l* or *ry*) unaccompanied by an eye color defect may have been induced but would not have been selected. The XDH of *Drosophila* probably contains

TABLE. III. Non-lethal maroon-like mutants.

Mutant	Mutagen	Reference
$ma\text{-}l^{1}$	X-ray	Lindsley and Grell (1967)
$ma\text{-}l^{2}$	X-ray	Schalet (1961)
$ma\text{-}l^{F1}$ ($bz;ma\text{-}l^{bz}$)*	Nitrogen mustard CB 3007	Fahmy and Fahmy (1958)
$ma\text{-}l^{F2}$ ($ma\text{-}l\ bz^{56k}$)*	Methyl Methanesulphonate	Fahmy and Fahmy (unpublished observations)
$ma\text{-}l^{F3}$ ($ma\text{-}l^{65c}$)*	N-ethyl-N-nitrosourethane	Fahmy and Fahmy (unpublished observations)
$ma\text{-}l^{F}$ (bz^{65c})*	N-ethyl-N-nitrosourethane	Fahmy and Fahmy (unpublished observations)
$ma\text{-}l^{14}$	X-ray	Schalet and Finnerty (1968a)
$ma\text{-}l^{20}$	2,4,6-triethyleneimino-1,3,5-triazine (TEM)	*ibid.*
$ma\text{-}l^{21}$	TEM	*ibid.*
$ma\text{-}l^{23}$	TEM	*ibid.*
$ma\text{-}l^{24}$	ethyl methanesulfonate (EMS)	*ibid.*
$ma\text{-}l^{25}$	EMS	*ibid.*
$ma\text{-}l^{26}$	TEM	*ibid.*
$ma\text{-}l^{27}$	TEM	*ibid.*
$ma\text{-}l^{28}$	TEM	*ibid.*
$ma\text{-}l^{29}$	TEM	*ibid.*
$ma\text{-}l^{30}$	EMS	*ibid.*
$y^{+}Yma\text{-}l^{106}$	X-ray	*ibid.*
$y^{+}Yma\text{-}l^{116}$	X-ray	*ibid.*

* Prior designations.

two distinct sites for substrate binding, one for purines and another for pteridines (Yen and Glassman, 1967). One might imagine that some of the mutations affecting the purine binding site need not necessarily affect the pteridine binding site. Similarly, any mutation leading to only a partial loss of XDH activity but a wild type eye color would not have been selected. The problems associated with the selection of such classes of mutations may be at least partially obviated in future studies by the use of the purine selective system. Moreover, the purine system offers the possibility of obtaining several types of mutational lesions at the low xanthine dehydrogenase (*lxd*, 3–33) locus (Keller and Glassman, 1964a) and perhaps some mutations for so far undefined loci involved in purine metabolism or in the final expression of XDH activity.

2. *The purine selective system*

Glassman (1965) first reported that flies lacking XDH activity reared on purine-enriched standard *Drosophila* medium would die before eclosion while wild types would survive. The concentration of purine necessary to kill a given genotype is directly proportional to the level of XDH present in that genotype. A purine-enriched media may provide the basis for a variety of either visual or lethal selective systems. The following are examples of some of the possibilities it presents: (1) For recombinational analysis of any locus deficient for XDH one may utilize the lethal effects of purine to select the exceedingly rare wild types arising from appropriate mutant heterozygotes (Finnerty *et al.*, 1970a; Chovnick *et al.*, 1970; Smith *et al.*, 1970). Further, spontaneous or induced wild type revertants arising from mutant homozygotes for such loci could be selected from

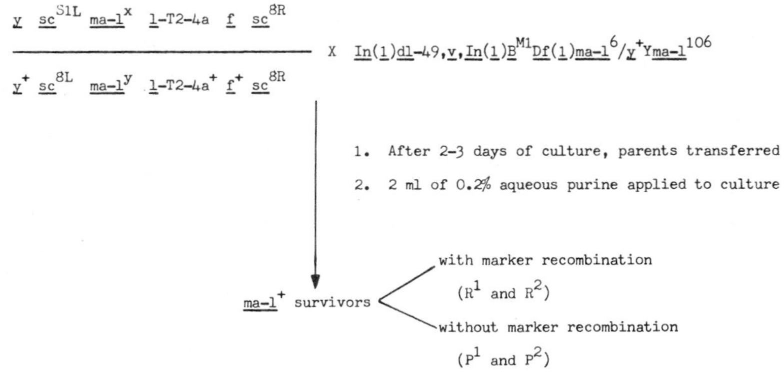

FIG. 4. Typical fine structure cross at *ma-l*.

purine-treated cultures. Various suppressors of XDH-negative mutants might also be selected in this manner. (2) Appropriately crossed individual wild types bearing mutagenized chromosomes may be cultured on normal media followed by a transfer to a replicate purine-treated culture. The absence of offspring (or a class of offspring) in the purine-treated culture would then indicate the presence of any newly induced mutation leading to a deficiency of XDH activity; the mutant (which need not display a mutant eye color) is then recovered from the untreated culture. Depending upon the arrangement of the crosses, this may be used to select recessive XDH negatives against known mutations for *ry*, *ma-l* or *lxd*, or for selecting dominant XDH negatives at any locus. Further, if the treated chromosomes are rendered homozygous, replicate cultures could be used to select XDH negatives for any locus. (3) An *in vivo* inhibitor of XDH (Pomales *et al.*,

TABLE IV. Surviving progeny in fine structure crosses

Series	Experimental cross	*ma-l*⁺ Chromosomes R^1	R^2	P^1	P^2	Total progeny X 10^{-3}	Map distance X 10^4
	ma-lF3/ma-l^2	0	5	1	1	1848	5·4
	ma-lF3/ma-l^{21}	0	3	0	1	765	7·8
	ma-l^2*/ma-l*^{21}	0	1	0	1	4760	0·4
A	*ma-lF4/ma-l*^{2}	2	0	0	0	511	7·8
	ma-lF4/ma-l^{21}	1	0	0	0	767	2·6
	ma-lF1/ma-l^{21}	3	0	3	2	8590	0·7
	ma-lF1/ma-l^2	0	0	1	0	1500	—
	ma-lF4/ma-lF1	2	0	0	1	3000	1·3
	ma-l^1*/ma-lF3*	2	0	1	5	2500	1·6
B	*ma-l*^{1}*/ma-l*^{2}	0	0	0	1	3389	—
	ma-lF4/ma-l^1	2	0	4	1	1922	2·1
	ma-lF1/ma-l^1	1	0	0	0	2071	1·0
	ma-l^2*/ma-l*^{20}	1	0	0	0	507	3·9
	ma-l^2*/ma-l*^{29}	1	0	0	2	3078	0·7
C	*ma-l*^{2}*/ma-l*^{25}	0	0	0	0	1675	—
	ma-l^2*/ma-l*^{23}	0	0	1	3	1701	—
	ma-l^2*/ma-lF2*	0	0	0	0	7970	—
	ma-l^1*/ma-lF2*	0	0	0	0	4460	—
	ma-lF3/ma-l^{20}	1	0	3	3	4025	0·5
D	*ma-lF3/ma-l*^{29}	0	0	0	0	4068	—
	ma-lF3/ma-l^{23}	0	0	1	0	500	—

R^1, a$^+$ *ma-l*$^+$ b recombinant; R^2, a *ma-l*$^+$ b$^+$ recombinant. P^1, *y ma-l*$^+$ *l T2–4a* parental; P^2, *y*$^+$ *ma-l*$^+$ *l T2–4a* parental.

1963), HPP (4-hydroxypyrazolo (3,4,-d) pyrimidine), when mixed with standard medium will effectively create phenocopies of the dull brown (*ry* or *ma-l*) eye color in individuals containing rather low levels of XDH activity; the concentration of HPP necessary for the phenocopy being directly proportional to the level of XDH activity present in the fly (Keller and Glassman, 1965). Here too, depending upon the specific arrangement of the crosses, HPP media may be used to visually select leaky alleles against known lesions at the *ry*, *ma-l* or *lxd* loci (Keller and Glassman, 1965). In addition, from mutagenized wild types it should be possible to select for dominant alleles at any locus which might lead to a lowered XDH activity. If the treated chromosomes were made homozygous, recessive mutations for any locus leading to a partial loss of XDH activity might be visually selected. A medium containing HPP alone, however, has some limitations as a selective tool since concentrations low enough to allow complete viability will permit some newly induced mutants with moderate XDH activities to escape the action of the HPP. A lethal selective system for extracting such mutant classes from any mutagenized XDH negative may be constructed via the use of a medium containing HPP plus purine along with a replicate culture of standard media. Although purine alone could be used for such purposes, its combination with HPP allows a finer control on the level of XDH activity necessary for survival. Further, increasing quantities of HPP in the media necessitate using less of the more expensive purine. Therefore, an HPP-purine media may be used to select flies which possess levels of XDH activity in excess of those normally found in wild type. Thus, all classes of purine-HPP resistant mutants and all mutations leading to greater than wild type levels of XDH activity may be selected. Certainly either purine or HPP alone might be used to select for mutations leading to resistance for one but not both of the two agents. Some of the uses outlined for the purine-HPP selective system have already met with success (Duck, 1973). The toxicity of purine is not fully understood, but it was suggested that XDH may convert the water-soluble purine to hypoxanthine; the relative insolubility of hypoxanthine crystals would then allow them to be segregated within the malphigian tubules where their toxic effects could be minimized (Glassman, 1965). In contrast to this is the finding that purine does not appear to act as a substrate for XDH, and will even inhibit the conversion of hypoxanthine to xanthine when assayed on acrylamide gels (McCarron, unpublished observations). Thus, the exact basis for the toxic effects of high levels of HPP or purine even on wild types is unknown. (4) Finally, the collection of large numbers of virgin females or males for almost any purpose may be accomplished with ease using purine-enriched media with stocks bearing appropriate *ma-l* or *ry* markers (Finnerty *et al.*, 1970b).

For the fine structural analysis of *ma-l* (Finnerty *et al.*, 1970a), exactly 15 pairs of parental flies were placed in half-pint creamers containing standard media for 2–3 days. Immediately after transfer aqueous purine is added to the culture. This procedure is then repeated for a series of five transfers. Under these conditions more than 90% of $ma\text{-}l^+$ zygotes will survive and egg hatchability for both $ma\text{-}l^+$ and *ma-l* is normal. An estimate of the total number of zygotes sampled for each cross was obtained by omitting purine from 1/60 of the cultures, and counting the progeny in those cultures.

3. *Experimental crosses*

A typical fine structure-cross is outlined in Fig. 4. The relative position of any pair of *ma-l* mutants is determined from the pattern of recombination of the outside markers borne by the surviving $ma\text{-}l^+$ offspring. For example, from heterozygous females, a $ma\text{-}l^x$ b/$a^+ ma\text{-}l^y$ b^+, $ma\text{-}l^+$ offspring of the type a $ma\text{-}l^+$ b^+ would indicate that $ma\text{-}l^x$ was to the right of $ma\text{-}l^y$; if the $ma\text{-}l^+$ recombinants were $a^+ ma\text{-}l^+$ b, $ma\text{-}l^y$ would be placed to the right of $ma\text{-}l^x$. From any given heterozygous *ma-l* female, all of the $ma\text{-}l^+$ progeny showing recombination of the outside markers displayed exclusively either one or the other (R^1 or R^2, Table IV) of the outside marker distributions, thus providing an unambiguous position in each case. In every case the *ma-l* allele listed on the left in the first column of Table IV entered the cross marked with the recessive alleles of the outside markers and the *ma-l* allele listed on the right was present on a chromosome carrying the wild type alleles of those outside markers. The exact genotypes of the parental flies and the crosses used to determine the outside marker distribution of the $ma\text{-}l^+$ offspring are given elsewhere (Finnerty *et al.*, 1970a). The pertinent feature of the genotypic constitution of the flies used for the fine structural crosses is that the outside markers and tester chromosomes were completely non-selective for $ma\text{-}l^+$ offspring, the only selective agent being the purine. All $ma\text{-}l^+$ offspring analysed in this study appeared as rare single individuals in a culture vessel; contaminations would appear as a burst of wild type progeny which were discarded.

Those $ma\text{-}l^+$ survivors which bore a recombination of the outside markers (R^1 and R^2, Table IV) comprised 41% of the total number of wild types recovered. In addition, 59% of the $ma\text{-}l^+$ survivors did not display a recombination for the outside markers (P^1 and P^2, Table IV); they represent a class of progeny frequently observed in recombinational studies involving tightly linked markers. The nature of the intragenic events which are reflected by such exceptional progeny was brought to light in a later study and is fully discussed in Chapter 8. Although such wild types, lacking recombination for the outside markers do not provide useful mapping data, they nevertheless represent the majority of the *ma-l*$^+$ offspring recovered in the study and some rather definite ideas concerning their mode of origin were ascertained from a consideration of the present data: (1) The crosses used to confirm and/or identify the outside markers carried by the *ma-l*$^+$ survivors were such as to allow dominant or recessive autosomal suppressors to segregate from the *ma-l*$^+$ chromosome. These crosses could not eliminate closely linked dominant suppressors or second site mutations within the *ma-l*$^+$ locus. However, such suppressors and second-site mutants should not lead to a uniform restoration of wild type levels of XDH activity. Enzyme assays of a random sampling of *ma-l*$^+$ survivors (recombinants and exceptionals) demonstrated that they behaved as if they were wild type with respect to XDH activity (Finnerty *et al.*, 1970a). Although a few of the *ma-l*$^+$ exceptionals could have arisen as a result of a second-site mutation or closely linked dominant suppressor, certainly the majority of the wild types did not originate in that manner. (2) Another possibility for the origin of the *ma-l*$^+$ exceptionals would invoke conventional two-strand double exchanges, one between the *ma-l* sites and the second between the *ma-l* cistron and one or the other outside marker. In that case, an extraordinarily high degree of negative interference (multiple exchanges within a short segment of the chromosome) would be required, since this putative double exchange leading to exceptional progeny would have to occur *more* frequently than the single exchanges leading to the recombinant progeny. If the origin of the *ma-l*$^+$ exceptionals were via classical double exchanges, one of the two crossovers must occur between the *ma-l* mutants If the second exchange occurred anywhere between the distal *ma-l* mutants and the distal outside marker, then a *ma-l*$^+$ exceptional would appear associated with the chromosome which originally bore that distal *ma-l* mutant. A second exchange between the proximal *ma-l* and the proximal outside marker should yield a *ma-l*$^+$ exceptional associated with the chromosome that originally bore the proximal *ma-l* mutant. The first line of Table IV describes a cross in which *ma-l*^{F3} yielded *ma-l*$^+$ recombinants in tests against *ma-l*^{2}, and their outside marker distribution identified *ma-l*^{F3} as the proximal allele and *ma-l*^{2} as the distal allele of that pair. Of the 2 *ma-l*$^+$ exceptionals, one (P^1) carried the flanking markers originally associated with the proximal allele, *ma-l*^{F3}, while the other (P^2) carried the markers associated with the distal allele, *ma-l*^{2}. Since the distal outside marker, *y*, is almost eight times further from *ma-l* than is the proximal outside marker, *lT2–4a*, the expectation would be that the distally derived exceptional should arise much more frequently than the proximally derived *ma-l*$^+$ exceptional. However, from Table IV it can be seen that a total of 15 proximally and 15 distally derived exceptionals were recovered in all, and it therefore appears unlikely that classical double exchanges play a significant role in the origin of the *ma-l*$^+$ exceptionals. (3) The origin of the *ma-l*$^+$ exceptionals is clearly associated with recombination. Considering Table IV, the fine structure experiments fell into 2 classes: (a) those yielding *ma-l*$^+$ recombinants and (b) those which failed to yield *ma-l*$^+$ recombinants. The frequency of *ma-l*$^+$ exceptionals in the first class is 29/34,344,000, while that for the second class is 7/25,263,000. The frequencies are significantly different ($P < 0{\cdot}01$) (Stevens, 1942). (4) If the *ma-l*$^+$ exceptionals arise by spontaneous reverse mutation, then the flanking markers present on the exceptional chromosome identify the mutant allele which "reverted". One may then compare the frequencies with which a given allele "reverts" in crosses yielding recombinants and in crosses not yielding recombinants. Since reversion has no necessary connection to recombination we would expect the frequencies to be the same in each case. Only one allele, *ma-l*^{F3}, was tested frequently enough for such a comparison; *ma-l*^{F3} is an excellent complementer (Table V), thus eliminating the prospect that it could be a small deletion which recombines well but would not be particularly revertable. Nine "revertants" of *ma-l*^{F3} were recovered from four crosses yielding *ma-l*$^+$ recombinants, while one "revertant" of *ma-l*^{F3} was recovered from the two crosses which failed to yield *ma-l*$^+$ recombinants. Since 1/2 of all zygotes sampled in each of those crosses contain the *ma-l*^{F3} allele, they then represent the number of opportunities in which *ma-l*^{F3} could revert. Thus, the frequency of spontaneous "reverse mutation" of *ma-l*^{F3} in crosses yielding *ma-l*$^+$ recombinants was 9/4,569,000 while that frequency in crosses which did not yield *ma-l*$^+$ recombinants was 1/2,284,000. The difference between the two frequencies is significant ($P < 0{\cdot}01$) and does not support the spontaneous mutation hypothesis.

Considering now the *ma-l*$^+$ survivors with outside marker recombination, the first cross in series A (Table IV) placed *ma-l*^{2} to the left of *ma-l*^{F3}. The second cross placed *ma-l*^{21} to the left of *ma-l*^{F3} and the third cross placed *ma-l*^{21} to the left of *ma-l*^{2}, establishing the order *ma-l*^{21} — *ma-l*^{2} — *ma-l*^{F3}. The remaining crosses of series A place *ma-l*^{F4} and *ma-l*^{F1} to the left of both *ma-l*^{2} and *ma-l*^{21}, with *ma-l*^{F4} to the left of *ma-l*^{F1}. The crosses of series B established the position of *ma-l*^{1}; *ma-l*^{25} and *ma-l*^{F2} are placed above *ma-l*^{2} on the basis of their failure to recombine with *ma-l*^{2}. The mutant *ma-l*^{23} is similarly placed because it failed to recombine with *ma-l*^{2} in a larger sample than when tested with *ma-l*^{F3}; *ma-l*^{22} is placed with *ma-l*^{F3} since it fell to the right of *ma-l*^{2} and was inseparable from *ma-l*^{F3}; *ma-l*^{20} fell to the right of *ma-l*^{F3}. Those recombinational tests where there was a failure of separation are interpreted as reflecting the proximity rather than identity of two mutational sites. In some cases the failure to observe

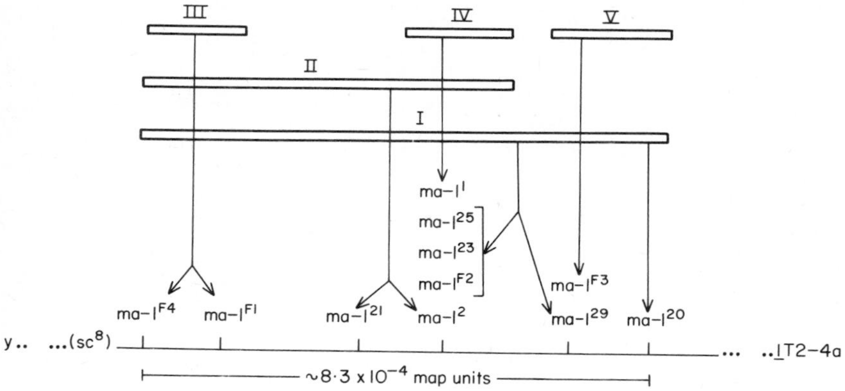

FIG. 5. Colinearity of genetic and complementation maps at *ma-l*.

recombination is quite obviously due to inadequate sampling: *ma-l*^{F1} failed to recombine with *ma-l*^{2} when $1{\cdot}5 \times 10^6$ zygotes were sampled, but *ma-l*^{F1} is clearly not identical to *ma-l*^{2} since it falls to the left of *ma-l*^{1} and *ma-l*^{21}. The entire series of crosses is summarized by the genetic map given at the bottom of Fig. 5. Map distances are estimated as 2 × (frequency of *ma-l*$^{+}$ recombinants) × 100.

The positions given for each of the six sites on the genetic map are unambiguous since each one was obtained from left-right recombination tests. Moreover, the map distances obtained were surprisingly consistent and therefore useful in predicting the left-right positions of various other sites. For example, the *ma-l*^{F3}/*ma-l*^{2} and *ma-l*^{F3}/*ma-l*^{21} crosses suggested that *ma-l*^{21} was further to the left of *ma-l*^{F3} than was *ma-l*^{2}. The *ma-l*^{2}/*ma-l*^{21} cross demonstrated that *ma-l*^{21} was indeed to the left of *ma-l*^{2}. When *ma-l*^{F1} and *ma-l*^{F4} were crossed to the middle sites, *ma-l*^{2} and *ma-l*^{21}, the recombination frequencies suggested that *ma-l*^{F4} was further to the left than *ma-l*^{F1}, and that indeed proved to be the case.

C. COMPLEMENTATION ANALYSIS

1. *Eye color*

When all possible heterozygotes of viable *ma-l* alleles are scored for eye color, certain of them are complementary, i.e. display the wild type eye color in sharp contrast to the dull brown of *ma-l* homozygotes. Such observations may be summarized by a complementation map wherein overlapping lines are used to indicate a lack of complementation and non-overlapping lines indicate complementation (Gillie, 1966). Figure 6 presents the complementation map of *ma-l* along with the mutants listed

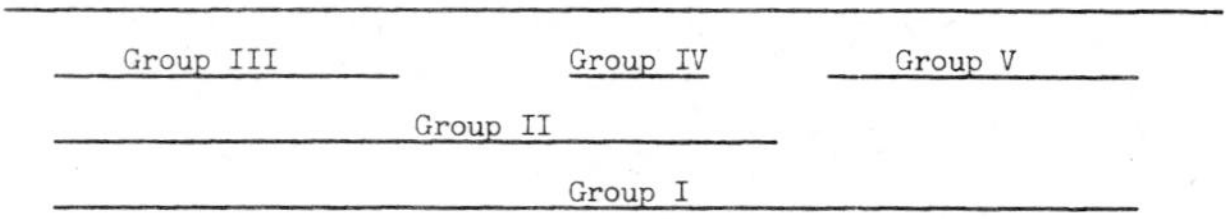

Group I	Group II	Group III	Group IV	Group V
ma-l^{F2}	ma-l^{2}	y^{+}Yma-l^{116}	ma-l^{1}	ma-l^{F3}
ma-l^{14}	ma-l^{21}	ma-l^{F1}		
ma-l^{20}	ma-l^{26}	ma-l^{F4}		
ma-l^{23}	ma-l^{27}			
ma-l^{24}	ma-l^{30}			
ma-l^{25}				
ma-l^{28}				
ma-l^{29}				
y^{+}Yma-l^{106}				

FIG. 6. Maroon-like complementation map.

according to their complementation group. Of the five groups, those of Group I, the complete non-complementers, are the most numerous while two of the groups, IV and V, are represented by a single mutant. Although *inter se* crosses involving any of the lethal *ma-l* mutants (Schalet and Finnerty, 1968a) produce no viable *ma-l* offspring, all of the lethal *ma-l*/viable *ma-l* heterozygotes are predictably non-complementary. The mutants of Group II complement only those of Group V while those of Groups III, IV and V are mutually complementary.

2. *Xanthine dehydrogenase, aldehyde oxidase and pyridoxal oxidase*

All of the *ma-l* heterozygotes complementary for eye color were found to possess varying levels of XDH activity while all of the non-complementary heterozygotes and the homozygotes lacked XDH activity. Table V summarizes the results of enzymatic assays of all possible viable *ma-l* heterozygotes and homozygotes (Finnerty, unpublished observations): complementary heterozygotes are found to possess 5–66% of the XDH activity seen in the wild type. Furthermore, such heterozygotes display a perfectly congruent complementation for aldehyde oxidase activity, with all of those flies lacking XDH activity being similarly deficient for aldehyde oxidase activity. The striking similarity in the degree to which complementary heterozygotes exhibit both activities suggests that the *ma-l* locus plays a similar if not identical role in the final expression of both enzymatic activities. Although not all of the possible *ma-l* heterozygotes were examined, none were found to be complementary for pyridoxal oxidase activity (Chovnick *et al.*, 1969), perhaps due to the insensitivity of that assay (Karam, 1965). The other general possibility would be that the role of the *ma-l* product in the final expression of PO activity is either a trivial one or is so far removed from its catalytic function that effective complementation would not occur.

3. *Simple cistron versus multicistronic models of organization*

The most interesting aspect of the *ma-l* complementation behavior is seen when the complementation map is compared to the genetic map as in Fig. 5, for the two are found to be perfectly colinear. Further, the Group I non-complementary mutants are found exclusively at the right side of the genetic map. This, taken with the colinearity, in terms of an acceptable hypothesis for the functional organization of *ma-l* would lead to consideration of an operon-like model with the mutants of complementation Groups III, IV and V representing each of three adjacent functionally related cistrons. The viable Group I and II mutants would include site mutants as well as deficiencies, the site mutants indicating the direction of translation of a polycistronic message. Thus, Group I site mutants might include lesions at sites concerned with the regulation or initiation of transcription or translation as well as polar translational mutants in the first cistron. Group II site mutants would be polar mutants in the second cistron. Although the polarized distribution of non-complementary mutants and the colinearity of genetic and complementation maps is indicative of a multicistronic organization, it does not *per se* constitute evidence for such a model. A variation of this model would consider *ma-l* as being composed of three adjacent cistrons separately transcribed and translated. All of the Group I mutants would then have to be aberrations involving the three cistrons. The mapping of Group I mutants, particularly *ma-l*^{20} and *ma-l*^{29} which behave as site mutants serves to eliminate this variation of the multicistronic model.

Many of the fine structural crosses involved combinations of *ma-l*^{1} or *ma-l*^{2} and Group I mutants since a Group I site mutant mapping to the left of *ma-l*^{1} or *ma-l*^{2} (and, therefore, clearly not in the first cistron) or a Group II site mutant mapping to the left of *ma-l*^{F1} would have provided evidence against a multicistronic model. It should be emphasized that intercistronic complementation in heterozygotes involves a restoration of activity based upon the wild type products of the loci in question (Schlesinger and Levinthal, 1965). In such instances, whether or not a polycistronic message were involved, it would be difficult to explain the fact that such Group I and II mutations fail to complement.

A second model for the organization of *ma-l* considers the locus a single cistron whose biologically active product, a homomultimer, consists of an aggregate of a single polypeptide. The complementation observed between various mutants would reflect the production of hybrid aggregates consisting of differently defective products of that single cistron (Fincham, 1966).

Although some of the complementary *ma-l* heterozygotes display high levels of XDH activity as would be expected for intercistronic complementation, other heterozygotes are extremely low. Since *ma-l* is fully recessive to wild type, with *ma-l*/+ having about the same XDH activity as +/+ (E. H. Grell, 1962), it is then difficult if not impossible to explain the low levels of complementation (Table V). The high levels of complementing activity in other heterozygotes are not unexpected, since as much as a 67% restoration of activity was reported for a well documented case of intracistronic complementation in *E. coli* (Garen and Garen, 1963).

TABLE V. Xanthine dehydrogenase and aldehyde oxidase in *ma-l* heterozygotes.

ma-l Heterozygotes		Activity[a]/fly, % of wild type	
		XDH	AO
Group I/Group II, III, IV or V		0	0
Group II/Group III or IV		0	0
Group III/Group IV		10	3
Group III/Group V		5	3
Group IV/Group V		25	28
Group II/Group V:	F3/2	11	9
	F3/26	58	58
	F3/27	66	71
	F3/30	54	62
	F3/21	46	45
(all *ma-l* homozygotes)		0	0

[a] XDH activity measured by the method of Glassman, 1962; AO activity by the method of Courtright, 1967. The preparation of extracts is described in Chovnick *et al.*, 1969.

In summary, the extraordinarily high levels of xanthine dehydrogenase and aldehyde oxidase activities in certain complementing heterozygotes while suggestive of intercistronic complementation are also compatible with intracistronic complementation. Only with some difficulty could intercistronic complementation explain the low levels of complementation in other heterozygotes. Moreover, if the lack of pyridoxal oxidase activity were the only biochemical lesion of which we were aware, then the complete lack of activity in those heterozygotes tested might be interpreted in terms of a single functional lesion. Thus, neither model for the organization of *ma-l* is firmly supported by these data; for the present, perhaps the chief value in these considerations lies in the fact that they serve to illustrate the caution necessary in attaching functional interpretations to such observations.

D. Studies concerning the Functional Organization of Maroon-like

1. Biochemical assay of non-complementary mutants

The single cistron-allele complementation model for *ma-l* predicts that the biologically active product of the locus should function in the form of a dimer or higher multiple aggregate. Since the XDH activity in complementary heterozygotes in some way reflects the presence of the *ma-l* product(s), it provides a means for studying their behavior. Specifically, a complementary *ma-l* heterozygote is ry^+ and is, therefore, potentially capable of possessing wild type levels of XDH activity, its limiting factor being the lesions at the *ma-l* locus.

Consider a group of three *ma-l* mutants, *ma-*l^x, *ma-*l^y and *ma-*l^z. *ma-*l^x and *ma-*l^y complement each other but *ma-*l^z complements neither of these two. The allele *ma-*l^z was believed to produce a product because it does complement other *ma-l* alleles. Assuming that the *ma-l* products are active in the form of dimer aggregates which form by random association of monomers and that only by hybrid dimer *x-y* is active, we have two general forms (see Fig. 7) of the allele complementation model which could apply to *ma-l*: (1) The dosage regulated model, which assumes an adjustment of activity of the various alleles to lead to a common finite number of monomers (and therefore dimers) produced by both *ma-*l^x/*ma-*l^y and *ma-*l^x/*ma-*l^y/*ma-*l^z. (2) The second model assumes a constant output of monomers per allele. Comparison of the number of active dimers produced by the *ma-*l^x/*ma-*l^y heterozygote (genotype A) with that produced by the *ma-*l^x/*ma-*l^y/*ma-*l^z heterozygote (genotype B) predicts that the presence of the *ma-*l^z mutant leads to a reduction in the number of biologically active hybrid aggregates. The two allele complementation models may be distinguished by the ratio, A/B, of active dimers expected in the two genotypes. Model I predicts a ratio of 2·25 while Model II predicts a ratio of 1·5. However, an operon-like model predicts that *ma-*l^z, being non-complementary with both *ma-*l^x and *ma-*l^y would be a polar mutant or deletion involving the cistrons represented by *ma-*l^x and *ma-*l^y. Therefore, no reduction in the number of active hybrid aggregates is expected and the XDH activity expected for the two genotypes would be the same, so A/B = 1.

Genotype	ma-1^x/ma-1^y (A)	ma-1^x/ma-1^y/ma-1^z (B)	Ratio A/B
Monomers produced	ma-1^x $\longrightarrow$ x ma-1^y $\longrightarrow$ y	ma-1^x $\longrightarrow$ x ma-1^y $\longrightarrow$ y ma-1^z $\longrightarrow$ z	
Random aggregation into dimers	$(x+y)^2$ $x\cdot x+\underline{2x\cdot y}+y\cdot y$	$(x+y+z)^2$ $x\cdot x+y\cdot y+z\cdot z+\underline{2xy}+2x\cdot z+2y\cdot z$	
If only x·y dimers are active	1/2 of dimers are active	2/9 of dimers are active	
<u>Model I</u> Dosage regulation to produce finite number, 2N, monomers in both genotypes	Total monomers =2N Total dimers = N Active dimers=1/2N	Total monomers=2N Total dimers=N Active dimers-2/9N	2.25
<u>Model II</u> Each allele produces N monomers	Total monomers =2N Total dimers = N Active dimers=1/2N	Total monomers-3N Total dimers=3/2N Active dimers=2/9·3/2N Active dimers=1/3N	1.5

FIG. 7. Two forms of the allele complementation model applied to maroon-like.

The experiment involves the use of attached-X females of the type *ma-l*^{F1}/*ma-l*^{1} (Group III/Group IV). In addition to this attached-X, the females bore certain Y chromosomes carrying X-duplications which in turn carried: *ma-l*^{2} (Group II; Table III); *ma-l*^{113}, or *ma-l*^{102} (Schalet and Finnerty, 1968a) or *ma-l*^{106} (Group I, Table III). Thus, attached-X females, *ma-l*^{F1}/*ma-l*^{1}, bearing the various Y-duplications were assayed for XDH activity. A complete description of the chromosomes and assay methods is given in a report by Chovnick, *et al.* (1969). The results of these experiments are given in Table VI; each experiment was performed 7 times and their average XDH activity is presented in the Table. The controls were either homozygous mutant, *ma-l*^{1}/*ma-l*^{1} or *ma-l*^{F1}/*ma-l*^{F1} to indicate that the assay is capable of recording null activity, and wild type

TABLE VI. XDH activity[a] of maroon-like heterozygotes bearing various Y-duplications.

	Attached-X female, $ma\text{-}l^{1}/ma\text{-}l^{F1}$				Controls			Ratio Genotype
	A		B					
	$ma\text{-}l^{102}$	$ma\text{-}l^{113}$	$ma\text{-}l^{2}$	$ma\text{-}l^{106}$	$ma\text{-}l^{1}/ma\text{-}l^{F1}$	$ma\text{-}l^{1}/ma\text{-}l^{1}$	+/+	A/B
Av. XDH activity	1·6	1·6	0·95	0·88	0	0	0	1·7

[a] Measured as cumulative change in fluorescence units/fly over a 35 min incubation at 30°C. XDH activity is the average of 7 experiments. Extracts were made from adult females which bore the attached-X as well as the indicated Y-duplication.

females to indicate that the assay is competent to detect high levels of XDH activity. The attached-X females bearing the *ma-l* deficiencies, *ma-l*^{113} or *ma-l*^{102}, serve as genotype A, while those attached-X females bearing *ma-l*^{2} serve as genotype B. The presence of *ma-l*^{2} depressed the XDH activity in each one of the 7 experiments. The A/B ratio, averaged for the 7 experiments, was 1·7, thus significantly greater than 1 and less than 2·25 but not different from the 1·5 expected for the allele complementation model assuming a constant output of gene product per allele.

The multicistronic model would predict that *ma-l*^{106} (Group I) be an aberration or deletion involving all three cistrons, a polar mutant in the first cistron or a mutant interfering with the initiation of transcription or translation. In any case *ma-l*^{106}, like *ma-l*^{2} should not produce a detectable product. The finding that *ma-l*^{106}, like *ma-l*^{2} does depress the XDH activity argues that they do produce some product and therefore the multicistronic model does not apply to *ma-l*.

2. *Genetic study of a doubly mutant chromosome*

Consider the mutants *ma-l*^{F4} (Group III), *ma-l*^{1} (Group IV) and *ma-l*^{F3} (Group V) which are mutually complementary. The complementation behavior of the double mutant, *ma-l*^{F4} *ma-l*^{F3}, offers a means of distinguishing between the intercistronic and intracistronic models of complementation, and, therefore, organization of the *ma-l* locus. Such a doubly mutant chromosome made heterozygous with either *ma-l*^{F4} or *ma-l*^{F3} would be homozygous for one of the sites and would therefore display the mutant phenotype. Intercistronic complementation predicts that a heterozygote of *ma-l*^{F4}*ma-l*^{F3}/*ma-l*^{1} should be complementary since this would be a triple heterozygote involving three distinct cistrons. Since *ma-l* is completely recessive to wild type, the model predicts that the presence of three hypothetical wild type products would lead to a detectable level of XDH activity. The single cistron-allele complementation model makes no prediction regarding the complementation behavior of such a double mutant. It is nevertheless reasonable to expect that if *ma-l* produces a single polypeptide, a double mutant, producing a polypeptide carrying two lesions would no longer form active homomultimers with the *ma-l*^{1} polypeptide. The double mutant would thus behave as a non-complementary mutant.

The *ma-l*^{F4}*ma-l*^{F3} doubly mutant chromosomes arose from a recombination experiment which employed a lethal selective system, one adaptable for the fine structural analysis of any sex-linked locus (Schalet, 1971a). This system allows survival of only male progeny of certain crossover classes involving the *ma-l* region, and it assumes the correctness of the map order of *ma-l* sites established earlier (Fig. 5). Females of the genotype given in Figure 6 were crossed to the indicated males on standard *Drosophila* medium. In addition to the lethals flanking *ma-l*, the females carried two inverted third chromosomes, one containing *Ultrabithorax* (*Ubx*^{130}, 3–58·8) and the other, *Stubble* (*Sb*, 3–58·2), both of which are lethal when homozygous. The male parents bore an unmarked X-chromosome which carries a third chromosome translocation marked with *Sb* and *Ubx*. All female offspring receive a third chromosome carrying either *Ubx*^{130} or *Sb* from the maternal parent in addition to a paternal X-chromosome bearing *Sb* and *Ubx*, and will die due to homozygosity for *Ubx* or *Sb*. Most of the male offspring die because of the lethality of one or the other of the flanking lethals. The only surviving male offspring are those which have become lethal-free by virtue of recombination in the *ma-l* region. Such recombinants may occur in any one of the three regions outlined in Fig. 8. Those in region 1 will carry *ma-l*^{F3} while those in region 3 will carry *ma-l*^{F4}. A doubly mutant chromosome, *ma-l*^{F4} *ma-l*^{F3} will result from recombination ih region 2.

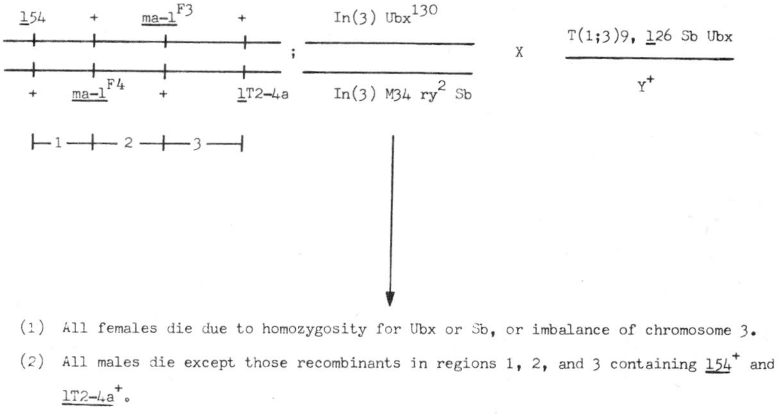

FIG. 8. Construction of a doubly mutant chromosome.

A total of 1778 fertile males were recovered from this cross. These survivors were individually mated to tester females heterozygous for *ma-l*^{1} and a balancer chromosome, and their offspring were then screened for complementation with *ma-l*^{1}. All but 4 of the 1778 males were found to be carrying an X chromosome complementary with *ma-l*^{1}, thus indicating that they bore either *ma-l*^{F4} or *ma-l*^{F3}. The 4 survivors which were non-complementary with *ma-l*^{1} were retested with an array of *ma-l* mutants and all 4 were found to behave as Group I completely non-complementary mutants. These 4 survivors are also completely deficient for xanthine dehydrogenase and aldehyde oxidase activities (Finnerty, unpublished results). In the case of rudimentary, a double mutant made from two complementary alleles was found to behave as a complete non-complementer (Carlson, 1971).

One of the 4 doubly mutant chromosomes was further analysed to verify that it in fact contained the *ma-l*^{F4} and *ma-l*^{F3} mutant sites along with the wild type configuration of the *ma-l*^{1} mutant site (Duck and Chornick, 1975). In a recombination experiment involving the heterozygote, *ma-l*^{F4}*ma-l*^{F3}/*ma-l*^{1}, Duck recovered progeny bearing only *ma-l*$^{1+}$ as well as others carrying only *ma-l*^{F3}. The failure to recover the *ma-l*^{F4} allele is attributed both to an insufficient sampling and to the possibility that the level of purine used would have killed such progeny.

Although the non-complementarity of the double mutant is not a *necessary* prediction of the allele complementation model, the recovery of such a *bona fide* non-complementary double mutant provides a definite contradiction to the complementary behavior predicted for such a mutant by intercistronic complementation. These genetic data taken with the finding that certain Group I and II mutants produce a detectable product lead to the conclusion that the *ma-l* locus behaves as a single cistron.

E. The maroon-like Function

1. The cofactor hypothesis

On the basis of his biochemical studies, Glassman (1965; Glassman *et al.*, 1968) proposed two general means by which the maroon-like locus could be involved with the activity of three so disparate enzymes: one, *ma-l* may contribute a polypeptide subunit to each enzyme; or two, *ma-l* may produce an activator or cofactor of common use to the three enzymes. The term "cofactor" is used in the present context to indicate any molecule (except a polypeptide subunit) which an enzyme might require for its proper function.

There is ample evidence to indicate that the three enzymatic activities deficient in *ma-l* mutants reside in separate molecules (Courtright, 1967; Collins *et al.*, 1971). Moreover, the *ma-l* locus does not appear to be a major structural gene for either xanthine dehydrogenase or aldehyde oxidase. A description of the evidence that the structural gene for XDH is at the rosy locus is given in the previous section. Similar evidence has been presented to show the location of the structural gene for aldehyde oxidase. The aldehyde oxidase gene was first localized to chromosome 3 using the electrophoretic differences in the enzyme from *D. melanogaster*/*D. simulans* hybrids as compared to the enzyme of either parental species (Courtright,

1967). An extensive survey of wild type stocks of *D. melanogaster* revealed both electrophoretic variants and negative alleles which mapped to the same area and behaved as alleles (i.e. were non-complementary) in complementation tests (Dickenson, 1970). These mutants were then used to map the aldehyde oxidase (*aldox*) structural gene at 3–56·6 ± 0·7. *Aldox* negative/*aldox*$^+$ heterozygotes have half the aldehyde oxidase activity associated with *aldox*$^+$ homozygotes, thus exhibiting a dosage effect for that locus (Dickenson, 1970). Further, the *aldox* negative mutant contained no material (CRM) capable of precipitating with antibody to the *aldox*$^+$ enzyme (Dickenson, 1970). The relationship of pyridoxal oxidase to a particular chromosomal site is less clear. The mutant low pyridoxal oxidase (*lpo*, 3–57±) when homozygous lowers the pyridoxal oxidase activity to 2% of the wild type level while the XDH and aldehyde oxidase activities remain at the wild type level. An *lpo*/*lpo*$^+$ heterozygote has about half of the pyridoxal oxidase activity of *lpo*$^+$/*lpo*$^+$, thus exhibiting a dosage effect (Collins and Glassman, 1969). Since no electrophoretic variants of this enzyme are known, the role of this locus as the structural gene for pyridoxal oxidase is still in doubt.

There is as yet no apparent explanation for the intriguing observation that *lpo* and *aldox* are so closely located on chromosome 3; however, the finding that immunological precipitation of aldehyde oxidase from a wild type extract removes less than 4% of the pyridoxal oxidase activity precludes the possibility that the two activities reside in a single molecule (Dickenson, 1970). Further, 200-fold purified aldehyde oxidase does not react with pyridoxal (Courtright, 1967), the only known substrate for pyridoxal oxidase (Forrest *et al.*, 1961). Pyridoxal oxidase is partially separable from aldehyde oxidase on DEAE-cellulose columns (Collins *et al.*, 1971) and is fully separable from XDH by this method (Karam, 1965). Rosy homozygotes contain wild type levels of aldehyde oxidase (Courtright, 1967) and *aldox*^{neg} homozygotes possess wild type levels of XDH (Dickenson, 1969), so that neither enzyme appears to require a product produced by the other locus for its own activity. Mutations at either locus contain wild type levels of pyridoxal oxidase activity. Further, XDH and aldehyde oxidase activities are partially separable by ammonium sulfate precipitation and DEAE-cellulose chromatography (Collins *et al.*, 1971) and are fully separable by gel electrophoresis (Glassman *et al.*, 1968). Finally, differences in the electrophoretic mobility of aldehyde oxidase from two *Drosophila* species and from their hybrid progeny were not correlated with equivalent differences in the mobility of their XDH molecules (Courtright, 1967).

It is then reasonable to conclude that the three enzymes exist as separable molecular species, although this fact *per se* does not permit us to distinguish

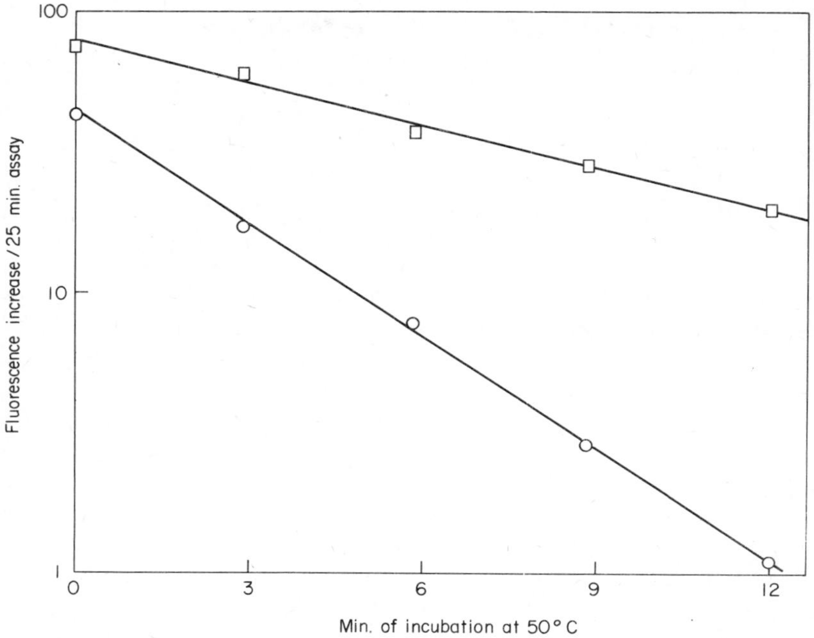

FIG. 9. Heat lability of complemented XDH. Preparation of extracts and XDH assay are given in Chovnick *et al.*, 1969. Mutant and wild type extracts, each containing 200 adults were incubated at 50°C. At the indicated intervals, aliquots were removed, chilled and subsequently assayed for XDH activity. The slope of the least squares straight line drawn through the experimental points was −0·049 for the wild type (□) and −0·135 for *ma-l*^{F3}/*ma-l*^{1} (○). A detailed presentation of these data will appear elsewhere.

between the polypeptide subunit model and the common cofactor model for the *ma-l* function. Two lines of evidence argue that the polypeptide subunit model is incorrect: first, the known electrophoretic variants for aldehyde oxidase and XDH are clearly not located at *ma-l*. Second, *ma-l* mutants contain both XDH (Glassman, 1965) and aldehyde oxidase CRM (Dickenson, 1970). Thus, the *ma-l* locus does not appear to make a substantial structural contribution to XDH or aldehyde oxidase. The cofactor hypothesis gains more credibility from studies of the properties of the XDH extracted from complementary *ma-l* heterozygotes. Two such heterozygotes possess an XDH which is considerably more heat labile than the wild type enzyme when assayed in partially purified extracts (Fig. 9). The comparative heat lability of a more purified form of XDH may be ascertained by electrophoresis of crude extracts on discontinuous gels, then heating the gels with a thiol reagent for various times prior to staining for enzymatic activity (McCarron, unpublished). In this instance, complementing XDH is found to increase in activity compared to wild type. Similarly, the wild type eye color of certain *ma-l* heterozygotes appears mutant if the flies are reared at elevated temperatures (Schalet, 1971b). All of these observations suggest that complemented XDH may have a less stable tertiary or quaternary structure than does the wild type XDH. There do not appear to be electrophoretic differences between wild type XDH and complemented XDH (McCarron, unpublished). Neither is there any indication of whether there may be differences in the heat stability of wild type aldehyde oxidase as compared to its complemented counterpart. Nevertheless, the differences in heat stability found when wild type XDH is compared to complemented XDH are taken to indicate that *ma-l* product is intimately associated with XDH (and may in fact be a peptide) yet it does not appear to make a major structural contribution to the molecule.

Another line of evidence concerning the role of *ma-l* in the expression of XDH activity comes from experiments involving the mixing of partially purified extracts of *ma-l* and *ry* to obtain a restoration of XDH activity (Glassman, 1962). The *ry* extract was thought to contribute the product of the *ma-l*$^+$ locus and the *ma-l* extract would donate the product of the *ry*$^+$ locus to the reaction. This intercistronic complementation reaction *in vitro* was found to involve large inactive multimers of about 250,000 daltons each, the same size as the molecules with XDH activity produced in that reaction or the XDH found in wild type flies (Glassman *et al.*, 1966). Although studies of the inactive multimers have not succeeded in identifying their components, it is possible that the cofactor is present in pyridoxal oxidase which may then donate it to the *ry*$^+$ factor during the complementation reaction (Glassman *et al.*, 1966). Comparisons of the properties of aldehyde oxidase and pyridoxal oxidase with those of the complementing factors are only of limited value since those properties assigned to the "cofactor" when associated with another molecule could differ considerably from those of such a molecule in a free state. Nevertheless, the important implication is that the manner in which two inactive multimers could interact to produce an active multimer of the *same* molecular weight would most likely be that one of the inactive multimers donates a rather small cofactor to the other multimer which is thenceforth active (Glassman *et al.*, 1966).

The recombination data for *ma-l* are consistent with the hypothesis that the *ma-l* cistron contains information for a relatively small molecule. The fine structural analysis of *ma-l* suggests that it spans $8{\cdot}3 \times 10^{-4}$ map units as compared to $8{\cdot}86 \times 10^{-3}$ map units for rosy (Chovnick *et al.*, 1964). Furthermore, all intragenic recombinational events between markers spanning *ma-l* are non-reciprocal (Smith *et al.*, 1970) whereas both reciprocal and non-reciprocal events are observed within the *ry* cistron (Chovnick *et al.*, 1971). The exclusive occurrence of non-reciprocal events clearly indicates that the markers involved are extremely close to one another (Chovnick *et al.*, 1971). Finally, attempts to produce viable *ma-l* mutants were always remarkably less successful than those producing viable *ry* mutants. This is taken to reflect the difference in the size of the target presented by each cistron to a given mutagen.

The *ma-l* cistron then, is apparently involved in the production of a relatively small homomultimeric molecule intimately associated with the structure and function of XDH, and at least with the function of aldehyde oxidase. The relationship of the *ma-l* product to pyridoxal oxidase activity is not clear.

2. *The relationship of xanthine dehydrogenase to aldehyde oxidase and pyridoxal oxidase*

The best known form of aldehyde oxidase (EC 1.2.3.1) extracted from rabbit liver is a flavoprotein containing molybdenum and iron (Mahler, 1955). Xanthine oxidase (EC 1.2.3.2) from a variety of sources is well characterized and also contains FAD, molybdenum and iron (Bray, 1963). The xanthine dehydrogenase from *Drosophila* is analogous to xanthine oxidase except that the insect (and avian) enzyme utilizes molecular oxygen at a very much slower rate (Glassman and Mitchell, 1959a). *Drosophila* XDH (Parzen and Fox, 1964; Karam, 1965) and aldehyde oxidase (Courtright, 1967; Dickenson, 1970) have not been purified to homogeneity and so little is known about their structural properties. The XDH and aldehyde oxidase from mammalian and avian sources have similar absorption spectra and at least *in vitro* have several substrates in common. *Drosophila* XDH with NAD can oxidize salicylaldehyde or benzaldehyde, but aldehyde oxidase may accomplish such oxidations directly using molecular oxygen and is therefore a true oxidase (Collins *et al.*, 1971). There are no reported studies of the oxidation of purines or pteridines by *Drosophila* aldehyde oxidase, but this may prove to be a possibility in view of the fact that rabbit liver aldehyde oxidase can use as substrate some of the non-aldehydic heterocyclic compounds such as purines and pteridines also used by XDH (Johns *et al.*, 1965). It should also be noted that there is presently no real evidence suggesting that unsubstituted purine serves as a substrate for *Drosophila* XDH either *in vivo* or *in vitro*. The reactions of *Drosophila* XDH discussed by Forrest are quite probably the ones catalysed *in vivo* (Forrest *et al.*, 1956, 1961; Glassman and Mitchell, 1959a); aldehyde oxidase is capable of oxidizing a number of aliphatic and aromatic aldehydes *in vitro* (Courtright, 1967) but its *in vivo* function is probably the oxidation of acetaldehyde. Pyridoxal oxidase is the least characterized of the three enzymes; *in vitro* it utilizes a single substrate, pyridoxal, which it converts to pyridoxic acid (Forrest *et al.*, 1961). The *in vivo* function of pyridoxal oxidase has not been investigated. Pyridoxal will protect XDH from heat inactivation in the presence of hypoxanthine and is thought to bind to both active sites of XDH since it competitively inhibits the oxidation of purines and pteridines (Yen and Glassman, 1967). This reaction may reflect the enzyme's known ability to bind competitively to a variety of cyclic compounds (Fridovitch, 1967), and since XDH does not use pyridoxal as substrate this binding may have little significance *in vivo*. Pyridoxal does not bind to 200-fold purified aldehyde oxidase (Courtright, 1967). Thus, there is no evidence at present which indicates that these three enzymes share substrates *in vivo* or that they catalyse reactions in metabolically interrelated pathways.

An interesting aspect of Glassman's (Glassman *et al.*, 1968; Collins *et al.*, 1970) studies of *Drosophila* XDH and aldehyde oxidase was the discovery that the enzymes could exist in two electrophoretically separable molecular forms. The one form predominates in crude extracts from flies raised on standard media and the other appears only after partial purification. If the flies are reared on an aseptic semi-defined synthetic media, a second form of XDH and of aldehyde oxidase is found even in crude extracts. The appearance of these other forms of XDH and aldehyde oxidase was accompanied by significantly higher levels of XDH, aldehyde oxidase and pyridoxal oxidase activities, but no increase in XDH CRM was found. Further, aside of the differences in electrophoretic mobility, no changes in other properties of XDH were discovered. In addition, the effect appears specific to XDH, aldehyde oxidase and pyridoxal oxidase since no changes were detected in an unrelated enzyme. Although XDH (Smith *et al.*, 1963) and aldehyde oxidase (Dickenson, 1970) appear to be composed of subunits, the appearance of the new enzymatic forms is believed to involve a mechanism other than a simple rearrangement of subunits. The lack of increase in CRM in flies raised on defined media indicates no *de novo* synthesis occurs and was interpreted as an indication that activation by a cofactor was involved. The conclusion from this work which is pertinent to this discussion is that there does appear to be an *in vivo* relationship between XDH, aldehyde oxidase and pyridoxal oxidase.

A second aspect of the relationship between XDH and aldehyde oxidase is summarized in Table V which demonstrates the perfectly parallel restoration of the two activities in certain *ma-l* heterozygotes. This finding was extended in another way by asking whether the dilution of XDH activity observed, for example, in $ma\text{-}l^1/mal^{F1}/ma\text{-}l^2$ heterozygotes compared to *ma-l*^{1}/*ma-l*^{F1}/*ma-l*^{113} (Chovnick *et al.*, 1969) is accompanied by a dilution of AO activity. Females with one X-chromosome bearing a *ma-l* duplication (*ma-l*^{F3}, *ma-l*^{1}) (Finnerty, 1968) and the other X-chromosome bearing one of the non-complementary *ma-l* alleles or a *ma-l* deletion were assayed for XDH and aldehyde oxidase activities. In every case, those non-complementers such as *ma-l*^{2} and *ma-l*^{24} which depressed the XDH activity below the level seen in the *ma-l*^{1}, *ma-l*^{F3}/Df(1)*ma-l*^{6} control also depressed the aldehyde oxidase activity below that of the control (Finnerty, unpublished observations).

The congruent restoration of XDH and aldehyde oxidase activity in complementary *ma-l* heterozygotes and the parallel depression of XDH and aldehyde oxidase activities found when a non-complementary allele is present with a pair of complementary alleles indicates that XDH and aldehyde oxidase are physiologically related to one another via the product of the *ma-l* locus.

3. *One possibility for the maroon-like function*

The exact biochemical function of the *ma-l* product is still a matter for conjecture. A truly promising approach to the problem is suggested by the elegant work of Nason and co-workers (Nason *et al.*, 1970) with the nitrate reductase system of *Neurospora*. The *nit-1* mutants of *Neurospora* lack activity for nitrate reductase, an enzyme complex of four activities normally present in constant proportions in a molecule of 228,000 daltons. The four activities (concomitantly induced by nitrate) are: NADPH-nitrate reductase, FAD-dependent NADPH-cytochrome *c* reductase, $FADH_2$-nitrate reductase and reduced methyl viologen (MVH)-nitrate reductase. At first they were able to show that hybrid nitrate reductase closely resembling the wild type enzyme could be formed *in vitro* by intercistronic complementation between an induced *nit-1* extract (which lacks both nitrate reductase and xanthine oxidase) and uninduced wild type or a non-allele *nit-2* mutant extract (Nason *et al.*, 1970). They then discovered that acidified bovine milk or intestinal xanthine oxidase, chicken liver XDH or rabbit liver aldehyde oxidase would also provide a component necessary for the formation of significant amounts of nitrate reductase in an induced *nit-1* extract (Ketchum *et al.*, 1970). In this case, too, the nitrate reductase formed regained its four activities and resembled the wild type enzyme in sucrose density gradient profile, substrate affinities, molecular weight, etc.

This component evidently shared by the XDH, aldehyde oxidase, and nitrate reductase from such diverse phylogenetic sources has been characterized as a small peptide (about 1000 daltons) involved in the binding of molybdenum. The implication that such a molecule could have remained relatively unchanged (Cook and Koshland, 1969) throughout so vast an evolutionary process is indeed fascinating. The obvious parallels between the behavior of the *ma-l* mutants, the *nit-1* lesion and still another series of mutants in *Aspergillus* (Pateman *et al.*, 1964) indicate this to be an important area for future research on the *ma-l* function.

4. *Other loci involved with maroon-like*

A low aldehyde oxidase allele (*lao*, 3–56±) extracted from a Swedish wild type population was reported to possess only 25% of the aldehyde oxidase normally found in Pacific wild type (Collins *et al.*, 1971). The *lao* mutant was not considered to be allelic to $aldox^{neg}$ (3–56·6) since $lao/aldox^{neg}$ heterozygotes have considerably more aldehyde oxidase activity than *lao* or $aldox^{neg}$ homozygotes (Collins *et al.*, 1971). Since the precise aldehyde oxidase activity of *lao*/*lao* was variable and the activity of $aldox^{neg}/+$ was not reported, it is really not possible to determine the type of complementation this represents. Thus, the possibility that the two loci are functionally related in some manner is not yet eliminated. The *lao* mutant is probably not an allele of *lpo* (3–57±) because *lpo* has wild type levels of aldehyde oxidase activity (Collins and Glassman, 1969). The *lao* homozygote has 200% of the pyridoxal oxidase activity normally found in Pacific wild type. The latter finding probably has little relationship to the *lao* allele *per se* since the levels of pyridoxal oxidase may, as do those of XDH, show a great deal of interstrain variation (Keller and Glassman, 1964a).

The *lxd* mutation is of particular interest since it is apparently responsible for the production of a molecule involved with all three enzymes: when homozygous, it has 25% of the XDH (Karam, 1965), 5–10% of the aldehyde oxidase (Courtright, 1967), and a trace of the pyridoxal oxidase activity (Collins and Glassman, 1969) found in the wild type. Immunological studies with the *lxd* mutant demonstrated that it produces a mixture of inactive and fully active XDH molecules and that the number of XDH molecules present is equal to that found in the wild type (Karam, 1965). The aldehyde oxidase molecules found in *lxd* mutants were similarly studied and were found not to be catalytically defective but probably present in fewer numbers than in the wild type (Courtright, 1967). These studies also demonstrated that both the XDH and aldehyde oxidase in *lxd* extracts were similar to the enzymes of wild type in size and electrophoretic mobility. Although *lxd* was once thought to control the production of the $ma\text{-}l^{+}$ product (Glassman *et al.*, 1964), it was later reported that *lxd* extracts contained an inhibitor of XDH activity (Glassman, 1966). It is possible that *lxd* acts to regulate the production of the *ma-l* product or, that it too produces a component commonly required by the three enzymes (Glassman *et al.* 1968). There is no compelling reason to suspect that the *lxd* product might not be the molybdenum cofactor previously discussed, and the *ma-l* product is still another cofactor required for the expression of the three enzymatic activities. At least two different loci are involved in the production and function of a cofactor common to XDH and nitrate reductase in *Aspergillis* (Scazzocchio *et al.*, 1973). The present *lxd* mutants, extracted from wild type populations could be leaky mutations for that locus. No genetic studies have been reported with *lxd.*

Recent work with eukaryotic systems has provided a body of evidence to indicate that there can be several separable loci involved in the final expression of a given structural gene. The functional properties of a gene product may depend upon other gene products such as enzymes affecting the synthesis and/or availability of effector or cofactor molecules necessary for its activity. Still other gene products may modify the properties of a protein following translation but prior to its becoming fully active (Kabat, 1970; Lazarides and Lukens, 1971). The final expression of a gene product may also depend upon its intracellular location (Ganshow and Paigen, 1967). The system of mutations at *ma-l*, *ry*, *lxd*, *aldox*^{neg}, *lao* and *lpo* may thus represent a significant portion of the total array of loci involved in the final expression of xanthine dehydrogenase, aldehyde oxidase and pyridoxal oxidase activities, and therefore offer numerous prospects for investigating the process of gene expression in eukaryotic organisms.

References

AMES, B. N. and MARTIN, R. G. (1964). Biochemical aspects of genetics: the operon. *A. Rev. Biochem.* **33,** 235–258.

BENZER, S. (1957). The elementary units of heredity, pp. 70–93. *In*: "The Chemical Basis of Heredity" (Eds. W. D. McElroy and B. Glass). Johns Hopkins Press, Baltimore, Md.

BRAY, R. C. (1963). Xanthine Oxidase. *In*: "The Enzymes," 2nd edition. **7,** 533–556.

CARLSON, E. A. (1959). Comparative genetics of the complex loci. *Q. Rev. Biol.* **34,** 33–67.

CARLSON, P. S. (1971). A genetic analysis of the *rudimentary* locus of *Drosophila melanogaster*. *Genet. Res. Camb.* **17,** 53–81.

CHOVNICK, A. (1966). Genetic organization in higher organisms. *Proc. Roy. Soc. London* **B164,** 198–208.

CHOVNICK, A. and SANG, J. H. (1968). The effects of nutritional deficiencies on the maroon-like maternal effect in Drosophila. *Genet. Res. Camb.* **11,** 51–61.

CHOVNICK, A., SCHALET, A., KERNAGHAN, R. P. and TALSMA, J. (1962). The resolving power of genetic fine structure analysis in higher organisms as exemplified by Drosophila. *Am. Nat.* **46,** 281–296.

CHOVNICK, A., SCHALET, A., KERNAGHAN, R. P. and KRAUSS, M. (1964). The rosy cistron in *Drosophila melanogaster*. Genetic fine structure analysis. *Genetics* **50,** 1245–1259.

CHOVNICK, A., FINNERTY, V., SCHALET, A. and DUCK, P. (1969). Studies on genetic organization in higher organisms: I. Analysis of a complex gene in *Drosophila melanogaster*. *Genetics* **62,** 145–160.

CHOVNICK, A., BALLANTYNE, G. H., BAILLIE, D. L. and HOLM, D. G. (1970). Gene conversion in higher organisms: Half-tetrad analysis of recombination within the rosy cistron of *Drosophila melanogaster*. *Genetics* **66,** 315–329.

CHOVNICK, A., BALLANTYNE, G. H. and HOLM, D. G. (1971). Studies on gene conversion and its relationship to linked exchange in *Drosophila melanogaster*. *Genetics* **69,** 179–209.

COLLINS, J. F. and GLASSMAN, E. (1969). A third locus (lpo) affecting pyridoxal oxidase in *Drosophila melanogaster*. *Genetics* **61,** 833–839.

COLLINS, J. F., DUKE, E. J. and GLASSMAN, E. (1970). Nutritional control of xanthine dehydrogenase. I. The effect in adult *Drosophila melanogaster* of feeding a high protein diet to larvae. *Biochim. Biophys. Acta* **208,** 294–303.

COLLINS, J. F., DUKE, E. J. and GLASSMAN, E. (1971). Multiple molecular forms of xanthine dehydrogenase and related enzymes. IV. The relationship of aldehyde oxidase to xanthine dehydrogenase. *Biochem. Genetics* **5,** 1–13.

COOK, R. A. and KOSHLAND, D. E., Jr. (1969). Specificity in the assembly of multisubunit proteins. *Proc. Nat. Acad. Sci. U.S.A.* **64,** 247–254.

COURTRIGHT, J. B. (1967). Polygenic control of aldehyde oxidase in Drosophila. *Genetics* **57,** 25–39.

DELAND, M. C. (1971). Genetic studies of a micro region of chromosome IIIR of *Drosophila melanogaster*. Ph.D. dissertation, Univ. of Connecticut, Storrs, Conn.

DEMEREC, M. and HARTMAN, P. E. (1959). Complex loci in microorganisms. *A. Rev. Microbiol.* **13,** 377–406.

DICKENSON, W. J. (1969). Developmental genetics of aldehyde oxidase in *Drosophila melanogaster*. Ph.D. dissertation, Johns Hopkins Univ., Baltimore, Md.

DICKENSON, W. J. (1970). The genetics of aldehyde oxidase in *Drosophila melanogaster*. *Genetics* **66,** 487–496.

DUCK, P. D. (1973). Structural and functional aspects of the maroon-like locus of *Drosophila melanogaster*. Ph.D. dissertation, Univ. of Connecticut, Storrs, Conn.

DUCK, P. and CHORNICK, A. (1975). Resolution of an equivocal genetic element in *Drosophila melanogaster*: organization of the maroon-like locus. *Genetics* **79,** 459–466.

FAHMY, O. G. and FAHMY, M. J. (1958). Report of new mutants. *Dros. Inf. Serv.* **32,** 67–78.

FINCHAM, J. R. S. (1966). "Genetic Complementation." W. A. Benjamin, Inc., New York.

FINNERTY, V. (1968). Fine structure and complementation at the maroon-like locus of *Drosophila melanogaster*. Ph.D. dissertation, Univ. of Connecticut, Storrs, Conn.

FINNERTY, V. and CHOVNICK, A. (1970). Studies on genetic organization in higher organisms. III. Confirmation of the single cistron-allele complementation model of organization of the maroon-like region of *Drosophila melanogaster*. *Genet. Res., Camb.* **15,** 351–355.

FINNERTY, V., DUCK, P. and CHOVNICK, A. (1970a). Studies on genetic organization in higher organisms. II. Complementation and fine structure of the maroon-like locus of *Drosophila melanogaster*. *Proc. Nat. Acad. Sci. U.S.A.* **65,** 939–946.

FINNERTY, V., BAILLIE, D. L. and CHOVNICK, A. (1970b). A chemical system for mass collection of virgin females or males. *Dros. Inf. Serv.* **45,** 190.

FORREST, H. S., GLASSMAN, E. and MITCHELL, H. K. (1956). Conversion of 2-amino-4-hydroxypteridine to isoxanthopterin in *D. melanogaster*. *Science, N.Y.* **124,** 725–726.

FORREST, H. S., HANLY, E. W. and LAGOWSKI, J. M. (1961). Biochemical differences between the mutants rosy-2 and maroon-like of *Drosophila melanogaster*. *Genetics* **46,** 1455–1463.

FRIDOVITCH, I. (1967). Xanthine oxidase, *In*: "The Encyclopedia of Biochemistry", pp. 852–854, (Eds. R. J. Williams and E. M. Lonsford, Jr.) Reinhold, N.Y.

GANSHOW, R. and PAIGEN, K. (1967). Separate genes determining the structure and intracellular location of hepatic glucouronidase. *Proc- Nat. Acad. U.S.A.* **58,** 938–945.

GAREN, A. and GAREN, S. (1963). Complementation for alkaline phosphatase in *E. coli*. *J. Molec. Biol.* **7,** 13–22.

GILLIE, O. J. (1966). The interpretation of complementation data. *Genet. Res., Camb.* **8,** 9–31.

GLASSMAN, E. (1962). Convenient assay of xanthine dehydrogenase in single *Drosophila melanogaster*. *Science, N.Y.* **137,** 990–991.

GLASSMAN, E. (1965). Genetic regulation of xanthine dehydrogenase in *Drosophila melanogaster*. *Fed. Proc.* **24,** 1243–1251.

GLASSMAN, E. (1966). Complementation *in vitro* between non-allelic Drosophila mutants deficient in xanthine dehydrogenase. III. Observations on heat stabilities. *Biochim. Biophys. Acta* **117,** 342–350.

GLASSMAN, E. and MCLEAN, J. (1962). Maternal effect of *ma-l*$^+$ on xanthine dehydrogenase of *Drosophila melanogaster*. II. Xanthine dehydrogenase activity during development. *Proc. Nat. Acad. Sci. U.S.A.* **48,** 1712–1718.

GLASSMAN, E. and MITCHELL, H. K. (1959a). Mutants in *Drosophila melanogaster* deficient in xanthine dehydrogenase. *Genetics* **44,** 153–162.

GLASSMAN, E. and MITCHELL, H. K. (1959b). Maternal effect of ma-l$^+$ on xanthine dehydrogenase of *Drosophila melanogaster*. *Genetics* **44,** 547–554.

GLASSMAN, E. and PINKERTON, W. (1960). Complementation at the maroon-like eye-color locus of *Drosophila melanogaster*. *Science, N.Y.* **131,** 1810–1811.

GLASSMAN, E., KARAM, J. D. and KELLER, E. C., Jr. (1962). Differential response to gene dosage experiments involving the two loci which control xanthine dehydrogenase of *Drosophila melanogaster*. *Z. indukt. Abstamm. VererbLehre.* **93,** 399–403.

GLASSMAN, E., KELLER, E. C., Jr., KARAM, J. D., MCLEAN, J. and CATES M. (1964). *In vitro* complementation between non-allelic mutants deficient in xanthine dehydrogenase. II. The absence of the *ma-l*$^+$ factor in *lxd* mutant flies. *Biochem. Biophys. Res. Comm.* **17,** 242–247.

GLASSMAN, E., SHINODA, T., MOON, H. M. and KARAM, J. D. (1966). *In vitro* complementation between non-allelic Drosophila mutants deficient in xanthine dehydrogenase. IV. Molecular weights. *J. Molec. Biol.* **20,** 419–422.

GLASSMAN, E., SHINODA, T., DUKE, E. J. and COLLINS, J. F. (1968). Multiple molecular forms of xanthine dehydrogenase and related enzymes. *A. N.Y. Acad. Sci.* **151,** 263–273.

GREEN, M. M. (1955). Pseudoallelism and the gene concept. *Am. Nat.* **89,** 65–71.

GRELL, E. H. (1962). The dose effect of *ma-l*$^+$ and *ry*$^+$ on xanthine dehydrogenase activity in *Drosophila melanogaster. Z. Indukt. Abstamm. VererbLehre.* **93,** 371–377.

HADORN, E. and SCHWINCK, I. (1956). A mutant of Drosophila without isoxanthopterine which is non-autonomous for the red eye pigments. *Nature* **177,** 940–941.

HEXTER, W. (1958). On the nature of the garnet locus in *Drosophila melanogaster. Proc. Nat. Acad. Sci. U.S.A.* **44,** 768–771.

HUBBY, J. L. and FORREST, H. S. (1960). Studies on the mutant maroon-like in *Drosophila melanogaster. Genetics* **45,** 211–224.

JOHNS, D. G., IANNOTTI, A. T., SARTORELLI, A. C., BOOTH, B. A. and BERTINO, J. R. (1965). The identity of rabbit-liver methotrexate oxidase. *Biochim. Biophys. Acta* **105,** 380–382.

KABAT, D. (1970). Phosphorylation of ribosomal proteins in rabbit reticulocytes. Characterization and regulatory aspects. *Biochemistry* **9,** 4160–4175.

KARAM, J. D. (1965). Studies on the three loci which control xanthine dehydrogenase in Drosophila melanogaster. Ph.D. dissertation, Univ. of N. Carolina, Chapel Hill, N. C.

KELLER, E. C. and GLASSMAN, E. (1964a). Xanthine dehydrogenase: differences in activity among Drosophila strains. *Science, N.Y.* **143,** 40–41.

KELLER, E. C. and GLASSMAN, E. (1964b). A third locus (lxd) affecting xanthine dehydrogenase in *Drosophila melanogaster. Genetics* **49,** 663–668.

KELLER, E. C. and GLASSMAN, E. (1965). Phenocopies of the *ma-l* and *ry* mutants of *Drosophila melanogaster*: Inhibition *in vivo* of xanthine dehydrogenase by 4-hydroxypyrazolo (3,4-d) pyrimidine. *Nature, Lond.* **208,** 202–203.

KETCHUM, P. A., CAMBIER, H. Y., FRAZIER III, W. A., MADONSKY, C. H. and NASON, A. (1970). *In vivo* assembly of *Neurospora* assimilatory nitrate reductase from protein subunits of a *Neurospora* mutant and the xanthine oxidizing or aldehyde oxidase systems of higher animals. *Proc. Nat. Acad. Sci. U.S.A.* **66,** 1016–1023.

LAZARIDES, E. and LUKENS, L. N. (1971). Collagen polypeptides: Normal release from polysomes in the absence of proline hydroxylation. *Science, N.Y.* **173,** 723–725.

LEFEVRE, G. (1971). Cytological information regarding mutants listed in Lindsley and Grell 1968. *Dros. Inf. Serv.* **46,** 40.

LEWIS, E. B. (1951). Pseudoallelism and gene evolution. *Cold Spring Harb. Symp. Quant. Biol.* **16,** 159–174.

LEWIS, E. B. (1967). Genes and gene complexes, pp. 17–47. *In*: "Heritage from Mendel," (Ed. A. Brink), Univ. of Wisconsin Press, Madison, Wis.

LINDSLEY, D. L. and GRELL, E. H. (1968). Genetic variations of Drosophila melanogaster. Carnegie Institute of Washington, Publication No. 627.

MAHLER, H. R. (1955). Flavin-linked aldehyde oxidase. "Methods in Enzymology" Vol. 1, 523–528. (Eds. S. P. Colowick and N. O. Kaplan). Academic Press, New York, London and San Francisco.

MITCHELL, H. K., GASSMAN, E. and HADORN, E. (1958). Hypoxanthine in rosy and maroon-like mutants of *Drosophila melanogaster*. *Science, N.Y.* **129,** 268–269.

MITCHELL, M. (1955). Further evidence of aberrant recombination in Neurospora. *Proc. Nat. Acad. Sci. U.S.A.* **41,** 935–937.

NASON, A., ANTOINE, A. D., KETCHUM, P. A., FRAZIER III, W. A. and LEE, D. K. (1970). Formation of assimilatory nitrate reductase by *in vitro* inter-cistronic complementation in *Neurospora crassa*. *Proc. Nat. Acad. Sci. U.S.A.* **65,** 137–144.

NOLTE, H. (1955). The eye-pigmentary system of Drosophila. IV. The pigments of the ruby and red groups of mutants. J. Genet. **53,** 1–10.

PARZEN, S. D. and FOX, A. S. (1964). Purification of xanthine dehydrogenase from *Drosophila melanogaster*. *Biochim. Biophys. Acta* **92,** 465–471.

PATEMAN, J. A., COVE, D. J., REVER, B. M. and ROBERTS, D. B. (1964). A common co-factor for nitrate reductase and xanthine dehydrogenase which also regulates the synthesis of nitrate reductase. *Nature, Lond.* **201,** 58–60.

POMALES, R., BIEBER, S., FRIEDMAN, R. and HITCHINGS, G. H. (1963). Augmentation of the incorporation of hypoxanthine into nucleic acids by the administration of an inhibitor of xanthine oxidase. *Biochim. Biophys. Acta* **72,** 119–120.

SCAZZOCCHIO, C., HALL, F. B. and FOGUELMAN, A. I. (1973). The genetic control of molybdoflavoproteins in *Aspergillus nidulans*. Allopurinol-resistant mutants constitutive for xanthine dehydrogenase. *Eur. J. Biochem.* **36,** 428–445.

SCHALET, A. (1961). Report of new mutants. *Dros. Inf. Serv.* **35,** 46–47.

SCHALET, A. (1963). Marked Y chromosomes. *Dros. Inf. Serv.* **38,** 82.

SCHALET, A. (1971a). Two modified crossover-selector systems of general application to fine structure analysis. *Dros. Inf. Serv.* **46,** 135–136.

SCHALET, A. (1971b). Temperature sensitivity of complementation at the *maroon-like* eye color locus in *Drosophila melanogaster*. *Molec. Gen. Genetics* **110,** 82–85.

SCHALET, A. and FINNERTY, V. (1968a). Report of new mutants. *Dros. Inf. Serv.* **43,** 65–66.

SCHALET, A. and FINNERTY, V. (1968b). The arrangement of genes in the proximal region of the X chromosome of *Drosophila melanogaster*. *Dros. Inf. Serv.* **43,** 128–129.

SCHALET, A. and FINNERTY, V. (1970). Is a deficiency for maroon-like lethal? *Dros. Inf. Serv.* **45,** 77.

SCHALET, A., KERNAGHAN, R. P. and CHOVNICK, A. (1964). Structural and phenotypic definition of the rosy cistron in *Drosophila melanogaster*. *Genetics* **50,** 1261–1268.

SCHALET, A. and LEFEVRE, G. Jr. (1973). The localization of "ordinary" sex-linked genes in section 20 of the polytene X chromosome. *Chromosoma* **44,** 183–202.

SCHLESINGER, M. J. and LEVINTHAL, C. (1965). Complementation at the molecular level of enzyme interaction. *A. Rev. Microbiol.* **19,** 267–284.

SMITH, K. D., URSPRUNG, H. and WRIGHT, T. R. F. (1963). Xanthine dehydrogenase in Drosophila: Detection of isozymes. *Science, N.Y.* **142,** 226–227.

SMITH, P. D., FINNERTY, V. and CHOVNICK, A. (1970). Gene conversion in *Drosophila*: Non-reciprocal events at the *maroon-like* cistron. *Nature, Lond.* **228,** 442–444.

STADLER, L. J. (1954). The gene. *Science, N.Y.* **120,** 811–819.

STEVENS, W. L. (1942). Accuracy of mutation rates. *J. Genet.* **43,** 301–307.

URSPRUNG, H. (1961). Weitere untersuchungen gu komplementaritat und nict-autonomei der augenfarb-mutaten ma-l und ma-l^{bz} von *Drosophila melanogaster. Z. indukt. Abstamm. VererbLehre.* **92,** 119–125.

WHITTINGHILL, M. (1950). Two crossover-selector systems: New tools in genetics. *Science, N.Y.* **111,** 377–378.

YEN, T. T. T. and GLASSMAN, E. (1965). Electrophoretic variants of xanthine dehydrogenase in *Drosophila melanogaster. Genetics* **52,** 977–981.

YEN, T. T. T. and GLASSMAN, E. (1967). Electrophoretic variants of xanthine dehydrogenase in *Drosophila melanogaster.* II. Enzyme kinetics. *Biochim. Biophys. Acta* **146,** 35–44.

ZIEGLER, I. and HARMSEN, R. (1969). The biology of pteridines in insects. *In*: "Advances in Insect Physiology" Vol. 6, pp. 139–203. (Eds. J. W. L. Beament, J. E. Treherne and V. B. Wigglesworth) Academic Press, London.

19. Genetic Units of Drosophila—Complex loci

B. H. JUDD

Department of Zoology
University of Texas
Austin, Texas, U.S.A.

I. Introduction

The analysis of the genetic structure of *Drosophila* has contributed a great deal to the understanding of some general principles of genetic organization in eukaryotes. Most of this knowledge has been gained through rather classical genetic and cytological operations even during the last two decades when the attack on the gene at the molecular level in prokaryotes was proving so fruitful. There is a rather impressive body of information about the genetic architecture of *Drosophila* that is only recently being exploited by molecular biologists in the search for an understanding of gene control in higher organisms.

There is little doubt that the fundamental properties of nucleic acids as the bearers of genetic information and the processes of nucleic acid replication, transcription and translation apply to eukaryotes as well as prokaryotes. The major genetic difference between these two groups appears to be in the way genes are organized in chromosomes and the mechanism by which genes are regulated.

A central question about the nature of the genetic unit of function in higher forms is whether the operon (Jacob and Monod, 1961), which has been rather convincingly demonstrated to be a module of genetic control in prokaryotes, has played any role in the evolution of control systems in eukaryotes. If it has, we might expect to find evidence of coordinately controlled, tightly linked cistrons in *Drosophila*. A logical place to begin our search is with an examination of some of the complex loci.

Operationally the fundamental unit of genetic function in *Drosophila* is the cistron. This is defined by the complementation test, the classical test for allelism, which involves the comparison of the phenotypes of the cis ($ab/++$) and trans ($a+/+b$) heterozygotes of two linked mutants, *a* and *b*. If the mutants fail to complement, thus producing a mutant phenotype in trans configuration but giving a wild type phenotype in cis, they are considered to be mutants of the same functional unit. Since the work of Benzer (1957) the term cistron has come to signify that sequence of bases in DNA which specifies a biologically active polypeptide. In most cases *Drosophila* gene products have not been identified and little is known about the relationship between the complementation unit and the structural gene sequence. Lewis (1967) has pointed out that usually the unit defined by the complementation test is unambiguous, but difficulties in interpretation arise in the case of inter-allelic complementation (Fincham and Pateman, 1957; Giles *et al.*, 1957), where two structurally abnormal gene products form a polymer which has some degree of normal function, and in the case of two or more cistrons under coordinate control as in the prokaryote operon. Examples of inter-allelic complementation are known in *Drosophila* in such cases as the rudimentary (P. Carlson, 1971) and dumpy (E. Carlson ,1959) loci. The gene product has not been identified in either case so it is not possible to determine whether polymers are being formed or not. There are of course a number of loci which appear complex in their organization and function and I wish to examine some of these in detail. As we shall see, however, there is no compelling evidence for coordinately controlled, tightly linked cistrons in *Drosophila* or, for that matter, in any eukaryote.

One of the most powerful tools used in the attack on the gene is recombination. Intragenic recombination is well known in *Drosophila*, for in fact it was discovered in this organism by Oliver (1940), but it was primarily from the work of Benzer (1957) on the rII gene of the bacteriophage T4 that a thorough understanding of the fine structure of genes emerged. Benzer's work provided strong evidence that recombination could occur between adjacent nucleotide pairs in DNA, a point which was later proven by Yanofsky *et al.* (1964) who showed that two mutations occurring in adjacent nucleotide pairs of the same triplet codon could be recombined. The gene appears to be a sequence of nucleotides which specifies a biologically active polypeptide. It is the nucleotide, however, which represents the unit of recombination and mutation.

As a number of loci in *Drosophila* were examined by recombination between mutant alleles, it appeared that the genetic organization of the cistron might be quite different from that of bacteria and viruses. First, the range in degree of linkage between allelic mutants in different loci is large.

Loci such as rosy or vermilion exhibit extremely tight linkage of mutant sites while others like Notch or dumpy are relatively loose indicating rather large size. Second, some loci seem to be organized as a continuum of mutant sites, for example Notch, while others such as bithorax appear to be grouped in a discontinuous cluster pattern. It is the latter type which Lewis (1948) considered to be a complex of genes that carry out related functions but which fail to complement with each other. These complexes were called "position pseudoalleles" and later in his analysis of the bithorax cluster Lewis (1963) drew parallels between this complex and the operon of prokaryotes. Though it is possible of course that a gene complex such as the bithorax cluster is organized in basically the same manner as the operon, there is also a possibility that it represents an organization which is unique to higher organisms.

From mutation studies still other facets of the genetic unit are exposed. The actions of various mutagens in forward and reverse mutation events and in the production of various chromosomal rearrangements have been excellent probes for discovering fundamental properties of nucleic acids at the molecular level (see Drake 1969 for review) and for discovering some interesting facts about genes and chromosomes at the higher levels of organization (Auerbach and Kilbey, 1971).

One rather striking observation that emerges from almost any mutation experiment is the speed with which complementation units are saturated. That is to say that rather quickly there appear mutants allelic to earlier identified loci. This means either that the number of loci capable of mutating is rather small or that there are classes of genetic units that mutate over a range of markedly different rates. Alikhanian (1937) used this observation to estimate the number of genes in the X chromosome of *D. melanogaster*. By determining the mutation rate in a selected segment and assuming that it is similar to all other segments of comparable size, the proportion of induced sex-linked lethals that occurred in that region led him to conclude that there are 968 genes in the X chromosome. That number corresponded reasonably well to the number of bands observed in the polytene X chromosome and supported the then accepted view that chromomeres represent genes.

This observation opens one of the central issues of gene organization in eukaryotes. Measurements of the amount of DNA found in a haploid X chromosome of *D. melanogaster* (Rudkin, 1965; Laird and McCarthy, 1969) show that it contains about 3×10^7 nucleotide pairs. There are approximately 1000 chromomeres in the X chromosome (Bridges, 1938) so the average chromomere has enough DNA to make up about 30 genes of 1000 nucleotide pairs each. Recent studies by Judd and co-workers (Judd *et al.*, 1972; Shannon *et al.*, 1972; Judd and Young, 1973) designed to approach this problem directly, show that as a general rule each chromomere contains a single complementation group or cistron. This observation creates a paradox and raises some fundamental questions about the genetic organization of chromosomes.

Judd's approach to the analysis of gene organization consisted of: (1) the selection of mutations that occur in a specific region of the X chromosome extending from band 3A2 to 3C2 inclusive. A deletion for this segment was employed in the genetic screen for mutations in such a way that, in theory, representatives of every functional group should have been recognized and recovered; (2) the grouping of mutations into complementation units by crossing the mutants *inter se*; (3) the determination of the cytological position of each complementation group by deletion mapping and by cytological determination of break points of the deletions and duplications. These studies identified 12 lethal and semi-lethal loci located between the *z* and *w* loci and two loci including lethal alleles of *gt* located to the left of *z* (Fig. 1). The mutation studies of Lim and Snyder (personal communication) have recently provided 3 lethal alleles at a new locus in

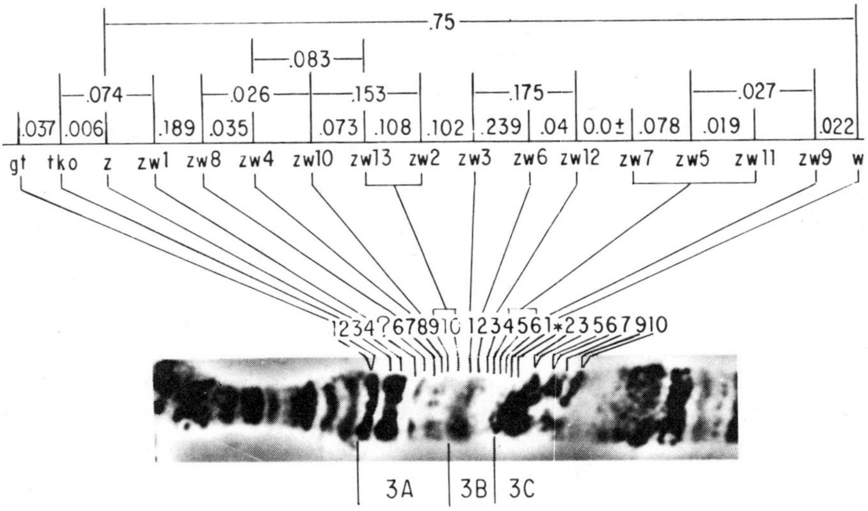

FIG. 1. The genetic and cytological map of the 3A to 3C2 region of the X chromosome of *Drosophila melanogaster*. The cytological position of each complementation group as determined by deletion mapping is indicated in so far as possible. Band 3A5 is designated by ? because it is extremely difficult to distinguish in most preparations. A new lethal locus discovered by G. Lefevre maps in this region and may be positioned in or near band 3A5. (From Judd, B. H. 1974 in *The Eukaryote Chromosome*, W. J. Peacock and R. D. Brock, eds. A.N.U. Press, Canberra.)

3A. The precise cytological location of the new locus is not yet known but recombination mapping shows that it is between *l(1)zw10 l(1)zw2*. This is the region where a band in addition to those described by Judd *et al.* (1972) has been described by Bridges (1938) and where possibly two more bands can be delineated in electron microscope pictures of the region (M. Sorsa, personal communication).

It is obvious then that a crucial point in these experiments is whether or not saturation of the region has been achieved. The genetic screen for detecting mutations picks up those causing lethal and morphological changes rather easily. A refinement of the screen makes it possible to detect mutants which cause delayed development, sterility and behavioral abnormalities. Konopka and Benzer (1971) have identified a locus in 3B in which mutants exhibit upset circadian rhythm. Its exact location is not yet known but preliminary tests show that it is not allelic to lethals *zw2*, *zw3*, *zw6*, or *zw12* (Konopka, personal communication) which are located in the region. This could represent a new locus. It remains to be seen whether or not it can be localized to a chromomere and whether or not it may prove to be an exception to the general rule of one function: one chromomere.

Another exception to this relationship may have been discovered during a study of mutations in the 3A–3C region which cause female sterility. A modification of the selection mechanism to recover such mutations produced seven mutants in the 3A–3C region among 14,430 mutagen-treated chromosomes tested (Judd and Young, 1973). These seven mutants fall into three complementation groups with one being allelic to *l(1)zw12* previously described in the region. The other two groups are both located between *l(1)zw7* and *l(1)zw5*. The recombination tests are not yet extensive enough to be definitive but these sterility mutants could represent a case where more than one functional unit is found in a chromomere. It is not yet clear whether these mutants complement because they are in different structural sequences or whether they represent an example of interallelic complementation. What is clear is that even if some cases of several functional groups per chromomere are found, the majority of chromomeres in the 3A–3C region appear to contain information that concerns a single essential function.

A question still exists, however, concerning types of mutations which do not exhibit any of the rather easily classifiable phenotypes. What proportion of genes are dispensable for normal development and, when mutated, show no detectable phenotype? Intuitively the answer is that there are few, but O'Brien (1973) has presented evidence that such genes may be rather frequent. Duplicate genes or genes that perform the same or similar functions almost certainly exist, but it seems unlikely that this category will increase the number of cistrons in a genome by the factor of at least 10 which is needed to reconcile the number of genes with the amount of DNA present in chromosomes.

Hochman (1971, 1973 and Chapter 22) has been carrying out studies of the genetic composition of the small fourth chromosome of *D. melanogaster* with results that strongly support the concept of one essential function per chromomere. He has examined more than 170 induced and spontaneous lethal and visible mutations which fall into 40 complementation groups. Thirty-three of these groups have lethal mutant representatives while the other seven have been identified by recessive visible mutations only. The polytene fourth chromosome contains about 50 chromomeres which is consistent with the idea that each band represents the site of a single vital function.

The work of Lifschytz and Falk (1968, 1969) on mutations confined to the proximal portion of the X chromosome indicates reasonably good correspondence between the number of functional groups and chromomeres when considered in the light of the cytological analysis of the region by Schalet *et al.* (1970).

Attention must be focused on the nature of the cistron and on the organization of the chromomere if a solution to this puzzle is to be found. A sizeable sample of loci which have mutant alleles causing morphological abnormalities have been studied, some in great detail. One of the most complex is an array of noncomplementing mutations that controls some of the steps in the development of the thoracic and anterior abdominal segments of *Drosophila*. The bithorax complex analysed by E. B. Lewis (1951, 1954, 1963, 1964, 1967, 1968) gives some insight to the genetic control of developmental pathways and at the same time gives some information about the organization of the functional units involved.

II. The Bithorax Locus

The bithorax cluster (*bx*) is located in the third chromosome at 58·8 and contains seven types of mutants, *a*, *B*, *C*, *d*, *e*, *F*, *G*. (Fig. 2). Mutants of the *a*- and *e*-types cause a transformation of metathoracic structures to those resembling the corresponding mesothoracic structures. The anterior part of the metathorax is affected by the *a*-type mutations (*bx*, bithorax) while *e*-type mutants (*pbx*, postbithorax) transform the posterior metathoracic portions. Double mutant homozygotes of extreme *a* and *e* mutants show almost complete transformation of the entire metathorax, resulting in an individual with tandemly repeated mesothoracic segments, each with a nearly normla set of wings.

A single dominant *B*-type mutant (*Cbx*, Contrabithorax) is known which

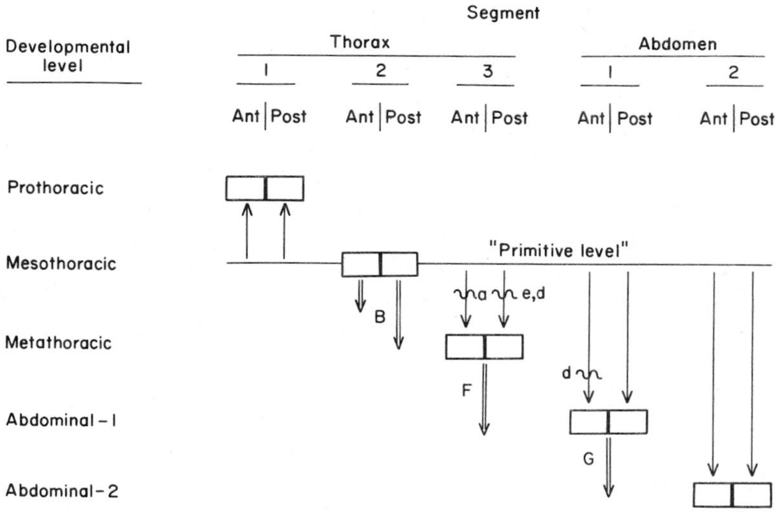

FIG. 2. A diagrammatic representation of the transformation effected by the thoracic and two abdominal segments of *Drosophila melanogaster* assuming that the most primitive level is the mesothoracic developmental state. The developmental paths presumed to be interrupted by mutants of types *a* (bithorax), *d* (bithoraxoid) and *e* (postbithorax) are indicated. The double line arrows show transformations caused by dominant mutants of types *B* (Contrabithorax), *F*, and *G*.

causes almost the reverse of the *a*- and *e*-types of transformations. Its action changes the mesothorax into a metathorax-like structure. The transformation is most ponounced in the homozygote. The *B* mutant in combination with *a* and *e* mutants suppresses their effects and *a* mutants in turn partially suppress the effect of *B*. The combination $a\ B/+\ +$ is more nearly wild type than is $B/+$ while $a\ +/a\ B$ has a suppressed *a* and *B* phenotype. The $B\ e/+\ e$ combination is indistinguishable from $B/+$ as is $B\ e/+\ +$. The *B* mutant in combination with homozygous *a* or *e* mutants suppresses their effects the suppression being greatest in the case of the *e*-type change.

C-type mutants (*Ubx*, Ultrabithorax) are weakly dominant. They cause enlarged halteres and all except one are recessive lethals. Despite this lethality, Lewis (1963) has been able to study the effects of homozygous *C* mutants by constructing individuals which are somatic mosaics composed of mixtures of wild-type and mutant tissues. This is accomplished by inserting bx^+ into a ring X-chromosome which is eliminated with rather high frequency at mitosis. The loss of the ring-X creates islands of mutant male tissue which have also lost bx^+, surrounded by female bx^+ tissue, thus exposing the effects of mutant *bx* alleles carried in the usual autosomal position. From the mosaic studies, *C* mutants appear to have the effects of *a*-, *d*- and *e*-types combined. It also interacts with the *B* mutant in a manner similar to that of *a*. The *B C*/++ combination results in a complete suppression of the *B* phenotype.

The first abdominal segment is transformed to a metathoracic segment by *d*-type mutations, which also have an *e*-type effect on the metathorax. The dominant *F* mutant causes almost the reverse effect, transforming the metathorax to a structure resembling the first abdominal segment. The *G* mutant also affects the first abdominal structures, causing them to resemble those of the second abdominal segment. A summary of the types of transformations affected by each of the mutant types is given in Table I and presented in diagrammatic form in Fig. 2.

TABLE I. Types of body segment transformations caused by mutants of the bithorax series.

Genotype	Segment Transformation Type
a/*a*	Type I (AMT → AMS)
e/*e*	Type II (PMT → PMS)
d/*d*	Type II and Type III (AB_1 → AMT)
C/*C*	Lethal (Type I, Type II, Type III)
B/+ and *B*/*B*	Type IV (PMS → PMT)
F/+	Type V (AMT → AB_1)
G/+	Type VI (AB_1 → AB_2)
a+/+*d*	wild type
a+/+*e*	wild type
d+/+*e*	Type II
a+/+*C*	Type I, Type II (trace)
C+/+*d*	Type I (trace), Type II, Type III
C+/+*e*	Type I (trace), Type II (strong)
a+/+*B*	Type IV (strong)
B+/+*d*	Type IV (strong)
B+/+*e*	Type IV (strong)
B+/+*C*	Type I (moderate), Type II (trace), Type IV
aB/++	Type IV (moderate)
aB/*a*+	Type I (moderate), Type IV (moderate)
Be/+*e*	Type IV
Be/++	Type IV
BC/++	Type I (trace), Type IV (trace)

AMT = Anterior Metathorax; AMS = Anterior Mesothorax; PMT = Posterior Metathorax; PMS = Posterior Mesothorax; AB_1 = First Abdominal Segment; AB_2 = Second Abdominal Segment. (From Lewis, E. B., 1955, *Amer. Nat.*, 89: 73–89.)

The multiple effects of this group of mutants appears at first sight to be very complex and unlikely to be explained as blocks in the synthesis or modifications of the structure of a single gene product. Particularly puzzling with respect to gene function and regulation is the phenomenon of "transvection" described by Lewis (1954). Transvection involves the enhancement of the mutant phenotype of some trans-heterozygotes by chromosome rearrangements which have break points proximal to the bithorax locus in the right arm of the third chromosome. The rearrangements which are effective in transvection cause disruption of pairing between homologues at the bithorax region, 89E, of the salivary gland chromosomes. Lewis interprets this to mean that there is some interaction of genes in homologous chromosomes which is somehow dependent on somatic pairing of homologues and which is upset if pairing is disturbed. This type of interaction is difficult to explain in conventional terms of gene regulation as it is understood from prokaryotic systems. Transvection may, however, be an important clue to some of the mysteries of gene control in eukaryotes. I shall return to this point later.

The complementation pattern among the recessive bithorax mutants can be interpreted to mean that more than one locus may be involved. Type *a* mutants complement with both type *d* and type *e* with the possible exception that there is a slight transvection effect in the bx^3/pbx heterozygote. On the other hand, C-type mutants, *Ubx*, fail to complement with all three recessive types, *a*, *e*, and *d*, which is rather strong evidence for either a single cistron with some intra-locus complementation or a coordinately controlled group of cistrons as in an operon. Lewis (1963) discusses two possible models, both of which are based on a multi-locus or pseudoallelic complex system. The sequential reaction model assumes that the bithorax genes are responsible for the elaboration of three bithorax substances needed to carry out the necessary transformations of the thoracic segments during their development. The cis-trans effects outlined in Table I and the transvection effects are most easily explained by assuming that these substances are produced on or near the chromosomes and that they are more easily transported along a chromosome than from one chromosome to its homologue. Lewis assumes that the substances are proteins produced by enzymatic activity, thus presenting a difficulty in the localization of the substances since protein synthesis takes place on cytoplasmic ribosomes. The model may have some value, however, if it is assumed that the substance(s) produced are not proteins but are direct RNA transcripts which are acting in some regulatory capacity. It is not difficult to understand the cis-trans effects and the transvection on this basis if it is assumed that portions of the RNA transcript function by binding specific sequences in DNA and that in those cases where transvection occurs this binding is at a closely linked site and is interrupted by chromosome rearrangements in the vicinity. There is no complelling reason to assume a multilocus system for the *bx* complex itself under this latter type of model.

Lewis discusses the operon model as a possible basis for explaining the bithorax system. He points out that the *C*, *d*, and *e* mutants exhibit a polarity in their interaction which in a sense parallels that of the genes in the lactose operon. The cis-trans effects can be accounted for by this model but the transvection effects can be explained only if there is some cooperative effort between homologues in the transcription process. Overall the support for the idea that the bithorax system is similar to an operon is rather weak. Regulatory mutants comparable to those of the i^- or o^c types in the lac operon are not available though Lewis does point out some similarity between the *B*-type mutant, *Cbx*, and o^c. The important point is that *a B*/+ + and *B C*/+ + mutant combinations result in a partial or complete loss, respectively, of the *B* phenotype.

Despite the complexity of function of the bithorax series of mutants, it is possible without great difficulty to conform the observations to the model that *bx* is a single locus responsible for specifying a single polypeptide. Such a model has been constructed by Kiger (1973) who postulates that the locus is the structural gene for an allosteric protein which interacts with an inducer molecule present in an anterior-posterior gradient in the egg. Depending on the number of reactive sites bound by the inducer, the bithorax protein is activated to one of a number of possible states. Each state is specific for binding a control element called an expressor. The expressor is postulated to be contiguous to the gene or genes that it controls. With the bithorax protein having the capacity to bind several expressors, it can thus activate a battery or batteries of genes that are actually responsible for the developmental transformations that occur in each segment.

It is rather interesting to note that the recessive mutations *a*, *e* and *d*, which might be looked on as the equivalent of loss of function of the *bx* locus essentially leave the thorax at the mesothoracic state of development. The *C* mutants appear from analysis of mosaics to behave in essentially the same way and are classified as dominants only because *C*/+ heterozygotes exhibit a very slight mutant effect on the anterior part of the metathorax. The remaining dominant mutations (*B*, *F*, and *G*) can be viewed as missense changes which function abnormally in the determination and transformation of the mesothoracic level to metathoracic or abdominal developmental states.

Lewis postulates that the mesothoracic stage is the most primitive in terms of the evolution of the thoracic developmental pathway. Suppression of abdominal leg formation is necessary to reach the mesothoracic state and Lewis speculates that an entire set of genes has evolved by duplication from an original gene which carries out this suppression. This sequence of events would result in the bithorax complex being a cluster of genes with related functions. As has already been pointed out, however, it may not be necessary to invoke multiple functional units to explain the effects of the mutants in this series even though some of the mutants do complement with others. The evolutionary steps then might be envisioned as changes affecting the regulation of this ancestral gene and how the gene interacts with other genes in differentiating cells.

An important point involves the cytological location of the bithorax complex. Whether there is one or as many as seven loci tightly linked, it is important to discover the relationship of the group to the chromomere or chromomeres in which it is located. Unfortunately the data do not allow precise positioning even though a rather sizeable number of rearrangements which result in changes of the bithorax phenotype have been analysed. It is clear that the bithorax mutants can be localized to section 89E. Lewis has postulated that the sites of the *a*- and *C*-types of mutants are located in the doublet 89E1–2 and that *bxd*, the type *d* mutants, are most likely in 89E3–4, a doublet very similar in appearance to 89E1–2. The repeat doublets are suggestive of adjacent duplications and thus give support to the idea of the evolution of the bithorax complex through a tandem duplication process. Lewis bases the positioning of *bxd* to the right of 89E1–2 on a rearrangement which has one of the break points between 89E1–2 and 89E3–4. A segment containing bands 89B6 to 89E2 is transposed to section 66C. This rearrangement, $Tp(3)bxd^{100}$, has an extreme *bxd* phenotype. The transposed section contains bx^+ but not *bxd*. A duplication derived by crossing over in region 66C–89B in a $Tp(3)bxd^{100}$,/+ heterozygote is apparently duplicated for bx^+ but shows no evidence of containing *bxd* (Fig. 3). The reciprocal deletion has a *Ubx* phenotype. Lewis has constructed a homozygous *Ubx* individual to which was added the bx^+ duplication either as one dose or as two. One dose offsets the lethal action of *Ubx* but gives an extreme bithoraxoid phenotype. Two doses of the duplication still allow an extreme bithoraxoid phenotype but there is a reduction in the enlargement of the anterior portion of the haltere. I would like to propose an alternative explanation based on the assumption that there is a single bithorax locus at 89E1–2 and that the break in this region has caused a bxd-type of mutation at the locus. The duplication derived by the crossover described above would then appear to be bx^+ but would also carry this extreme *bxd* allele and thus should complement with *Ubx* as if it carried only one wild-type bithorax locus. Also the reciprocal deletion would be expected to show a *Ubx* phenotype since, if my assumption is correct, it is deficient for the entire locus positioned in 89E1–2. As a

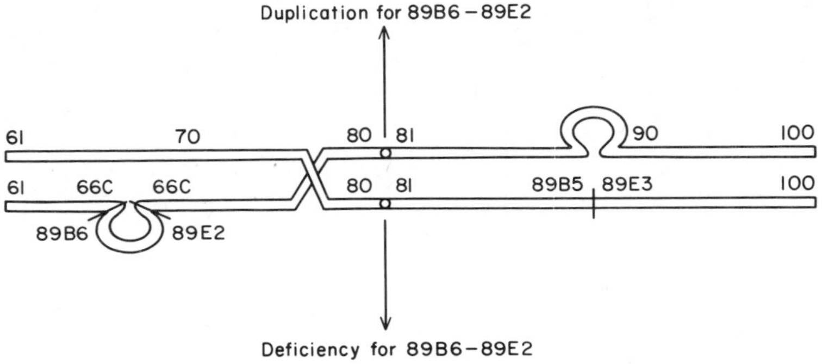

FIG. 3. The diagrammatic representation of the pairing at meiosis of a normal chromosome 3 with transposition *Tp(3)bxd*[100]. The rearranged chromosome causes an extreme bithoraxoid phenotype when homozygous. A crossover such as that shown in the interval between 66C and 89B generates duplication and deficiency products which are used to analyse the mutant complex. The duplication product appears to be duplicated for *bx* but not for *bxd*. The complementary deficiency expresses a *Ubx* phenotype. See text for details and an alternative explanation.

counter to this explanation, however, Lewis has observed that $Tp(3)bxd^{100}/R(bx^3)$, where R involves a break in the heterochromatin in the right arm of chromosome 3, shows a strong transvection effect while a break in the left arm heterochromatin does not. This might indicate that *bxd* is indeed still present in the right arm of 3 and not transposed to region 66 in 3L along with bx^+. A recent finding by Lewis and Shaw (personal communication) involving another rearrangement, $Tp(3)bxd^{110}$, also seems to offer strong evidence that several closely linked genes of the bithorax cluster occupy several bands in the 89E region. $Tp(3)bxd^{110}$ has a break point between 89E2–3 with the insertion of section 91D–92A between the 89E1–2 and 89E3–4 doublets. There is a *bxd* mutation associated with the rearrangement; moreover, the inserted segment contains the wild type allele of Delta, a gene which when mutant causes delta-like fusions of the tips of wing veins. Lewis and Shaw have used X-ray to try to delete the insertion 91D–92A section and restore, insofar as possible the original association of 89E1–2 and 89E3–4. One such deletion removed all but one or two bands of the insertion and it is noted that the mutant *bxd* phenotype is now reduced. The assertion could be made that there has been another mutation superimposed on the original *bxd* lesion and that the double mutant is less extreme in its phenotype than the original *bxd*. It may now be possible to determine whether the bithorax complex is separated into two parts by extracting by recombination the bithorax alleles and determining what, if any, mutant changes have occurred.

III. The White Locus

Another locus which has long been considered to be a prime example of a gene complex is that of white (w:1–1·5). The large number of alleles that represent this locus all form essentially a single complementation group but there are some aspects of their phenotypes, the genetic fine structure of the locus, and its mutation characteristics which point to an organization of some complexity.

The phenotype exhibited by the deletion for the locus and by the most extreme alleles is the absence of all but a trace of pigment in eyes, ocelli, larval malpighian tubules, and testes sheath of adult males. It is significant to note that the deletion of the locus does not cause lethality (Green, 1959a; Lefevre and Wilkins, 1966; LeFever, 1966), indicating that, in a developmental sense, the locus probably controls a terminal step in development, the interruption of which produces a rather striking morphological change but leaves viability and fertility essentially unimpaired. The normal brick-red pigmentation in the eyes of wild-type individuals involves the production and deposition of two distinctly different types of pigments. They are the drosopterins, or red pigments, derived from pteridine intermediates and the ommochromes, or brown pigments, synthesized from tryptophan. Pathways for the biosynthesis of these pigments are outlined in Fig. 4. Though the two pigments are quite unrelated in structure and appear to have no common intermediate in their formation, the white mutants reduce the amount of both types of compounds. A number of alleles which have phenotypes intermediate between the extreme mutant and the wild type allow some of one or both of these pigments to be produced.

While the majority of white mutations affect the quantity of the drosopterins and the ommochromes, there are four alleles occupying the rightmost position in the fine structure map of the locus (Fig. 5) which affect the distribution of pigment in the eyes as well. These are the w^{sp} mutants that cause a fine-grained mottling in the eye with the scattered pigmented facets ranging in color from yellowish to brown. The w^{sp} alleles complement somewhat with other alleles to produce a homogeneous brown eye color. This is the case in such heterozygotes as w^{sp}/wch or w^{sp}/w^{a}, but in combination with a deletion, w^{sp} produces the mottled phenotype typical of the homozygous w^{sp}/w^{sp}.

This pleiotropic effect on the formation and deposition of the two pigment types might provide a useful insight to the control mechanisms involved if the gene product for the white locus could be identified. This has not yet been possible though considerable work on the eye pigments, their biosynthesis and deposition has been carried out (see Ziegler, 1961, for review). Ghosh and Forrest (1967a, b) have provided a plausible model

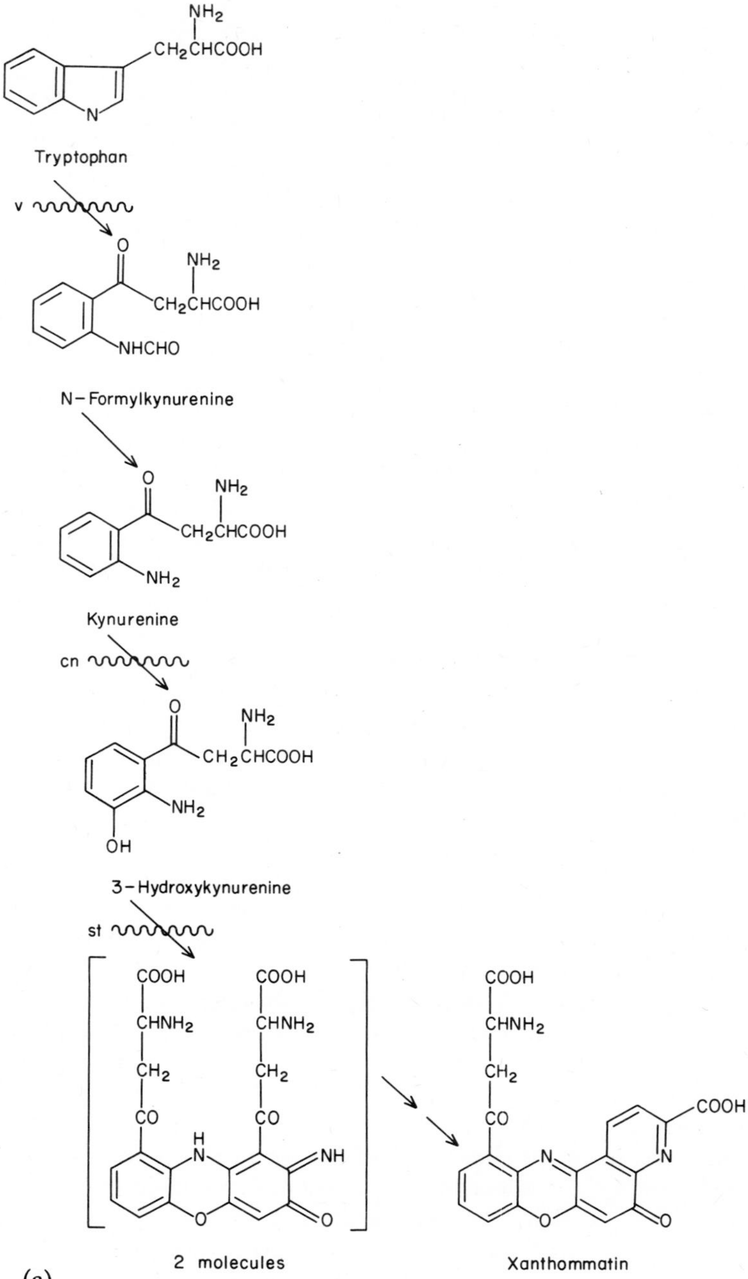
Tryptophan
v
N-Formylkynurenine
Kynurenine
cn
3-Hydroxykynurenine
st
2 molecules
Xanthommatin

(a)

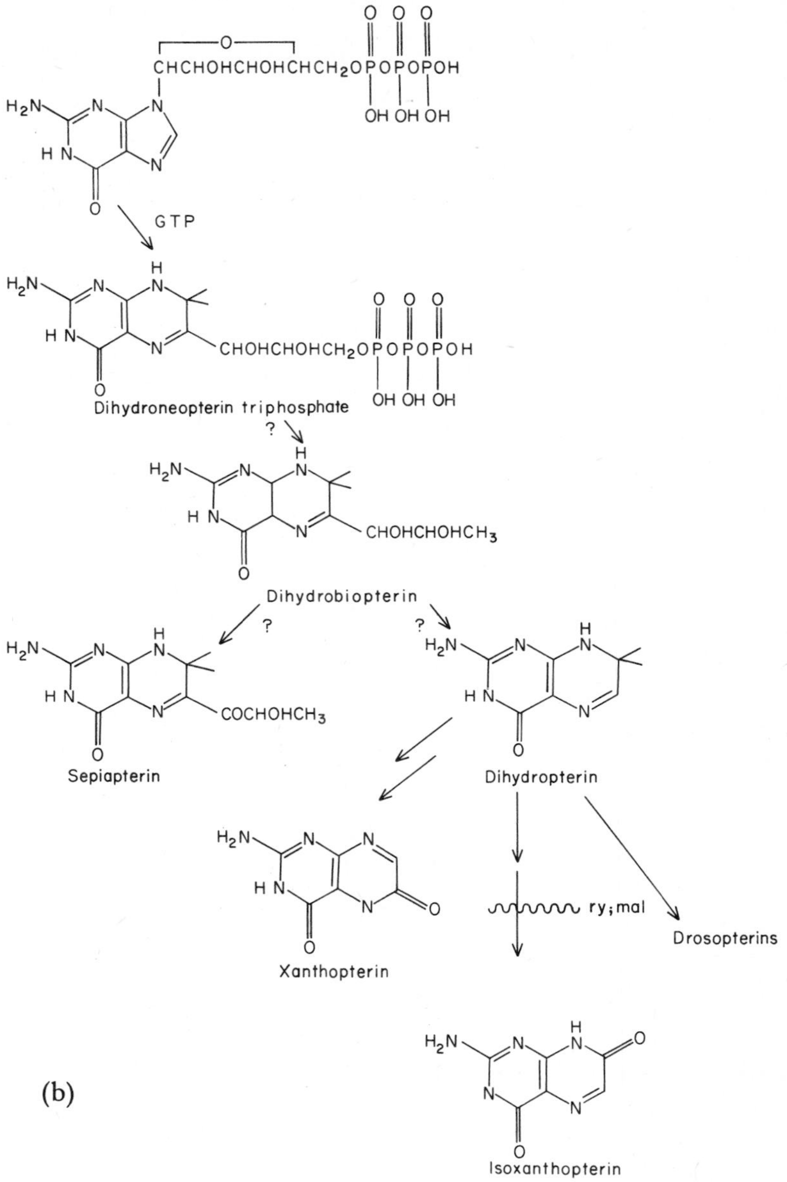

(b)

FIG. 4. Pathways for synthesis of the ommochrome (a) and drosopterin (b) pigments in *Drosophila*. The steps which are interrupted by mutant alleles of the vermilion (*v*), cinnabar (*c*) and scarlet (*st*) loci are indicated in the ommochrome pathway and the rosy (*ry*) and maroon-like (*mal*) loci in the drosopterin pathway. Considerable confusion remains concerning the step sequences in drosopterin synthesis as indicated by the question marks.

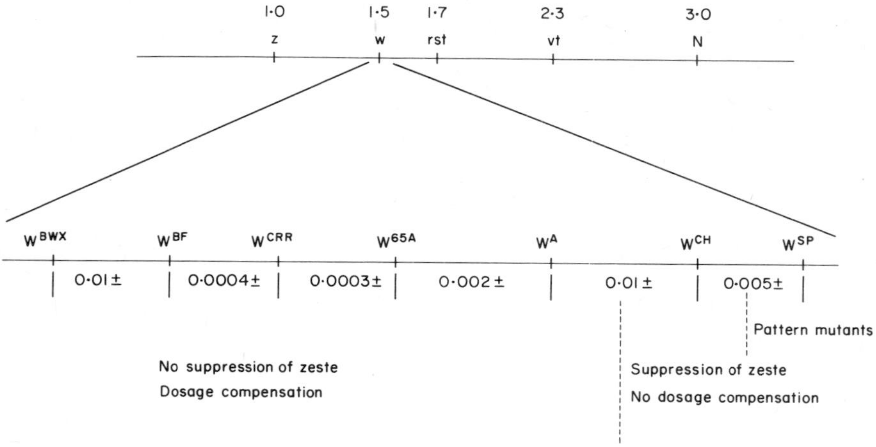

FIG. 5. Fine structure map of the white locus of *Drosophila melanogaster* showing positions of seven mutant sites separable by recombination. Map distances given for each interval have been reduced by a factor of 3 to correct for the increased crossing over in this interval caused by rearrangements present in heterozygous condition in the second and third chromosomes. The differences in phenotypes of mutants located in various positions within the locus are indicated. (Adapted from LeFever, H. M. 1973 *Dros. Inform. Serv.* 50: 109–110.)

for white locus function based on the observations that pteridines of the biopterin type inhibit the activity of tryptophan pyrrolase and that the activity of kynurenine hydroxylase, lacking in the cinnabar mutant, is reduced to about half of the wild-type level in the white mutant. The model they propose is based on the supposition that the kynurenine hydroxylase has a pteridine cofactor. The white locus lesion is envisioned to cause a malfunction of a redox enzyme involved in the reduction of a pteridine. This causes a shortage of the pteridine cofactor necessary for function of kynurenine hydroxylase and at the same time an accumulation of a biopterin compound which inhibits the activity of tryptophan pyrrolase. The result of these interactions would be to reduce or block both drosopterin and ommochrome biosynthesis.

Another equally logical model for white locus function stems from the observation by Ziegler (1960) that the pigment granules of white mutants have a different osmotic characteristic than those of wild type. It is, therefore, possible that a protein component of the pigment granule is missing or modified in white mutants. The terminal steps in synthesis and deposition of both the drosopterins and the ommochromes are thought to be carried out on the pigment granules and thus may depend on the structure of the granules themselves. The pleiotropic effect of white including the reduced activity of kynurenine hydroxylase and the reduction in quantity of both pigments could easily be accounted for in these terms.

A second aspect of white locus pleiotropism involves its interaction with the closely linked zeste locus (z:1–1·0). The zeste mutation produces a sex-limited phenotype resulting in lemon-yellow eye color in females. The mutant was discovered by Gans (1953) who analysed thoroughly the genetics and cytology of the locus. Gans discovered that the sex-limited nature of zeste depends on the number of w^+ genes the individual fly possesses. Females homozygous for zeste and carrying normal alleles of white ($z\ w^+/z\ w^+$) show a zeste phenotype while males of genotype $z\ w^+/Y$ are wild type. Gans noted that deletion of a white locus in z/z females to produce $z\ w^+/z\ w^-$ results in a suppression of the zeste phenotype and restores essentially a wild-type eye color. Similarly, duplicating the white locus in males ($z\ w^+/Dp\ w^+/Y$) causes expression of the mutant zeste phenotype.

Some white alleles act as suppressors of zeste in much the same manner as does a deletion of the locus; some other alleles on the other hand have no effect on zeste and interact with the zeste mutation in essentially an additive fashion such that the phenotype is that of the most extreme mutant whether it be a zeste or a white allele. There are two alleles which are non-suppressors but which act synergistically with zeste in males, however, These are w^i and w^a (Rasmuson, 1962). In $z\ w^a$ males the eye color is a dilute apricot, almost buff in color and w^i interacts with z^{59d15} in much the same way. This type of effect is similar to that of a presumed white locus duplication. Rasmuson conjectures that these two mutants may represent additional material at the white locus.

An interesting aspect of the suppression effect was discovered by Green (1959b) who noted that all those alleles which act as *Su-z* are located in the rightmost part of the white locus complex. The positions of the suppressor mutants are shown in Fig. 5 which depicts a fine structure map of the white locus constructed from recombination tests by Lewis (1952, 1956), Green (1959b), MacKendrick and Pontecorvo (1952), Judd (1959), Nicoletti (1960) and LeFever (1966 and 1973). Seven mutation sites can be distinguished by these tests and only the mutants located in the two rightmost positions act as dominant suppressors. Judd (1961) has demonstrated that a deletion of only a part of the white locus, which includes the wch mutation site but not that of w^a, is an effective z suppressor. The reciprocal duplication for the wch segment acts as an enhancer of z in the same fashion that duplication of the entire locus does. The group of suppressor alleles range in phenotype from white such as w^1 to rather heavily pigmented forms as in the case of w^e and also include the pattern alleles of which w^{sp} is an example. It may be of importance to the understanding of the white–zeste interaction to note that these alleles with partial function are just as effective as the deletion in causing the suppression of zeste. Green (1959b) has pointed out that those pigmented alleles which act as suppressors of zeste are the ones enhanced by the enhancer of eosin [$e(w^e)$].

Another characteristic of the white locus which allows two distinct groups of white locus alleles to be distinguished is dosage compensation. Those alleles which compensate so that the male with one gene copy produces as much pigmentation as the female homozygote with two are with one exception located in the leftmost part of the locus and are indeed those alleles which have no effect on zeste. The two exceptions are the w^h (honey) allele and w^i (ivory). White–honey originated as a partial reversion of w^1, it is a zeste suppressor, exhibits dosage compensation, and has proven inseparable from w^1 in moderately extensive recombination tests. It is quite likely that w^h is a double site mutation in the white locus. White–ivory occurred spontaneously as a cluster of males. It does not suppress zeste but also does not show dosage compensation. As pointed out above w^i is thought to be a duplication of a part of the white locus (Rasmuson, 1962a, b).

Possibly of great significance in characterizing the functional subdivisions that may exist within the white locus is the discovery by Forrest (1963; Ghosh and Forrest, 1967a) that the mutants can be divided into three distinct groups on the basis of their content of xanthurenic acid and 3-hydroxykynurenine. The divisions reflect a correlation between map position and presence of either or both of these compounds. Mutants mapping near the left end of the locus have both compounds. A second group including w^{bf} and w^a lacks xanthurenic acid, while the third group, mapping at the right, has neither compound. The significance of these subdivisions is not immediately obvious but does draw attention to the possibility of a tie between the drosopterin and ommochrome pathways. This was one of the observations that led to the theory stated above that a pteridine in the drosopterin pathway acts as a cofactor for kynurenine hydroxylase.

Consideration of the fine structure map of the white locus and some of the unusual recombinants that are generated in the mapping procedures gives support to the idea that the unit defined by the complementation test is something more complex than the nucleotide sequence specifying a single polypeptide. Attention has already been drawn to the correlation between spatial distribution of alleles and their particular functional characteristics. It is the rightmost portion of the locus that (1) interacts with zeste, (2) shows a lack of dosage compenstaion (3) contains the pattern producing alleles and (4) contains those mutants which do not accumulate either xanthurenic acid or 3-hydroxykynurenine. Further information about the organization of the locus can be gained by taking advantage of a rather unusual characteristic of the locus. With a low but regular frequency, the white loci of homologous chromosomes apparently pair with one another inaccurately. Such mispairing, when accompanied by exchange within the mispaired section, generates duplication (w^{rdp}) and deficiency (w^{rdf}) products.

One pair of such products known to be reciprocal because they were recovered from a single crossover event in attached-X chromosomes has been analysed by Judd (1961, 1964, 1965). Ordinarily it would be difficult or even impossible to detect a crossover event in attached-X chromosomes that resulted in a deletion in one chromosome and the complementary duplication in the other. In the case of the white locus this difficulty can be overcome, however, by using the fact that the expression of zeste is dependent on the genetic make-up of the white locus. Thus from $y\ sc\ z\ w^{a}\ ec/y^{2}\ w^{bf}\ spl$ attached-X females Judd was able to distinguish the $y\ sc\ z\ w^{a,rdf}\ spl/y^{2}\ w^{bf,rdp}\ ec$ by its almost white eye color. Even though zeste is heterozygous the duplication enhances its action to dilute the light buff color of the $w^{a,rdf}/w^{bf,rdp}$ to essentially white. The mutant w^{bf} is easily removed from the duplication chromosome by recombination and the duplication can be almost as easily combined with the w^{a} mutant. The phenotypes of the w^{bf} and w^{a} mutants in combination with the duplication show that neither of these mutant sites is included in the duplication. Recombination analysis showed that the duplicated segment does include the wch mutation site and probably that of w^{sp} as well.

It has been pointed out above that the deletion for wch acts as a suppressor of zeste while the duplication enhances zeste such that a $z\ w^{rdp}$ male is zeste while a $z^{+}\ w^{rdp}/z\ w^{+}$ female has a zeste-mottled phenotype. w^{rdf} is white in phenotype in homozygous females and hemizygous males. Quite surprising is the observation that w^{rdp} in both females and males is wild type unless it is in combination with z. This is difficult to understand if the exchange that created the deletion and duplication chromosomes occurred within a structural gene sequence. The deletion would be expected to have an extreme mutant phenotype and that is indeed the case. A duplication which begins within a cistron would also be expected to result in most cases in a frame shift mutation or, if the proper reading frame is retained, a gene product containing duplicate segments should be produced. The probability that such a repeat sequence in the polypeptide chain would allow it to function properly should be quite low. On the other hand, if the locus is made up of several subunits, two related but different subunits may have paired and undergone exchange. The resulting duplication chromosome might then be expected to include two complete copies of some of the subunits but not others. Normal functions would not be expected to be impaired even if the duplicated segment is a part of a coordinately controlled group of structural sequences. There might, however, be some upset of gene dosage relationships. Rasmuson (1962a, b) has studied the characteristics of w^{is} which appears to be a very similar duplication and has discovered that though the eye color is normal, males have greatly reduced amounts of isoxanthopterin in their abdomens. This indicates that normal function of the locus is indeed impaired but not in a way to cause visible change in the amount or type of pigment deposited in the eyes.

Another presumed duplication for a part of the locus is the mutant w^{zm} and several of its derivatives such as w^{zl} and w^{z}. w^{zm} originated as a single scute, mottled-eye male from females of genotype *sc z ec ct*/w^{bf}. Because females homozygous for the chromosome were zeste in phenotype, Green classified the change as a new mutant at the *z* locus. Judd (1963) showed, however, that it was a *w* locus mutation and probably arose as a duplication by unequal crossing over within the white region. The genotype of the original male is then *sc z* w^{zm}. The duplication maps to the right of w^{a} and in the absence of *z* (i.e. $z^{+}w^{zm}$) the eye color is wild type. w^{zl} which is a spontaneous derivative of w^{zm}, maps in the same position and also is wild type when combined with z^{+}. The two mottled mutants differ only in the pattern of mottling in males. The red to brown pigmented spots scattered on a zeste background are numerous and small in *z* w^{zm} and rather larger but fewer in *z* w^{zl}. These duplications and w^{is}, though mapping in the righthand portion of the locus, do not enhance zeste quite as strongly as the duplication derived by unequal exchange from w^{a}/w^{bf} or those of presumably the same origin from w^{a}/w^{a4} and $w^{a}/+$ described by Green (1963b). This might be taken to indicate that the duplications are similar but not identical. Green extended his analysis to the construction of the triplication (w^{rtr}) which in *z* $w^{rtr}/+$ females causes zeste to be almost completely dominant, producing a near-zeste phenotype.

If, as suspected, all of these types of duplication arose by unequal crossing over within the white locus, their particular characteristics appear to depend strongly on the genetic constitution of the parental females, particularly the white locus genotype. All, with the exception of w^{is}, which was found in a wild type strain, have been derived from females heterozygous for w^{a}. Attempts to discover anything unusual about w^{a} such as it being a double site mutation or a minute chromosome rearrangement have met with failure. Parental females of different genotypes may well produce unique duplication-deletion products which thus far remain undetected. It should be remembered that only through their interaction with *z* have those described come to our attention.

TABLE II. Eye color phenotypes expressed in males carrying a duplication for the proximal segment of the white locus in cis combination with various white and/or zeste locus mutants.

Genotype	Phenotype
w^{rdp}	wild type (red)
$z\ w^{+}$	wild type
$z\ w^{rdp}$	zeste (lemon yellow)
w^{a}, w^{rdp}	apricot
w^{bf}, w^{rdp}	buff
w^{e}, w^{rdp}	eosin
w^{rdp}, w^{e}	wild type
w^{rdp}, w^{ch}	wild type
$z\ w^{rdp}, w^{ch}$	fine-grained cherry mottle

w^{a} = white-apricot; w^{bf} = white-buff; w^{ch} = white-cherry; w^{e} = white-eosin; w^{rdp} = duplication for proximal segment of the white locus which includes the wch and w^{e} mutant sites; z = zeste locus.

Clues which give some guidance to conjectures about the organization of the white locus are obtained from combining the duplication and various white mutants in cis arrangement. Some of these are given in Table II. The combination $w^{a}\ w^{rdp}$ is apricot in phenotype and acts as an enhancer of zeste, while the combination $w^{rdp}\ w^{ch}$ is wild-type in phenotype unless combined in cis with z ($z\ w^{rdp}\ w^{ch}$) where it causes a fine-grain mottling similar to that of the w^{sp} alleles. The combination $w^{a}w^{ch}\ w^{rdp}$ which should be generated as the reciprocal product of the wild type recombinant recovered from $w^{a}\ w^{ch}/w^{rdp}$ is probably white in phenotype. This is the conclusion drawn from the fact that none of this class were recognized as recombinant products and, therefore, are probably like one of the parental phenotypes, most likely white like $w^{a}\ w^{ch}$. If this is the case, wch is expressed differently depending on whether it is in the right or the left position of the duplication. Green also combined various white mutants with the intralocus duplication derived from w^{a}/w^{a4} or w^{a}/w^{+} heterozygotes and was able to show rather conclusively that w^{e}, which maps along with wch to the right of w^{a} and thus is probably included in the duplicated region, is expressed differently depending on its position in the duplication. As with w^{ch}, the combination $w^{e}\ w^{rdp}$ is mutant in phenotype but $w^{rdp}\ w^{e}$ is wild type. For some reason the left segment of the duplication is dominant to the right and in this sense is an example of polarity of function otherwise not seen in this locus and indeed, seen rarely in any eukaryotic mutant expression.

Recombination experiments have uncovered other sets of unusual white locus products, the nature of which have not been determined. They are probably best classified as curiosities at this point since they do little to shed light on the organization of the locus. I will outline a few of the cases, however, for they may actually become rather important clues as our knowledge of the locus increases.

From females of genotype *y^2 w^a spl ec/w^{bf}*, Judd (1959, 1964) reported the recovery of two classes of white recombinants, *y^2 "w"* and *"w" spl ec*, but none which were *y^2 w^+* as would be expected from the results of Green's (1959b) experiments. Two distinct classes can be distinguished among the *y^2 "w"* group. One has the same characteristics as the intralocus deletion recovered from the attached-X experiment described above. The other group does not behave like a deletion in that it complements with *w^{sp}* to produce a uniformly pigmented brownish eye color and it does not act as a suppressor of zeste. The *"w" spl ec* class is expected to be the *w^{bf} w^a* double mutant but an attempt to extract either or both of the two mutants by recombination in *"w" spl ec/+* females yielded neither the expected *w^{bf}* nor *w^a*. About 48,000 offspring were examined from this cross, among which nine recombinants between *w^{bf}* and *w^a* are expected if the double mutant can be separated with the same frequency that it appears to be formed. Similarly, nondeficient *y^2 "w"/+* females failed to produce any offspring that would indicate that the *y^2 "w"* is a double mutant. The curious events occur when offspring from females carrying the two non-deficient white derivatives (*y^2 "w"/"w" spl ec*) are examined. Among 61,664 offspring, five *y^2 w^a spl ec* and eight *w^{bf}* individuals were found. It appears that the nondeficient *y^2 "w"* and the *"w" spl ec* are reciprocal crossover products but that possibly neither of them is truly the *w^{bf} w^a* double mutant. Even on the assumption that the *"w" spl ec* is the double mutant, the nature of the *y^2 "w"* type and the mechanism by which it is produced is difficult to understand. When the *y^2 "w"* deficiency type is used in a similar experiment, the *y^2 "w"/"w" spl ec* females produce only *y^2 w^a spl ec* as white locus recombinants (4/29, 875).

These results could possibly be explained if either *w^a* or *w^{bf}* or both were double site mutants to begin with. Tests to separate two mutant components by recombination have failed, however (Judd, 1964). Could it be that the recombination system is imprecise when mutants which are very closely linked are involved in the exchange segment. This would be equivalent to an allele-specific induction of a recombination error. This is essentially the interpretation that Green (1963a) uses to explain a similar set of unusual products from *w^{ch}/w^{sp}* or *w^e/w^{sp}* heterozygotes. Three classes of recombinants with non-parental eye color are found among the offspring of these females. Two of the classes are those expected if *w^e* is located to the left of *w^{sp}* (i.e. *w^e w^{sp}*, which is a very pale yellow in phenotype, and w^+, which has red eyes). The third class is lighter in color than either wch or w^e, being very similar to the w^e w^{sp} double mutant. It does not show dosage compensation, and it acts as a zeste suppressor. This pale yellow type (w^{dil}) always occurs as a recombinant carrying the left part of the w^{sp} chromosome and the right part of the w^e or wch chromosome. The mutant recombines with w^a, lying to its right. There is no evidence that it is a deletion or duplication. It is rather unusual that though w^{dil} is clearly associated with recombination, no reciprocal product is recognized. This means that either the reciprocal type has a phenotype that is inseparable from one of the parental types, i.e. w^e or w^{sp}, or it simply is not formed and thus w^{dil} may be, as Green points out, a case of directed or paramutation.

It has already been mentioned that w^i, which is an exception to the rule that those alleles which map to the left of w^1 show dosage compensation, is conjectured to be a duplication for a part of the white locus (Rasmuson, 1962b). Another unusual characteristic of this allele is its high rate of reversion to w^+ both in germinal and somatic cells. Lewis (1959) recovered 15 revertants among 290,000 offspring from w^i/w^i females and also reported them as occurring among the progeny of w^i/wch and w^i/w females. Reversion rate in males is about an order of magnitude lower than in females. Bowman (1965) reports a rate of $0{\cdot}3 \times 10^{-5}$ for males compared to $7{\cdot}0 \times 10^{-5}$ in homozygous females. Females heterozygous for a deletion of the white locus showed essentially the same reversion rate as the hemizygous male. Bowman favors as an explanation of these results a model based on w^i as a tandem duplication which undergoes intrachromosomal pairing and crossingover. It is rather interesting to note that in addition to w^i there are a number of white locus mutants that show extremely high mutation rates. Some of these are reviewed in this volume by M. M. Green so I will only point out that most of the highly mutable alleles have had their origin in chromosomes that are suspected of carrying at least a partial duplication of the white locus.

The cytological location and extent of the white locus has been a subject of investigation for a number of years and it appears that there still remain some questions about this. Lefevre and Wilkins (1966) have done the most comprehensive study of chromosome rearrangements involving the white locus and have concluded that the locus is included in band 3C2. Prior to this time, bands 3C1, 2, and 3 had each been ascribed the site of the locus by various investigators and in fact as late as 1963 there seemed to be sufficient evidence from cytological and recombination data to place the "pseudoalleles" of white in all three bands (Green, 1963a).

More recently the placement of the locus in 3C2 seemed to fit all available data as regions on either side of the locus were intensively studied

(Rayle and Green, 1968; LeFever, 1966; Judd *et al.*, 1972; Lefevre and Green, 1972) even though the putative intra-locus duplications such as w^{zm} and w^{zl} showed a faint band between *3C1* and *3C2* (Judd, unpublished observations) and a similar band was described by Lefevre and Green (1972) from an unusually well stretched salivary gland preparation of *y w spl*/*Tp* (*1*) *L2*. The existence of a thin band between 3C1 and 3C2 would also explain the recent results reported by Sorsa *et al.* (1973) who have used the electron microscope to examine *In* (*1*) z^{+64b9}, which in turn was obtained by inverting a section of an X chromosome carrying a triplication for the rightmost segment of the white locus. Sorsa and co-workers observed that the inversion has a breakpoint between 3C1 and 3C2 with the entire 3C2, 3 doublet inverted to a new position near 12C. The triplication of the white locus seemed to have been reduced to a single w^+ gene based on the way the white locus interacts with *z*. The curious fact they observed was that though 3C2, 3 was moved to a new position, w^+ still mapped in its original position and was now more than 40 map units from *N* which ordinarily is only 1·5 units away. The electron microscope pictures showed a thin gray band remaining in the uninverted segment just to the right of 3C1. Since such a band is not seen in most preparations of normal chromosomes, the first thought is to assume that it resulted from a break that passed through 3C2 transferring a major fraction of the band into a new position but leaving a small bit behind. The obvious conclusion then is that since the w^+ function is associated with a minor part of the chromomeric DNA, w^+ occupies only a very small fraction of the chromomere.

I would like to propose that w^+ is normally situated in a very small band between 3C1 and 3C2 which is visible only on rare occasions when an especially well stretched preparation separates the darkly staining 3C1 and 3C2 bands or in the case of duplications of the locus such as w^{zm} or those derived from other asymmetric exchange events. This proposal can possibly be tested by examining a large number of normal chromosomes by electron microscopy to determine whether such a very thin band is indeed normally present. If such proves to be the case, this leaves a question about what function or functions can be assigned to the 3C2, 3 doublet. The work of Lefevre and Green (1972) gives firm basis for believing that the 3C2, 3 and 3C5, 6 doublets may in fact be duplications arranged as tandem repeats. If this is correct, the genes may be carrying out related functions which might result in making one or the other of the duplicate elements appear genetically empty and dispensable.

Despite the extensive set of observations about the various characteristics of white locus, most of the evidence that points to complexity of the locus is quite indirect and inconclusive. Though the left and right portions of the locus do indeed appear to be functionally different, there is no evidence that more than one polypeptide product is specified by the nucleotide sequences in them. I propose that the complexity that apparently exists is based on the internal differentiation of the locus into a structural sequence that codes for a polypeptide and several regulatory sequences that act in the control of the production of the gene product and in the coordination of the function of the white locus with other genes in the genome.

The observations which point toward such an organization of the white locus are that all of the mutants that exhibit blocks in regulatory-like activity are localized in the rightmost portion of the locus. The putative regulatory mutants exhibit failure to compensate for gene dosage, upsets in the pattern and timing of pigment deposition, abnormalities in the interaction with the *z* locus (which may be looked upon as a dosage compensation interaction). All of the mutants located in the left-hand segment behave as if the polypeptide product has been altered but the activity and timing of the gene are unaltered.

Another observation that supports the internal differentiation of the locus is that mutants that are included within duplicated segments of the locus have a different phenotypic expression depending on whether they are in the left or right part of the tandemly repeated sections. An example given above is that $w^{e}\ w^{rdp}$ is mutant while $w^{rdp}\ w^{e}$ is wild type. Can this be taken as evidence that there is a polarity to the locus, at least in the right-hand portion that may play a regulatory role?

If there are indeed both structural and regulatory elements in this locus and if we accept the assumption that the mutants we observe are not limited to either type of element, it is important to remember that this series of mutants forms a single complementation unit. This means that regulatory and structural mutations act as cis-dominant lesions. Or to put it another way, there must be no exchange of some of the regulatory signals between alleles in homologous chromosomes. Much of the regulatory information must be used within the gene that generates it. This does not mean that signals from other elements of the genome cannot be received or transmitted. It means only that there are some information molecules that are used intragenically by cis-positioned sequences only.

IV. The Rudimentary Locus

The rudimentary locus (*r*:1–54·5) exhibits some characteristics which qualify it as one of the strongest contenders for a multifunctional complex. Its phenotype consists of an oblique truncation of the wings with sparse, irregularly spaced marginal bristles, a reduction in viability, and a severe reduction in fertility of r/r females when mated to r males. Rudimentary females mated to wild type males produce almost normal numbers of fully viable and fertile females ($r/+$) but fewer than 1% of the expected r/Y males (Lynch, 1919).

Complementation and recombination studies by Fahmy and Fahmy (1959) and by Green (1963c) showed a rather complex complementation pattern and at least three recombinationally separable sites within the rudimentary system. It was the very thorough and meticulously executed study of the locus by Carlson (1971) that has given the most complete picture of the fine structure of the locus and the relationship of the complementation map to the recombination map. Carlson showed that both the wing truncation and the female sterility phenes show identical complementation patterns. The complementation map is linear and shows seven complementation units, with some 45 mutations falling into 16 different complementation groups. This map is shown in Fig. 6 along with the genetic fine structure map constructed by recombination tests. An interesting aspect of the complementation pattern lies in the observation that though seven units are clearly delineated by the trans mutant combina-

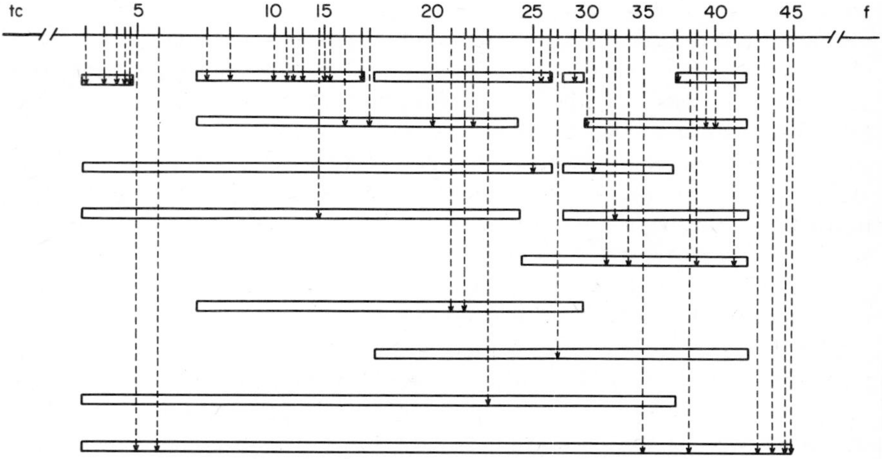

FIG. 6. A recombination and complementation map of the rudimentary locus of *Drosophila melanogaster*. The recombination map positions of 45 alleles are shown on the top line. Distances between mutant sites represent relative frequency of r^+ recombinants where the total recombination within the interval is about 35 recombinants per 10^5 offspring or about 0·07 map units. The complementation map is indicated by the open bars and the mutants occupying a particular complementation group are shown by the arrows drawn from map position to complementation group. (Adapted from Carlson, P. 1971 *Genet. Res.* (Camb.) 17: 53–81.)

tions less than half (18/45) of the mutants studied by Carlson behave as if they belong to only one of the complementation units. No mutants are known for group II only and the majority of mutations fail to complement with two or more of the seven units recognized. Eight of the 45 mutations fail to complement with all other *r* mutants tested. Carlson constructed double mutant combinations in cis-arrangement and noted that all of them exhibited total non-complementation even in those cases where, on the basis of the individual patterns, complementation would be expected. For example, mutants #23 and #39 complement with each other in trans configuration, but the double mutant combination fails to complement with all other *r* mutants, even those that complement both #23 and #39 individually. This may be an important clue about how this locus is organized.

The major reason that more than passing attention is focused on the *r* locus comes from the discovery by Norby (1970) that rudimentary mutants have a specific nutritional requirement for pyrimidines. Norby showed that an exogenous supply of pyrimidines or pyrimidine precursors is necessary for survival of rudimentary larvae. Since carbamyl aspartate is capable of satisfying this requirement, the conclusion from these observations is that *r* mutants are blocked in one of the first two steps of the pyrimidine biosynthetic pathway, either in the synthesis of carbamyl phosphate or carbamyl aspartate. The mutants could then be deficient for carbamyl phosphate synthetase and/or aspartate transcarbamylase. In those eukaryotes where these reactions have been studied, the two enzyme activities purify together and are found in a single high molecular weight enzyme complex. In *Neurospora* (Williams *et al.* 1970) and in yeast (Lue and Kaplan, 1971) it appears that either a single structural gene is specifying a protein capable of both enzymatic activities or that the two structural genes form a multicistronic system. The molecular weights of the *Neurospora* and yeast enzymes are about 650,000 and 800,000 respectively and in mammals it is 600,000–900,000.

Norby (1973) has examined the aspartate transcarbamylase (ATC) activities in wild-type *Drosophila* and in several of the *r* mutants. He discovered that ATC activity is low in the non-complementing mutants tested and in some of those that complement, while other complementing mutants show wild-type activity levels. Norby interprets this to mean that both the ATC and the carbamyl phosphate synthetase (CPS) enzymes are encoded by the *r* locus since the nutritional requirement of the non-complementing strain can be satisfied by supplementing with carbamyl aspartate. A good assay for CPS has not yet been worked out so it is not possible to measure this activity in *r* mutant individuals.

When the data on ATC activity of various *r* mutants (Norby, personal communications) are compared to the fine structure and complementation maps of Carlson (1971) a very interesting picture emerges. Mutants 1, 4, 9, 11, 15, 16, 19 and 20 show high levels of ATC while alleles 3, 22, 28, 29, 30, 36, 38, 39, 40 and 45 show little or no ATC activity. With the exception of mutant 3, all alleles with impaired ATC function are grouped near the proximal end of the locus. It is of great interest to determine whether this pattern holds up as more mutant alleles are assayed and whether those with normal ATC levels are indeed impaired in their CPS activity. As more is learned about the characteristics of each individual allele and its protein product, it should be possible to determine precisely the arrangement of the structural gene or genes in this locus and learn how it is regulated.

V. Conclusions

This survey of a few examples of "complex loci" in *Drosophila* leaves still unanswered some of the very important questions about the organization of the genetic material in this eukaryote. On the other hand, the picture which is gradually emerging contains some interesting and important highlights. The most obvious of these is that there seems to be close correspondence between the unit of complementation, the cistron, and the cytological unit of chromosome organization, the chromomere. The evidence is not yet sufficient to be more than tentative, but it does indicate that these units of organization are co-extensive. Some very important relationships emerge if this is indeed the case.

To begin with, the number of such units in *Drosophila* is probably between 5000 and 6000 and almost surely less than 10,000. Unless each of these units is composed of a number of structural gene sequences, as in a multicistronic operon, the number of proteins required to make a *Drosophila* is between 5000 and 10,000. Is this a reasonable figure? At the present time there is no good way to determine whether or not this is a valid estimate. If, however, each complementation unit does consist of several or many structural sequences, we must postulate that mutations in these different elements of a chromomere fail to complement with each other thus forming a cis-dominant group.

It then follows, that the module of function in *Drosophila* is quite different from the operon of prokaryotes. In *Drosophila* the complexity of the eukaryotic module appears to reside not in a grouping of related genes in tight linkage and under coordinate control as in an operon but in the arrangement of an extensive and possibly elaborate set of control sequences in union with each structural gene.

Though little is known about the transcription products of *Drosophila*, there is evidence from the study of other eukaryotes that the messenger RNA sequences are derived from significantly larger precursor molecules (Williamson *et al.*, 1973). These large heterogeneous nuclear RNA molecules have a size range that would be expected if a major part of the chromomeres were being transcribed. That such is the case for the chromomere that forms Balbiani Ring 2 in *Chironomus* is indicated by the results of Daneholt (1972) who found that the transcript formed from this chromomere has a molecular weight of about 35×10^6 while the DNA of BR 2 is about 60×10^6 molecular weight (Daneholt and Edström, 1967).

Most large nuclear RNAs undergo maturation in the nucleus, a process which appears to involve cleavage, with a good deal of the transcript turning over in the nucleus (Darnell, 1968; Darnell *et al.*, 1970; McCarthy *et al.*, 1970). That this is not the case with the giant transcript of BR 2 is shown by Daneholt and Hosick (1970) who offer evidence that the large 75S nuclear RNA is transported to the cytoplasm. This may mean that the protein molecule that is encoded by this message is unusually large (Grossbach, 1973) and possibly that the maturation process is rather simple compared to most other transcripts and involves very little turnover. Judd and Young (1973) have speculated that a basis for the observation of one complementation unit per chromomere might be due to the nature of the giant transcript and the manner in which it is processed. If the maturation of the transcript is an orderly stepwise sequence of interactions between the RNA and various proteins, it is not difficult to imagine that a mutation in that portion of the chromomere that is transcribed but which is not part of the structural sequence might upset the maturation process such that no mRNA is produced. Other mutations might interfere with the transcriptional step itself or with any of a number of steps involving the transport or translation of the messenger.

An interesting point to consider is whether some portions of the transcript that are released in the nucleus as the maturation of RNA progresses might play important regulatory roles. Such RNA sequences could combine with specific complementary DNA to activate other genes in a biosynthetic or developmental pathway. Activation by this method could assure an orderly sequential functioning of batteries of genes whose action is necessary at a particular time in the life of an organism.

We may then extend our summary to include the possibility that the chromomere and the unit of transcription are also coextensive. It is clear that the genetics of *Drosophila* is in an exciting phase as the way is now open for a molecular attack on the organization of the genome to be coupled with that provided by the several decades of work at the organismal, cellular and chromosomal levels.

References

ALIKHANIAN, S. I. (1937). A study of the lethal mutations in the left end of the sex chromosome in *Drosophila melanogaster*. *Zool. Zh.* (*Mosc.*) **16,** 247–279.

AUERBACH, C. and KILBEY, B. J. (1971). Mutation in eukaryotes. *A. Rev. Genet.* **5,** 163–218.

BENZER, S. (1957). The elementary units of heredity. *In*: "The Chemical Basis of Heredity" (W. D. McElory and B. Glass, eds.), pp. 70–93. The Johns Hopkins Press, Baltimore.

BRIDGES, C. B. (1938). A revised map of the salivary gland X-chromosome of *Drosophila melanogaster*. *J. Hered.* **29,** 11–13.

BOWMAN, J. T. (1965). Spontaneous reversion of the white-ivory mutant of *Drosophila melanogaster*. *Genetics* **52,** 1069–1079.

CARLSON, E. A. (1959). Allelism, complementation, and pseudoallelism at the dumpy locus in *Drosophila melanogaster*. *Genetics* **44,** 347–373.

CARLSON, P. (1971). A genetic analysis of the rudimentary locus of *Drosophila melanogaster*. *Genet. Res.* (Camb.) **17,** 53–81.

DANEHOLT, B. (1972). Giant RNA transcript in a Balbiani ring. *Nature New Biol.* **240,** 229–232.

DANEHOLT, B. and EDSTRÖM, J. E. (1967). The content of deoxyribonucleic acid in individual polytene chromosomes of *Chironomus tentans*. *Cytogenetics* **6,** 350–356.

DANEHOLT, B. and HOSICK, H. (1973). Evidence for transport of 75 S RNA from a discrete chromosome region via nuclear sap to cytoplasm in *Chironomus tentans*. *Proc. Natl. Acad. Sci. U.S.A.* **70,** 442–446.

DARNELL, J. E. (1968). Ribonucleic acids from animal cells. *Bact. Rev.* **32,** 262–290.

DARNELL, J. E., MADEN, B. E. H., SOEIRO, R. and PAGOULATOS, G. (1970). The relationship of nuclear RNA to cytoplasmic RNA in HeLa cells. *In*: "Problems in Biology: RNA in Development" (E. W. Hanly, ed.), pp. 315–329. Univ. of Utah Press, Salt Lake City.

DRAKE, J. W. (1969). Mutagenic mechanisms. *A. Rev. Genet.* **3,** 247–268.

FAHMY, O. G. and FAHMY, M. J. (1959). Complementation among the subgenic mutants of the *r* locus of *Drosophila melanogaster*. *Nature, Lond.* **184,** 1927–1929.

FINCHAM, J. R. S. and PATEMAN, J. A. (1957). Formation of anenzyme through complementary action of mutant "alleles" in separate nuclei in a heterocaryon. *Nature, Lond.* **179,** 741–742.

FORREST, H. S. (1963). Biochemical division of the white locus in *Drosophila melanogaster*. *Proc. 11th Intern. Congr. Genet.* **1,** 4.

GANS, M. (1953). Etude genetique et physiologique du mutant *z* de *Drosophila melanogaster*. *Bull. Biol. France Belg.* (*Suppl.*) **38,** 1–90.

GILES, N. H., PARTRIDGE, C. W. H. and NELSON, N. J. (1957). The occurrence of two dehydroquinases in *Neurospora crassa*, one constitutive and one inducible. *Proc. Natl. Acad. Sci. U.S.A.* **43,** 305–317.

GHOSH, D. and FORREST, H. S. (1967). Enzymatic studies on the hydroxylation of kynurenine in *Drosophila melanogaster*. *Genetics* **55,** 423-431.

GHOSH, D. and FORREST, H. S. (1967). Inhibition of tryptophan pyrolase by some naturally occurring pteridines. *Arch. Biochem. Biophys.* **120,** 578–582.

GREEN, M. M. (1959a). Non-homologous pairing and crossing over in *Drosophila melanogaster*. *Genetics* **44,** 1243–1256.

GREEN, M. M. (1959b). Spatial and functional properties of pseudo-alleles at the *white* locus in *Drosophila melanogaster*. *Heredity* **13,** 302–315.

GREEN, M. M. (1959c). Putative non-reciprocal crossing over in *Drosophila melanogaster*. *Z. indukt. Abstamm. Vererblehre* **90,** 375–384.

GREEN, M. M. (1963a). Genetic fine structure in *Drosophila*. *Genetics Today* **2,** 37–49.

GREEN, M. M. (1963b). Unequal crossing over and the genetical organization of the white locus of *Drosophila melanogaster*. *Z. indukt. Abstamm. Vererblehre* **94,** 200–214.

GREEN, M. M. (1963c). Interallelic complementation and recombination at the rudimentary wing locus in *Drosophila melanogaster*. *Genetica* **34,** 242–253.

GROSSBACH, U. (1973). Chromosome puffs and gene expression in polytene cells. *Cold Spring Harb. Symp. Quant. Biol.* **38,** 619–627.

HOCHMAN, B. (1971). Analysis of chromosome 4 in *Drosophila melanogaster*. II: Ethyl methanesulfonate induced lethals. *Genetics* **67,** 235–252.

HOCHMAN, B. (1973). Analysis of a whole chromosome in *Drosophila*. *Cold Spring Harb. Symp. Quant. Biol.* **38,** 581–589.

JACOB, F. and MONOD, J. (1961). On the regulation of gene activity. *Cold Spring Harb. Symp. Quant. Biol.* **26,** 193–211.

JUDD, B. H. (1959). Studies on some position pseudoalleles at the white region in *Drosophila melanogaster*. *Genetics* **44,** 34–42.

JUDD, B. H. (1961). Formation of duplication-deficiency products by asymmetrical exchange within a complex locus of *Drosophila melanogaster*. *Proc. Natl. Acad. Sci. U.S.A.* **47,** 545–550.

JUDD, B. H. (1963). The genetic fine structure of the mutants z^m and z^l in *Drosophila melanogaster*. *Genetics Today* **1,** 3–4.

JUDD, B. H. (1964). The structure of intralocus duplication and deficiency chromosomes produced by recombination in *Drosophila melanogaster*, with evidence for polarized pairing. *Genetics* **49,** 253–265.

JUDD, B. H. (1965). Chromosome pairing and recombination in *Drosophila melanogaster*. *Genetics* **52,** 1229–1233.

JUDD, B. H. and YOUNG, M. W. (1973). An examination of the one cistron: one chromomere concept. *Cold Spring Harb. Symp. Quant. Biol.* **38,** 573–579.

JUDD, B. H., SHEN, M. W. and KAUFMAN, T. C. (1972). The anatomy and function of a segment of the X chromosome of *Drosophila melanogaster*. *Genetics* **71,** 139–156.

KIGER, J. A., JR. (1973). The bithorax complex—a model for cell determination in *Drosophila*. *J. Theor. Biol.* **40,** 455–467.

KONOPKA, R. J. and BENZER, S. (1971). Clock mutants of *Drosophila melanogaster*. *Proc. Natl. Acad. Sci. U.S.A.* **68,** 2112–2116.

LAIRD, C. D. and MCCARTHY, B. J. (1969). Molecular characterization of the Drosophila genome. *Genetics* **63,** 865–882.

LEFEVER, H. M. (1966). Structure and function of the 3C, 2, 3 region of the X-chromosome of *Drosophila melanogaster*. *Dissertation,* Univ. of Texas at Austin. Pp. 1–47.

LEFEVER, H. M. (1973). Analysis of three White mutants resulting in two new recombination sites at the white locus in *Drosophila melanogaster*. *Dros. Inf. Serv.* **50,** 109.

LEFEVRE, G., JR. and WILKINS, M. O. (1966). Cytogenetic studies on the white locus in *Drosophila melanogaster*. *Genetics* **53,** 175–187.

LEFEVRE, G., JR. and GREEN, M. M. (1972). Genetic duplication in the white-split interval of the X chromosome in *Drosophila melanogaster*. *Chromosoma* (*Berl.*) **36,** 391–412.

LEWIS, E. B. (1948). Pseudoallelism in *Drosophila melanogaster*. *Genetics* **33,** 113.

LEWIS, E. B. (1951). Pseudoallelism and gene evolution. *Cold Spring Harb. Symp. Quart. Biol.* **16,** 159–174.

LEWIS, E. B. (1952). The pseudoallelism of white and apricot in *Drosophila melanogaster*. *Proc. Natl. Acad. Sci. U.S.A.* **38,** 953–961.

LEWIS, E. B. (1954). The theory and application of a new method of detecting chromosomal rearrangements in *Drosophila melanogaster*. *Am. Nat.* **88,** 225–239.

LEWIS, E. B. (1956). An unstable gene in *Drosophila melanogaster*. *Genetics* **41,** 651.

LEWIS, E. B. (1959). Germinal and somatic reversion of the ivory mutant in *Drosophila melanogaster*. *Genetics* **44,** 522.

LEWIS, E. B. (1963). Genes and developmental pathways. *Am. Zool.* **3,** 33–56.

LEWIS, E. B. (1964). Genetic control and regulation of developmental pathways. *In*: "The Role of Chromosomes in Development" (M. Locke, ed.), pp. 231–252. Academic Press, New York, London and San Francisco.

LEWIS, E. B. (1967). Genes and gene complexes. *In*: "Heritage from Mendel" (A. Brink, ed.), pp. 17–47. Univ. of Wisconsin Press, Madison.

LEWIS, E. B. (1968). Genetic control of developmental pathways in *Drosophila melanogaster*. *Proc. XII Int. Congr. Genet.* **1,** 96–97.

LIFSCHYTZ, E. and FALK, R. (1968). Fine structure analysis of a chromosome segment in *Drosophila melanogaster*. Analysis of X-ray induced lethals. *Mutation Res.* **6,** 235–244.

LIFSCHYTZ, E. and FALK, R. (1969). Analysis of ethyl methanesulfonate-induced lethals. *Mutation Res.* **8,** 147–155.

LUE, P. F. and KAPLAN, J. G. (1971). Aggregation states of a regulatory enzyme complex catalyzing the early steps of pyrimidine biosynthesis in baker's yeast. *Can. J. Biochem.* **49,** 403–411.

LYNCH, C. (1919). An analysis of certain cases of intra-specific sterility. *Genetics* **4,** 501–533.

MACKENDRICK, E. M. and PONTECORVO, G. (1952). Crossing over between alleles at the *w* locus in *Drosophila melanogaster*. *Experientia* **8,** 390.

MCCARTHY, B. J., SHEARER, R. W. and CHURCH, R. B. (1970). The unstable nuclear RNA of mammalian cells. *In*: "Problems in Biology: RNA in Development" (E. W. Hanly, ed)., pp. 285–313. Univ. of Utah Press, Salt Lake City.

NICOLETTI, B. (1960). w^{cf}: white-coffee. *Dros. Inf. Serv.* **34,** 52.

NORBY, S. (1970). A specific nutritional requirement for pyrimidines in rudimentary mutants of *Drosophila melanogaster*. *Hereditas*, **66,** 205–214.

NORBY, S. (1973). The biochemical genetics of rudimentary mutants of *Drosophila melanogaster*. I. Aspartate carbamoyltransferase levels in complementing and non-complementing strains. *Hereditas* **73,** 11–16.

O'BRIEN, S. J. (1973). On estimating functional gene number in eukaryotes. *Nature New Biol.* **242,** 52–54.

OLIVER, C. P. (1940). A reversion to wild type associated with crossing over in *Drosophila melanogaster*. *Proc. Nat. Acad. Sci. U.S.A.* **26,** 452–454.

RASMUSON, B. (1962a). An intragenic duplication in *Drosophila melanogaster* and its significance for gene function. *Hereditas* **48,** 587–611.

RASMUSON, B. (1962b). Evidence for a compound nature of the mutant alleles w^a and -w^i in *Drosophila melanogaster*. *Hereditas* **48,** 612–618.

RAYLE, R. E. and GREEN, M. M. (1968). A contribution to the genetic fine structure of the region adjacent to white in *Drosophila melanogaster*. *Genetica* **39,** 497–507.

RUDKIN, G. T. (1965). The relative mutabilities of DNA in regions of the X chromosome of *Drosophila melanogaster*. *Genetics* **52,** 665–681.

SCHALET, A., LEFEVRE, JR., G. and SINGER, K. (1970). Preliminary cytogenetic observations on the proximal euchromatic region of the X chromosome of *D. melanogaster*. *Dros. Inf. Serv.* **45,** 165.

SHANNON, M. P., KAUFMAN, T. C., SHEN, M. W. and JUDD, B. H. (1972). Lethality patterns and morphology of selected lethal and semi-lethal mutations in the zeste-white region of *Drosophila melanogaster*. *Genetics* **72,** 615–638.

SORSA, V., GREEN, M. M. and BEERMANN, W. (1973). Cytogenetic fine structure and chromosomal localization of the white gene in *Drosophila melanogaster*. *Nature New Biol.* **245,** 34–37.

WILLIAMS, L. G., BERNHARDT, S. and DAVIS, R. H. (1970). Co-purification of pyrimidine-specific carbamyl phosphate synthetase and aspartate transcarbamylase of *Neurospora crassa*. *Biochemistry* **9,** 4329.

WILLIAMSON, R., DREWIENKIEWICZ, C. E. and PAUL, J. (1973). Globin messenger sequences in high molecular weight RNA from embryonic mouse liver. *Nature New Biol.* **241,** 66–68.

YANOFSKY, C., CARLTON, B. C., GUEST, J. R., HELINSKI, D. R. and HENNING, U. (1964). On the colinearity of gene structure and protein structure. *Proc. Natl. Acad. Sci. U.S.A.* **51,** 266–272.

ZIEGLER, I. (1960). Zur Feinstruktur der Augengranula bei *Drosophila melanogaster*. *Z. indukt. Abstamm. Vererblehre* **91,** 206–209.

ZIEGLER, I. (1961). Genetic aspects of ommochrome and pterin pigments. *Adv. Genet.* **10,** 349–403.

20. The Bobbed Locus

F. Ritossa

Istituto di Genetica
Università di Bari
Bari, Italy

I. Introduction

The first bobbed (*bb*) mutant in *D. melanogaster* was described by Bridges (Morgan *et al.*, 1925). The mutant affected the bristle length and behaved as a sex limited recessive. First Bridges, and then Sturtevant, mapped the locus in the right end of the X chromosome. To explain the sex limited expression of *bb*, Burlingame (cited in Lindsley and Grell, 1968) suggested that a wild allele of *bb* was carried by the Y chromosome. Stern (1927) found, in agreement with this suggestion, that while *bb*/*bb* females and *bb*/0 males showed the *bb* phenotype, *bb*/*Y* males and *bb*/*bb*/*Y* females were phenotypically wild-type. The question of the homology between the *bb* locus on the X and that on the Y chromosome was settled by the discovery of many *bb* mutants on the Y chromosome (Morgan *et al.*, 1927) and by Stern's (1929) outstanding work on the additive effect of different *bb* mutants. Thus *bb*/*0* males had shorter bristles than *bb*/*Ybb* males; furthermore, a series of females were obtained in which the bristle length could be predicted according to the "strength" of the *bb* alleles introduced into the genotype. Similar results were later obtained by Spencer (1944) in *D. hydei*.

According to the terminology of Muller (1932), *bb* mutants are hypomorphic: they produce the same "type-effect" as the wild-type allele but to a lesser extent (Wagner and Mitchell, 1964). All the predictable members of the series were eventually obtained.

The weaker members of the series of *bb* alleles give a wild phenotype when homozygous and individuals with shorter bristles in *bb/0* males or, when heterozygous, in females with $In(1)sc^{4L,8R}$ which has a complete deletion of the locus (Lindsley and Grell, 1968). As the strength of a given member of the series increases, *bb/bb* individuals show smaller and smaller bristles, and pleiotropic effects become evident. The affected individuals are late in hatching and have an etched abdominal cuticle. In extreme cases external genitalia are completely missing and some adult males have larval testes. More extreme *bb* mutants are called deficiency sensitive (bb^{ds}) mutants (Stern and Ogura, 1931) and are lethal when heterozygous with $In(1)sc^{4L,8R}$. *bb* mutants also exist which can be shown

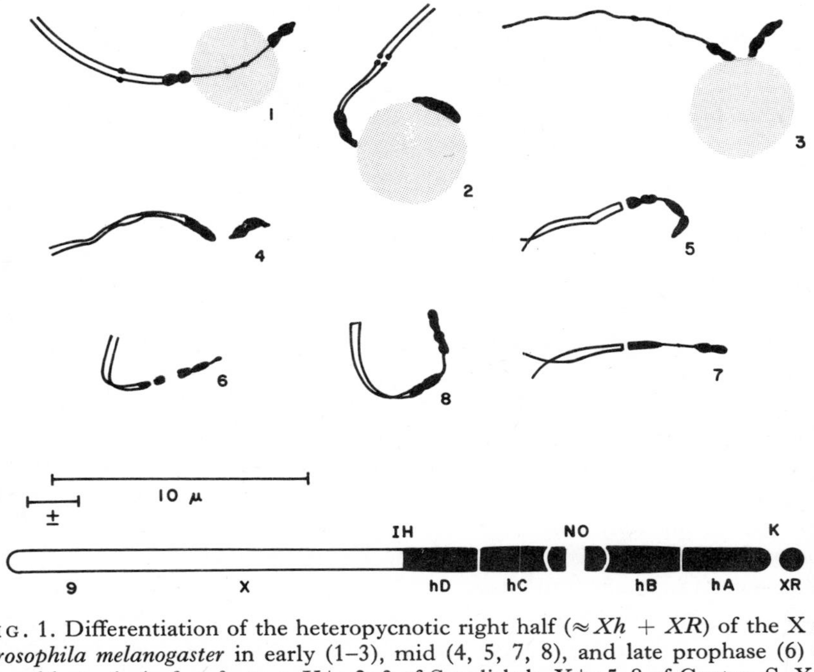

FIG. 1. Differentiation of the heteropycnotic right half ($\approx Xh + XR$) of the X of *Drosophila melanogaster* in early (1–3), mid (4, 5, 7, 8), and late prophase (6) of neuroblasts. 1, 4 of a y^2 *apr v*, X^+; 2, 3 of Swedish-b, X^+; 5–8 of Canton-S, X^+. 9, diagrammatic representation of X, heteropycnotic regions in grey: IH, junction of isopycnotic and heteropycnotic regions; hA–hD, main segments of *Xh* the "paranucleolar bodies" set off to each side of the nucleolus organizer; K, centromere; NO, nucleolus organizer; XR, genetic right limb of X. (From Cooper, 1959.)

to contribute some type-effect in combination with other members of the series but are themselves lethal when homozygous, these are called *bobbed lethal* mutations (bb^l) (Morgan *et al.*, 1926; Lindsley *et al.*, 1960).

The mapping of *bb* required a tremendous effort by many workers (for a detailed analysis see Cooper, 1959). Sturtevant placed *bb* in the X chromosome at position 66 (Bridges and Brehme, 1944). It was soon realized that the locus was located in the heterochromatic half of the X. Using free duplications, Dobzhansky (1932) located it to the left of the centromere at a physical distance which is 0·5–1·5 times the length of the fourth chromosome. Cooper (1958) by studying a series of inversions, mapped the *bb* locus near the nucleolus organizer. Lindsley's (1958) data were in agreement with this location. In Cooper's (1959) terminology, the *bb* locus lies between blocks hC and hB (Fig. 1).

Less settled is the question of the location of the *bb* locus on the Y chromosome. The location of bb^+ in Y "which offers the least complicated interpretation of all" (Cooper, 1959) is on the short arm of the chromosome, proximal to the fertility factors. Again, the most plausible location of *bb* coincides with that of the nucleolus organizer region (Kaufmann, 1933, 1934; Heitz, 1934).

Ritossa and Spiegelman (1965) showed that the heterochromatic region of the X between the right points of breakage of $In(1)sc^4$ and $In(1)sc^8$ contained all the genes that code for ribosomal RNA (rRNA). An amount of rDNA similar to that located in this region was shown to be normally present in the Y chromosome. This conclusion was obtained by rRNA/DNA hybridization experiments in which DNA preparations obtained from flies with varying dose of this region were saturated with rRNA (Figs. 2 and 3). The important point is that although this region, comprising 4–5% of the mitotic chromosomal complement, is about ten times larger than the size estimated for rDNA, it clearly includes, besides the rDNA, the *bb* locus and the nucleolus organizer.

This experiment was designed to obtain more direct evidence supporting numerous previous implications that the nucleolus is involved in ribosome formation (Edstrom *et al.*, 1961; Perry, 1962; Brown and Gurdon, 1964). The localization of rDNA in this region was elegantly confirmed by the use of cytological rRNA/DNA hybridization (Pardue *et al.*, 1970).

The presence of *bb* in a region implicated in rRNA synthesis led us to suspect an involvement of rRNA synthesis in the *bb* mutant phenotype. Following Atwood's suggestions, we tested the idea that *bb* mutants are partial deletions of the multiple copies of rRNA genes. The nucleolus organizer and the *bb* locus might be, respectively, the cytological and the genetic manifestations of the genes for rRNA.

The results presented in Table I provide evidence that that part of

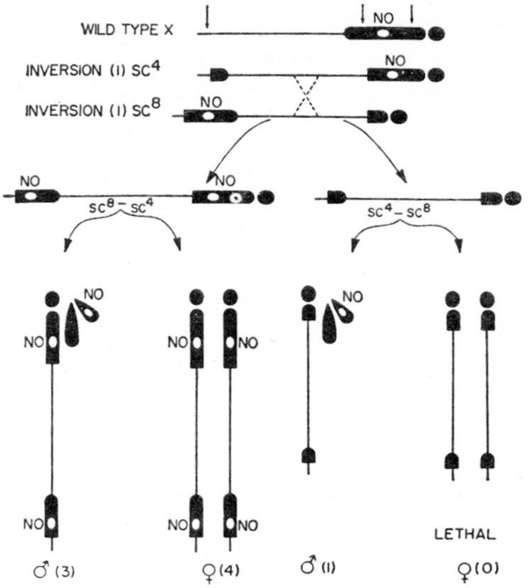

FIG. 2. Diagram illustrating the preparation of stocks carrying 1, 3 and 4 nucleolus organizer (NO) regions. Two inversions of the X chromosome are used: *In(1)sc*^{4} and *In(1)sc*^{8}. The two inversions have almost the same left point of breakage. The right point of one is situated to the left of the nucleolus organizer region, while the other is to the right of it. Crossing over in a female heterozygous for these inversions gives rise to one deleted (*sc*^{4}*sc*^{8}) and one duplicated (*sc*^{8}*sc*^{4}) chromosome with respect to the region included between the right points of breakage of the two original inversions. In fact, when chromosomes are used which have the duplication of the nucleolus organizer region, the left side of the chromosome is that of *In(1)sc*^{S1}, since the *sc*^{8L,4R} chromosome is deficient for *sc* (see Lindsley and Grell, 1968). As a source of individuals with two nucleolar organizer regions wild males and females are used. (From Ritossa *et al.*, 1966.)

the hypothesis which correlates *bb* and rDNA is correct. *bb* mutations are partial deletions of rDNA. The average saturation value after rRNA/DNA hybridization, using the DNA from wild-type flies, is 0·274% of the diploid genome. If adult flies have an rDNA content which is less than about 0·137% they will be phenotypically bobbed, and those combinations with less than 0·03–0·04% rDNA will be lethal. Additive effects are phenotypically observable between 0·04 and 0·137% rDNA. Generally, above such threshold the phenotype is wild. rDNA gene multiplicity will be discussed in detail later.

Whether the *bb* locus coincides with the nucleolus organizer is not so clearly established. I will list some points which support the idea that the *bb* locus and the nucleolus organizer are the same. There is the coincidence of their map positions (Cooper, 1958, 1959). Also, in some cases a correla-

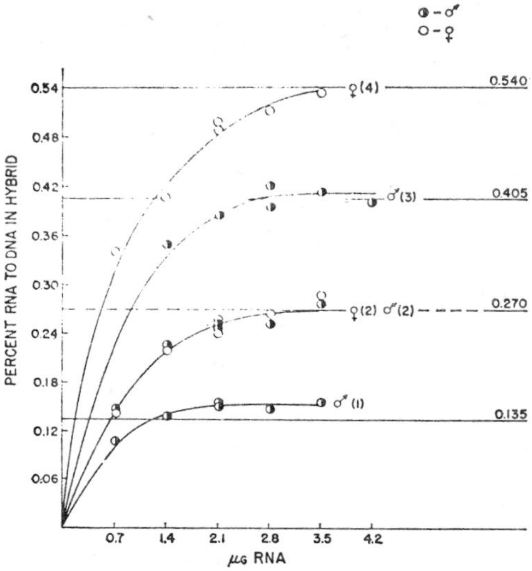

FIG. 3. Saturation levels of DNA containing different dosage of nucleolus organizer (NO) regions with rRNA. Dosage of NO is indicated by the number in parentheses. Dotted horizontal line at 0·27 is assumed to be a correct estimate for a dosage of 2, and solid horizontal lines represent predicted plateaus for dosages of 1, 3, and 4, respectively. Numerical values of the plateaus are given on right. Hybridizations were made according to the technique described by Gillespie and Spiegelman (1965). (From Ritossa *et al.*, 1966.)

tion between the length of the nucleolar constriction and the amount of rDNA has been noted; for example, Sturtevant (1929) has reported that in *D. simulans* the nucleolus organizer of the X is longer than that of *D. melanogaster*, and we could show (Ritossa and Atwood, 1966) that in *D. simulans* the amount of rDNA per bb^+ locus is generally higher than that of *D. melanogaster*. In amphibia, similar situations have also been observed (Miller and Brown, 1969). Particularly worth noting in this context is the case of rDNA produced by amplification in amphibia. Here, oocytes contain thousands of free nucleoli, which are perfectly functional and are not structurally dissimilar from normal nucleoli. Only rDNA repeating units are associated with such nucleoli (Brown and Dawid, 1968; Miller and Beatty, 1969; Gall, 1969; Birnstiel *et al.*, 1971).

Doubts, however, remain. In a remarkable study, Cooper (unpublished observations) challenged the point by studying a series of free X chromosome duplications and Y chromosomes. The *bb* strength of the elements was compared with their cytological characteristics. Whenever the chromosomal element had a functional *bb* locus it was able to give rise to a nucleolus. In two cases, (*Dp(1;f) 1514* and *Dp(1;f)1209*) in spite of

TABLE I. Summary of rRNA/DNA ratios obtained with DNA from bobbed and wild-type flies of various genetic constitution.

Source of DNA	Nucleolus organizer regions, + and *bb*	(r-RNA/DNA) × 100 at saturation	(r-DNA/DNA) × 100 per NO region[c]
♀ (4)	4 +	0·472	0·118
♂ (3)	3 +	0·393	0·131
		0·402	0·134
		0·399	0·133
		0·420	0·140
		0·368	0·123
♀ (2)	2 +	0·284	0·142
		0·317	0·159
♂ (2)	2 +	0·283	0·142
		0·244	0·122
♀ & ♂ (2)	2 +	0·251	0·126
		0·249	0·125
		0·253	0·127
♂ (1)	1 +	0·140	0·140
		0·188	0·188
			Average = 0·137 ± 0·018
car bb ♀	2 *bb*	0·122	0·061
		0·090	0·045
		0·136	0·068
car bb/Y ♂	1 +, 1 *bb*	0·199	0·064 *bb* only
		0·211	0·076 *bb* only
uco3 ♀	2 *bb*	0·098	0·049
		0·149	0·075
uco3 ♂	1 +, 1 *bb*	0·210	0·075 (*bb* only)
bb^{ds} ♀	2 *bb*	0·172	0·086
		0·184	0·092
bb^{ds}/Y ♂	1 +, 1 *bb*	0·250	0·115
bb^{ds}/Y^{Bs} ♂	1 +, 1 bb^{ds}	0·220	0·085 (bb^{ds})[ab]
$bbrt/bb^{l}$ ♀	1 bb^{ds}, 1 bb^{l}	0·125	0·040 (bb^{l})[ab]
$bb^{ds}/sc^{4}\ sc^{8}$ ♂	1 bb^{ds}	0·102	0·102 (bb^{ds})[a]
bb^{ds}/bb^{l} ♀	1 bb^{ds}, 1 bb^{l}	0·176	0·074 (bb^{l})[a]
$bb^{ds}/sc^{4}\ sc^{8}$ ♂	1 bb^{ds}	0·065	0·065 (bb^{ds})[ab]
bb^{ds}/bb^{l} ♀	1 bb^{ds}, 1 bb^{l}	0·098	0·033 (bb^{l})[ab]
			Average = 0·071 ± 0·022

[a] Parallel experiments. [b] Nondisjunctional Y chromosomes excluded. [c] In calculating r-DNA/DNA ratios for *bb*, the value for + was rounded to 0·135. (From Ritossa *et al.*, 1966.)

the presence of functional *bb* loci, no nucleolar constriction was evident. In one case, the Ybb^- chromosome of Schultz (see later), neither a functional *bb* locus was present, nor was the chromosome ever observed to be associated with a nucleolus, but a normal constriction was evident at metaphase. Although the Ybb^- chromosome was shown to carry a considerable amount of nonfunctional rDNA (Ritossa, 1968a), the relationship between *bb* and the constriction remains hypothetical.

II. The surroundings of bobbed

On both sides of the locus there are large heterochromatic blocks. According to Cooper (1959) two such blocks (hD and hC) are located to the left of bobbed, while two others (hB and hA) are on the right of it. These blocks are resolved in mitotic prophases of neuroblast cells (see Fig. 1). A modern interpretation of most heterochromatin is that it is rich in "repetitive DNA" (Rae, 1970; Gall *et al.*, 1971). It mostly remains, as Cooper (1959) ironically defined it, "the seat of the unorthodox" (Britten and Kohne, 1969). The heterochromatic blocks are susceptible to differential replication in different tissues. Rudkin (1969) has clearly shown that polytene nuclei contain less DNA than they would if the whole DNA content of a diploid cell were replicated during polytenization (Swift, 1962; Rasch *et al.*, 1971). In accord with previous cytological observations (Hinton, 1942), the hypothesis of Rudkin was that the DNA of the chromocenter, which contains most of the heterochromatin, was under-replicated. Gall *et al.* (1971) confirmed the hypothesis: the amount of heterochromatin DNA in a polytene chromosome is about the same as that of a diploid cell.

What then is the fate of rDNA which is surrounded by non-polytenizing blocks in an otherwise polytenic chromosome? This point was investigated by Hennig and Meer (1971). They hybridized ribosomal RNA to DNA obtained from polytene chromosomes of salivary glands of *D. hydei*, as well as to that obtained from adult males and females, which are considered a mixture of polytenic and non-polytenic tissues, and from embryos which are considered to have only diploid nuclei. The rDNA saturation levels were found to be lower when DNA from polytenic chromosome was used than when DNA from embryos was used. Intermediate values were obtained using adult DNA. Thus, in salivary glands, assuming (a) a level of polytenization of 1024C (b) the heterochromatin (which is normally 30% of the diploid genome) to be at a 4C level and (c) the block of genes for rRNA duplicated as a single entity then, they calculate, the rDNA block is present about 128 times. Similar results were obtained for *D. hydei* by Pardue *et al.* (1970), by means of cytological hybridization, and for *D. melanogaster* by Spear and Gall (1973).

The simplest interpretation of these results, at present, is that the block of genes for rRNA replicates autonomously, independently of the surrounding chromosomal regions. In spite of this independence, the presence of heterochromatin can, in certain circumstances, influence the expression of the block.

Baker (1971) considered a series of inversions where the *bb* locus was displaced from its normal position (sc^{V2}, sc^{8}, sc^{L8} and sc^{S1}, shown in Fig. 4). In appropriate genotypes these inversions lead to position-effect variegation of the genes situated on the extreme, uninverted tip of the X chromosome. Most are lethal as X/0 males. Lethality is overcome in $sc^{8}/0$ and $sc^{V2}/0$ males by the free duplication *Dp (1;f) 1337* which adds second copies of the genes situated at the tip of the X. This free duplication is ineffective in restoring viability to $sc^{S1}/0$ and $sc^{L8}/0$ males. In these last two cases, hence, lethality is not due to position-effect suppression of vital genes on the uninverted region of the X. That the rearrangement is

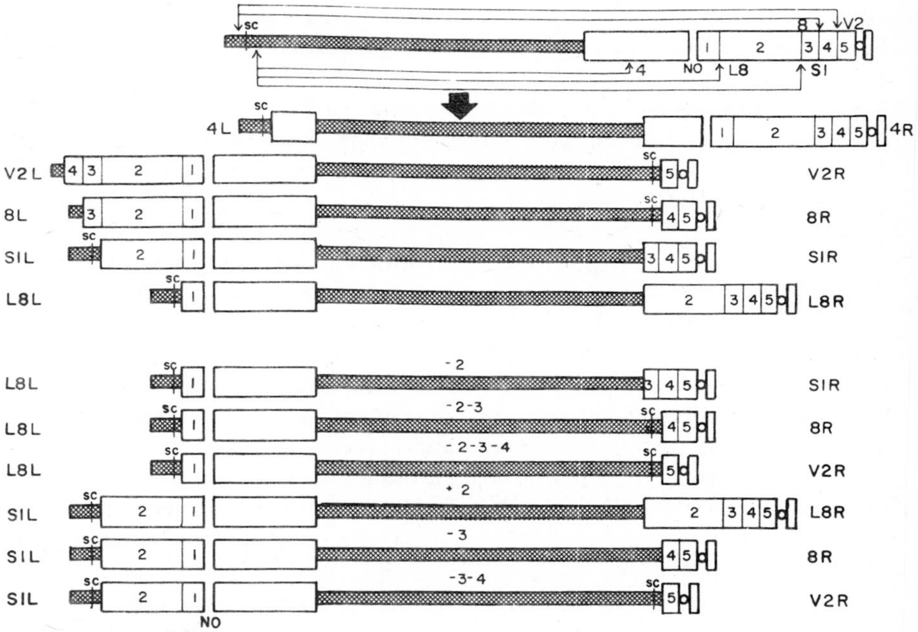

FIG. 4. Pictorial presentation of the X chromosome scute inversions. Euchromatic regions are shaded, heterochromatic regions are open. Each of the lower group of inversions was formed from two of the upper group by recombination. The right breaks of four of the inversions delimit the five numbered regions of heterochromatin between the nucleolus organizer (NO) and the centromere (small circle). The right sc^{8} and sc^{S1} breaks may be reversed in order. (From Baker, 1971.)

suppressing rDNA activity in these cases is supported by the effects of adding Y chromosomes carrying non functional genes for rRNA (*Ybb*$^-$ chromosomes). It is known that the addition of a Y chromosome inhibits variegated position effect. Baker (1971) observed that sc^{S1}/Ybb^- and sc^{L8}/Ybb^- combinations were partially viable in spite of the fact that the *Ybb*$^-$ chromosome contributes no functional rDNA. In passing, one should note that the possible combinations of the right and left parts of the inversions used by Baker (Fig. 4) will be very useful for the analysis of the DNA neighbouring *bb*. Indeed, their use might lead to the isolation of particular fractions of the X basal heterochromatin.

III. The organization of the rDNA block

The basic sequences making up the *bb* locus are, at least, those complementary to ribosomal RNA (Table I). We have seen evidence that all the sequences complementary to 28 and 18s ribosomal RNAs were included in the heterochromatic region between the right points of breakage of $In(1)sc^4$ and $In(1)sc^8$. This region accounts for much more DNA (about 4% of the diploid content) than that needed to code for ribosomal RNA (about 0·6% in double-stranded form). On this simple basis one might suppose that genes for rRNA are either clustered or dispersed within this region. However, *bb* mutants, whose rDNA content is lower than that of wild individuals, are not reported to be necessarily deficient for heterochromatin though, in some cases, they may be so (Lindsley and Grell, 1968). Furthermore, the mapping experiments (see above) localized *bb* in a region much smaller than that included between the right points of breakage of inversions sc^4 and sc^8.

The sequences complementary to 28s RNA are different from those complementary to 18s rRNA. This was shown by preparing tritium labelled 28s rRNA and P^{32} labelled 18s rRNA and hybridizing them separately to DNA. Each saturate DNA at a lower level than that obtained using a mixture of the two, labelled with the same isotope—a level which is proportional to their molecular weights (Ritossa *et al.*, 1966). When DNAs from *bb* mutants were used in similar experiments, the saturation values indicated that the deletion resulted in the loss of equal numbers of sequences complementary to both 28s and 18s molecules (Table II). These results favour the view that the two sequences are intercalated. These results were expected since Greenberg (1967), and later Tartof and Perry (1970), demonstrated that in *Drosophila*, as in other higher organisms, the ribosomal RNAs are transcribed as a single precursor RNA molecule. The molecular weight estimated for such a molecule in *Drosophila* is

TABLE II. Ratio of DNA complementary to 28 and 18 s rRNA in the wild type and in different mutants.

	a (rRNA/DNA) % in hybrid	b (28 s rRNA/ DNA) % in hybrid	c (18 s rRNA/ DNA) % in hybrid	$\frac{a}{c}$	$\frac{a}{b}$	$\frac{b}{c}$
Wild type	0·373 ± 0·013	0·247 ± 0·012	0·122 ± 0·002	3·05 ± 0·15	1·51 ± 0·12	2·02 ± 0·13
y w bb S1	0·165 ± 0·009	0·111 ± 0·004	0·053 ± 0·003	3·11 ± 0·28	1·48 ± 0·13	2·09 ± 0·23
y w bb S2	0·205 ± 0·006	0·138 ± 0·004	0·066 ± 0·003	3·10 ± 0·24	1·48 ± 0·09	2·09 ± 0·18
car bb S1	0·254 ± 0·006	0·170 ± 0·003	0·082 ± 0·003	3·09 ± 0·18	1·49 ± 0·06	2·07 ± 0·11
car bb S2	0·168 ± 0·006	0·109 ± 0·005	0·053 ± 0·002	3·17 ± 0·23	1·54 ± 0·13	2·05 ± 0·17
UCO3 bb S1	0·185 ± 0·006	0·123 ± 0·004	0·060 ± 0·002	3·08 ± 0·20	1·50 ± 0·10	2·05 ± 0·13

(From Quagliarotti and Ritossa, 1968.)

$2{\cdot}85 \times 10^6$ Daltons, while the molecular weights of the 28s and 18s molecules are estimated to be $1{\cdot}40 \times 10^6$ and $0{\cdot}65 \times 10^6$ respectively These data indicate first that the sequences complementary to the 28s and 18s rRNA's alternate along the DNA and second that the repeating unit is at least as long as a precursor RNA molecule (i.e. $2{\cdot}85\mu$, Miller and Beatty, 1969). Data showing in a direct way that at least a fraction of the sequences complementary to the two ribosomal RNA molecules are intercalated have been presented by Quagliarotti and Ritossa (1968). Use was made of the fact that nitrocellulose columns retain single stranded DNA, but not pure RNA/DNA hybrids, while partially hybridized DNA can, at least in part, be eluted from the columns by buffers of low ionic strength.

Thus, when broken DNA of a given molecular weight was used we could always recover a higher fraction of "pure" hybrid after hybridization with both 28s and 18s than after hybridization with 28s alone.

Hamkalo *et al.* (1973) have recently pictured active rRNA genes of *Drosophila* embryos. As shown in Fig. 5 the genes are also, in this case (Birnstiel *et al.*, 1971), separated by "spacer" regions. Hennig (personal communication) obtained similar results.

At this point, a proper calculation of the number of the genes for ribosomal RNA in a diploid cell of a wild type *Drosophila* can be attempted. After RNA/DNA hybridization using simultaneously 28s and 18s rRNAs, the saturation level of DNA from diploid cells from Oregon-R females, for example, is 0·469% (Spear and Gall, 1973). If we assume with Rudkin (1965) that the DNA content of a diploid cell is $0{\cdot}4 \times 10^{-12}$ g ($2{\cdot}4 \times 10^{11}$ Daltons), $1{\cdot}1256 \times 10^9$ Daltons of DNA are complementary to 28s and 18s rRNA's. Since we know that the two rRNA molecules are distinct and amount together to $2{\cdot}05 \times 10^6$ Daltons, the number of rRNA genes

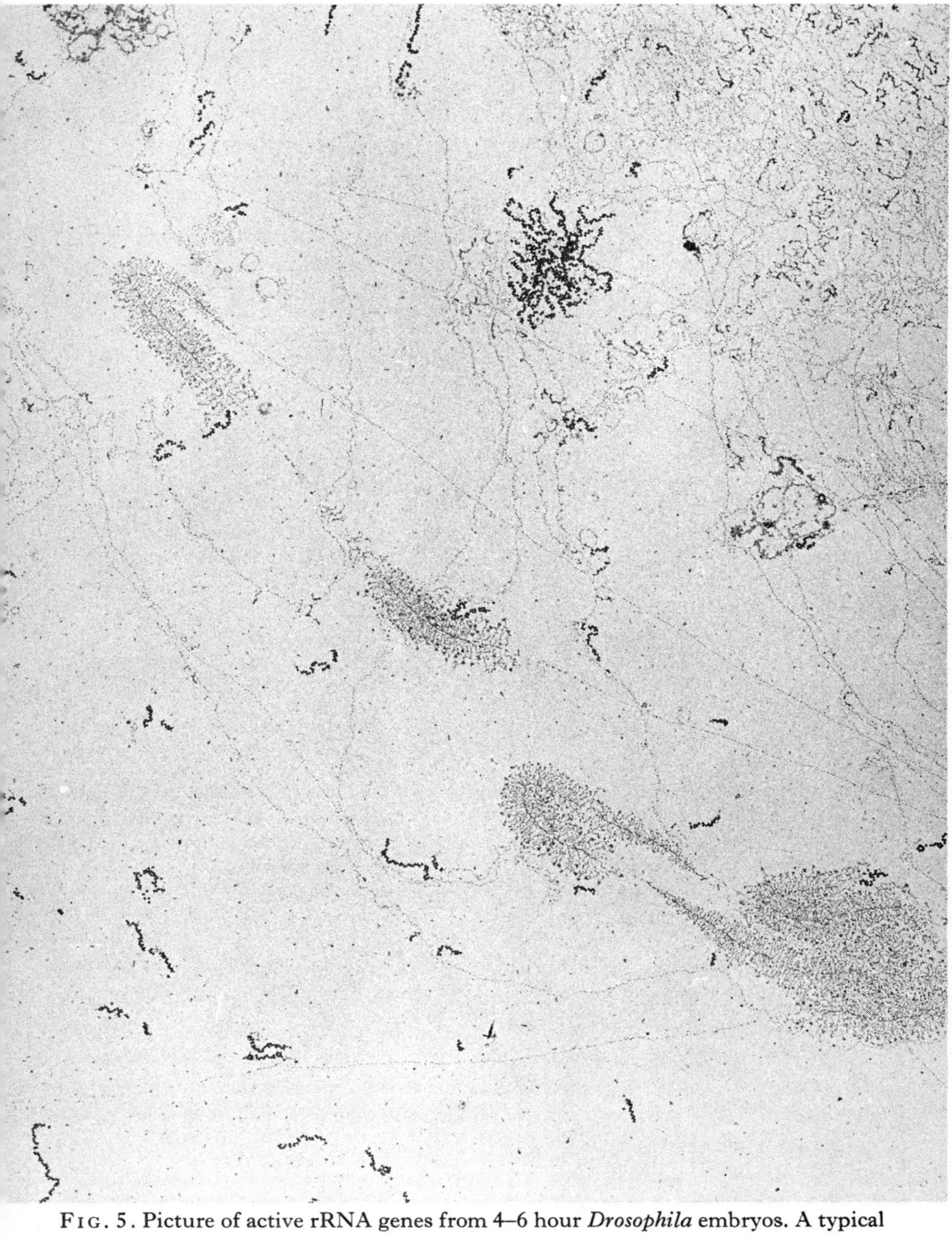

FIG. 5. Picture of active rRNA genes from 4–6 hour *Drosophila* embryos. A typical gene measures about 2·65 microns. "Spacer" regions have variable length, the shortest being around 0·4 microns. (Taken from Hamkalo *et al.*, 1973.)

per cell is 549. If the rRNA content of Urbana-S diploid cells is used (0·365 %), the number of rRNA genes per cell is 427.

Summing up, the best approximation is that each bb^+ locus is normally composed of about 200–300 clustered genes for ribosomal RNA, each intercalated with a spacer region. All of them, or at least the majority, are in tandem.

This last conclusion derives from a study of the relative orientation of the rRNA genes on the X and Y chromosomes with respect to their centromeres (Palumbo *et al.*, 1973). As shown in Fig. 6, the two loci

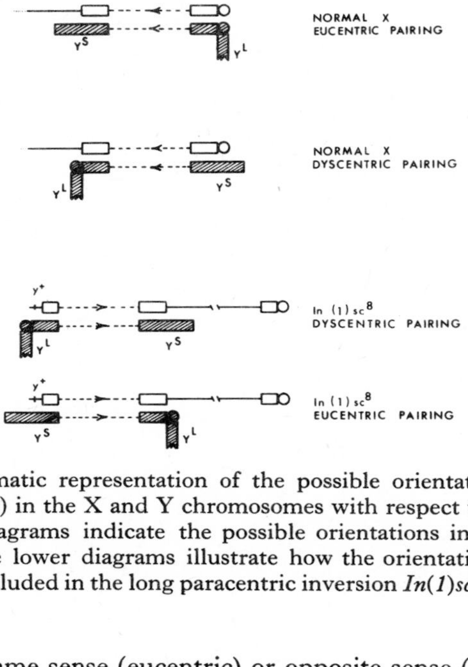

FIG. 6. Diagrammatic representation of the possible orientation of the rRNA genes (dashed lines) in the X and Y chromosomes with respect to the centromere. The upper two diagrams indicate the possible orientations in normal X and Y chromosomes. The lower diagrams illustrate how the orientations will be if the rRNA genes are included in the long paracentric inversion $In(1)sc^8$. (From Palumbo *et al.*, 1973.)

might have the same sense (eucentric) or opposite sense (dyscentric) with respect to the centromeres of X and Y. If *bb* loci are dyscentric in normal X and Y chromosomes, they will be eucentric in $In(1)sc^8$ and Y chromosomes since $In(1)sc^8$ carries a paracentric inversion of most of the X, including *bb* (Fig. 6). If the *bb* loci have the same sense with respect to the centromeres, exchange at the *bb* locus is possible. Since Schalet (1969) has shown that unequal exchange can occur in *bb* (see below), the criterion to score exchanges at the *bb* locus was the appearance of *bb* loci of intermediate redundancy out of a bb^+/bb^l heterozygote. Thus, X–Y exchange was studied in males of the following two combinations: $w^a bb^l/Ybb^+$ and $In(1)sc^8$, $bb^l\ cv/Ybb^+$. X–Y exchange at the *bb* locus in $w^a bb^l/Ybb^+$ males is expected to generate X·Y^L, w^a and Y^S. products (Neuhaus, 1936). X.Y^L, w^a crossovers were detected (Table III), and all of them were of the bb^+ type. Note that our selective procedure was such that crossovers carrying bb^l loci escaped detection, but those carrying *bb* loci were recoverable.

TABLE III. Outcome of the cross between $w^a bb^l/Ybb^+$ males and *C(1)RM*, *y v f*/Ybb^- females.

Males		Females	
$w^a bb^+$	*y v f*	*y v f*	$y^+v^+f^+$
16[a]	8	78,218	16[b]

[a] Six of these males were $w^a bb^l/Ybb^-/Ybb^+$; two died before analysis, while seven were $X.Y^L/Ybb^-$. Finally, one was X/Ybb^-. The $w^a bb^+$ bearing element in this case was indeed sterile with both Y^S and Y^L chromosomes, and was shown to be rod shaped by cytological analysis. It can be interpreted as a double crossover, either within *bb* or in the regions neighbouring *bb*. The 7 $X.Y^L$ chromosomes were single events. The rod-shaped $w^a bb^+$ chromosome was obtained together with 19 brothers of the same type which are not listed in the table. [b] One of the X chromosomes of such females is due to detachment of the X chromosomes in the mother. The *bb* phenotype of such females is variable.

X–Y exchange at the *bb* locus in $In(1)sc^8$, $bb^l cv/Ybb^+$ males is expected to lead to the formation of Y^{S}X. and y^+.Y^L products (Lindsley, 1955; Fig. 7). Our selective system was such that only y^+.Y^L crossovers could be detected. As shown in Table IV such crossovers were obtained and some of them carried *bb* loci instead of the bb^+ and bb^l loci carried by parental chromosomes. Thus X–Y recombination in this case was at the *bb* locus. The conclusion is that at least the majority of the rDNA of X

TABLE IV. Outcome of the cross between $In(1)sc^8 bb^l cv/Ybb^+$ males and *C(1)RM*, *y v f*/Ybb^- females.

Males		Females		
$cv\ bb^+$	$y\ v\ f^a$	*y v f*	$y^+v\ f$	$y^+v^+f^{+a}$
38[b]	20[c]	75,964	8[d]	15

Superfemales were not counted. [a] Such individuals originate from detachment of double X chromosomes; females were either *bb* or bb^+. [b] Nondisjunctional products. [c] 13 such males were from a single bottle, the others were single events. [d] All such females were shown to carry $y^+ \cdot Y^L$ crossovers. Four of these carried a bb^+ locus, one a bb^l locus, two a *bb* locus and one a bb^{ds} locus. (After Palumbo *et al.*, 1973.)

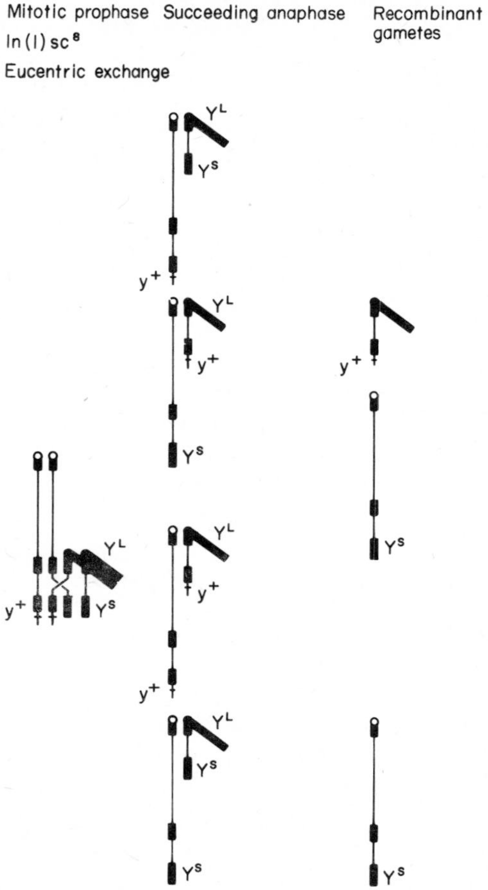

FIG. 7. Diagram showing recombination at *bb* loci of the *Y* and of the inverted X, *In(1)sc*^{8}, chromosomes. *bb* loci have the same sense with respect to the centromere in this case. The event is supposed here to be mitotic. A meiotic event of this type will generate the same recombinants. The figure is redrawn from Lindsley (1955).

and Y chromosomes have the same sense with respect to the centromere only when one of the loci is inverted. rRNA genes in normal X and Y are then inverted relative to each other with reference to their centromeres (see Palumbo *et al.* 1973 for a fuller discussion).

IV. On the regulation of rRNA transcription

At present, although little precise data is available we do have evidence that regulation of rRNA transcription exists. This comes from the observation that the number of ribosomes, hence the amount of rRNA is not necessarily proportional to the number of genes for rRNA present in a given cell. Schultz and Travaglini (1965) found no difference in the ribosome content of eggs produced by females carrying 2 or 3 nucleolus organizers. Kiefer (1968) measured the ribosome content in adult flies with 1, 2 or 3 bb^+ loci with similar results. Although different bb^+ loci might carry different numbers of rRNA genes, these data show that an excess of rDNA beyond a certain threshold does not contribute to the cells' content of ribosomes. The existence of other factors that might limit ribosome biosynthesis cannot be invoked since, in one of the experiments mentioned, only one bb^+ locus was present in an otherwise diploid complement (Kiefer, 1968). In the choice of a cell system to study regulation of transcription one must be particularly careful. The ribosomal RNA content of the egg, for example, is almost completely dependent on the activity of nurse cells. These are polyploid cells whose DNA content might rise as high as 1024 C (Dapples and King, 1970) and, *a priori*, one cannot exclude the differential duplication of particular DNA fractions. Using DNA from entire ovaries, however, rDNA percentages were found which were similar to those obtained from adults of the same genotype. Using excised ovaries from individuals having different numbers of genes for rRNA, Mohan and Ritossa (1970) were able to show that the rate of rRNA synthesis was proportional to rRNA gene number only up to a certain threshold; ovaries with higher gene dosages showed neither

TABLE V. *In vitro* RNA synthesis in ovaries of various genotypes.

Genotype	Specific activity (cpm/μg RNA) rRNA	tRNA	rRNA/tRNA
bb^+/bb^+ (0·370)	185	49	3·7
bb^+y^2eq/bb^+y^2eq (0·580)	151	41	3·7
bb^+/sc^4sc^8 (0·185)	182	43	4·2
$car\ bb/sc^4sc^8$ (0·085)	97	52	1·9
$XY^L \cdot Y^S\ bb/w^abb^l$ (0·120)	77	49	1·6
$XY^L \cdot Y^S\ bb/sc^4sc^8$ (0·090)	75	46	1·6

Flies were mated with X/0 males fo. 7 days before experiment. 30 minute pulses were made with excised ovaries in Ringer containing ^{3}H-uridine. The number in parenthesis after the genetic composition indicates probable rDNA content expressed as a percentage of diploid genome. In those combinations where one of the X chromosomes is the sc^4sc^8 chromosome, the rDNA content might be higher due to compensatory processes (see text). (From Mohan and Ritossa, 1970.)

increase in the rate of rRNA synthesis (Table V) nor in the number of ribosomes per egg. An analysis of rRNA synthesis in polytene cells (Krider and Plaut, 1972) leads to similar conclusions. Cells of the XX type carrying 1, 2, 3 and 4 nucleolus organizers synthesize similar amounts of RNA in polytene cell nucleoli. Although the rDNA content of polytene cells of females with one or two nucleolus organizers is practically identical (Spear and Gall, 1973), the conclusion appears warranted in this case too that some mechanism of control for rRNA synthesis must exist (see rDNA dosage compensation).

Sandler (1970) has reported that an autosomal gene (*abo* 2, ± 37) very probably affects embryo viability by influencing the activity of the bb^+ locus. The evidence is as follows. Eggs laid by *abo*/*abo* females, with 2 bb^+ loci, cannot support normal zygote development even if the genotype of the zygotes is bb^+/bb^+. The inability to support development by eggs laid by *abo*/*abo* females is much more evident if the zygotes have suboptimal rDNA contents ($Xbb^+/0$, Xbb^+/sc^4sc^8 and Xbb^+/Xbb were tested). As Sandler notes, however, more direct biochemical approaches are needed to support a regulatory role of the *abo* gene on rDNA.

Since the genes for rRNA are clustered, the question might be asked

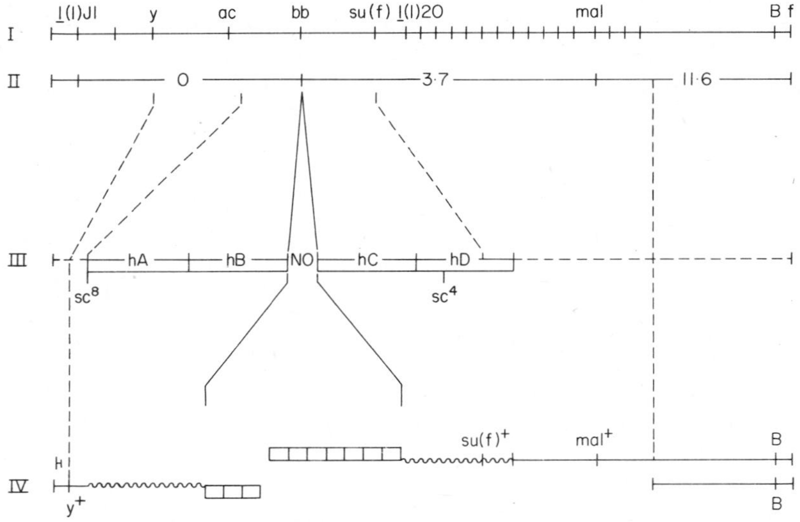

FIG. 8. I, Genetic makers; II, Linkage relations derived from $Df(1)y^{X2}$ sc^8 mal^1 f v cv/sc^8 mal^{F3} females crossed to Y/y v f mal^1 $su(f)$ males, mal^{F3}/mal^1 females have wild type eyes; III, Cytogenetic map of heterochromatic region of mitotic X (redrawn from Cooper, 1959). Placement of *su*(*f*) uncertain; IV, Schematic representation of parental *bb* chromosomes. Above ——$Df(1)y^{X2}$, below ——$Df(1)mal^{12}$. (From Schalet, 1969.)

as to whether clustering has a significance for the coordination of gene activity. The available evidence favours the idea that each gene of the *bb* cluster is capable of independent regulation. The pioneering work of McClintok (1934) in Maize and that of Beermann in *Chironomus* (1960) and Krivshenko in *D. busckii* (1959) have shown that the nucleolus organizer region can be split into several parts each of which remains perfectly capable of independent activity.

Of particular interest in this context are two mutants obtained by Schalet (1969). They were both obtained by X-irradiating $In(1)sc^{8}$ chromosomes, in which the bobbed locus is inverted (Lindsley and Grell, 1968) One mutant, $Df(1)y^{X2}$, lacks the left side of the inverted bobbed locus, as well as a number of genes for rRNA, the other, $Df(1)mal^{12}$, is missing the right part of the rDNA block (Fig. 8) (see chapter 21 by Schalet and Lefevre in this volume). Both of the deletions maintain functional rDNA. The analysis of these mutants reinforces the idea that each gene for rRNA can act independently from the other genes of the block. Cases exist, however, where nonfunctional rDNA has been reported (Ritossa, 1968; Marrakechi and Prud'homme, 1971). In one such case, the Ybb^{-} of Schultz (Bridges and Brehme, 1944), the presence of rDNA can be revealed by hybridization with labelled rRNA (see in particular Tables 1 and 4 in Henderson and Ritossa, 1970), and a constriction is cytologically evident (Cooper, unpublished observations) while the chromosome contributes no *bb* type activity. The mutation was also shown to be cis-

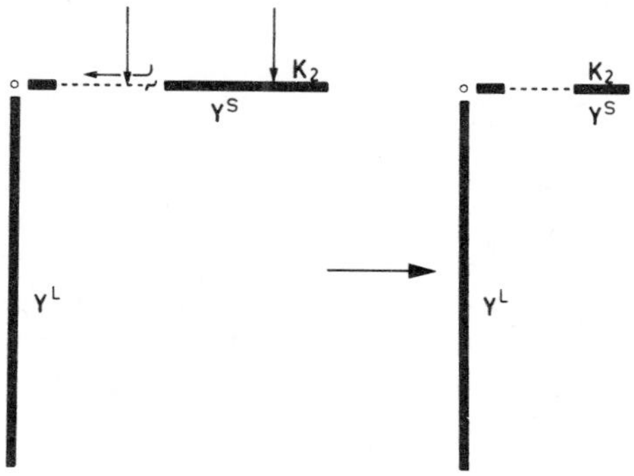

FIG. 9. Diagram showing a possible organization of the *bb* locus in the Y^{+} chromosome and of the events leading to the formation of the Ybb^{-} chromosome. The Ybb^{-} chromosome has a reduced short arm and carries a reduced number of rRNA genes which are non functional. The event leading to its formation is here supposed to be a two-break event, with the distal break occurring proximal to the arm fertility factors (KS) and the proximal break occurring in *bb*. According to such scheme, one of the sides of *bb* is missing. (From Ritossa, 1968.)

specific (in that the simultaneous presence of another *Ybb* chromosome did not produce rescue of the genes for rRNA in the Ybb^- chromosome). Its cytological description (Schultz in Bridges and Brehme, 1944) is consistent with the loss of one side of the bobbed locus (Fig. 9).

Recently Tartof (1973) has raised doubts on the nature of the Ybb^- chromosome. In his hands the Ybb^- chromosome carries 0·036% rDNA in adults instead of the 0·08–0·096% we had shown for one particular source. The source he used is not indicated and we had also shown (Ritossa, 1968) that certain lines of the Ybb^- mutation could be estimated to carry as low as 0·066% rDNA or to have changed their basic nature. But were the rDNA content of the Ybb^- chromosome that indicated by Tartof, and the deletion a normal deletion of rDNA, one would expect additivity with other *bb* loci. No such additivity is observed with the Ybb^- chromosome although bb^l loci, whose rDNA content is as low as 0·015%, do show additive effects. Thus, it seems justified to maintain the conclusion that the rDNA of Ybb^- is in some way "non-operative".

V. Variability in redundancy values

In order to study variability of the number of chromosomal genes for rRNA one has first to discuss the experimental parameters used in this study. At present such parameters are saturation values after rRNA/DNA hybridization, using DNA from adults and sometimes the "intensity" of the bobbed phenotype.

The first hybridization experiments between adult *Drosophila* DNA and rRNA were made using the Urbana wild type and gave saturation values of 0·27% for both males and females (Ritossa and Spiegelman, 1965; Vermeulen and Atwood, 1965). Assuming that adult *Drosophila* are composed of cells which are either diploid or which contain exact multiple haploid sets as estimated by Rudkin (1965) (i.e. $0{\cdot}2 \times 10^{-12}$g DNA), the number of genes for rRNA in a diploid cell can be estimated to be about 300. But we have seen that in *D. hydei* comparative hybridization values using DNA from embryos, which are supposedly made exclusively by diploid cells, and adult flies gave different saturation values; the DNA from embryos having the higher values (Hennig and Meer, 1971). Similar results have been obtained using DNA from imaginal disks (diploid) and salivary glands (polytene) in *D. melanogaster* (Spear and Gall, 1973). As we have already calculated, these results imply that the number of rRNA genes per cell is greater than 300, both in embryos and in adult flies, provided that the integrity of the chromosomal block of rRNA is maintained.

The hypothesis is hence that differential replication of different chromosomal fraction is the rule, the replication unit containing *bb* being under-replicated in some cells of the adult. Clearly, an alternative hypothesis might be that adjustment of redundancy occurs within the block of rRNA genes in the various tissues of the adult. That blocks and not genes are generally counted is shown by the proportionality between saturation values in DNA/rRNA hybridization experiments and number of similar bb^+ loci in DNA from adult flies (Fig. 10) (see also Henderson and Ritossa, 1970).

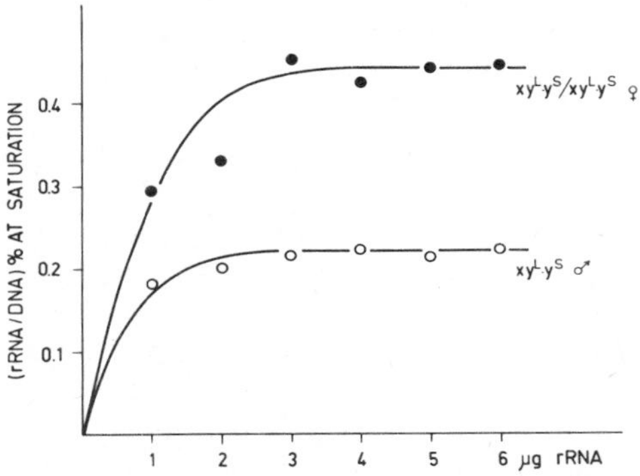

FIG. 10. Saturation levels in rRNA/DNA hybridization experiments using DNA from males and females carrying sex chromosomes in the form of attached X.Y. Males have one, and females two X.Y chromosomes. When corrections are made for excess DNA in females (two Y chromosomes more than a normal female), the saturation plateaus are directly proportional to the number of elements. (From Ritossa and Scala, 1969.)

Further evidence in favour of the above conclusion is the identification that *bb* mutations are partial deletions of rDNA. If the cell were able to regulate its rDNA content "at will", mutations of such regulatory mechanisms might have been phenotypically *bb*, but mapping apart from the sites where rDNA is located.

As far as the other parameter for variability is concerned, i.e. the "intensity" of the bobbed phenotype, one has to note that, until now, the stronger the *bb* phenotype, the lower the rDNA content of the locus considered, the only exception being the mutations of the bb^- type discussed previously.

After this, I assume here that differences in saturation values using DNAs from adults reflect differences in the number of genes for rRNA in the array which makes up the *bb* locus. Exceptions to this assumption are indeed observed and will be discussed later.

Another point worth mentioning in this respect is that hybridization experiments are often made using rRNA from wild type larvae. If larval cells transcribe different rRNA genes from those transcribed in the adult, a fraction of rDNA would escape detection. Similar errors would also be made if the rRNA genes were different in different stocks. However, when competition hybridizations were made using adult and larval rRNA and rRNAs from wild and bobbed flies of several stocks, perfect similarity between the RNAs was found (Ritossa, unpublished observations). Perfect similarity in competitive hybridization was also observed between rRNAs of different *Drosophila* species (Ritossa and Atwood, 1966; Laird and McCarthy, 1968) as well as between rRNAs from *bb* loci of the X and of the Y chromosomes. This is in accord with observations made in other organisms: rRNAs are conserved during evolution (Birnstiel *et al.*, 1971). Thus, variations of rDNA redundancy were studied using DNA from adults. The challenge of the experiments described below was double; on the one hand one wants to know the significance of rDNA redundancy and on the other, the mechanisms by which it is maintained and eventually changed. The literature contains very many instances where *bb* mutations changed to the wild condition (Bridges and Brehme, 1944), while on the other hand if natural populations, or laboratory stocks, are carefully tested many bobbed mutations are found (Spencer, 1944; Ritossa *et al.*, 1966). The reversion of bobbed mutants to the wild condition is often attributed to a "marked tendency to accumulate modifiers that suppress the phenotype" (Lindsley and Grell, 1968). This interpretation has been severely criticized by Atwood (1969). Furthermore, in my experience no case of *bb* expressivity has been found without a corresponding variation in the rDNA content. In our studies on rDNA variation (Ritossa and Scala, 1969), we started from the observation that there is normally an excess of rDNA over the minimum needed to give a visible wild phenotype. This excess is about one half the amount of rDNA present in wild type flies. To study what happens if the redundant rDNA is removed or allowed to go below that minimum amount of rDNA necessary to give a wild phenotype, *Drosophila* stocks were prepared having subnormal rDNA redundancy. In addition old stocks have been analysed and reference made to the description of their genetic constitution given in the literature.

If one of the partner loci is normal, while the other carries a partial (*bb*) or complete deletion of its rDNA, changes in rDNA redundancy in the stock are observed. These changes can occur in three possible directions:

(a) The partial deletion goes to a normal level of redundancy. This is possibly the case of several of the *bb* mutations reported to have reverted to wild type (Bridges and Brehme, 1944; Lindsley and Grell, 1968). One such case is shown in Table VI. The occurrence of this phenomenon has also been directly followed in a laboratory stock (Table VII).

(b) The redundancy of the partner locus increases. This was found in

TABLE VI. rDNA redundancy in stock Y^{bb}/v.

Starting condition		
	Y^{bb} X^{bb+} $(+)^a$	X^{bb+} X^{bb+} $(+)^a$
	$(?)^b$	$(?)^b$
now		
	Y^{bb+} X^{bb+} $(+)^a$	X^{bb+} X^{bb+} $(+)^a$
	$(0{\cdot}261)^b$	$(0{\cdot}246)^b$

[a] Phenotype. [b] Percentage of rRNA to DNA in hybrid. When this stock was constructed the Y chromosome was carrying a *bb* mutation. The X had a bb^+ isoallele. The rDNA content at the time of the stock's construction was unknown. The analysis of the stock, at present, showed a bb^+ locus in both X and Y chromosomes. The saturation value in rRNA/DNA hybridization experiments is given in parenthesis. (From Ritossa and Scala, 1969.)

some stocks carrying the Ybb^- chromosome which, as we have seen, carries non-functional rDNA and is hence equivalent to a complete deletion of rDNA.

TABLE VII. rDNA redundancy in stock *car bb*.

Starting condition		
	Y^{bb+} X^{bb} $(+)^a$	X^{bb} X^{bb} $(bb)^a$
	$(0{\cdot}205)^b$	$(0{\cdot}116)^b$
now		
	Y^{bb+} X^{bb+} $(+)^a$	X^{bb+} X^{bb+} $(+)^a$
	$(?)^b$	$(?)^b$
		some loci are still *bb*,
		the majority are bb^+,
		one of these is 0·127% in rDNA

[a] Phenotype. [b] Percentage of rRNA to DNA in hybrid. When the stock was made, all females had a strongly bobbed phenotype. The stock was maintained without selection for bobbed and, after about three years females drifted to the wild condition. After analysis of single loci, some were found to be still bobbed, but the majority were bb^+. One of these was selected and analysed for rDNA content. (From Ritossa and Scala, 1969.)

(c) A redundancy level is favoured which is normally suboptimal. This conclusion came from the analysis of a series of stocks carrying the *C(1)DX* chromosome. These attached Xs carry no nucleolus organizer (Cooper, personal communication). Genetically, females carrying this chromosome are not viable unless another *bb* locus is independently added (Lindsley and Grell, 1968). The rDNA content of this compound is zero (Ritossa *et al.*, 1971). A series of stocks of the general constitution

C(1)DX/Y and *X/Y* have been analysed. In none of these had the free X been reported to carry a *bb* mutant, while upon analysis many were revealed as carrying it. Successive observations substantiated this point.

With a number of reservations some conclusions were drawn that still hold:

(a) There is a tendency to establish a redundancy value of rDNA in adult flies which is around 0·27–0·3% of the diploid genome (although some stocks with different redundancy are found).

(b) Irrespective of the initial genetic constitution there is a tendency to establish an rDNA content which is similar in males and females.

(c) If the Y chromosome carries no rDNA (or non-functional rDNA) the X chromosome tends to accumulate genes to such an extent that males, even if carrying fewer genes than females, will have an amount of rDNA ranging around 0·27–0·3%.

One firm conclusion from this work is that the number of genes for rRNA per *bb* locus is not constant. This is contrary to the first evidence on this point (Ritossa and Spiegelman, 1965).

VI. Mechanisms for rDNA variation

A. Unequal Crossing Over

The possible involvement of unequal crossing over in variations of rDNA redundancy (Ritossa *et al.*, 1966) was a necessary deduction from the supposed organization of the genes for rRNA, the high frequency of appearance of *bb* mutations and what was known for a series of other tandemly duplicated loci (Sturtevant, 1925; Judd, 1961). Intrachromosomal exchange (Peterson and Laughnan, 1963) was also thought to be possibly responsible for variations of redundancy at the *bb* locus (Ritossa *et al.*, 1966).

The clever use of selective methods enabled Schalet (1969), to show unequal crossing-over at bobbed. Schalet made use of the y^{X2}/mal^{12} system previously illustrated (see Fig. 8). After crossing females of the y^{X2}/mal^{12} type with *X/Y* males, no male progeny survive unless crossing over occurs between the two lethal deletions. Since the only region of homology between these lethal deletions is bobbed, only crossing over in the *bb* region will give viable males. Both the y^{X2} and the mal^{12} chromosomes carry a *bb* mutation of known intensity, and unequal exchanges can be evidenced by the formation of *bb* loci which have a "strength" different from that of the parental loci. Thus, Schalet was able to identify unambiguously the generation of *bb* loci which had either a lower type-effect than the stronger of the parental loci and *bb* loci which had a higher type-effect than the weaker of the parental loci. The total frequency of exchange at *bb* in this system was estimated to be 0·4%.

Using this value together with Rudkin's (1965) estimate of the amount of DNA per map unit in the X chromosome ($4{\cdot}5 \times 10^5$ nucleotide pairs per unit) the size of the bobbed locus is quite similar to that estimated by molecular methods (Schalet, 1969). There are indications from recent experiments that the frequency of exchange at *bb* is lower when different selective systems are used (Schalet, personal communication).

Suggestions of unequal exchange at the *bb* locus can be also found in some extraordinarily rich older studies of exchange between X and Y chromosomes (Neuhaus, 1936; Lindsley, 1955) and as I mentioned previously, we have recently shown unequal exchange between bobbed loci on the Y and *In(1)sc*^{8} chromosomes (Palumbo *et al.*, 1973).

That variations of redundancy at the *bb* locus might also be due to intrachromosomal exchanges is indicated by some data of Schalet (1969). He observed the appearance of weaker *bb* loci than the parental ones in the absence of recombination of outside markers. Such a mechanism might also be responsible for the spontaneous appearance of *Ybb* chromosomes (we selected a series of such mutants from $\overline{XX}$/Y females). The

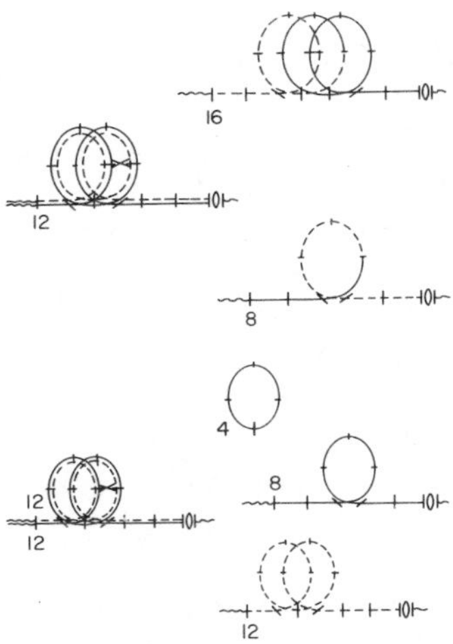

FIG. 11. Diagrammatic representation of intrachromosomal exchange. If the exchange occurs between different chromatids, one of the chromatids gains genes at the expense of the other (Upper). If the exchange occurs within the same chromatid, there is loss of genes in the form of a ring (Lower). (Redrawn from Peterson and Laughnan, 1963.)

events which might lead to variation of redundancy as the result of intrachromosomal exchange are illustrated in Fig. 11.

B. rDNA Magnification

rDNA magnification is observed in the progeny of phenotypically bobbed males. It involves the rapid accumulation of rDNA by unorthodox mechanisms. Fertile males, phenotypically bobbed, which have any one of the following genotypes have been shown to display the phenomenon: $XbbYbb$, Xbb/Ybb^o, Xbb^o/Ybb, $X.Y\,bb/0$, $X.Y^S$, bb/Ybb^o, $X.Y^Sbb/Y^L$. (By bb^o I mean the complete absence of rDNA or the presence of non-functional rDNA.) A certain fraction of *bb* loci transmitted by such males will be less extreme bobbed than their fathers; even wild type. For example, male progeny from the cross of $X.Ybb/0$ males (phenotypically strongly bobbed) to $\overline{XX}/0$ females are either less extreme bobbed than their fathers or wild type (Ritossa and Scala, 1969). This is called bobbed magnification. Similarly if $X.Ybb/0$ males are crossed to $bb^o/bb^o/B^SY$ females their $X.Ybb/bb^o$ daughters exhibit bobbed magnification. However, the progeny of $X.Ybb/bb^o$ females (which are bobbed in phenotype) do not show magnification. For example, when $X.Ybb/bb^o$ females are crossed to $X.Y$ males, their $X.Ybb$ sons will still be phenotypically bobbed (such sons, however, will, in their progeny, display magnification).

rDNA magnification is not restricted to X/Y bobbed male combinations. It occurs also in X/Y/Y, males and other combinations provided that they are bobbed in phenotype. In $Xbb/0$ males some steps of the process apparently occur, though the effect cannot be followed in the successive generation due to their sterility.

Any bobbed locus in a bb/bb^+ combination is stable: that is, it is subject to variations of redundancy only by mechanisms such as unequal crossing over or intrachromosomal exchange, described previously; their frequency is rather low. A *bb* mutant can be quite safely maintained by combining it with a bb^+ chromosome in such a way that the rDNA redundancy is almost similar in both males and females. (An *Xbb* chromosome can be maintained, for example, by crossing $\overline{XX},bb/Y$ females to Xbb/Y males while a *Ybb* chromosome is safely maintained in stock by crossing $\overline{XX}/Ybb$ females to X/Ybb males.)

For the study of rDNA magnification the *bb* bearing chromosome is taken from parental stock to generate phenotypically bobbed males. For example, Xbb/Y males are crossed to $\overline{XX}/Ybb^-$ females to give Xbb/Ybb^- (phenotypically bobbed) males; or X/Ybb males are crossed to $bb^o/bb^o/Y$ females to give bb^o/Ybb bobbed males.

It is in such bobbed males that magnification starts, although without any apparent phenotypic consequence. The first step consists, presumably, in the extra synthesis of rDNA which has no immediate phenotypic effect. This increase of rDNA is evidenced by comparing the percentages of rDNA in the DNA of such bobbed males and that attributable to the *bb* locus in the parental combination. Thus, a *Ybb* chromosome was estimated, in the parental combination (*Ybb*/*X*), to carry an amount of rDNA equal to 0·045% of the diploid genome, while in the sc^4sc^8/Ybb combination, where magnification starts, its rDNA content was considerably higher (0·08%))Boncinelli *et al.*, 1972).

For an *Xbb* chromosome its rDNA content in the parental combination (*Xbb*/*Y*) was estimated to be 0·086% of the diploid genome while in males of the *Xbb*/0 and Xbb/Ybb^- type, its rDNA contributions were higher (0·170 and 0·102% respectively) (Ritossa *et al.*, 1971). The greater increase in rDNA was observed in the *Xbb*/0 males. *X*/0 males have been shown to exhibit dosage compensation with respect to their rDNA content (Tartof, 1971). At least part of the increase in redundancy in *Xbb*/0 males is probably accounted for by dosage compensation (see below for discussion).

The rDNA accumulated during this first step of magnification, which we call premagnification, apparently does not contribute to any phenotypic effect. Normally, a fly whose DNA has 0·170% rDNA is perfectly wild type while one with 0·102% rDNA is weakly bobbed. Although more experiments are needed, it would seem that the increase of rDNA which occurs at premagnification is lower than, or at maximum equal to, the amount of rDNA of the *bb* locus before magnification.

To explain this increase in rDNA during premagnification we propose an "extra synthesis" of rDNA (Ritossa *et al.*, 1971; Boncinelli *et al.*, 1972). The hypothesis, still to be proven, is suggested by the following observations:

(a) If the same *Xbb*/*Y* males are mated to $\overline{XX}/Ybb^-$ and to $\overline{XX}/Y$ females, they will generate male progeny in which the rDNA content of the *bb* locus of the *X* will be respectively higher than and identical to that estimated in the parental combinations. Since different rDNA contents in sperm has no selective value (bb^l bearing sperm are as efficient as bb^+ bearing ones in fertilization) one can exclude differences in the parental male sperm population. Similar considerations clearly apply to *Ybb* chromosomes.

(b) To explain the higher rDNA content of males during premagnification one might postulate somatic events such as unequal crossing over between the partner bobbed loci or events of the intrachromosomal exchange type between sister chromatids (see Fig. 11), followed by somatic selection of the cells having the higher rDNA content (Ritossa, 1968b;

Ritossa and Scala, 1969; Atwood, 1969). In spite of the low expectation of such processes (Peterson and Laughnan, 1963), one should find, if they occur, a high incidence of mosaic individuals. Although the existence of some mosaicism has been reported in bobbed males undergoing premagnification (males G1 or Fig. 13) (Atwood, 1969), we could not detect any with certainty in a series of different males during premagnification (Ritossa, 1973). Also, such events should generate "stable" *bb* loci, yet a certain instability has been reported among newly magnified *bb* loci (see below).

Bobbed males, during premagnification, are also characterized by a high rate of RNA synthesis (Table VIII). The higher rates of RNA synthesis are not accounted for by an overall increase of RNA synthesis in the cell, but rather by the increased synthesis of a 38s precursor to rRNA (Ritossa *et al.*, 1971; Graziani, 1975).

TABLE VIII. Specific activity[a] of RNA, after 30 min of labeling with [^{3}H]uridine, of excised genitalia from males of different genetic composition.

$g^2ty\ bb/O$	$g^2ty\ bb/Ybb^-$	$g^2ty\ bb/Ybb^+$	bb^+/O	bb^+/Ybb^+	$g^2ty\ bb^{m23}Y/bb^-$	$XY^{L.S}Ybb$
strong *bb*[b]	strong *bb*	bb^+	bb^+	bb^+	bb^+	strong *bb*
210[c]				58		
178				34		
	215	59				
	243		45			
				80	85	217

[a] Specific activity is expressed as cpm/μg of total RNA. [b] Phenotype of male. [c] The results obtained from experiments done in parallel are indicated on the same line. (From Ritossa *et al.*, 1971.)

However, this RNA apparently has a high turnover since the bobbed tissues assayed exhibit a high rate of synthesis almost throughout the adult period, yet are always found to have a lower total RNA content than tissues from wild type flies (Ritossa *et al.*, 1971). Graziani (1975) has evidence that this precursor is not methylated (or is undermethylated), which might cause its failure to mature. Tarantino (1972) studied RNA synthesis during the successive steps of magnification and found that extra synthesis of the 38s precursor parallels magnification and fades down when the bb^m locus becomes wild.

The progeny of the bobbed males which undergo premagnification can exhibit magnification. This means that magnification is not necessarily observed in all progeny. Its efficiency was found to vary both with the

TABLE IX. Estimation of the percentages of magnification after one step.

Male genetic constitution	Female used in the cross	Parameter of magnification	Efficiency	Reference
$g^2ty\ bb/Ybb^-$	$y\ v\ f/Ybb^-$	Appearance of g^2ty males without etched abdomen	96%	Ritossa 1968b and subsequent observations
same	same	same	90%	same
same	same	same	84%	same
same	same	same	37%	same
$w^a bb^l/Ybb$ *su-var5*	$w^a bb^l/w^a bb^l/B^S Y$	Appearance of $w^a bb^+$ males	83%	Boncinelli *et al.*, 1972
$XY^L \cdot Y^S$, (108–9) $y^2 su(w^a)w^a bb/0$	$y^2 su(w^a)w^a/O$	Appearance of bb^+ males	54%	Ritossa and Scala, 1969
same	same	same	42%	
bb^l/Ybb	bb^l/bb^+	Magnification of *Ybb* is studied. Increase of survival of Ybb/bb^l males in respect to that of fathers	From 10–20% to 80–90%	Atwood, 1969
$y\ w\ bb^l/Ybb$	$sc^4sc^8, y\ cv/sc^4sc^8, y\ cv/B^S Y$	Magnification of *Ybb* is studied. Survival of sc^4sc^8/Ybb males is compared to that of same males after similar cross using bb^+/Ybb males	From 0·9% to 31%	Ritossa, 1972

different *bb* loci studied and in duplicate experiments. Table IX gives the percentages of magnification in some cases studied.

Similar results were obtained using single pair or mass crosses by Atwood (1969) but Locker and Prud'homme (1973) indicate that in single pair crosses, the number of flies showing the average frequency of magnification (as observed in mass crosses) varies. Using certain *bb* alleles, few single pairs do not magnify at all while the majority have a high frequency of magnification, while using other alleles the opposite situation was found.

Magnification is a stepwise process (Ritossa, 1968b; Atwood, 1969). As an example, with the continued backcrossing of g^2 *ty bb*/*Ybb*$^-$ males to *C(1)RM*/*Ybb*$^-$ females illustrated in Fig. 12, the rDNA contents of the *bb* locus on the X chromosome of the males, measured in the three successive generations, increased (Table X). Further generations of backcrossing did not lead to further consistent increases in rDNA content (Ritossa, 1968b).

A working model has been recently advanced for magnification (Ritossa, 1972). According to this idea, when male *Drosophila* are generated which are phenotypically bobbed "signals" accumulate in the cell which stimulate extra rDNA synthesis. The extra copies of rDNA do not exceed the amount of rDNA pre-existing in the *bb* locus undergoing magnification. The hypothesis assumes that the extra rDNA is free in the majority of somatic cells, but can be integrated into the chromosome in the germ line. Integration is visualized as due to crossing over between the chromosomal locus and the circularized extra copies of rDNA (Fig. 13).

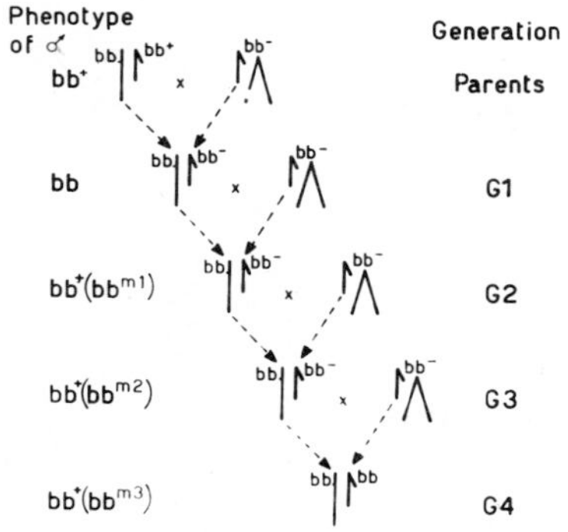

FIG. 12. Scheme of the crosses to produce bb^m loci. Males of composition g^2ty *bb*/*Ybb*$^+$ are crossed with females *C(1)*/*Ybb*$^-$. The males obtained after this cross show a strong bobbed phenotype (g^2ty *bb*/*Ybb*$^-$). When these males are crossed again to females *C(1)*/*Ybb*$^-$, males are obtained which are no longer bobbed in phenotype while relevant chromosomes are the same (g^2ty bb^m/*Ybb*$^-$). (From Henderson and Ritossa, 1970.)

TABLE X. rDNA content attributable to the *bb* locus of g^2ty *bb* chromosome before and during magnification.[a]

Generation	Genetic composition		Phenotype
P		$g^2ty\ bb/Ybb^+$ 0·295 (0·086)	Wild
G 1	$g^2ty\ bb/O$ 0·170 (0·170)	$g^2ty\ bb/Ybb^-$ 0·182 (0·102)	Strong bobbed
G 2	$g^2ty\ bb^{m1}/O$ 0·175 (0·175)	$g^2ty\ bb^{m1}/Ybb^-$ 0·195 (0·115)	Weak bobbed
G 3	$g^2ty\ bb^{m2}/O$ 0·252 (0·252)	$g^2ty\ bb^{m2}/Ybb^-$ 0·250 (0·170)	Wild

[a] The number under each genotype is the rRNA/DNA percentage at saturation found after rRNA/DNA hybridization with DNA from individuals of the indicated composition. The number in parentheses is the probable rDNA contribution of the g^2ty *bb* chromosome. (This is obtained by subtracting the rDNA content of the homologous chromosome.) (From Ritossa *et al.*, 1971.)

According to this hypothesis, only those loci where integration has occurred will show magnification in the succeeding generation.

If the zygote in which these happen to be still has an insufficient amount of rDNA, then a further step of magnification similar to that in the previous generation will start, but only if the combination is a phenotypically bobbed male. A similar working model has been recently proposed by Locker (1973). Also, Locker and Prud'homme (1973) could show that, parallel to magnification, few bb^l loci are produced from magnifying *bb* loci. This observation fits a working model where recombinational events are involved. Indeed, parallel to integrational events some excision events are to be expected.

Magnification of lethal bobbed mutants has also been observed (Atwood, 1969; Ritossa, 1972). To realize a phenotypically bobbed male, to start magnification, a bb^l deletion necessarily needs a helper *bb* locus (*1Hbb*) (Fig. 14). According to the hypothesis the first step of bb^l magnification is the extra synthesis of genes equal, at most, to the number of genes already existent in the bb^l locus. After this first step, and the successive integration of the rDNA, the bb^{lm1} locus is expected to be still lethal if tested against a full deletion of the genes for rRNA. It is then necessary to remove the

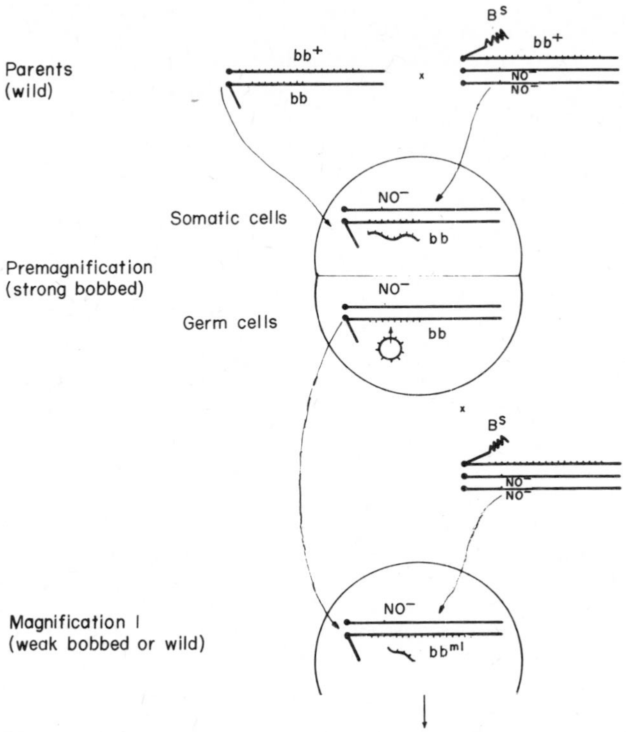

FIG. 13. Diagram illustrating a working hypothesis on the first steps of rDNA magnification. A bobbed male is here generated by crossing *Xbb*$^+$/*Ybb* males with *In(1)sc*^{4,8}/*In(1)sc*^{4,8}/*B*^{S}*Y* females. (The *In(1)sc*^{4,8} chromosome carries no gene for rRNA while the *B*^{S}*Y* has a wild bobbed locus.) In such bobbed male combination, magnification starts. It consists in the synthesis of rDNA not bound to the chromosome and unable to produce mature ribosomal RNA. Only in the germ line of such males can the extra copies of rDNA be anchored to the chromosome. The extra rDNA is here assumed to be in a circular form and anchorage is supposed to be an integration event. In the successive generation (magnification 1) in those zygotes which receive a *Ybb* chromosome where integration of extra rDNA has not occurred, the process will start all over again; while zygotes which receive a *Ybb* chromosome where rDNA integration occurred, will generate individuals (*In(1)sc*^{4,8}/*Ybb*^{m1}) whose phenotype will be normal or less severely bobbed than that of their fathers. In appropriate conditions a further step of magnification, similar to that occurred previously, can go on in this, magnification 1, generation. (From Ritossa, 1972.)

1Hbb locus and substitute it with another helper locus, *2Hbb*. The new helper has to be such that the combination *bb*^{lm1}/*2Hbb* is phenotypically bobbed male. *2Hbb* can be the same as *1Hbb* or another bobbed locus with a lower rDNA content; what is important is that the *bb*^{l} locus under

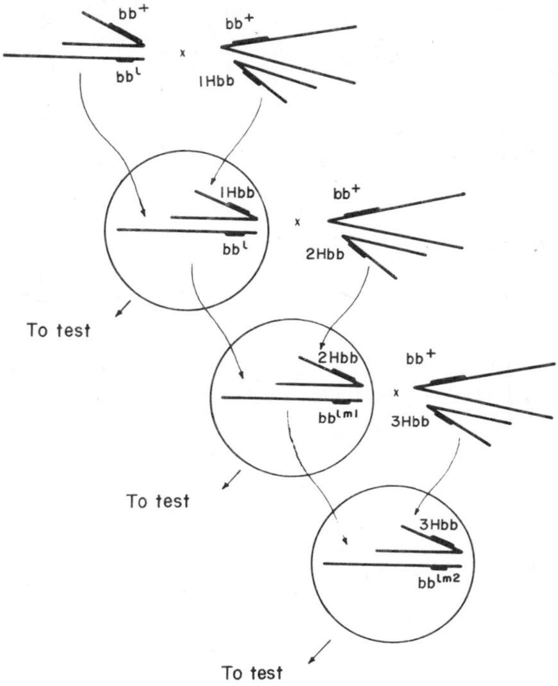

FIG. 14. The figure illustrates a way to maintain a bb^l deletion carried by the X chromosome in a bobbed male line to allow magnification of bb^l. Parent males, Xbb^l/Ybb^+, are crossed to $\overline{XX}/1HbbY$ females. Male sons, $Xbb^l/1HbbY$, phenotypically bobbed, are then crossed with $\overline{XX}/2HbbY$ females. The $2HbbY$ chromosome has to be such that male sons of this cross ($bb^{lm1}/2HbbY$) be again phenotypically bobbed. One can repeat this for several generations. Bobbed males so produced (enclosed in a circle in the figure) are also used to test for bb^l magnification. (From Ritossa, 1972.)

magnification remains in a phenotypically bobbed male. This process was followed for several generations, according to these rules, as illustrated in Fig. 14.

In accord with the hypothesis, quantitative magnification of bb^l loci, here operationally identified with the appearance of bb^{lm}/Ybb^- flies, was observed after two generations of association of the bb^l locus with helper loci (Table XI). A low number of bb^{lm} loci (able to support life without a *bb* bearing partner), were also generated after one generation of association of bb^l with a helper locus (Table XI, first row).

Atwood (1969) observed that such exceptions were almost wildtype. When several male combinations were studied of the kind illustrated in

TABLE XI. Outcome of the cross between *y w* bb^l/Ybb males and *C(I)RM*, *y v f*$/Ybb^-$ females.

Male parent	Phenotype	Progeny: Males[a] *y w bb*	Progeny: Females *y v f*
bb^l/Ybb	*bb*	4	1919
bb^{lm1}/Ybb	*bb*	189	1062
bb^{lm2}/Ybb^b	*bb*	87	758
bb^{lm3}/Ybb^b	*bb*	107	464
bb^{lm4}/Ybb^b	*bb*	14	470
bb^{lm5}/Ybb^b	*bb*	116	848

[a] The bobbed phenotype of such males is much stronger than that of their fathers.
[b] Some males at these steps of magnification appear which are either weak *bb* or wild. *bb* males were selected to obtain the next generation. (From Ritossa, 1972.)

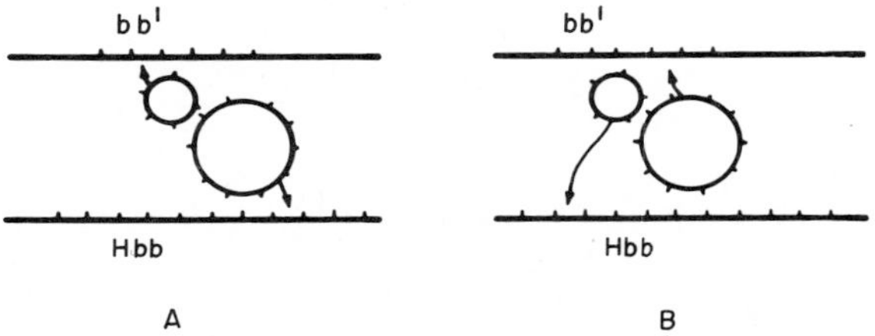

FIG. 15. Alternative ways of integration of extra copies of rDNA. In (a) each *bb* block was primer for an rDNA ring of the same length. Each rDNA ring is integrated in the same *bb* locus from which it was derived. In (b) the possibility is illustrated that rDNA rings, formed as described in Figure (a), are instead integrated into *bb* loci from which they were not derived. (From Ritossa, 1972.)

Fig. 14 we could confirm that the few bb^{lm1}/Ybb^- males had a phenotype much closer to wild type than that of the majority of bb^{lm2}/Ybb^- individuals. Such exceptions can be justified by our working hypothesis (Fig. 15). Alternative aspects of this same general working model have been discussed (Ritossa, 1972). Magnification continues in bb^{lm2}/Ybb^- individuals which are phenotypically bobbed, and stops only when the bb^{lm}/Ybb^- combination has reached the wild phenotype (Ritossa, 1973; Morea and Ritossa, in preparation).

According to our hypothesis, if integration of magnified rDNA is normally restricted to the *bb* locus from which it was originated, it can also occasionally be integrated at the homologous locus, then simultaneous integration events might occur. The frequency of such double events might be of the order of magnitude of the product of the frequencies of

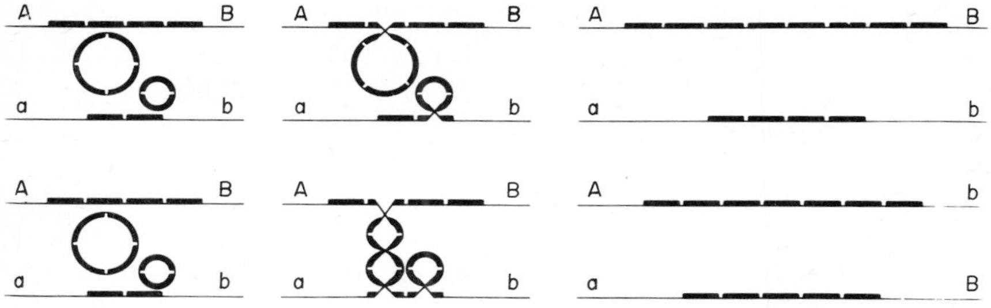

FIG. 16. A model proposing how integration of extra copies of rDNA might occur in combinations where two *bb* loci are present. In the upper part of the figure two extra copies are supposed to be separately integrated into both chromosomal loci. In the lower part of the figure one extra copy is supposed to be simultaneously integrated into both chromosomal loci. In this case, recombination of outside markers is expected. (From Ritossa, 1973.)

the single events. If cells undergoing magnification contain rDNA on the X and on the Y chromosomes (e.g. bb^l/Ybb and bb/Ybb^-), then crossover products involving the X and Y chromosomes should be obtained (Fig. 16).

To test this point, X–Y recombination was studied in $In(1)sc^8bb^lcv/Ybb$ males. They are phenotypically bobbed and magnification occurs both at the bb^l locus on the X and at the *bb* locus on the Y (Ritossa, 1973). Furthermore, *bb* loci on the $In(1)\ sc^8bb^lcv$ and *Ybb* chromosomes have the same sense with respect to the centromere. We have already seen that if X–Y

TABLE XII. Outcome of the following crosses.[a]

Cross	Reference	Progeny[b] Females y^+	Females y	Males y	Males y^+
$sc^8bb^l\ cv/Ybb$ X $XY^L.Y^S(108\text{–}9)\ y^2su(w^a)w^a$		6,903	22	5,444	18
sc^8B/Y X $y\ w\ In\ 49\ f$	Bart, 1958	33,735	2	32,779	—
$sc^8, f\ v\ cv/Y$ X $Y^SX.Y^L, In(1)EN, B\ y$	Lindsley, 1955	11,381	3	8,085	3
$sc^8, f\ v\ cv/Y$ X $Y^SX.Y^L, Ins(1)EN,dl49,car\ f\ v\ y$	Lindsley, 1955	93,675	6	85,818	—

[a] Magnification occurs only in males of first line. [b] Exceptional, yellow, females and yellow$^+$ males are due to the presence of crossovers between X and Y chromosomes. Exceptional, yellow females due to maternal non-disjunction are excluded.

recombination occurs in this case within the *bb* locus, $y^+.Y^L$ and $Y^SX.$ crossovers should be generated (see Fig. 7). Two kinds of crosses were made. In one case (Table XII), *In(1)sc⁸bbˡcv/Ybb* males were crossed to females homozygous for the $XY^L.Y^S$ (108–9), $y^2su(w^a)w^a$ chromosome. Formation of $y^+.Y^L$ crossovers in this case will lead to y^+ male progeny. Formation of $Y^SX.$ crossovers, which carry a deletion of the y^+ region, will lead to the formation of yellow females (Lindsley, 1955; Ritossa, 1973). In the other case (Table XIII), *In(1)sc⁸bbˡcv/Ybb* males, and other magnifying combinations, were crossed to *C(1)RM,y v f/Ybb⁻* females. Only $y^+.Y^L$ crossovers can be recovered from this cross—as y^+ females.

TABLE XIII. Female progeny after the following crosses.

Cross		Magnification[a] in males	Females $y\ v\ f$	Females $y^+\ v\ f$
sc^8bb^lcv/Ybb	$\times$ $C(1)RM,y\ v\ f/Ybb^-$	M	11,327	31
$sc^8bb^{lm1}cv/Ybb$	$\times$ $C(1)RM,y\ v\ f/Ybb^-$	M	2,300	12
$sc^8bb^{lm2}cv/Ybb^-$	$\times$ $C(1)RM,y\ v\ f/Ybb^-$	M	1,379	3
$sc^8bb^{lm7}cv/Ybb^-$	$\times$ $C(1)RM,y\ v\ f/Ybb^-$	L	19,437	3

[a] (M) indicates that magnification is occurring. (L) indicates that magnification is almost at its end.

The data presented in Tables XII and XIII show that during magnification of a sc^8bb^l/Ybb combination there is a marked increase of crossover products between the X and the Y chromosomes. This frequency is from 12 to 100 times greater than the frequency in the absence of magnification. Since the chromosomes used in the experiments summarized in Table XII might differ from those used in the reported controls, the data in Table XIII are more significant because they refer to the same chromosomes during and almost at the end of magnification. One can see that in those combinations where magnification occurs (M) the frequency of appearance of X–Y recombinants ($y^+v\,f$ females) is much higher than in the combination where magnification has been almost completed (L). A control of the frequency of X–Y recombination in non-magnifying males is also shown in Table IV.

All but one of the examined y^+ bearing crossovers listed in Tables XII and XIII were effectively shown to be of the $y^+.Y^L$ type and some of them could be shown to be products of recombination at the rDNA level. Furthermore, the majority of them do not appear in clusters (Ritossa, 1973). This observation favours the idea that such recombination is not gonial, but rather meiotic. Had recombination occurred in gonial cells, clusters of recombinants would be expected (Lindsley, 1955). Also, had X–Y recombination in magnifying males been mitotic, formation of Y^SX. crossovers would be twice as frequent as that of $y^+.Y^L$ crossovers (see Fig. 7). If the event is meiotic, however, the two kinds of crossovers are expected to appear in a 1:1 ratio.

As indicated in Table XII, the ratio between yellow females and y^+ males which we observed is close to 1:1. However, only 10 of the 18 yellow females we could examine were shown to carry effectively Y^SX. crossovers (Ritossa, 1973). These observations, together with other evidence (Ritossa *et al.*, 1974) favour the idea that X–Y recombination in males undergoing magnification occurs mostly at meiosis.

Another feature of magnification is the "instability" of some of the rDNA accumulated. Thus, when newly magnified bb^m loci were associated

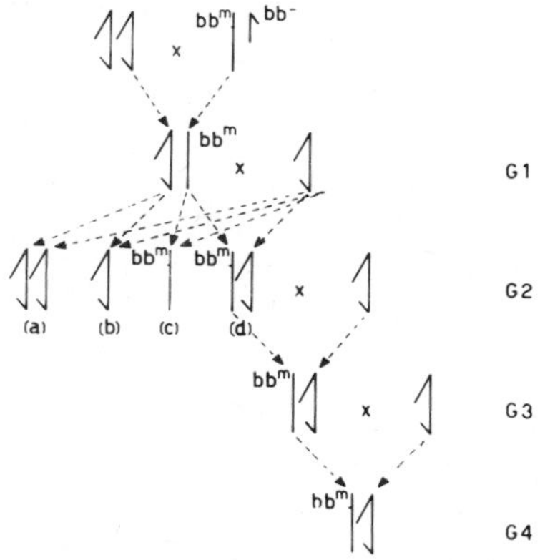

FIG. 17. Scheme of the crosses made to study the inheritance of rDNA of bb^m loci when associated with a bb^+ locus.$g^2ty\ bb^m/Ybb^-$ males are crossed to $Y^SX.Y^L/Y^SX.Y^L$ females. The X carried by the $Y^SX.Y^L$ chromosome is inverted (*In*(*1*)*EN*) and carries *y* and *B*. *y* is included in the inversion and practically cannot be removed from the $Y^SX.Y^L$ chromosome. F_1 females, which have Bar eye, are then crossed with $X^SX.Y^L$ males. Sons are obtained which are of two types, as far as body color is considered. y^+ ones, which carry the bb^m locus [males (c) of the figure], are of the $X/0$ type and are scored for reversion of the bb^m locus to the original expressivity. Yellow sons [males (b) of the figure] have the $Y^SX.Y^L$ chromosome and are counted to monitor possible abnormalities of segregation and for formation of *bb* alleles (none was found in our studies). Daughters are also obtained which are either *y* or y^+. Yellow daughters [females (a) of the figure] are homozygous for the reference chromosome and are counted for reference. y^+ ones [females (d) of the figure] are of the $bb^m/Y^SX.Y^L$ composition. They are mated with $Y^SX.Y^L$ males. Crosses are continued for many generations and the same analysis of the progeny is made as described here. (From Henderson and Ritossa, 1970.)

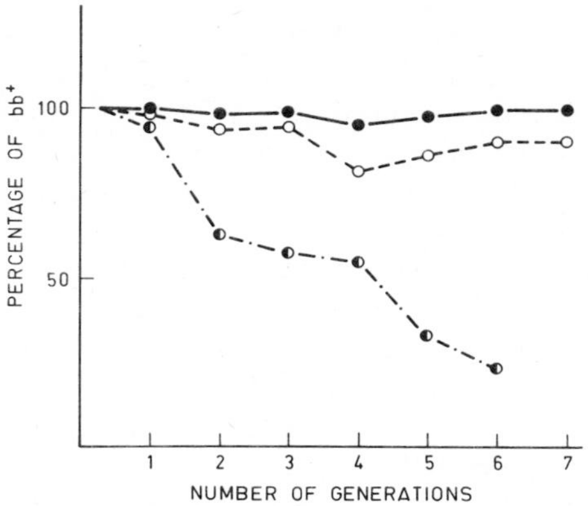

FIG. 18. Percentage of individuals maintaining the wild phenotype after the bb^m locus was associated with a bb^+ locus for a different number of generations. $g^2ty\ bb^m/Ybb^-$ males of different generation time after magnification (bb^{m2}, bb^{m4}, bb^{m7} of Fig. 11), were crossed to reference females as indicated in Fig. 17. bb^m/O males [males (c) of Fig. 17] were scored for *bb* phenotype after the bb^m locus was associated with the bb^+ locus of reference chromosome for an increasing number of generations, as shown in the abscissa. Etched abdomen was used as a parameter for *bb* phenotype. (Filled circles refer to bb^{m7}, open circles refer to bb^{m4}, half-filled circles refer to bb^{m2}.) (From Henderson and Ritossa, 1970.)

with bb^+ partners, a considerable reversion of the bb^m loci to *bb* was observed in appropriate tests (Ritossa, 1968; Henderson and Ritossa, 1969; Boncinelli *et al.*, 1972; Locker, 1973). An experimental plan followed to study reversion is shown in Fig. 17 and the frequencies of reversion of bb^{m2}, bb^{m4} and bb^{m7} loci observed are shown in Fig. 18.

Some points are worth mentioning on this particular question:

(a) Reversion of bb^m to *bb* is paralleled by the loss of rDNA (Boncinelli *et al.*, 1972).

(b) When newly magnified bb^m loci are associated with a series of *bb* loci of varying rDNA content, the rDNA contributed by the bb^m locus to the combination is inversely proportional to the rDNA content of the partner locus, but their rDNA content never returns to the starting value of redundancy (Malva *et al.*, 1972; Henderson and Ritossa, 1969; Boncinelli *et al.*, 1972).

(c) After some generations, bb^m loci loose their ability to revert (Henderson and Ritossa, 1970; Boncinelli *et al.*, 1972; Locker, 1973) (see behaviour of bb^{m7} in Fig. 18).

(d) If magnified *bb* lethal loci are associated with bb^+ there is not a consistent reversion to the lethal condition (Morea and Ritossa, in preparation).

(e) Reversion to *bb* of newly magnified bb^{m} loci occurs also in females where the only rDNA genes present are those of the bb^{m} locus. Thus, for example, if one tries to perpetuate the $g^{2}ty\ bb^{m2}/In(1)sc^{4,8}$ combination, starting with phenotypically wild females, a progressive increase in phenotypically bobbed progeny is observed. One has to note that in this case individuals are formed which are not selectively favoured (Caputi, 1972). Clearly, if *bb* loci magnify to such a point as to be able to support a wild phenotype and afterwards, upon association with a bb^{+} partner, can revert to a *bb* condition, then some of the rDNA produced during magnification has to become functional without chromosomal integration. However, the fact that bb^{lm} loci do not revert to the lethal condition and that the rDNA content of the bb^{m} loci, after association with bb^{+} never returns to the original content, is in favour of an initial integration of rDNA, as is the fact that after some generations bb^{m} loci lose their ability to revert. Thus it would seem that during magnification some rDNA is integrated within the chromosome and some "goes along" with it in some other manner, but is ultimately integrated.

The loss of non integrated rDNA might be responsible for the occasional appearance of mosaics in the steps of magnification that follow premagnification.

In the presentation of magnification here, I have intermingled a part of the data with the model we currently use to justify them. This presentation is coherent with the development of the studies in the field and has the ambition of making understandable otherwise complicated and unorthodox data. I wish to emphasize, however, that the model represents only a testable working hypothesis.

C. Dosage Compensation

Tartof (1971) found that $Xbb^{+}/0$ males and $Xbb^{+}/In(1)sc^{4,8}$ females had rDNA contents much higher than half the rDNA content of Xbb^{+}/Xbb^{+} females, a combination homozygous for the same locus. Tartof also reported that the combination $In(1)sc^{4,8}/Ybb^{+}$ did not show any increase of rDNA with respect to the expected value for the Ybb^{+} chromosome. The rDNA accumulated in $Xbb^{+}/In(1)sc^{4,8}$ females is not inheritable (Tartof, 1971).

A molecular explanation for dosage compensation has been proposed recently by Spear and Gall (1973). They calculated rDNA percentages, relative to total cell DNA, in diploid cells (imaginal disks) and polytene cells (salivary glands) of *D. melanogaster* larvae. They could show that in diploid cells the amount of rDNA is proportional to the number of nucleolus organizer regions. Thus, DNA from imaginal disks of $Xbb^{+}/$

Xbb^{+} females and *Xbb*$^{+}$/0 males showed saturation values, after rRNA/DNA hybridization, of 0·469 and 0·264% respectively (*Xbb*$^{+}$ was in this case from Oregon-R). However, when DNA was obtained from salivary glands of *Xbb*$^{+}$/*Xbb*$^{+}$ females and *Xbb*$^{+}$/0 males, it showed saturation values with rRNA which were respectively 0·078 and 0·074%. Thus, the rDNA content of polytene cells is not proportional to the number of nucleolus organizer regions.

Polytene cells exist also in the adult (Ashburner, 1970). If rDNA polytenization proves to be independent of the number of nucleolus organizer regions in these cells (at least within the limits of one versus two), then the rDNA content per *X* of *Xbb*$^{+}$/0 males is expected to be higher than that of females, if total adult DNA is considered (see also the calculation of rRNA gene redundancy previously made in this chapter).

In an attempt to understand something more of the control of dosage compensation, it was recently tested whether the mechanism starts to operate when the rDNA content is below a certain threshold and/or when there is only one nucleolus organizer region of the *X* per cell. Thus *X*/0 males were made with a *bb*$^{+}$ locus whose rDNA content, in homozygous females, was estimated to be as high as about 0·3% and *X*/0 males were made which had two nucleolus organizer regions (*sc*^{S1L,4R}/0). The results indicate that compensation occurs in both cases. Thus, a check between homologues seems a possible prerequisite to compensation. If one is alone or has a partner quite different from itself the mechanism starts. The observation that the extent of compensatory increase of rDNA is directly correlated to the rDNA content of the particular *bb* locus studied (Tartof, 1973; Barsanti, in preparation) favours the idea of Spear and Gall (1973) that compensation might concern the extent of polytenization of the chromosomal block of rDNA, rather than the attainment of a particular rDNA content independent from the rDNA content of the chromosomal block.

It is important to emphasize that magnification and compensation are quite different processes (contra Tartof, 1973):

(a) magnification (and premagnification) can involve a *bb* locus of the Y chromosome, while *bb*$^{+}$ loci on Y chromosomes apparently do not show compensation phenomena (Atwood, 1969; Boncinelli *et al.*, 1972).

(b) $XY^{L}.Y^{S}$, *bb*/0 males can show magnification but not compensation (Ritossa and Scala, 1969).

(c) Associated with premagnification there is a high rate of rRNA synthesis, at least in extracted genitalia, while this seems not to be the case in compensation. Thus, *bb*$^{+}$/0 males show a rate of rRNA synthesis which is the same as that found in *Xbb*$^{+}$/*Ybb*$^{+}$ males (Table VIII). One has to note, however, that Krider and Plaut (1972) have shown that polytene cells of $Xbb^+/0$ males show a higher rate of nucleolar RNA synthesis than those of $Xbb^+/In(1)sc^{4,8}$ and Xbb^+/Xbb^+ females.

(d) *Xbb*/*Ybb* males can magnify rDNA, while Xbb^+/Ybb^+ combinations do not compensate for rDNA (Atwood, 1969a; Ritossa, 1972). All of this adds to the fact that rDNA accumulated in compensation is not inheritable, while that accumulated in magnification is inheritable.

VII. Possible significance of magnification

Genes for ribosomal RNA clearly evolve (Amaldi, 1969). Recently, Brown *et al.* (1972) have shown that although the sequences which will generate mature rRNAs are very similar (if not identical) in different *Xenopus* species, the sequences which make up the spacer and the transcribed spacer regions are very different. Within a species all spacer regions are identical. Kinetic identity of rDNA was also observed within one species of *Xenopus* (Birnstiel *et al.*, 1969). As I have mentioned, no sign of competition was observed between rRNAs of bobbed and wild type individuals. Furthermore, every *bb* locus studied could, by magnification or in other ways, give rise to a bb^+ locus. All of this favours the idea that in *Drosophila* all the genes for rRNA are identical or almost so.

Magnification hence offers a model to explain rapid "horizontal" evolution of genes for rRNA (Brown *et al.*, 1972; Ritossa, 1972). Thus, unequal crossing over or sister strand, intrachromosomal, crossing over might lead to the formation of partial deletions of the block or to blocks of increased redundancy. The latter might be selected against (Ritossa and Scala, 1969) while partially deleted blocks, when in an appropriate genotype, can suddenly increase their multiplicity by magnification. Since the increase of multiplicity occurs by the formation of new copies from the copies left in the block, there will be an increase of homogeneity in the reformed block. This homogeniety will be greater the lower the starting number of genes. I have reviewed the data showing that bb^l loci can also magnify and reach finally the bb^+ condition. In one such case, for example, there were originally about 15 genes in the bb^l block and about 200 such genes after magnification. Homogeneity of the block at the end was therefore at least 10-fold higher with respect to a "normal" block similarly large. The mechanism can also account for a fast parallel evolution of rRNA genes in the X and the Y chromosomes (see Fig. 15), and for a rapid attainment of proper redundancy values.

VIII. Genesis of the bobbed phenotype

The hypothesis is that bobbed flies synthesize a subnormal amount of ribosomes, so that the cell's translating machinery is impaired and proteins are not synthesized in sufficient amounts to give a normal phenotype (Ritossa *et al.*, 1966). The traits expected to be most affected by the mutation are those characterized by an intense rate of protein synthesis.

When the rate of rRNA synthesis in ovaries, which are the most active organ of adult females, was measured *in vivo* and *in vitro* it was found that the rate of synthesis of rRNA precursor was lower in bobbed than in wild type females (Mohan and Ritossa, 1970). The RNA:DNA ratio of eggs layed by normal or bobbed females was almost the same. Perhaps there are triggering mechanisms which do not allow the laying of an egg until it has a normal content of ribosomes.

Weinman (1972) has studied ribosomal and 5s RNA synthesis in adult females. He has shown that bobbed mutants synthesize less rRNA than wild type flies. Furthermore, he could observe that there is a direct correlation between the intensity of the *bb* phenotype, measured as the length of the bristles, and the rate of rRNA synthesis.

RNA/DNA ratios of bobbed flies are similar to those of wild flies (Mohan and Ritossa, 1970). Thus, the idea started taking root that the lower rate of rRNA synthesis is compensated by the longer developmental time of bobbed flies. Taken to its extreme this idea would lead to the prediction that no trait should be effected by the mutation. Indeed, every tissue could reach its optimum ribosomal content in a time inversely proportional to the number of genes for rRNA present in the genome. The only limit to this would be the "half-life" of the ribosome. However, although certain tissues are never found to be affected by the mutation, others clearly show it. A plausible compromise is to consider that the attainment of a threshold number of ribosomes conditions developmental time in some tissues only. Thus, these tissues will have to have a normal, or almost normal, ribosomal content to proceed in development, while others will proceed even if their content is subnormal. Mohan and Ritossa (1970) explained the normal RNA/DNA ratios of bobbed females with the assumption that the relative proportion of cells with a normal ribosome content was rather high with respect to those with a subnormal content.

In contrast to the above data, and in accord with the original hypothesis, Howell (1972) has found that larvae, pupae and adult *Drosophila* carrying a bobbed mutation had a lower RNA/DNA ratio than control flies. Furthermore the RNA yield from the same number of male internal genitalia was constantly lower from bobbed than from wild type individuals (Ritossa *et al.*, 1971). It is not to be excluded that a major role in the outcome of such experiments is the "strength" of the bobbed mutation used in any given experiment. Cell interactions have also to be considered in the genesis of the bobbed phenotype. For example Dapples and King

(1970) sharply focused the idea that the role of nurse cells in the ovary can be viewed as an equivalent to the rDNA amplification observed in other insects (Gall *et al.*, 1969; Lima de Faria *et al.*, 1969) and amphibia (Brown and Dawid, 1968; Evans and Birnstiel, 1968; Gall, 1968).

References

AMALDI, F. (1969). Non-random variability in evolution of base composition of ribosomal RNA. *Nature, Lond.* **221,** 95–96.

ASHBURNER, M. (1970). Function and structure of polytene chromosomes during insect development. *Adv. Insect. Physiol.* **7,** 1–95.

ATWOOD, K. C. (1969). Some aspects of the bobbed problem in *Drosophila. Genetics* **61,** Suppl. 1, 319–328.

BAKER, W. K. (1971). Evidence for position-effect suppression of the ribosomal RNA cistrons in *Drosophila melanogaster. Proc. Nat. Acad. Sci. U.S.A.* **68,** 2472–2476.

BART, C. (1958). A retest of the frequency of spontaneous loss of the yellow$^+$ region of the scute-8 chromosome. *Dros. Inf. Serv.* **32,** 111–112.

BEERMANN, W. (1960). Der Nukleolus als lebenswichtiger bestanteil des zellkernes. *Chromosoma* **11,** 263–296.

BIRNSTIEL, M. L., GRUNSTEIN, M., SPEIRS, J. and HENNIG, W. (1969). Family of ribosomal genes in *Xenopus laevis. Nature, Lond.* **223,** 1265–1267.

BIRNSTIEL, M. L., CHIPCASE, M. and SPEIRS, J. (1971). The ribosomal RNA cistrons. *Prog. Nucl. Acid Res. Mol. Biol.* **11,** 351–389.

BONCINELLI, E., MALVA, C., GRAZIANI, F., POLITO, L. and RITOSSA, F. (1972). rDNA magnification at the bobbed locus of the Y chromosome in *Drosophila melanogaster. Cell Differentiation* **1,** 133–142.

BRIDGES, C. B. and BREHME, K. S. (1944). The mutants of *Drosophila melanogaster.* Carnegie Inst. Washington Publ. 552.

BRITTEN, R. J. and KOHNE, D. E. (1969). Implication of repeated nucleotide sequence. *In*: "Handbook of Molecular Cytology." (Lima-de-Faria, ed.), North-Holland Pub. Co. Amsterdam, pp. 159.

BROWN, D. D. and DAWID, I. B. (1968). Specific gene amplification in oocytes. *Science, N.Y.* **160,** 272–280.

BROWN, D. D. and GURDON, J. B. (1964). Absence of ribosomal RNA synthesis in the anucleolate mutant of *Xenopus laevis. Proc. Nat. Acad. Sci. U.S.A.* **51,** 139–146.

BROWN, D. D., WENSINK, P. C. and JORDAN, E. (1972). A comparison of the ribosomal DNA's of *Xenopus laevis* and *Xenopus mulleri*: the evolution of tandem genes. *J. Molec. Biol.* **63,** 57–74.

CAPUTI, I. (1972). Biol. Doctor thesis, University of Bari.

COOPER, K. W. (1958). A probable heterochromatic deficiency in *In(1)sc*^{L8}, the approximate location of bobbed, and the size of block A. *Dros. Inf. Serv.* **32,** 118–119.

COOPER, K. W. (1959). Cytogenetic analysis of major heterochromatic elements (especially Xh and Y) in *Drosophila melanogaster* and the theory of "heterochromatin". *Chromosoma* **10,** 535–588.

DAPPLES, C. C. and KING, R. C. (1970). The development of the nucleolus of the ovarian nurse cell of *Drosophila melanogaster. Z. Zellforsh.* **103,** 34–47.

DOBZHANSKY, T. (1932). Cytological map of the X-chromosome of *Drosophila melanogaster*. *Biol. Zbl.* **52,** 493–509.

EDSTROM, J. E., GRAMPP, W. and SCHOR, N. (1961). The intracellular distribution and heterogeneity of ribonucleic acid in starfish oocytes. *J. Biophys. Biochem. Cytol.* **11,** 549–557.

EVANS, D. and BIRNSTIEL, M. (1968). Localization of amplified ribosomal DNA in the oocyte of *Xenopus laevis*. *Biochim. Biophys. Acta* **166,** 274–276.

GALL, J. G. (1968). Differential synthesis of the genes for ribosomal RNA during amphibian oogenesis. *Proc. Nat. Acad. Sci. U.S.A.* **60,** 553–560.

GALL, J. G. (1969). The genes for ribosomal RNA during oogenesis. *Genetics* **61,** Suppl. 1, 121–132.

GALL, J. G., MACGREGOR, H. C. and KIDSTON, M. E. (1969). Gene amplification in the oocytes of Dytiscus water beetles. *Chromosoma* **26,** 169–187.

GALL, J. G., COHEN, E. H. and POLAN, M. L. (1971). Repetitive DNA sequences in Drosophila. *Chromosoma* **33,** 319–344.

GILLESPIE, D. and SPIEGELMAN, S. (1965). A quantitative assay for DNA-RNA hybrids with DNA immobolized on a membrane. *J. Molec. Biol.* **12,** 829–842.

GRAZIANI, F. (1975). RNA transcription products during the first spets of magnification in *Drosophila melanogaster*. *J. Molec. Biol.* in press.

GREENBERG, J. R. (1967). Sedimentation studies on *Drosophila virilis* salivary gland RNA. *J. Cell. Biol.* **35,** 49A.

HAMKALO, B. A., MILLER, JR., O. L. and BAKKEN, A. H. (1973). Ultrastructural aspects of genetic activity. In Molecular Cytogenetics, B. A. Hamkalo and J. Papaconstantinou Eds. Plenum Publ. Co.

HEITZ, E. (1934). Eine beziehung zwischen der genischen und strukturellen Langsdifferenzierung des X-chromosome von *Drosophila melanogaster*. *Z. indukt. Abstamm. Vererbungshehre* **67,** 216–217.

HENDERSON, A. and RITOSSA, F. (1970). On the inheritance of rDNA of magnified bobbed loci in *Drosophila melanogaster*. *Genetics* **66,** 463–473.

HENNIG, W. and MEER, B. (1971). Reduced polyteny of ribosomal RNA cistrons in giant chromosomes of *Drosophila hydei*. *Nature New Biol.* **233,** 70–71.

HINTON, T. (1942). A comparative study of certain heterochromatin regions in the mitotic and salivary gland chromosomes of *Drosophila melanogaster*. *Genetics* **27,** 119–127.

HOWELL, A. J. (1972). Levels of RNA and DNA in *Drosophila melanogaster*. at different stages of development: a comparison between one bobbed and two phenotypically non-bobbed stocks. *Biochem. Genet.* **6,** 217–230.

JUDD, B. H. (1961). Formation of duplication-deficiency products by asymmetrical exchange within a complex locus of *Drosophila melanogaster*. *Proc. Nat. Acad. Sci. U.S.A.* **47,** 545–550.

KAUFMANN, B. P. (1933). Interchange between X- and Y-chromosomes in attached X females of *Drosophila melanogaster*. *Proc. Nat. Acad. Sci. U.S.A.* **19,** 830–838.

KAUFMANN, B. P. (1934). Somatic mitoses in *Drosophila melanogaster*. *J. Morph.* **56,** 125–155.

KIEFER, B. I. (1968). Dosage regulation of ribosomal DNA in *Drosophila melanogaster*. *Proc. Nat. Acad. Sci. U.S.A.* **61,** 85–89.

KRIDER, H. M. and PLAUT, W. (1972). Studies on nucleolar RNA synthesis in *Drosophila melanogaster*. *J. Cell Science* **11,** 675–687.

KRIVSHENKO, J. (1959). The divisibility of the nucleolus-organizer and the structure of the nucleolus in *Drosophila busckii*. *Genetics* **44,** 520–521.

LAIRD, C. and MCCARTHY, B. (1968). Magnitude of interspecific nucleotide sequence variability in *Drosophila*. *Genetics* **60,** 303–322.

LIMA-DE-FARIA, A., BIRNSTIEL, M. and JAWORSKA, H. (1969). Amplification of ribosomal cistrons in the heterochromatin of *Acheta*. *Genetics* **61,** Suppl. 1, 145–159.

LINDSLEY, D. L. (1955). Spermatogonial exchange between the X and Y chromosomes of *Drosophila melanogaster*. *Genetics* **40,** 24–44.

LINDSLEY, D. L. (1958). Spermatogonial exchange involving the X but not the Y chromosome in *Drosophila melanogaster*. *Z. indukt. Abstamm. VererbLehre.* **89,** 103–122.

LINDSLEY, D. L. and GRELL, E. H. (1968). Genetic variations of *Drosophila melanogaster*. Carnegie Inst. of Washington, Publ. No. 627.

LINDSLEY, D. L., EDINGTON, C. W. and VON HALLE, E. S. (1960). Sex-linked recessive lethals in *Drosophila* whose expressions in suppressed by the Y chromosome. *Genetics* **45,** 1649–70.

LOCKER, D. and PRUD'HOMME, N. (1973). Etude de plusieur facteurs faisant varier la frequence de reversion au locus bobbed chez *Drosophila melanogaster*. *Molec. gen. Genet.* **124,** 11–19.

LOCKER, D. (1973). Doctor de 3e Cycle These, Université de Paris VI.

MALVA, C., GRAZIANI, F., POLITO, L., BONCINELLI, E. and RITOSSA, F. 1972). Check of gene number during the process of rDNA magnification. *Nature New Biol.* **239,** 135–136.

MARRAKECHI, M. and PRUD'HOMME, N. (1971). A study of bobbed mutants induced by ethyl-methane-sulfonate in *Drosophila melanogaster*. *Biochem. Biophys. Res. Commun.* **43,** 273–277.

MCCLINTOK, B. (1934). The relation of a particular chromosomal element to the development of the nucleoli in *Zea mays*. *Z. Zellfosch. Mikrosk. Anat.* **21,** 294–328.

MILLER, O. J. JR. and BEATTY, B. R. (1969). Extrachromosomal nucleolar genes in amphibian oocytes. *Genetics* **61,** Suppl. 1, 133–143.

MILLER, L. and BROWN, D. D. (1969). Variation in the activity of nucleolus organizers and their ribosomal gene content. *Chromosoma* (*Berl.*) **28,** 430–444.

MOHAN, J. and RITOSSA, F. M. (1970). Regulation of ribosomal RNA synthesis and its bearing on the bobbed phenotype in *Drosophila melanogaster*. *Devl. Biol.* **22,** 495–512.

MORGAN, T. H., BRIDGES, C. B. and STURTEVANT, A. H. (1925). "The Genetics of *Drosophila*." s-Gravenage, M. Nijhoff.

MORGAN, T. H., STURTEVANT, A. H. and BRIDGES, C. B. (1926). The constitution of the germ material in relation to heredity. *Carnegie Inst. Washington Year Book* **25,** 308–312.

MORGAN, T. H., STURTEVANT, A. H. and BRIDGES, C. B. (1927). The constitution of germ material in relation to heredity. *Carnegie Inst. Washington Year Book* **26,** 284–288.

MULLER, H. J. (1932). Further studies on the nature and causes of gene mutation. *Proc. 6th Int. Congr. Genet.* **1,** 213–255.

NEUHAUS, M. J. (1936). Crossing over between the X and the Y chromosomes in *Drosophila melanogaster*. *Z. indukt. Abstamm. VererbLehre.* **71,** 265–275.

PALUMBO, G., CAIZZI, R. and RITOSSA, F. (1973). Relative orientation with respect to the centromere of Ribosomal RNA genes of the X and Y chromosomes of *Drosophila melanogaster Proc. Nat. Acad. Sci. U.S.A.* **70,** 1883–1885.

PARDUE, M. L., GERBI, S. A., ECKARDT, R. A. and GALL, J. G. (1970). Cytological localization of DNA complementary to ribosomal RNA in polytene chromosomes of *Diptera. Chromosoma* (*Berl.*) **29,** 268–290.

PERRY, R. P. (1962). The cellular sites of synthesis of ribosomal and 4S RNA. *Proc. Nat. Acad. Sci. U.S.A.* **48,** 2179–2186.

PETERSON, H. M. and LAUGHNAN, J. R. (1963). Intrachromosomal exchanges at the Bar locus in *Drosophila. Proc. Nat. Acad. Sci. U.S.A.* **50,** 126–133.

QUAGLIAROTTI, G. and RITOSSA, F. M. (1968). On the arrangement of genes for 28S and 18S ribosomal RNA's in *Drosophila melanogaster. J. Molec. Biol.* **36,** 57–69.

RAE, P. (1970). Chromosomal distribution of rapidly reannealing DNA in *Drosophila melanogaster. Proc. Nat. Acad. Sci. U.S.A.* **67,** 1018–1025.

RASCH, E. M., BARR, H. J. and RASCH, R. W. (1971). The DNA content of sperm of *Drosophila melanogaster. Chromosoma* **33,** 1–18.

RITOSSA, F. (1968a). Non-operative DNA complementary to ribosomal RNA. *Proc. Nat. Acad. Sci. U.S.A.* **59,** 1124–1131.

RITOSSA, F. (1968b). Unstable redundancy of genes for ribosomal RNA. *Proc. Nat. Acad. Sci. U.S.A.* **60,** 509–516.

RITOSSA, F. (1972). A procedure for magnification of lethal deletions of genes for ribosomal RNA. *Nature New Biol.* **240,** 109–111.

RITOSSA, F. (1973). Crossing-over between X and Y chromosomes during rDNA magnification in *Drosophila melanogaster. Proc. Nat. Acad. Sci. U.S.A.* **70,** 1950–1954.

RITOSSA, F. M. and ATWOOD, K. C. (1966). Unequal proportions of DNA complementary to ribosomal RNA in males and females of *Drosophila simulans. Proc. Nat. Acad. Sci. U.S.A.* **56,** 496–500.

RITOSSA, F. and SCALA, G. (1969). Equilibrium variations in redundancy of rDNA in *Drosophila melanogaster. Genetics* **61,** Suppl. 1, 305–317.

RITOSSA, F. M. and SPIEGELMAN, S. (1965). Localization of DNA complementary to ribosomal RNA in the nucleolus organizer region of *Drosophila melanogaster. Proc. Nat. Acad. Sci. U.S.A.* **53,** 737–745.

RITOSSA, F. M., ATWOOD, K. C., LINDSLEY, D. L. and SPIEGELMAN, S. (1966). On the chromosomal distribution of DNA complementary to ribosomal and soluble RNA. Nat. Cancer Monograph No. 23: 449–472.

RITOSSA, F. M., ATWOOD, K. C. and SPIEGELMAN, S. (1966). A molecular explanation of the bobbed mutants of *Drosophila* as partial deficiencies of "ribosomal" DNA. *Genetics* **54,** 819–834.

RITOSSA, F., MALVA, C., BONCINELLI, E., GRAZIANI, F. and POLITO, L. (1971). On the first steps of rDNA magnification. *Proc. Nat. Acad. Sci. U.S.A.* **68,** 1580–8584.

RITOSSA, F., SCALENGHE, F., DI TURI, N. and CONTINI, A. M. (1974). On the cell stage of X–Y recombination during rDNA magnification in *Drosophila melanogaster. Cold Spring Harb. Sym. Quant. Biol.* **38,** 483–490.

RUDKIN, G. F. (1965). The relative mutabilities of DNA in regions of the X chromosome of *Drosophila melanogaster. Genetics* **53,** 665–681.

RUDKIN, G. T. (1969). Non-replicating DNA in Drosophila. *Genetics* **61,** Suppl. 1, 227–238.

SANDLER, L. (1970). The regulation of sex chromosome heterochromatic activity by an autosomal gene in *Drosophila melanogaster*. *Genetics* **64**, 481–493.

SCHALET, A. (1969). Exchanges at the bobbed locus of *Drosophila melanogaster*. *Genetics* **63**, 133–153.

SCHULTZ, J. and TRAVAGLINI, E. (1965). Evidence for homeostatic control of ribosomal content in *Drosophila melanogaster* eggs. *Genetics* **52**, 473.

SPEAR, B. B. and GALL, J. G. (1973). Independent control of ribosomal gene replication in polytene chromosomes of *Drosophila melanogaster*. *Proc. Nat. Acad. Sci.* **70**, 1359–1363.

SPENCER, W. P. (1944). Iso-alleles at the bobbed locus in *Drosophila hydei* populations. *Genetics* **29**, 520–536.

STERN, C. (1927). Ein genetischer und zytologischer Beweis fur Vererbung in Y-chromosome von *Drosophila melanogaster*. *Z. Indukt. Abstamm. Vererb.* **44**, 187–231.

STERN, C. (1929). Uber die additive Wirckung multiplier allele. *Biol. Zbl.* **49**, 261–290.

STERN, C. and OGURA, S. (1931). Neue untersuchungen uber aberrationen des Y-chromosoms von *Drosophila melanogaster*. *Z. Indukt. Abstamm. VererbLehre* **58**, 81–121.

STURTEVANT, A. H. (1925). The effects of unequal crossing over at the Bar locus in *Drosophila*. *Genetics* **10**, 117–147.

STURTEVANT, A. H. (1929). The Genetics of *Drosophila simulans*. Carnegie Inst. Wash. Publ. 399, 5–62.

SWIFT, H. (1962). Nucleic acids and cell morphology in dipteran salivary glands. *In*: "The Molecular Control of Cellular Activity". (Ed. J. M. Allen), McGraw-Hill Book Co., New York, pp. 73–125.

TARANTINO, E. (1972). RNA synthesis and rDNA content during magnification in *Drosophila melanogaster*. *Atti Ass. Genet. Ital.* **17**, 97.

TARTOF, K. D. (1971). Increasing the multiplicity of ribosomal RNA genes in *Drosophila melanogaster*. *Science, N.Y.* **1971**, 294–297.

TARTOF, K. D. (1973). Regulation of ribosomal RNA gene multiplicity in *Drosophila melanogaster*. *Genetics* **73**, 57–71.

TARTOF, K. D. and PERRY, R. P. (1970). The 5S RNA genes in *Drosophila melanogaster*. *J. Molec. Biol.* **51**, 171–183.

VERMEULEN, C. W. and ATWOOD, K. C. (1965). The proportion of DNA complementary to ribosomal RNA in *Drosophila melanogaster*. *Biochem. Biophys. Res. Commun.* **19**, 221–226.

WAGNER, R. P. and MITCHELL, H. K. (1964). "Genetics and Metabolism." John Wiley and Sons Inc., New York.

WEINMAN, R. (1972). Regulation of ribosomal RNA and 5S RNA synthesis in *Drosophila melanogaster*: I Bobbed mutants. *Genetics* **72**, 267–276.

Notes in Proof

(1) While this paper was in proof, a paper appeared (Spear, 1974) claiming that the Ybb^- chromosome carries no rDNA at all. DNAs from diploid tissues (brains and imaginal discs) obtained from X/Ybb^- and X/0 males gave saturation levels with rRNA which were $0{\cdot}391 \pm 0{\cdot}014$ and $0{\cdot}371 \pm$

0·017% respectively. If corrections are made for the different DNA contents of the cells used (Henderson and Ritossa, 1970), which Spear apparently did not do, one can conclude that the rDNA content of the *Ybb*⁻ chromosome is about 0·057±0·015% in diploid cells. Furthermore it has been shown that recombination can occur between the X and the *Ybb*⁻ chromosome. At least some of this recombination is at the rDNA level (Ritossa, 1973).

(2) Tartof (1974) has revived the hypothesis that unequal sister strand crossing over explains magnification. The data to support it are: presence of bristle mosaic in magnifying males; inability of *bb* loci to magnify if located on ring chromosomes and inability of newly magnified bb^m loci to revert to the *bb* condition. We looked for mosaic bristles and, indeed, found them in large numbers. In agreement with Tartof (1973), however, their frequency was similar in magnifying bobbed males and non-magnifying bobbed females. For this reason and for those described by Tartof (1974), the relevance of this observation to an understanding of the mechanisms of magnification appears doubtful. Also, it appears that the stability test was not properly applied by Tartof (1974). However, without special assumptions the inability of *bb* loci to magnify when located on ring chromosomes cannot be explained by our working model.

References

HENDERSON, A. and RITOSSA, F. (1970). On the inheritance of rDNA of magnified bobbed loci in *Drosophila melanogaster*. *Genetics* **66,** 463–473.

RITOSSA, F. (1973). Crossing-over between X and Y chromosomes during rDNA magnification in *Drosophila melanogaster*. *Proc. Nat. Acad. Sci. U.S.A.* **70,** 1950–1954.

SPEAR, B. B. (1974). The genes for ribosomal RNA in diploid and polytene chromosomes of *Drosophila melanogaster*. *Chromosoma* (*Berl.*) **48,** 159–179.

TARTOF, K. D. (1973). Unequal mitotic sister chromatid exchange and disproportionate replication as mechanisms regulating ribosomal RNA gene redundancy. *Cold Spring Harb. Symp. Quant. Biol.* **38,** 491–500.

TARTOF, K. D. (1974). Unequal mitotic sister chromatid exchange as the mechanism of ribosomal RNA gene magnification. *Proc. Nat. Acad. Sci. U.S.A.* **71,** 1272–1276.

21. The Proximal Region of the X Chromosome*

ABRAHAM SCHALET AND GEORGE LEFEVRE, JR.

Department of Radiation Genetics and Chemical Mutagenesis
State University of Leiden
Leiden, The Netherlands

and

Department of Biology
California State University, Northridge,
California, U.S.A.

* Investigations of the authors were carried out in part within the framework of the Association between Euratom and the University of Leiden, Contracts 052–64–I BIAN and 102–72–a–I BIAN, and with support from the J. A. Cohen Institute for Radiopathology and Radiation Protection; and a research grant from the U.S. Public Health Service, GM 13631.

I. Introduction

In *The Genetics of Drosophila* (1925), Morgan, Bridges and Sturtevant took notice of E. G. Anderson's freshly obtained, but then unpublished, experimental observations on a new stock of *D. melanogaster* females that carried attached-X chromosomes heterozygous for 5 mutant markers. According to their account, "A curious relation was discovered with respect to the frequency with which the various heterozygous mutants emerge as homozygotes. . . . that is, the further to the right the locus, the greater is the difficulty in becoming homozygous . . ." From this relation Anderson concluded that the point of attachment of the two X's is to the right, beyond forked, and that the free ends are the left ends. In other words, the spindle-fiber attachment to the X chromosome is at the extreme right end (presumably beyond the locus of bobbed) and not (as previously supposed to be the case) at the left end where yellow is located.

Soon thereafter, a number of additional singular relations were manifested at the right end of the X chromosome, so that matters became "curiouser and curiouser". To this day the list of unusual relations seems not to have been exhausted, nor have the earlier discovered remarkable associations been completely clarified. To begin with, there was the interesting observation that, in contrast to some 150 other mutants assigned by Morgan, Bridges and Sturtevant to the X chromosome, only the bobbed (*bb*) locus proved to have a normal allele on the Y chromosome (Stern, 1927). In addition, Morgan, Bridges and Sturtevant noted that the relative genetic lengths of the X, second, third and fourth chromosomes were "roughly the same as the lengths of the actual chromosomes as observed in the metaphase plate", and concluded that "the maps of the mutant genes cover approximately the entire length of the chromosomes". Then Muller and Painter (1932) and Dobzhansky (1932) showed that the right-hand half of the actual mitotic X chromosome did not carry any known gene except *bb*, and that in this half of the chromosome there was little or no crossing over. At this point, a significant level of comprehension was restored when Heitz (1934a) and Kaufmann (1934) noted that the region which Muller and Painter had characterized as "relatively inert genetically" appeared to correspond to that portion of the X chromosome which exhibited the cytological properties that Heitz had earlier described as heterochromatic. At the same time it was established that the nucleolus was associated with both the X and Y chromosomes. Specifically, the secondary constriction in the X concerned with nucleolar development was in the proximal heterochromatic region.

Meanwhile, Muller (1930) had reported numerous cases of variegated position-effect mutants. Although Muller recognized that these mutants were connected with chromosomal rearrangements, it was not until Schultz (1936) subjected such cases to the newly introduced method of polytene chromosome analysis that it became clear that the chromosome rearrangements involved at least one breakpoint in what was believed to be the salivary gland chromosome equivalent of a mitotic heterochromatic region. For the X chromosome, Painter's (1934) initial cytogenetic correlations had already indicated that, in the polytene nuclei, a region homologous to the mitotic heterochromatic X was not clearly evident. However, Muller and Prokofyeva's (1935) analysis indicated that at least the region designated as section 20 on Bridges' (1935) detailed map of the polytene X chromosome was heterochromatic. To account for the difference in the relative lengths of the heterochromatic region in the mitotic chromosome as compared with the salivary gland chromosome, Muller and Gershenson (1935) suggested that the heterochromatic region seen in the mitotic X chromosome consisted "essentially of non-genic material derived from a very few specific active genes", and that "the salivary gland chromosomes, therefore, give a truer picture of the chromonema".

From the bare account presented thus far, the more elaborate history (see Cooper, 1959, for references), and subsequent investigations, it is obvious that most of the attention showered upon the proximal X region was drawn off into studies of the structure, function, and phenomena associated with the elements of the proximal heterochromatic region of the X chromosome. Furthermore, there was no particular reason to suppose that the proximal euchromatic region differed in any interesting way from the remainder of the euchromatic X. As a consequence, although the proximal euchromatic portion of the X chromosome to the right of *car* was known to be well populated with genes from early studies on the distribution of X-ray-induced sex-linked lethals (see data of Harris and also Oliver in Rudkin, 1965), only in recent years have attempts been initiated to chart the region accurately (Schalet and Finnerty, 1968b). Yet, some of the basic uncertainties that bore directly upon the attributes of the heterochromatic region arose precisely because of the difficulty in delineating the proximal euchromatic and heterochromatic regions. Specifically: (1) What point on Bridges' (1938) map of the salivary X chromosome corresponds to the euchromatic-heterochromatic (E–H) junction as seen in the mitotic X chromosome? (2) Do ordinary sex-linked genes (those with no alleles on the Y chromosome) extend into the proximal heterochromatic region of the X chromosome? (3) With which salivary gland chromosome band is the nucleolus associated? (4) Are bands in the most proximal region of the salivary gland X chromosome, section 20, equivalent in their genetic significance to those found in more distal regions, such as section 19, particularly with regard to a one-to-one relationship of genes to bands? (5) Is crossing over completely absent in the proximal heterochromatic region?

Cooper's (1959) analysis of the heterochromatic elements in the X and Y chromosomes has been valuable, not only because of the synthesis of a vast amount of experimental work, but also because he stressed uncertainties and gaps. Although subsequent information has negated some of Cooper's arguments and conclusions, his insistence that the versatile functions of heterochromatic regions should be considered as based upon diverse genetic elements located in heterochromatic regions, not as aspects of heterochromatin, remains valid. However, in common with most *Drosophila* geneticists, Cooper accepted the view that the proximal sections of the salivary gland chromosomes were polytene representations of at least parts of the mitotic proximal heterochromatic regions. Thus, he was able to argue, on the basis of the comparable ratio of loci to bands in centric *vs.* not-centric regions, that heterochromatic regions were not genetically inert nor notably lacking in genes. The argument that the centric basal portion of the X chromosome (including at least the 17 most proximal bands of Bridges' 1938 map) is populated by genes of an ordinary sort has been borne out by subsequent work (Schalet and Lefevre, 1973), but the cytogenetic correlations have also provided evidence that most, if not all, of the base region of the polytene X chromosome does not correspond to the heterochromatic portion of the mitotic X. (In accord with this point of view, we have adopted Cooper's terms Xh = heterochromatic X and Xe = euchromatic X to signify the parts of the X chromosome which are so distinguished on the basis of their mitotic appearance.) These results were foreshadowed by the evidence presented in earlier experiments which indicated that the reason for the different proportions of euchromatic and heterochromatic regions in mitotic *vs.* salivary gland chromosomes was the failure of the centric heterochromatic regions to polytenize in the salivary gland nuclei (Rudkin, 1969; Gall *et al.*, 1971). The absence of a replicated Xh in the salivary gland chromosome explains many old "errors" of interpretation of breakpoints in the proximal sections of the X-chromosome.

As fascinating as the cytogenetic properties of the proximal Xh may be, this chapter will be mainly concerned with clarifying some of the basic distinctions between the proximal Xe and Xh, and to that end the fundamental cytogenetic structure of the proximal Xe region will be emphasized.

II. Genetic Mapping of the Proximal Xe Region

A. Methods

Genetic mapping of the proximal X region has been facilitated by the production of altered Y chromosomes (*Ymal*$^+$ and *y*$^+$*Ymal*$^+$) bearing sections of the X that include the interval from *ot*$^+$ to *su(f)*$^+$ (Brosseau *et al.*, 1961; Schalet, 1963). The cytological extent of the proximal X-chromosome region included in these altered Y chromosomes has been established directly for *y*$^+$*Ymal*$^+$ (and inferred from the genetic data for *Ymal*$^+$) as consisting of the entirety of salivary gland chromosome sections 19 and 20 (Schalet and Lefevre, 1973). Some other useful altered Y chromosomes carry subsegments of the *ot*$^+$–*su(f)*$^+$ interval. In addition to the B^SY and B^SYy^+ chromosomes (Brosseau *et al.*, 1961), a series of altered Y chromosomes (*y*$^+$*Ymal*^{102}, *y*$^+$*Ymal*^{108}, *y*$^+$*Ymal*^{113}, *y*$^+$*Ymal*^{118}, *y*$^+$*Ymal*^{126}) bearing subsegments of different sizes were obtained by irradiating *y*$^+$*Ymal*$^+$ (Chovnick *et al.*, 1969; Schalet and Finnerty, 1968a). Another derivative, *y*$^+$*Ymal*^{106}, recovered from the irradiation of *y*$^+$*Ymal*$^+$, carries a mutant allele of *mal*, covers all the proximal X lethals covered by *y*$^+$*Ymal*$^+$, and has been frequently used in place of *y*$^+$*Ymal*$^+$.

Some difficulties in mapping can be largely avoided by instituting relatively simple procedures when the mutations to be used for subsequent analysis are initially isolated and tested to determine whether they are, in fact, located in the proximal region. (1) Care should be taken to discriminate between complete lethals and semilethals ("escapers" or "leaky" mutants). (2) Care should be taken to minimize the possibility that a culture, isolated because it appears to contain a lethal chromosome, does not include females that are germinally heterogeneous with respect to possible lesions induced in a single chromosome of the treated parent. (3) Mutations in the proximal regions should be covered or balanced by altered Y chromosomes that carry a dominant marker in order to recognize the presence of a covering Y chromosome in stock females or female progeny in complementation tests.

1. *Semilethal mutations*

In a conventional lethal test, a chromosome initially isolated as carrying an ostensible lethal mutation may in fact have a semilethal in the proximal region, or the apparent lethality may be the product of two semilethals only one of which is in the proximal region. The presence of two mutations is not unlikely when a potent mutagen such as ethyl methanesulphonate is used. Whether or not the mutant-bearing X chromosome is maintained in a stock with a covering Y chromosome, the true nature of the lethal effect may go undetected under conditions of mass culture. However, in an allelism test, an unrecognized semilethal mutation may yield a relatively small number of females carrying the two chromosomes being tested against one another and lead to the incorrect conclusion that the mutations are in different functional units. Thus far in our experience with semilethal mutations that were initially classified as lethals, all have shown visible phenotypes when survivors are examined (Schalet, 1972b; Schalet and Lefevre, 1973); however, according to other studies (Hochman, 1971) such semilethals may be ostensibly normal. Apparent lethals that permit development to proceed at normal rates and kill just prior to eclosion are especially suspect and should be checked under controlled conditions of crowding to insure that they are not semilethals. There are other semilethals in which development time may be so retarded that mutant individuals eclose late in the hatch or even fail to eclose under overcrowded conditions. This type of mutation may be scored initially as a lethal but in subsequent complementation tests produce offspring whose significance is misinterpreted.

2. *Lethal mosaics*

We have encountered several cases in which tests of individual females from a stock containing a proximal lethal showed that some females carried an additional uncovered distal lethal, but others did not. Although the distal lethal may have arisen spontaneously during maintenance of the stock, there is reason to believe that some such cases originated as mosaic lethals after ethyl methanesulphonate treatment and persisted in the stock. The high frequency with which complete and mosaic lethals arise following chemical treatments (Carlson and Oster, 1962; Alderson, 1965; Epler, 1966) indicates that where a culture from a conventional recessive sex-linked lethal test lacks males carrying the chemically treated chromosome, then all F_2 females bearing the treated chromosome may not be uniform with respect to the presence of the genetic lesions responsible for the absence of males. As Alderson (1965) points out, "The misclassification of an F_2 culture as a complete lethal is statistically possible, though the culture may be, in fact, either F_1 lethally mosaic, semilethal, or even completely non-lethal." Furthermore, Epler (1966) presented evidence that after ethyl methanesulphonate treatments an F_2 culture classified as a complete lethal may be, in fact, a double mosaic gonadal lethal. For these reasons, when a suspected lethal-bearing chromosome is saved for subsequent genetic analysis, it is advisable to continue the line by using only one F_2 female per culture as the parent of the next generation and to cross such females immediately to males carrying a covering Y chromosome. The simple expedient of crossing single F_2 females to males carrying a Y chromosome which does not cover a proximal mutation and maintaining a confirmed lethal stock by selecting the appropriate offspring from a single F_2 culture will eliminate practically all chances of heterogeneity for sex-linked induced mutations among the females carrying a derivative of the treated chromosome. This procedure will not necessarily detect all induced semilethals, nor will it permit the detection of more than one mutation on the treated chromosome, but such discriminations can be made in subsequent tests.

3. *Covering Y chromosomes*

The dominant B^S marker in B^SY or B^SYy^+ and the dominant *Hw* effect associated with the y^+ region of B^SYy^+ and y^+Ymal^+ or its derivatives (see above) permit the detection of a Y chromosome in potential parental and pertinent progeny females of a complementation test cross. As a consequence, the use of dominantly marked covering Y chromosomes rather than $Ymal^+$ permits the recognition of spurious cases of complementation between allelic mutants. In our experience, such cases are not infrequent. In tests of proximal X mutants spurious complementation presents a special hazard because Xe deficiencies extending into Xh, especially those that extend to the right to include at least part, if not all, of the *bb* locus, often produce high frequencies of primary non-disjunction in males when such males are fertile, e.g. *Df(1)X–1*, *Df(1)A209*. The same difficulty is encountered when $Df(1)sc^{4L}sc^{8R}$ males or males carrying certain *bb* lethal deficiencies (Lindsley *et al.*, 1960) are used to test for the presence of the *bb* locus in lethal-bearing chromosomes.

Another problem not specifically related to structural changes in Xh arises from the observation that high primary nondisjunction in females has been reported for reciprocal X;2 and X;3 translocations (Lindsley *et al.*, 1960; Chandley, 1965). When viable, such translocations are usually male sterile. Consequently, if a proximal X lethal happens to be associated with a reciprocal translocation and is maintained in a stock with a covering Y chromosome, then such a stock would be expected to contain, in addition to lethal/balancer females, numerous covering Y/lethal/balancer females. In the absence of a dominant marker for the covering Y chromosome, as in the $Ymal^+$ chromosome, the covering Y/lethal/balancer females might be chosen for a complementation test cross and thereby yield a result which could be misinterpreted. If, in the above example, the covering Y chromosome is marked only with the dominant *Hw* effect, it is still possible to distinguish females with a covering Y chromosome, despite the fact that balancer chromosomes of the $sc^{S1L}sc^{8R}$ type also express a dominant *Hw* effect associated with the sc^{S1L} end of the chromosome. Such females tend to show extra hairs and extra vein spurs in the wings, which have been described for flies carrying two doses of the y^+ region (Lindsley and Grell, 1968; Williamson, 1968).

Finally, in crosses involving two different lethal stocks, even when there is no special reason to expect a high frequency of paternal or maternal nondisjunction, there are instances where a parental female will carry a covering Y chromosome because of nondisjunction in the stock from which she came, or from nondisjunction in the parental male of the cross. In these cases, occasional female offspring can carry both lethal chromosomes, even though the lethals are allelic. By using a dominantly marked Y chromosome, such cases can be recognized. In any event, the occurrence of nondisjunction, whether frequent or relatively rare, cannot be discounted in complementation tests, and may have contributed to some of the differences which we have noted (Schalet, 1972b) between our mapping results with y^+ *Ymal*$^+$ and those reported for experiments which utilized the unmarked *Ymal*$^+$ chromosome. This is suggested from the fact that in the latter work, "Two lethals were considered alleles only when they did not produce a single normal female progeny" (Lifschytz and Falk, 1968, 1969).

B. Results

Figure 1 presents our current view of the genetic map of the proximal Xe region covered by the y^+ *Ymal*$^+$ and *Ymal*$^+$ chromosomes. Near the top of the figure the lethal and semilethal mutants, which thus far appear to involve only single functional units, have been divided into two groups. Above the line listing the visible phenotypes associated with mutations in the region (see Table I) are placed the lethal and semilethal mutants originally analysed by Lifschytz and Falk (1968, 1969) as mutations in the proximal region that were covered by the *Ymal*$^+$ chromosome. The lethal and semilethal mutants presented below the visible phenotypes have been analysed by Schalet and Finnerty (1968a), Schalet and Singer (1971), and Munoz and Schalet (unpublished observations). The arrangement of loci is based principally upon the results of *inter se* crosses of visible and lethal mutants; the latter class includes the lethal deficiencies also presented in the figure. The tests of allelism were supplemented by tests for coverage by various Y-borne and free-X duplications of subsegments of the proximal X region. Both of these methods were described by Alikhanian (1937).

With the exception of the examples listed in Table I, the allelic relationships shown in Fig. 1 are based on crosses carried out at 24–25°C. Although the cited cases were sufficient to indicate that the 24–25°C crosses alone can give an incorrect reading of the true allelic relationship between two apparently adjacent single functional unit lethals, or between a single functional unit lethal and a rearrangement (usually a deficiency) with a breakpoint abutting the single functional unit lethal, no systematic effort was made to repeat the tests at temperatures other than 24–25°C.

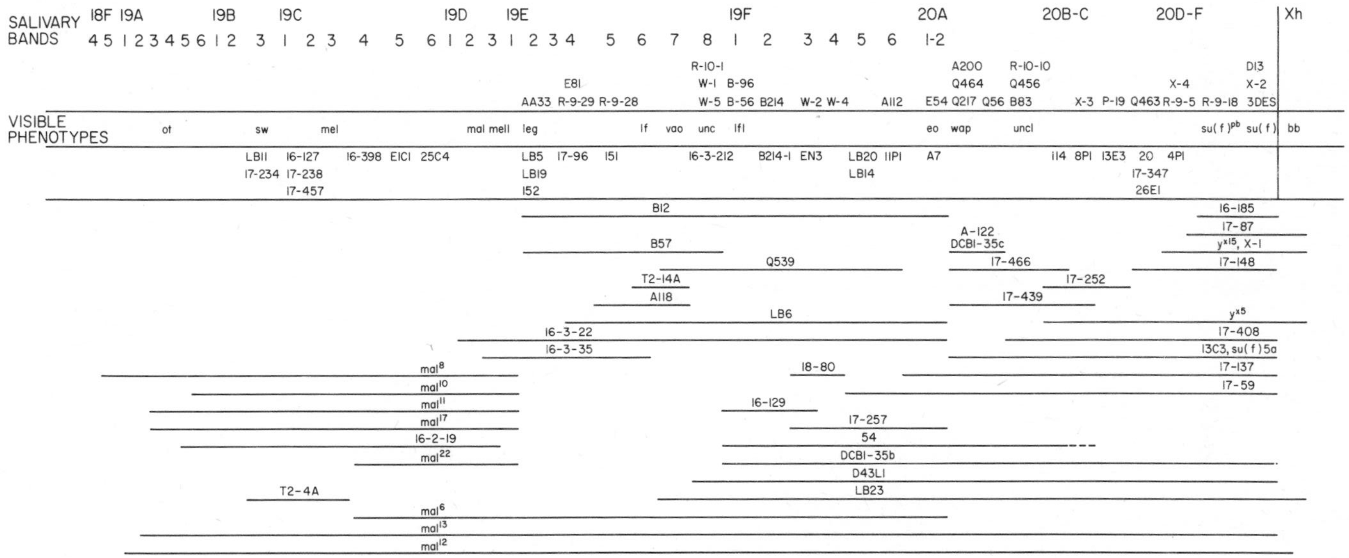

FIG. 1. Cytogenetic map of the proximal Xe region.

TABLE I. Visible phenotypes associated with mutations in polytene chromosome sections 19 and 20 of the X chromosome.

Gene locus	Symbol	Band position	Phenotypes and comments supplement descriptions in Lindsley and Grell (1968)
outheld	*ot*	19A3–5	
short wing	*sw*	19B3–19C3	*sw l(1)17–234* ♀♀ show *sw* at 29–30°C but apparently not at 24–25°C.
melanized	*mel*	19C2 or 19C3	Abdominal tergites have slight transverse wrinkles.
maroonlike	*mal*	19D	mal^{1}/mal^{bz} is mal^{+} at 24–25°C, *mal* at 29–30°C; *Df(1)16–2–19/Df(1)16–3–22* is *mal.*
melanizedlike	*mell*	19D3 or 19E1	Abdominal tergites have slight transverse wrinkles, perhaps thorax darker than normal, flies somewhat smaller with slightly broader wings, eyes of ♂♂ slightly rough, wings of ♀♀ variably wrinkled or curled. Shows in $y^{+}Ymal^{102}$*/Df(1)16–3–35* or *16–3–22* ♂♂ and *Df(1)16–3–35* or *16–3–22/Df(1)*mal^{8}, mal^{10}, mal^{11}, or mal^{17} ♀♀. All compounds are *mal.*
legless	*leg*	19E	*l(1)17–169/l(1)AA33* or *l(1)LB19* ♀♀ which survive usually have one or both hind legs absent.
little fly	*lf*	19E6 or 7	Eclosion generally delayed.
varied outspread	*vao*	19E7–8	Eye pigment unevenly distributed, best seen in pupal eyes and young imago, wings somewhat wrinkled, "material" often protruding from vagina. Shows in *Df(1)T2–14a* or *A118/Df(1)Q539* or *LB23* ♀♀, and *l(1)17–169/Df(1)T2–14a, A118,* or *LB6* ♀♀. *Df(1)B57/Df(1)Q539* ♀♀ are *vao unc* but at 17–18°C eyes appear normal.

			Name adopted from lost mutant, *In(1)vao*, described by Fahmy as variegated for an eye color and having a proximal breakpoint at 19E7–8.
uncoordinated	*unc*	19E8–19F1	Name adopted because phenotype is similar to lost mutant described by Fahmy which may have been allele of this or *uncl* locus.
littlefly-like	*lfl*	19F1–3 (inferred)	*lfl* = *l(1)B–56*, semilethal. ♂♂, ♀♀ and *lfl*/deficiency ♀♀ developmental time at 24–25°C is 13 days or more and eclose as small flies. lfl^2 = *l(1)B–96* survival extremely rare. lfl^2/lfl or deficiency ♀♀ show much better survival and have rough eyes, absent bristles, sparse thoracic hairs, abnormal wings.
extra organs	*eo*	20A1–2	In extreme cases a leg may be branched or completely duplicated, an antenna or arista duplicated or triplicated, eyes and wings malformed. Usually only eye effect present. Shows in $y^+ Ymal^{126}/l(1)A7$ ♂♂.
wings apart	*wap*	20A, to right of 20A2	*wap* = *l(1)A200*, *Q217*, *Q464*, semi-lethal. ♂♂, ♀♀ and *wap*/deficiency ♀♀ usually have wings set slightly apart, thorax darker than normal, may have one or more extra crossveins. Phenotype more extreme at 29–30°C.
uncoordinatedlike	*uncl*	20A, to right of 20A2	See *unc*. *uncl* = *l(1)B83*, *Q456*, *R–10–10*, semi-lethal. ♂♂, ♀♀ and *uncl*/deficiency ♀♀ which eclose have uncoordinated leg movements and die soon after eclosion.
sparse hairs	*sph*	20D or 20EF	Thoracic hairs sparse, variable eye roughening, wings extended and wing margins incised. Overlaps wild-type at 24–25°C, but shows in all flies at 29–30°C. Shows in *Df(1)17–87/l(1)4P1*, *R–9–5*, or *X–4*.

TABLE I.—(*continued*)

Gene locus	Symbol	Band position	Phenotypes and comments supplement descriptions in Lindsley and Grell (1968).
suppressor of forked-pale bristles	$su(f)^{pb}$	20D or 20EF	Bristles and hairs are pale yellow and thread-like, dark pigment on thorax usually concentrated at dorsal anterior region, wings curled or wrinkled. $su(f)^{pb} =$ *l(1)R–9–18* which is fully viable but weak at 17–18°C provided overcrowding is prevented. Phenotype is partially expressed in $su(f)^{pb}/su(f)^{D13}$ ♀♀ at 17–18°C and $su(f)^{pb}/su(f)^{X-2}$ ♀♀ at 24–25°C. $su(f)^{pb}$/deficiency ♀♀ which die just prior to eclosion at 17–18°C shows extreme $su(f)^{pb}$ phenotype. In $f\ su(f)^{pb}/f\ su(f)$ ♀♀, *f* is suppressed at all temperatures.
suppressor of forked	$su(f)$	20D or 20EF	$su(f)$ is Minute-like at 29–30°C. $su(f)$/deficiency is Minute-like at 24–25°C and lethal at 29–30°C. $su(f)/su(f)^{D13}$ or $su(f)^{X-2}$ is Minute-like at 24–25°C and lethal at 29–30°C. $su(f)/su(f)^{3DES}$ and $su(f)^{ts}/su(f)^{3DES}$ or $su(f)^{pb}$ are Minute-like at 29–30°C. $w^{a}su(f)$ has white eyes at 24–25°C or lower but apricot eyes at 29–30°C. $w^{a}\ su(f)/su(f)^{bp}$ has white eyes at 24–25°C; $w^{a}\ su(f)/su(f)^{3DES}$ has eyes between white and apricot at 24–25°C but nearly white at 17–18°C. $su(f)$ enhances lz^{37h} and suppresses lz^{1} at all temperatures. $su(f)^{pb}$ at 17–18°C and $su(f)^{ts}$ at 24–25°C enhance lz^{37h}.

Genotypically *mal* progeny of *mal*⁺ heterozygous or homozygous mothers exhibit a maternal effect and often appear to be phenotypically wild type. However, the effect is not as pervasive when heterozygous mothers are used, so that sometimes genotypically *mal* progeny which appear early in a hatch are phenotypically *mal*. Nevertheless, whenever possible, deficiencies that were suspected to involve the *mal* locus were used as male parents in crosses to females homozygous for a *mal* mutant.

The map shown in Fig. 1 supplements, refines, changes and corrects earlier maps of the region (Lifschytz and Falk, 1968, 1969; Lifschytz, 1971; Schalet and Finnerty, 1968b; Chovnick *et al.*, 1969; Schalet and Singer, 1971). Justification for most of the alterations can be found in Schalet and Singer (1971), Schalet (1972b) and Schalet and Lefevre (1973). Contrary to Schalet and Singer (1971), *l(1)E1C1* is located to the left of *mal*.

A number of ambiguities in the map should be noted:

(1) *sw* and its lethal alleles, *mel*, and the three allelic lethals between *sw* and *mel* are all included in *Df(1)T2–4A*; *sw* has been placed to the left of *mel* on the basis of a single crossover between *sw* and *mel* (Schalet, 1969a). However, the position of the three allelic lethals with respect to *sw* and *mel* is not known.

(2) The relative positions of the three lethals between *mel* and *mal* are not known.

(3) The left–right orientation has not been determined for the *lfl* alleles *vs. l(1)B214*; *l(1)LB20* and its allele *l(1)LB14 vs. l(1)11P1* and its allele *l(1)A112*; the *wap* alleles *vs. l(1)Q56*.

(4) The relative positions have not been determined for *l(1)R–9–18* and *l(1)3DES*. These lethals are completely viable with each other at all temperatures, but both appear to belong to a complex *su(f)* locus so that they may represent an instance of allelic complementation.

On our map the relative positions of a number of visible loci do not always agree with the linkage map positions given by Lindsley and Grell (1968): *ot* (65·7), *sw* (64·0), *mel* (64·1), *mal* (64·8), *lf* (68·1), *su(f)* (65·9), *bb* (66·0). However, Lindsley and Grell recognized the unreliability of linkage map positions. This is especially true because the linkage map values for visibles and lethals in this region were usually not obtained from single crosses in which two relatively new mutants are mapped against one another and in relation to crossover values with "older" mutants with "fixed" positions on the standard map. For these reasons (see also below) we have chosen not to append linkage map values to Fig. 1 and Table I.

It is probable that the map which we have presented has not saturated the region for functional units. There is no quantitative evidence from the literature to suggest this possibility. In fact, it is likely that we have omitted some previously described functional units. This is suggested from the complementation map positions of some lethal mutants, *l(1)4P1* in Schalet and Singer (1971) and *l(1)R–9–15* in Lifschytz and Falk (1969) which have been lost and thus are unavailable for retesting. Furthermore, there are some newly obtained single and multiple functional unit lethals which have not been completely tested with the mapped lethals or with one another, but give some indication of representing additional functional units. A number of previously described visible mutations, most of which unfortunately have been lost, whose descriptions do not seem to match the visibles listed in Table I and whose linkage map positions suggest the possibility that they may actually belong to this region, have not been tested. Of course, some may have represented visible alleles of lethals on the map.

There are 32 complementation units depicted on the map. Thirty of these are represented by mutations which appear to involve single functional units. The *mell* and *vao* loci were recognized because some deficiency compounds yielded a visible phenotype (see Table I). Polytene chromosome analysis of the deficiencies which showed the *mell* phenotype indicated that the phenotype was associated with the absence of band 19D3 or 19E1. Similarly, the *vao* phenotype was shown to involve the loss of bands 19E7–8. Since most of the mutations used to construct the map were obtained in experiments where visibles would have been discarded, *mell* and *vao* mutations involving single functional units would not have been saved.

In addition to the *mell* and *vao* loci, genetic tests of overlapping deficiencies, confirmed by polytene chromosome analysis, indicate that deficiencies for the *mal* and *unc* loci are not lethal (Fig. 1; Tables I and II). However, flies lacking the *vao* or *unc* loci have reduced viabilities.

Figure 1 does not list all of the single functional unit mutations which we have observed at the 32 loci indicated by the map. For instance, at what appears to be the most mutable locus, *l(1)A7*, we have found 6 additional radiation-induced (X-ray or gamma ray) alleles. (The 5 alleles which we tested with y^{+} *Ymal*^{126} showed the *eo* phenotype, see Table I.) The additional alleles at this and other loci, which are not presented in the figure, have not all been tested against one another. Aside from the *su(f)* locus, there are only one or two instances which suggest the possibility of allelic complementation between lethal or semilethal mutants. The question has not been pursued rigorously. However, examples of allelic complementation between lethal mutants have been reported for chromosome 4 mutants (Hochman, 1971).

As compared to the maps of Lifschytz and Falk (Lifschytz and Falk, 1969; Lifschytz, 1971), the present map has reduced the number of functional units. This was principally because we were able to recognize that a number of mutations originally classified as multifunctional unit lethals were, in fact, semilethals (Schalet, 1972b; Schalet and Lefevre, 1973) and not because all-or-none tests for allelism placed partially complementing lethals into separate functional units.

III. Cytogenetic Mapping of the Proximal Xe Region

A description of the banded structure in the most proximal portion of the polytene X chromosome first appeared in the detailed map of Bridges (1935) and in the work of Prokofyeva-Belgovskaya (Muller and Prokofyeva, 1935; Prokofyeva-Belgovskaya, 1935). Bridges (1938) regarded section 20 as the most difficult region of the chromosome to analyse, and this opinion has been abundantly documented by later efforts to describe the region (Viinikka *et al.*, 1971) or to assign rearrangement breakpoints there (Cooper, 1959). Until recently, only a single proximal cytogenetic element, the nucleolus organizing region or *bb* locus, had been generally thought to be correlated with a definite band position on the polytene chromosome map. Lindsley and Grell's (1968) invaluable compilation of genetic variations gives no gene localization other than *bb* in sections 19 or 20. Yet, most of the evidence for an association of the *bb* locus with a banded subsection of the polytene chromosome map was based on its genetically determined position between the breakpoints of inversions such as sc^4 and sc^8, whose proximal breaks were reported to be in sections 19 and 20. Yet, cytologists courageous enough to assign a position for the nucleolus organizing region to a specific subsegment of 20 invariably used qualifying descriptions, such as "seems most often to be dependent" or "appears to be associated".

Recently, however, careful study has shown that, in contrast to the 20B–F region, 20A and all of section 19 is sufficiently amenable to cytological analysis that in most cases breakpoint determinations for deficiencies are accurate within an error of no more than one band (Schalet and Lefevre, 1973). Therefore, the relative precision in identifying salivary gland chromosome breakpoints in 19 and 20A may be considered to be on a par with most of the remaining polytene X chromosome (see Chapter 2). In contrast to earlier work in the proximal region, this study combined polytene and mitotic cytological analysis with the genetic positioning of ordinary sex-linked mutants by means of complementation mapping. It also took advantage of many newly available visible and lethal mutants of diverse origin. The ability to correlate the position of mutants on the genetic map with reference to the positions of deficiency breakpoints on the polytene chromosome map permitted the localization of ordinary

TABLE II. Cytologically analysed deficiencies in Sections 19 and 20.

Deficiency	Left breakpoint[a]	Right breakpoint[a]
mal-8	18F4–5	19E1
mal-12	19A1	Far to the right of 20A
mal-3	19A1 or 2	Far to the right of 20A
mal-11	19A2 or 3	19E1
mal-17	19A2 or 3	19E1
16–2–19	19A5	19D3
mal-10	19A5–6	19E1
T2–4A	19B3	19C4
mal-6	19C3	20A2
mal-22	19C3	19E1
16–3–22	19D1	20A2
16–3–35	19D2 or 3	19E6 or 7
B57	19E1–2	19F1
LB6	19E4	20A2 or 3
A118	19E4 or 5	19E8
T2–14A	19E5	19E7–8
Q539	19E6	19F6
LB23	19E6 or 7	Far to the right of 20A
D43L1	19E8	Far to the right of 20A
54	19F1 or 2	20B–D
DCB1–35b	19F1 or 2	Far to the right of 20A
su(f)5A	20A3	Far to the right of 20A
13C3	20A3	20EF
y^{x5}	20A4–5	Deficient for the rest of 20
y^{x15}	20D1–2	Deficient for the rest of 20

[a] Unless otherwise indicated, any listed breakpoint may be in error by as much as one band, right or left.

sex-linked mutants in section 20. In turn, this permitted a clearer distinction of breakpoints assigned to the right of 20A.

Figure 1 presents the cytogenetically and genetically determined extents of 40 deficiencies in sections 19 and 20. In so far as possible, Fig.1 also depicts visible and lethal genes as being associated with specific polytene chromosome bands. Twenty-six deficiencies have been analysed cytologically, the others only genetically; their breakpoints are arbitrarily depicted as occurring between localized genes. However, our effort to represent the genes as located within bands has led in some cases to cytological impasses. For instance, the left breakpoint of *Df(1)16–3–22* is presented in Fig. 1 as between 19D1 and 2; whereas, the left breakpoint of *Df(1)16–3–35* is shown as between 19D2 and 3. The figure also shows the right breakpoint of *Df(1)16–2–19* as between 19D3 and 19E1. However, all three deficiencies are *mal* when heterozygous with *mal* mutants, and

Df(1)16–2–19/Df(1)16–3–22 females are also *mal*. (Males carrying *16–3–35* or *16–2–19* and a Y chromosome such as y^{+} *Ymal*^{106}, which covers the lethal effects, are *mal* but sterile.) Therefore, according to the deficiencies in Fig. 1, *mal* ought to be associated with 19D3, but an examination of the deficiency breakpoints given in Table II would permit the conclusion that *mal* was associated with 19D2 or 3. Actually, since any breakpoint considered here may be in error by as much as one band, right or left, the best that can be said is that *mal* is probably associated with one of the bands or interbands of 19D and is so listed in Table I.

Table II lists the breakpoints of the 25 cytogenetically analysed deficiencies. Of the 26 lethal mutations initially diagnosed genetically as deficiencies and then subjected to salivary gland chromosome analysis, only one (*Df(1)DCB1–35c* in Fig. 1) has failed to show the detectable absence of bands. The only serious discrepancy between the cytological and genetic analysis, which has not yet been worked out, concerns the right breakpoint of *Df(1)16–3–35*. Cytologically, the right breakpoint is at 19E6 or 7. Nevertheless, *16–3–35* is viable and phenotypically normal with *Df(1)A118* and *Df(1)T2–14A* which have left breakpoints at 19E4 or 5 and 19E5 respectively. Thus far, the only genetic difference found between *A118* and *T2–14A* is that the former is lethal with *l(1)151* and *l(1)R–9–28*, while the latter is not. *Df(1)16–3–35* is viable with *l(1)R–9–28*, but lethal with *l(1)LB19*, *l(1)AA33*, *l(1)R–9–29*. (Males carrying *16–3–35* or *l(1)151* and a covering Y-chromosome are sterile.) The possibility that a minute section (19E5?) has been transposed to another part of the *16–3–35* X chromosome has not been tested.

IV. The Position on the Polytene Chromosome Map of the Mitotic Euchromatic–heterochromatic Junction and the Proximal Limit of "Ordinary" Sex-linked Genes (those with no Alleles on the Y-chromosome)

"Of the 1024 bands which Bridges (1938) has represented in the polytene map of the X-chromosome, no more than 25 to 30 . . . lie proximally to the leftmost limit of Xh perhaps located at 19EF . . . and of these only about 17 are truly chromocentral" (Cooper, 1959). "The polytene X consists of just over 1,000 bands of which 25–30 correspond to the region that is heteropycnotic in the mitotic X" (Lindsley and Grell, 1968). These statements embody a concept to which few researchers with *D. melanogaster*, least of all ourselves, would have taken exception. However, a few years ago evidence began to accumulate that during the transformation of mitotic-type chromosomes into polytene chromosomes of salivary glands the proximal heterochromatic regions of chromosomes are not replicated

(Rudkin, 1964, 1969; Gall *et al.*, 1971). It was early recognized that Xh in the mitotic chromosome comprised between a third and a half of the entire X, but the segment in the polytene chromosome believed to be homologous to the mitotic Xh constituted only about 5% of the polytene X. Thinking about the basis for this discrepancy was greatly influenced by the idea (Muller and Gershenson, 1935; Muller and Prokofyeva, 1935; Muller *et al.*, 1937; Muller, 1944, 1954; Wagoner, 1965, 1968) that most of the mitotic Xh was the "temporary product of individual genes" (Muller and Gershenson, 1935). Consequently, the "real" sizes of Xe and Xh were represented by the polytene chromosome segments thought of as homologous to the mitotic chromosome Xe and Xh. Muller's explanation for the different proportions of Xe and Xh in mitotic chromosomes as compared to their supposed equivalents in polytene chromosomes was in some sense a simplified reversal of the interpretation presented by Heitz (1934b) to account for similar discrepant proportions between euchromatic and heterochromatic regions in the mitotic and polytene chromosomes of *D. virilis*. Applying Heitz's argument to the Xe and Xh of *D. melanogaster*, we would say that during polytenization the salivary chromosome equivalent of the mitotic Xe was enlarged, while the equivalent of the mitotic Xe essentially was not (cf. Rudkin, 1965, 1969; Gall *et al.*, 1971). Thus, contrary to Muller's concept, the "real" proportions of Xe and Xh were indeed seen in the mitotic chromosomes.

The picture we have presented here is of course an over-simplification of Heitz's ideas (see Beermann, 1962). For instance, Heitz discriminated between "alpha" and "beta" heterochromatin, and only the former was thought not to grow during polytenization. However, it is important to realize that much work with *D. melanogaster*, especially studies on radiation and chemical mutagenesis, has not made this discrimination. Therefore, whether one followed Muller's view that the "real" dimensions of Xe and Xh were given by the polytene chromosomes, or one was of the opinion that the "real" dimensions of Xe and Xh were given by the mitotic chromosomes (for instance, Kaufmann, 1954; Lefevre *et al.*, 1953), the essential idea contained in the statements quoted at the beginning of this section still held: in the proximal portion of the polytene X chromosome is a segment represented by bands and interbands of Bridges' map homologous to the Xh of the mitotic X. Consequently, the leftmost limit of Xh at the E–H junction of the mitotic X should have an identifiable counterpart on the polytene map.

Intimately allied to this notion was the thought that the proximal limit of ordinary sex-linked genes, that is, genes not covered by the Y chromosome, probably corresponded to the mitotic E–H junction. It was known that ordinary sex-linked genes did not extend proximally beyond the right breakpoint of *In(1)sc*^{4} (see below), so that the proximal limit of such genes could not extend into more than about 20% of the mitotic Xh (see Cooper, 1959). In any case the proximal limit of ordinary sex-linked genes should also have a counterpart on the polytene chromosome map, and cytogenetically analysed lethals should not be associated with the absence of bands to the right of the proximal breakpoint of *In(1)sc*^{4}. Conversely, if it were possible to localize, with any degree of assurance, ordinary sex-linked genes to a position on the polytene chromosome map proximal to the assigned right breakpoint of *In(1)sc*^{4}, or for that matter to the right of assigned right polytene chromosome breakpoints of any other inversions that on the basis of genetic or mitotic cytological analysis were to the right of that of *In(1)sc*^{4} (for instance w^{m4}, rst^3, sc^8), then the polytene chromosome assignment of such breakpoints could be called into question. A similar argument applies to any assigned polytene chromosome position for the *bb* locus.

By 1935 it was recognized that the proximal region of the mitotic X that had been earlier characterized as "relatively inert genetically" by Muller and Painter (1932) corresponded to the region which was cytologically characterized as heteropycnotic (Heitz, 1934a; Kaufmann, 1934). Muller and Prokofyeva (1935) at first identified the inert region with at least 5 or 6 of the most proximal bands of the polytene X. Later, when Bridges' (1935) detailed map was published, it was initially concluded that the inert region corresponded to 19EF and 20A–D (Prokofyeva-Belgovskaya, 1935). Subsequent work of various investigators, including Prokofyeva-Belgovskaya (1937), produced different opinions concerning the exact number of polytene bands homologous to Xh, but this equivalent became widely accepted.

The essential genetic correlation depended upon the position of *bb* in both the mitotic X and the polytene X. The work of Muller and Painter (1932), Dobzhansky (1932), and Gershenson (1933) showed that the *bb* locus was located medially in the mitotic Xh. By using inversions with genetically determined proximal breakpoints in Xh on either side of *bb* and combining such information with the polytene chromosome analysis of the proximal breakpoints, different workers assigned the position of the *bb* locus to the 19F–20D1 interval on the polytene chromosome map. Cooper (1959), although recognizing the high degree of uncertainty in making breakpoint assignments in this polytene region, nevertheless attempted to reconcile the divergent opinions and tentatively placed *bb* at "20C2 or 20C1?" and the E–H junction at 19E. The vital point here is that the medial placement of *bb* in polytene section 20 and in the mitotic Xh permitted the reasonable inference that salivary gland chromosome bands proximal to the position of *bb* were homologous to the portion of the mitotic Xh proximal to *bb*, and that some number of bands distal to *bb* were equivalent to the portion of the mitotic Xh distal to *bb*. Accordingly, the polytene equivalent of the mitotic E–H junction should be located in the distal portion of Section 20 or even in the proximal portion of 19. Consonant with this concept were observations that rearrangements with proximal breakpoints assigned to proximal Section 19 and distal 20 (as well as to proximal 20) were capable of producing variegated position effects associated with the placement of euchromatically located genes in proximity to Xh (Schultz, 1936; Hannah, 1951).

Possible flies in the ointment, about which most workers must have been unaware, were "hidden" in three reports (Slizynski, 1942; Slizynska and Slizynski, 1947; Bird and Fahmy, 1953). These papers described at least 8 cytogenetically localized sex-linked lethals that were believed to be associated with the absence of bands entirely located within polytene section 20. They included deficiencies for bands 20B1–2, 20C1–2 and 20B–F. In addition, there were at least 3 deficiencies limited to bands in 19E or 19F. In view of the differing opinions concerning the polytene chromosome position of the E–H junction, the position of the *bb* locus, and the positions of the proximal Xh breakpoints of the inversions mentioned above, there was no compelling reason at that time for these workers to consider the positions assigned to the lethals as especially significant. Furthermore, owing to the difficulty of establishing the true band situation because of the confused nature of the banding pattern in section 20, the relationship between the lethal mutants and the apparent absence of bands in section 20 may have been spurious.

In another approach to the question of whether ordinary sex-linked genes were located in the mitotic Xh, Cooper (1959) stated that *su(f)* was definitely located in Xh on the basis of the analysis of 4 free duplications of Xh. Cooper's analysis, as reported in Lindsley and Grell (1968), indicated that these duplications lacked "only the distalmost heterochromatic segment hD". The polytene chromosome proximal breakpoints for 2 of the duplications (*Dp(1;f)3* and *52*) were determined by Gersh as being in sections 19–20. Schalet and Finnerty (1968b) found that at least 4 additional proximally located lethal loci distal to *su(f)* were covered by *Dp(1;f)3* and pointed out, in accord with Cooper's determination, that these loci might be located in the proximal heterochromatin.

Subsequently, a combined genetic complementation and polytene chromosome study (Schalet *et al.*, 1970) that included deficiencies extending into section 20 from section 19 indicated that there were at least 9 loci in section 20, among which were 7 lethals distal to *su(f)* on the genetic map and proximal to bands 20A1–2 on the polytene chromosome map. These results indicated that the 19F assignment for the proximal breakpoint of *In(1)sc*^{4} was too far to the left, and suggested that the proximal breakpoints of *In(1)w*^{m4} and *In(1)rst*^{3} might be closer to the more proximal positions that Prokofyeva-Belgovskaya (1939) originally assigned to them than to the 20A and 20B positions suggested by Cooper (1959). In addition, these results confirmed the earlier indications that the proximal limit of ordinary sex-linked genes on the polytene chromosome map was actually further to the right than would have been permitted were the breakpoint of *In(1)sc*^{4} actually at 19F. Furthermore, if the mitotic analysis of *Dp(1;f)3* was correct, the fact that the 8 loci located proximally to 20A1–2 were covered by *Dp(1;f)3*, but a lethal localized to 20A1–2 was not, implied that the mitotic E–H junction corresponded to a position on the polytene chromosome map "just to the left of salivary bands 20A1–2 or to a slightly more distal point" (Schalet, 1970). Since none of the 8 genes just considered, not even the most proximal *su(f)*, is included within *Df(1)sc*^{4L}*sc*^{8R}, it was inferred that they were located in the distal half of the mitotic heterochromatic segment hD. As much as Schalet would have wished to be correct, succeeding work (Schalet and Lefevre, 1973) has demonstrated that this particular conjecture concerning the polytene chromosome position of the mitotic E–H junction was in error. Most, if not all, of the sex-linked genes covered by *Dp(1;f)3* are not in the heterochromatic segment hD.

A mitotic examination of *Df(1)y*^{x5} and *Df(1)y*^{x15} (Table II and Fig. 2) showed the complete absence of heterochromatic material which had been present at the telomere end of these *In(1)sc*^{8} chromosomes prior to the induction of the deficiencies. The fact that the mitotic heterochromatic segments hD–hB and almost all of hA (Cooper, 1959; Lindsley and Grell, 1968) were now missing, yet in *Df(1)y*^{x15} proximal genes up to and including *l(1)20* were present and, in *Df(1)y*^{x5}, the genes up to and including *uncl* were present, demonstrates that *l(1)20* and all of the genes distal to it (in the order presented by the normal uninverted chromosome) cannot be in Xh. Moreover, the fact that *Dp(1;f)3* covered the genes up to and including the *wap* locus, which is distal to *uncl*, suggested that the original characterization of *Dp(1;f)3* as being broken in the distal portion of Xh, that is, in the heterochromatic segment hD, was incorrect. Actually, a mitotic re-examination of *Dp(1;f)3* has convinced us that none of Xh is deleted. In passing, we may mention that one of the other free duplications, *Dp(1;f)52*, which lacked only the distal-most heterochromatic segment hD according to Cooper and which had earlier been reported to carry the wild-type allele of *su(f)* (Lindsley and Sandler, 1957), was found by us some years ago to lack *su(f)*$^{+}$.

Polytene chromosome analysis of *Df(1)y*^{x5} and *Df(1)y*^{x15} (Fig. 2) reveals that they were broken at or just to the left of 20B1–2 and at or adjacent

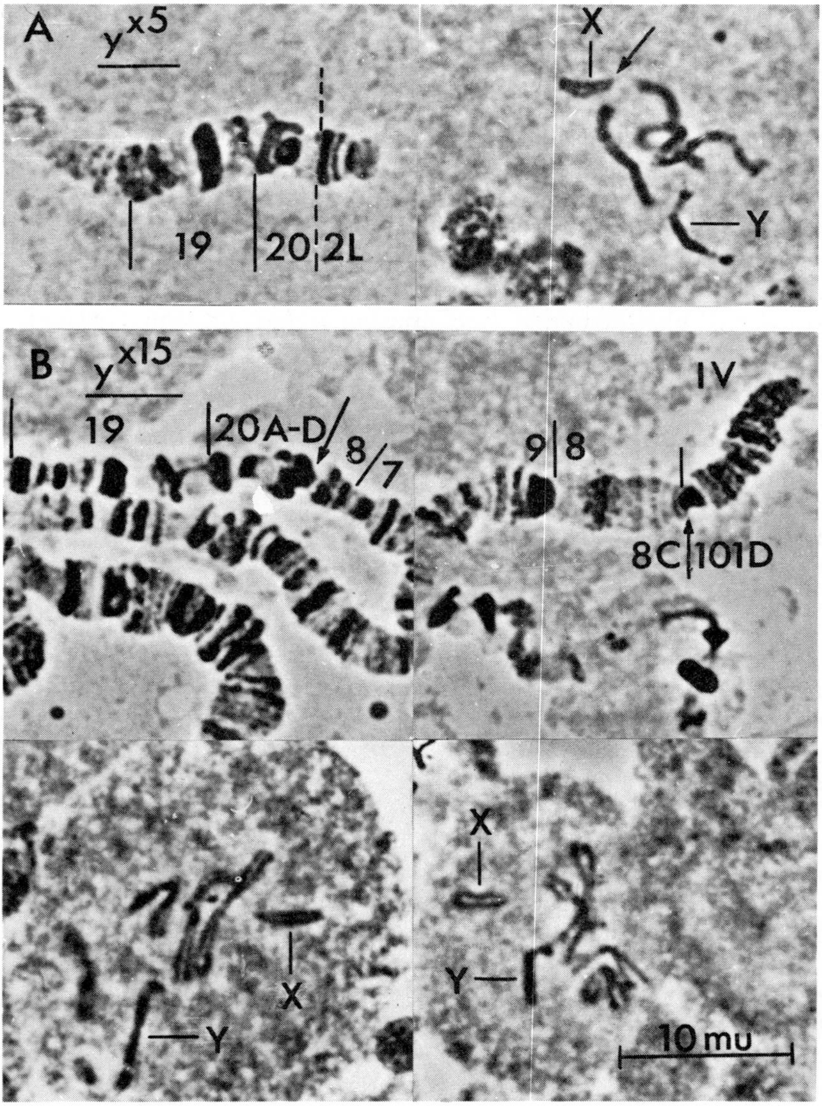

FIG. 2. The cytology of deficiencies y^{x5} and y^{x15}. (A) y^{x5}: Left, a male salivary gland chromosome preparation showing sections 19 and 20 at the base of the X chromosome. At 20A, the chromosome is capped with a short segment, possibly the tip of 2L. The breakpoint in 20A follows 20A3 (the dark round band). Right, a larval ganglion mitosis showing no heterochromatin at the telomere end of y^{x5} (arrow), although a short segment representing the sc^8 centromere region is present

to 20D1–2, respectively. Furthermore, an examination of the B^SY chromosome, which covers the loci to the right of *l*(*1*)*114*, suggests the presence of section 20 bands at least from 20B or C to the right. Therefore, *l*(*1*)*20* has been securely placed in 20B–C, if not in 20C, and the *sph* and *su*(*f*) loci in 20D or 20EF (Fig. 1). Since loci at least as far to the right as *l*(*1*)*20* cannot be in Xh (see previous paragraph), the polytene chromosome position of the E–H junction can be no further to the left than 20C. Since ordinary sex-linked genes can be placed in 20D, the proximal limit of such genes must be in 20D or even farther to the right. As a consequence of these results, the polytene chromosome position of the *bb* locus, which is genetically to the right of *su*(*f*), cannot be to the left of 20D. Since the earlier placements of the E–H junction and the *bb* locus, which had been inferred from the polytene chromosome breakpoint assignments of inversions judged to be broken in the mitotic Xh on the basis of genetic and mitotic cytological analysis, were in conflict with the deficiency analysis, we undertook a re-examination of the proximal polytene chromosome breakpoint positions of inversions sc^4, sc^8 and w^{m4}. The results of this analysis, discussed and illustrated in Schalet and Lefevre (1973) (see also Chapter 2), are in accord with the evidence from the deficiency analysis which had led us to conclude that all of these inversions must actually be broken to the right of 20D, that is, in 20EF or even to the right of 20F in the unpolytenized portion of the X chromosome.

Thus, conventional cytogenetic methods, pushed close to their limits, have permitted us to reach conclusions previously suggested by the work of Rudkin (1964, 1969) and Gall *et al.* (1971). As applied to the proximal region of the X-chromosome, the information that heterochromatic regions as seen in mitotic chromosomes are not polytenized in the salivary gland chromosomes is compatible with the argument from our evidence that the identification of the mitotic Xh with any of the polytene X

---

at the other end. (The Y chromosome is atypical and carries a duplication for both the tip and base of the X chromosome, which allows y^{x5} males to survive.) (B) y^{x15}: Upper left: A male salivary gland chromosome preparation showing the inversion breakpoint joining 20D with 8C. Note the heavy bands, just to the left of the arrow, representing the 20B–D region. Upper right: Virtually the entirety of chromosome 4, broken at 101D, caps the X at 8C (arrow). Lower left: A colchicine-treated larval ganglion mitosis at prophase. The X chromosome shows heterochromatin both at the centromere end from the sc^8 inversion and at the telomere end from chromosome 4. A slight suggestion of heterochromatin is seen in the middle where 20A–D should be (arrow), but a similar condition occurs in the y^{x5} chromosome above and is probably not significant. Lower right: Another cell showing y^{x15}. Here, the X chromosome appears circular, held together at both ends by heterochromatin, but shows no indication of heterochromatin in the middle. (The doubly duplicated Y chromosome provides for survival of y^{x15} as well as y^{x5} males.) (From Schalet and Lefevre, 1973.)

chromosome bands is incorrect. Consequently, ordinary sex-linked genes may well extend to the rightmost limit of Bridges' map, i.e. 20F, the mitotic E–H junction may not exist in the salivary gland X chromosome, and the *bb* locus-nucleolus organizing region may not be represented by any section 20 bands.

V. Band–gene Relationships in Sections 19 and 20

The information presented in Fig. 1 provides the foundation for ascertaining some elementary facts about band–gene–crossover relationships in the proximal Xe. In this connection it must be recognized that some basic data are still lacking, including the "correct" band count (see Chapter 2) and convincing evidence that the array of detected mutations, at least the obvious morphological changes and lethals, has saturated the functional units in this region. It is not likely that polytene cytology will clearly establish the number of bands in section 20. The difficulties in cytological analysis of this segment have been recently reaffirmed (Viinikka *et al.*, 1971), and we will not venture to give a "correct" band count. We can neither verify nor absolutely refute Bridges' (1938) estimate of 19 bands for section 20.

Since the long-studied and thoroughly analysed euchromatic 3A3–3C7 (*z*–*N*) interval (Slizynska, 1938; Judd *et al.*, 1972; Lefevre and Green, 1972; Berendes, 1970) is still subject to uncertainty with respect to the band count, it would not be surprising if the proximal interval from 18F4–5 through 20A is subject to revision. For the interval from 18F4–5 through 20A, Bridges' (1938) estimate of 39 bands is suspect on two counts. This interval has a very high proportion of doublets as compared to single bands (16/7). Beermann (1962) has argued that many doublets may be fixation artifacts, and for the polytene chromosome region 1A–4E, Berendes' (1970) electron microscopic observations failed to resolve many of Bridges' doublets. Berendes also states that, "Observations on the regions 4E5–20 indicate that here too the number of doublets is greatly reduced as compared with Bridges' map." Accordingly, we are not convinced that 19D1–2 is double, and we strongly suspect that 19E1–2 and 19E3–4 are genetically duplicate. On the other hand, our observations suggest that both 19E5–8 and 19F3–6 have more faint bands than Bridges drew. Furthermore, in 20A we see 3 faint bands after 20A3, not 2 (see also Slizynski, 1942), and band 20A3 seems to be truly double.

With these considerations in mind, we emphasize the limitations and uncertainties placed on our designations of the polytene chromosome positions for visible and lethal mutants presented at the top of Fig. 1 and in Table I. Using Bridges' 1938 map as a standard, cytologically analysed deficiency breakpoint determinations in 18F4–5 through 20A can be in error by ± one band, and in some places, especially in 19E5–8 and 19F3–6, possibly by more than one band. For 20B–F, breakpoint determinations are even less precise.

For convenience, in the linear representation of deficiency extents in Fig. 1, breakpoints are indicated as occurring between bands and the uncertainties indicated by Table II are largely omitted. We consider it useful to attempt to place as many genes as possible in a one-to-one correspondence with the bands of Bridges' map, but it should be noted that not a single lethal mutant can unambiguously be delimited to a single band or adjacent interband on the basis of the cytogenetically analysed deficiencies. Perhaps the best localization is the positioning of *l(1)E54* and *A7* at 20A1–2. On the other hand, the 5 unequivocal lethal loci between *unc* and *eo* are simply restricted to a cytologically defined segment to the right of 19F1 and to the left of 20A3, and the one-to-one correspondence with the bands of Bridges' map is inferred from the genetic (complementation) analysis of additional deficiencies. Similar limitations apply to the correspondence of most visible mutants to particular bands. The restriction of *vao* and *unc* to a segment defined by the bands and associated interbands of 19E7–19F1 provides a good example of gene localization in this region.

There is no persuasive evidence that the mutations thus far detected in the portion of Xe covered by $Ymal^{+}$ and y^{+} $Ymal^{+}$ have fully saturated the functional units in the segment. It is worthwhile examining, however, why the data of Lifschytz and Falk (1968, 1969) should have been considered as indicating that saturation was being approached (Hochman, 1971; Beermann, 1972) or even achieved (Lifschytz, 1971). Curiously, Lifschytz and Falk (1970) and Lifschytz (1971) assumed saturation without presenting any new data and thereby disregarded their earlier caveat (Lifschytz and Falk, 1969) concerning the observation that in the later experiments most lethals affected already identified units. Accordingly, "this would indicate that we are approaching the stage where most functional units have been discovered". But this was not considered to be conclusive, since it was stated, "such a conclusion must, however, be made with reservation in view of the non-random distribution of the lethals induced by EMS, until it is shown that with another type of mutagen not many more units can be discovered". We would make three additional points based on the presentation of the 1969 map: (1) Of the 32 functional units defined by lethal effects, 7 (22%) are inferred from overlapping deficiencies and are not represented by lethals affecting single functional units. (2) It is stated that the number of functional units delineated by 70 lethals induced by chemical mutagens was less than the number delineated by the 35 X-ray-induced lethals analysed earlier (Lifschytz and Falk, 1968). This observation overlooks the fact that, in the construction of the earlier map, 9 additional X-ray and chemical mutants were used, and these alone defined 5 functional units on the 1968 map. Furthermore, corrections presented by the 1969 paper, if applied to the earlier map, would have removed 3 additional functional units. Thus, the 35 X-ray-induced lethals actually defined only 12 functional units, so that the 21 additional functional units defined by the 65 new chemically induced lethals do not encourage the belief that saturation was being approached. Falk (1970a) also refers to 2 more functional units that were identified since the publication of the 1969 map, but these are not included in Lifschytz's (1971) analysis. (3) If the formula from the Poisson distribution that Alikhanian (1937), Hochman *et al.* (1964), and Hochman (1971) used to estimate the number of loci that did not mutate to lethality or semi-lethality in the segments they studied were applied to the 1969 data of Lifschytz and Falk, which for the purpose of this calculation is assumed to be correct, then it can be calculated that 10 additional essential loci remained to be detected.

When Alikhanian and Hochman initially applied the formula to the segments they were studying, the regions were far from exhausted for the number of loci detected. Nevertheless, the estimated total number of loci for each segment, 47 lethal and semi-lethal loci for Alikhanian's region at the tip of the X chromosome and 38 for the number of lethal loci for chromosome 4 in Hochman's case, show some fair correlation with current ideas concerning the relationship between genes and salivary chromosome bands. For the segment studied by Alikhanian, the number of bands has been estimated as 35 by Berendes (1970) but as 55 by Bridges (1938); for the fourth chromosome the number of bands is considered to be about 50 (Hochman, 1971). Hochman's (1972) data puts the number of loci in chromosome 4 at 44, 37 being essential loci and 7 which were identified only through recessive visible mutants.

Beyond the objections outlined above, what has not been appreciated in considering the question of saturation in the proximal X region is the fact that the system used by Lifschytz and Falk (as well as by Munoz, see below), whereby only lethals are scored in the initial screening generation, clearly did not allow for the detection of even obvious morphological mutations unless they so drastically reduced viability that they initially simulated a sex-linked lethal. Thus, nonessential loci would not have been detected, and loci capable of mutating only to semi-lethality (which thus far in our analysis of this region have always shown visible effects) would have been detected only haphazardly. This contrasts with the methods employed by Alikhanian (1937), Hochman (1971) and Judd *et al.* (1972) that were competent to detect most, if not all, of these kinds of mutations. The proportion of such loci in any particular segment cannot be predicted in advance, but our data suggest that in the proximal X these loci represent a significant fraction, perhaps as much as 1/3 of the detected loci (see Fig. 1 and below). In chromosome 4, 7/44 of the loci thus far identified have been recognized only by their recessive visible effects, and in the region between *z* and *w*, 2/12 of the loci yield only semilethal mutants with visible phenotypes.

For the reasons outlined above, we tend to discount the numerical comparisons which have been made between the proximal X region and other studied segments, especially with respect to the question of the relationship between salivary gland chromosome bands and genes (Hochman, 1971; Beermann, 1972; Judd *et al.*, 1972). In addition, there is some uncertainty concerning the cytological extent of the region covered by $Ymal^+$ in the studies of Lifschytz and Falk (1968, 1969). We question the security of the evidence in support of the one band-one gene concept in the proximal portion of the X chromosome presented by Lifschytz (1971).

Without denying the cogency of the evidence from other segments of the genome, part of the problem is that the attractiveness of the one band-one gene concept has perhaps promoted an eagerness to find supportive evidence. During the course of this study, we have found ourselves susceptible to this contagion. For the record, we are of the opinion that because of the variability in the banding pattern, it will be perhaps impossible to prove an exact one-to-one correspondence, even should it exist, between genes and the bands of section 20. However, it should be possible to show that the number of mutants is of the same magnitude as the number of bands in Bridges' 1938 map, not a number significantly larger or smaller. As for the more distal region, it is sufficient to point out that in what seems to be the most populated portion of the map, 19D1–2 through 20A1–2, it has, as yet, not been necessary to squeeze more than one of the 15 identified functional units there into any one band (and/or the adjacent interband) of Bridges' map, which for this segment presents 3 single and 8 double bands.

VI. Sterility Effects in the Proximal Xe and Xh

Of the large number of single and multiple functional unit mutations which have been studied in the proximal X region, a considerable proportion proved to be male sterile in the presence of a covering Y chromosome. In our material, we have made no systematic attempt to define the basis of the sterility effects exhibited by each mutant or to ensure that this phenotype was associated with a change involving the proximal Xe or Xh. The literature is not lacking for hypotheses, ongoing or abandoned, that have attempted to relate male sterility to factors in the proximal Xe or Xh

(Lindsley *et al.*, 1960; Lindsley, 1965; Lifschytz and Falk, 1968, 1969; Lifschytz and Lindsley, 1972; Lindsley and Lifschytz, 1972).

There can be no single locus or segment in the proximal Xe region encompassed by y^+ *Ymal*$^+$ or *Ymal*$^+$ whose absence confers dominant sterility on males or females. The fertility of covered *Df(1)mal*^{12} males and heterozygous females is by itself sufficient to prove the point. For females, the length of the region whose absence imposes no complete sterility can be extended to include all of Xe proximal to salivary gland chromosome bands 18A3–4 and all of Xh up to the proximal breakpoint of *In(1)sc*^{8}, as attested to by the fertility of individuals heterozygous for *Df(1)y*^{4L}*sc*^{8R} (Lindsley and Grell, 1968). Moreover, males carrying a Y chromosome that includes a section of Xe extending distally at least as far as the *car* locus, and therefore to 18D1–2 on the polytene chromosome map, are fertile enough to be useful.

Recently the region between *su(f)* and *bb* has received specific attention in connection with more general ideas concerning X-chromosome activity during spermatogenesis. According to Lifschytz and Lindsley (1972), "in a large collection of proximal deficiencies, those that are deficient for both *su(f)* . . . and *bb* . . . are invariably male sterile, while deficiencies for *su(f)* but not *bb* and *bb* but not *su(f)* are in every instance male fertile. These results show that sterility is caused by deficiency for a region and cannot be attributed to the absence of a particular gene locus." And later, "We interpret these observations as indicating that the distal segment of the proximal X heterochromatin plays an important role in regulating X-chromosome activity during spermatogenesis." Lindsley and Lifschytz (1972) repeat the statements concerning the fertility and sterility of males carrying a *Ymal*$^+$ chromosome and the three types of deficiencies described above. Their interpretation is phrased as follows, "We have entertained the idea that *su(f)–bb* deficiencies are in some way involved with the site of control of precocious X-chromosome inactivation".

Schalet (1972b), however, described a number of *su(f)–bb* deficiencies that were male fertile in the presence of a covering Y chromosome. These included: (1) *Df(1)mal*^{12} (Schalet and Finnerty, 1968a), (2) *Df(1)A209* and *Df(1)X–1* (Lifschytz and Falk, 1968, 1969; Lifschytz, 1971). Lifschytz (1971) described *Df(1)A209* as deficient for the *su(f)–bb* interval, but our tests have shown that both chromosomes are *su(f)–bb* deficiencies and are male fertile when covered by y^+ *Ymal*$^+$, (3) at least 7 of the 14 deficiencies which include *su(f)* and *bb* shown in Fig. 3 are male fertile with *Ymal*$^+$ (Munoz, unpublished observations). Finally, a most instructive example is provided by *Df(1)y*^{x5}, which has been analysed cytogenetically. This deficiency arose in an X-rayed *In(1)sc*^{8} chromosome and in addition to being deficient for the proximal genes indicated by Fig. 1, genetic tests

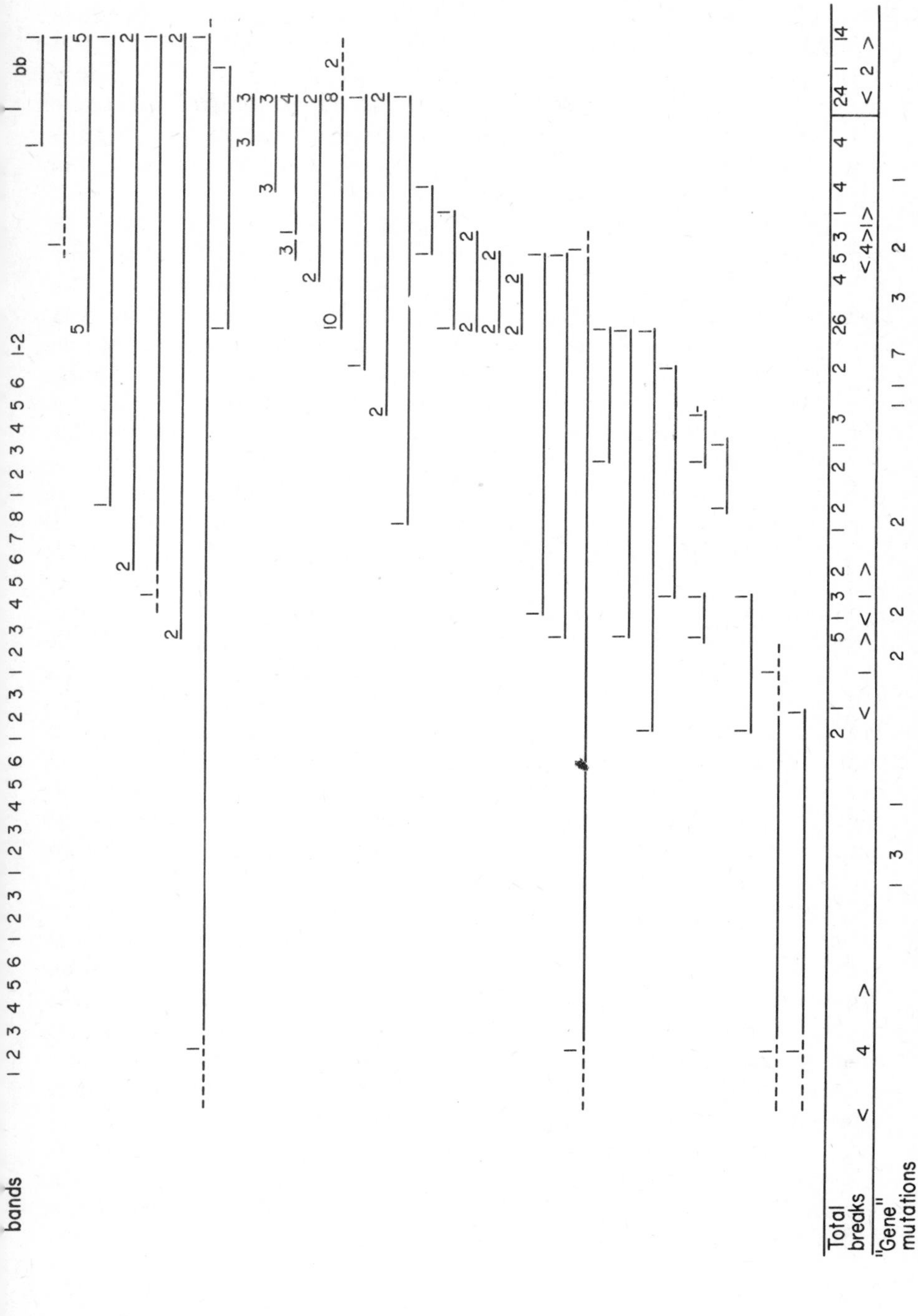

FIG. 3. Distribution of neutron-induced deficiency breakpoints in sections 19 and 20.

showed a deficiency for the distal markers from *l(1)J1* to *ac*. Polytene chromosome analysis shows a break at, or just to the left of, 20B1–2 and the chromosome is capped with a very short tip of about 3 bands, possibly consisting of material from 2L. The mitotic X shows no heterochromatic material at the telomere end, but the appropriate amount of heterochromatin of *In(1)sc*^{8} occurs at the centric end. *Df(1)y*^{x5} is male fertile with y^{+} *Ymal*$^{+}$.

The above results demonstrate that males with a covering Y chromosome can be fertile even though they lack the *su(f)–bb* interval. However, the report that males deficient only for the *bb* locus are invariably fertile is supported by an observation of Kogan (1966), who indicated that at least 33, if not all 34, X-ray-induced *bb* lethal mutations on the X chromosome detected in one of his experiments were male fertile. Since the loss of the *su(f)–bb* interval does not necessarily produce a sterile effect, we consider it prudent not to extend speculations concerning the basis for the male sterility that does occur in some such mutants.

VII. The Relative Susceptibility of Xe and Xh to Radiation-induced Breakage

As we have seen, it is inappropriate to consider polytene chromosome section 20 as homologous to the mitotic Xh. Yet, the apportionment of induced breaks into euchromatin and heterochromatin has been a feature of numerous studies (Bauer *et al.*, 1938; Bauer, 1939; Kaufmann, 1939, 1946; Nicoletti and Lindsley, 1960; Slizynska, 1957, 1969) in which section 20 was arbitrarily taken to represent heterochromatin. It is likely that many of the breakpoints which these workers placed in section 20 were not actually in the heterochromatic region, so that the proportion of euchromatic to heterochromatic breaks must have been underestimated to some degree. In some studies, such as that of Slizynska (1969), where the proportion of triethylene melamine-induced breaks in heterochromatic regions increased drastically with storage, the underestimate could not have affected the data significantly. (Slizynska actually scored breaks in all chromosomes, so that salivary gland chromosome sections 20, 40, 41, 80, 81 and 101 were all considered to be heterochromatic.) In terms of the relative susceptibility of euchromatic *vs.* heterochromatic regions to undergo rearrangement, however, any overestimate of breaks assigned to heterochromatic regions because of their supposed identity to section 20 and the other proximal polytene chromosome sections may be important.

Muller (1954) and Kaufmann (1954) summarized two contrasting interpretations of the observation that there appeared to be a correspondence between the apportionment of X-ray induced breaks in Xe and Xh and their respective lengths in mitotic chromosomes. Both interpretations assumed polytene chromosome section 20 of Bridges map was equivalent to the proximal heterochromatic region of the mitotic X chromosome, but Muller believed that the polytene chromosomes presented the "real" relative sizes of Xe and Xh, that Xh in mitotic chromosomes consisted mostly of "adventitious nongenetic material", the virtually unbreakable "blocks", and that the remaining genic heterochromatin was some 20 times more susceptible to having structural changes induced in it than equivalent lengths of euchromatin. Kaufmann, on the contrary, accepted the mitotic chromosome as presenting the real picture. He concluded that euchromatin and heterochromatin were identically susceptible to breakage, length for length.

Cooper (1959) challenged the idea of large unbreakable blocks. His mitotic analysis of about 40 X chromosome duplications with proximal breakpoints in Xh (listed in Lindsley and Grell, 1968) showed that Xh was breakable at many points along its length, i.e. there were no large unbreakable "blocks". Furthermore, evidence presented by Rudkin (1964, 1969) and Gall *et al.* (1971) indicates that DNA located in the centric regions of the chromosomes does not replicate during polytenization. The proportion of unreplicated DNA and its centric location pointed to its identity with the heterochromatic portions of the mitotic chromosomes. Accordingly, not the polytene, but the mitotic chromosomes present a more accurate picture of the proportions of the "gene string" (DNA) in Xe and Xh.

It follows that Muller's concept of yellow-lethal mutations in $In(1)sc^8$ chromosomes as being minute rearrangements is incorrect. The high frequency with which such mutations arise following irradiation (Belgovsky, 1938) may not properly be regarded as supporting the idea that the heterochromatic region adjacent to the yellow locus in sc^8 chromosomes, because of its high susceptibility to structural change, is responsible for the high frequency of such mutations in normal chromosomes. Rather, the interpretation put forth to account for the relatively high recovery of Notch mutations in $In(1)rst^3$ and $In(1)w^{m4}$ chromosomes, if applied to the yellow-lethal mutations in sc^8, seems more reasonable (Lefevre *et al.*, 1953). According to this interpretation, the types of mutations just mentioned are recovered more frequently because the loss of even large segments of the adjacent heterochromatic region does not lead to the haplo-insufficiency (dominant lethality) that the loss of equally large segments of an adjacent euchromatic region would produce.

Even if these particular ideas of Muller concerning the heterochromatic region must be abandoned, there are two interesting observations which require re-interpretation: (1) In $In(1)sc^8$ chromosomes, the frequency of yellow-lethal mutations induced by X-rays shows a linear relationship to dose (Belgovsky, 1939; Muller 1940, 1959). (2) As reported by Muller (1944) and confirmed by Wagoner (1965, 1968), after irradiating males from two special stocks in which there was a two-fold difference in the mitotic length of the X-chromosomes, the frequency of X autosome translocations was the same in both stocks. The difference in length was brought about by diminishing the size of the heterochromatic region in one chromosome to about 1/4 the normal value, and increasing its size in the other to nearly twice the normal value.

In support of the concept that X-ray-induced breaks are distributed in proportion to chromosome length, regardless of the euchromatic or heterochromatic properties of its segments, Kaufmann (1946) noted that the 30% of the X chromosome breaks in Xh corresponded closely to the estimated length of Xh as one-third of the entire X. Actually, only 23% of the breaks were observed in polytene chromosome section 20, believed to be equivalent to the mitotic Xh. The figure of 30% was achieved by (1) alloting to Xh a proportion of the total breaks in sections 20, 40, 41, 80, and 81 that could not specifically be assigned any individual chromosome, and (2) estimating the number of cytologically undetectable X-chromosome rearrangements confined entirely to the proximal heterochromatic region.

Even though Kaufmann's figure of 30% for Xh may be in error, it is impossible to judge what proportion of the 321 breaks which Kaufmann (1946) actually observed in section 20 were not really in the heterochromatic region. If the 19–20 bands of section 20 responded to X-ray-induced breakage in a manner comparable to some of the subdivisions in sections 1–19 (Table 2, Kaufmann, 1946), the proportion of breaks would be considerable. For instance, a "breakability" comparable to that of 19EF (14 bands, 33 breaks) would yield 45 breaks for section 20. Note, too, in our Fig. 3, there are approximately 23 breaks in 19EF as compared with 52 breaks in section 20 to the left of *su(f)*.

Although Kaufmann estimated the length of Xh as one-third of the entire X, Cooper's (1959) calculations suggest a range from 30 to 50%. For the present purpose, DNA content offers a better base line than chromosome length. According to Rudkin (1965 and personal communication) 32% of the DNA content of the entire X is contained in the heterochromatic segment deleted in *Df(1)*$sc^{4L}sc^{8R}$. Consequently, the entire Xh should contain about 40% of the total X DNA. If Xe and Xh undergo X-ray-induced rearrangement in proportion to their DNA contents, then the ratio of Xe/Xh breaks should be 60/40. This appears to be somewhat lower than observed, so that, although X-ray-induced mutation and breakage in euchromatic segments is proportional to DNA content (Rudkin, 1965; Lefevre, 1969), the relative susceptibility of Xe and Xh to undergo radiation-induced breakage and rearrangement must remain an open question.

VIII. Analysis of Radiation-induced Lethal Mutations in the Proximal Xe

A. X-RAY AND NEUTRON-INDUCED MUTATIONS

A quantitative study of radiation-induced mutations in the proximal Xe region covered by *Ymal*$^+$ was reported by Lifschytz and Falk (1968). Recessive sex-linked lethal mutations induced in predominantly post-meiotic germ cells were obtained from adult males of a wild-type stock exposed to an X-ray dose of 3,200 R. This exposure produced 8% sex-linked lethals, as detected by the *Basc* test, and 10% of these lethals proved to be covered by the *Ymal*$^+$ chromosome. Complementation analysis of these lethals, as well as 9 additional lethal mutants obtained in other experiments, indicated that 30/35 (86%) of the covered lethals involved more than one functional unit. Ordinarily, this type of analysis does not discriminate between point lethals affecting one functional unit, and those associated with rearrangements such as inversions or translocations. Thus, among the 5 single functional unit mutants, some may have been rearrangements. Much has been made of the significance of these observations with regard to the nature of X-ray-induced mutations in post-meiotic male germ cells of *Drosophila*.

It is desirable to mention the results of a recent study comparable to the analysis of X-ray-induced lethals. The data presented represent a collaborative effort with Dr. Enzo Munoz, who has kindly given permission for their inclusion here. Recessive sex-linked lethal mutations induced in mature spermatozoa were obtained from adult males of an Oregon-K stock exposed to about 2,200 Rads of 3 MeV neutrons. There were 7·6% sex-linked lethals detected by the *Basc* test, and 10% of the lethals tested (100/982) proved to be covered by the *Ymal*$^+$ chromosome, a result that is in complete agreement with the proportion of X-ray-induced lethals covered in the work of Lifschytz and Falk (1968). Of 93 covered lethals analysed by complementation tests, 64 proved to involve 2 or more contiguous functional units and were considered to be genetic deficiencies. Since 3 of the deficiencies produced a *mal* phenotype in combination with viable *mal* alleles, they were selected for cytological analysis and proved to be cytological deficiencies which overlapped for at least 19D2 on the polytene chromosome map (*16–2–19*, *16–3–35* and *16–3–22* in Fig. 1). There were 3 additional lethals that may be deficiencies, but seem to involve no more than 2 contiguous functional units. One more lethal

(*17–169*) appeared to involve 2 noncontiguous functional units, *leg* and *vao*. Cytological analysis was difficult, but indicated the occurrence of an insertion of a segment from about 19E5–8 to 20 into chromosome 3L at 78A. There remained 26 lethals affecting only 1 functional unit that were distributed among 12 loci. It is interesting to note that 7 of the 26 lethals were alleles of *l(1)E54*, and mutations at this locus arose at a rate of about 1/1900. Lifschytz and Falk (1969) reported that after ethyl methanesulphonate treatment the highest frequency of mutations also occurred at this locus. About one-fifth of their single functional unit lethals were alleles of *l(1)E54*. It can be calculated from their data that mutations at this locus arose at a rate of about 1/370. Since their overall lethal frequency of about 37% following the ethyl methanesulphonate treatments was approximately 5 times higher than in the neutron treatments, the mutational response of this locus appears to be about the same for both mutagens.

B. Distribution of Deficiency Breakpoints in sections 19 and 20

Figure 3 presents the distribution of breakpoints for 64 established deficiencies. Based on the cytogenetic analysis of the 24 deficiencies listed in Table II and Fig. 1, as well as the genetic analysis of the additional deficiencies presented in Fig. 1, the genetically determined breakpoints of the deficiencies may be correlated with the polytene chromosome map positions presented at the top of Fig. 3.

There are 31 deficiency breakpoints in section 19 (including 3 which may be in 18F) as compared to 52 in section 20 to the left of *su(f)* and 41 in Xh, i.e. to the right of *su(f)*. The frequency of section 20 breakpoints in the X-ray data from post-meiotic sperm was approximately 0·34% among the chromosomes tested for recessive sex-linked lethals as compared to approximately 0·39% from the neutron experiments. There is no ready way to determine the frequency of breakpoints involved in deficiencies located entirely within Xh. However, on the assumption that each heterochromatic lethal (bb^- lethal) represents 2 deficiency breakpoints in Xh, then a minimum estimate is available from the information presented by Lindsley *et al.* (1960), Edington *et al.* (1962) and Epler and Eddington (1963). Their data indicate that for 3000–4000 R there are approximately as many breakpoints producing bb^- lethals as Xh breakpoints (0·30%) involved in deficiencies producing ordinary sex-linked lethals. Therefore, there are, at a minimum, twice as many deficiency breakpoints in Xh as in section 20.

The neutron results confirm the presence of a "hot-spot" for radiation-induced breakage between *l(1)E54* (*eo*) and *l(1)A200* (*wap*), which we have identified on the polytene chromosome map as 20A3. Lifschytz (1971) and Falk (1973) regard *l(1)E54* and *l(1)A200* as straddling the mitotic E–H junction, and Falk stated that Schalet and Singer (1971) made this identification. A careful reading of Schalet and Finnerty (1968b), Schalet (1970), and Schalet and Singer (1971) will show that Schalet did not identify this position as the mitotic E–H junction, but rather regarded, albeit incorrectly as subsequent evidence proved, the tests with *Dp(1;f)3* as indicating only that loci proximal to *l(1)A7*, an allele of *l(1)E54*, were in the mitotic Xh.

C. The Proportion of Deficiencies in Relation to the Nature of Radiation-induced Mutations

A number of additional comparisons can be made between the data obtained from neutrons and the X-ray data of Lifschytz and Falk (1968). However, the complementation map for the X-ray data, as well as the later analysis of EMS-induced lethals (Lifschytz and Falk, 1969), was restricted to a proximal subsegment of the Xe region covered by the $Ymal^+$. This subsegment was bounded on the left by the distal breakpoint of *Df(1)B57*, i.e. the locus of *lethal(1)AA33* on the genetic map and, according to our analysis, band 19E1–2 on the polytene chromosome map. For these comparisons, we have made some modifications of the originally reported X-ray data that are necessitated by the corrections in the extent of some deficiencies reported by Lifschytz and Falk (1969) and by our own analysis (Schalet, 1972b; Schalet and Lefevre, 1973).

The data from both X-ray and neutron irradiations agree in showing that approximately 3/4 of the lethals consist of mutants affecting more than one complementation unit, i.e. deficiencies. However, about 2/3 of the deficiencies, or about 45% of all the lethals, possess a right breakpoint proximal to *su(f)*, namely, in Xh. If deficiencies with a breakpoint in Xh are excluded from the sample, then about 50% of the lethals consist of mutants involving only one complementation unit. For the neutron data, this proportion holds whether we include the lethals for the entire segment covered by $Ymal^+$ or exclude from the sample those mutants entirely or partially within the subsegment to the left of the distal breakpoint of *Df(1)B57*.

Lifschytz and Falk (1968) state that the "over-representation" in the sample of deficiencies with breakpoints in Xh (to the right) "would be compensated, however, by the loss of extensive lethals that reach beyond the regions covered by $Ymal^+$ to the 'left' ". However, it should be recognized that after preselecting a chromosome segment "whose length was defined by its homologous fragment which had been translocated to the Y-chromosome", the published analysis of X-ray lethals was limited to a proximal subsegment of this region. Therefore, the left limit of the defined segment was not preselected, but chosen as the distal breakpoint of *Df(1)B57*. This excluded from the analysis some lethals in the distal subsegment of the proximal Xe region covered by *Ymal*$^+$. From Fig. 1 it can be seen that the uncharted "left" subsegment in the X-ray analysis includes at least 20 bands, 18F4–5 and the 18 bands of 19A–D on the polytene chromosome map, and at least 9 complementation units on the genetic map. Be that as it may, the crucial point is not that any deficiency lethals were lost because they extend distally beyond the portion of Xe covered by *Ymal*$^+$, but whether, in calculating the proportion of lethals involving single complementation units within a defined segment, it is valid to include in the analysed sample any deficiencies with breakpoints outside the defined segment.

Properly speaking, the scoring of such deficiencies represents a selective sampling of multiple complementation unit lethals from a differently defined interval; at the same time, some of the possible single complementation unit lethals from this second interval, those beyond the limits of the defined segment, are excluded from the sample. More specifically, deficiencies with a breakpoint outside of the defined segment are produced in part by radiation-induced "hits" in the segments which flank the defined segment. Some other "hits" in the *proximal* flanking segment, i.e. in Xh, could produce alterations in the DNA of Xh which are identical with alterations in Xe, but because the DNA in Xh does not code for ordinary genes, these changes are not expressed as sex-linked lethals limited to single complementation units. Consequently, deficiencies with a breakpoint in Xh are properly excluded from the analysed sample because, whatever the number of complementation units they involve in the defined segment, deficiency producing "hits" in Xh can contribute to the score of lethals in the defined segments, but other Xh "hits" cannot. This argument holds whatever the relative "breakability" or Xh *vs.* Xe (see above). Some other "hits" in the *distal* flanking euchromatic segment would be capable of producing alterations in DNA that would have caused genetic changes limited to single complementation units, but these would map as ordinary sex-linked lethals in the left flanking segment. Therefore, the inclusion in the analysed sample of deficiencies with one breakpoint distal to the limit of the defined segment permits deficiency-producing "hits" from the left flanking segment to be scored as belonging to the defined segment, but the contribution of nondeficiency producing "hits", i.e. single complementation unit mutants, are recorded as lethals outside of the defined segment. Consequently, for the purpose of calculating the proportion of lethals involving single complementation units within the proximal segment of Xe adjacent to Xh, it is necessary to exclude deficiencies with a breakpoint beyond either boundary of the segment. The inclusion of such deficiencies illegitimately enriches the sample of lethals with genetic events involving more than one complementation unit.

Moreover, in the sample of 42 X-ray-induced lethals recovered by Lifschytz and Falk (1968), there were no deficiencies covered by $Ymal^+$ that extended from the left into the analysed segment, as they defined the segment. In the sample of 93 neutron-induced lethals, there were 4 deficiencies of this type (see Fig. 3). Furthermore, there is evidence to indicate that few lethals were missed because they represented deficiencies which extended distally beyond the region covered by $Ymal^+$. Kaufmann's (1946) analysis of polytene chromosome breakpoint distribution obtained from F_1 offspring of X-ray treated males showed that the frequency of breakage in the adjacent polytene chromosome sections 17 and 18 was much lower than that in section 19. If there were many X-ray-induced deficiencies that extended into the region analysed by Lifschytz and Falk from beyond the distal limit of Xe covered by $Ymal^+$, then such deficiencies would uncover the *sw* and *mal* loci. Accordingly these deficiencies would be observed in the F_1 as *sw* and *mal* mutants in specific locus tests, and would breed as male lethal mutations. Sobels (1962) recorded no male-lethal *sw* mutations following the exposure of mature sperm in adult males to 5000 of X-rays. He did detect 1 male viable *sw* mutant among 13,000 progeny scored. Fahmy and Fahmy (1959) recorded 8 male lethal *mal* mutations among 44,000 progeny following the exposure of largely post-meiotic sperm in adult males to 2,990 R of X-rays. Thus, in the experiment of Lifschytz and Falk (1968), in which largely post-meiotic sperm in adult males were exposed to 3200 R of X-rays and 5300 chromosomes were subjected to recessive lethal tests, not a single deficiency that reached beyond the region covered by $Ymal^+$ would have been expected.

Deficiencies that span almost the entire Xe segment covered by $Ymal^+$ or $y^+ Ymal^+$, such as $Df(1)mal^3$ and mal^{12} (Fig. 1), yields females of good viability and fertility. Among several hundred cytologically analysed X-ray-induced lethals distributed throughout the X chromosome, we have observed deficiencies involving section 18, but we have yet to find a deficiency that extends from 18E into section 19. This suggests that *M(1)n*, which is to the right of *car* at 18D1–2 on the polytene chromosome map, is located in section 18E or F. Females heterozygous for *M(1)n* have low viability and fertility; females heterozygous for a deficiency that includes all but the first two bands of section 18 and all of sections 19 and 20 (for example, $Df(1)y^{4L}sc^{8R}$) are poorly viable (Lindsley and Grell, 1968). Consequently, it is not surprising that deficiencies extending distally beyond the region covered by the *Ymal*$^{+}$ chromosomes are not readily recovered in radiation experiments, since females with such deficiencies are likely to be relatively inviable and poorly fertile as well.

The proximity to Xh of a euchromatic segment enriches with deficiency mutants any sample of radiation-induced mutants drawn from such a segment. Therefore, we have not considered, as Lifschytz and Falk have, that the high proportion of X-ray-induced lethals involving more than one complementation unit in the subsegment they analysed can be extrapolated to characterize the aberrational nature of most post-meiotic X-ray-induced mutations in the genome as a whole (Lifschytz and Falk, 1968, 1969; Falk, 1970b). Our re-evaluation of their data reduces the proportion of lethals involving more than one complementation unit from 86% to about 50% (10/19). The latter figure agrees with the neutron data (26/52).

The proportion of single and multiple functional unit lethals obtained from other defined segments in the genome has been analysed by combining complementation tests with cytogenetic tests for rearrangements. In a pioneering analysis of this type, Alikhanian (1937) studied 22 lethals and semi-lethals induced in the left end of the X-chromosome. Following the exposure of adult males to X-ray doses of 3500 R, 4000 R and 5000 R, Alikhanian found that 54% (12/22) of the mutations affected single functional units and showed no detectable chromosomal change in their polytene chromosomes. There were 10 rearrangements: 7 deficiencies, 1 translocation, 1 inversion and 1 undecipherable minute rearrangement. Hochman (Hochman *et al.*, 1964; Hochman, 1971) carried out a cytogenetic analysis on 41 X-ray induced lethals in chromosome 4. The lethals were obtained from adult males exposed to X-ray doses of 3000 R or more. Although no details are given, it is likely that most of the lethals came from post-meiotic germ cells. The later work increased the number of essential loci from the earlier figure of 22 to 33 and increased the number of analysed X-ray-induced mutants to 41. The final results showed: 30 lethals affecting single functional units and unconnected with rearrangements, 4 cytologically confirmed deficiencies, 3 suspected deficiencies and 4 translocations. Thus, 73% (30/41) of the X-ray-induced mutations were not rearrangements. For ethyl methanesulphonate-induced lethals, the proportion was 97% (70/72).

We believe that the analysis performed by Lifschytz and Falk does not permit sound inferences concerning the nature and proportion of X-ray-induced mutations confined to single complementation units. However, there is evidence on this point from the analysis of mutations within genetic units that can be categorized as single cistrons or complex loci. At the *ry* locus, all of the essentially unselected sample of 14 X-ray-induced mutants used in recombination studies proved to involve lesions that must have been considerably smaller than the entire cistron, since they were capable of intracistronic recombination (Chovnick *et al.*, 1964). Furthermore, there were 5 X-ray-induced mutants used in allele complementation and recombination analysis in the *mal* cistron. Three of the mutants showed allele complementation, and the two mutants which failed to complement shared this property with half of the 14 chemically induced mutants that were studied (Chovnick *et al.*, 1969). In fine-structure mapping, the 2 X-ray-induced mutants studied recombined as readily as did the chemically induced mutants (Finnerty *et al.*, 1970).

Additional evidence is provided by genetic studies on the *w* (Green, 1960) and *r* (Carlson, 1971) loci. All 13 X-ray-induced *w* mutants utilized in recombination analysis recombined in a manner that was indistinguishable from the spontaneous mutants tested. At the *r* locus, all 7 X-ray-induced mutants displayed recombinational behavior and complementation properties which were no different from those of 38 chemically induced and spontaneous mutants. Consequently, whatever the nature of the intracistronic and intra-locus lesions produced by X-rays in *Drosophila*, the above described operations failed to differentiate them from genetic changes produced by more than a dozen chemical mutagens, including ethyl methanesulphonate. As a result, we fail to see how the observation that the vast majority of ethyl methanesulphonate mutations induced in the proximal X region involved single complementation units can be claimed to "support our previous conclusion that X-ray-induced lethals were nearly always aberrations" (Lifschytz and Falk, 1969). Furthermore, the observations at the *ry*, *mal*, *w* and *r* loci cited above demonstrate that, if one desires to infer that "visible mutations induced by X-rays were deficiencies at nonessential loci" (Lifschytz and Falk, 1968), then such deficiencies must involve only a small fraction of the genetic length of the loci and differ in no manner from chemically induced mutations used in the same experiments.

D. A Possible Influence of the Method of Detection on the proportion of Deficiency Mutations

Mutant alterations in more than 50% of the genes thus identified in the proximal X region are capable of being expressed as morphological changes in adult flies. Most of these are by no means subtle changes. This observation indicates that the manner in which mutations are initially recognized can influence the accuracy of conclusions concerning mutation frequency and the nature of induced mutations. In the work where such analyses have been attempted (Lifschytz and Falk, 1968, 1969; Lifschytz, 1971), the mutants used for genetic tests were originally chosen from a population of sex-linked recessive lethals distributed along the entire length of the X chromosome. These lethals were obtained by conventional tests, and there is no indication in the published reports that visible mutants with or without semi-lethal effects, which may have been observed in the original F_2 test generation, were saved for possible coverage by the *Ymal*$^+$ chromosome. Such visible mutants were not included in the sample of neutron-induced mutants detected by Munoz, who used essentially the same procedures. Although a number of mutants originally scored as lethals have turned out to be visible mutants with reduced viabilities, many mutants of loci with dispensable functions must have been missed. In the subsequent complementation analysis some such loci may be detected, but this will depend on the chance occurrence that two deficiencies will overlap by only a single nonessential gene. Other mutants of this sort have been placed in our complementation map, but this was possible only because pre-existing visible mutants, whose linkage map positions suggested their proximal location, were available for testing.

If the type of screening described above is not competent to identify loci capable of producing visible or even semi-lethal mutants, methods originally described by Shapiro (1937) are available for this purpose. These methods or their modifications have been applied to segments at or near the end of the X chromosome (Alikhanian, 1937; Judd *et al.*, 1972) and to the rosy region of the third chromosome (Schalet *et al.*, 1964) to cite just a few examples.

Aside from the fact that the proximity of a segment to Xh produces an enrichment of aberration-related mutants in any sample of lethal mutants produced by mutagens such as X-rays and neutrons, which are "efficient" in the production of aberrations, a process of selection which excludes visible mutations in the initial screening generation will by itself increase the relative proportion of deficiencies among the analysed mutants. This is because recessive sex-linked visibles and lethals detected by a conventional *Basc* type test do not represent subsamples from the same population of various types of genetic events. Ordinarily, a lethal phenotype will be produced either by a change limited to a single essential gene (included here are changes associated with inversions and translocations) or by a deletion of two or more adjacent genes. In the latter event, when even as few as two genes are involved, neither need necessarily be an essential gene, provided the absence of both functions is sufficient to produce a lethal effect. By contrast, a visible phenotype will usually be limited to a change in a single gene (included here are changes associated with inversions and translocations). Only infrequently will two nonessential genes lie adjacent to one another and their double loss lead to no important impairment in viability. The *y* and *ac* loci provide a classical example of this type (Muller, 1935). In *w* and *rst*, as well as in *mal* and *mell*, we have other examples. The viability of the deficiency for both *vao* and *unc* is approximately 15%, but only when special care is taken to prevent overcrowding. Thus, when the sample of mutants to be analysed by complementation tests is restricted to mutants that behave as lethals in screening generation, there must be selection against mutants limited to single complementation units. The degree of this selection can be ascertained only by determining the proportion of nonessential genes in the segment, the proportion of mutant changes in essential genes which produce an obvious morphological change without significant impairment in viability, and the relative mutability of each gene in the segment. However, the fact that more than 50% of the genes in the proximal X region can produce visible mutant forms suggests that the selection against single unit mutants may not have been inconsiderable.

IX. Crossing Over in the Proximal Xe-Xh Region

A. Crossing Over in the Proximal Xe in Normal and Inverted Sequences

Our knowledge about linkage relationships in proximal Xe and Xh is still primitive. A considerable portion of the linkage data for the region derives from control values for experiments designed for diverse purposes. In a study having the avowed purpose of examining "recombinational patterns" in the region (Lifschytz and Falk, 1970; Lifschytz, 1971), the analysis is, for the most part, defeated because of errors in the positioning and characterization of many mutants (Schalet, 1972b; Schalet and Lefevre, 1973) and the lack of effective internal controls.

As far as it can be ascertained, *su(f)* is the most proximal ordinary sex-linked mutant and accordingly may serve as a close marker for the E–H junction. Recombination proximal to *su(f)*, whatever its nature, is ordinarily well below 0·1%. Consequently, for most purposes, measurements of crossing over in all or part of Xe proximal to *car* may properly utilize either *su(f)* or $Dp(1;1)sc^{V1}y^{+}$ to mark the centromere end of the chromosome. In contrast to other *Dp(1;1)* fragments that have been used in the past, $Dp(1;1)sc^{V1}y^{+}$ has no detectable effect on crossing over in proximal Xe or Xh. The standard recombination values of 5·8% for the *f–car* interval and 3·5% for the *car*–centromere interval were established some forty years ago. Although such values are encountered in the subsequent literature, significantly higher values, up to 7·5% (and sometimes higher) for *f–car* and 4·7% for *car*–centromere, have frequently been reported in comparable experiments performed under essentially standard conditions (for example, R. F. Grell, 1962; Hinton, 1965; Williamson, 1966; Roberts, 1969; see also Herskowitz *et al.*, 1962; Schalet and Finnerty, 1968b). Comparably high values, 7·4% for *f–car* and 4·4% for *car–bb*, can be calculated from the very extensive data of Bridges for the entire X chromosome used by Weinstein (1936).

In view of these results from carefully performed experiments, it would appear that standard linkage values for the proximal X are unreliable and that the true values are significantly higher. Thus, it is not surprising that in the absence of a marker for the centromere end of the chromosome, the common practice of reckoning linkage map positions for newly discovered, proximally located, visible and lethal mutants by adding their recombination values with *car* or *f* to their standard map positions can lead to serious errors in the actual position of the new mutant. For example, compare the positions of *lf* and *su(f)* as given in Fig. 1 with their linkage map positions of 68·1 and 65·9, respectively, as given by Lindsley and Grell (1968). Furthermore, linkage map positions for *rfr* and *gr* are given as 67·9 and 72·,0 respectively; yet, both mutants must be to the left of *ot* since they are not covered by either $mal^{+}Y$ or $y^{+}Ymal^{106}$. We heartily agree with Lindsley and Grell that the map (based on linkage values) should be treated only as a rough guide to the relative positions of loci.

When it is desired to compare recombination values from different crosses involving cytologically normal lethal (or visible) mutants, it is essential that in each cross a measurement be made of a flanking interval common to all crosses. Accordingly, a four point cross such as $y\ car\ l^{1}/y + l^{2}.\ Dp(1;1)sc^{V1}y^{+}\ X\ y\ car/Y$ would seem to be a minimum requirement for a proper study. Thus, for a comparison of the crossover frequencies between lethals 1 and 2 in one cross and lethals 1 and 3 in another cross, the values actually observed might have to be adjusted according to possible differences in crossover values for the entire *car–Dp* interval. If recombinants are scored only among male progeny in crosses between two tightly linked lethals, the use of flanking markers is essential for the correct interpretation of events responsible for the occurrence of individuals which appear to be lethal-free males. This is especially necessary when only a few such flies are recovered. Even in chromosomal regions where extraneous influences do not appear to inhibit recombination, crossover values of 0·02% or less have been reported between closely linked, apparently unrelated loci (Schalet *et al.*, 1964, for the *ry* region; Lefevre, 1971, for the *v* region; Judd *et al.*, 1972, and Rayle and Green, 1968, for the *z–w* region). For example, males representing one-half of the crossovers between two loci have been observed at the rate of 0·0075% (12/159,000, Rayle and Green, 1968). Therefore, it is not unreasonable to consider the extent to which rare events that occur at a frequency of

0·01%, or even higher, can produce flies which may be mistaken for recombinants, but are actually unconnected with recombination between two lethal loci. In the absence of appropriate outside markers, rare 2X:3A individuals can be misclassified as recombinants. Upon careful examination the intersex characteristics of such individuals are usually discernible. However, sometimes these flies cannot be distinguished from normal males on the basis of external morphology; therefore, fertility tests of otherwise vigorous "male recombinants" should be mandatory. Although flies resulting from either spontaneous recessive sex-linked or dominant autosomal suppressors or reverse mutations would likely be even less frequent than intersexes, in large-scale experiments which fail either to use flanking markers or to test the few exceptional progeny, the possibility of such events cannot be excluded.

Unfortunately, most of the reported recombination data for the proximal Xe segment covered by y^+ *Ymal*$^+$ and *Ymal*$^+$, and represented in the polytene chromosomes by sections 19 and 20, has been accumulated in experiments which for one or another of the reasons cited above do not permit valid comparisons between the recombination frequencies found in different crosses. The results, such as they are, indicate that recombination values in the *mal*–centromere interval may differ by as much as 1·0%. For instance, Lifschytz and Falk (1968) stated that the recombination frequency between *lethal(1)AA33* and *lethal(1)D13* was 1·5%; whereas, the frequency between their respective alleles, *lethal(1)P235* and *lethal(1)R–9–18*, was 2·2%. The frequency for the somewhat shorter interval between *lethal(1)P235* and *lethal(1)Q463* was given as 2·3% by Lifschytz (1971). For the *mal-su(f)* interval, Schalet (1972a) reported a value of 1·5%. Aside from the figure of 1·5% between *AA33* and *D13*, for which no data were presented, each of the above determinations was based on an assay of more than 10,000 gametes. This variance in recombination values, previously noted for the *f–car* and *car*–centromere intervals (see similar results for the centric region of chromosome 3, Arajärvi and Hannah-Alava, 1969) has restrained us from assigning linkage map positions to the visible mutants listed in Table I.

Based on the standard map lengths and the higher recombination values mentioned above, the observed lengths of the *f–car* (5·8–7·4%) and *car*–centromere (3·5–4·7%) intervals yield percent crossing over/band values of 0·046–0·058 and 0·049–0·065 respectively. If crossing over in these segments occurred as freely as in the long central portion of the X from *w–f*, where the percent crossing over/band is 0·078 (Lefevre, 1971), then the map lengths would be 9·9% for *f–car* and 5·6% for *car*–centromere. This calculated length of approximately 15% for the *f*–centromere interval is in fact achieved when the equivalent euchromatic interval is placed distally, as in the *In(1)sc*^{8} chromosome (see below). Consequently, it is legitimate to consider that the lower percent crossing over/band values in the *f*–centromere interval reflect an inhibition of crossing over associated with proximity to the centromere.

In so far as can be judged from the paucity of and the proportionately higher variance in available crossover data for the *mal*–centromere region, the percent crossing over/band values appear to be about the same as for the longer *car*–centromere interval. On at least two counts, it is difficult to determine whether significantly lower values are to be found in the most proximal segment, the region to the right of *l(1)A7*, which is represented on the polytene chromosome map by the bands proximal to 20A1–2. First, it is practically impossible to resolve the actual number of bands in 20B–F. Second, as the number of bands in an interval becomes smaller, then, provided crossing over occurs in proportion to DNA content (Lefevre, 1971), the quality of the bands, i.e. their DNA content, not the band number becomes the important consideration. In comparisons of two long intervals, the relative proportion of thick and thin bands in each interval is likely to be about the same, but this does not necessarily apply to comparisons between short and long segments.

Data interpreted as indicative of a possible influence of the centromere on crossing over was presented by Beadle (1932), who compared crossing over in normal third chromosomes with crossing over in a homozygous 3–4 translocation. In the translocation, the most proximal segments studied in 3L were closer to the centromere (of chromosome 4) than in the normal third and showed a very marked reduction in crossing over. Similarly, Offermann and Muller (1932) and Stone (1934) reported that segments of the X chromosome placed closer to the centromere (of the X or 4) in flies homozygous for X–4 translocations showed reductions in crossover values. Furthermore, when Offermann and Muller (1932) followed crossing over in females homozygous for *In(1)sc*^{8}, whose proximal break is in Xh, they found not only that there was reduced crossing over in the normally distal segments placed close to the centromere end, but also that segments normally close to the centromere showed increased crossing over in their new distal positions. Most of the subsequently reported data for normally distal segments placed close to the centromere have involved *In(1)sc*^{8} (Stone and Thomas, 1935; Sturtevant and Beadle, 1936; Mather, 1939; Roberts, 1969), but data from other inversions with proximal breakpoints in Xh, including sc^{4}, bb^{Df}, $sc^{4L}sc^{8R}/sc^{8L}sc^{8R}$ (Sturtevant and Beadle, 1936; Mather, 1939; Novitski, 1951) agree in showing a consistent reduction in crossing over. Likewise, subsequently obtained data for normally proximal segments placed distally in the tested inversions, sc^{4}, sc^{8}, rst^{3}, w^{m4}, $sc^{S1L}sc^{8R}$, $sc^{4L}sc^{8R}$, $sc^{4L}sc^{8R}/sc^{8L}sc^{8R}$ (Stone and Thomas, 1935; Grüneberg, 1935; Sturtevant and Beadle, 1936; Mather, 1939; Novitski, 1951; Falk, 1955; Braver, 1956, 1957; Schalet, 1969b and unpublished data) have generally shown an increase in crossing over, even when comparison is made with the higher than standard frequencies of 7·4% for the *f–car* interval and 4·7% for the *car*–centromere interval. One clear exception to the foregoing results is Roberts' (1969) failure to find an increase in the distal *y–car* and *car–f* intervals of *In(1)sc*^{8}, even though in a separate experiment with *In(1)sc*^{8} he showed that the displacement to the centromere region of the *w*^{a}*–cv* interval resulted in recombination values of about one-third the normal value.

In the papers referred to in the previous paragraph, extensive data obtained for distal segments in the *sc*^{8} inversion indicated that in the *y–f* interval, equivalent to the *f*–centromere interval in the uninverted chromosome, there was 15% or more crossing over. Less extensive data were obtained for the *y–car* and *car–f* subsegments. For *In(1)rst*^{3}, values of 9·8%, 8·8% and 10·1% were observed for the *car–f* interval (Grüneberg, 1935; Mather, 1939; Braver, 1956) as compared to 6·5% and 8·8% (Stone and Thomas, 1935), 9·5% (Sturtevant and Beadle, 1936) and 10·8% (Mather, 1939) for *car–f* in *In(1)sc*^{8}. In the earlier experiments of Grüneberg and Mather, the high values for the *y–car* interval, 18·6% and 15·6%, later confirmed by Braver (1956, 1957), permitted Mather to infer that a substantial portion of the increased crossing over occurred in the Xh subsegment, which in its distal portion was free from the inhibiting effect of the centromere. In *In(1)rst*^{3}, the *w–car* interval is essentially comparable to *y–car* in *In(1)sc*^{8} with respect to its euchromatic content. Nevertheless, as Braver showed, crossing over in the *w–car* interval measured 10·8% and 10·1% in two experiments, or about twice the value which was reported for the *y–car* interval in *In(1)sc*^{8} by Stone and Thomas (1935) and Mather (1939).

B. Crossing Over in Distally Located Xh

Cooper's (1959) mitotic analysis of *In(1)rst*^{3} and *In(1)sc*^{8}, showed that the distal Xh segment of *In(1)sc*^{8} is about four times the length of the distal Xh segment of *In(1)rst*^{3}. Although the data for *y–car* is relatively scanty, the possibility cannot be discounted that the difference in recombination values between *In(1)rst*^{3} and *In(1)sc*^{8} is real and that there is a substantial amount of crossing over in the distal Xh of *In(1)rst*^{3}, but little in the distal Xh of *In(1)sc*^{8}, despite its relatively greater length. Indeed, Schalet (1972a, see below) found that crossing over in the distal Xh of *In(1)sc*^{8} ordinarily does not exceed 0·05%. However, it is possible to ascribe this low value to an inhibitory effect associated with the telomere of the X. In normal chromosomes, this is expressed as a low crossing over/band ratio extending from the telomere to the *z* locus at the map position of 1·0 (Slizynska, 1938; Redfield, 1955). The data of Judd *et al.* (1972, Fig. 4) show that the percent crossing over/band in the *z–w* interval is close to if not identical with the figure of 0·078% calculated by Lefevre (1971) for the long central portion of the X in which crossing over is free from inhibition by the telomere or centromere. Since the distal breakpoint of $In(1)rst^3$ is to the right of the *w* locus at 1·5, in contrast to the distal breakpoint of $In(1)sc^8$ between *ac* and *sc* immediately to the right of *y* at 0·0, telomere suppression of crossing would not be expected to affect the distal Xh of $In(1)rst^3$. In any event, measurement of crossing over in the distal Xh of $In(1)rst^3$, which would be possible by marking the segment with *w* and *su(f)*, could provide a decisive answer to the question of whether crossing over occurs in the distal Xh of $In(1)rst^3$.

A proper marking of the limits of the distal Xh segment has been achieved for $In(1)sc^8$ by introducing *y* and *su(f)*. For the *y–su(f)* interval, combined results of four experiments yielded a recombination frequency of 0·033% (27/82,000, Schalet, 1972a, experiments 2a, 3a, b and 4). This frequency was about one order of magnitude lower than the 0·41% (19/4,587) reported earlier for the *bb* locus alone in the $In(1)sc^8$ chromosome (Schalet, 1969b). However, this last value was obtained in a special system that utilized two deficiencies, $Df(1)y^{X2}$ and $Df(1)mal^{12}$, each of which lacked part of the *bb* locus and extended into the euchromatic region on one or the other side of the distal Xh, thereby permitting the selection of exchanges in Xh confined to the *bb* locus. Such exchanges occurred in this system even though crossing over distal to *B* was reduced to about 1–2%, as compared to the usual 15% in $In(1)sc^8$ chromosomes. Even more curious was the observation that, after visible markers had been inserted into the segments to the right of *B* in the original $In(1)sc^8$ chromosomes carrying $Df(1)y^{X2}$ and $Df(1)mal^{12}$, the frequency of *bb* locus exchange dropped to about 0·024%, i.e. there were only 5 possible crossovers in approximately 21,000 gametes assayed.

C. Crossing Over in Normally Located Xh

At the time of the initial observations that an extensive proximal portion of the X chromosome, as seen in mitotic figures, did not appear to contain any of the then known sex-linked genes (except for *bb*, which was also present on the Y chromosome), it was appreciated that there was little or no crossing over in this segment (Muller and Painter, 1932; Dobzhansky, 1932). The complete absence of ordinary sex-linked genes in a proximal segment of considerable size was confirmed by the synthesis (Gershenson,

1933) and detection (Sivertzev–Dobzhansky and Dobzhansky, 1933) of *bb*-deficient X chromosomes, $In(1)sc^{4L}sc^{8R}$ and $In(1)bb^{Df}$, which were viable and fertile as X/Y males, but were reduced cytologically to approximately 2/3–3/4 of the length of the normal mitotic X. Heitz (1934b) and Kaufmann (1934) pointed out that the proximal region, which Muller and Painter had characterized as "relatively inert genetically", seemed to correspond to the region which cytologically had been characterized as heteropycnotic. Accurate tests to determine whether there was any crossing over in Xh would have required the proper identification of the most proximal gene on the linkage map (other than *bb*), and its relationship to the E–H junction. Such a task was perhaps beyond the state of the cytogenetic art of the time; even now our designation of *su(f)* at that locus is subject to some reservation.

In the absence of a genetic marker for the E–H junction, the medial position of *bb* in Xh and the availability of special duplications attached to the right of the X centromere permit the measurement of crossing over between *bb* and the centromere. Indeed, Muller and Painter (1932) and Dobzhansky (1932) noted that the work of Stern (1929) had already given evidence on this point. Stern's experiment had shown that in the presence of a part of the Y chromosome containing bb^{+} attached to the proximal end of the X, there were no crossovers to the right of *bb* among some 4,000 offspring in which such crossovers could have been detected. In the same experiment, crossing over between *B* and *bb* appeared to be normal. In an experiment of comparable magnitude where the centromere end was marked by a duplication derived from the X chromosome, Dobzhansky (1932) recovered two apparent crossovers to the right of *bb*, but he could not distinguish them from spontaneous detachments of the duplication. In a similar, but smaller experiment involving several hundred offspring, Muller and Painter (1932) failed to detect any crossing over proximal to *bb*, although crossing over between *f* and *bb* was reported to be normal.

No doubt the best work providing evidence for crossing over between *bb* and the centromere was presented by Brown (1940). From a cross of *f car bb; ey*/+++*T*(*1;4*)females to *Y*/*f car bb; ey* males, female progeny were scored for apparent crossovers between *bb* and the centromere marked by *ey*. Scrupulous tests were performed to eliminate those flies which appeared to be crossovers between *bb* and the centromere, but were actually derived from other recognized genetic events. Among 20,000 flies scored, there were 15 cases considered to be verified crossovers. These included 5 individuals believed to represent a simultaneous additional crossover between *car* and *bb*, and one individual thought to have resulted from an additional crossover between *f* and *car*. However, only recently has it been appreciated that the structure of the *bb* locus itself is such as to invalidate the use of a *bb* marker in experiments of this type, or in experiments designed to detect the possibility of crossing over in Xh distal to the *bb* locus. Since the *bb* locus is organized as a set of linearly repeated genes capable of undergoing inter- and intra-chromosomal exchange with one another and the *bb* phenotype is usually dependent upon the number of such genes present (Ritossa *et al.*, 1966; Schalet, 1969b), in Brown's experiment some crossovers within the *bb* locus could have produced progeny with *bb* or bb^+ phenotypes that would have been indistinguishable from flies derived from crossovers in Xh to the left or to the right of the *bb* locus. Accordingly, of the 15 flies observed by Brown, 9 (8 bb^+ *ey*, 1 *f* bb^+ *ey*) could just as well have come from inter-chromosomal *bb* locus crossovers, 4 (3 *f car* bb^+ *ey*, 1 *car* bb^+ *ey*) could have been generated by intra-chromosomal *bb* locus exchanges, and 2 *bb* individuals could have been derived from either intra-chromosomal *bb* exchanges or partial deletions of the *bb* locus. Similarly, the two cases found by Dobzhansky (1932) would have originated as *bb* locus exchanges. Therefore, Brown's work actually demonstrated that crossing over could occur either within the *bb* locus or between *bb* and the centromere.

There are two additional reports in the literature which bear on the question of crossing over between the *bb* locus and the centromere, but as before the interpretation of the results is ambiguous. In both experiments females of the type *y car* +. *Dp* $y^+/y+bb^l$ were crossed to males bearing a Y^{bb-} chromosome. Atwood (1969) found no *y* males among approximately 30,000 male offspring and regarded this result as indicating that no exchanges occurred proximal to *bb*. (In another experiment which employed the same *Dp(1;1)112*, Atwood noted that when the female parents possessed a bb^+ locus in both X chromosomes, recombination between *car* and y^+ was only 2·1%.) However, in the controls for experiments concerned with induced crossing over in the proximal region, Hayashi and Suzuki (1968) reported that 12–15 *y* males appeared among 103,545 male offspring. These numbers include 5 or 6 males among 38,000 male offspring from parental females heterozygous for autosomal inversions, but as these data showed and Roberts (1965) had reported earlier, such inversions have no effect upon exchanges in Xh. These experiments utilized *Dp(1;1)*sc^{V1}, and the recombination frequency between *car* and bb^l (in the absence of the inversions) was 3·5%. Again, the *y* males noted in these experiments may have originated (1) as *bb* locus exchanges in which pairing was polarized so that the shorter bb^l segment paired at the proximal end of the longer bb^+ segment to produce a bb^+ recombinant chromosome, (2) as exchanges in Xh proximal to the *bb* locus, or (3) as spontaneous losses of the y^+ marker in the duplication.

Experiments have been designed to detect crossing over within the *bb* locus in normal chromosomes (Atwood, 1969; Schalet, 1972a). Starting with parental females which carried a bb^+ locus in each X chromosome, Schalet tested about 50 offspring which were recombinant for the *su(f)* to *Dp(1;1)sc*^{V1}*y*$^+$ interval. There were two independent cases including one apparent cluster, in which the recombinant chromosome was mutant at the *bb* locus. The test permitted the detection of only those *bb* locus exchanges which resulted in a sufficiently reduced number of *bb* genes to produce a *bb* or lethal phenotype over a bb^- ($sc^{4L}sc^{8R}$) chromosome. The reciprocal crossover class could not have been identified as a *bb* exchange, nor could symmetrical *bb* locus exchanges that produce no change in the number of *bb* genes have been detected. Atwood directly selected for *bb* mutants among F_1 males that possessed a Y^{-bb} chromosome. He detected 5 *bb* mutants, but none of these were associated with the exchange of flanking markers. However, Atwood's method of selection was such as to prevent the recovery of *bb–lethal* alleles or alleles which did not severely retard development. Under these conditions, Atwood would have missed the two cases like those found by Schalet which showed only a slight retardation of developmental time.

Although it has not been determined whether crossing over in Xh distal to the *bb* locus occurs in a normal chromosome, the measurement of recombination between *su(f)* and *Dp(1;1)sc*^{V1}*y*$^+$ in experiments where the adjacent distal region, *car–su(f)* or *mal–su(f)*, shows no obvious reduction in crossing over should provide a maximum estimate of the amount of crossing over in the entire Xh. From experiments in which the condition of the *bb* locus in the parental females was not readily known, combined values yielded a frequency of 0·027%, 13/47,000 (Herskowitz *et al.*, 1962; Roberts, 1965, 1969). For parental females with bb^+ in both X chromosomes, Schalet (1972a, experiment 1b) found 0·019% crossing over among about 50,000 gametes assayed. In experiment 1a, 0·12% crossing over occurred among some 53,000 gametes assayed from females (sisters of the females in experiment 1b) which had inadvertently been placed at 17°C for three or four days prior to eclosion. In the experiments just cited, the equality of the complementary recombinant classes indicated that the spontaneous loss of the y^+ marker of *Dp(1;1)sc*^{V1}, which would have produced a fly simulating a recombinant, made no appreciable contribution to the observed recombination frequencies.

The foregoing results on recombination in the proximal region of the X chromosome may be summarized as follows: In females with free X chromosomes, crossing over occurs in Xh in normal and *In(1)sc*^{8} chromosones at frequencies that generally range betweeen 0·01% and 0·1%. At least some exchange takes place within the *bb* locus. If *su(f)* is actually within Xh, another class of exchange in Xh occurs either within *su(f)* or between *su(f)* and *bb*. In any case, the evidence presented thus far has neither convincingly demonstrated nor assuredly eliminated the possibility that some of the observed crossovers between *su(f)* and the centromere (or the equivalent interval in *In(1)sc*^{8}) are in the Xh segments flanking the *bb* locus. Furthermore, it is not known to what extent the inhibition of crossing over attributed to the presence of the centromere contributes to the rarity of crossing over in Xh. However, in contrast to crossing over in the adjacent Xe, the presence of autosomal inversions has no effect on crossing over in Xh. This lack of effect is perhaps associated with indications that at least some Xh exchanges in free X chromosomes are of premeiotic origin (Schalet, 1972a). These observations are in accord with earlier reports that spontaneous detachments of compound-X chromosomes which involve Xh sometimes occur in clusters.

References

ALDERSON, T. (1965). Chemically induced delayed germinal mutation in *Drosophila*. *Nature, Lond.* **207,** 164–167.

ALIKHANIAN, S. I. (1937). A study of the lethal mutations in the left end of the sex-chromosome in *Drosophila melanogaster*. *Zool. Zhur.* **16,** 247–278. (Russian with English summary.)

ARAJÄRVI, P. and HANNAH-ALAVA, A. (1969). Cytogenetic mapping of *in* and *ri*. *Dros. Inf. Serv.* **44,** 73–74.

ATWOOD, K. C. (1969). Some aspects of the *bobbed* problem in *Drosophila*. *Genetics* **61,** Suppl. 1, 319–327.

BAUER, H. (1939). Röntgenauslösung von Chromosomenmutationen bei *Drosophila melanogaster*. I. Bruchhäufigkeit,-Verteilung und -Rekombination nach Speicheldrüsenuntersuchung. *Chromosoma* **1,** 343–390.

BAUER, H., DEMEREC, M. and KAUFMANN, B. P. (1938). X-ray induced chromosomal alterations in *Drosophila melanogaster*. *Genetics* **23,** 610–630.

BEADLE, G. W. (1932). A possible influence of the spindle fibre on crossing-over in *Drosophila*. *Proc. Natl. Acad. Sci. U.S.A.* **18,** 160–165.

BEERMANN, W. (1962). Riesenchromosomen. Protoplasmologia. "Handbuch der Protoplasmaforschung" Vol. 6 D, 1–161. Springer-Verlag, Wien.

BEERMANN, W. (1972). Chromomeres and Genes. *In* "Results and Problems in Cell Differentiation", Vol. 4, "Developmental Studies with Giant Chromosomes" (W. Beermann, H. Ursprung and J. Reinert, eds.), pp. 1–33. Springer-Verlag, Heidelberg.

BELGOVSKY, M. L. (1938). Influence of inert regions of chromosomes on the frequency of occurrence and type of changes in adjacent activite sections. *Izv. Akad. Nauk SSSR*, Ots. mat.-est., Ser. biol., 1017–1036. (Russian with English summary.)

BELGOVSKY, M. L. (1939). Dependence of the frequency of minute chromosome rearrangements in *Drosophila melanogaster* upon X-ray dosage. *Izv. Akad. Nauk SSSR*, Ser. biol., 2, 159–170. (Russian with English summary.)

BERENDES, H. D. (1970). Polytene Chromosome Structure at the Submicroscopic Level. I. A Map of Region X, 1–4 E of *Drosophila melanogaster*. *Chromosoma*, **29,** 118–130.

BIRD, M. J. and FAHMY, O. G. (1953). Cytogenetic analysis of the action of carcinogens and tumour inhibitors in *Drosophila melanogaster*. I. 1:2, 3:4-diepoxybutane, *Proc. Roy. Soc.* (*Lond.*), **B 140,** 556–578.

BRAVER, G. (1956). Crossing over in the distal euchromatin of homozygous *In(1)rst*^{3}. *Dros. Inf. Serv.* **30,** 105.

BRAVER, G. (1957). Crossing over in *In(1)rst*^{3}. (Abstr.) *Rec. Genet. Soc. Amer.*, **26,** and *Genetics* **42,** 361.

BRIDGES, C. B. (1935). Salivary chromosome maps. With a key to the banding of the chromosomes of *Drosophila melanogaster*. *J. Hered.* **26,** 60–64.

BRIDGES, C. B. (1938). A revised map of the salivary gland X-chromosome of *Drosophila melanogaster*. *J. Hered.* **29,** 11–13.

BROSSEAU, G. E., NICOLETTI, B., GRELL, E. H. and LINDSLEY, D. L. (1961). Production of altered Y chromosome bearing specific sections of the X chromosome in *Drosophila*. *Genetics* **46,** 339–346.

BROWN, M. S. (1940). Chiasma formation in the *bobbed* region of the X chromosome of *Drosophila melanogaster*. *Univ. Texas Publ.*, *No.* **4032,** 65–72.

CARLSON, E. A. and OSTER, I. I. (1962). Comparative mutagenesis of the dumpy locus in *Drosophila melanogaster*. II. Mutational mosaicism induced without apparent breakage by a monofunctional alkylating agent. *Genetics* **47,** 561–576.

CARLSON, P. S. (1971). A genetic analysis of the *rudimentary* locus of *Drosophila melanogaster*. *Genet. Res.* **17,** 53–81.

CHANDLEY, A. C. (1965). Application of the "distributive pairing" hypothesis to problems of segregation in translocation heterozygotes of *Drosophila melanogaster*. *Genetics* **52,** 247–258.

CHOVNICK, A., SCHALET, A., KERNAGHAN, R. P. and KRAUSS, M. (1964). The rosy cistron in *Drosophila melanogaster*: Genetic fine structure analysis. *Genetics* **50,** 1245–1259.

CHOVNICK, A., FINNERTY, V., SCHALET, A. and DUCK, P. (1969). Studies on genetic organization in higher organisms: I. Analysis of a complex gene in *Drosophila melanogaster*. *Genetics* **62,** 145–160.

COOPER, K. W. (1959). Cytogenetic analysis of major heterochromatic elements (especially Xh and Y) in *Drosophila melanogaster* and the theory of "heterochromatin". *Chromosoma* **10,** 535–588.

DOBZHANSKY, T. (1932). Cytological map of the X-chromosome of *Drosophila melanogaster*. *Biol. Zbl.* **52,** 493–509.

EDINGTON, C. W., EPLER, J. L. and REGAN, J. D. (1962). The frequency-dose relation of X-ray-induced Y-suppressed lethals in *Drosophila*. *Genetics* **47,** 397–406.

EPLER, J. L. (1966). Ethyl methanesulphonate-induced lethals in *Drosophila*—frequency-dose relations and multiple mosaicism. *Genetics* **54,** 31–36.

EPLER, J. L. and EDINGTON, C. W. (1963). Y-suppressed lethals in immature germ cells of *Drosophila melanogaster*. *Dros. Inf. Serv.* **38,** 61.

FAHMY, O. G. and FAHMY, M. J. (1959). Differential gene response to mutagens in *Drosophila melanogaster*. *Genetics* **44,** 1149–1171.

FALK, R. (1955). A chromosome for the detection of the locus of lethals induced in the Muller-5 chromosome. *Dros. Inf. Serv.* **29,** 115.

FALK, R. (1970a). Evidence against the one-to-one correspondence between bands of the salivary gland chromosome and genes. *Dros. Inf. Serv.* **45,** 112.

FALK, R. (1970b). Induced recessive lethals in the ring X-chromosome of *Drosophila. Mutation Res.* **10,** 53–60.

FALK, R. (1973). Breakage and rejoining in a short segment of the X-chromosome of *Drosophila melanogaster. In*: "Chromosomes Today" (J. Wahrman and K. R. Lewis, eds.) vol. 4, pp. 283–296, Israel Universities Press, Jerusalem.

FINNERTY, V. G., DUCK, P. and CHOVNICK, A. (1970). Studies on genetic organization in higher organisms, II. Complementation and fine structure of the *maroon-like* locus of *Drosophila melanogaster. Proc. Natl. Acad. Sci. U.S.A.* **65,** 939–946.

GALL, J. G., COHEN, E. H. and POLAN, M. L. (1971). Repetitive DNA sequences in *Drosophila. Chromosoma* **33,** 319–344.

GERSHENSON, S. (1933). Studies on the genetically inert region of the X-chromosome of *Drosophila.* I. Behavior of an X-chromosome deficient for a part of its inert region. *J. Genet.* **29,** 297–313.

GREEN, M. M. (1960). Comparative mutability of wild-type isoalleles at the white loci in *Drosophila melanogaster. Genet. Res.* **1,** 452–461.

GRELL, R. F. (1962). A new model for secondary nondisjunction: The role of distributive pairing. *Genetics* **47,** 1737–1754.

GRÜNEBERG, H. (1935). A new inversion of the X-chromosome in *Drosophila melanogaster. J. Genet.* **31,** 163–184.

HANNAH, A. (1951). Localization and function of heterochromatin in *Drosophila melanogaster. Advanc. Genet.* **4,** 87–125.

HAYASHI, S. and SUZUKI, D. T. (1968). A comparative study of induced increases in proximal recombination in *Drosophila melanogaster* females. *Can. J. Genet. Cytol.* **10,** 276–282.

HEITZ, E. (1934a). Eine Beziehung zwischen genischen und strukturellen Längsdifferenzierung des X-Chromosoms von *Drosophila melanogaster. Z. indukt. Abstamm. VererbLehre* **67,** 216–217.

HEITZ, E. (1934b). Über α und β-Heterochromatin sowie Konstanz und Bau der Chromomeren bei *Drosophila. Biol. Zbl.* **54,** 588–609.

HERSKOWITZ, I. H., SCHALET, A., REUTER, M. DEL VAL (1962). Induced changes in female germ cells of *Drosophila.* VII. Exchanges induced in different X chromosome regions after X-raying oocytes and oogonia. *Genetics* **47,** 1663–1678.

HINTON, C. W. (1965). The effects of heterozygous autosomal translocations on recombination in the X chromosome of *Drosophila melanogaster. Genetics* **51,** 971–982.

HOCHMAN, B. (1971). Analysis of chromosome 4 in *Drosophila melanogaster.* II: Ethyl methanesulphonate induced lethals. *Genetics* **67,** 235–252.

HOCHMAN, B. (1972). The detection of four more vital loci on chromosome 4 in *Drosophila melanogaster.* (Abstr.) *Genetics* **71,** s71.

HOCHMAN, B., GLOOR, H. and GREEN, M. M. (1964). Analysis of chromosome 4 in *Drosophila melanogaster.* I: Spontaneous and X-ray-induced lethals. *Genetica* **35,** 109–126.

JUDD, B. H., SHEN, M. W. and KAUFMAN, T. C. (1972). The anatomy and function of a segment of the X chromosome of *Drosophila melanogaster. Genetics* **71,** 139–156.

KAUFMANN, B. P. (1934). Somatic mitoses of *Drosophila melanogaster*. *J. Morph.* **56,** 125–155.

KAUFMANN, B. P. (1939). Distribution of induced breaks along the X-chromosome of *Drosophila melanogaster*. *Proc. Natl. Acad. Sci. U.S.A.* **25,** 571–577.

KAUFMANN, B. P. (1946). Organization of the chromosome. I. Break distribution and chromosome recombination in *Drosophila melanogaster*. *J. Expl. Zool.* **102,** 293–320.

KAUFMANN, B. P. (1954). Chromosome aberrations induced in animal cells by ionizing radiations. *In*: "Radiation Biology", 1 (A. Hollaender, ed.) Vol. 1, pp. 627–711. McGraw-Hill, New York.

KOGAN, Z. M. (1966). Occurrence of lethal mutations in the heterochromatic region of *Drosophila melanogaster* X-chromosome depending on pre-radiational development temperature. *Genetika* **4,** 38–44. (Russian with English summary.)

LEFEVRE, G., JR. (1969). The eccentricity of *vermilion* deficiencies in *Drosophila melanogaster*. *Genetics* **63,** 589–600.

LEFEVRE, G., JR. (1971). Salivary chromosome bands and the frequency of crossing over in *Drosophila melanogaster*. *Genetics* **67,** 497–513.

LEFEVRE, G., JR. and GREEN, M. M. (1972). Genetic duplication in the *white-split* interval of the X chromosome in *Drosophila melanogaster*. *Chromosoma* **36,** 391–412.

LEFEVRE, G., JR., RATTY, F. J., JR. and HANKS, G. D. (1953). Frequency of Notch mutations induced in normal, duplicated and inverted X-chromosomes of *Drosophila melanogaster*. *Genetics* **28,** 345–359.

LIFSCHYTZ, E. (1971). Fine structure analysis of the chromosome recombinational patterns at the base of the X-chromosome of *Drosophila melanogaster*. *Mutation Res.* **13,** 35–47.

LIFSCHYTZ, E. and FALK, R. (1968). Fine structure analysis of a chromosome segment in *Drosophila melanogaster*. Analysis of X-ray-induced lethals. *Mutation Res.* **6,** 235–244.

LIFSCHYTZ, E. and FALK, R. (1969). Fine structure analysis of a chromosome segment in *Drosophila melanogaster*. Analysis of ethyl methanesulphonate-induced lethals. *Mutation Res.* **8,** 147–155.

LIFSCHYTZ, E. and FALK, R. (1970). Fine structure analysis of the chromosome. Recombination values in the *ma-l* region. *Dros. Inf. Serv.* **45,** 144.

LIFSCHYTZ, E. and LINDSLEY, D. L. (1972). The role of X-chromosome inactivation during spermatogenesis. *Proc. Natl. Acad. Sci. U.S.A.* **69,** 182–186.

LINDSLEY, D. L. (1965). Chromosome function at the supragenic level. *Natl. Cancer Inst. Monogr.* **18,** 275–290.

LINDSLEY, D. L. and GRELL, E. H. (1968). Genetic variations of *Drosophila melanogaster*. Carnegie Inst. Wash. Publ. 627, 472 pp.

LINDSLEY, D. L. and LIFSCHYTZ, E. (1972). The genetic control of spermatogenesis in Drosophila. *Proc. Int. Symp. The Genetics of the Spermatozoon*, 203–222.

LINDSLEY, D. L. and SANDLER, L. (1957). The meiotic behavior of grossly deleted X chromosomes in *Drosophila melanogaster*. *Genetics* **43,** 547–563.

LINDSLEY, D. L., EDINGTON, C. W. and VON HALLE, E. S. (1960). Sex-linked recessive lethals in *Drosophila* whose expression is suppressed by the Y chromosome. *Genetics* **45,** 1649–1670.

MATHER, K. (1939). Crossing over and heterochromatin in the X chromosome of *Drosophila melanogaster*. *Genetics* **24,** 412–435.

MORGAN, T. H., BRIDGES, C. B. and STURTEVANT, A. H. (1925). The genetics of *Drosophila*. *Bibliogr. genet.* **2,** 1–262.

MULLER, H. J. (1930). Types of visible variations induced by X-rays in *Drosophila*. *J. Genet.* **22,** 299–334.

MULLER, H. J. (1935). A viable two-gene deficiency phaenotypically resembling the corresponding hypomorphic mutations. *J.* Hered. **25,** 469–478.

MULLER, H. J. (1940). An analysis of the process of structural change in chromosomes of *Drosophila*. *J. Genet.* **40,** 1–66.

MULLER, H. J. (1944). The non-equivalence of the blocks and the salivary "heterochromatin". (Abstr.) *Rec. Genet. Soc. Amer.* **13,** 28; and *Genetics* **30,** 15.

MULLER, H. J. (1954). The manner of production of mutations by radiation. *In*: "Radiation Biology" (A. Hollaender, ed.) Vol. 1, pp. 475–626. McGraw-Hill, New York.

MULLER, H. J. (1959). Advances in radiation mutagenesis through studies on Drosophila. *In*: "Progress in Nuclear Energy", Ser. VI, Biol. Sci. 2, 146–160.

MULLER, H. J. and GERSHENSON, S. M. (1935). Inert regions of chromosomes as the temporary products of individual genes. *Proc. Natl. Acad. Sci. U.S.A.* **21,** 69–75.

MULLER, H. J. and PAINTER, T. S. (1932). The differentiation of the sex chromosomes of *Drosophila* into genetically active and inert regions. *Z. indukt. Abstamm. VererbLehre* **62,** 316–365.

MULLER, H. J. and PROKOFYEVA, A. A. (1935). The structure of the chromonema of the inert region of the X-chromosome of *Drosophila*. *C.R.* (*Dokl.*) *Acad. Sci. U.R.S.S.*, N.S. **1,** 658–660.

MULLER, H. J., RAFFEL, D., GERSHENSON, S. M. and PROKOFYEVA-BELGOVSKAYA, A. A. (1937). A further analysis of loci in the so-called "inert region" of the X chromosome of *Drosophila*. *Genetics* **22,** 87–93.

NICOLETTI, B. and LINDSLEY, D. L. (1960). Translocations between the X and Y chromosomes of *Drosophila melanogaster*. *Genetics* **45,** 1705–1722.

NOVITSKI, E. (1951). Non-random disjunction in *Drosophila*. *Genetics* **36,** 267–280.

OFFERMANN, C. A. and MULLER, H. J. (1932). Regional differences in crossing over as a function of the chromosome structure. *Proc. 6th Int. Congr. Genet., Ithaca,* **2,** 143–145.

PAINTER, T. S. (1934). The morphology of the X chromosome in salivary glands of *Drosophila melanogaster* and a new type of chromosome map for this element. *Genetics* **19,** 448–469.

PROKOFYEVA-BELGOVSKAYA, A. A. (1935). The structure of the chromocenter. *Cytologia* **6,** 438–443.

PROKOFYEVA-BELGOVSKAYA, A. A. (1937). Observations on the structure of chromosomes in the salivary glands of *Drosophila melanogaster*. *Izv. Akad. Nauk SSSR., Otd. mat.-est., Ser. biol.*, 719–724. (Russian with English summary.)

PROKOFYEVA-BELGOVSKAYA, A. A. (1939). Cytological study of the breaks at the white locus of the X-chromosome of *Drosophila melanogaster*. *Izv. Akad. Nauk SSSR., Otd. mat.-est., Ser. biol.* **2,** 215–227. (Russian with English summary.)

RAYLE, R. E. and GREEN, M. M. (1968). A contribution to the genetic fine structure of the region adjacent to *white* in *Drosophila melanogaster*. *Genetics* **39,** 497–507.

REDFIELD, H. (1955). Recombination increase due to heterologous inversions and the relation to cytological length. *Proc. Natl. Acad. Sci. U.S.A.* **41,** 1084–1091.

RITOSSA, F. M., ATWOOD, K. C. and SPIEGELMAN, S. (1966). A molecular explanation of the bobbed mutants of *Drosophila* as partial deficiencies of "ribosomal" DNA. *Genetics* **54,** 819–834.

ROBERTS, P. A. (1965). Difference in the behavior of eu- and hetero-chromatin: crossing-over. *Nature, Lond.* **205,** 725–726.

ROBERTS, P. A. (1969). Some components of X ray-induced crossing over in females of *Drosophila melanogaster*. *Genetics* **63,** 387–404.

RUDKIN, G. T. (1964). The structure and function of heterochromatin. *In*: "Genetics Today", *Proc. XI Int. Congr. Genet.*, The Hague, Vol. 2, pp. 359–374. Pergamon Press.

RUDKIN, G. T. (1965). The relative mutabilities of DNA in regions of the X chromosome of *Drosophila melanogaster*. *Genetics* **52,** 665–681.

RUDKIN, G. T. (1969). Non replicating DNA in *Drosophila melanogaster*. *Genetics* **61,** Suppl. 1, 227–238.

SCHALET, A. (1963). Marked Y chromosomes. *Dros. Inf. Serv.* **38,** 82.

SCHALET, A. (1969a). Additional data concerning genes in the proximal region of the X chromosome of *Drosophila melanogaster*. *Dros. Inf. Serv.* **44,** 96.

SCHALET, A. (1969b). Exchanges at the bobbed locus of *Drosophila melanogaster*. *Genetics* **63,** 133–153.

SCHALET, A. (1970). Some observations on the proximal euchromatic-heterochromatic region of the X chromosome in *Drosophila melanogaster*. (Abstr.) *Genen en Phaenen* **14,** 16–17.

SCHALET, A. (1972a). Crossing over in the major heterochromatic region of the X chromosome in normal and inverted sequences. *Dros. Inf. Serv.* **48,** 111–113.

SCHALET, A. (1972b). Lethal, semilethal, and male sterile mutants in the proximal region of the X chromosome of *Drosophila melanogaster*. *Dros. Inf. Serv.* **48,** 65–66.

SCHALET, A. and FINNERTY, V. (1968a). New mutants: Report of A. Schalet and V. Finnerty. *Dros. Inf. Serv.* **43,** 65–66.

SCHALET, A. and FINNERTY, V. (1968b). The arrangement of genes in the proximal region of the X chromosome of *Drosophila melanogaster*. *Dros. Inf. Serv.* **43,** 128–129.

SCHALET, A. and LEFEVRE, G., JR. (1973). The localization of "ordinary" sex-linked genes in Section 20 of the polytene X chromosome of *Drosophila melanogaster*. *Chromosoma* **44,** 183–202.

SCHALET, A. and SINGER, K. (1971). A revised map of genes in the proximal region of the X chromosome of *Drosophila melanogaster*. *Dros. Inf. Serv.* **46,** 131–132.

SCHALET, A., KERNAGHAN, R. P. and CHOVNICK, A. (1964). Structural and phenotypic definition of the rosy cistron in *Drosophila melanogaster*. *Genetics* **50,** 1261–1268.

SCHALET, A., LEFEVRE, G. and SINGER, K. (1970). Preliminary cytogenetic observations on the proximal euchromatic region of the X chromosome of *D. melanogaster*. *Dros. Inf. Serv.* **45,** 165.

SCHULTZ, J. (1936). Variegation in *Drosophila* and the inert chromosome regions. *Proc. Nat. Acad. Sci. U.S.A.* **22,** 27–33.

SHAPIRO, N. I. (1937). The method of studying the process of mutation in a limited region of the chromosome. *Dros. Inf. Serv.* **7,** 94–95.

SIVERTZEV-DOBZHANSKY, N. P. and DOBZHANSKY, T. (1933). Deficiency and duplications for the gene bobbed in *Drosophila melanogaster. Genetics* **18,** 173–192.

SLIZYNSKA, H. (1938). Salivary chromosome analysis of the white-facet region of *Drosophila melanogaster. Genetics* **23,** 291–299.

SLIZYNSKA, H. (1957). Cytological analysis of formaldehyde induced chromosomal changes in *Drosophila melanogaster. Proc. Roy. Soc.* (*Edinb.*), **B 66,** 288–304.

SLIZYNSKA, H. (1969). The progressive approximation, with storage, of the spectrum of TEM-induced chromosomal changes in *Drosophila* sperm to that found after irradiation. *Mutation Res.* **8,** 164–175.

SLIZYNSKA, H. and SLIZYNSKI, B. M. (1947). Genetical and cytological studies of lethals induced by chemical treatment in *Drosophila melanogaster. Proc. Roy. Soc.* (*Edinb.*), **B 62,** 234–241.

SLIZYNSKI, B. M. (1942). Deficiency effects of ultra-violet light in *Drosophila melanogaster. Proc. Roy. Soc.* (*Edinb.*), **B 61,** 297–315.

SOBELS, F. H. (1962). Rates of forward and reverse mutation in *Drosophila* after exposure to mustard gas and X-rays. *Genetica* **33,** 31–44.

STERN, C. (1927). Ein genetischer und zytologischer Beweis für Verenbung im Y-Chromosom von *Drosophila melanogaster. Z. indukt. Abstamm. Vererb-Lehre* **44,** 187–231.

STERN, C. (1929). Untersuchungen über Aberrationen des Y-Chromosoms von *Drosophila melanogaster. Z. indukt. Abstamm. VererbLehre* **51,** 253–353.

STONE, W. S. (1934). Linkage between the X and IV chromosomes in *Drosophila melanogaster. Genetica* **16,** 506–520.

STONE, W. S. and THOMAS, I. (1935). Crossover and disjunctional properties of X chromosome inversions in *Drosophila melanogaster. Genetica* **17,** 170–184.

STURTEVANT, A. H. and BEADLE, G. W. (1936). The relations of inversions in the X chromosome of *Drosophila melanogaster* to crossing-over and disjunction. *Genetics* **21,** 554–604.

VIINIKKA, Y., HANNAH-ALAVA, A. and ARAJÄRVI, P. (1971). A reinvestigation of the nucleolus-organizing regions in the salivary gland nuclei of *Drosophila melanogaster. Chromosoma* **36,** 34–45.

WAGONER, D. E. (1965). The frequency of effective breakage of heterochromatin in *Drosophila melanogaster. Diss. Abstr.* **26,** 2938.

WAGONER, D. E. (1968). The frequency of effective breakage of heterochromatin in *Drosophila melanogaster. Proc. XII Int. Congr. Genet.*, Tokyo, Vol. 1, 191.

WEINSTEIN, A. (1936). The theory of multiple-strand crossing-over. *Genetics* **21,** 155–199.

WILLIAMSON, J. H. (1966). Interchromosomal effects of autosomal translocations on recombination in *Drosophila melanogaster. Genetics* **54,** 1431–1440.

WILLIAMSON, J. H. (1968). Identification of Y fragments with two doses of y^+ or B^S. *Dros. Inf. Serv.* **43,** 157.

22. The Fourth Chromosome of *Drosophila melanogaster**

BENJAMIN HOCHMAN

Department of Zoology
The University of Tennessee
Knoxville, Tennessee, U.S.A.

I. Introduction

Several years ago a popular American song included the line, "I know a little bit about a lot of things". It is hoped that a conscientious perusal of the sections which follow will enable the reader to rearrange this phrase to, "I know a lot of things about a little bit". The "little bit", of course, refers to the fourth chromosome of *Drosophila melanogaster*. Even the most thorough reading, however, will not gain one a full knowledge or appreciation of this autosome. Limitations of space and of the writer

* Supported in part by the Faculty Research Fund, The University of Tennessee and National Science Foundation Research Grant GB 8466.

necessitate the omission of certain topics and a superficial coverage of others. The reader will have to look elsewhere in this and other volumes for discussions of nondisjunction, preferential segregation, position effect and gene dosage studies as they relate to chromosome 4.

Genetic studies of chromosome 4 began in 1914 when the first two microchromosomal mutants were found; bent (*bt*) by Muller (1914) and eyeless (*ey*) by Hoge (1915). In 1935 Bridges published two reviews (1935a, b), one covering the cytology and the other the mutants of 4.

A. The 1935 Reviews by Bridges

Since cytological descriptions are presented in this and other chapters, there would be little purpose served by here recounting Bridges on the normal 4. However, two aberrations of 4 delineated by Bridges deserve mention. The Minute-4 deficiency (now symbolized *Df(4)M*) was depicted as lacking at least four major bands between the spindle fiber attachment and line G (now 102B9–10). There are still some uncertainties as to the breakpoints of this deletion (the cytology of proximal 4R is difficult) but my best estimate is that 11–15 of the 50 4R bands are missing.

Bridges' description of the eyeless-Dominant duplication closely parallels what this reviewer has personally observed. Inserted near line O (102 D1–2) is a reversed repeat of some 10–12 bands of a texture coarser than that noted elsewhere in 4R. I have suggested (1971 and earlier) that 4L was the source of the duplication; Bridges was unable to locate the source nor did he ever report seeing 4L. The symbol ey^D, which indicates allelism with recessive eyeless, is a misnomer based on the interaction between the duplication and *ey*. As Bridges points out, the allele ey^2 enhances the reduction in eye size of L^2 heterozygotes (as well as ey^D—duplication heterozygotes) without any supposition of allelism between ey^2 and L^2.

Most of the visible mutants of 4 had already been discovered by 1935 and were included by Bridges in his second review (1935b). An enumeration is practicable as the list is short. There were two recessive alleles of bent (*bt*) and bt^D, five *ey* alleles, two shaven (*sv*) alleles, two of abdomen rotatum (*ar*), cubitus interruptus (*ci*) and ci^D, and one allele each of grooveless (*gvl*) and Scutenick (*Scn*), plus the aforementioned aberrations *Df(4)M* and ey^D. In the years to follow only sparkling (*spa*) and its presumed alleles spa^{pol} and spa^{Cat}, Cell (*Ce*) and alleles, and gouty (*gy*) would be added to the list of visibles. Obscure mutants such as *su(B)4* and *Mal* shall be ignored in this review.

I cannot refrain from commenting on the serial order of loci presented at the end of Bridges' compilation. The map was based on very limited data, mostly that of Bolen (1931) on the white-mottled-5 translocation, and it was almost altogether incorrect. Nevertheless, it appeared in Bridges and Brehme (1944) and its errors may still be found in recent textbooks of genetics, e.g. Burns (1969), Singleton (1962) and others. In view of the fact that Sturtevant published a corrected map of 4 in 1951, the continued persistence of such mistakes in print is somewhat disturbing.

II. Characteristics of 4

A. Size and Band Number

Chromosome 4 at ordinary mitotic metaphase (neuroblasts, gonia) measures 0·2–0·3μ in length (a similar diameter giving it a dot-like appearance) and accounts for approximately 0·04 of the total length (7·9μ) of the haploid complement in *D. melanogaster*. One arm (4R) is all that is usually observed although a small, thin limb (4L) on the other side of the centromere can be seen (Kaufmann, 1934). In salivary gland preparations, if squash pressure has been inadequate, both ends of 4 remain attached to the chromocenter. A moderately stretched salivary gland 4 may extend 10–15μ from the chromocenter but the left arm and typically the centromere remain embedded. Excessive pressure during squashing can stretch 4R to 30μ and more and render 4L and the centromere visible. In most instances the band pattern in division 101 (4L and the proximal 4R) is extremely difficult to discern. Measurements of the lax and stretched lengths of all salivary gland chromosomes and the number of bands in each given by P. N. Bridges (1942) may be employed to estimate the relative amount of genetic material embodied in 4. Table I presents these estimates, most of which lie close to 1%.

Of the more than 5000 bands noted in the salivary gland polytene chromosomes, 50 (*ca* 1%) are microchromosomal. If doublets are scored

TABLE I. Estimates of the length and number of bands of the polytene salivary gland 4th chromosome.

	Length (μ)			Number of bands	
	Lax	Moderately stretched	Greatly stretched	Doubles = 2	Doubles = 1
Chromosome 4	9	15	15[a]	50	33
Haploid set	765	1175	2188	5062	3795
4's share (%)	1·2	1·3	0·7	1·0[b]	0·9

[a] Bridges' (1942) figures are used although Slizynski (1944) and Hochman (1971) have stretched 4 over 30μ. This would increase 4's share to at least 1·4% (30/2203).
[b] Employing Slizynski's report of 137 bands in 4 raises this to 2·7% (137/5149).

as one band each, the total drops to 3795 and chromosome 4's share (33) remains about 1%. Only Slizynski (1944) reports more bands (137) in 4. Some 26 of these bands were placed in 4L by Slizynski. According to my own preparations, and the published figure in Griffen and Stone (1940), this number of bands in 4L is too high. I have seen the dark bands which begin subdivisions A–D in 101 as well as a few other light lines between them, perhaps a dozen bands in all. Regardless of the contribution of 4L, the microchromosome's size and band number suggest that it contains at least 1% (and possibly 3–4%) of the genes in *D. melanogaster*.

Evidence that most of what has been called 4L is actually located to the right of the centromere has recently been presented by Roberts (1972). A translocation, *T(3;4)10*, induced with X-rays, involves breakpoints "considerably to the left of 101 D" (the presumed site of the centromere of 4) and near the tip of 3R according to Roberts. The larger segment of 4 has capped the broken 3R and the end piece of 3R has combined with the remainder of 4. Since the stock has retained both elements of the translocation for at least 70 generations, it appears certain that no dicentric chromosome (or acentric fragment) was formed originally. The stability of both elements and the examination of the relevant salivary gland chromosome banding indicate that the centromere is to the left of both 101 D and the breakpoint in 4. Roberts finds it probable "that 4 is acrocentric rather than submetacentric".

Bands 101 D 3,4 [whose vesicle or ring structure was interpreted as a possible spindle-fiber attachment by Bridges (1935a)] have been translocated to the tips of other chromosomes by Roberts. None of these rearrangements exhibit the instability of dicentrics. Of special interest in these translocations is the observation that the width, and presumably the polyteny, of 101A–D (or "basal 4R" as Roberts terms the region) has increased perhaps three-fold from the thin state seen in structurally normal 4's to approximately the same size as the rest of 4R.

B. Heterochromatin

The literature is replete with contradictory statements regarding the presence of heterochromatin in the fourth chromosome. Since Heitz (1928) introduced the term heterochromatin (to describe specific chromosomal regions which remain condensed throughout the cell cycle), its meaning has been extended considerably to include all sorts of cytological and genetical conditions. The wisdom of such broad usage of a term might be questioned (see for example, Ris and Kubai, 1970) but this shall not occupy us here. I think the evidence presented below (especially the recent cytological findings) justifies the assertion that chromosome 4 contains heterochromatin.

The absence of heteropycnotic regions in chromosome 4 in mitotic cells led Heitz (1933) to conclude that it lacks detectable heterochromatin. Kaufmann (1934) has also been cited as claiming this but a careful examination of his paper reveals no clear-cut statement on heterochromatin in 4. It is true that pycnotic areas are described in the text only for the large autosomes and the X and Y. However, in Figs. 2 and 4 of Kaufmann, the fourth chromosomes are shown as darkly stained as the pycnotic regions of X, 2 and 3. His fig. 4, which shows clearly both arms of 4, depicts one darkly stained and one lightly stained microchromosome. In any event, as Hannah (1951) notes, the small size of 4 may hamper the detection of heterochromatic blocks on both sides of the centromere as they appear in the large autosomes.

Recently, three independent studies utilizing quinacrine staining (Vosa, 1970; Ellison and Barr, 1971; and Adkisson *et al.*, 1971) have agreed that the dot-like fourth displays a brilliant fluorescence in neuroblast cells. That this stain detects heterochromatin is indicated by the fact that the Y chromosome (heterochromatic by all criteria) is the brightest element in quinacrine-treated metaphase cells.

Early reports about heterochromatin in the salivary gland fourth chromosome disagreed. Griffen and Stone (1940) found none in either arm, whereas Slizynski (1944) placed it on the free ends of both arms and in the proximity of the centromere. Bridges (1935a), while not employing the term heterochromatin, reasoned that there were "inert" regions at the basal and terminal portions of 4 which were responsible for both ends of the microchromosome typically being embedded in the chromocenter ("both of which fuse with the inert regions of the other chromosomes to give a collective chromocenter").

The three quinacrine-staining studies cited above obtained similar results with respect to the polytene 4. Intensely fluorescent regions at 101F and 102F were found on the polytene 4R after treatment with various quinacrine compounds in all three laboratories. There were some differences noted, e.g. Vosa (1970) observed a fluorescent band at 102B (not seen by the others) and Ellison and Barr (1971) and Adkisson *et al.* (1971) detected a brilliant region at 102D not present in Vosa's preparations. Mr. A. J. Calandra in my laboratory, employing quinacrine dihydrochloride to stain the chromosomes of several different stocks, finds that 101 (F?) and 102D invariably fluoresce intensely (Fig. 1). Bands 102B and 102F do not appear to be significantly brighter than other nonfluorescent areas. Ellison and Barr do not believe differences in staining methods can account for these discrepancies. They invoke the possibility that genetic variation

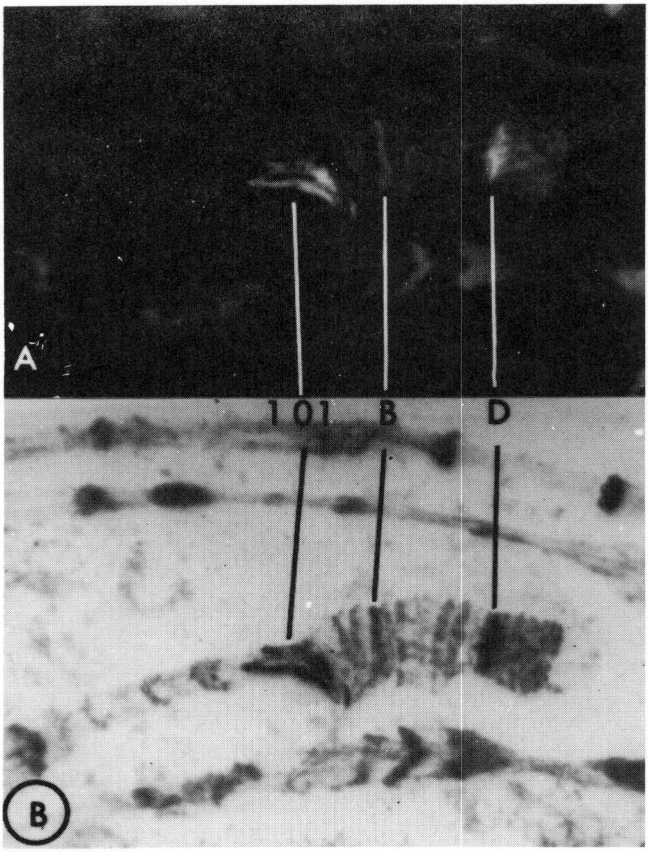

FIG. 1. A quinacrine dihydrochloride treated pair of salivary fourth chromosomes from the Oregon-R stock. (A). Fluorescent regions seen in dark field using UV illumination. Division 101 and the first bands of subdivisions 102 B and F are indicated by lines. (B). A "negative" print of the same chromosome pair to illustrate a band-interband pattern which is essentially like that obtained with orcein staining. The chromosomal material to the left is probably not part of 4. Photographs courtesy of A. J. Calandra.

between the stocks tested may be responsible for the fluorescent dissimilarities. These differences notwithstanding, if one grants that quinacrine stains heterochromatin (or one of the postulated types of heterochromatin), the location of this "substance" on the right arm of the polytene 4 is established.

Barigozzi *et al.* (1966), in their study of DNA replication patterns in embryonic cells, found that chromosome 4 was often labelled with incorporated tritiated-thymidine together with the Y, the proximal X, and the centromeric sections of 2 and 3 at late stages in the S period when the euchromatic portions of 2, 3 and X were unlabelled. The pattern of late DNA replication thus coincided approximately with the gross distribution of heterochromatin based on other cytological criteria.

Two "genetic" properties associated with heterochromatin (relative inertness and a role in the position effect phenomena) may also bear on the question. Some, and perhaps most of, the left arm of 4 can be considered genetically inert; it is dispensable as demonstrated by the viability of *C(4)RM/0* flies. In polytene cells, 4L usually remains within the chromocenter, a behavior expected of centromeric heterochromatin.

The position effects characterizing the *ci* locus in 4 are atypical. Whereas most V-type position effects are the result of a gene being transferred from its euchromatic site to heterochromatin, the reverse appears true for *ci*. A complete description of this phenomenon is to be found in Chapter 24 of volume 1 by Spofford.

On the basis of the foregoing, I should like to suggest that 4R is primarily euchromatic (as attested by its many essential genes to be discussed later) with proximal heterochromatin and intercalated heterochromatic regions at 102D, 102F and perhaps elsewhere, while 4L is mainly or solely heterochromatic.

C. Number of Loci

The number of distinct loci found on chromosome 4 will be presented first followed by estimates based on my own mutation work and on the amount of DNA calculated for the microchromosome from the published reports of others.

My stock collection now includes one or more alleles at 37 separate vital loci on chromosome 4. By vital is meant a locus capable of mutating to a form which is either lethal, semilethal or sterile when homozygous. Most of the mutations detected are completely lethal, although at loci *24* and *33* semilethality of various degrees is the rule. One mutation, *fs(4)34*, has exposed the first locus on 4 whose sole function appears to be essential for female fertility.

In addition to the essential loci there are 6–8 others identified from recessive visibles. Two of the eight, eyeless and shaven, may be identical to vital loci *33* and *40*, respectively. The other six are *ci*, *ar*, *gvl*, *bt*, *gy* and *spa*. Dominant visibles which are also lethal when homozygous such as ci^{D}, Ce^{2}, bt^{D}, spa^{Cat}, and *Scn* are not added to the list of loci because the first four interact lethally with one or more recessive lethals, and the last (and lost) mutant *Scn* may have been allelic to Ce^{2}. On the other hand, *M*, a presumed point mutation which does not interact with other lethals or visibles, is counted as a separate locus. Figure 2 is a map of the loci based on cytological mapping (deficiencies) and complementation tests.

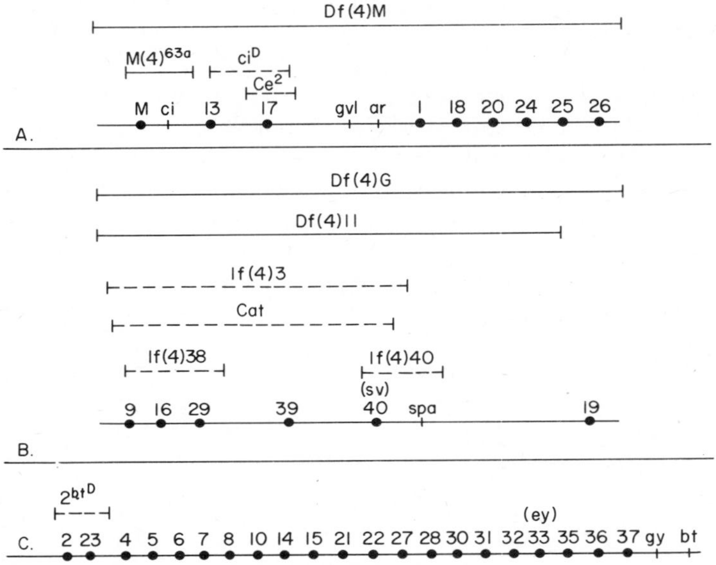

FIG. 2. (A). Genetic factors located within the region delimited by the proximal 4R deficiency *Df(4)M*. See text for explanation of *M–17* sequence. No sequence intended for *gvl–26*. ● = vital loci. (B). Complementation map of factors located within the region delimited by the terminal deficiency *Df(4)G*. *Df* = cytologically verified deficiency, *lf* = deficiency suspected on genetic grounds. (C). Loci situated outside *Df(4)M* and *Df(4)G*. No sequence intended.

The total number of essential loci to be expected on 4 can be estimated from the mutation data by employing a formula derived from the Poisson distribution. If n_1 is the number of loci that mutated once and n_2 is the number that mutated twice, then $n_1^2/2n_2$ estimates n_0, the number of loci failing to mutate. At the time of this writing n_0 equals 30 which, when added to the 37 loci already exposed, gives an estimate of 67 vital loci on 4. Owing to the rather haphazard nature of the mutation detection work, n_0 has fluctuated widely in the course of my studies with 30 being its highest value to date.

As to loci revealed through recessive visibles, one can be reasonably sure that very few, if any, remain undetected. Between 1914, when Muller found the first one, *bt*, and 1965, when he reported *gy*, only eight such loci were uncovered. Moreover, no new major visibles have been disclosed in the past decade. There have been reports of minor genes on 4 affecting such things as sternopleural bristle number and abdominal pigmentation (Osman and Robertson, 1968), ether resistance (Ogaki *et al.*, 1967), the penetrance of witty (Whitten, 1968), etc. Chromosome 4 may carry genes which are part of polygenic systems but I shall ignore them in my consideration of the number of loci.

The expected number of major loci is therefore approximately 75. Earlier published estimates (Hochman *et al.*, 1964; Hochman, 1971) were closer to 50. At any rate, the number is probably less than 100 and conflicts sharply with the expectations based on DNA measurements. Based on Rudkin's (1965) calculation of the amount of DNA in the average band of the polytene X (per chromosome strand), chromosome 4 with its 50 bands has about $1{\cdot}5 \times 10^6$ nucleotide pairs. Laird and McCarthy (1969) found enough DNA in the haploid genome of *D. melanogaster* to account for 10^8 nucleotides; a 1% share for 4 is 10^6 nucleotides. Regardless of which of these estimates is the more accurate, the presumed DNA content of the microchromosome far exceeds that expected for a chromosome with 50–100 genes, if the average gene in *Drosophila*, like those in micro-organisms, consists of 1000–1500 nucleotide pairs. One hundred genes averaging 1500 nucleotide pairs would constitute a chromosome whose DNA content is still an order of magnitude below the estimates derived above!

I have commented elsewhere (Hochman, 1971) on the disparity in these estimates of microchromosomal gene number. The explanations offered included: (1) errors in the DNA measurements (rejected because of the basic accord of the two independent appraisals); (2) genetic redundancy in 4 [at best only a partial answer since Robertson *et al.* (1969), Laird and McCarthy (1969), Rae (1970) and Gall *et al.* (1971) all agree that the reiterated fraction in *D. melanogaster* is only about 10%]; (3) chromosome 4 carries a large number of genes affecting viability too slightly to be detected by my screening procedures [rejected on the grounds that Kenyon (1967) estimates that the maximum number of viability-affecting loci on 4 is 50 relative to a presumed 400 on chromosome 2]; and (4) that most of the DNA on 4 does not perform the genetic functions of structural or regulatory genes [doubtful from an evolutionary (natural selection) standpoint]. To the above arguments should be added the possibility that 4 might carry more reiterated DNA sequences than the 10% average for *D. melanogaster* (see Jones and Robertson, 1970). R. F. Grell (1971) also suggests that the lack of fourth chromosome exchange could result in the accumulation of varying amounts of genetic material (originating through duplication) on existing 4's.

Chromosome 4 might have 10^3 genes and the entire genome might contain 10^5, but this seems excessive. For want of a better alternative, I favor at this time the idea that each band of the polytene chromosome (or better, each chromomere) is the site of a long, integrated chain of DNA which normally controls one function. Independent mutations of these functional units for the most part do not complement one another in the *trans* state, and they are therefore considered allelic although they may impair widely separated portions of the long DNA chain. (The example of partial complementation at locus 2, to be discussed later, may be the exception that proves the rule.)

It may be propitious to resurrect "the classical idea that chromomeres are the elementary functional entities of chromosomes" (Ris and Kubai, 1970). Three independent studies of sections of X chromosomes and my own work agree so far that the number of vital loci or functional units found does not exceed the number of polytene bands observed (or estimated) in the section being scrutinized (see Lifschytz and Falk, 1969; Judd *et al.*, 1972; and Rowan [personal communication]).

D. Unique Features

In addition to its small size, two properties set chromosome 4 apart from the other members of the complement. First, in marked contrast to the situation encountered in X, 2, 3, there is a lack (or virtual lack) of recombination between homologous 4's in normal diploid females cultured at ordinary temperatures. (Techniques for circumventing this barrier to mapping will be described later.)

Secondly, while aneuploidy for chromosomes 2 and 3 invariably results in death, flies will survive with only one fourth chromosome (haplo-4) or three 4's (triplo-4). Even a proportion of tetra-4 adults live (E. H. Grell, 1961; Moore and R. F. Grell, 1972). Nullo-4 individuals die as embryos (Li, 1927). Haplo-4's are weak with reduced fertility and they exhibit various abnormalities, chief of which is a Minute phenotype. Triplo-4 flies are hard to distinguish from ordinary diploids but tetra-4's have wings which are slightly longer and more pointed than those of diplo-4's.

Both of these unique properties of chromosome 4 have significance with respect to natural populations and their evolution, the recombinational block probably more so than the viable aneuploids. As far as laboratory work is concerned, one advantage accruing from the lack of crossing over in 4 is the stability it confers on balanced-lethal stocks. The experimental value of viable aneuploids extends to studies of gene dosage effects (Schultz, 1935; Stern, 1948) and chromosomal pairing and segregation (Sturtevant, 1936; R. F. Grell, 1959).

III. Methods of Analysis

A. Detection of Mutants

Recessive fourth chromosome mutations, induced by mutagens or present in natural populations can be detected by screening procedures extending one, two, three or four generations. In the past, I have (1) crossed treated (or trapped) wild-type males to ci^D/ey^D females, (2) mated individual $ey^D/+$ (or $ci^D/+$) F_1 males back to ci^D/ey^D females, and (3) intercrossed the generation 2 $ci^D/+$ flies within each line. If no morphological or viability mutation was present on the "+"-chromosome transmitted by his father to a given F_1 male, the generation 3 progeny contain ci^D and non-ci^D flies in about a 2:1 ratio. Recessive visible mutations on 4 cause all (or some, if penetrance is less than 100%) of the non-ci^D individuals to appear phenotypically abnormal. Recessive lethal or semilethal mutations lead to the absence or reduced frequency, respectively, of the non-ci^D (+/+) class in generation 3. Temperature sensitive (*ts*) mutations can be uncovered by raising a generation 3 progeny of each line at two temperatures (29°C and 21°C). Sterility mutations (*ms* or *fs*) can be discerned by providing the +/+ flies of each line with normal flies of the opposite sex and noting if larvae appear in the fresh culture vials. Finally, the occurrence of mutations which specify electrophoretically separable proteins can be revealed by comparing individual +/+ and $ci^D/+$ flies of each non-lethal bearing line by means of appropriate techniques.

Thus, in the space of two months or so, providing ample technical assistance is available, a rather extensive survey of possible recessive mutations can be accomplished. If one wishes to concentrate only on visibles, the time interval may be reduced to a single generation by utilizing one of the attached-4 stocks, *C(4)RM/0*, constructed by E. B. Lewis. A compound-4 strain also simplifies the search for viability mutants. The F_1 (ey^D/"+") males mentioned above, when crossed to *C(4)RM/0* females, produce triplo-4($ey^D/+/+$ and "+"/+/+) and non-ey^D haplo-4 offspring if the "+"-chromosome does not contain a lethal. If the monosomics fail to appear, the suspected lethal may be extracted from the unmarked triplo-4's.

B. Characterization of Mutants

Recovered mutants are subjected to genetic and cytological tests to determine their allelism and position with respect to verified and putative deletions of 4. It should be mentioned that the usual method of localizing new mutations in *Drosophila* has not been employed because of the recombinational difficulties discussed elsewhere in this review. The mapping procedures followed may be illustrated using a newly detected lethal as the example.

The new lethal is first made heterozygous with the two large deficiencies, *Df(4)M* (in the proximal region of 4R) and *Df(4)G* (located distally in 4R). If it is lethal with either deficiency it is crossed to the other smaller deficiencies and "point" mutation loci previously mapped to the region in question. A lethal which is not localized by the above crosses is next tested against the most non-complementing members of the *2–23* complex, i.e. 2^{btD} and 2^{c}. Failure to obtain interaction with these means that the lethal has to be crossed to at least one representative at each of the 20 unlocalized vital loci and the loci identified earlier by their visible mutations. When these various tests are completed one is able to conclude tentatively that the lethal chromosome being examined contains either (1) a single lethal mutation at a new or previously known locus, or (2) a deficiency (or inactivation) for two or more adjacent loci, or (3) independent mutations at two distinct and probably widely separated loci. The possibility that the lethal effect is associated with a translocation is tested genetically (see Patterson *et al.*, 1934) and salivary gland chromosome examinations are utilized both to verify suspected translocations and to uncover other aberrations.

As pointed out below, some of the existing translocations involving 4, as well as those induced in the future, may prove extremely useful in the cytological mapping of microchromosomal loci. Loci currently placed within sections delimited by known deficiencies may be seriated further and the unlocalized group may be sequenced.

All of the lethal (and semilethal) mutations found to date have been characterized as to the period they arrest development. To ascertain this, a lethal under study (*l*) is made heterozygous with normal fourth chromosomes from both the Oregon-R (O-R) and Canton-S (C-S) wild-type stocks. Following their being mated with *l*/C-S males, the *l*/O-R females oviposit in stender dishes containing a grape juice-fortified standard medium. An egg count (facilitated by the darkened medium) is followed at appropriate times by counts of larvae, pupae and adults. Since 25% of the zygotes are expected to die as a result of homozygosity for the lethal, these counts usually enable one to classify the lethal as monophasic (acting in either embryonic, larval or pupal stages) or as polyphasic. Most of the lethals found on 4 are monophasic and an unexpectedly high proportion (39%) act solely or partly during the pupal period (Hochman, 1968 and unpublished observations). The X chromosome of *D. melanogaster* is also "rich" in pupal lethals (42% according to Medvedev, 1938 and Oster, 1952) but only 8% of chromosome 2 lethals die as pupae (Seto, 1961).

C. Analysis of a Large Unit of Inheritance

Since individual fourth chromosomes rarely cross over, the whole autosome tends to be inherited as a single block of genes, with variations between 4's originating primarily through mutation and chromosomal aberration. Moreover, the small size of 4 and its presumed paucity of loci makes feasible the attempt to discover all of its genes (the "major" genes especially). Such an undertaking is also possible for certain short regions of other *Drosophila* chromosomes (as described elsewhere in this volume, see Chapter 19), but entire chromosomes in this species are too large to make such a project practicable. (The Y of *Drosophila* is probably an exception but its importance to the fly outside of its role in male fertility is questionable.)

The indispensability of chromosome 4 cannot be questioned. Nullo-4's die at about the sixth hour of embryonic development (Li, 1927). At least one dose of more than 30 genes (and perhaps all of 4R) must be present if development is to proceed through emergence of the imago. A complete map of all microchromosomal loci and knowledge of the function of each normal gene (with respect to developmental effects at least) could provide answers for such questions as: (1) How many genes can be "crowded" into an eukaryotic chromosome which measures less than $0{\cdot}3\mu$ at its contracted metaphase state? (2) What is the average size of eukaryotic genes in terms of linear chromosomal dimensions and DNA content? (3) Is there a correlation between the sequence of certain loci and the effects these genes have on the development of the organism? (4) Are there examples of two or more structural genes under the control of an adjacent regulator? and (5) Is 4 derived from the X of some ancestral form?

IV. Problems of Mapping

A. Crossing Over

Crossing over in the fourth chromosome occurs so infrequently under "normal" genetic and environmental conditions that Sturtevant (1951) expressed doubt that "as many as five crossovers have ever been detected from diploid females". The first undisputed example of exchange in 4 was provided by Curry (reported in Bridges, 1935b). Earlier cases recorded by Tiniakov and Terentieva (1933) and Bridges (unpublished observations) were subsequently explained by Bridges (1935b) as probable examples of nondisjunction or mutation.

Curry's early attempts to get crossovers in 4 were unsuccessful despite the utilization of five heterozygous inversions (involving the other three chromosomes). She achieved her objective by using high temperatures to increase crossing over. Curry raised *ci* ey^R/gvl females at 30°C, mated them with *ci* ey^R males and allowed oviposition to occur at the high temperature. The progeny were reared at 19°C to enhance the expression of *ci*. Two crossovers (one *ci* and the other ey^R), appearing in a total progeny of 5273 (a frequency of 0·0004) were demonstrated, by appropriate testing, to be genetically *ci* + + and + *gvl* ey^R, respectively. Crossing over between the *gvl* and ey^R loci was responsible for both recombinants. Bridges' plans to do additional testing of 4 at 30°C either failed to materialize or the findings were never published.

If an elevated temperature of 30°C promotes crossing over in 4, heat shocks of 32°C and 35°C are even more potent inducers of exchange as shown by R. F. Grell (1971). Heat treatments of 12 and 24 h durations, when given to female pupae aged 120–150 h after oviposition, induced crossing over between the loci of ci^D and spa^{pol}. Animals 132–144 h old when treatment was initiated were the most responsive to the heat shocks, giving some 0·2–0·3% crossovers (17/7488). R. F. Grell reports that heat-induced exchange in 4, and in the X and 2, occurs in a period which is coextensive in part with the time of DNA synthesis in the oocyte.

The appreciable amount of fourth chromosome crossing over in diplo-4 triploid females, reported in Morgan *et al.* (1945), was used by Sturtevant (1951) to map five genes (*ci*, *gvl*, *bt*, *ey* and *sv*) on this autosome. In two separate 4-point linkage crosses Sturtevant obtained 63 single and 3 double crossovers among 2388 offspring, a crossover frequency of about 3%. Two interesting aspects of these experiments are (1) the unexpected high frequency of doubles and (2) the sequence of loci that they reveal differs markedly from that deduced earlier from the behavior of translocations (Bridges, 1935b). No explanation of the high coincidence was offered but the overall correctness of the map positions was confirmed by Fung and Stern (1951). These investigators seriated, by means of variously deficient 4's and the phenomenon of pseudo-dominance, the recessive visibles of 4 into three groups; a proximal cluster (*ar*, *ci*, *gvl*, *Scn*), a middle trio (*bt*, *ey*, *Mal*), and a distal pair (*sv*, *spa*).

The recent literature includes two other accounts of "recombination" in the fourth chromosome. Williamson *et al.* (1970a, b) induced exchanges in 4 with X-rays but, on consideration of the kinetics of induction and the meiotic properties of a large sample of the recombinant chromosomes, they concluded that radiation-induced recombination is actually a translocational process. Induced crossovers, unlike spontaneous ones, apparently are frequently unequal, giving rise to products containing small duplications or deficiencies. The segregational properties of these recombinants, as judged in females carrying a compound X, varied widely (0·41 to 0·72 segregation from *C(1)RM*) instead of exhibiting the bimodality (0·50 and 0·66) of the original parental 4's.

Somewhat more difficult to explain is Thompson's report (1963) of six chromosome 4 exchanges among 6808 progeny of females heterozygous for a structurally normal 4 and a translocation [*T(3;4)86D*]. During meiotic pairing of the 4's in the above heterozygote, only the free fourth's centromere is involved. According to Thompson, this releases the crossing over normally inhibited by paired 4 centromeres. In this experiment the free 4 carried *ci gvl* and spa^{Cat}, and the translocated 4 contained the respective wild-type alleles. Four of the six recombinants were normal in phenotype; if correctly classified they represent either four separate exchanges between *ci*(101 F–102 A) and the breakpoint of the translocation (101 F), or some sort of double exchange. Neither alternative is very likely. R. F. Grell (personal communication) has raised the interesting possibility that the four normal flies were the result of double nondisjunction, i.e. the eggs in question lacked a 4 while the sperm transmitted both 4's of the unmarked (as far as 4 was concerned) father. Grell has observed that such patroclinous diplo-4 progeny occur when properly marked male parents are crossed to *T(3;4)86D* heterozygous females.

The other two recombinants were *ci gvl*, the exchange taking place between *gvl* and spa^{Cat}. Since spa^{Cat} overlaps wild type and is lethal when homozygous, the only sure proof of crossing over would have been the establishment of a homozygous stock from each recombinant. This apparently was not accomplished and so, in this reviewer's mind, the question of the effect of an unpaired centromere on exchange in 4 remains open.

The virtual or actual absence of chromosome 4 crossing over in completely diploid females cultured at the usual temperatures remains an enigma; one is presently forced to invoke the centromeric interference suggested by Beadle (1932) and Mather (1939). Answers as to why such interference is relaxed in diplo-4 triploids or at temperatures of 30°C and higher may aid in the elucidation of crossover mechanisms in general. One might speculate that, if the paired centromeres normally block crossing over in 4, perhaps one member of the pair is occasionally "peeled away" by an unpaired X or large autosome in diplo-4 triploid females and a similar centric separation is promoted by high temperatures.

B. Cytological Mapping

The refractory nature of the microchromosome to recombinational mapping has compelled the author to rely mainly on deletion mapping for the localization of lethal mutants detected on 4. This technique combines a cytological approach (examination of the salivary gland chromosomes of suspected deficiencies) with genetic findings (complementation tests of individual lethals with the deficiencies). Given a sufficient number of overlapping deficiencies, it will be possible to assign each lethal mutant (i.e. each vital locus) to a specific band in the polytene 4th chromosome. Figure 2(b) shows the present status of the complementation map of the eight loci situated within *Df(4)G*, a deficiency which covers the distalmost 8–9 bands of 4R. In order to confirm the apparent linearity of the complementation pattern and the colinearity of band location with gene function, a few more deletions will have to be induced and the polytene chromosome extents of the putative deficiencies will have to be established.

Cytological mapping of microchromosomal genes may also be effected through the use of translocations involving 4 and the other members of the complement. This technique, suggested to me by D. L. Lindsley and E. H. Grell, utilizes chromosomes consisting of various-sized pieces of 4 and relatively small amounts (to minimize the problems of hyperploidy) of either the X, Y, 2, or 3. Appropriate crosses yield individuals which possess a lethal- or visible-bearing 4 of normal length and, as partner to this 4, a half-translocation which lacks a certain defined part of the microchromosome. If the lethal is situated within the segment missing in the translocated 4, adults of this genotype will not appear. In the case of visibles so tested, emerged adults will express the mutant phenotypes. Some of the extant translocated 4's should prove useful, although in most cases their breakpoints in 4 need to be identified more precisely. Newly induced rearrangements will doubtless be required for a definitive mapping of all recognized loci.

V. Genetic Composition and Significance

A. Distribution of Loci

Table II lists the lethal and semilethal mutations detected at 36 essential loci on chromosome 4. The total number of alleles recovered at each locus and the lethal period of mutants at the loci is also shown. One additional vital locus, revealed by mutant *fs(4)34*, and 6–8 loci identified by recessive visibles increase the number of recognized loci to 43–45. Since two of the eight visibles, eyeless and shaven, may be coincident with vital loci *33* and *40*, respectively, the lower number of 43 will be employed in the calculations below.

The distribution of loci on chromosome 4 is as follows:

(A) Nine vital loci (*1*, *13*, *17*, *18*, *20*, *24*, *25*, *26* and *M*) and three loci recognized from recessive visibles (*ci*, *gvl* and *ar*) are within the limits of the deficiency *Df(4)M*. This comprises about 27–32% of the right arm

TABLE II. Chromosome 4 lethals and semilethals analysed to 1971.

Region	Locus designation	Effective lethal phase[a]	Total alleles	Sources: Spont.	X rays	EMS	ICR–170	Melphalan
	1	L	11	2	6	3		
	13	E–L	1		1			
	17	E–L	2		2			
	18	P?	1			1		
Df(4)M	20	P	4	1		3		
	24	L–P?	10			10		
	25	L	5	1		3		1
	26	L	2			1	1	
	M	L	1		1			
	9	P	4	2		2		
	16	E–L	9	4		4	1	
	19	P	8			2	4	2
Df(4)G	29	P	3	3				
	39	E–L	1			1		
	40[b]	L	0					
"bt^D"	2	E	35	3	6	23	3	
	23	E	8	1		6	1	
	4	L	15	2	3	9	1	
	5	E–L	11	1	1	9		
	6	P	7	1	3	3		
	7	E	4		1	3		
Between	8	L–P	3		3			
M and *G*	10	E	3	1	1	1		
or	14	L	7	1	2	4		
proximal	15	P	3	3				
to *M*	21	P	5	1		4		
	22	P	1	1				
	27	L	1			1		
	28	L	3			3		
	30	L	1			1		
	31	P?	1			1		
	32	P	1			1		
	33	P	4	1		3		
	35	L	1			1		
	36	P	4			4		
	37	L	4			4		
Total	**36**		**184**	**29**	**30**	**111**	**11**	**3**

[a] Based on the developmental arrest caused by mutations at each locus. E (embryonic), L (larval), P (pupal), E–L, L–P (in two adjacent stages or their boundary). [b] Locus deduced from behavior of suspected deficiencies.

of the microchromosome (4R near the centromere) in stretched salivary gland chromosomes.

(B) Six vital loci (*9, 16, 19, 29, 39* and *40*) and two others (*sv* and *spa*) map within a terminal deficiency, *Df(4)G*, which occupies about 19–24% of 4R.

(C) Vital loci numbering 22 (including loci *2* and *23*) and *bt, ey* and *gy* probably are situated between *Df*'s(*4*)*M* and *G*, although one or more might be to the left of *M*.

There is no evidence in the above figures against the idea that loci on 4R are distributed more or less at random. As indicated in Table III, the proportions of loci detected, salivary gland chromosome bands counted and relative lengths measured for the three microchromosomal regions in question (*Df(4)M*, *Df(4)G* and *M–G* interval) are in good agreement.

TABLE III. The number of loci detected in the three regions of the right arm of chromosome 4 compared to estimates of the length and band content of the regions in salivary gland chromosomes.

	Regions			
	Df(4)M	*Df(4)G*	Between *M* & *G*	Total[a]
Number of Loci	12	7	24	43[b]
	(0·28)	(0·16)	(0·56)	(1·0)
Number of Bands	11–15	8–9	26–31	50
	(0·22–0·30)	(0·16–0·18)	(0·52–0·62)	(1·0)
Relative Length				
A.	0·27	0·24	0·49	1·0
B.	0·32	0·19	0·49	1·0

[a] The small segment proximal to *Df(4)M* and 4L are ignored. [b] The identity of locus *33* and *ey* and of *40* and *sv* is assumed. A. and B. refer to chromosomes stretched to 15 μ and 30 μ, respectively.

1. The Df(4)M *Region*

Mapping of the loci within *Df(4)M* has lagged as a consequence of the scarcity of fourth chromosomes lacking shorter critical segments within the large deficiency. *M, ci, 13* and *17* are grouped together on the basis of complementation tests and the small $M(4)^{63a}$ deletion. This latter is lethal when homozygous or heterozygous with the presumed point mutation *M*, and it uncovers recessive *ci*. The dominant visible, recessive lethal ci^D survives over $M(4)^{63a}$ but dies in combination with lethals at independent loci *13* and *17*. Ce^2/ci^D and $Ce^2/17$ heterozygotes are inviable as are Ce^2-

homozygotes. Ce^2/ci^D individuals die mainly in the pupal stage while the respective homozygotes perish as embryos or, in the case of Ce^2, occasionally as larvae. The delayed lethality of the heterozygote may be viewed as partial complementation and taken as an indication of non-allelism. On the basis of the greater deviation from normal wing venation in ci^D/ci flies as compared to $ci^D/+$ and ci/ci, the two factors are shown as adjacent on the map. The finding that $M(4)^{63a}$ interacts with *ci* but not ci^D (in particular the viability of $M(4)^{63a}/ci^D$) casts doubt on a conclusion of simple allelism between the dominant and recessive vein mutants. No sequence for *gvl*, *ar* and the six vital loci *1–26* can be offered at this time.

2. *The* Df(4)G *Region*

The availability of several smaller deficiencies, some verified cytologically and others suspected from genetic data, within *Df(4)G* has permitted a more detailed mapping of the seven distinct loci found therein. Locus *19* is assigned the most distal site thus far detected on 4R because it is viable with *Df(4)11* but lethal over *Df(4)G* and, while these two deficiencies have apparently the same left breakpoints, *11* retains terminal bands of 102F which are missing in *G*.

Interactions occurring between the mutants within *Df(4)G* have yielded a complementation map of the region which is "linear" for the most part. Putative deficiencies *38* and *40* separate two groups of genes; *9*, *16*, and *29* forming one cluster and *40*, *sv*, and *spa* the other. Loci *39* and *19* are excluded from the two groups, *19* being distal and *39* either between them or to the left of *38*. Additional mapping will be required to seriate *9*, *16*, and *29*, to establish firmly *39*'s place, etc.

3. *The 2–23 Region* ("bt^D")

More than half of the loci detected on 4 (24 of 43) lie outside the large deficiencies *M* and *G*. Most or all of them lie between *M* and *G* but the possibility of loci proximal to *M* cannot be eliminated at this time. The order of these loci is not yet known and I shall dwell at length only on two of them, *2* and *23*. The lethal alleles of both genes interact lethally with two X-ray-induced factors, 2^c and the so-called bt^D. Schultz (reported in Bridges, 1935b) named the recessive lethal, dominant visible he induced in 1933, "bent-Dominant" because of phenotypic similarities to, and interactions with, recessive bent. The lethality of the chromosome remains but the visible effects are no longer observed.

Locus *2* has an exceptionally high mutation rate; over 20% of the lethals found on chromosome 4 are alleles of *2*. All but six of these alleles are

TABLE IV. Results of crosses ($l_1/ci^D \times l_2/ci^D$) involving the complementing alleles of locus *2*

Cross	Progeny		
	ci^D	non-ci^D	% non-ci^D
$2^f \times 2^h$	287	0	0
$2^f \times 2^t$	203	0	0
$2^h \times 2^t$	683	0	0
$2^b \times 2^k$	1375	27	1·93[a]
$2^b \times 2^{ii}$	976	33	3·27[a]
$2^b \times 2^f$	366	105	22·29[a]
$2^b \times 2^h$	228	79	25·73[a]
$2^b \times 2^t$	730	110	13·10[a]
$2^k \times 2^f$	405	102	20·12[a]
$2^k \times 2^h$	431	85	16·47[a]
$2^k \times 2^t$	841	43	4·86[a]
$2^k \times 2^{ii}$	1311	4	0·30[a]
$2^{ii} \times 2^f$	737	202	21·51[a]
$2^{ii} \times 2^h$	979	224	18·62[a]
$2^{ii} \times 2^t$	420	105	20·00[a]
$2^b \times 23$	133	64	32·49
$2^k \times 23$	332	154	31·69
$2^{ii} \times 23$	97	59	37·82
$2^f \times 23$	69	51	42·50
$2^h \times 23$	138	60	30·30
$2^t \times 23$	426	225	34·56
Total for 2 × 23 crosses	1195	613	33·90

[a] Chi-square tests give $P < 0{\cdot}01$ for 2 ci^D:1 non–ci^D ratio.

embryonic lethals in homozygous and all pairwise heterozygous combinations. The six exceptional alleles fall into four complementation units. One group of three (2^f, 2^h, 2^t) kills embryos when homozygous or heterozygous with each other or with the 29 alleles already mentioned. However, when 2^f, 2^h, or 2^t are combined with 2^b, 2^k or 2^{ii}, non-ci^D surviving adults, e.g. $2^f/2^b$, $2^h/2^k$, etc., appear. The proportions of these non-ci^D flies are in all cases significantly below the approximate 33% found in crosses of nonallelic lethals such as *2* and *23* (see Table IV). Lethals 2^b, 2^k, and 2^{ii} kill larvae when homozygous; this property marks them as unique from all other *2* alleles. They also complement each other to the extent that surviving adults such as $2^b/2^k$ and $2^b/2^{ii}$ appear. However, the proportions of such flies (0·3–3·3%) are much lower than the examples of complementation described earlier for $2^b/2^f$, etc. In all these instances complementation is only partial as indicated by both the frequences of survival and by the phenotypes of the survivors; they are characterized by abdomens clearly narrower than normal. The evidence of high mutation rate, partial complementation, and divergent developmental effects leads to the conclusion that locus *2* is a complex (pseudoallelic) one. A complementation map of *2* is given in Fig. 3.

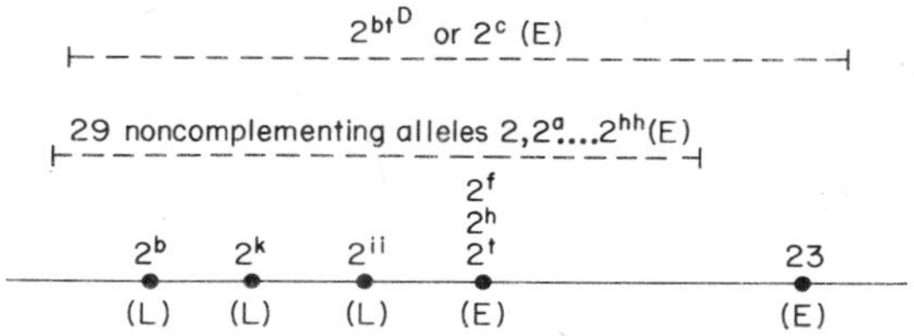

FIG. 3. Complementation map of the *2–23* ("b^{tD}") region. (E) and (L) indicate that death of homozygotes occurs in embryonic or larval period, respectively.

Fig. 3 also shows the presumably adjacent locus *23*. Seven completely lethal mutations and one semilethal have occurred at *23*. Only the lethal alleles can be properly classified; they are embryonic lethals when homozygous or heterozygous with each other or with 2^{btD} and 2^{c}. As shown in Table IV, *23* is fully viable with the other *2* alleles. One interpretation of these findings is that 2^{btD} and 2^{c} are mutations of a regulatory gene which controls two adjacent loci, *2* and *23*, both of which normally function in the embryonic stage. Salivary gland polytene chromosome analyses have not revealed any aberrations in the 2^{btD} or 2^{c} chromosomes. Additional study of these lethals from the cytogenetic point of view, as well as the biochemical (e.g. examination of electrophoretic patterns of proteins), may help to clarify the situation. Crossing over obstacles in chromosome 4 make difficult the attempt to separate by recombination the sub-units of *2* or locus *2* from *23*.

B. THE ROLE OF 4

The analysis of lethal mutants at the vital loci of 4 demonstrates that this autosome, despite its small size and relative paucity of genetic material, performs essential functions at all three pre-adult stages of the insect. Additionally, some involvement in adult fertility is indicated by the female sterile mutant *fs(4)34*. One might also mention that certain adult structures and organs such as eyes, wing veins and bristles are controlled in part by genes on 4. One negative finding of interest, reported by Donady (personal communication), is that five microchromosomal loci (*2, 5, 7, 23* and ci^{D}) do not influence the differentiation of nerve and muscle cells. *In vitro* cultures, homozygous for embryonic lethal mutants at any of these loci, are indistinguishable from wild-type cultures in their ability to generate axons, ganglia and pulsating spindle-shaped muscle cells.

One of the 45 or so loci in *D. melanogaster*, whose mutations or deletions are responsible for the Minute phenotype, is located on 4. $M(4)^{57g}$ is probably a point mutation at this locus judging from the normality of its salivary gland polytene chromosomes and the failure of the mutant to uncover the recessive *ci*. Individuals homozygous for $M(4)^{57g}$ die as larvae whereas embryonic death occurs for *Df(4)M* homozygotes. To be sure, there are many loci absent in the *Df(4)M* chromosome including ci^D, *Ce*, *13* and *17*, all four of which operate to some extent during embryogenesis. The M^+ gene *per se*, whether it specifies a tRNA (Ritossa *et al.*, 1966) or not, seemingly is unnecessary until larval life commences. Experiments conducted in my laboratory, attempting by means of free amino acid analysis to determine the species of tRNA encoded by the M^+ gene on 4, have not yet yielded conclusive evidence on this point.

A minor role in sex determination has been ascribed to chromosome 4. Bridges (1925) noted that 2X, 3A intersexes showed considerable variation and seemingly formed a bimodal distribution of male-like and female-like individuals. A correlation with the number of fourth chromosomes in the karyotype was observed, i.e. flies with three 4's were more female-like while those with two 4's were more male-like. This led Bridges to postulate the presence of female determiners on 4. Support for this idea has been provided by Fung and Gowen (1960).

C. Relationship to X

There are several independent lines of evidence which suggest a closer kinship of chromosome 4 with the X chromosome than with the other autosomes. The preceding section mentioned the presence of female-determiners on 4. Earlier in this review I contrasted the relatively high frequency of pupal lethals observed on X and 4 (about 40%) with the low incidence (<10%) reported for chromosome 2. Genetic evidence of homology between X and 4 has been gathered by Sandler and Novitski (1956). They observed a higher frequency of X-chromosome nondisjunction in triplo-4 females as compared to diplo-4's. The assumption is that the extra 4 occasionally pairs with X, thereby causing a disturbance in the usual segregation of the X's. Sandler and Novitski suggest that the proximal heterochromatin may be the area of affinity between X and 4. The idea that proximal heterochromatic regions are responsible for non-homologous pairing has been examined and discredited by R. F. Grell (1967 and earlier). According to Grell, "Recognition at distributive pairing is correlated with the total size of the chromosome, is independent of homology, and is restricted to chromosomes which have not undergone exchange with an independent homologue." (For a fuller discussion see R. F. Grell, Chapter 10 in volume 1c.)

To these genetic arguments can be added some cytological evidence of homology between X and 4. Kaufmann and Gay (1969) observed that the distal tip of 4R (in two different X-ray-induced *2;4* translocations) paired end-to-end more frequently (59% of the associations recorded) with the tip of the X than with the other autosomes. One interpretation of this mutual attraction is that it reflects structural (and possibly genetic?) similarities between the microchromosome and X.

Krivshenko (1959 and earlier) has postulated a homology between the microchromosome of *D. melanogaster* (and presumably of other species such as *D. simulans*) and the proximal euchromatic section of the X in *D. busckii. D. busckii* (n = 3) lacks a dot-like chromosome but contains two metacentric autosomes and a rod X (Patterson and Stone, 1952). In Xp, the section of the X between the centromere and the heterochromatic area (which includes a nucleolus organizer), Krivshenko has found loci whose mutants mimic closely *Ce*, ci^D, *gvl* and *sv*, all of which are on chromosome 4 in *D. melanogaster*. A student of Krivshenko, Rowan (personal communication), has detected two additional visibles in Xp which resemble *ey* and *ar*, respectively, of the *D. melanogaster* 4. Rowan reports some 26 loci (mainly disclosed through lethal mutations) on Xp, which, incidentally, has an estimated 44 bands in the polytene chromosome. Krivshenko (1959) has drawn some general phylogenetical conclusions (from some of the above information and other considerations) among which is the notion that "the microchromosome of *D. melanogaster* was in the past evidently a part of the X chromosome . . ." If this hypothesis is correct, the evolutionary divergence between X and the erstwhile sex chromosome turned autosome, 4, has not been extreme. Chromosome 4 has retained significant attributes of its X ancestry, namely a high proportion of genes which act during the pupal stage and a dosage compensation mechanism which permits monosomics to survive, albeit not as well as XO individuals. Can the "little bit" I alluded to in the Introduction be an ex-X?

References

ADKISSON, K. P., PERREAULT, W. J. and GAY, H. (1971). Differential fluorescent staining of *Drosophila* chromosomes with quinacrine mustard. *Chromosoma* **34,** 190–205.

BARIGOZZI, C., DOLFINI, S., FRACCARO, M., REZZONICO RAIMONDI, G. and TIEPOLO, L. (1966). *In vitro* study of the DNA replication patterns of somatic chromosomes of *Drosophila melanogaster*. *Expl. Cell Res.* **43,** 231–234.

BEADLE, G. W. (1932). A possible influence of the spindle fibre on crossing-over in *Drosophila. Proc. Natl. Acad. Sci., U.S.A.* **18,** 160–165.

BOLEN, H. R. (1931). A mutual translocation involving the fourth and the X-chromosomes of *Drosophila. Am. Nat.* **65,** 417–422.

BRIDGES, C. B. (1925). Sex in relation to chromosomes and genes. *Am. Nat.* **59,** 127–137.

BRIDGES, C. B. (1935a). Cytological data on chromosome four of *Drosophila melanogaster. Trud. Dinam. Razvit.* **10,** 463–474.

BRIDGES, C. B. (1935b). The mutants and linkage data of chromosome four of *Drosophila melanogaster. Biol. Zh.* (*Mosc.*) **4,** 401–420.

BRIDGES, C. B. and BREHME, K. S. (1944). The mutants of *Drosophila melanogaster.* Carnegie Inst. of Wash. Publ. 552, Washington, D.C.

BRIDGES, P. N. (1942). A new map of the salivary gland 2L-chromosome of *Drosophila melanogaster. J. Hered.* **33,** 403–408.

BURNS, G. W. (1969). "The Science of Genetics: An Introduction to Heredity." MacMillan, New York.

ELLISON, J. R. and BARR, H. J. (1971). Differences in the quinacrine staining of the chromosomes of a pair of sibling species: *Drosophila melanogaster* and *Drosophila simulans. Chromosoma* **34,** 424–435.

FUNG, S.-T. C. and GOWEN, J. W. (1960). Role of autosome-IV in *Drosophila melanogaster* sex balance. *Genetics* **45,** 988–989.

FUNG, S.-T. C. and STERN, C. (1951). The seriation of fourth chromosome loci in *Drosophila melanogaster. Proc. Natl. Acad. Sci., U.S.A.* **37,** 403–404.

GALL, J. G., COHEN, E. H. and POLAN, M. L. (1971). Repetitive DNA sequences in *Drosophila. Chromosoma* **33,** 319–344.

GRELL, E. H. (1961). The tetrasomic for chromosome *4* in *Drosophila melanogaster. Genetics* **46,** 1177–1183.

GRELL, R. F. (1959). Non-random assortment of non-homologous chromosomes in *Drosophila melanogaster. Genetics* **44,** 421–435.

GRELL, R. F. (1967). Pairing at the chromosomal level. *J. Cell. Physiol.* **70,** 119–146.

GRELL, R. F. (1971). Heat-induced exchange in the fourth chromosome of diploid females of *Drosophila melanogaster. Genetics* **69,** 523–527.

GRELL, R. F. and GRELL, E. H. (1960). The behavior of non-homologous chromosomal elements involved in nonrandom assortment in *Drosophila melanogaster. Proc. Natl. Acad. Sci., U.S.A.* **46,** 51–57.

GRIFFEN, A. B. and STONE, W. S. (1940). The second arm of chromosome *4* in *Drosophila melanogaster.* Univ. Texas Publ. **4032,** 201–207.

HANNAH, A. (1951). Localization and function of heterochromatin in *Drosophila melanogaster. Adv. Genet.* **4,** 87–125.

HEITZ, E. (1928). Das Heterochromatin der Moose. I. *Jahrb. wiss. Bot.* **69,** 762–818.

HEITZ, E. (1933). Die somatische Heteropyknose bei *Drosophila melanogaster* und ihre genetische Bedeutung. (Cytologische Untersuchungen an Dipteren. III.) *Z. Zellforsch.* **20,** 237–287.

HOCHMAN, B. (1968). The developmental time of action of recessive lethal mutations on the fourth chromosome of *Drosophila melanogaster.* Proc. XII Int. Cong. of Genetics **1,** 147.

HOCHMAN, B. (1971). Analysis of chromosome *4* in *Drosophila melanogaster.* II. Ethyl methanesulfonate induced lethals. *Genetics* **67,** 235–252.

HOCHMAN, B., GLOOR, H. and GREEN, M. M. (1964). Analysis of chromosome *4* in *Drosophila melanogaster*. I. Spontaneous and X-ray-induced lethals. *Genetica* **35,** 109–126.

HOGE, M. A. (1915). Another gene in the fourth chromosome of *Drosophila*. *Am. Nat.* **49,** 47–49.

JONES, K. W. and ROBERTSON, F. W. (1970). Localization of reiterated nucleotide sequences in *Drosophila melanogaster* and mouse by *in situ* hybridization of complementary RNA. *Chromosoma* **31,** 331–345.

JUDD, B. H., SHEN, M. W. and KAUFMAN, T. C. (1972). The anatomy and function of a segment of the X chromosome of *Drosophila melanogaster*. *Genetics* **71,** 139–156.

KAUFMANN, B. P. (1934). Somatic mitoses of *Drosophila melanogaster*. *J. Morph.* **56,** 125–155.

KAUFMANN, B. P. and GAY, H. (1969). The capacity of the fourth chromosome of *Drosophila melanogaster* to establish end-to-end contacts with the other chromosomes in salivary gland cells. *Chromosoma* **26,** 395–409.

KENYON, A. M. (1967). Comparison of frequency distributions of viabilities of second with fourth chromosomes from caged *Drosophila melanogaster*. *Genetics* **55,** 123–130.

KRIVSHENKO, J. (1959). New evidence for the homology of the short euchromatic elements of the *X* and *Y* chromosomes of *Drosophila busckii* with the microchromosome of *Drosophila melanogaster*. *Genetics* **44,** 1027–1040.

LAIRD, C. D. and MCCARTHY, B. J. (1969). Molecular characterization of the *Drosophila genome*. *Genetics* **63,** 865–882.

LEWIS, E. B. (1950). The phenomenon of position effect. *Adv. Genet.* **3,** 75–113.

LI, J.-C. (1927). The effect of chromosome aberrations on development in *Drosophila melanogaster*. *Genetics* **12,** 1–58.

LIFSCHYTZ, E. and FALK, R. (1969). Fine structure analysis of a chromosome segment in *Drosophila melanogaster*. *Mutation Res.* **8,** 147–155.

MATHER, K. (1939). Crossing over and heterochromatin in the X-chromosome of *Drosophila melanogaster*. *Genetics* **24,** 412–435.

MEDVEDEV, N. N. (1938). Studies in genetics of development. II. Influence of lethal genes on the development of characters as studied by transplantation. *C.R.* (*Dokl.*) *Acad. Sci., U.R.S.S.*, N.S. **20,** 319–321.

MOORE, C. M. and GRELL, R. F. (1972). Factors affecting recognition and disjunction of chromosomes at distributive pairing in female *Drosophila melanogaster*. I: Total length vs. arm length. *Genetics* **70,** 567—581.

MORGAN, T. H., STURTEVANT, A. H. and MORGAN, L. V. (1945). Investigations on the constitution of the germinal material in relation to heredity. *Yearb. Carnegie Instn. Wash.* **44,** 157–160.

MULLER, H. J. (1914). A gene for the fourth chromosome of *Drosophila*. *J. Exp. Zool.* **17,** 325–336.

OGAKI, M., NAKASHIMA-TANAKA, E. and MURAKAMI, S. (1967). Inheritance of ether resistance in *Drosophila melanogaster*. *Jap. J. Gen.* **42,** 387–394.

OSMAN, H. E. S. and ROBERTSON, A. (1968). The introduction of genetic material from inferior into superior strains. *Gen. Res.* **12,** 221–236.

OSTER, I. I. (1952). A study of ultraviolet induced lethal mutations in *Drosophila melanogaster*. *Heredity* **6,** 403–407.

PATTERSON, J. T. and STONE, W. S. (1952). "Evolution in the genus *Drosophila*." MacMillan, New York.

PATTERSON, J. T., STONE, W. S., BEDICHEK, S. and SUCHE, M. (1934). The production of translocations in *Drosophila*. *Am. Nat.* **68,** 359–369.

RAE, P. M. (1970). Chromosomal distribution of rapidly reannealing DNA in *Drosophila melanogaster*. *Proc. Natl. Acad. Sci., U.S.A.* **67,** 1018–1025.

RIS, H. and KUBAI, D. F. (1970). Chromosome structure. *In* "Annual Review of Genetics" (H. L. Roman, L. M. Sandler and A. Campbell, eds.) Vol. 4, pp. 263–294. Annual Reviews, Inc., Palo Alto, Calif.

RITOSSA, F. M., ATWOOD, K. C. and SPIEGELMAN, S. (1966). On the redundancy of DNA complementary to amino acid transfer RNA and its absence from the nucleolar region of *Drosophila melanogaster*. *Genetics* **54,** 663–676.

ROBERTS, P. A. (1972). A possible case of position effect on DNA replication in *Drosophila melanogaster*. *Genetics* **72,** 607–614.

ROBERTSON, F. W., CHIPCHASE, M. and MAN, N. T. (1969). The comparison of differences in reiterated sequences by RNA–DNA hybridisation. *Genetics* **63,** 369–385.

RUDKIN, G. T. (1965). The relative mutabilities of DNA in regions of the *X* chromosome of *Drosophila melanogaster*. *Genetics* **52,** 665–681.

SANDLER, L. M. and NOVITSKI, E. (1956). Evidence for genetic homology between chromosomes *1* and *4* in *Drosophila melanogaster*, with a proposed explanation for the crowding effect in triploids. *Genetics* **41,** 189–193.

SCHULTZ, J. (1935). Aspects of the relation between genes and development in *Drosophila*. *Am. Nat.* **69,** 30–54.

SETO, F. (1961). A developmental study of recessive lethals from wild populations of *Drosophila melanogaster*. *Am. Nat.* **95,** 365–373.

SINGLETON, W. R. (1962). "Elementary Genetics." Van Nostrand, Princeton, N. J.

SLIZYNSKI, B. M. (1944). A revised map of salivary gland chromosome *4*. *J. Hered.* **32,** 322–325.

STERN, C. (1948). The effects of change in quantity, combination and position of genes. *Science, N.Y.* **108,** 615–621.

STURTEVANT, A. H. (1936). Preferential segregation in triplo-IV females of *Drosophila melanogaster*. *Genetics* **21,** 444–466.

STURTEVANT, A. H. (1951). A map of the fourth chromosome of *Drosophila melanogaster* based on crossing over in triploid females. *Proc. Natl. Acad. Sci., U.S.A.* **37,** 405–407.

THOMPSON, P. E. (1963). Centric pairing and crossing-over in *Drosophila melanogaster*. *Genetics* **48,** 697–701.

TINIAKOV, G. G. and TERENTIEVA, E. L. (1933). Cubitus-interruptus, a new genovariation of the fourth chromosome of *Drosophila melanogaster*. *Genetics* **18,** 117–120.

VOSA, C. G. (1970). The discriminating fluorescence patterns of the chromosomes of *Drosophila melanogaster*. *Chromosoma* **31,** 446–451.

WHITTEN, M. J. (1968). Genetic control of penetrance and evolution of dominance in *Drosophila*. *Heredity* **23,** 263–278.

WILLIAMSON, J. H., PARKER, D. R. and MANCHESTER, W. G. (1970a). X-ray-induced recombination in the fourth chromosome of *Drosophila melanogaster* females. I. Kinetics and brood patterns. *Mutation Res.* **9,** 287–297.

WILLIAMSON, J. H., PARKER, D. R. and MANCHESTER, W. G. (1970b). X-ray induced recombination in the fourth chromosome of *Drosophila melanogaster* females. II. Segregational properties of recombinant fourth chromosomes. *Mutation Res.* **9,** 299–306.

23. Mutable and Mutator Loci

M. M. GREEN

Department of Genetics
University of California
Davis, California, U.S.A.

I. Introduction

During the six or so decades of genetic research with *Drosophila*, a number of sporadic occurrences of extraordinarily high spontaneous mutation have been reported. When considered collectively, the individual cases of increased spontaneous mutation appear to fall into one or the other of three discrete classes. One class of increased mutations can be ascribed to mutable genes. Mutable genes are specific alleles at recognized gene loci which manifest the property of mutational instability. By and large the mutational events associated with mutable genes are intragenic in nature and thus delimited to the specific gene locus involved. A second class of increased spontaneous mutation is associated with mutator genes. Mutator genes, as a consequence of their altered function, "induce" mutations among a wide spectrum of gene loci. Thus, in contrast to mutable genes, the action of mutator genes is intergenic. Mutator genes can be mapped to specific loci. A third class of increased spontaneous mutation has been ascribed to extrachromosomal factors or agents. Here, it has not been possible to correlate the observed mutations with any chromosomal gene or genes and thus extrachromosomal factors are invoked as responsible for mutational events.

In the discussion which follows specific examples of mutable genes, mutator genes and extrachromosomal mutator factors will be considered with particular emphasis on (1) their origin, (2) their genetic properties, and (3) their possible modes of action.

II. Mutable Genes

Mutation is herein arbitrarily defined as an intragenic process disassociated from recombination events such as meiotic crossing over, gene conversion, etc. This definition restricts mutable genes to those examples where recombination has been excluded as a factor in the mutation process. From the historical point of view this definition excludes from consideration what has been considered to be the first mutable gene found in *Drosophila*, viz. the yellow-reddish-alpha body color mutant (y^{ra}) of *D. virilis* described by Demerec (1926a, 1928a). The genetic conditions under which y^{ra} reverted to wild type strongly suggest that recombination was intimately involved with reversion. Thus reversions occurred in females and not males and then only in heterozygous females, e.g. y^{ra}/y or y^{ra}/y^{r} but not in y^{ra}/y^{ra} females. In addition a disproportionate number of reversions were associated with recombination in the *y–sc* (*sc* = scute) interval. Taken together these facts strongly suggest that reversion of y^{ra} is a recombination correlated event akin to what is currently called gene conversion.

A. Mutable Miniature-3 alpha (*mt-3α*) of *D. virilis*

Spanning a period of 15 years of research, Demerec pioneered the study of mutable genes with his detailed investigations of several mutable genes in *D. virilis* especially *mt-3α*. The properties and vagaries of *mt-3α* will be considered in some detail because thus far among mutable genes of *Drosophila* they have been described in the greatest detail and because they provide a frame of reference for subsequent studies of mutable genes.

1. The Origin of mt-3α.

"A single miniature male was found among 177 flies of an experiment with reddish and from this male all miniature-α flies were derived." So

Demerec (1926b) described the origin of *mt-3α*. Because reddish (y^{re}) is unrelated to *mt* except for loose linkage to the X chromosome, it can be concluded that the origin of *mt-3α* represents a unique spontaneous event.

2. *The Mutability of* mt-3α

Breeding experiments with the original *mt-3α* male and his descendants established the following facts (Demerec, 1926b). Recessive *mt-3α* is linked to the X chromosome and allelic to the standard recessive miniature allele, *mt-1*. Mutations of *mt-3α* to wild-type occur frequently and occur in *mt-3α* males, homozygous *mt-3α* females and heterozygous females, e.g. *mt-3α/mt-1*. Reversions of *mt-3α* to wild type in females are not associated with crossing over. Wild type reversions of *mt-3α* are mutationally stable. Mutations of *mt-3α* to wild type occur both germinally and somatically—the latter manifest as mosaic flies.

Attempts to estimate rates of reversion of *mt-3α* to wild type established that the reversion process was amenable to selection. Selection within *mt-3α* (Demerec, 1928b) led to the establishment of three lines: (1) a low mutable line in which no germinal mutations occurred and somatic reversions, as mosaics, were found in 3·5% of the flies; (2) a high mutation line where among the progeny *ca* 30% were wild type, 50% were mosaics and the remainder miniature; and (3) a mosaic line where all individuals were mosaics but no germinal mutations were recovered. Genetic analysis of these lines established several significant facts. The low mutable line resulted in a "change of state" in *mt-3α* to a new allelic form, *mt-3γ* which was germinally stable but somatically mutable. The mosaic line resulted from the interaction between *mt-3γ* and *S-1*, a second chromosome dominant which increases the somatic mutability of *mt-3γ*. The high mutation line resulted from the interaction of *mt-3α* and *M*, an autosomal dominant gene which increases the mutability of *mt-3α*. Subsequently (Demerec, 1929a), two other autosomal factors, recessive *s-2* and dominant *S-3*, were isolated and were shown to stimulate the somatic mutability of *mt-3γ*. Finally, yet another change of state, designated *mt-3β*, was isolated (Demerec, 1929b) as a derivative of *mt-3α* and shown to be mutationally stable somatically as well as germinally. At least one instance of *mt-3β* changing to *mt-3γ* was isolated from a mass culture of *mt-3β* (Demerec, 1929b).

3. *The Basis of Mutability of* mt-3α

The facts bearing on the mutability of *mt-3α* speak for themselves. Little of relevance can be extracted from these data which throws light on the underlying cause of mutation of *mt-3α*. At this juncture the fact that this mutation process can be influenced by other genetic factors is of interest but adds little to an understanding of the causal mechanism.

B. Mutable Magenta-alpha (*m-α*) of *D. virilis*

Concurrent with the finding of *mt-3α*, a mutable allele of the sex-linked recessive eye color mutant, magneta (*m*) was described by Demerec (1927).

1. The Origin of Mutable m-α

Two *m-α* males were recovered among the 120 progeny of a pair mating. One male crossed to four sisters produced an F_1 consisting of 469 wild type and 46 *m-α* females, and 365 wild type, 19 *m-α* and 1 mosaic males suggesting that one female was heterozygous. Since *m-α* individuals, especially females, are near wild type in phenotype they could have been overlooked in the stock for several generations. Allelism of *m-α* to standard *m* was established by mapping *m-α* since *m-α/m* often is near wild type in phenotype.

2. The Mutability of m-α

Crosses of *m-α/m f* (*f* maps 4 units from *m*) females to *m f* males resulted in the recovery of numerous wild type non-*f* males suggesting *m-α* was reverting to wild type. Such reversions appear to be mutationally stable. Reversions to wild type were also recovered from homozygous *m-α* females and males. Individuals with eyes mosaic for *m-α* and wild type were infrequently recovered indicating the somatic reversion of *m-α*.

3. The basis of mutability of m-α

The published information on *m-α* are too scanty to conjecture the cause of *m-α* mutability. No further information on *m-α* was published and it can be presumed the stock was inadvertently lost.

C. Mutable White-crimson (w^c) of *D. melanogaster*

For a period of some thirty years the mutable genes described by Demerec represented the only examples in *Drosophila*. A probable exception in *D. melanogaster* was suppressor of black, a sex-linked recessive which frequently reverted to wild type (Plough, 1928). Because of this property, it was lost before a detailed genetic analysis could be made. One attempt to induce mutable genes in *D. virilis* by X-irradiation was unsuccessful

(Girvin, 1949). Meanwhile, the study of mutable genes in maize flourished. McClintock (1950, 1951) with her remarkable cytogenetic analysis of controlling element conditioned mutable genes in maize reopened the field and there followed a series of studies in maize by McClintock, Brink, Peterson and others. The hiatus in *Drosophila* research ended in 1967 with the discovery of the mutable w^c to be followed by other cases of mutable genes at the white locus which will be discussed below.

1. The Origin of Mutable w^c

In one of a series of experiments designed to measure the frequency with which w^i (white-ivory) reverts to wild type following X-irradiation, attached-X females homozygous for w^i *spl* (*spl* = split) were treated with 4000 R X-rays (w^i itself reverts spontaneously to wild type at a low frequency). One female was recovered whose eye color phenotype suggested that she was heterozygous for w^i and a partial reversion of w^i. Subsequent breeding tests established the partial reversion to be the mutable w^c (Green, 1967).

2. The Mutability of w^c

Shortly after the recovery of w^c it became clear that this was no ordinary reversion but a mutation with unique properties. A systematic study of the mutability of w^c (Green 1967) disclosed facts which are summarized as follows: (1) w^c mutates spontaneously at an inordinately high rate to a number of different states as judged by the concomitant phenotype change. (2) Mutation occurs in both females and males and appears to be primarily premeiotic as judged by the frequent clustering of recovered mutants. New mutants occur among the progeny of *ca* one in four w^c females and *ca* one in eight w^c males. (3) Mutation occurs in the absence of recombination, meiotic or mitotic, inter or intrachromosomal. (4) Mutational derivatives of w^c are of two types: stable and unstable. Stable types include reversion to wild type and some pure w mutants. Unstable types include those as mutable as the original w^c, e.g. w, w^{dc} (dark crimson), w^{di} (dark ivory), $w^{\text{``}+\text{''}}$ (near wild type) and those inseparable from the original w^i, both in phenotype and revertability to wild type. (5) From females and males homozygous for w^c or its mutable derivatives, deficiencies of varying lengths have been recovered. All begin at the w locus and extend either to the left or to the right, but do not overlap w. Deficiencies may include only the w locus or may extend over a distance of 4 map units (i.e. beyond the mutant *ec*) to the right. (6) Transpositions of a segment of the w gene including w^c to different sites in chromosome 3 have been recovered from both w^c females and males and retain their w^c mutability. (7) w^c maps at the w^a site of the *w* locus (Green, 1969a) and like w^i (Bowman and Green, 1966) reduces interallelic crossing over.

3. The Basis of w^c *Mutability*

Any explanation of the fundamental causes of w^c mutability must account for the unusual genetic features of this mutable gene. These are the production of chromosome deletions in the proximity of the *w* locus and the transposition and integration of small segments of the *w* locus into the third chromosome with the retention of mutability. It has been argued that mutability as an autonomous genic event seems unlikely especially as an explanation for the occurrence of deficiencies and transpositions. Rather, it is suggested, a more likely explanation relates these changes to the behavior of a virus-like foreign agent integrated at the *w* locus (Green, 1967, 1969b). The plausibility of this and other explanations for mutable gene behavior will be assessed *in extenso* below.

D. Mutable White-zeste-mottle (w^{zm}) of *D. melanogaster*

The phenotypic expression of the sex-linked mutant zeste (*z*) provides an unusually sensitive assay for genetic changes at the white locus. The zeste-white interrelationship will not be discussed here in detail except to note that the zeste phenotype depends upon dosage at the white locus and specifically of the right-most, the so-called w^e and w^{sp}, sites of this locus. Thus a female homozygous for both *z* and w^+ is zeste in phenotype because she has 2 w^{e+} and 2 w^{sp+} sites while a *z* male is wild type in eye color because he has only 1 w^{e+} and 1 w^{sp+}. If the number of w^{e+} and w^{sp+} sites in a *z* male is increased by duplication, the phenotype becomes zeste and if the number of w^{e+} and w^{sp+} sites in a homozygous *z* female is halved by deletion the phenotype becomes wild type. In this way site dosage at the w^+ locus can be assayed through the resultant *z* phenotype.

1. The Origin of Mutable w^zm

Among the progeny of a female of the genotype *sc z ec ct*/w^{bf} there occurred one exceptional male *sc z* in genotype but variegated (dark spots on a yellow salt and pepper background) in eye color (Green, cf. Becker, 1959). A homozygous stock was established and the subsequent demonstration of high mutability at the w^+ locus in this stock was the subject of a series of investigations by Judd (1963, 1967, 1969), and by Kalisch and Becker (1970) and Kalisch (1970).

2. *The Mutability of* w^{zm} *and derivatives*

Kalisch and Becker (1970) described a number of exceptional types isolated from the w^{zm} strain as spontaneous changes at the w^+ locus which are expressed in z males as greater and greater phenotypic departures from wild type or conversely more and more zeste in eye color. The mutant z acts as the phenotypic indicator for the several strains; in its absence all males are wild type in eye color. In phenotypic sequence they are denoted as: w^{zl} (spontaneous as one male in the w^{zm} stock), w^{zmz} (once as several males in the $z\ w^{zm}$ stock) and w^{zmzz} (as one male in the $z\ w^{zmz}$ stock). Among these four strains one, w^{zl}, is stable and the others mutable. Because of the comparative ease in the phenotypic scoring of exceptional males, Kalisch and Becker concentrated their mutability studies on the $z\ w^{zmz}$ and $z\ w^{zmzz}$ strains although they demonstrated that w^{zm} was also mutable.

A number of critical facts emerge from these studies. Both w^{zmz} and w^{zmzz} are highly mutable in males and females. Mutants were often recovered as clusters indicating a premeiotic origin. None of the mutations was to w^+ but the most frequent class of mutation recovered from $z\ w^{zmz}$ (1/250–1/300) was designated w^{zm+} and results in a male eye color intermediate between those of $z\ w^+$ and $z\ w^{zm}$. At a lower frequency (*ca.* 1/4000) w^{zmz} reverted to w^{zm} and to a white-eyed type designated w^{zmzw} (*ca.* 1/2000). In males, w^{zmzz} reverted to w^{zmz} at a rate of 1/721 gametes tested. Several interesting facts emerge from these experiments. Strains of the types w^{zm} and w^{zmz} derived by reversion from mutable w^{zmz} and w^{zmzz} were not mutable. A restudy of the mutability of the w^{zmz} strain two years after the initial study showed that it was mutable but at a much reduced level.

Using the same $z\ w^{zm}$ strain, Judd (1967, 1969) isolated mutant derivatives which Kalisch and Becker did not find. The most frequent changes were to w^{zl} and two different white-eyed types, one designated w^z which did not suppress z and the other designated w^{zs} which did suppress z. It was found that w^{zl} and w^{zs} mapped at the wch site and w^z at the w^a site of the w locus. In his brief reports, Judd noted that mutants often occurred in clusters, crossing over was not involved, and the mutation rate was greater in females than males. All changes were reversible. Most interesting is his finding that from w^z he could recover $w\ N$ females. Three independent N types were studied in detail and were found to be *bona fide* mutants not deficiencies of the w–N interval. Especially significant is the finding that two of the three N mutants proved to be mutable with the recovery of viable w males.

Kalisch (1970) isolated from strain $z\ w^{zmz}$ an interesting and puzzling white-eyed mutant designated $z\ w^w$. This mutant is associated with a short inversion extending from the w locus (3C1–2) to salivary gland chromosome bands 4B4–C1. A detailed study of w^{m} showed it to possess a low order mutability (higher in females than males) to derivatives with pigmented eyes. Seventeen independent derivatives were studied cytologically and genetically and fell into two classes. One class included 11 derivatives manifesting one or the other of the phenotypes $z\ w^{zm+}$, $z\ w^{z1}$, $z\ w^{zmz}$ and $z\ w^{zwzz}$. All were cytologically normal, i.e. were reinversions, and among the 11 some were mutationally stable (e.g. 2 w^{zmz}, 1 w^{zm+}, and 1 w^{zml}) while others were mutationally unstable (e.g. 4 w^{zmz} and 1 w^{zmzz}). The second class included 6 derivates whose eye pigment phenotype is unlike that of the w^{zm}–w^{zmzz} series. All 6 possessed the short inversion cytologically unchanged. Within this class some mutants were mutable, some stable. Precisely what mutational process is taking place is not clear but it seems fairly clear that mutability and reinversion are not causally associated. Since reinversion occurred in both females and males some intrachromosomal rather than an interchromosomal event must be involved.

3. The basis of w^{zm} *mutability*

To explain the origin and mutability of the w^{zm}–w^{zmzz} series, Kalisch and Becker (1970) reasoned that the increased departure from wild type at the zeste locus was a function of the increased dosage of those w locus sites (w^{e+} and w^{sp+}) which are involved in the differentiation of the z phenotype. Mutation then occurs as either an increase or decrease in the dosage of these sites by some kind of intrachromosomal recombination event. Meiotic crossing over is ruled out because mutation occurs in males as well as females. While this explanation has plausibility, it fails to account for one significant fact, the mutational stability of the type w^{zmz} derived by reversion of w^{zmzz} which had itself arisen from a mutable w^{zmz}. In other words if the two w^{zmz} types are in fact identical, the dosage hypothesis cannot account for the mutational instability of one and the mutational stability of the other. An alternative point of view is that the gene dosage explanation is correct and that while the two w^{zmz} types produce inseparable phenotypes, they are nonetheless structurally different and it is this structural difference which makes for mutability on the one hand and mutational stability on the other.

Judd (1969) concluded that his mutable derivatives of w^{zm} could better be explained by the presence of a controlling element. Two sets of facts appear to have motivated this conclusion. First, w^{zs} and w^{z} mutable derivatives of w^{zm} map at different sites, the former to the wch site, the later to the w^{a} site. Since the w^{a} site is not involved in the w–z interaction, it is difficult to understand how it can be mutable by changing its gene dosage. The second and more compelling observation is the recovery of mutable *N* types from w^z. *N* maps at least one map unit to the right of *w* and the origin of mutable *N* types through transposition of a controlling element from w^z to the *N* locus seems more likely than intragenic recombination of the *w* locus.

E. Mutable Wild Type White Allele (w^{+u}) of *D. melanogaster*

Quite another mutable system, w^{+u} with genetic features which distinguish it from both the w^c and w^{zm} mutable systems, has recently been described be Gethmann (1971). The properties of this system follow.

1. *The origin of mutable* $\mathrm{w}^{+\mathrm{u}}$

All mutable flies are descended of a single attached-X (*C(1)RM*) female carrying a new sex-linked mutation *Etd* (eye tissue determiner). The attached-Xs were detached and *Etd* mapped. In the course of mapping *Etd* which was linked to a w^+ allele, several unexpected white-eyed males were recovered. Since these exceptional males were noncrossovers, they arose from the w^+ linked to *Etd*. This chromosome is the source of the mutable w^{+u}.

2. *The mutability of* $\mathrm{w}^{+\mathrm{u}}$

Mutable w^{+u} mutates frequently to a recessive *w* producing the standard white eye phenotype both in homozygous and heterozygous females and in males. Crossing over is not involved. The recovery of *w* mutants in clusters implies premeiotic origin of the mutational event. Mutations appear to be limited almost exclusively to the germ line. The frequency of mutation is sensitive to the genetic background. Thus in one line of homozygous w^{+u} 24 of 64 females tested produced at least one *w* mutant offspring; in another line 14 of 77 females produced at least one *w* mutant offspring. Subsequent tests of both lines showed the mutation frequency to have decreased somewhat more. Mapping experiments localized w^{+u} to the w^e site of the *w* locus.

All *w* mutants derived from w^{+u} appear to be the same deficiency in which both the w^e and w^{sp} sites are removed. Cytologically the *w* mutants are normal. In experiments designed to recover transposition of the deleted chromosome segment, none was found. In addition, there is no evidence that w^{+u} affects interallelic crossing over.

3. *The basis of* w^{+u} *mutability*

Based on the aforementioned data, Gethmann (1971) suggests that neither the controlling element hypothesis nor the intrachromosomal recombination hypothesis fits the w^{+u} situation. He suggests that w^{+u} causes a malfunctioning in the replication of the white region leading to deletion. In some way w^{+u} occasionally causes a premature termination of DNA replication resulting in the *w* deficiencies.

F. Résumé

The three distinctive white mutable gene systems in *D. melanogaster* reviewed, make it amply clear that the drouth in this realm of genetic research has happily come to an end. When considered collectively, it is obvious that parallelisms in genetic behavior and properties exist between the mutable *w* genes and those mutable genes described in *D. virilis* by Demerec and in maize by McClintock and others. For the compelling question, what makes a gene mutable, there is presently no good answer and, in fact, there are no attractive suggestions. Mutable gene mediated deletions and transpositions motivated the suggestion that high mutability rests with a virus-like "controlling element" or "foreign agent" whose rare integration at a specific site in the chromosome results in a mutable gene at the site. How could such an agent become integrated into the chromosome? Obviously, integration would be facilitated by a chromosome break and in this connection there appears to be a significant coincidence. All three examples of mutable genes at the *w* locus were recovered subsequent to a presumed chromosome break, either as the result of X-irradiation or of crossing over. However, before going overboard on the "foreign agent" hypothesis, it is important to recall the genetic behavior of the male sex determiner ("sex realizer") in the Phorid fly, *Megaselia scalaris*, described by Mainx and his associates (cf. Mainx, 1964, 1966). The "sex realizer" which maps to the end of a chromosome regularly transposes itself from one chromosome end to a nonhomologous chromosome end without change in its sex determination capabilities. The transpositions appear to be premeiotic and often appear in clusters. The implications of this transposition phenomenon for the "controlling element" hypothesis are self-evident.

Cytogenetic studies with tandem duplications in *D. melanogaster* show that intrachromosomal exchanges do occur (Peterson and Laughnan, 1963; Green, 1968) and that the exchange event is not confined to females but can occur in males as a premeiotic event (Peterson and Laughnan, 1964;

Gabay and Laughnan, 1970). These findings lend credence to the intrachromosomal recombination hypothesis of mutability but it remains to be seen what relationship, if any, exists between the length of a tandem duplication and the frequency of intrachromosomal exchanges.

Finally, one may ask, why have the most recent examples of mutable genes in *D. melanogaster* been limited to the white locus? Is there something unique and different about this locus which makes for mutable genes? There seems little reason to believe that the white locus is unique. Rather the phenotypes associated with white are easily scored and thus the detection of mutable *w* genes is facilitated.

In a conversation some years ago, Barbara McClintock expressed the opinion that mutable genes will be discovered when investigators are mentally prepared to discover them. Mutable genes at the white locus have now provided the mental preparation for the discovery of mutable genes at other loci and for the experimental demonstration of their etiology and mechanisms of action. There is little doubt that the flies will generate the genetic information. It remains only for the investigator to keep his eyes open and report what the flies have done.

III. Mutator Genes

In *Drosophila* the phenotype of increased mutation frequency has been more or less refractory to genetic analysis. When undertaken, the genetic analysis has been limited to establishing that a specific chromosome is involved. That a specific mutator gene is responsible has been inferred rather than conclusively established. Thus in *D. melanogaster* where at least five independent cases of high mutation have been described, four have been associated with a specific chromosome. In two instances chromosome 2 has been implicated (Demerec, 1937; Ives, 1945, 1950) and in two other instances chromosome 3 has been implicated (Neel, 1942; Green, 1970). Unequivocal demonstration of a specific mutator gene was possible in only one case where the mutator gene was mapped at *ca.* 57 in chromosome 3 (Green, 1970).

In *D. persimilis* (*D. pseudoobscura*, race B) two presumably separate types of high mutation have been associated with chromosome 2, the homologue of 3L in *D. melanogaster* (Mampell, 1943, 1945).

Two examples of high mutation have been reported as due to extragenic factors or agents. In *D. robusta* increased chromosome breakage is maternally transmitted (Levitan, 1962) and in *D. melanogaster* the extrachromosomal element called delta was found to increase the spontaneous mutation rate (Minamori and Ito, 1971).

The properties of those mutator genes in *D. melanogaster* which have been studied in more detail will be presented below together with additional information on the extrachromosomal mutators.

A. Mutator Gene *hi* of *D. melanogaster*

1. The origin of hi

Ten lines homozygous for second chromosomes extracted from wild flies collected in Florida were tested for the production of spontaenous second chromosome recessive lethal mutations. One line produced an inordinate increase in lethals, and this line was the source of *hi* (Ives, 1945, 1950).

2. The genetic properties of hi

Linkage tests assigned *hi* to the second chromosome. That *hi* is a single gene is inferred, for no further linkage analysis was undertaken. Mutator *hi* increases spontaneous recessive frequencies in both females and males although most of the genetic analysis was centered on *hi* males. By assaying sex-linked recessive lethals with a modified *ClB* method which permitted the identification of XXY females, Ives (1950) was able to show that *hi* was semidominant in its action. As a heterozygote *hi* effected a near five-fold increase in the sex-linked recessive lethal frequency and as a homozygote the increase was nearly ten-fold. The recovery of frequent clusters suggests that *hi* induces lethals primarily in gonial cells. Genetic mapping of *hi*-induced X chromosome lethals uncovered the unexpected finding that a large proportion *ca.* 5 % of these are associated with chromosomal rearrangements (Ives, 1950). Salivary gland chromosome studies of 13 X chromosome rearrangements (Hinton *et al.*, 1951) showed 12 to be inversions in which 11 had the right chromosome break in the proximal heterochromatin and the left break more or less randomly located but at a site of presumed interstitial heterochromatin. One rearrangement was a transposition of an X chromosome segment (5C to 7E) to the proximal heterochromatin. A comparison of the genetic map distribution of mutator induced and ionizing radiation induced sex-linked lethals shows the two to be differently distributed (Ives, 1959). The radiation series is correlated with the DNA distribution (as indicated by the salivary gland chromosome bands), the *hi* series is not. This suggests that *hi* mutates some loci more specifically.

Are *hi* and the second chromosome mutator from the Florida stock (Demerec, 1937) the same? Ives (1950) suggests two reasons for their not being identical. First *hi* is more effective in inducing lethals. Second, the

Florida mutator caused a high frequency of recessive *y* mutants to occur, a feature not associated with *hi*.

3. *The mode of action of* hi

The available information does not permit anything but the rankest speculation concerning the action of *hi*. The high frequency of rearrangements with heterochromatic breaks suggests some kind of specificity but since *hi* has been lost, little more than this can be stated.

B. Mutator Gene *mu* of *D. melanogaster*

1. *The origin of* mu

In an experiment designed to test the pattern of mutation in w^c males, these males were individually crossed to successive harems of females of the genotype y^2 w^- *spl* sn^3. Among the progeny there were regularly found males y^+ w^- *spl* sn^3. The detailed analysis of the y^2w^- *spl* sn^3 stock established that it contained the mutator gene, *mu*, responsible for the reversions of y^2 to y^+ (Green, 1970). This stock has a somewhat varied history and thus the source of the mutator is obscure. Clearly it has existed in the stock unnoticed for a long time.

2. *The genetic properties of* mu

Because it causes y^2 to revert to y^+ at an enormous rate (1/3000 chromosomes), the formal genetics of *mu* could be studied (Green, 1970). This mutator gene functions only in females having no detectable effect in males. It is semidominant as measured by reversions of y^2 to y^+ and linked to chromosome 3. Reversions occur in clusters suggesting premeiotic actions of the mutator gene. It maps within the limits of the deficiency sbd^{105} (within which the *Sb* and *c(3)G* loci are also found) and thus is located to map position 57 of chromosome 3. In addition to reverting y^2, it also increases the reversion frequencies of f^{3N} and of w^{bf} and the forward mutation frequencies of y^2 to *y* and w^a to *w* (Green, 1970 and unpublished observations).

The sex-linked recessive lethal mutation frequency of homozygous *mu* females is *ca.* three times greater than that of homozygous *mu* males or wild type females. Roughly half the *mu* induced lethals are associated with cytologically demonstrable deficiencies (Green and Lefevre, 1972).

In addition to its mutator action, *mu* influences both chromosome disjunction and crossing over (Green, unpublished observations). Thus primary nondisjunction of both the X and fourth chromosomes is significantly increased and crossing over at the tip of the X (from *y–sn*) is significantly decreased in homozygous *mu* females. Crossing over at the base of the X (from *v–car*) is not altered.

The genetic relationship of *mu* and *c(3)G* is rather enigmatic. While both map within $Df(3R)sbd^{105}$ and affect chromosome disjunction and crossing over in a parallel manner, in compound they are complementary. In addition *c(3)G* appears not to be a mutator as measured by reversion of y^2 (Green, 1970) and by assaying sex-linked recessive lethal mutation induction (Hall 1971). Either *c(3)G* and *mu* are alleles which complement one another or they are nonallelic genes but part of a gene cluster ("super-gene") whose members are associated in the control of crossing over and disjunction.

3. *The mode of action of* mu

Any hypothesis designed to explain the action of *mu* must accommodate the fact that *mu* acts premeiotically to induce mutations and meiotically to influence crossing over and chromosome disjunction. This implies that *mu* must, in all likelihood, affect a process common to both mitosis and meiosis. Two processes come to mind: DNA replication and DNA repair. As a basis for further study of *mu*, it is suggested that one or the other process is associated directly with *mu* action. For the moment the fact that *mu* can produce both back mutations to wild type and forward mutations associated with deletions favors the idea that *mu* alters DNA repair. The added fact that *mu* works only in females means that this DNA repair system is one peculiar to females and not possessed by males.

C. Extrachromosomal Mutators

1. *Chromosome breaker of* D. robusta

In a series of reports Levitan and associates (Levitan, 1962, 1963, 1967; Levitan and Schiller, 1963; Levitan and Williamson, 1965) have described an unusual situation in *D. robusta*. In a stock designated *STy*, homozygous for the standard gene arrangement, a high frequency of spontaneous chromosome aberrations was found. The aberrations, which include translocations, para- and pericentric inversions and transpositions, occur among the progeny of *STy* females crossed to essentially any male. Well over 2000 aberrations have been scored. Whatever the factor responsible, three properties are well documented: (a) it is maternally transmitted; (b) it causes aberrations in progeny of either sex; and (c) aberrations occur exclusively in chromosomes of paternal origin. The female transmission suggests that the agent or factor involved is cytoplasmically transmitted.

The occasional disappearance of the factor in some lines and reappearance on outcrossing suggests that the agent is episome-like in character. However, at this juncture one can only speculate on the nature of the agent involved.

2. *Increased mutability by "infection"*

In *D. persimilis* (*D. pseudoobscura*, race B) a recessive autosomal mutator gene was reported whose mutational effects were manifest by an increased frequency in the occurrence of Minute mutants or Minute mosaics (Mampell, 1945, 1946). The mutator functioned only in males. This specificity was attributed to the Y chromosome, a claim which was not convincingly established. It was reported that XXY females homozygous for the mutator gene yield an increased frequency of Minute mosaics as compared to XX females homozygous for the mutator. Data to support this claim were not given. Moreover, in a parallel experiment the yield of mutations derived from XYY mutator males was statistically no greater than that derived from XY mutator males.

There is the further claim of the "infectious" transfer of increased mutability by breeding *D. melanogaster* males and females in the presence of *D. persimilis* males. The experimental basis for this claim is unconvincing. Increased mutation is scored as "mosaic Minutes". Careful examination of the data presented in these papers does not support the author's conclusions as firmly as one would hope. In fact, it would appear in retrospect that the phenomenon would have been more firmly established if Mampell had presented a more rigorous statistical analysis based upon more objective criteria for scoring mutations.

3. *Mutator effect of extrachromosomal element delta in* D. melanogaster

Minamori and associates have described an extrachromosomal element which kills zygotes homozygous for certain chromosomes. The arguments for the extrachromosomal nature of delta lie outside the scope of this discussion. It will suffice here to note that delta has a mutagenic action as studied by the frequency of second chromosome lethals (Minamori and Ito, 1971). The average rate of spontaneous second chromosome recessive lethals is increased 3–4 times in the presence of delta. Mutation clustering was frequently detected implying a premeiotic origin of the recessive lethals. In addition delta appears to increase the frequency of visible mutants as evidenced by the frequent recovery of yellow and white mutants. For the time being the mode of action of delta can only be conjectured.

D. Résumé

There can be little doubt that specific mutator genes exist in *Drosophila*. There can also be little doubt that this branch of genetic research with *Drosophila* has lagged behind others. However, genetical techniques, e.g. conditional lethals and specific auxotrophic mutants, are now available which permit the ready and easy study of the phenotype "mutation". The progress with the mutator *mu* demonstrates that there is a wealth of basic genetic information to be mined from the study of mutator genes. It remains only for the miners to begin their work.

Acknowledgement

This review was prepared at the Department of Genetics, University of Umeå, Sweden. The author is grateful to Professor B. Rasmuson for the hospitality and facilities extended.

References

Bowman, J. T. and Green, M. M. (1966). X-ray induced reversion of the white-ivory mutant of *Drosophila melanogaster*. *Genetica* **37,** 7–16.

Demerec, M. (1926a). Reddish—a frequently "mutating" character in *Drosophila virilis*. *Proc. Natl. Acad. Sci. U.S.A.* **12,** 11–16.

Demerec, M. (1926b). Miniature-alpha—a second frequently mutating character in *Drosophila virilis*. *Proc. Natl. Acad. Sci. U.S.A.* **12,** 687–690.

Demerec, M. (1927). Magenta-alpha—a third frequently mutating character in *Drosophila virilis*. *Proc. Natl. Acad. Sci. U.S.A.* **13,** 249–253.

Demerec, (1928a). Mutable characters of *Drosophila virilis*. I. Reddish-alpha body character. *Genetics* **13,** 359–388.

Demerec, M. (1928b). The behavior of mutable genes. *Z. indukt. Abstamm. VererbLehre*. Suppl. **1,** 183–193.

Demerec, M. (1929a). Genetic factors stimulating mutability of the miniature-gamma wing character of *Drosophila virilis*. *Proc. Natl. Acad. Sci. U.S.A.* **15,** 834–838.

Demerec, M. (1929b). Changes in the rate of mutability of the mutable miniature gene of *Drosophila virilis*. *Proc. Natl. Acad. Sci. U.S.A.* **15,** 870–876.

Demerec, M. (1937). Frequency of spontaneous mutations in certain stocks of *Drosophila melanogaster*. *Genetics* **22,** 469–478.

Gabay, S. J. and Laughnan, J. R. (1970). Genetic analysis of the aberrant behavior of an X-chromosome duplication in the germ line of *Drosophila melanogaster* males. *Genetics* **65,** 249–265.

Gethmann, R. C. (1971). The genetics of a new mutable allele at the *white* locus in *Drosophila melanogaster*. *Molec. Gen. Genet.* **114,** 144–155.

Girvin, E. C. (1949). X-ray produced mutations, deletions and mosaics in *Drosophila virilis*. Univ. Texas Publ. 4920, 42–56.

Green, M. M. (1967). The genetics of a mutable gene at the white locus of *Drosophila melanogaster*. *Genetics* **56,** 467–482.

GREEN, M. M. (1968). Some genetic properties of intra-chromosomal recombination. *Molec. Gen. Genet.* **103,** 209–217.

GREEN, M. M. (1969a). Mapping a *Drosophila melanogaster* "controling element" by interallelic crossing over. *Genetics* **61,** 423–428.

GREEN, M. M. (1969b). Controlling element mediated transpositions of the *white* gene in *Drosophila melanogaster. Genetics* **61,** 429–441.

GREEN, M. M. (1970). The genetics of a mutator gene in *Drosophila melanogaster. Mutation Res.* **10,** 353–363.

GREEN, M. M. and LEFEVRE, G. (1972). The cytogenetics of mutator gene induced X-linked lethals in *Drosophila melanogaster. Mutation Res.* **16,** 59–64.

HALL, J. C. (1971). The failure of two alleles of c(3)G to increase frequencies of X-linked lethals. *Dros. Inf. Serv.* **47,** 62.

HINTON, T., IVES, P. T. and EVANS, A. T. (1952). Changing the gene order and number in natural populations. *Evolution* **6,** 19–28.

IVES, P. T. (1945). The genetic structure of American populations of *Drosophila melanogaster. Genetics* **30,** 167–196.

IVES, P. T. (1950). The importance of mutation rate genes in evolution. *Evolution* **4,** 236–252.

IVES, P. T. (1959). Chromosomal distribution of mutator- and radiation-induced mutations in *Drosophila melanogaster. Evolution* **13,** 526–531.

JUDD, B. H. (1963). The genetic fine structure of the mutants z^m and z^l in *Drosophila melanogaster*. Proc. XI. Int. Congr. Genet. **1,** 3–4.

JUDD, B. H. (1967). Intrastrand exchange as a possible mechanism for instability of some *white* mutants of *Drosophila melanogaster. Genetics* **56,** 569.

JUDD, (1969). Evidence for a transposable element which causes reversible gene inactivation in *Drosophila melanogaster. Genetics* **62,** s29.

KALISCH, W.-E. (1970). Über eine mutable white-Inversion bei *Drosophila melanogaster. Molec. Gen. Genet.* **107,** 336–350.

KALISCH, W.-E. and BECKER, H. J. (1970). Über eine Reihe mutabler Allele des *white*-Locus bei *Drosophila melanogaster. Molec. Gen. Genet.* **107,** 321–335.

LEVITAN, M. (1962). Spontaneous chromosome aberrations in *Drosophila robusta. Proc. Natl. Acad. Sci. U.S.A.* **48,** 930–937.

LEVITAN, M. (1963). A maternal factor which breaks paternal chromosomes. *Nature, Lond.* **200,** 437–438.

LEVITAN, M. (1967). Evidence for episomal properties of a chromosome-breaking agent. *J. Cell. Biol.* **35,** 80A–81A.

LEVITAN, M. and SCHILLER, R. (1963). Further evidence that the chromosome breakage factor in *Drosophila robusta* involves a maternal effect. *Genetics* **48,** 1231–1238.

LEVITAN, M. and WILLIAMSON, D. L. (1965). Evidence for the cytoplasmic and possibly episomal nature of a chromosome breaker. *Genetics* **52,** 456.

MAINX, F. (1964). The genetics of *Megaselia scalaris* Loew (Phoridae): A new type of sex determination in Diptera. *Am. Nat.* **98,** 415–430.

MAINX, F. (1966). Die Geschlechtsbestimmung bei *Megaselia scalaris* Loew (Phoridae). *Z. indukt. Abstamm. VererbLehre* **98,** 49–60.

MAMPEL, K. (1943). High mutation frequency in *Drosophila pseudoobscura*, Race B. *Proc. Natl. Acad. Sci. U.S.A.* **29,** 137–144.

MAMPEL, K. (1945). Analysis of a mutator. *Genetics* **30,** 496–505.

MAMPEL, K. (1946). Genic and nongenic transmission of mutator activity. *Genetics* **31,** 589–597.

McClintock, B. (1950). The origin and behavior of mutable loci in maize. *Proc. Natl. Acad. Sci. U.S.A.* **36,** 344–355.

McClintock, B. (1951). Chromosome organization and genic expression. *Cold Spring Harb. Symp. Quant. Biol.* **16,** 13–47.

Minamori, S. and Ito, K. (1971). Extrachromosomal element delta in *Drosophila melanogaster* VI. Induction of recurrent lethal mutations in definite regions of second chromosomes. *Mutation Res.* **13,** 361–369.

Neel, J. V. (1942). A study of high mutation rate in *Drosophila melanogaster. Genetics* **27,** 519–536.

Peterson, H. M. and Laughnan, J. R. (1963). Intrachromosomal exchange at the Bar locus in *Drosophila melanogaster. Proc. Nat. Acad. Sci. U.S.A.* **50,** 126–133.

Plough, H. H. (1928). Black suppressor—a sex linked gene in *Drosophila* causing apparent anomalies in crossing over in the second chromosome. *Z. indukt. Abstamm. VererbLehre.* Suppl. II, 1193–1200.

Appendix to Chapter 23

THE BEHAVIOUR OF A TRANSPOSING ELEMENT IN *DROSOPHILA MELANOGASTER*

G. Ising and C. Ramel

Institute of Genetics, University of Lund and Wallenberg Laboratory, University of Stockholm, Sweden

Since the analysis by Green (1969) of the transposing property of the white allele white-crimson (w^c), further cases of a similar episome-like behaviour of chromosome segments in *Drosophila* have been found (Green, 1973). The present investigation deals with a system in *Drosophila* which also involves spontaneous transpositions of a segment of X, including at least a part of the white locus. The system is in many respects similar to the one reported by Green, but there are also certain differences which may be of interest. The transposing element is in our case considerably larger involving not only the white locus but also roughest to the right of white. It contains a white mutant, most probably white-apricot. Although spontaneous mutational changes from apricot to other eye colours do occur like in Green's case the frequency of these changes is much lower. The greater mutational stability of this transposing element is of value experimentally. It has enabled the maintenance and analysis of various transpositions and mutants without running the risk of loosing them through mutational changes.

The transposing element was originally discovered in a cross of attached *y w sn* females to Muller-5 males (Ising, 1964). As Muller-5 carries w^a all sons from that cross are expected to be w^a and all daughters white. However, 8 apricot-eyed daughters were found and they were shown to carry a dominant gene in chromosome 2 at 59·5, which functioned as a partial suppressor of white giving them apricot eyes. The gene was therefore designated suppressor of white. The gene also carried a recessive lethality and it was kept balanced against the Curly inversions. This "suppressor of white" was subsequently used in a population experiment in order to study the selection against it when occurring in a genetic background of white as compared to wild type (Ramel, 1966).

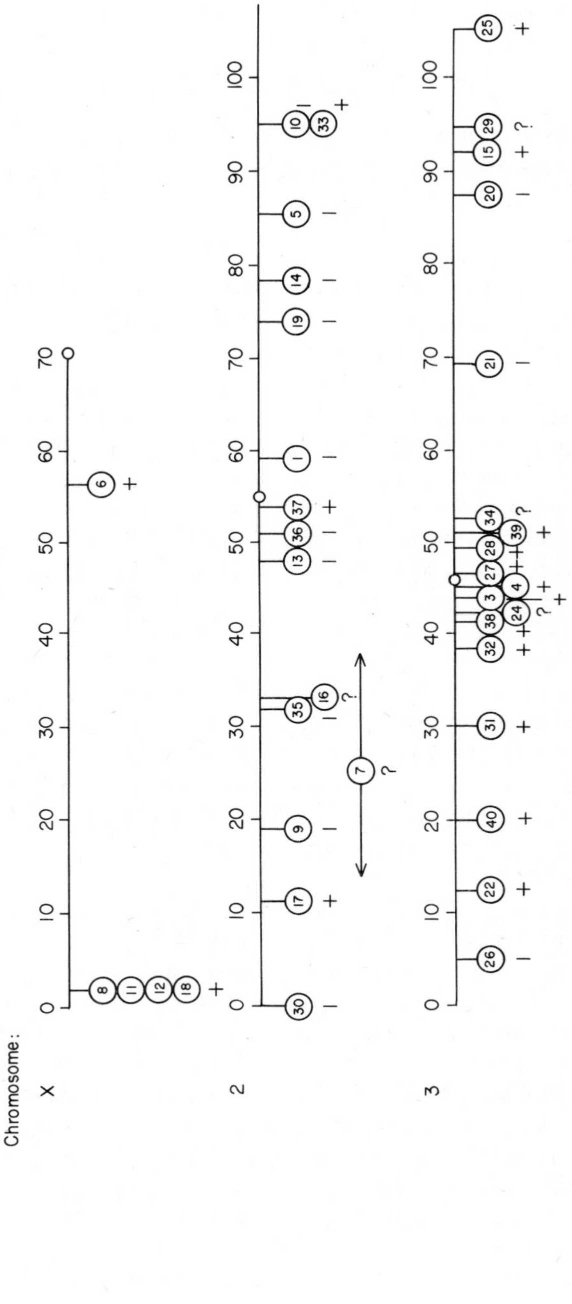

FIG. 1. Localized transpositions in the chromosomes of *Drosophila melanogaster*. Recessive lethal positions are indicated with 1. An additional position is localized in the long arm of chromosome Y.

The transposing property was revealed when a male was found where the suppressor gene had changed its position from the right to the left arm of chromosome 2.

Transposition Experiments

A systematic search for new transpositions was started with different crosses. So far around 40 transpositions have been established. The positions of those, which have been localized are shown in Fig. 1.

It should be mentioned that there is no appropriate term in *Drosophila* nomenclature to cover transpositions like these, as the denotation Tp (transposition) has been used for intrachromosomal events (Lindsley and Grell, 1968). We therefore have used the term "Transposing element" with the abbreviation TE, followed by a serial number.

As can be seen in Fig. 1 the transpositions are well scattered over the whole genome. In the autosomes there is only one case when two transpositions may have an identical position, that is TE 10 and TE 33 at 96 in the right arm of chromosome 2. There is, however, one preferential site for the transpositions and that is the white locus itself in the X chromosome. In at least five cases transpositions have occurred from the autosomes to the white locus.

The transposing element has in several cases changed position repeatedly, for instance from the original position in 2R (TE 1) to 2L (TE 7), from there to X at forked (TE 6) and further to chromosome 3 (TE 20).

The search for transpositions has involved different crosses, some with the transposing element in the second chromosome (TE 1 and TE 7) and one with the transposing element in the X chromosome (TE 6):

1. *w; al In(2L)Cy* TE 7 *In(2R)Cy/dp b* ♀♀ × *w; dp b* ♂♂
2. *C(1)RM,y w f/y*$^+$*.Y* ♀♀ × *y w rst*$^-$*; T(Y;2) In(2L)Cy In(2LR:36C–51D)* TE 1/+ ♂♂ (cross 2A: with apricot TE 1, cross 2B: with wild type TE 1)
3. *y w rst*$^-$*;* TE 1 (apricot type)/+ ♀♀ × *y w rst*$^-$*; T(Y;2)In(2L)Cy In(2LR:36C–51D)* TE 1 (wild type)/+ ♂♂
4. *C(1)RM, y w f/Y* ♀♀ × *w* TE 6 ♂♂

In the first of these crosses transpositions are identified as non-white *dp b* offspring. In the regular offspring of the second cross TE 1 is distributed only to the daughters because of the Y;2-translocation while regular sons will carry a deficiency including the roughest loci, which is, under the present experimental conditions, almost completely lethal without the transposing element present. Therefore among the male offspring the test system will select for new transpositions which can be transferred to the sons.

TABLE I. Estimated frequency of transpositions. Clusters are counted as one event.

Cross		Frequency of transpositions[a]	Frequency per 10^5
1. $\frac{w\ al\ In(2L)Cy\ TE\ 7\ In(2R)Cy}{w\ \ dp\ b} \times \frac{w\ dp\ b}{7\ \ dp\ b}$		1/49700	2·0
2. y w f f w y y⁺ (attached-X) $\times \frac{y\ w\ rst^-}{7}\ \frac{T(Y;2)\ In(2L)Cy\ In(2LR{:}36C\text{–}51D)\ TE\ 1}{+}$	A. apricot TE1	4/143000	2·8
	B. wildtype TE 1	4/82500	6·1
3. $\frac{y\ w\ rst^-\ TE\ 1}{y\ w\ rst^-\ \ +} \times \frac{y\ w\ rst^-}{7}\ \frac{T(Y;2)\ In(2L)Cy\ In(2LR{:}36C\text{–}51D)\ TE\ 1}{+}$ (♀♀ apricot TE 1, ♂♂ wild type TE 1. Only wild type TE collected)		10/118000	8·5
4. y w f f w y (attached-X) $\times \frac{w\ TE\ 6}{7}$		2/366000	0·5

[a] The total number corrected for lethality of males in cross 2 and for lethality of females in cross 3, due to rst⁻.

In the third cross only transpositions in the males were screened for and they were identified as red-eyed daughters. In the fourth cross regular daughters will be white-eyed and regular sons apricot-eyed. Transpositions are discovered as non-white daughters, while white-eyed sons indicate a loss of the transposing element.

Only a limited number of transpositions were picked up from crosses performed to actually measure the frequency of transposing events. The results of these crosses are shown in Table I. It should be pointed out that suspected transpositions were noticed in a couple of cases during the collecting of the parental flies for the experimental crosses. Although vials showing such an indication of previous transpositions were avoided, it cannot be ruled out that in some cases a transposition from a previous generation can have remained undetected. Most likely the error introduced by this is small, however, and it can hardly have influenced the estimation of the transposition frequency in a major way.

In cross three, where transpositions of wild type TE 1 in the males were screened for, the presence of the apricot form of TE 1 in the females could theoretically interfere with the result, if a mutational change to wild type occurred in the female in combination with a transposition. Such a combination of transposition and mutation is, however, according to our experience, very rare.

As is shown in Table I the frequency of transpositions is low—roughly one in a hundred thousand with the apricot type of the transposing element. However, the data from cross 2B and 3 indicate a somewhat higher frequency of transpositions of the wild type form of TE 1. The reason for this difference, if real, is not clear.

The transpositions occur as clusters in both sexes indicating that they occur mitotically just as the transpositions of w^c.

The Size of the Transposing Element

Considering the extent of the transposing element, it obviously contains at least a part of the white locus and from the expression and chromatographical characteristics, it most probably carries white-apricot. This would also be in accordance with the origin from a cross with Muller-5. It was found to suppress zeste in combination with w^{is} and this suggests that it contains at least the right part of the white locus. Further to the right it covers also *rst* as mentioned above, but not facet or split. To the left it does not cover sparse arista located just left of the white locus. Tentatively, the transposing element thus covers a segment from white-apricot to *rst*, which would mean a length of at least 0·7 map units, if *rst* is located at position 2·2, as indicated by Lefevre and Green (1972).

Although it is not sure that entirely the same length of chromosomal segment takes part in all the transpositions, most of them have been picked up by means of a system which is based on the presence of both the white allele and rst^+.

Cytological investigations of salivary gland chromosomes have not given sufficiently conclusive results as yet, although an extra band was observed with a transposing element located at the left tip end of the second chromosome.

Mutational Changes

The white allele in the transposing element mutates spontaneously to wild type or near wild type forms, corresponding to the back mutations of w^a (cf. Rasmusson *et al.*, 1960). Changes occur likewise in the other direction from dark eyes to lighter. The white allele in our system is far more stable than w^c in Green's system. However, there evidently is a variation of the mutational stability between different transpositions in our material. Thus TE 30, located in the second chromosome (Fig. 1) mutated at a frequency of roughly 0·2% which is about fifty times the rate in most of the other cases.

Loss of the Transposing Element

There is one type of change of the eye colour which presumably is of a different nature and that is the change to white. This change most probably involves a loss of the transposing element. In one tested case it has been observed that, when the second chromosome had lost TE 1, it no longer suppressed the lethal effect of rst^-, i.e. it had also lost rst^+. The occurrence of white-eyed flies may therefore be interpreted as an intitial step to transpositions, that is, the segment has left its position without being incorporated at other positions. Some investigations were therefore performed to study the frequency of such presumed losses. Attempts were made to increase the frequency with X-irradiation, temperature shocks and interchromosomal effects of inversions on recombination, but without any effect.

The frequency of losses, however, varies between experiments, presumably due to some modifying genetic influence. Some data on this was obtained with TE 6 located at 57·3 in the X chromosome. Although the analysis of the frequency of losses of the transposing element is complicated by the fact that it is a mitotic event showing clustering, a consistently higher frequency of loss was recorded when TE 6 was kept in a chromosome carrying rudimentary and Bar (see Table III). The neighborhood of the Bar duplication was not the cause of this as other chromosomes with Bar or double Bar did not give such a high frequency (see Table II).

TABLE II. The frequency of loss of the transposing element.

Cross	Number of loss	Total number	% Loss
$\frac{y\ w\ sn}{y\ w\ sn} \times \frac{w\ TE\ 6}{y^{+}\rightharpoonup}$	13	46902	0·03
$\frac{y\ w\ sn}{y\ w\ sn} \times \frac{w\ TE\ 6}{B\quad y^{+}\rightharpoonup}$	27	65467	0·04
$\frac{y\ w\ sn}{y\ w\ sn} \times \frac{w\ r\ B\ TE\ 6}{\rightharpoonup}$	278	53654	0·52
$\frac{y\ w\ sn}{y\ w\ sn} \times \frac{w\ r\ B\ TE\ 6}{\rightharpoonup}$	38	4591	0·83
$\frac{w}{w} \times \frac{y\ w\ sn\ B\ TE\ 6}{\rightharpoonup}$	0	12007	0
$\frac{w}{w} \times \frac{y\ w\ sn\ BB\ TE\ 6}{\rightharpoonup}$	4	25666	0·03
$\frac{w\ r\ B\ TE\ 6}{w\ +\ +\ TE\ 6} \times \frac{y\ w\ sn}{y^{+}\rightharpoonup}$	33 B⁺ 918 B	49396	0·07 1·86
$\frac{y\ w\ sn\ B\ TE\ 6}{y\ w\ sn\ +\ TE\ 6} \times \frac{w}{\rightharpoonup}$	43 B⁺ 72 B	31850	0·14 0·20
$\frac{y\ w\ sn\ B\ TE\ 6}{y\ w\ sn\ B\ TE\ 6} \times \frac{w}{\rightharpoonup}$	38	33104	0·12
$\frac{y\ w\ sn\ TE\ 6}{y\ w\ sn\ TE\ 6} \times \frac{w}{\rightharpoonup}$	114	46103	0·25

INDUCTION OF LETHALS

There is no conclusive evidence that the transposing element has any effect outside the white locus, indicating the occurrence of a more general controlling property. It is, however, possible that the induction of a lethality at the site of a transposition may indicate such an effect. Many of the transpositions bring about a recessive lethality, but the lethals are not allelic between different transpositions. When the transposing element has been lost as indicated by the occurrence of white-eyed flies, the lethality remains. New spontaneous lethality has also occurred in connection with loss of the transposing element from a non-lethal position. Thus, TE 4 in the third chromosome marked with threat (*th*) and radius incompletus (*ri*) on either side of the centromere was lost and replaced by a recessive lethal in the same short interval. A similar case was observed in connection with a spontaneous colour change in TE 6 from apricot to a weak yellow eye colour, when a recessive lethal of a Minute type occurred. This seems to be inseparable from the position of TE 6.

It should be mentioned that the induction of recessive lethality by the transpositions shows a peculiar distribution between the chromosomes. Of 13 analysed transpositions in the second chromosome, 10 were lethal, while the corresponding value for 17 transpositions in the third chromosome was three ($\chi^2_3 = 8{\cdot}3$, $P < 0{\cdot}005$).

Conclusions

In conclusion it may be said that while the most remarkable aspect of Green's w^c was the high rate of mutational changes, the peculiarity with the present system is not such changes, but transpositions. It is evident that a chromosomal segment for some reason can start to drift and behave as an episome. The mechanism for the insertion of the transposing element is somewhat difficult to envisage. The lack of preferential sites for the transpositions does not indicate that the insertion of the DNA segment is based on some specific nucleotide sequence which is recognized by the transposing element. It rather seems as if the insertions occur by means of some other mechanism. A counterpart may be found in the Mu-1 DNA in *Escherichia coli* which is inserted randomly without recognition of a common nucleotide sequence (Bukhari and Zipser, 1972).

References

Bukhari, A. I. and Zipser, D. (1972). Random insertion of Mu–1 DNA within a single gene. *Nature, New Biol.* **236,** 240–243.

Green, M. M. (1969). Controlling element mediated transpositions of the white gene in *Drosophila melanogaster. Genetics* **61,** 429–441.

Green, M. M. (1973). Some observations and comments on unstable and mutator genes in *Drosophila. Genetics* **73,** Suppl. 187–194.

Ising, G. (1964). A recessive lethal in chromosome 2, which in single dose has an effect on the eye colour of white animals. *Dros. Inf. Serv.* **39,** 74.

Lefevre, G. and Green, M. M. (1972). Genetic duplication in the white-split interval of the X chromosome in *Drosophila melanogaster. Chromosoma* **36,** 391–412.

Lindsley, D. L. and Grell, E. H. (1968). Genetics variations of *Drosophila melanogaster.* Com. of Wash. Publ. No. 627.

Ramel, C. (1966). The interaction of white and a dominant suppressor of white on viability in *Drosophila melanogaster. Hereditas* **56,** 113–130.

Rasmusson, B., Green, M. M. and Ewertson, G. (1960). Qualitative and quantitative analyses of eye pigments and pteridines in back-mutations of the mutant w^a in *Drosophila melanogaster. Hereditas* **46,** 635–650.

AUTHOR INDEX

The numbers in italics refer to the reference pages at the end of the chapters where the full reference appears.

C

Q

R

S

T

U

SUBJECT INDEX

Compiled by Dr. R. and Mrs. B. Woodruff.

Page numbers in bold type indicate pages on which figures and tables appear.

D

O

P

T

U

V

W

X

Y

Z

SPECIES INDEX

In the *Species Index* neither *Drosophila* (with no specific name) nor *D. melanogaster* are indexed since both appear in almost every page of this volume. With few exceptions only latin names are indexed, their English equivalents, as quoted in the text, being noted in brackets after the main headings.

INDEX OF GENETIC VARIATIONS

In the *Index of Genetic Variations* mutants are indexed alphabetically by their full names; their standard abbreviations follow in brackets. Except in a few cases (e.g. ca^{nd}, *w*) alleles are not separately indexed.

Followng the mutant index chromosome aberrations are indexed in the order of Lindsley and Grell's "Genetic Variations of *Drosophila melanogaster*" (1968, Carnegie Institution, Washington); i.e.: Deficiencies (*Df*), Duplications (*Dp*), Inversions (*In*), Rings (*R*), Translocations (*T*) and Transpositions (*Tp*). There then follows, in order, Balancers and special chromosomes, Compound chromosomes (*C*), Free chromosomes (*F*), X-Y combinations and Y derivatives.

We have adhered to Lindsley and Grell's practice as closely as possible for abbreviations and for the order within sections. We have avoided extensive cross indexing and all but a few questions of synonymy. Unless noted all mutants and aberrations are of *D. melanogaster*.

Mutants

M